PRINCIPLES OF INTEGRATED MARKETING COMMUNICATIONS

AN EVIDENCE-BASED APPROACH

SECOND EDITION

Marketing in the digital age poses major challenges for traditional and established practices of communication. To help readers meet these challenges *Principles of Integrated Marketing Communications: An Evidence-based Approach* provides a comprehensive foundation to the principles and practices of integrated marketing communications (IMC). It examines a variety of traditional and digital channels used by professionals to create wide-reaching and effective campaigns that are adapted for the aims of their organisations.

This edition has been thoroughly revised, and it introduces a 'consumer decision journey' as a framework for implementing communications to best meet the demands of a business and its consumers. Essential concepts such as synergy and IMC planning, uncovering insights and brand positioning, creativity and share of voice, social influence and content marketing, as well as system 1 and system 2 advertising pre-testing methods, are discussed in a clear and comprehensive way, and there is a strong focus on implementation of IMC strategies in digital and social contexts.

Each chapter includes:

- case studies of significant and award-winning campaigns from both Australian and international brands that illustrate the application of explored concepts

- discussion and case study questions that enable readers to critically evaluate concepts and campaigns

- a managerial application section that illustrates how concepts can be applied effectively in a real situation

- a 'further thinking' section that expands knowledge of advanced concepts and challenges readers to think more broadly about IMC.

Lawrence Ang is Associate Professor at Macquarie University. Prior to entering academia, he was a marketing research consultant. He has a keen interest in advertising effectiveness, customer relationship management, consumer behaviour and media studies.

Advance praise for *Principles of Integrated Marketing Communications*

Lawrence Ang provides a comprehensive, insightful and thoroughly enjoyable treatment of the subject. *Principles of Integrated Marketing Communications* is a real treasure trove for students and will make them smarter and better marketers.

Professor Kevin Lane Keller, Tuck School of Business, Dartmouth College, USA

I have never read such an accessible but still really complete and insightful introduction to integrated marketing communications. Who else than our highly esteemed colleague Lawrence Ang could have written this book that is strongly recommended to students and practitioners.

Professor Peter Neijens, University of Amsterdam, Netherlands

The world of marketing communications books would be a better place if all books were like Lawrence Ang's. It strikes a perfect balance between academic rigour and practical relevance, with a distinct focus on state-of-the art insights from both the academic and the professional advertising field. And maybe most importantly: it reads like a novel!

Professor Patrick De Pelsmacker, University of Antwerp, Belgium

Lawrence Ang has produced an original and insightful explanation of creativity in advertising based on his cutting-edge knowledge of advertising strategy. With wit and candour, he writes with authority showing how managers should approach creativity

Professor Scott Koslow, Macquarie University, Australia

Lawrence Ang did it again! The second edition again addresses practical suggestions but with comprehensive scientific evidence and intriguing examples ... [I]n light of the COVID-19 crisis Lawrence demonstrates the importance of timing for communication and he shows how the three elements of communications: message – media – time relate to each other.

Professor Martin Waiguny, IMC University of Applied Sciences Krems, Austria

The second edition of Lawrence Ang's essential book *Principles of Integrated Marketing Communications* is even better than the first. It aligns relevant theory that is clearly explained with fascinating examples of IMC in practice, vividly bringing the subject to life ... It's a brilliant and welcome contribution to this important topic.

Professor Francis Buttle, Macquarie University, Australia, Principal Consultant at Francis Buttle and Associates

The book provides a powerful compilation of creative executions in marketing communications. It's written in a convincing and accessible style and promises to engage and entertain its readers.

Professor Martin Eisend, European University Viadrina, Frankfurt (Oder), Germany

The book's exposition on social influence is a really interesting and balanced introduction to the complexities of social media marketing. It is wide-ranging, accessible and thoughtful.

Emeritus Professor Robert East, Kingston University London, UK

This book covers work in the branding domain more thoroughly than any other advertising book on the market ... The integration of COVID-19 lessons is highly topical and encourages students to critically analyse recent short-term tactical decisions against long-term strategic brand priorities.

Associate Professor Jasmina Ilicic, Monash University, Australia

This book gives an excellent overview. The explicitly formulated learning goals are key for students.

Associate Professor Eva van Reijmersdal, University of Amsterdam, Netherlands

This book is packed with real-world applications and examples. It will provide a solid platform for those who strive to get an edge within the marketing sphere. A thorough yet easy read, this book will broaden students' thinking across both current and future marketing concepts – a must-read!

Melissa Airs, Senior Account Manager, Media & Digital, Kantar, Australia

Lawrence Ang brings a wealth of hands-on experience to this comprehensive book on advertising and research.

Dr Max Sutherland, author of *Advertising & the Mind of the Consumer*

This is an absolute must-read! It is full of marketing knowledge and practical applications, while still being very easy to read. I highly recommend it!

Damaris Boisne, Associate Director, Kantar, Australia

PRINCIPLES OF INTEGRATED MARKETING COMMUNICATIONS

AN EVIDENCE-BASED APPROACH

SECOND EDITION

LAWRENCE ANG

CAMBRIDGE UNIVERSITY PRESS

WITHDRAWN

CAMBRIDGE
UNIVERSITY PRESS

University Printing House, Cambridge CB2 8BS, United Kingdom

One Liberty Plaza, 20th Floor, New York, NY 10006, USA

477 Williamstown Road, Port Melbourne, VIC 3207, Australia

314–321, 3rd Floor, Plot 3, Splendor Forum, Jasola District Centre, New Delhi – 110025, India

79 Anson Road, #06–04/06, Singapore 079906

Cambridge University Press is part of the University of Cambridge.

It furthers the University's mission by disseminating knowledge in the pursuit of education, learning and research at the highest international levels of excellence.

www.cambridge.org
Information on this title: www.cambridge.org/9781108703116

© Cambridge University Press 2014, 2021

This publication is copyright. Subject to statutory exception and to the provisions of relevant collective licensing agreements, no reproduction of any part may take place without the written permission of Cambridge University Press.

First published 2014
Second edition 2021

Cover designed by Sardine Design
Text designed by TDSM Design Media
Typeset by SPi Global

Printed in Malaysia by Vivar Printing, December 2020

A catalogue record for this publication is available from the British Library

A catalogue record for this book is available from the National Library of Australia

ISBN 978-1-108-70311-6 Paperback

Additional resources for this publication at www.cambridge.org/highereducation/isbn/9781108703116/resources.

Reproduction and communication for educational purposes

The Australian *Copyright Act 1968* (the Act) allows a maximum of one chapter or 10% of the pages of this work, whichever is the greater, to be reproduced and/or communicated by any educational institution for its educational purposes provided that the educational institution (or the body that administers it) has given a remuneration notice to Copyright Agency Limited (CAL) under the Act.

For details of the CAL licence for educational institutions contact:

Copyright Agency Limited
Level 12, 66 Goulburn Street
Sydney NSW 2000
Telephone: (02) 9394 7600
Facsimile: (02) 9394 7601
E-mail: memberservices@copyright.com.au

Cambridge University Press has no responsibility for the persistence or accuracy of URLs for external or third-party internet websites referred to in this publication and does not guarantee that any content on such websites is, or will remain, accurate or appropriate.

This book is dedicated to Dr NO (my darling wife, Nesrin Ozsarac, PhD)

Cambridge University Press acknowledges the Aboriginal and Torres Strait Islander peoples as the traditional owners of Country throughout Australia.

Cambridge University Press acknowledges the Māori people as *tangata whenua* of *Aotearoa* New Zealand.

We pay our respects to the First Nation Elders of Australia and New Zealand, past, present and emerging.

CONTENTS

CASE STUDIES

ABOUT THE AUTHOR

Lawrence Ang is an Associate Professor of Marketing at the Macquarie Business School, Sydney, Australia. He graduated with first-class honours and obtained his PhD from the Australian Graduate School of Management, University of New South Wales. Prior to entering academia, he was a marketing research consultant. His research interests include advertising effectiveness, customer relationship management, consumer behaviour, media studies and decision-making. An award-winning academic, an oenophile and a popular MBA teacher, he has published in the *International Journal of Management Reviews*, *Journal of Advertising*, *International Journal of Advertising*, *Journal of Advertising Research*, *Celebrity Studies*, *European Journal of Marketing*, *Journal of Marketing Management*, *Journal of Economic Psychology*, and *Journal of Behavioral and Experimental Finance*, among others.

Lately, he has discovered the art of social distancing.

ACKNOWLEDGEMENTS

When Lucy Russell, Senior Commissioning editor at Cambridge University Press, approached me to write the second edition, I thought it should be a piece of cake. Well, that was what I told my wife. But of course, writing a book never is. So, first and foremost, I want to thank Nesrin for her support (again), displaying amazing patience through it all. I am truly blessed.

A book is never a solo intellectual effort, even though only my name appears on the cover. I have been intellectually enriched over the years by the conversations, collaborations and late-night exchanges (over countless pints) between myself and my colleagues. It is on their shoulders that I stand.

In particular, I would like to thank Kevin Keller, Peter Neijens, Patrick De Pelsmacker, Scott Koslow, Martin Eisend, Martin Waiguny, Robert East, Francis Buttle, Jasmina Ilicic, Eva van Reijmersdal, Melissa Airs, Haydn Northover, Damaris Boisne and Max Sutherland for taking the time to read or comment on my manuscripts. I thank you all for your generosity and suggestions.

Of course, any omissions, short-sightedness, misinterpretations or cribbing are entirely my fault (I blame it on *that* virus).

Finally, the book would not have been possible without the encouragement and hard work of the editorial team at Cambridge University Press: thank you to Lucy Russell who agreed to take a punt on me (again); to Jodie Fitzsimmons who shepherded the manuscript to final production; and to Lauren Magee who among other things, kept me disciplined – but ever so politely! And to Karen Jayne who copyedited my writing so that I come across more cultured than I truly am. (Of course, all grammatical mistakes are entirely her fault!)

We are grateful to the following individuals and organisations for permission to use their material in *Principles of Integrated Marketing Communications*.

Figure 1.6: Courtesy of Casella Family Brands; **1.7**: Courtesy of Unilever; **2.3**: Photo used with permission. © 2020 The LEGO Group. All information in this material is collected and interpreted by its authors and does not represent the opinion of the LEGO Group; **2.6**: © Getty Images/anankkml; **2.7**: © Getty Images/Elena_Garder; **2.8**: © Getty Images/pikepicture; **2.9**, **12.20**: © Getty Images/CSA Images; **2.10**: © Getty Images/Michael Blann; **3.2**: Courtesy Burger King/INGO; **3.6**: Courtesy Johnnie Walker; **3.7** (left), **5.9**, **7.15**, **7.16**, **8.14**: Trade marks of The Coca-Cola Company are used with permission; **3.7** (centre): Courtesy Volvo Car Corporation; **3.7** (right): Courtesy Audi Australia Pty Ltd; **3.8**: From Appendix A, Complete and Incomplete Typeface Logos Used as Stimuli in Studies 1–3. A: Stimuli Used in Study 1 (Experiments 1a–1c) in H Hagtvedt, 'The Impact of Incomplete Typeface Logos on Perceptions of the Firm', *Journal of Marketing*, 75(4), 2011, p. 92; **3.9**: Figure 1. Examples of logo pairs used in Studies 1 and 2, Logo Pair D: Study 1b in J Luffarelli, A Stamatogiannakis and H Yang, 'The Visual Asymmetry Effect: An Interplay of Logo Design and Brand Personality on Brand Equity', *Journal of Marketing Research*, 56(1), 2019, p. 91; **3.10**: Yuwei Jiang, Gerald J. Gorn, Maria Galli and Amitava Chattopadhyay, 'Does Your Company Have the Right Logo? How and Why Circular- and Angular-Logo Shapes Influence Brand Attribute Judgments', *Journal of Consumer Research*, 42(5), 2016, p. 723, by permission of Oxford University Press; **3.12**: Reprinted from SM Baxter and J Ilicic, 'May the force drag your dynamic logo: The brand work-energy effect', *International Journal of Research in Marketing*, 35, 2018, pp. 509–523, with permission from Elsevier; **3.13**: Coach Horse and Carriage ® and Copyright (2020) Coach IP

Holdings LLC. Permission is granted to Lawrence Ang and his publisher Cambridge University Press solely for academic purposes and for inclusion on page 78 of this publication. No other authorisations are granted by Coach IP Holdings LLC; **3.14** (left): Courtesy Konica Minolta; **3.14** (right): Courtesy Texas Instruments; **3.16**, **3.17**: Tourism Australia; **3.18**: Courtesy Patek Philippe SA Geneve; **3.19**: Courtesy Qantas Airways Ltd; **3.20**: © Singapore Airlines; **Page 91**: © Getty Images/pop_jop; **Figure 4.3**: © Getty Images/Bethany Clarke/Stringer; **4.7** and **Tables 4.2**, **4.3**, **4.4**: 'The gift that keeps on giving: John Lewis Christmas advertising, 2012–2015', 2016 IPA Effectiveness Awards Grand Prix Winner; **Figure 4.17**: IPA Touchpoints UK 2019; **5.8**: Courtesy Posterscope; **5.10**: Courtesy Hanes Australasia; **5.12**, **5.13**: © 2018 Google LLC, used with permission. Google and the Google logo are registered trademarks of Google LLC; **5.14**: Courtesy Tourism Queensland; **5.16**: © Getty Images/Ksenia Omelchenko; **5.17**: © www.qkies.de; **5.18**, **5.19**: Courtesy Australia Post; **6.1**: © Wizard Co, Inc./Avis; **6.4**: Courtesy Zebco Brands; **6.8**: © Getty Images/GlobalP, © Getty Images/ALAMA; **6.9**: Courtesy Reckitt Benckiser; **6.11**, **6.22**: By courtesy of Heineken Brouwerijen B.V., Amsterdam; **6.12**: Courtesy Action on Smoking and Health; **6.14**: © Ansell Ltd 1999; **6.15**: With permission from Yalumba and kwp!; **6.18**: Courtesy Coopers Brewery; **6.19**: © Getty Images/kyoshino; **6.20**: Courtesy Polycell UK; **6.21**: © 2010 WWF (panda.org). Some rights reserved; **6.23**: © Getty Images/claudiodivizia; **6.24**: Courtesy Orlando Pardo DC Chiropractic Centre; **6.25**: Courtesy Remedy Drinks; **6.26**: Courtesy Henkel; **6.27**: Courtesy Heinz; **6.28**: Courtesy McCann Australia; **6.29**: Courtesy Corri Fetman & Associates; **6.31**: © Commonwealth of Australia; **6.32**: Courtesy of International Business Machines Corporation, © International Business Machines Corporation. IBM, the IBM logo, ibm.com, and SPSS are trademarks or registered trademarks of International Business Machines Corporation, registered in many jurisdictions worldwide. Other product and service names might be trademarks of IBM or other companies. A current list of IBM trademarks is available on the Web at 'IBM Copyright and trademark information' at www.ibm.com/legal/copytrade.shtml; **6.33**: Courtesy Kodak; **6.34**: Courtesy TAC; **7.1**, **11.2**: © Procter & Gamble; **7.2**: Courtesy Honda; **7.3**: Courtesy McCann Bristol; **7.4**: © Absolut Company AB; **7.7**, **7.8**, **7.9**: Courtesy KFC UK; **7.10**: © Winerytale; **7.11**: Courtesy My Wine Guy; **7.13**: Courtesy Mondelez; **7.14**: Courtesy Bega Foods; **7.17**: Pexels/Steven Gomez; **7.18**: Courtesy IKEA; **7.19**, **7.20**: Serviceplan France; **7.23**: Courtesy Lindt & Sprungli/Stuart Alexander; **8.4**: © Getty Images/Barcroft Media; **8.6**, **8.7**, **11.9**: Courtesy McDonald's Australia; **8.8**: Courtesy Ogilvy Singapore & Health Promotion Board, Singapore; **8.12**: Courtesy Zonination; **8.15**: Courtesy WineSquare; **9.2**: Courtesy Edelman Co.; **9.3** (on jetski): Wikimedia Commons/D@LY3D, Richard Branson, https://commons.wikimedia.org/wiki/File:Richard_Branson_(pic_2).jpg, licensed by CC BY 2.0, https://creativecommons.org/licenses/by/2.0/; **9.3** (pride float): © Getty Images/Noam Galai/Stringer; **9.3** (marathon): Nick Webb, Flickr, licensed by CC BY 2.0, https://creativecommons.org/licenses/by/2.0/; **9.3** (plane): © Getty Images/Patrick Riviere/Staff; **9.5**: Wikimedia Commons/Gade Skidmore, Donald Trump speaks at a campaign event in Fountain Hills, Arizona, before the March 22 primary, Hippocrates, https://commons.wikimedia.org/wiki/File:Donald_Trump_by_Gage_Skidmore_6.jpg, licensed under CC BY-SA 2.0, https://creativecommons.org/licenses/by-sa/2.0/deed.en/; **9.6**: Courtesy SPC; **9.7**: Courtesy Jess Gallagher; **9.8**: Wikimedia Commons/Анна Нэсси, Ronaldo in 2018, https://commons.wikimedia.org/wiki/File:Cristiano_Ronaldo_2018.jpg, licensed under CC BY-SA 3.0, https://creativecommons.org/licenses/by-sa/3.0/deed.en; **9.9**: Figure 1 Serial mediation model of advertising recognition effects, in BW Wojdynski, 'The Deceptiveness of Sponsored News Articles: How Readers Recognize and Perceive Native Advertising', *American Behavioral Scientist*, 60(12), 2016, pp. 1475–1491; **9.10**: Red Bull Stratos/Red Bull Content Pool; **10.1**: Getty Images/

Feverpiched; **10.12, 10.13**: Photo © Milton Wordley; **10.15**: © Getty Images/duncan1890; **11.1**: Getty Images/neirfy; **11.7**: Coles Group Limited; **11.8**: Courtesy Mondelez Australia Pty Ltd; **12.4**: Courtesy Meat and Livestock Australia; **12.12, 12.23**: © Affectiva; **12.19**: © Getty Images/William Taufic; **12.24, 12.27, 12.28**: Source: BBC Global; **12.25**: Michael J Apter, *Reversal theory: The dynamics of motivation, emotion and personality*, 2nd edition, 2007, Oxford, UK; **12.26**: © Getty Images/Andreus; **13.3**: Courtesy Menulog.

Every effort has been made to trace and acknowledge copyright. The publisher apologises for any accidental infringement and welcomes information that would rectify the situation.

CHAPTER 1
INTEGRATED MARKETING COMMUNICATIONS AND ITS SYNERGISTIC EFFECTS

CHAPTER OVERVIEW

This chapter begins with a message about the importance of diagnoses before developing a marketing communications (marcoms) campaign. We then use the idea of communication barriers to help explain why creating an effective marcoms campaign is so challenging, before providing a broad understanding of what integrated marketing communications (IMC) is and why it is used.

The chapter discusses both the theory and practice of achieving integration and synergy, and how synergistic effects come about. The managerial application of integration is also discussed, and its complexity is brought to life with the award-winning case of 'Magnum Gold?!' This chapter also provides a nine-step IMC planning model, including the importance of understanding how consumers make decisions. The consumer decision journey is suggested as a useful model, illustrated with another award-winning case involving the Korean car maker Hyundai, which broke into the consideration set of United States (US) car buyers during the global financial crisis (GFC).

Learning goals

After reading this chapter, you will understand:

- the importance of diagnoses before developing a campaign
- what IMC is, why it is used and how to integrate it
- what communication barriers are
- what synergies are and their psychological explanations
- how to integrate campaigns and levels of integration
- the IMC planning process.

IS MARKETING COMMUNICATIONS THE ANSWER?

Before planning any campaign, a marcoms manager should ask whether a marketing communications campaign is really the solution that is needed. Often, the product may not be ready, the distribution may be inadequate, or the service may not be up to scratch. In fact, there might be a host of reasons why a manager may not necessarily need to start a marcoms program immediately. For instance, if the product is not ready, a great marcoms program can destroy the brand faster than if there were no campaign at all. We often say 'nothing kills a bad product faster than a great campaign' – a gentle reminder to always step back and study the situation before starting the campaign.

Or consider the case of two brands of potato chips. Both brands may be of equal quality and price, and equally well known (i.e. similar level of brand awareness), but somehow one brand consistently outsells the other. If this is the case, then it is likely that this brand has better distribution and not because it has superior value or awareness. Under such circumstances, it may be more efficient for the competing brand to improve distribution *first* before embarking on a marcoms campaign. In fact, a marcoms campaign may *not* be necessary, especially if marcoms is not the cause of poor sales. Figure 1.1 suggests starting with diagnosis before developing strategies and tactics. In chapter 2 (uncovering insights), we will learn more about diagnosis.

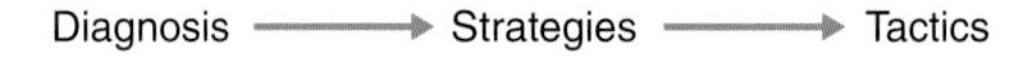

Figure 1.1 Three fundamental steps in planning a campaign

Assuming there are no other problems with the marketing mix, and the solution is solely communication based, there are a host of other challenges to be considered.

THE CHALLENGE: OVERCOMING COMMUNICATION BARRIERS

A communications campaign may fail for many reasons. Communication barriers may impede our acceptance of the message (implicitly or explicitly) and so decrease the probability that we will buy the brand. Figure 1.2 shows some of the major communication barriers we need to overcome.

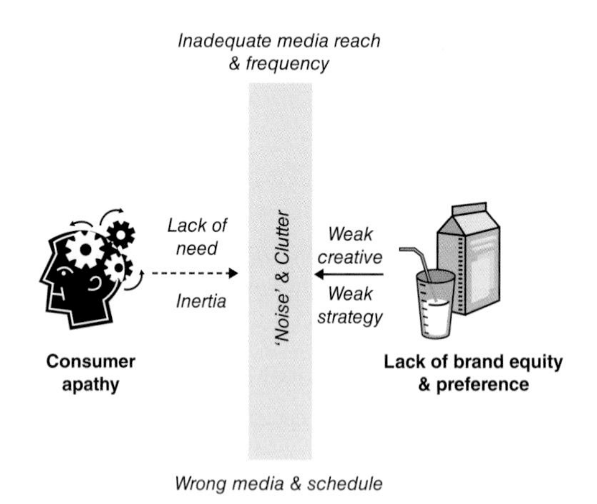

Figure 1.2 Barriers to marketing communications

Noise and clutter

The terms 'noise' and 'clutter' refer to two major communication barriers. Noise is any ambient stimulus (e.g. a radio playing or people chatting) that distracts attention from the message. Clutter, on the other hand, refers to the sheer number of ads we see in the media or in our environment. Competitive clutter (such as another brand's advertising or promotion) creates memory interference.[1]

Consumer apathy

Another major challenge for any marcoms campaign is overcoming the apathy of the target audience. There are a number of reasons why consumers may be apathetic.[2] First, they may simply not be interested (i.e. they are not really 'in the market') or they may be too busy (we all lead busy lives), and so consumers tend to filter out excess environmental stimuli while they concentrate on activities more closely aligned to their goals. In other words, they exhibit selective attention and will only 'tune in' if they find something of interest in the content.

Second, even if a consumer is in the market, they may not be aware of the brand; that is, they may have no 'brand awareness'. We are brand aware when a brand comes to mind when thinking of a product category. People tend to buy brands they know, and they buy out of habit. If this is the case, it is necessary to get the new brand into their evoked set (a list of brands we recall when we think of a product category; in other words, a mental 'shortlist').

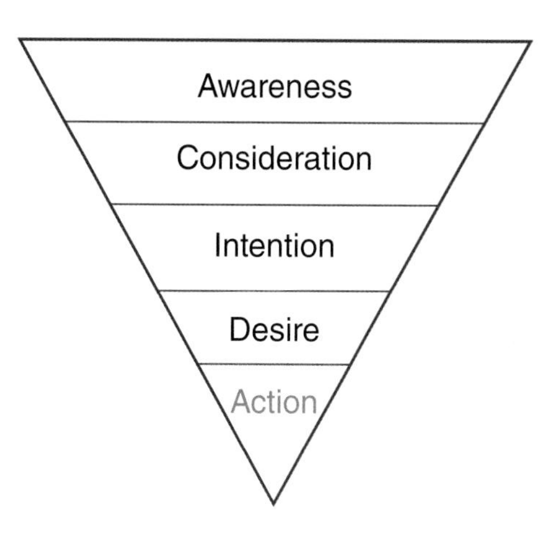

Figure 1.3 Sales funnel

Third, even if people are aware, there may not be enough incentive to drive them to want to take the next step. In marketing, this is often called the 'sales funnel' (see figure 1.3). Many barriers can impede the movement from awareness down the funnel towards action or sales. For instance, people may misunderstand the benefit and never consider the brand, they may fail to translate their intention to desire because it is too difficult to buy, or they may fail to translate desire to action (purchase) because it is too expensive. Good quantitative research can reveal the percentage of the target audience who fall into each of these bands (in comparison with competitors), and the reasons why translation down the funnel fails to occur. In chapter 4, we will revisit this funnel and see how it can be 'reverse-engineered' when developing a media plan.

Brand parity

Brand parity is another significant communication barrier. Brand parity means that a brand is not differentiated from its competition, leading consumers to develop no brand preference and, thus, buy based on price. The aim of marcoms, especially in relation to advertising, is to build a predisposition in consumers so that brand preference and ultimately brand equity will develop over time (see chapter 3). This involves building brand strength (knowledge and esteem) and brand stature (differentiation and relevance).

Weak creative ideas or strategies

The barriers described so far present a major challenge to the advertiser. Given the apathy of consumers, the clutter and noise in the environment, and the dangers of brand parity, advertisers have no choice but to ensure that their creative ideas and selling strategies are second to none.

These barriers, while considerable, are not insurmountable if the right solutions are applied. But there is yet another challenge, and that is the ever-increasing complexity of the business environment. This is where IMC can help.

WHAT IS IMC AND WHY DO WE NEED IT?

There are many definitions of IMC.[3] In this text, we adopt the following definition:

> IMC is defined as a research-based, audience-focused, result-driven communication planning process that aims to execute a brand communication program over time so that there is clarity and consistency in the positioning of the brand. This is achieved by coordinating different communication tools and channels and integrating multiple pieces of creative content across different media in order to create synergistic effects. The aim is to achieve short-term financial gain and long-term brand equity.[4]

Although this definition is long, it covers several key points a marcoms manager should know in order to develop an effective marcoms program.

First, IMC is a planning process rather than a concept. It aims to achieve a coordinated execution of a marcoms program. This means much thinking must be done up-front. Second, the communication tools chosen for an IMC campaign – for example, advertising, direct response, sales promotion, marketing-oriented public relations (PR), sponsorship and content marketing – must complement each other, so that the strength of one tool makes up for the weakness of another.

Third, IMC must be supported by research, and not guesswork. This means using diagnostics or other forms of research to help increase the probability of success. Fourth, it must take the target audience into consideration. This means understanding their decision process, motivations for buying (or not buying) and their media usage habits.

Fifth, it must be results-driven, which entails being accountable and ensuring a fair return on investment (ROI). Sixth, it must aim for clarity and consistency in the 'look, feel and voice'[5] of the brand over time, so that there is no confusion in people's minds. This demands clear and consistent brand positioning across all communication content. If there is a campaign, then it must also be consistent with the creative idea of the campaign.

Seventh, the media channel and creative content must support each other in this endeavour to create synergistic effects (to be discussed later). This means that the creative content must be appropriate for the medium and the use of multiple pieces of content geared to achieve a synergistic effect. All of these must also support the communication tool employed so that there is a seamless brand experience.

Several studies have shown that having an IMC orientation is correlated with market performance.[6] Generally, the more different channels used, the more effective the campaign.[7] For instance, a television-led campaign achieves the highest ROI (+126%) when combined with digital and outdoor (see figure 1.4).[8] However, there are downsides to IMC too. Consumers complain there are too many advertisements and less than half of the campaigns (46%) are well integrated and customised to the channel or device.[9]

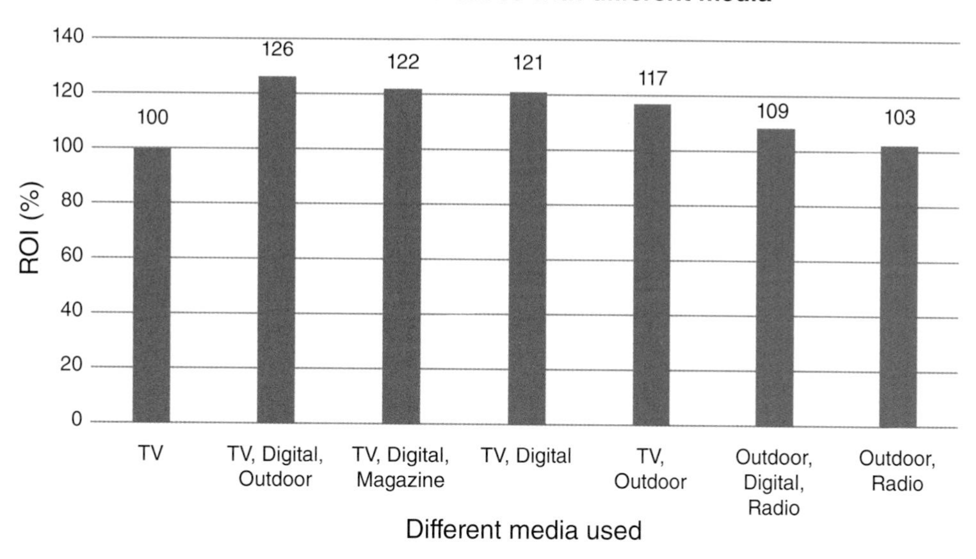

Figure 1.4 Synergistic effects of different media combinations

Now that we know what IMC is, we can consider when it should be used. IMC is only needed when there is complexity, which may come from having:

- many communication tools (sales promotions, direct marketing, personal selling and so on)
- many brand touch points
- more than one target audience
- more than one message to be communicated
- target audiences that habitually use different media
- different geographical areas to target
- the need for trade support.

IMC is generally more relevant for large businesses because of its complexity. However, with the growing number of channels and technology, small businesses may also take a leaf out of the IMC playbook. Take the example of brand contact points. Today, a customer can contact an organisation (small or large) in a range of ways, from a simple telephone call to a message sent through the brand's social media pages. Further, customers have all this literally at their fingertips, using their smartphones. With the advent of voice assistance, a simple voice command (e.g. 'Hello Alexa') is all that is needed to send a message, search the internet, schedule an event, play music, and control the devices in your home. As communication technologies expand, more coordination of activities will be needed even for a small business.

What are synergistic effects?

One of the hallmarks of IMC is to create synergistic effects, which are the incremental effects above and beyond the expected summative effects. We can illustrate this with a simple mathematical example. For instance, when we add 1+1, we expect the total to be 2. But if we get a total of 3, then there is an incremental effect. This is called positive synergy where the total is more than the sum of its parts.

There is no guarantee, however, that the interactive effects will always be positive. One study into four fast-moving consumer goods in Europe found that when advertising and company-sponsored word of mouth (WOM) activities are simultaneously deployed (see buzz agents in chapter 8), the effectiveness of the latter actually dropped.[10] This means that advertising has interacted negatively with WOM, decreasing its effectiveness. In fact, for every 1% increased spend on advertising, WOM equivalent effectiveness in increasing sales decreased by between 0.6% and 2.3%. Generally, when the expected summative effects are reduced, antergy (i.e. 1 + 1 = 1.5)[11] is said to occur (see also the Further Thinking section later in this chapter).

Ideally, we want the interactions to be positively synergistic. This means when different channels (or communication tools) are used in a campaign, the effects are stronger than when only one channel (or communication tool) is used. For instance, when an internet display ad is combined with search advertising, the sales for a retailer climbed by 199%. On the other hand, use of the internet display ad alone increased sales by only 16% and use of search advertising alone by 82%.[12] Another study into a retailer for home improvement shows that shifting the radio advertising to the same week as when exhibitions are held or when there is heavy advertising generated 891 *additional* leads, 548 *more* appointments and 140 *extra* sales for the retailer.[13]

Since positive synergistic effects are never guaranteed, the IMC manager *must* always evaluate the interactive effects of the various channels (or communication tools) campaign (see chapter 12). Only then can one be confident that an optimal mix is achieved.

Explanations of synergy

Why then does synergy work? What is the underlying process that causes synergy? The following are some psychological explanations.[14]

1. Encoding variability – when a message is seen in a different context (e.g. channels or creative asset), consumers may form different memory traces or pathways for easier retrieval later.
2. Central processing – when a message is seen in different variants across channels, consumers are more likely to pay attention and think more deeply about it.
3. Forward interest encoding – the message in one channel primes or arouses interest or curiosity in the brand for consumers when it is subsequently exposed in a different channel.
4. Mental playback – the message in one channel (e.g. radio ad) triggers a mental playback because consumers remember a related message in another channel (e.g. related television (TV) ad).
5. Multiple source credibility – when consumers see a message from different sources, the information is perceived to be more credible because the sources are thought to be independent.
6. Financially healthy perception – when a brand is advertised across different channels, consumers see the brand as financially fit and strong.[15]

Synergy is therefore a complex psychological effect. This is not to be confused with the notion of extended reach. In IMC, different channels often are used to reach different segments of the market, leading to extended reach. Figure 1.5 illustrates this notion. For instance, with TV alone, one can reach 60% of the target audience, but by including radio and newspaper, one might increase the reach to 70%. There may be audience overlap, but it is the non-overlapping audience that extends the reach.

However extended reach does not create synergy. This is because extended reach is about reaching more *unique* audiences, while synergy is about getting the *same* audience to be exposed to the same message (or its variant) in different channels. In other words, synergistic effects can only come from the overlapping of media (see bubbles in figure 1.5).

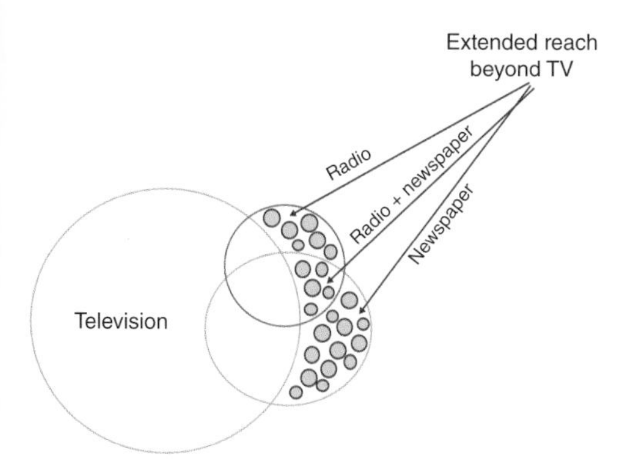

Figure 1.5 Using additional channels, like radio and newspaper, extends the reach beyond TV

How do you integrate?

According to the English Oxford dictionary, the word integration is derived from the Latin word *integrat*, meaning to 'make whole'. In IMC, this means combining different communication tasks to fulfil the communication objectives. IMC planning involves five tactical components: (1) select complementary marcoms tools; (2) select channels to maximise affordable reach; (3) create a consistent 'look, feel and voice'; (4) develop amazing, shareable content; and (5) synchronise activities.[16] We will now discuss each of these tactics in greater detail.

1. SELECT MARCOMS TOOLS WITH A CLEAR ROLE AND COMPLEMENTARY STRENGTHS

Different tools tend to have different strengths. Depending on the communication objectives, investment should only be in those that have a clear role to play. For instance, if the objective is to sell new products which require the use of moving images and sound, then the use of an electronic dynamic medium like TV or online video may be more suitable than say radio or print. An electronic medium, however, may be poor in closing purchase, which can be compensated by including a sales promotion using a print medium (e.g. promotion brochure). Each communication tool (i.e. dynamic videos and sales promotion) must have a clear role to play.

2. SELECT COMMUNICATION CHANNELS THAT MAXIMISE AFFORDABLE REACH

Regardless of the communications forms chosen, one must still try to get the selling message to the target audience as efficiently as possible. Since many communication channels are available, the critical question is how to achieve maximum reach within an affordable budget. Trade-offs may have to be made. If, for instance, one cannot afford TV as the primary channel, even if it has excellent reach and the communication form is ideal (i.e. dynamic video to sell a new product), then this communication channel is out. One then chooses the next best affordable media option (or some combination thereof), subject to its ability to support the communication objectives discussed above.

However, it should be noted that when a combination of media is used, the extended reach with the added secondary channels may not be substantial. One study across nine countries in the alcoholic beverage category found that 60% of the target audience in the second channel is duplicated. This is quite a substantial duplication. This means if a campaign were to be successful, primary reach cannot be ignored. In fact, the authors went on to argue that the reach of the *primary* channel used in the campaign is probably the most important factor in any multi-channel campaign.[17]

3. STRIVE FOR CONSISTENT 'LOOK, FEEL AND VOICE' ACROSS ALL CHANNELS

At a very basic level, integration means ensuring all the communication collaterals (including touch points) have the same look, feel and voice. This means at the very minimum all communication content should have the same brand cues (e.g. brand logo, brand name, slogan, corporate colour and sound effects). This should always be the case even if there is no active campaign so that the brand image will be consistent across all touch points.

When there is a campaign, however, something else is added other than the brand cues, and that is a selling message. Here, every piece of content should be amazing, but still coherently linked together in selling the brand. A simple way is to use similar cues across multiple executions. This can be the music, a scene from an ad, a colour scheme, a character, a motif or symbol and so forth. A good example is the Budweiser campaign in China. The selling message is 'This Bud's for you', and the campaign features Eason Chan, a popular Chinese singer and actor. All the ads use similar cues including the use of electronic music (where possible). They all aim to convey the impression that Budweiser is a young, passionate and forward-looking beer. Another example is the Toyota Vitz campaign in Japan. All the executions including TV ads, online video, Instagram video, online banner and magazine play on the distinctive design and aesthetic features of the car. Having the same cues across multiple pieces of content is often called 'matching luggage', or cosmetic integration, which consumers seem to appreciate in a campaign.[18]

4. DEVELOP AMAZING, SHAREABLE CONTENT AND/OR CREATIVE ASSETS, CENTRED AROUND A WINNING CAMPAIGN IDEA

Besides having a consistent image, the integration should have amazing content. That way it is more likely to be shared. Even better, the content should include creative assets that the company owns. These are recognisable properties which can be deployed and customised for each channel (online or offline). It brands the content and makes the campaign more distinctive. For instance, Disney might have the target message that its new Disney Cruise Line is family-oriented, fun and value for money. Here, Disney may decide to use Mickey Mouse as a moniker in the launch campaign. The campaign might include TV advertising featuring Mickey Mouse followed two weeks later by radio advertising in the voice of Mickey Mouse. Simultaneously, Disney could run a nationwide price promotional offer (e.g. 15% introductory offer) using the image of Mickey Mouse for its downloadable e-brochure.[19]

But what if a company is yet to develop a suite of creative assets? One solution is to creatively weave the brand cues (e.g. brand logo, brand name, colour, slogan and packaging) into the message. Brand cues are distinctive codes the company owns and thus can still be exploited to make the ad distinctive. For instance, the Australian wine company '[yellow tail]' has a kangaroo as a logo. For its TV ad campaign in the US (see figure 1.6), it uses an animatronic kangaroo and a yellow-suited man to spruik the wine to great success (volume purchase jumped 19%).[20]

Figure 1.6 Brand cues (logo and brand name) can be weaved into a TV ad (left)

Yet another solution, which is more long term, is to develop new assets. For instance, in 2012, Melbourne Metro's safety campaign 'Dumb Ways to Die' created new assets using funny bean-like cartoon characters (see figure 6.28). The ad showed how these characters get killed performing dangerous activities (e.g. setting fire to your hair). Set to a catchy tune with hilarious lyrics, the campaign quickly became a worldwide sensation, with 350 million views on YouTube. Having created these memorable assets, Melbourne Metro then developed various games around the theme of train safety using the same characters and humour as the original ad. These games have been downloaded 375 million times.[21] Creative assets that are recognisable and consistently used are far more effective in stimulating learning.[22]

Finally, always strive for a winning idea for the IMC campaign. Sometimes called the big idea, it is a unique and compelling way of selling the brand in a campaign (see chapter 6). Once the winning idea is found, different content can be developed around this idea in a single-minded fashion, with amazing multiple pieces of execution, each customisable for the selected channels. But all of these should be seamless – every piece of content counts toward the effectiveness of the integration.[23] This form of integration is therefore very strategic (see case study 1.1). We can call this strategic integration.

5. SYNCHRONISE ACTIVITIES TO ACHIEVE SYNERGY

Finally, synergy does not happen by accident. Activities must be coordinated between different parties to ensure that the campaign is run seamlessly and on time. This includes tactics like the overlapping of exposures, sequencing of exposures, interlinking of creative content/assets, cross-publicising of products and complements, and timeliness and support (see figure 1.8). All these synchronising tactics will be discussed in greater detail later under managerial applications.

CASE STUDY 1.1 MAGNUM GOLD?!

To illustrate the idea of integrating around a single-minded winning idea, consider the case of Magnum Gold ice-cream. When Unilever wanted to sell their limited edition Magnum Gold?! ice-cream in Europe, their advertising agency came up with an idea of a spoof trailer, called the Heist. Filmed like a Hollywood blockbuster movie (2.5 minutes), it starred celebrities Benicio Del Toro and Caroline Correa.[24]

Figure 1.7 The launch of Magnum Gold?! ice-cream starring two celebrities

It told the story of a couple planning to break into a high security vault and steal 75 million pieces of gold, except that in reality she played him because they were actually stealing Magnum Gold?! ice-creams. The teaser for this film was seeded on various entertainment sites and blogs before the TV launch and generated a great amount of buzz because of its unusual format (i.e. a spoof trailer). Real ads were also made showing a different side of this couple to fuel interest into their relationship. The launch was also supported by outdoor billboards. Furthermore, throughout the cities in Europe, armoured trucks and security vaults were used as street props to create curiosity.

For online activities, the agency created a special face-texturing feature that allowed consumers to superimpose their face in a video and customise the clip, which they could then share online. In terms of PR activities, there were competitions and special events where reporters (and a few consumers) met the glamorous couple, who were blowing up safes and dodging laser beams. The integrated campaign was a runaway success with Unilever selling €80 million worth of ice-cream, exceeding the target of €53.5 million.

DISCUSSION QUESTIONS

1. What was the theme of this campaign? Speculate what drove the advertising agency to come up with this creative idea.
2. Explain how the Magnum Gold?! campaign integrates around the target message.
3. Determine the ways in which the Magnum Gold?! campaign is simple and/or complex.

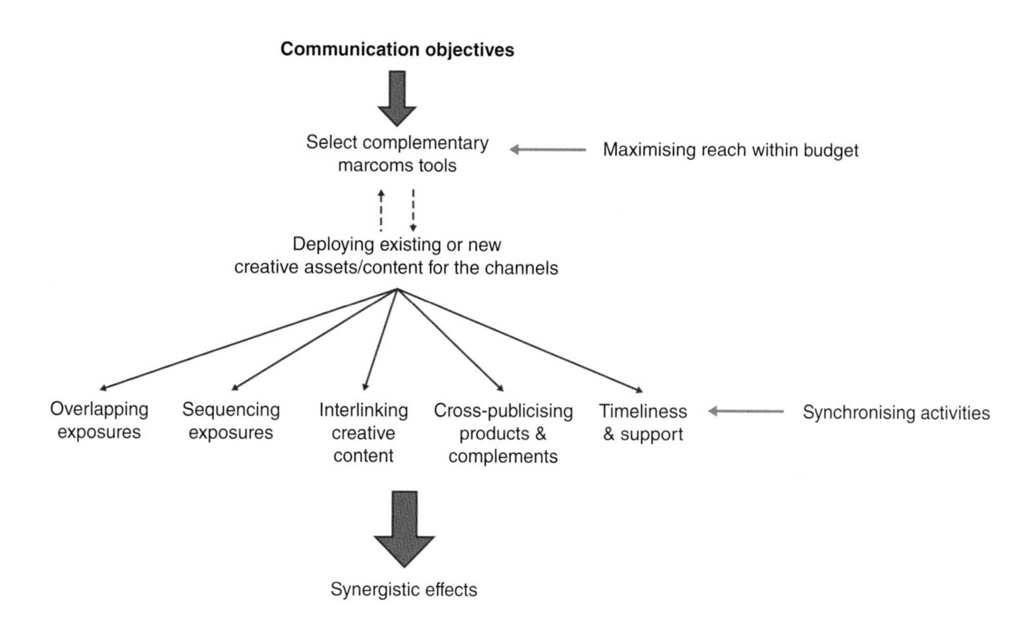

Figure 1.8 Summary of key managerial principles of integration

Thus, running an IMC campaign is a complex business. The deployment of existing or new creative content/assets must be tactically knitted properly to achieve synergy. This is an important point, because traditionally integration is simply to ensure that all the touch points have the same look, feel and voice for the brand (or company), often using the same ad or key visual. This form of integration is cosmetic in nature. More resources are required when a campaign involves numerous *different* creative content/assets (new or established), all strategically deployed in *different* channels, synchronising various activities to deliver the same message. This is far more complex than simply repeating the same ad in different channels (see case study 1.1).

Finally, for a company with a portfolio of products, selling to diverse groups of customers, multiple campaigns can be simultaneously carried out, each with different messages. In this situation, the integration is not around a single target message but rather around multiple messages using different subsets of the creative assets. For instance, a major airline may have a campaign in the Asia–Pacific with target message A, using four different creative content/assets integrated around message A. At the same time, the airline may also be running another campaign for South America with target message B, using a different set of creative content/assets. Here, it is more akin to an orchestration of diverse activities across two different campaigns. Such complexity may require the organisation to find multiple partners with different expertise to make the orchestration work smoothly. Figure 1.9 summarises the different levels of complexity in integration.

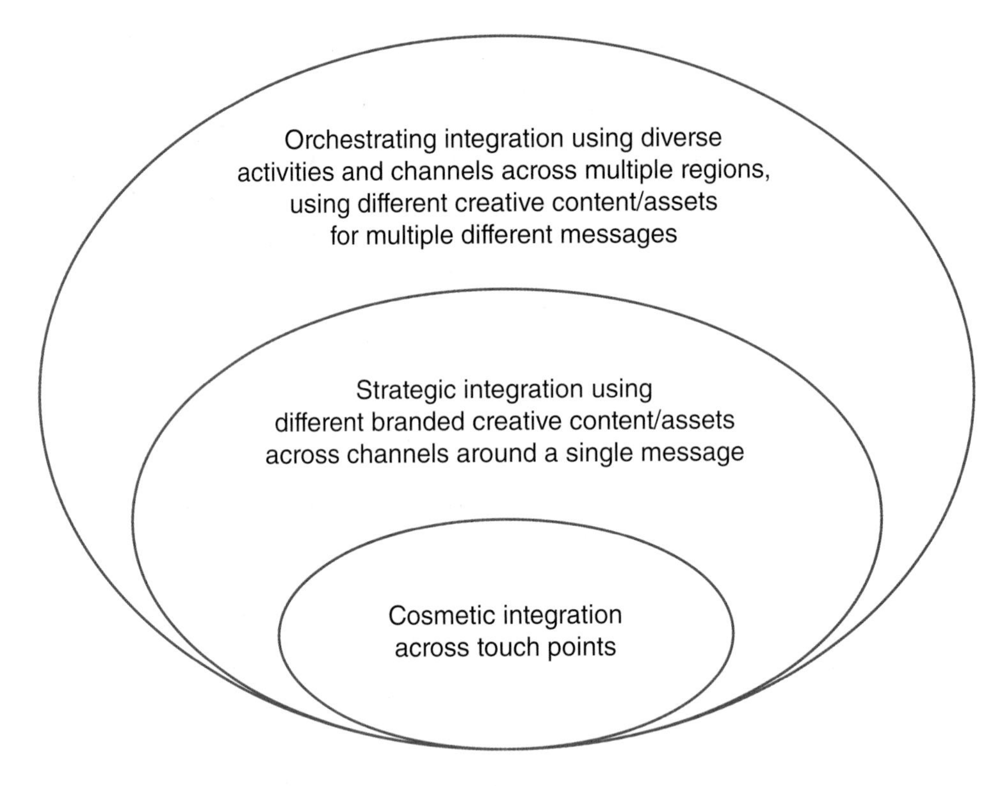

Figure 1.9 Different levels of complexity in integration

The IMC planning process[25]

How does one go about planning an IMC campaign? The process can be divided into nine steps, discussed over the next several pages. Figure 1.10 summarises the process.

1. UNDERSTAND THE BUSINESS ISSUES

The first step is to understand the business issues driving the campaign. An organisation will not embark on a campaign without a reason. The better we understand the business issues, the clearer the task becomes.[26] Usually, the business imperative revolves around increasing sales or addressing barriers that might be affecting sales. Here, the definition of one's market, its size and the target audience become important.

2. UNDERSTAND HOW DECISIONS ARE MADE BY THE TARGET AUDIENCE

Consumers do not buy capriciously. Usually, they are activated by some needs and wants. But once activated, we want to ensure that our brand will be considered. Now, unless it is a repeat

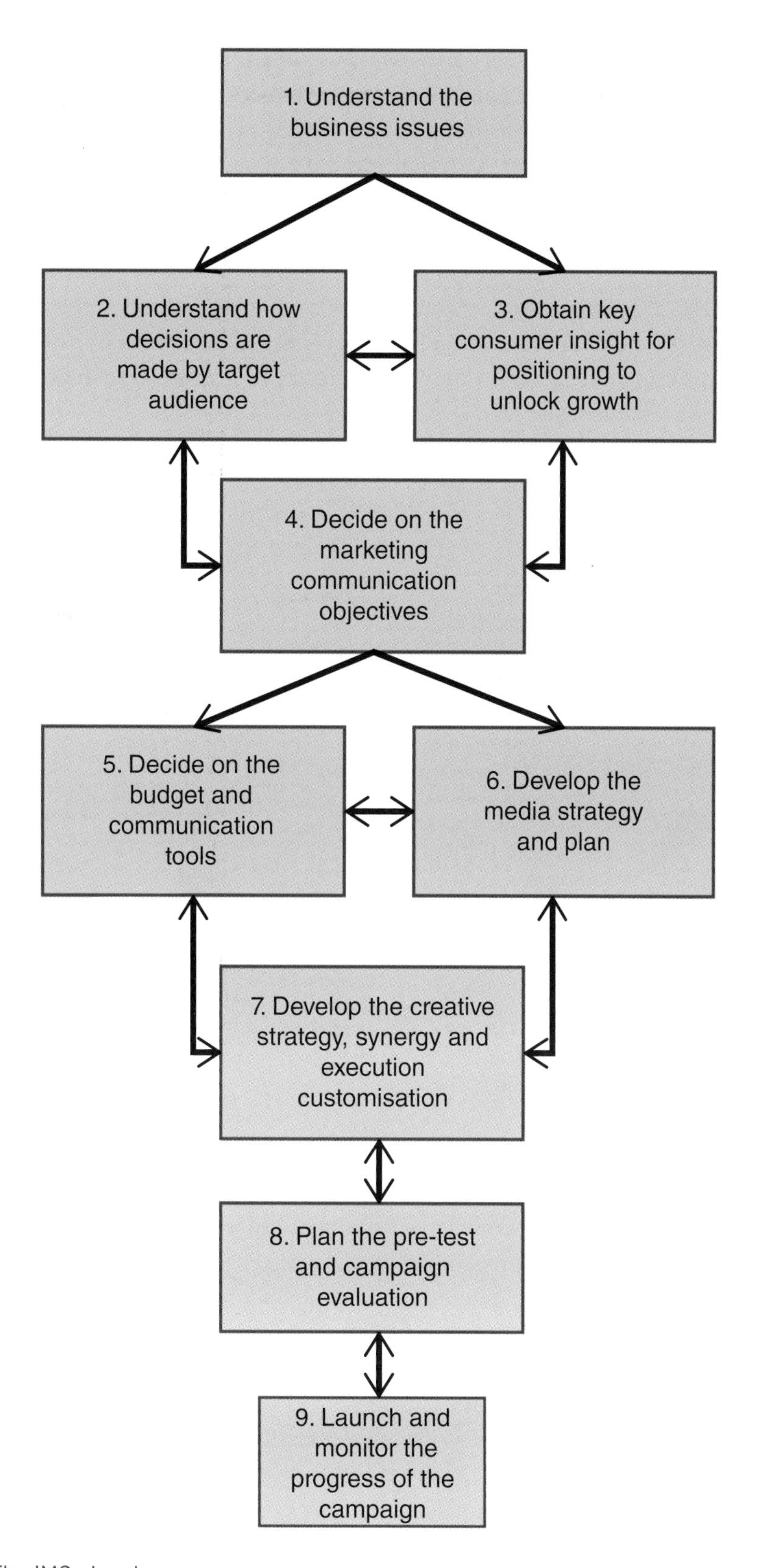

Figure 1.10 The IMC planning process

ASKHAM BRYAN
COLLEGE
LEARNING RESOURCES

purchase from a satisfied customer, a naïve consumer will search and evaluate the many competing brands available before deciding. So, one important source of competitive advantage is to give our customers a wonderful consumption and service experience. This should lead to more affection and bonding for the brand such that when it comes to repurchase and recommendation, our brand becomes the only brand for the target audience.

This is essentially the consumer decision journey. It is simply the end-to-end decision process consumers go through as they move from need activation to purchase and then repurchase of a brand. The consumer decision journey can be generalised into five stages: (1) need or want activation, (2) search and evaluation, (3) consideration, (4) purchase and (5) post-purchase and bonding. Figure 1.11 details what a consumer decision journey looks like.[27] It can be considered to be a more sophisticated version of the funnel.

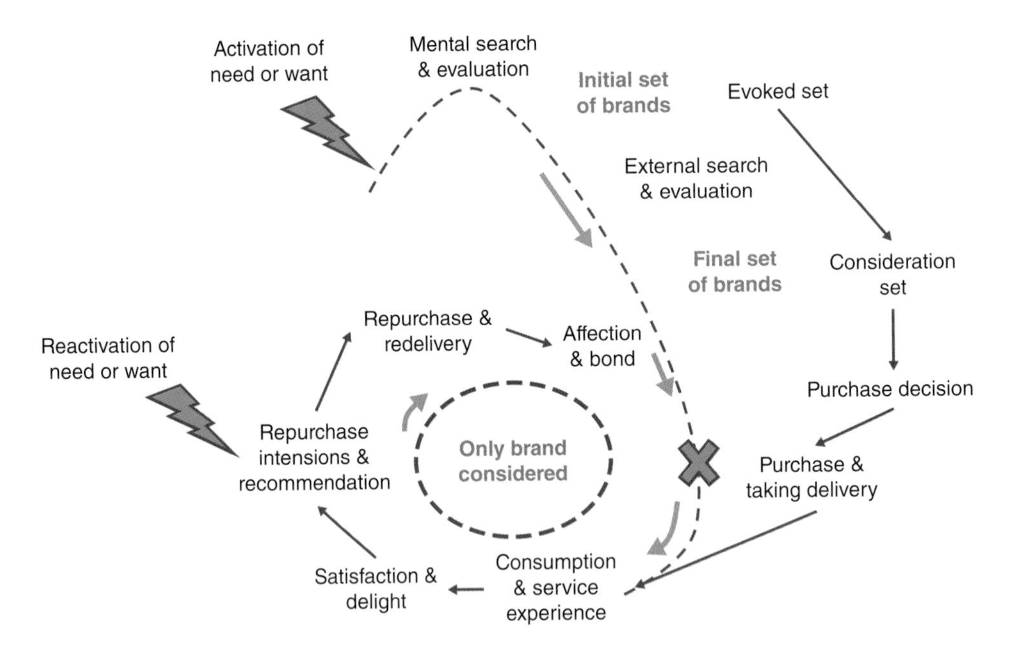

Figure 1.11 Consumer decision journey

The specifics of the journey will differ across product categories, consumer segments and mode of purchase. Every marcoms manager should know intimately how their different customer segments make their decisions and by what means. The data can then be translated into specific efficiency metrics, hence highlighting where the journey can be improved. For instance, one insurance study found that although people were aware of its brand, they tended to show little interest. Only a small percentage (7%) visited its website. Most went to the competitor's website (72%) or comparison websites (21%).[28]

As a general principle, to acquire new customers, marcoms activities should concentrate on the front end of the decision journey using channels that have wide reach; but for established customers, the activities tend to shift towards the back end of the journey using more focussed and targeted channels.

CASE STUDY 1.2 HOW HYUNDAI BROKE INTO THE CONSIDERATION SET OF US CAR BUYERS

During the GFC of 2008–2009, no one in the US was buying cars. This was expected as US consumers were gripped by the collapse of banks and financial institutions and increasing unemployment, so consumer confidence plunged. The US economy was in dire straits. Yet amidst this gloom, Hyundai managed to sell more cars than any other American car maker. Hyundai sales shot up 14%, while the entire US automobile industry dropped 37%! Its market share jumped from 3.1% in the first 10 months of 2009 to 4.3%. What is even more extraordinary is that Hyundai was not a well-known brand compared to, say, General Motors or Chrysler. So how did a poorly reputable Korean car brand, like Hyundai, become an automobile to be considered? The answer: improved product quality coupled with a bold marketing campaign.

When Hyundai first entered the US market in 1986 with a small car, Excel, quality was an issue. It took years of product improvement and hard work for Hyundai to catch up. But the turning point ironically happened during the GFC, when Hyundai managed to gain an unexpected advantage over their US rivals. During the GFC, sales dropped across the auto industry and Hyundai's initial advertising campaign in 2008, called 'Think Again', did not quite spark any excitement in the market-place. Then in January 2009, Hyundai launched the Hyundai Assurance program with its Genesis model, which allowed buyers to return the car even after using it for a year should they suddenly become unemployed. The voice-over said, 'Now finance or lease any new Hyundai, and if you lose your income in the next year, you can return it with no impact on your credit.'[29]

The campaign was launched with TV advertising during the 2009 Super Bowl game. There was also a second TV ad called 'Bosses', which touted Hyundai's Genesis being awarded the North American Car of the Year at the Detroit Auto Show – it showed German and Japanese car executives screaming at underlings because Genesis had just won the award. This was followed by nine spots during the Academy Awards; and Hyundai also agreed to sponsor and advertise in Fox's TV series, '24'. Those spots were vacated by General Motors and Ford, respectively, when they pulled out due to financial distress. But for Hyundai, the campaign was a resounding success; it caught the competitors flatfooted as they had all slashed their advertising budgets to stay afloat.[30] The TV campaign was also supported by online advertising with the headlines, 'We've got your back for one full year' and 'Assurance: certainty in uncertain times'. Besides being bold, Hyundai also displayed agility. From concept to advertising, the campaign only took 37 days to execute.[31]

The campaign succeeded because it showed that Hyundai cared about people.[32] It gave the American people comfort in troubling times. The press exposure and publicity that followed from the campaign was overwhelmingly positive. At the same time, the competitors were not advertising, which allowed Hyundai to better cut through the clutter with greater share of voice (see chapter 4). As a result, brand awareness of Hyundai jumped to 60% from 40% two years previously. Hyundai dealers also saw other makes being traded in for Hyundai Genesis, including Acuras, BMWs and Mercedes, a sure sign that Hyundai was eroding the equity of other brands. Consideration for Genesis also jumped to 59% in the first two months of 2009. Hyundai is now on the shopping list (i.e. consideration set) among US car buyers.

DISCUSSION QUESTIONS

1. What is the main lesson of this case in relation to competing on the consumer decision journey?
2. Why do you think Hyundai succeeded in getting into the consideration set of US car buyers even though they were in the midst of the GFC?
3. Since the assurance program was a runaway success, why do you think other car makers did not come up with the same idea first?

3. OBTAIN KEY CONSUMER INSIGHT FOR POSITIONING TO UNLOCK GROWTH

The objective here is to find a piece of information that can unlock growth for the brand. Typically, this means changing behaviour. If consumers are not buying (or are not buying enough), or in the case of social marketing not adopting a healthy lifestyle (e.g. quit smoking), there is a reason for their decision.

Study the success or failure of previous campaigns of the brand. Use the communication barrier framework (see figure 1.2) as a starting point. It will help trigger hypotheses for further investigation. Whenever possible, these hypotheses should be tested using marketing, attitudinal or behavioural data gleaned from databases or from previous studies; if necessary, commission new research to understand the situation better. This may include various aspects of the buying behaviour during the decision journey and the media usage habits of the target audience.

Changing behaviour often requires the target audience to think and feel differently about the brand. Therefore, any new insight that can be discovered (see chapter 2) will be beneficial.

4. DECIDE ON THE MARKETING COMMUNICATION OBJECTIVES

The marketing plan, which cascades down from higher corporate goals, guides communication objectives. The communication objectives should be measurable, linked to target market segments and achievable within a defined time period and geographical area.

Figure 1.12 shows that the objectives can take many forms. For instance, they can be:

- need- or category-oriented (e.g. activating a need)
- brand-oriented (e.g. increasing brand awareness)
- social-oriented (e.g. stimulating social media conversations)
- pre-purchase-oriented (e.g. generating enquiries)
- purchase-oriented (e.g. encouraging trial or repeat purchase)
- post-purchase-oriented (e.g. recommending to others).

The ultimate goal in most commercial situations is to stimulate purchase.

In advertising, where the charter is to build brands, objectives oriented around those brands take precedence. Of these, the most important is brand awareness, along with brand differentiation, if the brand is new.

Brand awareness allows the target audience to link the brand to the product category. For example, if we are in the personal computer (PC) hardware business, our target audience should be able to recall or recognise our brand (such as Dell) when they think of a PC. Brand differentiation, on the other hand, means that the target audience should think that our brand is different or unique. For a new product this is very important. Of course, whether a brand is new or

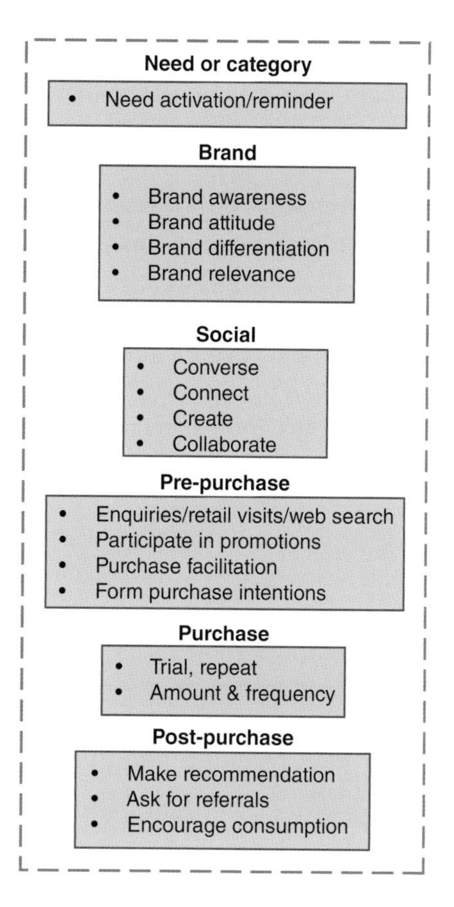

Figure 1.12 Marketing communications objectives

established, it is always good to be well regarded (brand attitude) and important in customers' lives (brand relevance).[33]

For established brands, sometimes the objective is to create a community using social media, in which case the focus of the creative content will be about encouraging community to converse and connect with each other around a targeted message or to create or collaborate with each other on a project. Many social marketing campaigns use this tactic. (See case study 8.2 on the Singapore Quit Smoking campaign).

Although the marketing plan dictates what the communication objectives should be, it should be guided by what we learn about from the consumer decision journey (end to end). For instance, if we learn that recommendation is an important source of acquiring new customers, but our established customers are not doing enough of this, then this should be quickly rectified and 'recommending a friend' now should become an important objective for the campaign.

5. DECIDE ON THE BUDGET AND COMMUNICATION TOOLS

The next step is to decide which communication tools can best deliver the communication objectives. For example, choose sales promotion or direct mail if the objective is behaviour-oriented (see chapter 10). The tools selected will be constrained by the budget, which is often imposed by higher management. Very often using marketing-oriented PR, or sponsorship, or content marketing with social media can be cost effective (see chapters 8 and 9).

6. DEVELOP THE MEDIA STRATEGY AND PLAN

All the planning will come to nought if we cannot get the message to our target audience. The principle here is to choose a medium that the target audience uses most frequently. This is the primary medium. For example, if the target audience spends much time on social media (e.g. Facebook, Instagram), then this medium would be ranked first. Then choose a secondary medium that the target audience uses the next most frequently, and so on.

Although this principle seems logical, it must be tempered by whether the media can also deliver on the desired communication objectives. For instance, social media may afford vast reach, but it has not been found to be effective in stimulating brand-related communication among friends (see chapter 8). Perhaps in time, this will change with the deployment of more effective social communication tools. Thus, more than just understanding the media consumption habits of our target audience, one has to ask if such habits can aid in fulfilling the desired communication objectives.

In developing a media strategy, one should also consider the timing of the campaign. The purchase of goods and services can be influenced by seasonality, so it is important to plan when the campaign will start. For instance, if one-third of all chocolates are bought during the lead-up to Christmas and Easter, then the campaign should start in time for that. All the stages of the planning should work back from the launch date.

7. DEVELOP THE CREATIVE STRATEGY, SYNERGY AND EXECUTION CUSTOMISATION

Once the date of the launch for the marcoms campaign is known, creative work can be scheduled to begin. It is important to set aside enough time to develop and execute the creative work (such as an ad, point-of-sale material or brochure and sales presentation).

The aim is to develop multiple pieces of amazing content that can effectively communicate the target message in a synergistic way, discussed above. The execution must always be customised. For instance, if it is decided that an app is to be used with the campaign, then it must be compatible with all mobile phone platforms. Steps 5, 6 and 7 are probably the most complex because they interact with each other, which is why they have double-arrows to each other in the IMC planning process. For instance, very often the budget is imposed by higher management and one must work within this limit.

However, if the campaign idea is good, extra resources can be negotiated. Alternatively, new solutions can be found which may turn out to be just as effective. For instance, media agencies are now becoming as creative as traditional advertising agencies because of the growth in technology and availability of media-related spend information (see chapter 5).

8. PLAN THE PRE-TEST AND CAMPAIGN EVALUATION

This step is relevant to accountability and should not be overlooked. Regular evaluation of campaigns also helps build a learning organisation. Figure 1.13 suggests that by planning (P), executing (E), evaluating (E), and learning (L) from each campaign, a marcoms manager will become smarter.[34] This is known as the PEEL cycle and it is an important principle because by using data we can refine our assumptions about human behaviour, which makes us more knowledgeable over time.

Evaluation involves pre-testing the communication collateral (e.g. TV ads) as well as tracking the effectiveness of its deployment in the field. Pre-testing means evaluating whether the creative

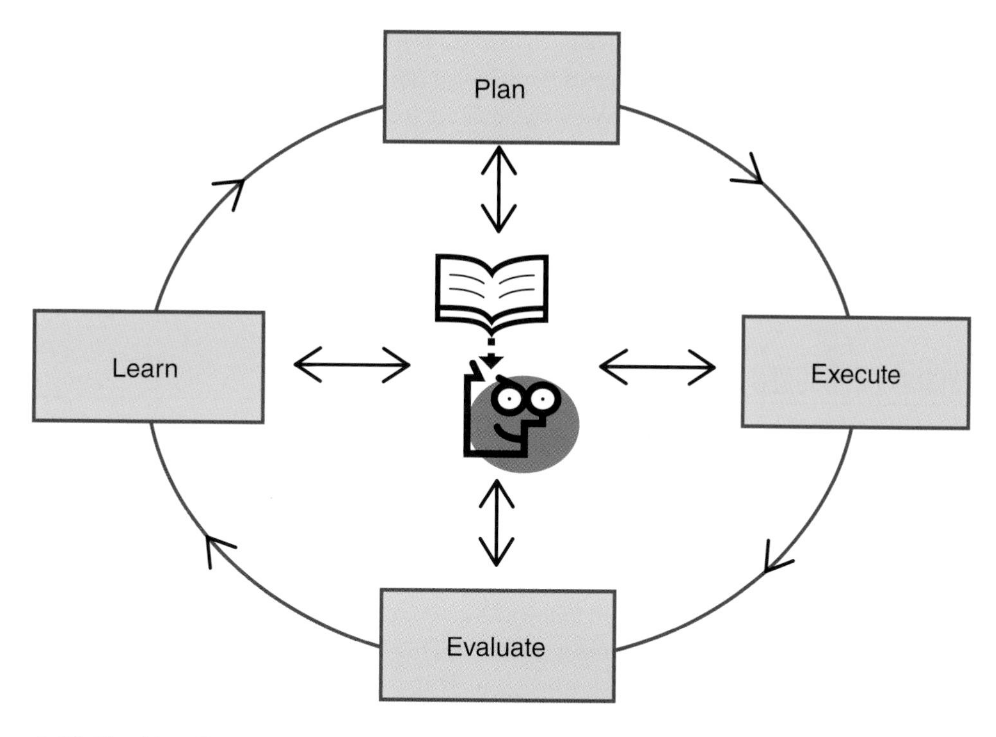

Figure 1.13 The Plan-Execute-Evaluate-Learn (PEEL) cycle

work is effective in communicating the desired message before committing more resources to it. This usually means producing a rough finish of the creative work and then getting unbiased reaction to it. For a campaign that involves substantial media spend – for example, TV advertising – pre-testing of the ad is quite a formal process involving large numbers of participants. Tracking the campaign means evaluating whether the progress of the campaign is delivering the objectives. If it is not progressing well, in-field adjustments can be made. Return on investment should be calculated (chapter 12). Finally, since it takes time to plan a campaign evaluation (e.g. to design a questionnaire or recruit a sample), it is important that evaluation is allowed for in the planning phase.

9. LAUNCH AND MONITOR THE PROGRESS OF THE CAMPAIGN

The campaign launch is often quite exciting because it marks the beginning of the battle for the minds and wallets of our target audience.

MANAGERIAL APPLICATION: PUTTING IT TOGETHER

How does one go about creating synergy, the cornerstone of IMC? The following tactics are recommended: overlapping exposures, sequencing exposures, interlinking creative content, cross-publicising of products and complements, and timeliness and support (see figure 1.8).

OVERLAPPING EXPOSURES

Synergy essentially requires an exposure from a minimum of two different pieces of content. This means, during the campaign, the exposure from two different creative assets must overlap. For instance, the campaign may involve TV and radio advertising. The radio advertisement may use some of the audio track of the TV ad, so that when consumers listen to the radio ad (after seeing the TV ad), the audio track will create a mental replay of the TV ad. This makes the audience less critical of the radio ad because it is now more involving.[35]

Generally, overlapping of exposures increases the probability of seeing another variation of the message, but in a different context. This encourages learning and elaborative processing, and the target audience is less likely to get bored. Hence seeing variation is important. If there is no variation, attention and learning are less likely to occur.[36]

SEQUENCING EXPOSURES

Sequencing exposures refers to the order in which the different pieces of content are exposed. This is important because some sequence of exposure may be more persuasive than others. For instance, one study found that it is more effective to run a PR campaign for a tourist resort *before* advertising it because the PR campaign gives the subsequent advertising more credibility.[37] Yet another study found that for high-involvement goods (e.g. smartphones), the message is more trustworthy and the ad more likeable, if the sequence of exposure is an internet ad followed by a TV ad rather than the reverse. One explanation is that showing the internet ad first encourages consumers to engage in more detailed evaluation, which is effective in reducing risk for high-involvement goods.[38,39]

Sequencing of exposure is trackable if the creative assets are digital in nature. For instance, when Adidas launched its soccer boots called Nemeziz, it decided to use several videos to showcase the new product, but in a controlled sequential manner.[40] For those who searched for this product online, Adidas could reliably track those who had watched the initial long-form video (more than three mins) featuring soccer stars on YouTube. This was the first long-form 'hero' piece related to this new product. (They could also track those who had skipped.) For those who watched this initial video, they were then showed a shorter six-second unskippable video about the product, followed by another long-form hero piece (about 46 seconds), then a 30-second product ad, and finally back to the six-second product video. This sequence of controlled video exposure among those who showed an initial interest lifted their product interest by 317%.

INTERLINKING CREATIVE CONTENT

Interlinking means using one creative content to direct attention to another. For instance, at the end of a TV ad, the URL can appear on screen to encourage viewers to visit the brand's website. Similarly, the brand's website can host an online video which viewers can click. Such linkages encourage the target audience to have multiple viewings of different creative assets which helps enforce the selling message.

One can see the same tactic applied in content marketing (see chapter 9), where one might start with a big hero piece which can be broken down into smaller pieces of content but distributed to different channels. For instance, if a nutritionist is interested in helping people reduce obesity, she might research and write a piece of content about this problem. This hero piece can appear on her website, but parts of it can be distributed to other channels (e.g. magazine, newspapers and other affiliated websites), encouraging readers to make contact with her through her website.

This interlinking tactic can also apply to old creative assets. Sometimes old content can be recycled and linked together to form a new campaign. When BMW wanted to communicate that its pre-owned

BMW could be as good as the new ones, they ran a campaign using old BMW ads – those that launched a particular model years ago. A new voice-over was added to say that 'a pre-owned BMW (of that model) can be as good as the new one if it is serviced by a certified BMW engineer'. Therefore, like an old ad being refurbished to become a new ad, a pre-owned BMW could also be refurbished to run like a new BMW. The TV ad ends with a tag line, 'Certified BMW – Like New Again'. The advertising agency went through five years' worth of BMW ads, including those on TV, radio, billboards, and social media tweets to create a new integrated campaign for less than the cost of a standard TV ad.[41]

CROSS-PUBLICISING OF PRODUCTS AND COMPLEMENTS

Interlinking is easier if there are complementary products to sell. For instance, instead of having a campaign for a single product (e.g. a ham), why not have a campaign that features a range of products (e.g. hams, sausages and bacon). Thus, instead of telling one story for one product, we can now tell multiple stories for different products yet linked together under the same theme. This is exactly what Denny, the Irish manufacturer of meat products, did with their 'Taste of Home' campaign. It showed a series of vignettes (of real stories) of how the Irish people live – like preparing for a wedding, mothers at home with their children, family around a breakfast table. This clever approach enabled Denny to sell a range of products across different occasions leveraging on the common theme of 'being home' regardless of where the Irish person might be. The campaign won a marketing effectiveness award.[42]

Yet another possibility is to consider whether a product is divisible. When the US rap artist Jay-Z launched his autobiography, he employed an agency to help him.[43] Instead of just using a straight campaign, the agency came up with an idea of a scavenger hunt using an online game. It was publicised using TV, Facebook, billboards, bus shelters and Twitter, but non-media sites like restaurants and swimming pools were also used, which is unusual. The following is how the campaign worked.

Each day, a single page of the book was released in different locations around the world but was chosen carefully to correspond with some content on the page. For instance, the page that talked about Jay-Z's restaurant was printed on a particular restaurant menu. Clues of these pages were revealed daily through social media, and participants could search for these using Microsoft's Bing search engine. The participant who could assemble the whole book digitally would win two lifetime passes to all of Jay-Z's concerts. The campaign worked brilliantly, and the book debuted at number three in the *New York Times* best-seller list. It generated one billion media impressions and returned twice the amount invested. It also helped Microsoft establish Bing as a search engine (in competition to Google).

TIMELINESS AND SUPPORT

This refers to the actual time in which the message delivery is made and how the message can be supported with other activities. This is important because without support, the effects of synergy will be lost. For instance, one study into fashion[44] found that internet shopping is highest on Mondays, and this was more likely to occur during the evenings (after 8 p.m.). Furthermore, desktop devices were more likely to be used during weekdays. However, on weekends, smartphones were the preferred devices when consumers were on the go. Knowing which day and time your online store is being visited will help you time the message delivery and use the correct platform. For instance, interactive videos will be more effective for desktop when consumers are more likely to shop on weekdays (especially Mondays) but less so for mobile phones (during weekends). This knowledge helps synchronise other supporting activities like employing more staff and other associated activities at the right time.

TIMING IS FATALLY CRITICAL

In this chapter, we discussed the concepts of integration and the orchestration of activities in a campaign. During a health crisis the timing of such executions is critical. For instance, even after COVID-19 was confirmed by Chinese scientists on 4 January 2020,[45] many governments around the world still did not take the disease seriously, sending mixed messages about herd immunity, mask wearing, closing of schools, border control, social distancing, mass gathering and lockdowns. Much of the dithering was due to ignorance, uncertainty, conflicting priorities, incompetence, and the fear of attracting bad publicity[46] (see also chapter 9 on PR).

But even if one is decisive, effective orchestration must still follow. In this regard, the Taiwanese government was exemplary, implementing no less than 124 measures as early as 20 January.[47] (Note: Taiwan had the lowest infection growth rate in the world at this point in time.) A National Epidemic Command Centre was activated which oversaw all inter-ministerial coordination. Nation-wide, the health care system was boosted (e.g. increase in personal protective equipment, testing stations and regimes). This was supported by a hotline to aid the reporting of cases. At the same time, a smartphone application was created to help publicise the availability of masks in pharmacies nationwide. Leveraging on the power of big data analytics, the government also integrated national health insurance data with that of immigration and the travel history of suspect individuals, followed by aggressive contact tracing of those who might be infected and, if so, they were quickly isolated.[48] The key was to lower the infectivity rate (see also chapter 2 on insight and chapter 13 on the application of artificial intelligence).

At the same time, public education with regards to social distancing, handwashing, wearing of masks, measuring of body temperature, and home quarantine were carried out, using different creative assets to convey these messages on TV, radio and social media (see also chapter 5 on digital and non-digital integration). The simplest was the use of print to explain the different preventive measures.[49] There were also daily press updates and regular press conferences given by the vice president, Chen Chien-jen, to instil public confidence and promote transparency in the government's decision-making. The fact that Chen is a well-known epidemiologist made him credible and hence persuasive (see also chapter 7 on credibility and chapter 10 on persuasion).

On the social media front, punitive measures for spreading misinformation about COVID-19 were also implemented[50] (see also chapter 8 on social influence). At the same time, the Ministry of Health and Welfare collaborated with LINE, a popular smartphone application (like WhatsApp), to produce chatbots for their website to help disseminate official information (e.g. travel restriction).[51] The government also leveraged popular cartoon-like characters or stickers to help increase interest.

In times of crisis, coordination becomes extremely complex. Here, the application of IMC principles takes on a special urgency – its successful orchestration can mean the difference between life and death.

FURTHER THINKING: PROCESSING EFFECTS

This section provides a theoretical overview of processing effects in the context of marcoms and its managerial application.

LEARNING GOALS

After reading this section, you will understand:

- processing effects and its relationship to managerial input.

A THEORETICAL FRAMEWORK OF PROCESSING EFFECTS

A marcoms campaign should have a theoretical framework of processing (with inputs and outputs), as shown in figure 1.14. The first step is to figure out which communication tools (such as advertising, personal selling or other communication tools) are the most appropriate for a campaign, based on one's objectives and how they can best be coordinated. Then, depending on the decisions made, the next decision is to develop a good campaign idea and decide how various creative content or assets can be integrated around this idea. Then decide which chan-

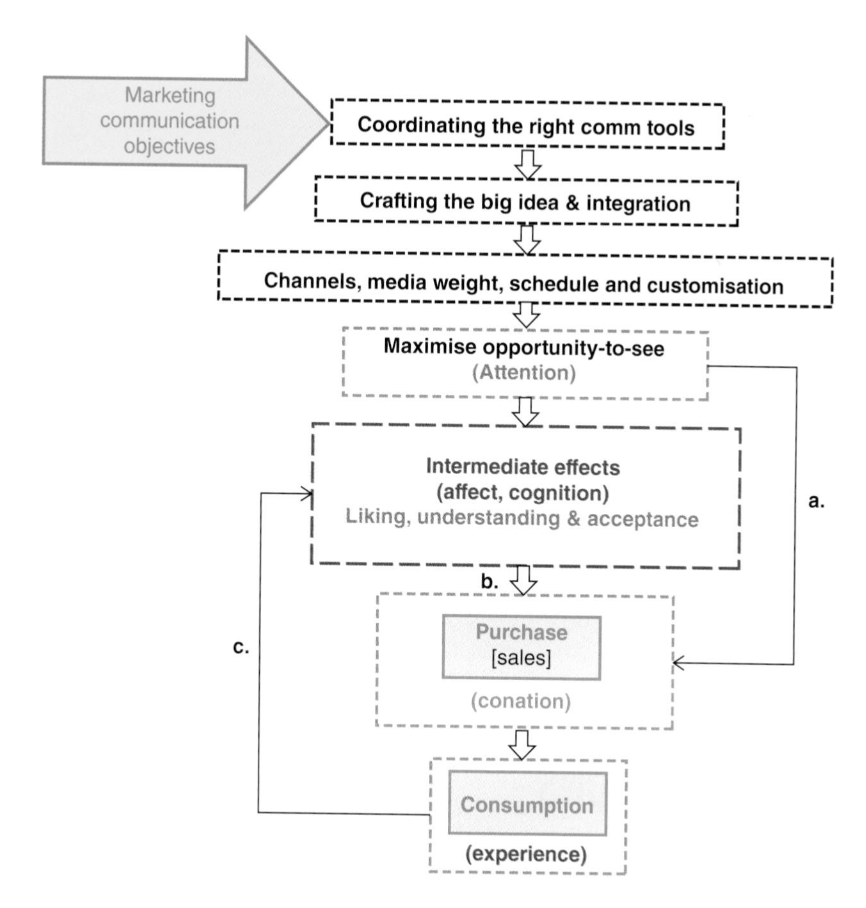

Figure 1.14 A theoretical framework for a marketing communications campaign

nels and media to use. This will be constrained by one's budget. All creative content should be customised for the channel.

By selecting the right media (see chapter 5) and deciding on the schedule and weight of the message, we maximise the opportunity for the target audience to see or hear it (see chapter 4). If the message is based on true consumer insights (see chapter 2) and embodied in a well-crafted creative idea (the 'big idea'), it should gain the attention of the target audience (see chapters 6 and 7). If this does not lead to immediate purchase (via path a) – which is what one would expect with sales promotions, direct response and personal selling (see chapters 10 and 11) – then, at a minimum, the communications should leave some impression in their minds; that is, the message should make the target audience feel and believe something positive about the brand. To put it another way, the audience's feelings (affect) and thinking (cognition) about the brand, in the form of associative memories, should become stronger and more positive.

These associations created can be thought of as the intermediate effects of the communications. Although we cannot 'see' these effects (just as we cannot see magnetic waves), we can measure them. We can also verify if these effects are due to our liking, understanding and acceptance of the message (see chapter 12) or perhaps the influence of others in our social networks (see chapter 8).

If these brand associations grow to be strong, it will increase the probability of purchase (via path b) (see chapter 3). The observable manifestation of this behaviour (called 'conation') is sales. However, these brand associations can also be learned, probably more strongly, from our consumption experience (via path c).

In the theoretical framework shown in figure 1.14, the green areas and words represent the individual's mental representations or memories of the brand (e.g. feelings, beliefs, experience about and of the brand), while the area shown in red represents their actions (e.g. purchase and consumption). The purple words represent their specific reactions to the message (e.g. attention to, liking, comprehension and acceptance of the branded message), while the black areas represent the managerial steps we can take to communicate that message (e.g. coordinating the right communication tools, crafting the creative idea and integrating it across different medium, and determining media weight and schedule).

Although the figure represents a very general model of communications, its application should not be too rigid. For instance, the crafting of a creative idea may be essential for advertising and marketing-oriented PR (see chapter 9) but not needed for sales promotion or personal selling. Similarly, acceptance of the message may be more important for a high-risk purchase but less so for a low-risk one. In social media, the focus may be on generating and spreading excitement about the brand, and not necessarily on closing a sale. Finally, as new digital tools are developed, they can be applied to enhance the effects of any of these stages.

DISCUSSION QUESTIONS

1. Choose a brand you are familiar with. Discuss some of the barriers to effective marketing communication for this brand.
2. What is integrated marketing communications (IMC)? Under what circumstances is IMC essential?
3. What are synergistic effects in an IMC? What are the underlying psychological processes that can explain this?

4. Although the concepts of integration and synergy are often used interchangeably, they are not the same. What is the difference between these two concepts?
5. Integration can be simple or complex. Explain the levels of complexity.
6. Figure 1.8 shows there are many ways of integration. Relay one recent example you can remember that uses one of these tactics.
7. Think about a new product you bought recently. Can you recall the decision journey you went through? How does the internet influence your journey?
8. This chapter suggests nine steps for planning an IMC campaign. Which do you think is the most interesting step and why?

NOTES

1 RR Burke and TK Srull, 'Competitive interference and consumer memory for advertising', *Journal of Consumer Research*, 15(1), 1988, pp. 55–68.

2 As humans we naturally gravitate to the 'default' option, sometimes even thinking blindly and settling for an option simply because it is easier. Thaler and Sunstein's fascinating book explores and catalogues human biases and how they can affect our lives. See RH Thaler and CR Sunstein, *Nudge*, Yale University Press, New Haven and London, 2008.

3 JG Kliatchko has traced the different definitions over the years. However, none of the definitions drew a distinction between coordinating different communication tools and integrating media with creative content. See JG Kliatchko, 'Revisiting the IMC construct: a revised definition and four pillars', *International Journal of Advertising*, 27(1), 2008, pp. 133–60.

4 This definition is adapted from a number of authors – see Kliatchko (2008), 'Revisiting the IMC construct', note 3.

5 This chapter is very much inspired by Larry Percy and particularly his way of expressing media integration – the 'look and feel' being consistent across all communication collateral. In this book, I have added another element to Percy's expression, that of 'one voice'. See L Percy, *Strategies for implementing integrated marketing communications*, NTC Business Books, American Marketing Association, Chicago, 1997.

6 G Low, 'Correlates of integrated marketing communications', *Journal of Advertising Research*, 40(3), 2000, pp. 27–39; M Reid, 'IMC–performance relationship: further insight and evidence from the Australian marketplace', *International Journal of Advertising*, 22(2), 2003, pp. 227–48; T Reinold and J Tropp, 'Integrated marketing communications: how can we measure its effectiveness?', *Journal of Marketing Communications*, 18(2), 2012, pp. 113–32. For a review see also L Ang, 'Integrated marketing communications', in P Moy (ed.), *Oxford bibliographies in communication*, Oxford University Press, New York, 2018.

7 K Cox, 'Integrated channel planning: effective integration', *Admap*, June, 2011, pp. 22–5.

8 From C Moldrich, CEO of Outdoor Media Association, personal communication, September 2019.

9 Kantar Millward Brown, 'AdReaction: the art of integration', *Global Report*, 2018. Accessed May 2019 at www.millwardbrown.com/documents/reports/The_art_of_integration/default.aspx?access=yes.

10 F Dost et al., 'Seeding as part of the marketing mix: word-of-mouth program interactions for fast-moving consumer goods', *Journal of Marketing*, 83, 2019, pp. 62–81.

11 Ehrenberg-Bass, 'Planning for synergy: harnessing the power of multi-platform media', Institute for Marketing Science, University of South Australia, 2012.

12 G Fulgoni and A Lipsman, 'Numbers, please: digital game changers: how social media will help usher in the era of mobile and multi-platform campaign-effectiveness measurement', *Journal of Advertising Research*, 54(1), 2014, pp. 11–16.

13 TM Smith, S Gopalakrishna and R Chatterjee, 'A three-stage model of integrated marketing communications at the marketing-sales interface', *Journal of Marketing Research*, 43(4), 2006, pp. 564–79.

14 P Neijens and H Voorveld summarised some of these theories in 'Cross-platform advertising: current practices and issues for the future', *Journal of Advertising Research*, 55(4), 2015, pp. 362–67. I have added two more and changed some of their labelling to aid comprehension.

15 T Ambler and EA Hollier, 'The waste in advertising is the part that works', *Journal of Advertising Research*, 2004, pp. 375–89.

16 Nowak and Phelps (1994) suggested very similar principles except they did not emphasise the importance of synergy. Their emphasis was more on coordination. Of course, this was more than 24 years ago. I have updated these principles and shifted the emphasis to achieving synergy, which is the cornerstone of IMC. GJ Nowak and J Phelps, 'Conceptualizing the integrated marketing communications phenomenon: an examiniation of its impact on advertising practices and its implications for advertisting research', *Journal of Current Issues & Research in Advertising*, 16(1), 1 March 1994, pp. 49–66. See also Ang (2018), 'Integrated marketing communications', note 6.

17 J Romaniuk, V Beal and M Uncles, 'Achieving reach in a multi-media environment: how a marketer's first step provides the direction for the second', *Journal of Advertising Research*, 53(2), 2013, pp. 221–30.

18 See Kantar Millward Brown (2018), 'AdReaction: the art of integration', note 9.

19 Disney actually used all its characters in its TV ad, not just Mickey. Accessed September 2019 at www.ispot.tv/ad/wmNe/disney-cruise-line-maya.

20 S Falewée, 'More Yellow Tail TV ads to come', *Wine spectator*, March 2017. Accessed September 2019 at www.winespectator.com/articles/more-yellow-tail-tv-ads.

21 Mumbrella, 'Metro Trains' Dumb Ways to Die launches superheroes video game', 2 June 2020. Accessed June 2020 at https://mumbrella.com.au/metro-trains-dumb-ways-to-die-launches-superheroes-video-game-629998?utm_source=.

22 See Kantar Millward Brown (2018), 'AdReaction: the art of integration', note 9.

23 Research shows that each piece of content is important, and the more it can be customisable for the channel, the more effective it will be. For instance, a TV ad should be modified to fit into the online format. See Kantar Millward Brown (2018), 'AdReaction: the art of integration', note 9.

24 E Flores, J Dorsett and M Warty, 'Magnum Gold?! How one golden integrated idea sold 130 million ice-creams', *Institute of Practitioners in Advertising, Silver, IPA Effectiveness Awards*, 2012. Accessed September 2019 at www.warc.com/content/paywall/article/Magnum_Gold!_How_one_golden_integrated_idea_sold_130_million_ice-creams/97384.

25 We take a practical approach towards IMC planning with a special emphasis on creating synergy. This is in contrast to other models like Batra and Keller (2016) which is more theoretical and does not emphasise synergy. R Batra and K Keller, 'Integrating marketing communications: new findings, new lessons, and new ideas', *Journal of Marketing*, 80(6), 2016, pp. 122–45.

26 For a non-commercial organisation (e.g. charity), the issues may not be business related, but just the same it is important to understand why it is embarking on a campaign.

27 There are many versions of the consumer decision journey, some extremely complex. This version is modified from a simpler model of D Court et al., 'The consumer decision journey', *McKinsey Quarterly*, 3, 2009, pp. 1–11. One should also note that the decision journey is far more complex than previous planning models, and in the digital age, behavioural data along the journey often have to be stitched together from different sources to yield a more complete picture.

28 R Pardini, personal communication, September 2019.

29 J Halliday, 'Marketer of the Year: Hyundai', 9 November 2009. Accessed February 2018 at http://adage.com/article/special-report-marketer-of-the-year-2009/hyundai-marketer-year-2009/140380/.

30 See J Halliday (2009), 'Marketer of the Year: Hyundai', note 29.

31 Ibid.

32 Knowledge@Wharton, 'How Hyundai sells more when everyone else is selling less', 2009. Accessed February 2018 at http://knowledge.wharton.upenn.edu/article/how-hyundai-sells-more-when-everyone-else-is-selling-less/.

33 The concept of brand salience has also been discussed in the literature (see also chapter 9). The concept of brand salience refers to the propensity of the brand being triggered by a host of cues, not just the product category. However, to be competitive, the brand also needs to be different and relevant. See J Samuel, 'The power of being meaningful, different, and salient', Millward Brown Point of View. Accessed May 2019 at www.millwardbrown.com/docs/default-source/insight-documents/points-of-view/Millward_Brown_POV_The_Power_of_Being_Meaningful-Different-Salient.pdf.

34 The most prominent example of this principle is in customer relationship management (CRM) where an organisation like a bank can conduct hundreds of mini-campaigns in a year (e.g. using direct mail). Learning from each campaign is important, as advocated by F Buttle, *Customer relationship management*, 2nd edition, Elsevier, Oxford, 2009.

35 JA Edell and KL Keller, 'The information processing of coordinated media campaigns', *Journal of Marketing Research*, 26, 1989, pp. 149–63.

36 HAM Voorveld and SM Valkenburg, 'The fit factor: the role of fit between ads in understanding cross-media synergy', *Journal of Advertising*, 44(3), 2015, pp. 185–95.

37 MD Loda and B Carrick Coleman, 'Sequence matters: a more effective way to use advertising and publicity', *Journal of Advertising Research*, 45(4), 2005, pp. 362–72.

38 HAM Voorveld, PC Neijens and EG Smit, 'The interacting role of media sequence and product involvement in cross-media campaigns', *Journal of Marketing Communications*, 18(3), 2012, pp. 203–16.

39 Another study found that the format of the message has an important effect in determining the sequence of the device used. If a message is in a form of an interactive video, then its exposure should be personal computer first, then the mobile phone. This is because the personal computer is more suited to creating interactivity. So, when an interactive video is subsequently used on the mobile phone, the added difficulty caused the consumers to try harder. This extra effort results in superior memory of the interactive video when the exposure is affected in this sequence. See D Varan et al., 'What works best when combining television sets, PCs, tablets, or mobile phones? How synergies across devices result from cross-device effects and cross-format synergies', *Journal of Advertising Research*, 53(2), 2013, pp. 212–20.

40 M Haller, 'How to create a product story that unfolds over time — and drives results', Think with Google, January 2019. Accessed January 2019 at www.thinkwithgoogle.com/advertising-channels/video/adidas-marketing-case-study/.

41 D&AD Award winner, 'The Like New Campaign', 2019. Accessed September 2019 at www.dandad.org/awards/professional/2019/integrated/230798/the-like-new-campaign/.

42 What is interesting is that these are real stories canvassed from the Irish people all over the country using postcards, social media (i.e. Facebook, Flicker, Twitter), as well as iPhone and on-pack and point-of-sale messages. There was even a mobile home travelling around the country, stopping at fairs and events to collect the stories. These stories thus resonated with the target audience.

43 B Anand, *The content trap: a strategist guide to digital change,* Random House, New York, 2016, p. 292.

44 J Zhang 'Trends: when do people shop online?' Work area, August 2017. Accessed September 2019 at https://blog.workarea.com/trends-when-do-people-shop-online.

45 WHO, 'Timeline – COVID-19'. Accessed April 2020 at www.who.int/csr/don/12-january-2020-novel-coronavirus-china/en/.

46 One of the reasons why many governments were hesitant about a lockdown was that it would have a devastating effect on the economy. For a critique of the Trump administration, see E Lipton et al., 'He could have seen what was coming: behind Trump's failure on the virus', *New York Times*, 11 April 2020. Accessed April 2020 at www.nytimes.com/2020/04/11/us/politics/coronavirus-trump-response.html.

47 N Smith, 'Taiwan's Vice-President Chen Chien-jen on his country's fight with Covid-19', *The Telegraph*, 18 April 2020. Accessed April 2020 at www.telegraph.co.uk/global-health/science-and-disease/taiwans-vice-president-chen-chien-jen-countrys-fight-covid-19/.

48 CJ Wang, CY Ng and RH Brook, 'Response to COVID-19 in Taiwan: big data analytics, new technology, and proactive testing', *JAMA*, 323(14), 2020, pp. 1341–2. Accessed April 2020 at https://jamanetwork.com/journals/jama/fullarticle/2762689.

49 You can see many of these at www.mofa.gov.tw/cp.aspx?n=4B97B267EBBDC9F2. Accessed April 2020.

50 If found guilty, a person can be jailed for up to three years and fined US$1000. See F Wang, C Liu and P Hsiao, 'Individuals caught spreading virus-related misinformation', *Focus Taiwan*, 13 March 2020. Accessed April 2020 at https://focustaiwan.tw/society/202003130021.

51 MH Liang, 'How Taiwan use technologies to fight coronavirus?'. Accessed April 2020 at www.interhacktives.com/2020/03/17/how-taiwan-uses-technologies-to-fight-coronavirus/amp/. See also CC Tung, 'Lessons from Taiwan's experience with COVID-19', New Atlanticist, Atlantic Council, 7 April 2020. Accessed April 2020 at https://atlanticcouncil.org/blogs/new-atlanticist/lessons-from-taiwans-experience-with-covid-19/.

CHAPTER 2
UNCOVERING INSIGHTS

CHAPTER OVERVIEW

This chapter examines the effective use of research to assist in the creative development of marketing communications. By this, we do not mean dry quantitative statistics (although this too can yield insights) but rather a thorough understanding of the relationship of the target audience with the brand or category. In this chapter, we assume that qualitative research, when conducted well, will yield workable insights, but when conducted badly, will yield misleading results that lead to disastrous outcomes. The ability to uncover workable insights is an important skill to develop so we will focus on how to achieve this competence.

Learning goals

After reading this chapter, you will understand:

- what an insight is and how it works to unlock growth
- what creative development research is and how it is different from evaluative or confirmatory research
- the role of the account planner in the creative development process
- the sources of consumer insights
- the level of accessibility consumers have to their own thoughts and feelings
- a range of methods for obtaining consumer insights, including qualitative and quantitative research, observation-based studies, deprivation studies, means–end laddering, levels of accessibility and projective techniques
- how to establish the reliability and validity of a key insight.

This chapter is about finding consumer insights, which become more important as brands edge towards parity, accompanied by declining loyalty. As a result, research is increasingly called upon to find that 'nugget of gold' that can help differentiate a brand from others. In the context of marcoms, this usually means finding a key consumer insight that can be turned into a winning creative idea.

Unfortunately, marketing research tends to be conducted (and taught) in a narrow way, emphasising the use and analysis of individualised, verbal self-reporting (such as a questionnaire). This often leads to a frustrating lack of richness in the researcher's understanding of consumers or their relationships with brands.[1] The dominant paradigm of marketing research is a rigid, rational–cognitive view of consumer behaviour, which assumes that the mental life of consumers is always objective and fully accessible.

In the normal scheme of things this may not matter if we are happy simply to maintain the status quo. However, if we are searching for competitive advantage or trying to reverse declining sales, new insights are needed.[2] For instance, more often than not, the advertising has to resonate with the target segment or segments to have any chance of changing the status quo and setting a new, improved direction for the brand (or organisation). Insights can emerge from anywhere including our experience, our understanding of human behaviour or observations, and sometimes it comes from plain old logic. Therefore, research is not purely data driven but is guided by a theory we might have (no matter how vague it may initially be) about how consumers behave and how they relate to brands. In this chapter, we demonstrate how to use research productively to obtain and translate workable insights into business opportunities. We also highlight how research can be used for the creative development of advertising concepts and the role of the planner in this process.

WHAT IS INSIGHT?

The concept of insight actually dates to the seminal work of Wallas,[3] who in 1926 suggested that problem solving occurs in four stages: (1) preparation, (2) incubation, (3) illumination and (4) verification. Insight is in fact illumination, the third stage of the problem-solving process. Insight then is the sudden realisation of how a problem can be solved.[4] The classic example we learnt in school is when Archimedes suddenly realised that the volume of water displaced by an object can represent its mass; he ran down the streets of Syracuse half naked, shouting Eureka! Eureka! This 'Aha' moment came to him while he was having a bath.[5]

Since this pivotal work, much research into insights has been carried out in psychology.[6] Using simple but testable insight problems with a definite solution, researchers have established certain *characteristics* about solving insightful problems. First, a person experiences a sudden jump from the impasse to the solution. That is, the solution comes suddenly and not simply the next step in a deliberate problem-solving process. Second, there is an 'Aha!' moment, an emotional response when the solution is found. Third, the initial problem often becomes reinterpreted or redefined in the light of this sudden realisation. However, this insight still needs to be verified; that is, to check whether the discovered solution can indeed solve the problem. This is the last stage of the problem-solving process according to Wallas.

But marketing problems are complex because there is a greater level of uncertainty and very often the cause of the problem is not clear and may be multifactorial in nature. Or the problem may also be tied to larger issues of the business (e.g. mergers with another corporation and new competing technologies). Furthermore, there may be more than one solution, and the optimal one may be difficult to ascertain.

Insight as a route to unlock growth for the brand

In marketing, there are essentially two main kinds of challenges. They are either associated with declining or stagnant sales or finding new sales opportunities for the brand. Therefore, one can view a marketing insight as the sudden realisation of how these issues can be solved. Since this often requires a change of consumer perception or behaviour, one can define a marketing insight as the sudden discovery of a motivational drive hitherto overlooked or not well communicated that can unlock sales for the brand. For instance, when ice-cream manufacturer Ben & Jerry's observed that the amount of 'chatter' on social media about their ice-cream increased during wet and rainy weekends, just as much as during hot and sunny weekends (as expected), they were stumped. There must be an explanation *why* the ice-cream was just as popular during wet and rainy weekends. Follow-up interviews discovered that consumers ate their ice-cream for an emotional lift over the weekend (regardless of the weather). This led to changes in their media strategy, focusing on pre-weekend exposures, resulting in an improvement of ROI.[7]

Thus, the sudden discovery of a motivational drive is only the beginning. The next step is to explore ways in which this insight can be actioned by the company. If not, this piece of new information is only interesting. One way of separating useful information from material that is only interesting is to ask, 'So what?'[8] Asking 'So what?' moves one step closer to understanding how the brand can be linked to this new motivational drive and hence unlock its growth.

In marcoms, this often involves communicating a promise that is uniquely linked to the brand. Usually this means promising to fulfil an unmet need, reinforcing a usage experience or correcting a mistaken belief. The linkage can be to the brand's image, attributes or benefits, and may involve changing its media plan. Asking 'So what?' helps focus the thinking on finding this link.

Let's consider another example. Workout wear started out as unfashionable attire, where T-shirts and sweatpants were the main fare for decades. Then with the invention of new synthetic materials like Spandex (or Lycra) and Gore-Tex, athletic giants like Nike, Adidas and Reebook began to manufacture workout clothes from this material. But it was Canadian company Lululemon, in the late 1990s, who repositioned the whole category, by making yoga pants a *fashionable lifestyle* brand among its loyal and cult followers who were willing to pay a premium for it. The triggering motivator was that women wanted to look good all the time (not just during yoga lessons), which the company actioned because of its breakthrough material technology. Lululemon yoga pants are made with form-fitting Luon material (composed of 86% nylon and 14% lycra). This is not only comfortable but also allows women to show off their bodies,[9] and of course project the image that they are also healthy! Yoga pants are now worn everywhere by women like a pair of jeans. They have evolved into fashionable everyday active wear, and the market is huge. Of course, other competing brands have jumped into this opportunity, but it was Lululemon who understood the underlying motivation, actioned it and in the process transformed the category. Today, the company continues to grow, leveraging on social media like Instagram to proselytise the brand.[10]

But finding the hidden motivator that can be actionable is challenging. This is because one must first have the ability to uncover this motivator. This requires a certain kind of skill set, whether it is qualitative research (to be discussed later) or having the analytical quantitative skill to interrogate consumer behaviour data. Second, one must then translate this finding into a brand trigger that the audience finds compelling, thereby overcoming any inhibitors. This requires creative thinking. In disruptive new business ventures, the search for a creative solution must involve ways of overcoming the entrenched mind-sets of investors who are biased by the lack of data.[11] In marcoms, it is usually the search for a creative idea that can uniquely express this motivation that will overcome any inhibitors. One way is to show the gap between 'what is' and 'what is possible'. This is easy when it is a new product with superior performance (see the example of Polaroid below). But it is more challenging if it is an established brand that has lost its uniqueness.

Consider Febreze.[12] Although it had sales of over one billion dollars worldwide, sales had been declining since 2009, and by June 2011, sales had reached their lowest point. This was because competing brands like Glad and Airwick had copied Febreze's advertising and product benefit, which was providing consumers with odour elimination. Essentially, Febreze had lost its uniqueness and now all three brands were perceived to be similar and consumers could not tell the difference between the ads of the different brands; that is, they all looked the same, and the brands were easily substitutable.

But before this problem could be solved, a key insight needed to be found to help develop the creative campaign. Using a number of different qualitative research data, Febreze uncovered a few pieces of information but the most important was this: consumers did *not* believe that a dirty house could smell good. So, here was a gap or tension between 'what is' and 'what is possible', which Febreze could potentially close. This therefore represented an opportunity. If Febreze could turn this tension into something useful (i.e. closing the gap between what is and what is possible), then the key insight for the campaign would have been found, which in Febreze's case was this: Febreze needed to demonstrate that it was so powerful that it could even make the filthiest place smell nice!

Armed with this key insight (i.e. a sudden realisation of a solution), the advertising agency came up with a creative idea demonstrating that people who are blindfolded sitting in the filthiest room imaginable still cannot tell it is smelly – provided it is sprayed with Febreze. The tag line was 'Breathe Happy'. The creative idea demonstrated how Febreze could close the gap between what is and what is possible. The campaign was extremely successful. Sales rebounded, and up to 80% of the target audience attributed the ad to Febreze and up to 84% to odour elimination. Note in this case, the technology or ingredients of Febreze had not changed; it was the way it had been communicated that had changed. The campaign had re-established the brand's position.

CREATIVE DEVELOPMENT RESEARCH

Finding an actionable insight is not easy and the search is very much a creative process.[13] But once a quality insight is found, the next challenge is to position the brand carefully with a message proposition. This is where creative development research comes in. Creative development research is not well understood, but it can be defined as a form of exploratory research, usually qualitative, which can spark the imagination of the creative team and hence assist them in coming up with the 'big' idea. Let's look at two examples.

Polaroid instant camera

Long before digital cameras were invented, advertising agency Goodby, Silverstein & Partners[14] was tasked with increasing the sales of the Polaroid camera, an instant camera that allowed the user to take a picture and see it develop before their eyes. To understand more deeply how consumers used the camera, the agency asked owners and non-owners of Polaroid cameras to take some pictures, and followed up a week later with a group discussion. The Polaroid owners received two packs of film, and the non-owners received a Polaroid instant camera and two packs of films.

What they discovered was that 90% of the pictures taken were pictures of friends, people at parties and in parks, cats and dogs and so on – the kinds of images that an ordinary 35-millimetre film camera would probably have taken better. The other 10% were of unusual situations, such as a picture of a dinged car, taken to accompany the user's insurance claim. One female participant took pictures of herself wearing different spectacles, so that she could show them to her husband at home. A male participant even took pictures of his naked girlfriend – something he couldn't do using a film camera without others seeing it at the film processing laboratory. In other words, Polaroid's instant camera allowed users to take pictures one at a time and see them develop right in front of their eyes – instant evidence! The account planner, Kelly Evans-Pfeifer, suggested many ideas to the creative team, including the ones reproduced in the information box '"Polaroid, the picture is only the beginning" ideas'.[15]

'POLAROID, THE PICTURE IS ONLY THE BEGINNING' IDEAS

1. Maybe highlight innovative or unusual ways in which people are using Polaroid – at home and at work.
2. Show Polaroid as a participant . . . a means, not an end.
3. Perhaps focus on the effects of a Polaroid picture . . . the chain of events that it sets in motion.
4. I took the picture so something would happen, for a certain reason, to achieve a particular objective.
5. Think about how Polaroid is a tool for communication, how the pictures can be a language in and of themselves.

As you can see in this example, Kelly Evans-Pfeifer had suggested many creative ideas that could help spark imagination in the creative team. Her suggested message proposition was this: 'Polaroid, the picture is only the beginning'. It is not difficult to imagine the many scenarios that could be created with such a proposition.

Bodywash for teenage boys

For another example, consider the case of a brand of bodywash targeting teenage boys. The insight uncovered was that boys are sexually aspirant but socially insecure; that is, teenage boys want sex but are socially awkward in approaching girls. There is thus an unspoken tension between 'what is' and 'what is possible'. The solution is to sell the bodywash as a means to embolden the social confidence of teenage boys with the imaginative message proposition: 'Your best first move'.[16] One can imagine the creative team coming up with lots of creative ideas in reaction to this clever message proposition.

In summary, one can quickly surmise that creative development research is exploratory. This is very different from research that seeks to confirm an outcome. The characteristics of creative development research can be summarised as follows:

1. It is not 'dry', based solely on statistical data.
2. It is not confirmatory in nature; the process is exploratory.
3. It should be transformative.
4. It should lead to a message proposition that can spark the imagination of the creative team.
5. It should inspire the creative team to strive for the best.
6. It is a means to unlock growth for the brand.

THE ROLE OF THE ACCOUNT PLANNER

Although the emphasis in this chapter is on research, not all advertising agencies believe in research. Advertising agencies that value research tend to have an account planner who distils all the important information from the client (e.g. the details of the business issue) and the market (e.g. purchase motivation) to come up with a key insight. This makes the work of the creative team more efficient and effective, which in turn improves the quality of their work. This is not surprising since problems are often complex, ill-defined, and exacerbated by poorly written briefs.[17] One early study suggests that advertising agencies that have an account-planning department tend to have more accounts, higher billings and win more creative awards.[18]

The role of the account planner was invented by Stanley Pollitt in 1965 because he felt that traditional marketing research was not pragmatic enough and often too late to assist in the creative development process.[19] The task of the account planner is to ensure that 'all data relevant to key advertising decisions should be properly analysed, complemented with new research, and brought to bear on judgements of creative strategy and how the campaign should be appraised'.[20] The account planner therefore adds value to traditional market research by being the 'voice of the consumer' in the accounts team and in essence ensures that consumer insights are integrated throughout the creative development process.[21]

Strategically, the account planner also gives the creative team realistic objectives setting out what the advertising needs to deliver and by when – whether the goal is to increase purchase rates or get the brand into the consideration set (defined as a list of brands that come to mind when a person is considering a purchase). To achieve this, the account planner has to clearly understand the buying motivation of the target segment and must give clear direction on how the message should be framed to give the campaign the greatest chance of success. The task of the account planner is therefore transformational, driven by a clear objective of coming up with a winning message proposition, which is why a key insight is so important.

The account planner is uniquely positioned in the advertising agency to perform this transformational role. On the one hand, the account planner metaphorically plays the role of the target audience, with intimate knowledge of consumers derived from a deep immersion in their lives. On the other hand, the account planner understands the creative process well enough to be able to guide research. For this reason, the account planner looks at research not as a dispassionate outsider but from a position that helps 'tweak' the concept to make it more effective for the campaign. In many ways, the account planner serves as a built-in quality controller of the campaigns. In chapter 6, we will return to the role of the account planner in the creative development process.

However, the traditional role of account planner may be changing. This is because consumers using digital technologies can become immediately immersed in the milieu of the brand with just one click. For example, by accessing a QR code (see chapter 5), consumers can be transported to the brand's online 'destination' – giving consumers a peek 'behind the scenes' of an event – even though they might be sitting in their living room. This means that being able to craft a positive consumer experience will become increasingly important for the account planner as brand custodian. In the future, account planners may evolve into architects of an integrated brand experience across the many contact points of the brand.

SOURCES OF CONSUMER INSIGHTS

There are many sources of consumer insights, and much of what we want to know about our consumers may be found in our existing knowledge base. Therefore, the knowledge base is the starting point, as a cheap secondary information source. For instance, the supermarket chain Tesco found, when it examined data from its loyalty program across its four store formats (i.e. Tesco Express, Metro, Extra and Supermarket), that young mothers tended to buy more baby products from pharmacies because they have greater trust in them. Tesco then launched Baby Club, which provided advice about parenting and coupons for related products. Within three years, Tesco's market share in baby products rose from 16% (in 2000) to 24% (in 2003).[22]

Insights can also be gained from primary research as well as from existing data (as seen above). Figure 2.1 shows that there are essentially two primary ways to do this: observation-based and interview-based research. In observational research, insights can come from mechanical means, such as broadcast ratings, which provide information about the viewing habits of households. In the era of big data, insights can also come from clever combinatory analyses of existing customer data sets. The example of Narellan Pools, which we discuss in case study 2.1, illustrates this point succinctly.

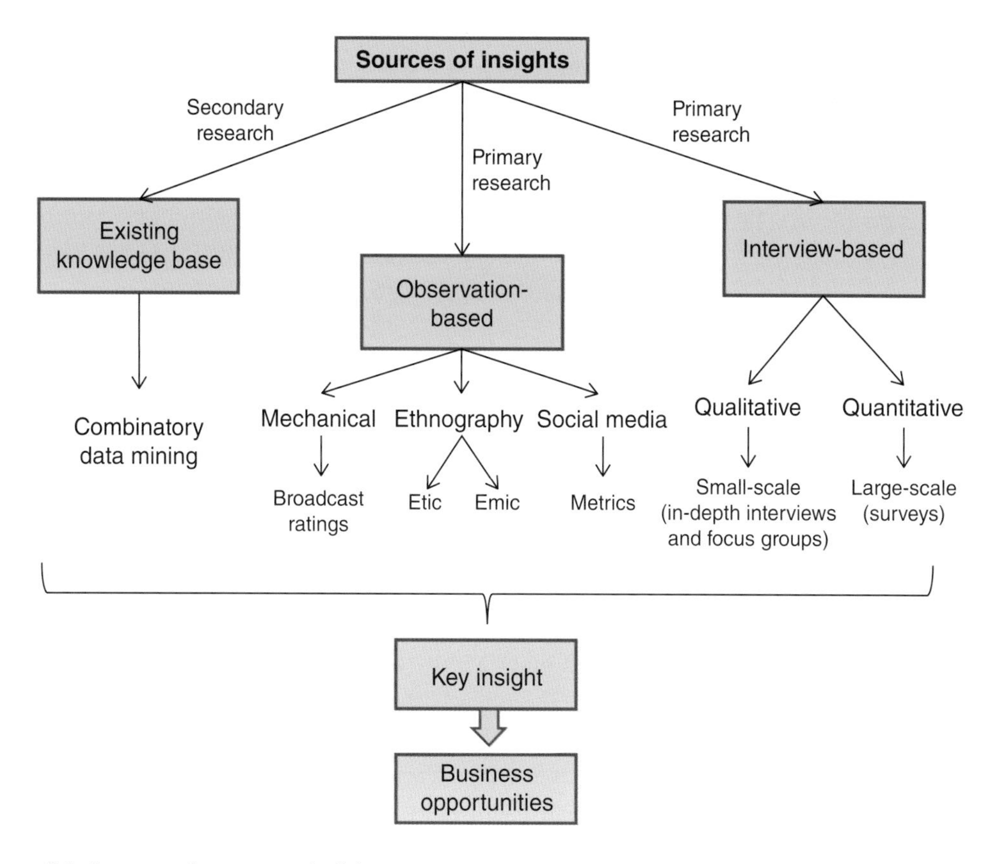

Figure 2.1 Sources of consumer insights

Observational insights can also come from making ethnographic observations of consumers in action. Interview-based insights can come from either qualitative or quantitative methods, using in-depth interviews and focus-group discussion or surveys, respectively.

CASE STUDY 2.1 NARELLAN POOLS

Narellan Pools had been experiencing a long-term decline in sales since 2007.[23] Selling family pools was becoming increasingly difficult in Australia, because of the rise in apartment living, increased household debt, decreasing housing affordability and increasing competition. It was also expensive to build a pool, each costing about $50 000 to build. It was therefore a daunting challenge because unless a solution was found to arrest or reverse declining sales, Narellan Pools would not survive.

Interestingly, Narellan Pools had traditionally invested in mass media advertising using TV and print to increase awareness and stimulate sales. The budget was about $900 000 but by 2014, this had been slashed to $495 000. However, the strategy was not working and the company did not know why. They then turned to an organisation called Affinity to gain better insights. The organisation first conducted qualitative research to find out what inspired a homeowner to build a pool. The key discovery was that owners remember having their 'first dive' as the most inspirational. This creative concept, called 'dive-in' moments, became the basis of a video. Affinity then conducted an audit of all their customer relationship management (CRM) data and discovered (a) the consumer decision journey ranged over 3–9 months, (b) with most sales occurring in the summer, and (c) being able to convert leads was the most efficient path to success.

But Affinity also discovered something curious. The conversion rate did not occur uniformly during summer. There were certain periods where conversion rates soared (up to 800%), but there were other periods with no conversions at all. To understand this anomaly, Affinity analysed five years of data (across 49 territories) comprising of leads, sales, conversion rates, promotional expenditure, website analytics, and time on site, and overlaid them with other data like weather, building approvals, consumer confidence, interest rates, CPI, building approvals and search volume. Their analysis found that the single most important driver of lead conversion was two consecutive days of hot temperatures above the rolling monthly average. When this occurred, prospects were more likely to pick up the phone and make enquiries or ask for a web-based quote. In the end, the consumers also took a shorter time to make a decision and were more likely to buy a pool. But this propensity only lasted for four days (including the two days of above average monthly temperature). This meant there was only a small window of opportunity for the company to act.

The solution was to automatically activate the campaign in any of the 49 sales territories every time the temperature reached the specified condition (using weather-polling apps). The marcoms activities included a pre-roll video, banner ads, search-engine advertising and social media using the 'dive-in' concept as the main message, all automatically activated by programmatic buying (see chapter 4 on programmatic media buying). This allowed the campaign to be seamlessly managed, coming on and off in real time based on specific weather conditions; that is, at a time when consumers were most likely to buy. This led to a significant increase in efficiency in the use of the marketing funds. Sales increased by 23% (and leads by 11%), even while the budget was reduced by 30%. The ROI was 54:1; that is, every dollar invested in the campaign led to a phenomenal return of $54.

DISCUSSION QUESTIONS

1. Is it necessary to spend millions of dollars on a campaign to be successful? Argue your case in the context of this case study (or others you may know).
2. If Narellan Pools had five years of CRM data, why didn't they look for insights in this data earlier?

METHODS FOR UNCOVERING INSIGHTS

Qualitative and quantitative research

To harness insights, it is important to learn how to combine qualitative and quantitative research. The principle is this: when we possess little or no idea about the focal topic under investigation, we should *always* start with qualitative research. For instance, if we are tasked to launch a new product in Shanghai and we have no idea how Shanghai consumers will react to it, then it pays to do research. But what sort of research should we do?

After we have conducted preliminary secondary research, the first major activity is qualitative research followed by a large-scale quantitative survey. This is simply because if our surveys are not asking the right questions, all the answers obtained from the surveys will be invalid, no matter how large the sample. In other words, if the input is invalid, so will be the output (colloquially known as 'garbage in, garbage out' or GIGO).

Therefore, the strengths of qualitative research should first be actioned to establish the validity of the phenomenon. This means interviewing the right participants – people whose behaviour is most germane to the issue under investigation. If not, we are at risk of GIGO. For instance, if we want to find out why some adults continue to play with LEGO® bricks, it makes sense to find and interview such adults *first* before carrying out any large-scale quantitative survey.

Qualitative interviews can be carried out one-to-one with a person, called in-depth interviews, or they can be carried out in a group (usually 6–8 people), called focus groups. In-depth interviews are more suited for understanding buying situations which are high involvement and individual-based, or when respondents do not have time to gather in one location. In business-to-business research, where interviews are being conducted with high-powered executives, the interviewers will often go to the executive's office and conduct the interview face-to-face. Such in-depth interviews are expensive. Focus groups are more suited when purchase decisions are simple and are influenced by social interactions with others. In such a group setting, the interviewing skills of the moderator are important because he/she needs to control the group dynamics and not let one person dominate to the detriment of others. If it is a mixed group of consumers – two competing groups of loyal customers of different brands, like Nike versus Adidas – then the moderator must keep track of what is being said, by whom and why. Putting opposing loyal members in one group can often uncover new information. Often, we are also interested in establishing the motivating and inhibiting factors that characterise the phenomenon. In-depth interviews and focus groups are increasingly being adapted for the online environment through the use of live chat, discussion forums and insight communities. These are lower in cost and becoming more common as online activities grow, accelerated by the COVID-19 pandemic.

Once the validity and cause of the phenomenon are established, quantitative research with large sample sizes can be used to establish the phenomenon's reliability. We are also interested in assessing the viability of a business opportunity through market sizing. For example, in our LEGO bricks example, we might ask: why do some adults still play with LEGO bricks while others do not? And how large is this segment of the market?

In many ways, carrying out qualitative research first in order to understand the phenomenon brings us closer to the scientific truth. It sensitises us to how this phenomenon should be measured. Accordingly, the route of investigation must go from (a) to (b) to (c) (see figure 2.2).

In our context, route (c) serves to confirm the key insight found using qualitative research (via path [b]). This means that we do not carry out quantitative research before we have explored the issues using qualitative research and, in the context of advertising, until we have uncovered actionable insights. Unless we are very confident about all the issues surrounding a phenomenon (at point [a]), it is not advisable to go straight to quantitative research (i.e. from path [a] to [d]). If we were to take the risk, and the quantitative results turned out to be inconclusive (via paths [a], [d] and [e]), then we may need to start all over again with qualitative research (via path [f]) to try to understand the anomaly in the survey. This would make the whole research process less efficient.

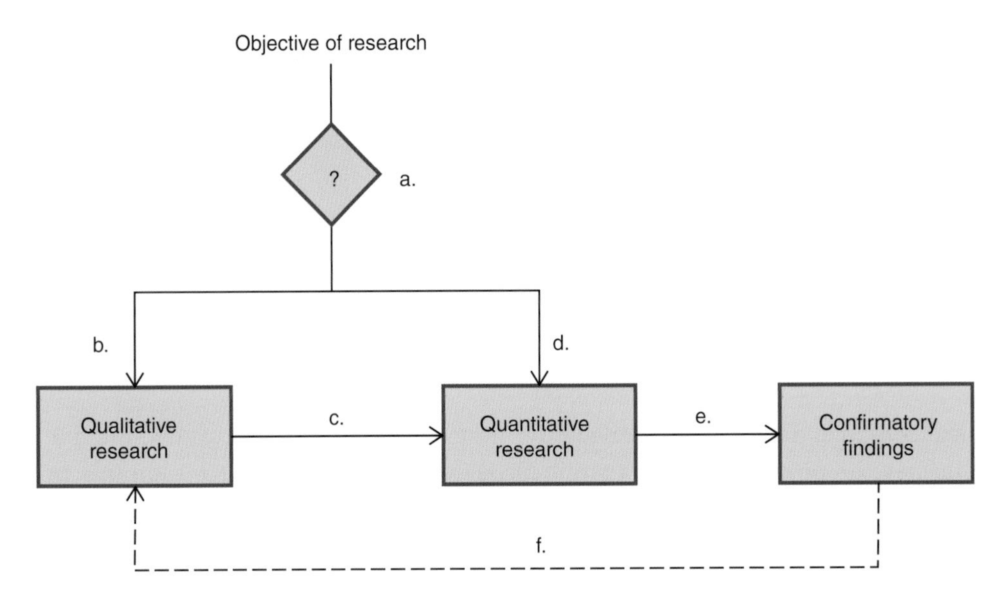

Figure 2.2 How qualitative and quantitative research can be fruitfully used jointly

The importance of qualitative research cannot be underestimated, as the following 'New Coke' case study[24] illustrates.

CASE STUDY 2.2 'NEW COKE'

In April 1985, The Coca-Cola Company launched 'New Coke' in the US, with much fanfare. 'New Coke' had a slightly sweeter formulation than original 'Coke' – but the reformulated product failed miserably, despite the fact that the company conducted more than 200 000 consumer interviews at a cost of US$4 million. It is said to have been the most expensive and exhaustive marketing research project ever, at the time.

Interestingly, before the launch, blind taste tests with 'New Coke' consistently showed that it was preferred over the original recipe by 55% of participants. Loyal 'Coke' drinkers also preferred 'New Coke' (53% of participants). Even in an identified taste test, where the brands were shown to participants, the new formulation still did better than the old, at 61%. All the quantitative testing clearly showed that 'New Coke' was superior to the original. What went wrong?

A few weeks after the new product's launch, a group of 'Coke' loyalists who did not like 'New Coke' and felt emotionally attached to the original 'Coke' sponsored their own grassroots campaign to boycott 'New Coke' across several cities. Fuelled by intense media attention, the boycott spread like wildfire across the US.

On 10 July 1985, The Coca-Cola Company capitulated and agreed to reinstate the old recipe (now renamed 'Coca-Cola Classic') to sell alongside 'New Coke'. It was the beginning of the end for 'New Coke'. With the rebranded classic product now in the market, sales of the new formula plummeted and, by 1986, 'Coca-Cola Classic' was outselling 'New Coke' by 8 to 1. By 1990, the market share of 'New Coke' had fallen to a negligible 0.6%.

So, what can we learn from this debacle, in the context of consumer insights?

First, the debacle could not be due to the quality of 'New Coke' since its taste was superior. Second, it could not be due to brand image, since the taste tests showed people preferred 'New Coke' over the old one, even when the products were identified. Third, it could not be the lack of advertising, since The Coca-Cola Company had spent US$48 million on advertising its new product.

What could be the reason for the failure? The top management blamed the inadequacy of the marketing research methodology for failing to detect the emotional response of the brand's loyalists. The Coca-Cola Company's president Donald Keough said that 'you cannot measure [loyalty] any more than you can measure love, pride, or patriotism'.[25] But we know this is not true, since methods for the detection of emotional response are well established.[26] Another explanation given was that the company asked the wrong questions in its research. Instead of just concentrating on the results of the taste tests (blind or identified), it should have asked consumers how they would feel if the old recipe were replaced with a new one. But subsequent investigation[27] revealed that this was not the reason either: it turned out that the company had asked this question.

In fact, in 1982 a study with 2000 respondents in 10 US markets was conducted using story-boards that explored this theme. In one mock commercial, it said that the cola had a new ingredient that would make it taste smoother. This was then followed by a series of questions that gauged the respondents' reactions – whether they would be upset, whether they would try 'New Coke', and whether they would switch. The result was that an estimated 10–12% of brand loyalists would be upset. Subsequent focus groups also consistently found that consumers did not look kindly on a change in the flavour of the original version. So negative emotional reactions to the change were already detected at least two years before the launch.

So why did the company's management ignore the negative findings of the qualitative research and consider only the positive findings of the taste test? One could speculate that they had already long decided to change the formulation of the original, in the light of the negative impact of their competitor Pepsi's highly successful 'Pepsi Challenge' campaign on its market share. It is also possible that management placed more weight on large-scale, quantitative studies (200 000 inter-views) compared to small-scale focus groups, since numbers and percentages looked more 'scien-tific', 'objective' and 'representative'.

Schindler[28] argues that the real lesson from this debacle is that focus-group discussions can help detect social influence, which is very useful. Since interviews, like taste tests, are individual based, they are deficient in detecting the social influence consumers might have on each other in the real world. This is critical if the purchase or usage decision is highly visible, risky and difficult to evaluate before purchase. Under such circumstances, the results of focus groups should be given more weight.

Although this debacle occurred in the mid-1980s, the power of social influence may in fact be even more important today because of the rise of social media (see chapter 8). Although the case of the 'New Coke' debacle is a classic, it also serves to remind us that we are social animals who like to share. This means that it is important for organisations to always monitor the 'social chatter' and look out for actionable insights that can unlock growth as we saw earlier in the case of Ben & Jerry's ice-cream. Social listening may be a new source of actionable insights (see figure 2.2).

DISCUSSION QUESTIONS

1. The Coca-Cola Company is a huge organisation with ample resources, yet they made mistakes when launching 'New Coke'. What kinds of bias were at work in the case?
2. What lessons could be learned about the use of focus-group vis-à-vis quantitative research?

Observation-based studies

Mechanical observations can often be far more accurate than self-report. For instance, in the mid-1980s, the Hoover Company conducted a survey asking respondents how much time they spent vacuuming. The answer given was about an hour a week. But when Hoover installed timers in some models, the result was only 30 minutes, half of what was reported![29] In the early 1980s, the United Kingdom (UK) broadcaster the BBC conducted an observation study[30] in which a video camera was installed in the TV. The objective was to understand the TV-watching behaviour of viewers. The finding was surprising at that time. People did not spend much time at all concentrating on the programs, but instead read, talked, ate, walked in and out of the room and so on. More recent studies seem to confirm the same observation. In an ethnography study (involving hundreds of hours of mechanical videotaping) into how people behave in their living rooms, Jayasinghe and Ritson found that during commercial breaks, viewers tended to engage in conversations where family values were discussed in reaction to the ads shown during the commercial breaks.[31] The lack of attention to the ads due to such social interactions can lower their effectiveness.[32]

The word 'ethnography' is derived from the words *ethnos* (from Greek) meaning 'people, race or cultural groupings' and *graphy* (from Latin *graphia*) meaning the 'field of study' or the 'study of'. Therefore, ethnography is the study of people and their cultures.

There are two approaches to ethnography – etic and emic.[33] An etic approach means we are observing from the outside in. The objective is to find a generalisation of human behaviour (or beliefs) that can be applied to another culture. In practical terms, this usually calls for observation research, in which the researcher adopts a dispassionate view of how consumers behave and then seeks to generalise this to another culture. For instance, if we are interested in cafe behaviour, we can tabulate and analyse how long consumers spend in a cafe at different times of the week, the number of cups of coffee consumed, and whether consumers come into the cafe singly, in pairs or as a group, whether they are having fun, and so on. In some European countries (e.g. Italy, France and Spain), the neighbourhood cafe is more than just a place to have a cup of coffee. It is also a meeting point where friends and acquaintances gather and socialise – a place to hang out. It is often referred to as the 'third place': the place you go when you are not at home or work. It is this observation that led Howard Schultz to position Starbucks as the 'third place' in the US.[34]

In the emic approach, on the other hand, the researcher becomes immersed in the social milieu of the participants, observing how they live and shop. This is because this approach emphasises the importance of a person's culture (or subculture) in influencing his or her behaviour or beliefs. In practical terms, this means that emic methods involve participant observation research, actually engaging with people in the target segment while they go about their daily lives. The rationale for this approach is that this immersion helps the researcher to understand the cultural perspective of the consumers more deeply. In one common technique, called accompanied shopping, the researcher accompanies the person while he or she shops. Questions are asked 'on the run', to capture how participants make decisions and choices at the precise moment they make them.

Another variation is to be immersed in the habitat of the target audience. In one ethnographic study by Kraft Foods,[35] the consumer insights team visited the homes of their most important target segments and discovered that these mothers were extremely house-proud (e.g. keeping a neat home and attaching sentimental value to furniture). The key insight unearthed was that when a mother shared the Kraft product with her child, it was a bonding moment; the Kraft product was seen as a means for the mother to pass her values to the child, which was deemed very important by the mothers.

However, this kind of knowledge comes at a cost: ethnographic studies are expensive for two main reasons. First, they are time-consuming, since it takes time for the researcher to gain the trust of the participants. Participants tend to behave differently when they are being observed; however, with time, their behaviour will revert to normal as trust is established. Second, detailed work is needed to document the lives of these consumers (e.g. the use of photographs, videos and transcription of interviews). This is often labour-intensive.

But sometimes, it may be worth the expense. For instance, through careful ethnographic studies, The LEGO® Group has finally cracked the girls' market through the creation of 'Mini-dolls' centred on five characters called LEGO Friends (see figure 2.3). This is an impressive feat given that its traditional customer base is 90% boys, and that The LEGO Group almost went broke in 2003 because of a series of corporate missteps.[36] One key reason for this success is that The LEGO Group spent an enormous amount of resources observing how children play. Since children may not be very articulate, there is little point asking them what they think.[37] It may be more fruitful to observe how they play – on their own, with their friends and siblings – and how they interact with their favourite and not-so-favourite toys and so on. 'We call it "camping with consumers"', says Anne Flemmert Jensen, senior director of its Global Insights group. In a worldwide study, she said, 'My team spends all our time travelling around the world, talking to kids and their families and participating in their daily lives.'[38] Mini-dolls have become a worldwide hit among the girls from China to the US. The LEGO Group is said to conduct the world's largest ethnographic study of children.[39]

Figure 2.3 LEGO's Mini-dolls

Source: Photo used with permission. © 2020 The LEGO Group

Insights can also be obtained in social media. In the age of social media, insights can also be mined 'real time' by listening carefully to what is being shared by the target audience across a range of social media platforms. This is called social listening, and information can be systematically sampled, coded and analysed to form metrics (e.g. amount of mentions, likes and sentiments).[40] But to increase the probability that a key insight can be found, the account planner must move beyond simple metrics and be guided by an overarching interesting research question (e.g. How do the millennials watch TV and interact online?). This means knowing who to listen to, spotting a trend and understanding the context of their conversations.[41]

Deprivation studies

Imagine you are asked not to use your mobile phone, to watch TV or to drink your favourite beer for the next 7–10 days. How would you feel? In that period, you also have to fill in a diary, write a blog, or create a video documenting your thoughts and feelings. This in essence is what deprivation studies are.[42]

Deprivation studies are extremely useful when studying consumers who automatically buy the same product every time. By suddenly depriving these consumers of their favourite products, the researcher hopes to bring to the surface any inner feelings consumers might have. This is usually carried out with a panel of consumers.

One successful application of this technique was the 'Got Milk?' campaign for the California Fluid Milk Processors Advisory Board, whose mandate was to increase milk consumption in the state.[43] During the 1980s, the consumption of milk declined among Californians (dropping about 20%). Various campaigns that directly advocated 'milk is good for you' did not arrest the decline, even though the percentage of Californians who agreed with the statement 'I should drink more milk than I do' increased from 40% (in 1982) to 52% (in 1992). However, although attitudes towards milk improved, sales did not. So, for more than 10 years, the milk board did not know what to do. Reams of quantitative attitudinal data collected over the decade did not offer a solution.

To find the key insight that helped change behaviour, the account planner, Jon Steel, conducted a deprivation study for seven days using a group of milk consumers. What Steel discovered was that consumers only realised they needed milk when it was missing. Further, he also discovered that consumers enjoyed certain food items, such as cereal and chocolate cookies, much less without milk. Deprivation studies not only revealed this key insight but also provided clues as to how the ad should be framed. This was how the successful 'Got Milk?' campaign was born. One ad showed how what could have been a great, savouring moment with a cookie was destroyed because there was no milk; another showed how the absence of milk could be used as a form of torture in hell. In chapter 6, we will further discuss the idea of the creative frame.

Means–end laddering

At the reflective level, one technique that has proven to be very useful in gaining insights is the means–end laddering method. Invented by Jonathan Gutman,[44] the idea behind this method is to understand the real reason why consumers are buying a certain brand. While information about why consumers are *not* buying a brand is easy to obtain (it is usually because of price or a mismatch of needs), understanding why they are buying may be more difficult. This is because when consumers are asked, they often give surface-level answers (i.e. focusing on product attributes such as the taste or variety or price or quality). However, these are not personally relevant reasons. Therefore, to go 'deeper', Reynolds and Gutman[45] suggest that we keep asking 'why?' until we get to the point when consumers reveal their personal values.

For instance, figure 2.4 shows the means–end ladder for a brand of upmarket ice-cream from Sweden. If you were to ask a consumer segment why they buy this brand of ice-cream, they might give surface-attribute answers about its ingredients, taste or flavour, or about its packaging. But if you were to probe further and systematically ask why these attributes are important, you would uncover the personal reasons. For example, for taste, we would probe, 'So why is taste important?' And the response might be 'Quality'. We then continue, 'And why is quality important?' and the response might be 'To reward myself'. We continue to probe, 'And why is rewarding yourself important?' and the response might be 'Because it gives me a sense of accomplishment'. So, by systematically probing, we can begin to see how each attribute is linked first to consequences (benefits) and then to values. Or, to put it another way, we can create a 'mental map' of how values (i.e. ends) are being attained by the surface attributes (i.e. means) of the brand.

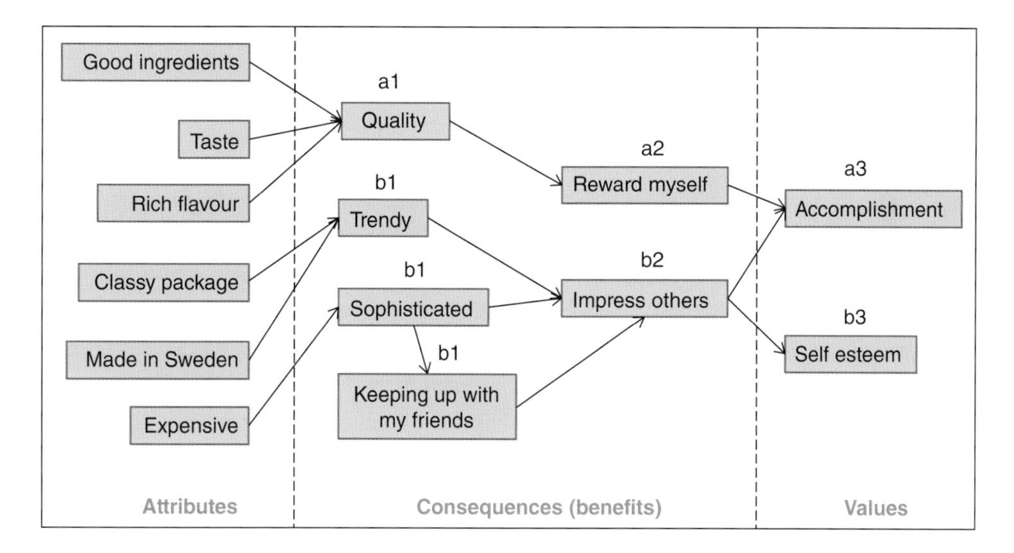

Figure 2.4 A means-end laddering result

There are a number of advantages to this methodology. It is considerably cheaper than ethnography. It takes about 30–40 minutes of in-depth questioning to complete an interview and usually, for each brand, an average of approximately 2.2 values are revealed.

Kahle and colleagues[46] found eight values influenced purchase behaviour, while Wansink[47] found seven, many of which overlapped with those identified by Kahle and colleagues. Nevertheless, these small numbers are practical. The seven values Wansink found are: accomplishment, belonging, self-fulfilment, self-esteem, family, satisfaction and security.

By relating the brand attributes to the consequences (benefits) and then values, the insight becomes more workable. The linkages can assist in the creative development of the advertising campaign; they can also ensure that the creative concept taps into the right values by having an appropriate tagline or slogan and by creating ad scenarios that creatively amplify the values.

Aggregating and analysing 'mental maps' of a number of consumers can provide clues on how the market can be segmented and the brand positioned; for example, in the ice-cream example above, further research might reveal that there are two distinct segments: the 'foodies' and the 'trendies'. The 'foodies' might be quality-driven (via path [a1], [a2], [a3]), while the 'trendies' want to impress others (via path [b1], [b2], [b3]). This means that we have the option of positioning the brand in two different ways, and we also know why this is.

Levels of accessibility

As humans, we suffer from bias and bounded rationality.[48] For instance, we may not have time to think through issues carefully, we may say things we do not mean, and at other times we may not say what we mean. We hesitate, stumble, feel embarrassed, pretend, exaggerate and tell lies, sometimes for nothing more than to gain social approval. In searching for the key insight, we should be sensitive to these human foibles, so that the key insight we hope to uncover is valid. How consumers respond freely to an interviewer is represented in figure 2.5.[49] Let's discuss this in greater detail.

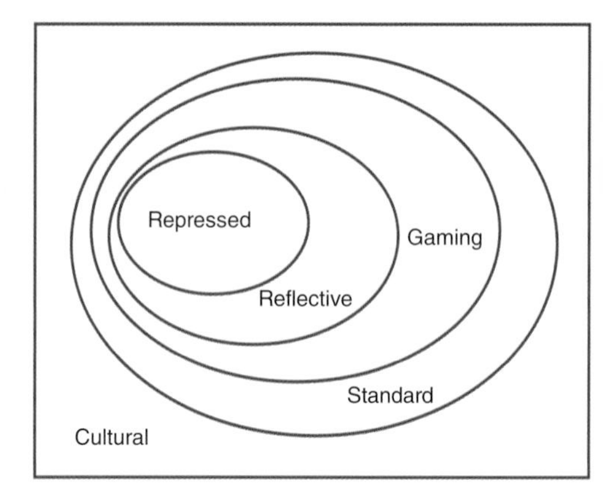

Figure 2.5 Concepts of different levels of accessibility

Consumers' responses are embedded in the culture they live in. For instance, Japanese consumers are more likely to want to avoid offending an interviewer than Western consumers, typically yielding fewer extreme scores in surveys than Western respondents.[50] In seven-point rating scales, for instance, Japanese surveys typically yield less variance because Japanese consumers tend not to give extreme scores. Ethnography, discussed above, is one way of understanding the cultural milieu of the consumers. But beyond the confines of the culture, it is also important to understand the different levels of revelation a consumer is willing to give. At the surface level, consumers' responses may be of the standard kind, as they give responses based on what is expected. For example, consumers often say they want more variety in the flavour of potato crisps, yet the biggest sellers are still cheese and onion, salt and vinegar, and salted. We also know from behavioural research that the more choices there are, the less likely consumers will buy, because they get more confused; this is also called the 'paradox of choice'.[51] Yet it is not uncommon for consumers to say they want more choices (in everything!).

Beyond the superficial level, consumers may start playing games. This behaviour is known as 'gaming responses', and we can see it in research into pricing. For instance, it has been observed that consumers will opt for the lower price even though, in reality, they are more than willing to pay more.[52] We also know that men tend to lie about their career and women about their age.[53]

After gaming responses comes the reflection level. This level is where consumers reflect more deeply and where qualitative research techniques become useful. Using various questioning techniques (e.g. gentle probing and pausing),[54] the moderator hopes to directly elicit responses that come from this deeper level. The means–end laddering technique, discussed above, is one example of this.

The next level is the most difficult to assess and it is the repressed level. At this level, consumers repress feelings, which they themselves may not know they have. Asking them directly may be useless because of what is known as the 'introspection problem'. This means that consumers are not sufficiently cognisant to express their innermost thoughts and feelings (simply because they are unable to do so). For instance, in direct marketing, people may say that they are not influenced by small gifts like free pens. But gifts are extremely effective. Similarly, we often hear consumers say that they are not influenced by advertising, and yet we know that advertising can influence purchases even with only one exposure.[55]

In social cognitive science, we can even uncover implicit stereotypical views people hold about certain races, which they may not admit (or even know) they hold. For example, due to growing up in a society that perpetuates negative and inaccurate stereotypes about black people and favours positive stereotypes of white people, people might (implicitly) associate black people with laziness and white people with intelligence. One way to test for this unconscious network of associations would be to first briefly show a group of people a photograph of a person of a particular race, and then show them a picture of a word stereotypically thought to be associated with that race. Respondents are told to indicate as rapidly as possible whether the word is positive or negative. Research has found that people who hold high levels of implicit racial stereotyping tend to respond quicker to the words 'lazy' and 'intelligent' if they are paired with a photograph of a black person and white person respectively.[56] If you ask most respondents directly if black people are lazy, the chances are that they will say no. This is not necessarily because they are lying but because they are unaware that they hold those views.[57] They may also be aware that the views they hold are considered racist and may not be well received by others. For this reason, it is important to realise that sometimes we cannot always take what consumers say at face value.

Now that we understand there are different levels of accessibility to the human psyche, we will discuss the various methods to access the deeper human psyche using projective techniques.

Projective techniques

Ordinarily, one assumes that consumers are always able and willing to express themselves freely. What if the subject matter is a sensitive topic like erectile dysfunction (for men) or sexual habits (for women)? Will participants be just as candid and honest in their responses? Probably not – we suffer from all sorts of biases (e.g. social desirability) that prevent us from necessarily telling the whole truth all the time. We might also simply be reluctant to disclose, for fear of embarrassment or retribution. And yet, at other times, we may not be able to disclose, even if we want to.

Consider the following.[58] Table 2.1 shows the percentage of consumers who preferred Diet Pepsi and Diet Coke in a blind taste test and when the brand was identified. In a blind taste test, there were slightly more consumers preferring Diet Pepsi (51%) to Diet Coke (44%). However, when the brands were identified, suddenly more consumers preferred Diet Coke to Diet Pepsi by a large margin (65% to 23%). Now, if you were to ask respondents why they preferred Diet Coke when the brands were identified, you would get the usual standard responses such as 'It tastes better!' Yet we know this is not true, as indicated in the blind taste test.

Table 2.1 Percentage preference of brands tasted blind or identified

Brands	Blind (%)	Identified (%)
Diet Coke	44	65
Diet Pepsi	51	23
Equal/Don't know	5	12
	100	100

ASKHAM BRYAN
COLLEGE
LEARNING RESOURCES

Although this example demonstrates the power of branding, it also demonstrates that our perception of objects is very powerful. Perception can even influence how we taste. For such reasons, we need to understand consumers and go beyond what they would normally say. A class of techniques known as 'projective techniques' provide a way of doing this.

Projective techniques have their roots in psychoanalysis, developed by Sigmund Freud in the 1900s. His major contribution was to point out the existence of the unconscious. According to Freud, certain parts of our consciousness are 'off limits' – for example, due to a past transgression – but we suppress these thoughts in order to survive. Although many of Freud's theorisations about sexuality and instinct are now questioned, his notion of the unconscious is highly influential. In the 1940s, Ernest Ditcher imported this idea into marketing research and established what was then called 'motivation research'. This became very popular because Freudian psychology was at its height, and organisations also thought this was a great way of segmenting the market.[59] It is now safe to say that Ditcher overstated its power.[60] Contemporary qualitative research now realises the limitations of motivation research and has evolved to capture only the best of its qualities.

Projective techniques can be defined as a class of techniques that encourage or enable participants to spontaneously express their thoughts and feelings without any fear of repercussions such as embarrassment or retribution. This is accomplished by:

- minimising anything that might lead participants to censor their thoughts
- allowing participants to freely transfer their thoughts and feelings (called projections) to a third party.

For example, instead of asking directly what participants think of Porsche drivers, we might ask them to complete the following sentence:

Porsche drivers are ____________________.

There are five different kinds of projective techniques,[61] which can be used either singly or in combination:

- association (words and pictures association, thought or speech bubble completion, metaphor elicitation and obituary writing)
- completion (sentence completion)
- construction (projective questioning, stereotype imagery and shopping list completion)
- expression (psychodrama and role-playing)
- choice ordering (timelines and ordering by degree of intensity).

ASSOCIATION

These techniques aim to tap into the first thing that comes to a participant's mind when they are shown a stimulus (the stimulus may be words or pictures). By expressing the first thing that comes to mind, researchers hope to circumvent participants' tendency to self-censor. The most famous example of picture association is the ink blot test, in which a person is asked to freely associate what comes to mind when they see an ink blot (see figure 2.6).

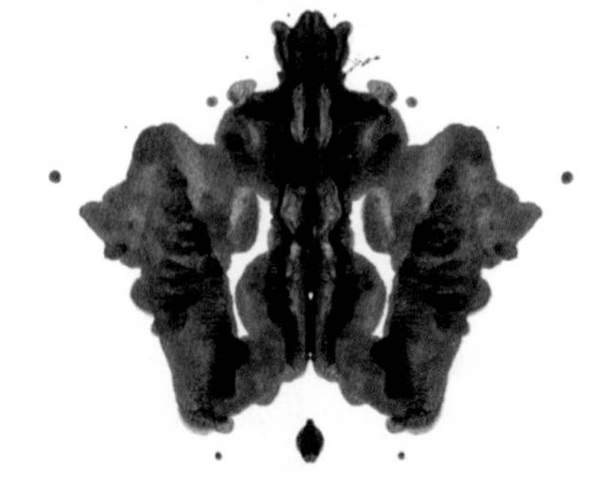

Figure 2.6 An ink blot test stimulus

Word and picture association

Advertising research often uses word association, with the brand as a stimulus (again, the stimulus may be in words or images). For instance, answer this question quickly: 'What comes to mind when you think of McDonald's?' As we will see in chapter 3, these associations are the basis of a brand's image. Sometimes participants are given a list of words and simply asked to tick the words that come closest to representing the brand (or the topic under discussion).[62]

Thought or speech bubble completion

Another association technique is to ask participants to complete a bubble drawing. The idea is to let participants spontaneously express their thoughts on paper as if they come from a third party, in this case the characters in a diagram. For instance, figure 2.7 can be used to study what people think about Facebook. The prompt can be as follows: 'Imagine this person just finished looking at her Facebook page. What might this person be thinking?'

This technique can also be used to understand social interactions. In the example shown in figure 2.8, a mother and a daughter at a kitchen table are depicted. Participants are asked to complete the speech balloon of a conversation between mother and daughter about a brand of cake mix. The moderator can use the following prompt: 'What do you think the mother and daughter are saying about baking the cake using Betty Crocker's cake mix?'

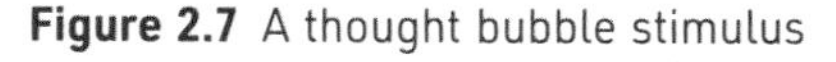

Figure 2.7 A thought bubble stimulus

Figure 2.8 A speech bubble stimulus

We can also combine speech and thought bubbles, as shown in the example in figure 2.9. This is useful when we want to investigate an awkward situation. We might say one thing but think another. The moderator could use the following prompt: 'Look at this picture. Imagine the person on the left is being audited by a tax officer from the government. What do you think both parties might be saying to each other?' When the speech bubbles are completed, the moderator can ask the participants to complete the thought bubble: 'Now, write what you think the person on the left might be thinking.' Usually the thought bubble yields more interesting ideas than the speech bubble.

Figure 2.9 A speech and thought bubble stimulus

Metaphor elicitation

Yet another association approach is metaphor elicitation, in which we ask respondents to imagine what the brand would be like if it were another object such as a car, a person or an animal. The idea behind metaphor elicitation is that the participants will use the most salient aspect of the object to represent the most important attribute of the brand image. For instance, we can ask a group of business students to imagine:

- What would a particular business school be like as a person?
- What gender would this person be?
- Where would the person live?
- What would the person's lifestyle be like?

This might be their response:

> If this business school were a person, he would be a man in his mid-50s, rich and successful. He would drive a Mercedes, eat in expensive restaurants and live in the posh eastern suburbs of Sydney. He would be very conservative, married with two grown-up children who no longer live at home, and so his only creative outlet would be his work. He would not have a social life, would go to sleep early but wake up at the crack of dawn to get to the office. He would be obsessed with wealth and reputation.

If we changed the name of this particular business school to another one, we might get a very different picture, for example, of a much younger or more dynamic male.

Obituary writing

A related technique to metaphor is the obituary technique. This technique is good for understanding brand heritage. Participants are asked to write an obituary for a brand as if it no longer exists. As in any obituary, participants have to outline what the achievements of the brand are (if any). They also write about any regrets, failures or missed opportunities, and essentially focus on what the brand wants to be remembered for (its legacy). This technique works well in focus-group discussion – participants enjoy poking fun at brands (as if they were people). This technique also works well for studying corporate reputation (see chapter 9).

COMPLETION

In completion tasks, participants are given an incomplete stimulus and told to complete it. Very often, this is in the form of an incomplete sentence. By asking respondents to complete the sentence, the moderator hopes to uncover a key element that is most meaningful to the participant about the focal topic. For example, if we are interested in studying solar energy, we can create sentences such as:

- I think solar energy is …
- Solar panels can be very …

This technique also lends itself to being provocative,[63] which may be useful for social marketing messages. For example, if we are developing an anti-smoking campaign, we might be interested in understanding how non-smokers feel about smokers, and the following provocative sentences may be used:

- Smokers deserve to be treated as outcasts because …

CONSTRUCTION

Construction tasks require participants to tell a story or create a scenario, in which only a minimum amount of information is given. Unlike association methods and completion tasks, this can be quite demanding. Many construction techniques are based on the building blocks of projective questioning.

Projective questioning

Projective questioning allows a participant to express their thoughts and feelings and yet also 'disown' them. This will make them feel less anxious about expressing their thoughts. For instance, instead of asking a business executive, 'What do you think about salary bonuses?', we might ask, 'What do you think the *average* executive might think about salary bonuses?' Since there is no such thing as an 'average business executive', what is revealed is likely to be the participant's true feelings on this issue.

Projective questioning with images (stereotype projection)

Projective questioning can also be carried out using pictures. One technique is to show the respondent pictures of different people and ask the respondent which person is likely to use the brand. Sometimes called 'stereotype projection', this technique is very useful for user imagery research (see chapter 3). Participants are also encouraged to construct background stories for these people.

For example, the moderator could show the picture (see figure 2.10) and ask 'This picture shows a driver of a ________ [car name, for example, Ferrari or BMW 5 series]. Can you briefly describe what he is like?' Participants might describe this person as a playboy, who probably cheated on his tax returns, is boastful, and so on. You might get different user imagery if another make of car is substituted.

Figure 2.10 An image that can be used with projective questioning

Shopping list evaluation

In the 1940s, Nescafé launched its brand of instant coffee to disappointing sales results. When management asked the target group what they disliked about the product, they said that the flavour was not good. However, this was not consistent with blind taste tests, which had found the flavour acceptable. This was perplexing. So, in a very clever experiment, a behavioural scientist called Mason Haire showed one target group of 50 women a shopping list (List 1) and another group of 50 women a different shopping list (List 2).[64] Each list contained:

- 1½ lbs hamburger
- 2 loaves of Wonder bread
- Bunch of carrots
- 1 can Rumford's Baking Powder
- 2 cans Del Monte peaches
- 5 lbs potatoes.

Only one brand was different in the two lists: Maxwell House coffee was included in List 1 and Nescafé in List 2.

The task for the participants was to write a brief character description of the shopper who used each list. But first, the respondents were given specific instructions to read the shopping list and then 'try to project yourself into the situation as far as possible until you can more or less characterise the woman who bought the groceries'. The results were startling. When the responses were tabulated into frequently mentioned categories, it emerged that respondents perceived a shopper with the Nescafé instant coffee (list 2) as lazy (48%), failing to plan household purchases and schedules well (48%), and not a good wife (16%)!

However, this was not all. To ascertain that the result was not because of the Nescafé brand name, Haire repeated the experiment. This time, he substituted the Nescafé brand with a fictitious brand and got the same result. In other words, it was not the Nescafé brand that was causing the negative association but the 'instantaneousness' that consumers attached to it.

Finally, just to be sure, Haire conducted a third study presenting list 2 (i.e. the Nescafé list) to 50 women in their homes and asking them to write a short description, as before. But at the same time, the researchers also looked inside the pantries of these 50 women. What they found confirmed their hypothesis. Women who wrote unfavourably did not have Nescafé in their pantries, but those who wrote favourably did. So, what Nescafé management thought to be a competitive advantage (i.e. the product's ability to instantly dissolve) turned out to be a liability. To solve the problem, Nescafé's management devised a campaign to change the perception of instant coffee. They repositioned the brand as more convenient so that there was time left to do other more important tasks at home. The concept of repositioning is discussed in chapter 3.

EXPRESSION

This is one of the most difficult techniques to use because participants not only have to reveal something about themselves but also express it in a way that reflects their personality.

Psychodrama and role-playing

In psychodrama, or role-playing, participants have to take on a role and act it out. Usually one person will play a certain focal role under investigation, and the other will play the supporting role. This technique is useful for obtaining insights into service encounters (or role conflicts) and works well with focus groups. For instance, we might want to find out how best to raise the service quality of a retailer. Two people can create and act out a good and bad incident while the rest of the group members watch. This is followed by discussion.

One of the challenges of this technique is that not all participants are comfortable with play acting; shy people may not want to be in the limelight. On the other hand, others will take the opportunity to show off their Oscar-winning performance. The dialogue used during the role play is an important value of this technique. It is often very realistic and usefully feeds into the creative development process.

CHOICE ORDERING

This technique is considered the simplest. Participants do not have to come up with or manipulate any associations; they just have to respond to what is given and then discuss. Commonly, participants are asked to place objects in a certain order. This may be in order of intensity, from low to high, or in the form of a timeline. In fact, any criterion can be used as the basis of the ordering task.

For example, we can ask participants to place three brands on a timeline, ranging from being an old-fashioned brand to being one with a future. In figure 2.11, we see that brand Y (e.g. Pinterest) is perceived as a future brand, while the other two brands, especially brand X (e.g. Facebook), are perceived as old-fashioned. To avoid group influence in the task, each participant first responds individually before showing their result to others. We can also combine this technique with that of metaphor elicitation, where each brand becomes a person.

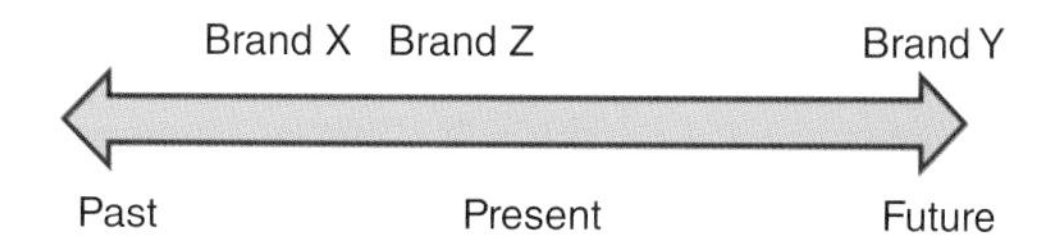

Figure 2.11 The ordering technique with brands

MULTI-METHOD PROJECTIVE

Although we have presented the different types of projective techniques individually here, they can also be used in combination. The important point is not to rush the participants – they should be relaxed and having fun. The Zaltman Metaphor Elicitation Technique (or ZMET) is one methodology that cleverly combines some of these techniques in a meaningful and fun way.[65]

ESTABLISHING THE VALIDITY AND RELIABILITY OF KEY INSIGHTS

The veracity of the key insight needs to be carefully established if a campaign hinges on it. By veracity, we mean that the insight has to be valid and reliable. 'Valid' means the insight is correctly interpreted, while 'reliable' means the insight is consistently observed. Reliability is an issue because insights are usually unearthed using qualitative research, which is often exploratory in nature, with small sample sizes. Validity is also an issue, especially with projective techniques, because the moderator may project their own bias on the findings. To establish the veracity of the insights uncovered, we can follow these steps:

1. Establish data redundancy – this means observing the same key insight over and over again within the same segment.
2. Observe whether there is a consistent response towards the stimulus across groups or participants, when visual stimuli are used.
3. Use a second researcher to independently examine and interpret the results and compare these results with those of the first researcher.
4. Get one or two participants in a focus-group situation to present the results back to the group using a visual aid (e.g. a flip chart) explaining the reasoning, then get the whole group to summarise the findings. Within-group 'playback' helps eliminate any misinterpretations.
5. Debrief participants at the completion of an ethnographic study about what was found and ask for their feedback. If participants disagree or seem puzzled by this (e.g. looking quizzical), then further investigation is needed, but if they agree (e.g. nodding in recognition), then one's interpretation is correct.
6. Replicate the phenomenon, as Mason Haire did in his shopping list studies.
7. Involve behavioural data as part of the replication, as in Mason Haire's third study, when he found that women who projected a negative perception of the instant coffee also did not stock it.
8. Confirm insights with quantitative data – for instance, if we find that the user imagery of brand A is working class, this can be confirmed by examining the demographic and usage data of the brand users.

MANAGERIAL APPLICATION: PUTTING IT TOGETHER

The thrust of this chapter has been about searching for the key consumer insights that will make a difference to the campaign (principally using qualitative research). Since the key insight is not immediately obvious and people may not be able to verbalise their motivation, projective techniques are also discussed.

But what happens if, despite much effort, no genuine key insight is uncovered? In this case, all we can do is to execute a great creative idea; that is, why the creative brief should always be inspiring (see chapter 6).

INTEGRATING RESEARCH INTO THE SEARCH FOR INSIGHTS

Figure 2.12 presents one view of how consumer insights can be integrated into the marketing research process to yield profitable business solutions at point (j), which is our ultimate objective.

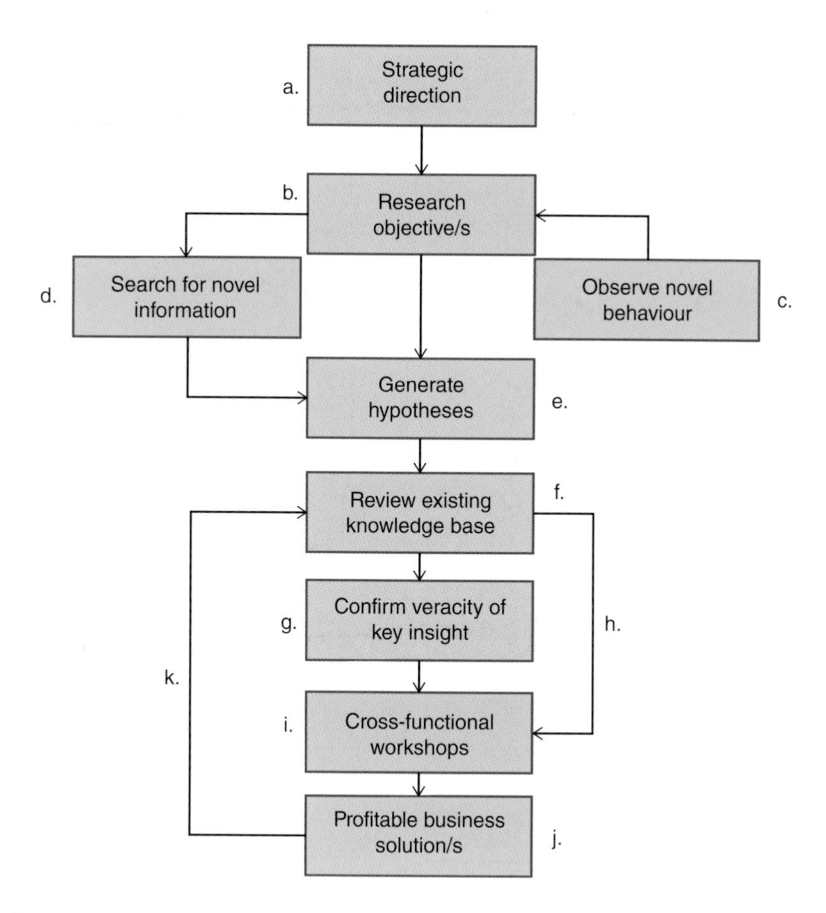

Figure 2.12 The role of research in generating, verifying and translating insights into profitable business solutions

It is most important to understand that a consumer insight can come from anywhere.[66] In this diagram, we posit that it can come from our observation (at point [c]) or from our deliberate search (point [d]). Since insights are by definition novel or unexpected, their occurrence should pique our interest, especially if we hope to capitalise on them. To do so, we want to understand *why* the phenomenon is occurring by generating some hypotheses (point [e]). As we have discussed in this chapter, the phenomenon can also be negative, for example when trying to explain why sales have been declining. Whether the search for insights is triggered by positive or negative events, it should always be guided by research objectives (point [b]). This in turn is dictated by the strategic direction of the organisation (point [a]).

To be cost-effective, we start the investigation by reviewing our existing knowledge base (point [f]), followed by new primary research to confirm the veracity of the insight (point [g]). Unless we are very confident, it is advisable not to skip this stage (via path [h]). When we have confirmed the insight's veracity, we should use cross-functional workshops to try to capitalise on the key insight (point [i]). Cross-functional workshops are useful because they bring together personnel with different expertise to brainstorm how the insight can be translated into profitable business solutions (point [j]).[67] Finally, whatever is learned from this investigation should be carefully documented to form part of the firm's knowledge base (via path [k]). Figure 2.13 shows some examples of the types of knowledge base that may exist in an organisation.

Figure 2.13 Types of knowledge base in an organisation

FURTHER THINKING: ACQUIRING KEY INSIGHTS

In this section we discuss how a manager can be sensitive to the emergence of insights during the planning process using 11 guided questions.

LEARNING GOALS

After reading this section, you will understand:

- the importance of motivation and media usage habits in guiding the IMC planning process
- how to use the 11 guided questions to look for key insights.

GUIDED QUESTIONS TO LOOK FOR KEY INSIGHTS

Since insights can come from anywhere, we must be sensitive to its possible fruition from any source. This means during the IMC planning process, hypotheses about purchase motivations and inhibitions should be entertained. Questions about the target market and its size will inevitably rise since they are linked to the issue of generating growth, and unlocking growth is *the* reason we look for insights. The important points are to acknowledge what we do not know and to keep an open mind. This will allow new insights to emerge from anywhere as we search for the solution. The following questions will help a marcoms manager think through the IMC planning process, and in the process sensitise themselves to possible sources of insights.

1. Where is the revenue coming from? Who is your target audience and what motivates them?
2. Who else influences the target audience's decision-making, and what motivates them?
3. How big is the target audience, and how much of it can we reach?
4. What other channel supports are needed?
5. How is the target audience's decision-to-purchase made for this brand?
6. What inhibitions are likely to prevent the target audience deciding in favour of the brand?
7. What are the communication objectives and tasks needed to overcome customer inhibitions and so induce the desired actions?
8. What purchase-decisive factors must be triggered in customers' minds to overcome these inhibitions?
9. What is the creative idea (if required), and how many exposures to the message are needed to trigger purchase-decisive factors?
10. What other communication options are available to overcome customer inhibitions?
11. How can all of the communication options be efficiently synchronised to create synergy?

Notice that most of these questions (1, 2, 4, 5, 6, 7 and 8) are about understanding the buying behaviour of the target audience. The information from these questions is important for effective planning, but questions 5 and 6 are especially pertinent for uncovering insights. Questions 8 and 9 should be considered jointly since they are about manifesting a motivating trigger that will increase sales. Let's now consider each of these questions in more detail.

1. Where is the revenue coming from? Who is your target audience and what motivates them?

Most of the time, an organisation is driven by the need to increase revenue. Typically, this means doing some or all the following marketing activities more efficiently:

- getting a lot of people to try the brand
- encouraging people to buy the brand at a higher price than the competition
- convincing current customers to keep buying
- finding ways of encouraging current customers to buy more (or buy more frequently)
- encouraging new usage
- winning back lost customers.

Therefore, the first step is to understand where business is likely to come from. The marketing plan with its situational and competitive analyses should help clarify our main target audience.

2. Who else influences the target audience's decision-making, and what motivates them?

This is an important question because human beings are social animals. When a risky purchase is involved, a person is likely to enlist the help of others, including their friends on social media. This means there is usually a primary and secondary target audience.

3. How big is the target audience, and how much of it can we reach?

When the target audience is known, the next stage is to figure out how large it is. Again, the marketing plan is a guide. The larger the target audience, the larger will be the number of responses, provided we can reach them and the response rate is good. The response rate is determined by a number of factors (such as the quality of the creative idea, effectiveness of the sales team, value of the offer and effective frequency), while the percentage of the target audience we can reach depends on selecting the right communication channels and media vehicles. The conceptual formula in figure 2.14 illustrates this idea.

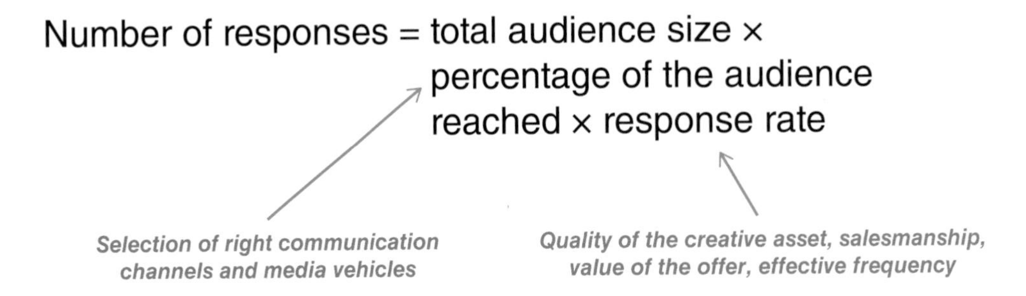

Figure 2.14 A conceptual formula for calculating number of responses

To reach as large a percentage of our target audience as possible, it pays to understand their media usage habits. The media vehicles they are exposed to (e.g. magazines and TV programs) can spark ideas about how to coordinate the campaign. Start with the most important vehicle first, and then build others around it. The objective is to maximise reach without exceeding the budget.

4. *What other channel supports are needed?*

In some product categories, such as consumer-packaged goods or electronics, channel members play a vital role. The organisation needs to 'sell into' these intermediaries before they can 'on sell' to the end user. Sometimes the marketing strategy requires channel members to 'push' the product through the channel, while advertising is used to 'pull' the market through by stimulating the interest of the end user. At other times, channel members need to offer a service that is part of the offering in order to stimulate sales. In these circumstances, the channel members should also be targeted in the communications. For instance, if there is a tourism campaign to attract visitors to Australia, then having travel agents as partners will be helpful. Again, the marketing plan is a useful guide for a marcoms manager.

5. *How is the target audience's decision-to-purchase made for this brand?*

This question is challenging to answer because it requires careful mapping. It is also challenging because the marketing plan does not normally include information about decision-to-purchase. It should therefore be carefully researched, using the consumer decision journey discussed in chapter 1 (see figure 2.15). But these stages should be customised for each business.

6. *What inhibitions are likely to prevent the target audience deciding in favour of the brand?*

While researching the audience's purchase decision, we should try to understand the inhibitors as well. The following are typical inhibitors:

- too expensive
- too risky (i.e. not trustworthy)
- not urgent or important
- poor image

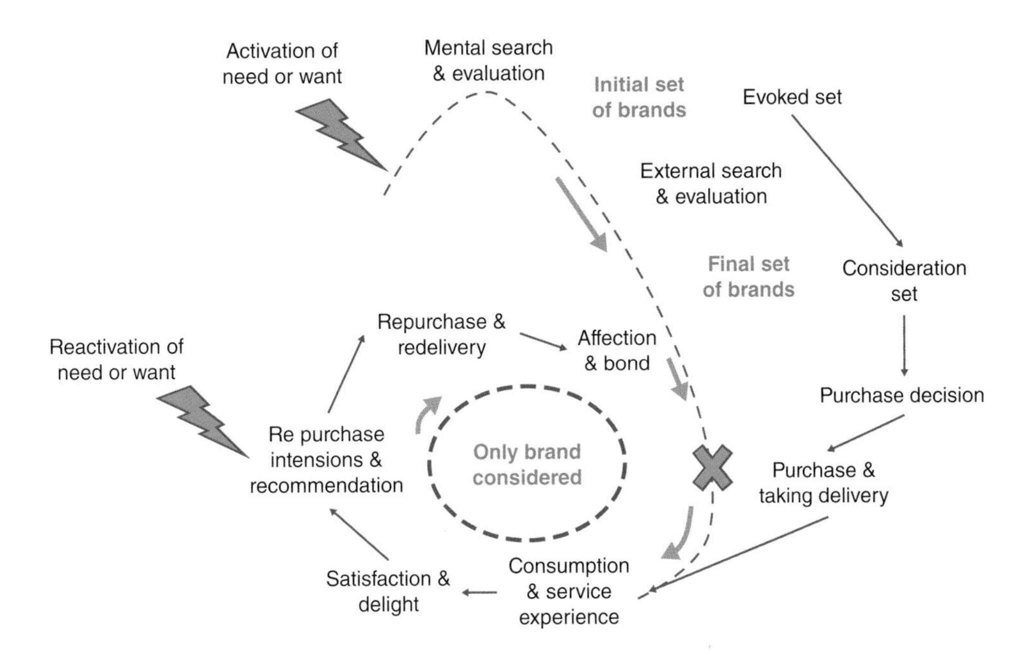

Figure 2.15 Consumer decision journey

- mistaken beliefs
- too complicated to buy
- too much effort needed to buy.

Answering this question will gives us an idea about the inhibitors that occur at each stage of the decision journey. One useful way of thinking is to consider the conversion ratios between each of the earlier stages in the decision-making process. In other words, we want to find out where the attrition is. For instance, Australia as a holiday destination is considered by a considerable number of US holiday makers (i.e. Australia is in their consideration set of holiday destinations), but only a small percentage (8%) will actually develop an intention to visit because Australia is too far away and hence too expensive to visit.[68]

7. ***What are the communication objectives and tasks needed to overcome customer inhibitions and so induce the desired action?***

Once we have discovered the audience's inhibitions, we need to think of ways to reduce these and induce the desired action. We start by understanding what exactly we want to communicate to the target audience. This forms the objectives, and from these objectives flow the tasks. For instance, if the objective is to raise brand awareness for a new product, the tasks involved may be to use print advertising (such as newspapers) and publicity (such as social media) simultaneously to achieve this objective. In the case of Tourism Australia, since only 8% of US visitors intend to visit Australia, increasing intention to visit will be a clear communication objective. This then influences subsequent tasks.

It should be noted that giving information may not be enough. For instance, we all know that physical exercise is good for us, yet many do not exercise enough (due to inertia or other reasons). Thus, more often than not, communication objectives need to include specific actions we want consumers to take.

8. *What purchase-decisive factors must be triggered in customers' minds to overcome these inhibitions?*

Once the inhibitors are discovered, then it is a matter of addressing them systematically. For instance, if the tyranny of distance and expense is a barrier for US holiday makers, then one can target the high-value US travellers – those willing to spend – and put out countervailing reasons why the long distance can be viewed positively (e.g. lots of onboard movies, lots of wine to drink onboard). One can also use the list of seven common motivators and values (see table 2.2) to brainstorm other ways of overcoming these inhibitors. For instance, if travelling to Australia is expensive, then the deciding factor might be a price deal. This will essentially remove the problem. Furthermore, since travelling to Australia may be on the bucket-list for many US travellers, the campaign can also communicate the end value of self-fulfilment, and perhaps have a social media campaign where US travellers can post stimulating images of their trip and win a prize.

Table 2.2 Common motivators and end values

Common motivators[69]	Common end values[70]
Sensory gratification	Family
Social approval	Belonging
Intellectual stimulation	Self-fulfilment
Normal depletion	Self-esteem
Dissatisfaction	Satisfaction
Problem removal	Accomplishment
Problem avoidance	Security

9. *What is the creative idea (if required), and how many exposures to the message are needed to trigger purchase-decisive factors?*

Question 9 is about creating the 'magic' that will actually trigger the behaviour. It is one thing to understand why people may not buy: it is quite another to find the actual motivational trigger that the target audience will pay attention to and find compelling. Creative thinking is required. It also requires thinking about the number of exposures needed. If the creative idea (or theme) is complex, repetition is generally needed. However, the greater the frequency, the greater the budget that is needed. Chapter 4 will discuss exposure frequency and continuity in greater detail.

Questions 8 and 9 are probably the most difficult to answer, as they require lateral thinking. Sometimes the solution is unearthed while searching for consumer insight (see earlier discussion); sometimes it comes from management team brainstorming. More often than not, the final creative solution will come from the creative team in an advertising, PR or promotion agency. Chapters 6 and 7 will discuss creative ideas and execution.

10. *What other communication options are available to overcome customer inhibitions?*

Although answering question 3 reveals what media vehicles to use, answering this question can suggest other communication options or channels as well. As new forms of communications are invented every day, there are now much greater opportunities to tackle inhibitors. In the case of Tourism Australia, the campaign has been supported by other amazing content of interviews posted online.

	April				May				June				Cost
	1	2	3	4	1	2	3	4	1	2	3	4	
Australian Financial Review (AFR) print ad with QR codes													10,000
AFR website banner and online (video) ad													24,000
Sydney Morning Herald (SMH) print ad with QR codes													10,000
SMH website banner and online (video) ads													20,000
Training print ad (for HR managers) with QR codes													4,500
Website activities (e.g., update testimonials)													3,000
Search engine optimisation and social media activities													2,000
Public seminars with Professors													300
Information evenings													8,000
University Open Day													500
												Subtotal	82,300

	November				December				January				Cost
	1	2	3	4	1	2	3	4	1	2	3	4	
Australian Financial Review (AFR) print ad with QR codes													10,000
AFR website banner ad and online (video) ad													24,000
Sydney Morning Herald (SMH) print ad with QR codes													12,000
SMH website banner ad and online (video) ad													20,000
Training print ad (for HR managers) with QR codes													3,000
Website activities (e.g., testimonials)													2,000
Search engine optimisation and social media activities													2,000
Public seminars with Professors													200
Information evenings													4,000
University Open Day													500
												Subtotal	77,200
												Grant total	159,500

Figure 2.16 Example of an IMC activity plan

11. How can all of the communication options be efficiently synchronised to create synergy?

The last question helps pull everything together. In practice, this question is not easy to answer since it involves many parts of the organisation. In chapter 1, we have already discussed the many ways in which marcoms activities can be synergised.

In summary, by asking these key questions, the marcoms manager will go a long way in understanding how an integrated media plan can be created. Notice how the planning moves 'outside-in' and that we choose the media that is best suited to reach the target audience without any preconceived bias towards any particular medium. Following this process will also help give the manager an idea of the budget required for the campaign. Finally, this preparatory work will also guide the development of the creative idea, which may in turn suggest other media options.

IMC ACTIVITY PLAN

It is important to put together an IMC activity plan as shown in figure 2.16 in order to time and execute all the planned activities in the right sequence. Once a preliminary plan – let's call it plan A – is in place, we can begin to think of better options, or a combination of options, that can be set up alternatively as plans B, C, D and so on. This is where debate and analysis of assumptions about consumer behaviour become important. This will then encourage us to revisit the 11 questions again. Throughout this text, we emphasise the importance of research in honing our understanding in developing a solid IMC activity plan. Figure 2.16 is an example of an IMC activity plan for our business school when we have a campaign to attract MBA students.

DISCUSSION QUESTIONS

1. What is a workable consumer insight? How is it different from an insight that is merely interesting?
2. What is the difference between qualitative and quantitative research? How can we combine these in a productive way?
3. What is creative development research? How is this different from confirmatory or evaluative research?
4. Why is qualitative research more appropriate for creative development research when you are trying to come up with a creative idea?
5. If you were to run an advertising agency, would you employ an account planner to help your creative team? Explain your answer.
6. What are deprivation studies? When is this technique most useful?
7. What is the means–end laddering technique? How is it useful to the creative advertising team?
8. What is the key defining characteristic of a projective technique? What assumptions guide its use?
9. Projective questioning is one of the techniques described in this chapter. Give an example of a projective questioning task.
10. What is the difference between the completion and construction projective techniques?
11. Marketing research does not have a good reputation among senior managers. Why do you think this is?

NOTES

1 L Soley, 'Projective techniques in US marketing and management research', *Qualitative Market Research:* An International Journal, 13(4), 2010, pp. 334–53.

2 L Fortini-Campbell, *Hitting the sweet spot*, Copy Workshop, Hudson, Chicago, 2001. This book outlines many case studies of using research to uncover consumer insights.

3 Wallas, Graham, *The art of thought*, Harcourt Brace, New York, 1926.

4 R East and L Ang, 'Making progress in marketing research', *Australasian Marketing Journal (AMJ)*, 25(4), November 2017, pp 334–40.

5 This story is not likely to be true, but it makes a good story. See Armand D'Angour's TEDEd explanation, 'The real story behind Archimedes' Eureka!' Accessed May 2018 at www.youtube.com/watch?v=0v86Yk14rf8.

6 RE Mayer, 'The search for insight: grappling with Gestalt psychology's unanswered questions', in *The Nature of Insight*, RJ Sternberg and JE Davidson (eds), MIT Press, Cambridge, MA, 1995, pp. 3–32.

7 D Taylor, 'Rebooting brand strategy for the digital age', *Market Leader*, Quarter 1, 2017. Accessed May 2017 at www.warc.com/content/paywall/article/mkt/rebooting-brand-strategy-for-the-digital-age/109882.

8 I would like to thank Judith Meyers, planner extraordinaire from Pepsico, for suggesting this quote as a way to foster clearer thinking.

9 A Lutz, 'How Lululemon brainwashes women into spending $98 on sweatpants', *Business Insider*, 2 April 2012. Accessed August 2019 at www.businessinsider.com.au/lululemon-brainwashes-women-2012-4?r=US&IR=T.

10 D Gajsek, 'Lululemon Athletica – How to beat Nike by creating a new category', 1 July 2018. Accessed August 2019 at https://dgajsek.com/growth-study-lululemon/.

11 N Hollis, 'Why so many companies fail to disrupt and grow', *Kantar Straight Talk*, 31 July 2019. Accessed 2 August 2019 at www.millwardbrown.com/global-navigation/blogs/post/mb-blog/2019/07/31/why-so-many-companies-fail-to-disrupt-and-grow?utm_source=Email.

12 'Febreze: Breathe Happy', Cannes Creative Lions Winner, Creative Effectiveness Lions, 2012. Accessed August 2019 at www.warc.com/Content/a9bc8b24-1869-4291-873d-8812b51c19ca.

13 J Parker, L Ang and S Koslow, 'The creative search for an insight in account planning: an absorptive capacity approach', *Journal of Advertising*, 47(3), 2018, pp. 237–58.

14 This is an example of a rare case where insights to message proposition are laid out. See J Steel, *Truth, lies and advertising*, John Wiley & Sons, New York, 1998, pp. 133–4; 173–4.

15 Quoted in J Steel (1998), *Truth, lies and advertising*, p. 174, note 14.

16 This example is taken from J Parker, L Ang and S Koslow, 'The creative search for an insight in account planning: an absorptive capacity approach', *Journal of Advertising*, 47(3), 2018, pp. 237–58.

17 J-M Dru, *Disruption: overturning conventions and shaking up the marketplace*, Wiley, New York, 1996.

18 A Maxwell, W Wanta, KB Sheehan and C Bentley, 'The effectiveness of account planners at US advertising agencies', in MA Shaver (ed.) *Proceedings of the 2000 Conference of the Academy of Advertising*. East Lansing: Michigan State University, 2000, pp. 149–54.

19 S Pollitt, 'How I started account planning in advertising agencies', in H Weichselbaum (ed.) *Readings in account planning*, 2008, The Copy Workshop, Chicago, IL. (Previously published in *Campaign Magazine*, April 1979.)

20 See S Pollitt (2008), 'How I started account planning in advertising agencies', note 19.

21 C Hackley, 'From consumer insight to advertising strategy: the account planner's integrative role in creative advertising development', *Marketing Intelligence and Planning*, 21(7), 2003, pp. 446–52.

22 JE Forsyth, 'Capitalizing on customer insights', *McKinsey Quarterly*, 3, 2006, pp. 42–53.

23 This case is based on L Brown, A Shar and A Smith, 'Narellan Pools: diving into big data for Narellan Pools', Gold winner of 2016 Small Budget, IPA Effectiveness, 2016.

24 S Fournier, 'Introducing New Coke', Harvard Business School Case Study [case number 9-500-067], 31 October 2001.

25 Quoted in J Greenwald, 'Coca-Cola's big fizzle', *Time*, 22 July 1985, pp. 48–52.

26 MJ Schlinger, 'A profile of responses to commercials', *Journal of Advertising Research*, 19(2), 1979, pp. 37–46.

27 T Oliver, *The real Coke, the real story*, Random House, New York, 1986.

28 R Schindler, 'The real lesson of New Coke: the value of focus groups for predicting the effects of social influence', *Marketing Research*, December, 1992, pp. 22–7.

29 J Koten, 'You aren't paranoid if you feel someone eyes you constantly', *Wall Street Journal*, 29 March 1985, p. 1.

30 R Wynberg and M Synnivig, 'Watching you, watching us, watching you', MRS Conference, 1986.

31 L Jayasinghe and M Ritson, 'Everyday advertising context: an ethnography of advertising response in the family living room', *Journal of Consumer Research*, 40(1), 2013, pp. 104–21.

32 S Bellman et al., 'How coviewing reduces the effectiveness of TV advertising', *Journal of Marketing Communications*, 18(5), 2012, pp. 363–78.

33 H Marvin, 'History and significance of the emic/etic distinction', *Annual Review of Anthropology*, 5, 1976, pp. 329–50.

34 H Schultz and DJ Yang, *Pour your heart into it: how Starbucks built a company one cup at a time*, Hyperion, New York, 1997.

35 M Fernandez and M Agui, 'To know you is to love you: a case study on how to uncover relevant consumer insights to build strong brands', *ESOMAR Excellence in Consumer Insights*, April, 2004.

36 J Ringen, 'How Lego became the Apple of toys', Fast Company, 1 August 2015. Accessed May 2018 at www.fastcompany.com/3040223/when-it-clicks-it-clicks.

37 LEGO's target group is children aged 5–11 years.

38 Quoted in J Davis 'How Lego clicked: the super brand that reinvented itself', *The Guardian*, November, 2017. Accessed May 2018 at www.theguardian.com/lifeandstyle/2017/jun/04/how-lego-clicked-the-super-brand-that-reinvented-itself.

39 J Davis (2017), 'How Lego clicked: the super brand that reinvented itself', note 38.

40 K Smith, 'Social media metrics: how you should be measuring success', Brandwatch, 23 March 2016. Accessed May 2018 at www.brandwatch.com/blog/social-media-metrics-measure-success/.

41 W McInnes, 'How to gain insight from social listening', World Advertising Research Centre (WARC). Accessed May 2018 at www.warc.com/content/paywall/article/how-to-gain-insight-from-social-listening/111763.

42 It is also possible to do the opposite with inundation studies or both. See B Urbick, 'Deprivation and inundation: paths to deeper brand insight', *Admap*, 506, 2009, pp. 50–1.

43 J Steel, *Truth, lies and advertising*, John Wiley & Son, New York, 1998, Chapter 7.
44 J Gutman, 'A means–end chain model based on consumer categorization processes', *Journal of Marketing*, 46(20), 1982, pp. 60–72.
45 TJ Reynolds and J Gutman, 'Laddering theory method, analysis and interpretation', *Journal of Advertising Research*, October/November, 1988, pp. 61–71.
46 LR Kahle, B Poulos and A Sukhdial, 'Changes in social values in the United States during the past decade', *Journal of Advertising Research*, February/March, 1998, pp. 35–41.
47 B Wansink, 'Using laddering to understand and leverage a brand's equity', *Qualitative Market Research*, 6(2), 2003, pp. 111–18.
48 H Simon, 'A behavioral model of rational choice', in *Models of man, social and rational: mathematical essays on rational human behavior in a social setting*, Wiley, New York, 1957.
49 Wendy Gordon's model on structure of consciousness (p. 166) influenced the development of this model. See W Gordon, *Good thinking: a guide to qualitative research*, Admap Publications, Oxfordshire, 1999.
50 T Johnson, A Holbrook and S Shavitt, 'Cross-cultural research methods in psychology', in D Matsumoto and F van de Vijver (eds), *Cross-cultural search methods in psychology*, Cambridge University Press, Cambridge, 2011, pp. 130–78. See also M Zax and S Takahashi, 'Cultural influences on response style: comparisons of Japanese and American college students', *Journal of Social Psychology*, 71(1), February 1967, pp. 3–10.
51 B Schwartz, *Paradox of choice*, Harper Perennial, New York, 2004.
52 S Needel, 'When good researchers go bad: cautionary tales from the front line', *ESOMAR Consumer Insights*, November, 2005.
53 According to a poll of 19 500 respondents from the US by online dating auction site WhatsYourPrice.com, 27% of women and 19% of men lie on their dating profiles. Interestingly, women are most likely to lie when they are aged between 25 and 30 years old, while men are most likely to do so between the ages of 24 and 39. And what do they lie about most? Their age and career, respectively. See PR Web, 'New dating study reveals which city's singles lie the most?'. Accessed August 2013 at www.prweb.com/releases/2013/prweb10502006.htm.
54 ASC Ehrenberg, GG Goodhardt and TP Barwise, 'Double jeopardy revisited', *Journal of Marketing*, 54(3), 1990, pp. 82–91.
55 JP Jones, 'How much advertising works?' in JP Jones (ed.), *How advertising works*, Sage Publications, Thousand Oaks, CA, 1998, pp. 291–6.
56 AA Cunningham, KJ Preacher and MR Banajo, 'Implicit attitudes measures: consistency, stability and convergent validity', *Psychological Science*, 12, 2001, pp. 163–70.
57 RH Fazio et al., 'On the automatic activation of attitudes', *Journal of Personality and Social Psychology*, 50, 1986, pp. 229–38.
58 L de Chernatony and S Knox, 'How an appreciation of consumer behaviour can help in product testing', *Journal of Market Research Society*, 32(3), July 1990, p. 333.
59 R Piirto, 'Measuring minds in the 1990s', *American Demographics*, 12(12), 1990, pp. 30–5.
60 W Gordon, *Good thinking: a guide to qualitative research*, Admap Publications, Oxfordshire, 1999.
61 L Gardner, 'On the classification of projective techniques', *Psychological Bulletin*, 15, 1959, pp. 158–68.
62 E Ramsey, P Ibbotson and P McCole, 'Application of projective techniques in e-business research context', *International Journal of Market Research*, 48(5), 2006, pp. 551–73.

63 E Mosicheva and T Ziglina, 'Provocative discourse as an insight generator', *ESOMAR Qualitative Research*, Barcelona, November, 2005.

64 E Fram and E Cibotti, 'The shopping list studies and projective techniques: a 40-year view', *Marketing Research*, December, 1991, pp. 14–20.

65 G Zaltman, *How customers think: essential insights into the mind of the market*, Harvard Business School Publishing, Boston, 2003.

66 S Wills and P Williams, 'Insight as a strategic asset: the opportunity and the stark reality', *International Journal of Market Research*, 46(40), 2004, pp. 393–410.

67 For recent examples of using consumer insights and cross functional team see A Narayanan, A Padhi and J Williams, 'Designing products for value', *McKinsey Quarterly*, October, 2012. Accessed July 2013 at www.mckinsey.com/insights/innovation/designing_products_for_value.

68 Effie, 'Tourism Australia: Dundee: The Son of a Legend Returns Home', 2019. Accessed August 2019 at www.effie.org/case_database/case/ME_2019_E-3994-659.

69 JR Rossiter, L Percy and L Bergkvist, *Marketing communications*, Sage Publications Ltd, 2018.

70 B Wansink, 'Using laddering to understand and leverage a brand's equity', *Qualitative Market Research*, 6(2), 2003, pp. 111–18.

CHAPTER 3
BRAND POSITIONING

CHAPTER OVERVIEW

The chapter is about brand positioning, one of the most important concepts in advertising. We can think of positioning as akin to impression management, first discussed by sociologist Ervin Goffman in the 1950s.[1] Impression management means that we present a certain image of ourselves to others, which serves a functional (or instrumental) purpose. In Goffman's terms, brand positioning is an impression we want to evoke in the mind of the target audience about the brand. In creating this impression, we also sometimes recreate an impression of competing brands, and this is where the topic of positioning becomes especially interesting. Ultimately, positioning is about creating an impression that allows a brand to differentiate itself from its competition.

However, whatever impressions that we try to create for a brand need to be fulfilled, or else they will not last long – competition will easily see to that. This means that before we take a position, we need to do much strategic thinking. In this chapter, therefore, we conceptualise positioning at two levels – a higher strategic level and a lower promotional level. Once this is understood, then all the positioning tactics make sense. The objective is to create brand associations that will predispose people to choose the brand over others, and ultimately to build brand equity. If all subsequent executions are well implemented, then consumers will come to prefer a brand over the competition. This, in essence, is the ultimate goal of positioning and branding.

Learning goals

After reading this chapter, you will understand:

- what brand positioning is
- why it is important to segment first before positioning the brand
- how targeting the right segment can affect profitability
- why positioning of a brand can also mean repositioning of competing brands
- the difference between strategic and promotional positioning
- tactics for brand positioning, and their advantages and disadvantages
- the challenges of repositioning a brand
- the concepts of point of difference, point of parity and frame of reference
- ways of conceptualising brand equity
- the relationship between brand associations, brand 'building', brand positioning and brand equity.

This chapter is about playing mind games. Let's start with an example.

The soft drink 7-Up[2] started life as a medicinal product to cure hangovers, and it was then presented as a soda-like mixer for whisky-based drinks. It was in 1967 that the advertising agency J Walter Thompson (JWT) was tasked with changing the position of 7-Up from a tonic to a soft drink. The only problem was that at that time cola was the only type of soft drink available and unfortunately 7-Up was a medicinal drink, not a cola. To change this perception, the agency had to come up with an idea that could link it to a cola even though it was not a cola. The creative team hit upon the idea of distancing 7-Up from cola, at the same time positioning itself as a soft drink. They came up with the brilliant tagline: '7-Up. The Uncola'. With that single tagline, JWT managed to reposition 7-Up as a 'cola' – a soft drink.

Consider the following quote about the mouthwash brand Listerine from Levitt and Dubner:[3]

> Listerine, for instance, was invented in the nineteenth century as a powerful surgical antiseptic. It was later sold, in distilled form, as both a floor cleaner and a cure for gonorrhea. But it was not a runaway success until the 1920s, when it was pitched as a solution for 'chronic halitosis' – a then obscure medical term for bad breath. Listerine's new ads featured forlorn young women and men, eager for marriage but turned off by their mate's rotten breath. 'Can I be happy with him in spite of that?' one maiden asked herself. Until that time, bad breath was not conventionally considered such a catastrophe. But Listerine changed that. As the advertising scholar James B Twitchell wrote, 'Listerine did not make mouthwash as much as it made halitosis.' In just seven years, the company's revenues rose from $115 000 to more than $8 million.

These examples illustrate one important concept – a brand adopting a certain position in people's minds. Since a brand cannot be all things to all people, taking a definite stand helps create clarity. This was most clearly articulated by Reis and Trout,[4] who first pointed out the importance of positioning as it relates to the mind. Since positioning occurs in the minds of the target audience, it follows that its success or failure also depends on how desirable the resulting mental associations are. We can thus define positioning as follows:

> Brand positioning is the creation of strong and favourable associations[5] in the mind of the target audience, so that the brand comes to represent something different and relevant and hence stands apart from competition. Successful positioning means being able to achieve a 'monopoly' of the desirable mind-space for the chosen audience.

PRINCIPLES OF BRAND POSITIONING

Principle 1: Segment first, then position

If positioning is all in the mind of the target segment, how can we assess this? Assessment is important because if we need to reposition an existing brand, we want to be able to tell whether the repositioning is successful after the campaign. The same applies to the positioning of a new brand.

One way of representing where a brand sits in the 'mental space' is to compare it with other brands using a perceptual map. Figure 3.1 is a simple example of a two-dimensional map of the car market, as rated by students. We can see that Mercedes SL is grouped with Porsche and is perceived to be sporty and luxurious. On the other hand, Mercedes E-class, BMW 7-series and Rolls Royce Ghost tend to be perceived as more conservative, although still luxurious. The other brands can be similarly interpreted.

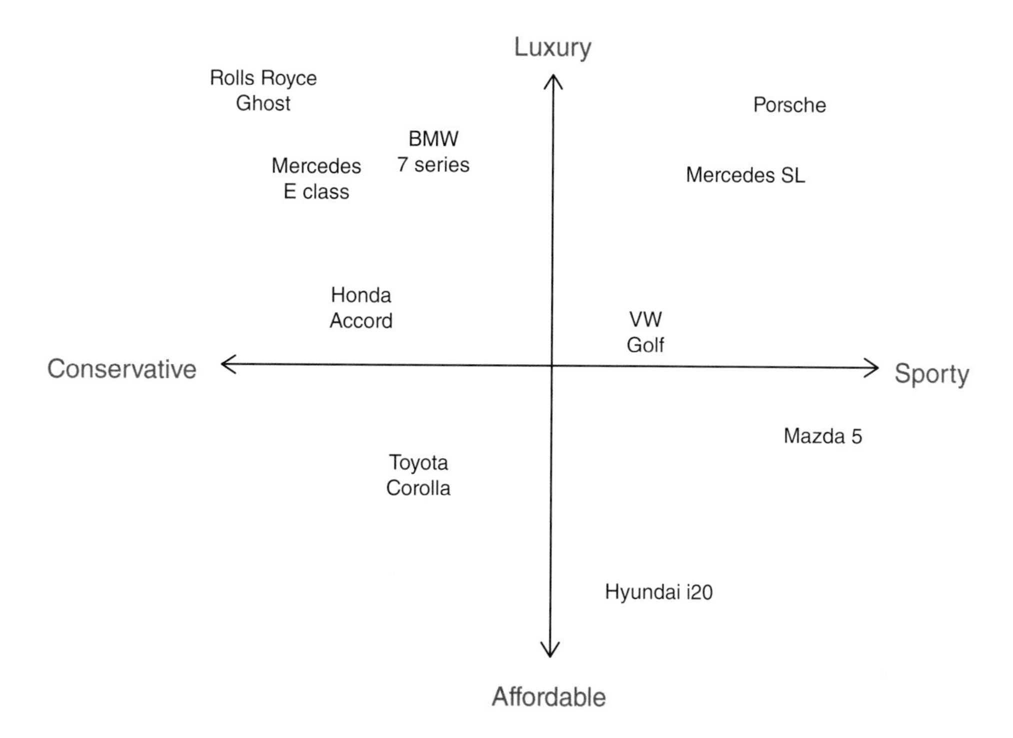

Figure 3.1 Perceptual map of cars

However, this map was derived from the input of students. It will change with another segment, such as business executives, and even with different types of business executive (e.g. finance executives or administrative executives). Therefore, the important point is to decide which segment or segments to target before contemplating how the brand should be positioned for the chosen segments. Sometimes the chosen segments may be too small to be profitable. Therefore, it may be necessary to broaden our targets to be profitable.

Another point to note is that perceptual maps must accurately reflect the 'mental space' of the chosen segments. This can be contentious because if it does not reflect the 'mind' of the target segments – or what they consider to be important – then it is not managerially useful. This often means going beyond two dimensions. For instance, three dimensions will help if it can further refine the mental representations of the brand. But the more important point is that the dimensions of the axes (whether two or three) are nothing more than a summary of a set of associations (which is why we call the axes 'dimensions'). It is important to interpret the map carefully, with an understanding of what associations make up each dimension.

Principle 2: Brand positioning is not the same as brand image

The concept of brand positioning is not the same as brand image. Brand image is essentially the associations that are attached to the brand. For instance, if you ask people what comes to mind when they think of McDonald's, they might say 'fast food, Big Mac, golden arches, unhealthy, greasy, cheap and artificial'. These words represent possible associations consumers have about the brand. But this is not McDonald's positioning. Positioning refers to the perception of the brand in relation to its competitors. While these associations represent

McDonald's, different associations may represent another brand of fast food, such as Subway (e.g. Subway has no golden arches or Big Mac). In order to compare McDonald's with Subway, we must find a common set of associations for these two brands so that their mental location in people's minds can be mapped relative to each other (see the car example in figure 3.1).

Principle 3: Positioning is hard work

Although the notion of brand positioning seems straightforward, it is by no means simplistic. It involves searching for that market (i.e. the segment) and mental space where the brand can dominate and prosper. To appreciate the complexity of a positioning task, consider the new product scenario described below.

Imagine you are tasked to develop a new ice-cream brand for the Shanghai market. After studying, you realise that there is a gap in the market for an up-market, expensive, rich luxury brand. No such brand currently exists in Shanghai.

This is surprising – that is, an insight – because the trend towards health consciousness would suggest there should be no demand for such a product. Yet your research suggests a niche exists. There is a distinct group of female consumers who view ice-cream as an indulgent treat. These are single, professional women in their late twenties and early thirties, who are financially independent. They like traditional flavours such as chocolate, vanilla and strawberry but will also occasionally try new, exotic flavours such as coconut, hazelnut, lychee and mocha.

In terms of their psychology of consumption, these women feel a little guilty every time they eat ice-cream, but always rationalise it by saying that they deserve it. Going to the gym at least three times a week to 'exercise the fat away' also helps relieve their guilt. You have established this by using projective interview techniques (discussed in chapter 2). In terms of lifestyle, they live alone and are single, but lead very active social lives. They feel free to indulge in whatever they desire.

As a manager, your immediate task may be as follows: to come up with (1) a brand name, logo, slogan and packaging; then decide on (2) the price point; (3) choice of distribution, and a website for the brand; and finally in terms of communication, (4) a creative concept that will resonate with this niche. It is a challenge.

After reading this 'new ice-cream' scenario, we can quickly appreciate the complexity of a positioning task. For instance, a product's new brand name, logo, slogan, packaging and website must be on message. This means that all elements must convey the same desired associations in a creatively integrated way (to be discussed later).

Principle 4: If possible, reposition the competition in a way that they cannot counter

Positioning of one's brand can often mean repositioning the competition. When 7-Up repositioned itself as a non-cola soft drink, it also effectively repositioned the 'Coca-Cola' and Pepsi-

Cola brands to appear more similar to each other. The 7-Up ad then pointed out that, unlike the other colas, it did not leave an aftertaste, instead offering a 'crisp, fresh, clean, wild' taste. This subtly implied that all colas were the same and, even more, did not taste good. The ad was saying '7-Up is different!'

Another classic example can be seen in Avis' 1962 campaign against Hertz (then the market leader in the US car-rental market). Avis' market share was just 11% and the company was unprofitable. Bill Bernbach of DDB created the 'We try harder' campaign. This tagline not only suggested that Avis had to work harder in order to survive but also cleverly implied that Hertz, as the market leader, did not provide as good a service as Avis. Within a year, Avis became profitable and by 1966 its market share rose to 35%.[6]

Both classic examples show that by positioning our brand, we can also end up repositioning the competition in a way that they cannot easily counter. A more recent example shows how Burger King (Sweden) tried to reposition McDonald's as inferior by directly comparing the Big Mac with its own burgers in their menu; for example, the menu would read, 'Like a Big Mac but juicier and tastier' or 'Like a Big Mac but actually big' or 'Big Mac-ish but flame-grilled of course' (see figure 3.2, and also the discussion later in the chapter on competitor comparison). Burger King could get away with this because McDonald's lost the exclusive right to use the Big Mac trademark in Europe.[7] It is fortuitous for Burger King, but McDonald's is appealing the EU ruling.

Figure 3.2 How Burger King (Sweden) repositioned McDonald's Big Mac as inferior

STRATEGIC ISSUES OF POSITIONING

That is not the end of the complexity. Complicating the issue is the need to decide what the organisation should be doing. For instance, the ice-cream scenario above assumes that developing a new brand is the correct strategic direction for the firm; it also assumes that the organisation has the capability to deliver that sort of product. But what if the organisation is not capable of doing this, due to a lack of resources or expertise? Or what if the CEO does not believe that there is a long-term future for a product positioned in this way (e.g. given the trend towards healthy living)?

All these strategic-level issues will affect lower-level positioning decisions. We might argue that the ice-cream example is about a new product, which may make the positioning task more difficult, but the same principle applies to repositioning an existing brand. In fact, in many ways, the repositioning of an old brand is harder because it is more difficult to change consumer perceptions than to create new ones. But from a managerial point of view the positioning of brands involves decisions in two areas: the strategic and the promotional.

Profitability of the brand

The first strategic question is to ask where the revenue of the new or repositioned brand is going to come from. It may come from new users, switchers from another brand or lapsed current users. Since the competition is also going after the same market, it is important to answer this strategic question. The answer will also affect decisions such as where to place the ad in order to reach the (new) chosen target segments. It will also help determine what level of penetration is needed or, alternatively, whether the current penetration level is satisfactory. Trade promotion may also be needed to secure or increase penetration (see chapter 11 for more discussion of trade promotion).

Once the revenue question is settled, the next step is to estimate the profitability that will be derived from the chosen segments, assuming that the positioning will be well executed. Profitability can be difficult to determine because of ambiguity in how costs are allocated in company records. But even so, an effort should be made to understand it. The option of at least increasing price should be considered since this will increase profitability.

We should also consider category dynamics.[8] If the brand falls into the value (cheap) category, where all the competing brands are also cutting prices, there may not be any funds left for differentiation activities. If so, then brand differentiation, if desired, may have to take a back seat. Usually such low-value, cheap brands are not operationally well managed (e.g. suffering from a bloated cost structure). The imperative is to cut costs to free up money for differentiation activities. This may involve making difficult operational decisions, such as closing facilities, standardising components, consolidating or forming alliances with suppliers or vertical integration, so that these funds can be ploughed into brand differentiation (e.g. innovation and image advertising). Brand differentiation is more likely to pay dividends if the brand is already in a category where the competing brands are not simply price-cutting (as in products such as beers, athletic footwear or cars).

A modern-day example of a successful and profitable brand differentiation is that of Apple. Over the years, it has successfully positioned itself as being simple, creative and human. In 2015, even though it had a global market share of only 15% of smartphones, they made up an incredible 79% of its global profits.[9]

Deliverable brand positioning

Effective execution of brand positioning also depends on the capability of the firm. This is the second strategic issue – can the organisation deliver on the promise? This may mean fulfilling the functional or experiential attributes promised in the positioning campaign. For instance, we might want to position the ice-cream as an up-market, indulgent brand, but if we cannot technically achieve the richness of taste and smoothness of texture we have promised, the campaign will be a waste of money. This means the organisation has to solve any product issues first, remembering that nothing kills a bad product faster than a great campaign (see chapter 1, and also case study 3.1 on Edsel).

The same principle applies to service organisations. For instance, if we want to position a bank as friendly and courteous, then we want to make sure that the service personnel are indeed friendly and courteous before the campaign starts. This may not be so easy to deliver if the staff require retraining to achieve a change in attitude. Much then depends on the distinctive competency of the firm.

Long-term strategic direction

This brings up the third strategic issue in positioning – the direction of the organisation in setting itself apart from its competitors. Note that the strategic direction of a firm is not the same thing as its competency. A firm may not be able to fulfil a strategic direction now, but that does not mean it cannot in the future. For instance, if senior managers think that service quality is critical for the future prosperity of the firm, then this is the strategic direction the firm should be pursuing, and it then drives the delivery of the brand. If a firm does not have the competency to move in a new direction but wants to, then that new competency has to be built or bought (resources permitting). Conversely, even if the firm has the competency but considers the proposed direction futile for whatever reason, there is no point pursuing such a positioning for the brand.

A virtuous triangle

We can see from these strategic issues how positioning decisions made at the corporate level (i.e. strategic positioning) will drive positioning at the lower level (i.e. promotional positioning). Yet the successful positioning of the brand at the promotional level, targeting the right target segments, will earn the company profits to sustain the strategic positioning. One can therefore think of strategic positioning as a statement of ambition, and promotional positioning as a means of getting there. For instance, Google's stated mission is to 'organize the world's information and make it universally accessible and useful'. This statement did not come from consumer insight (see chapter 2), but from a vision the organisation holds, made possible by a supporting promotional strategy to help achieve this mission.[10]

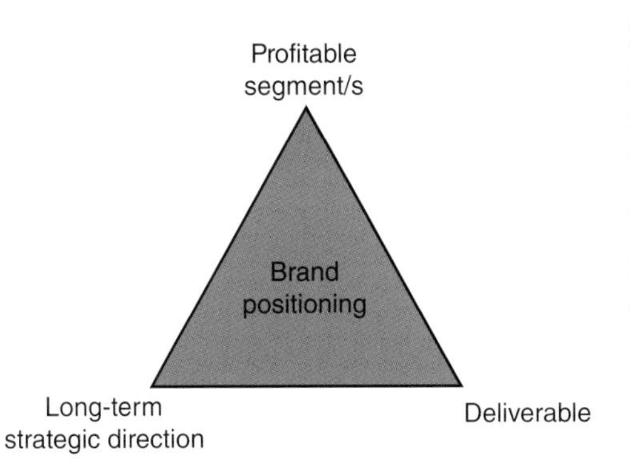

Figure 3.3 The three strategic issues that govern brand positioning

Figure 3.3 summarises this virtuous triangle. At the centre is brand positioning. When successfully applied, brand positioning helps articulate what the brand has to deliver to earn profits from the right target segments, and so to support the direction of the firm that will set it apart from its competitors in the long run. All of these points of the triangle are connected.

AFTERPAY AND THE KARDASHIAN SISTERS

A recent example of this interplay between strategic and promotional positioning is how Afterpay broke into the US market. Afterpay is an Australian start-up, which allows consumers to buy products now and pay later in instalments. Paying off a bill in smaller chunks periodically is extremely attractive (especially to millennials who do not like to get into debt, incurring interest payments), and Afterpay's technology can facilitate this between the consumer and retailers. But to launch in the US, Afterpay needed to create awareness among the millennials. So they enlisted the help of the Kardashians, who already had a huge following of millennials buying their makeup online. One day before Thanksgiving in 2018,[11] the Kardashians provided their customers with an additional form of payment, Afterpay, to take advantage of Black Friday (29 Nov) – a public holiday in the US that is considered the start of their Christmas shopping period. Afterpay now has a very successful business in the US.

MARKET SPACE AND MENTAL SPACE

Now that we understand the issues governing strategic positioning, let's look at its relationship with promotional positioning. One way of thinking about this relationship is that strategic-level questions are principally about deciding in which markets the firms want to gain profit from in the long term (i.e. which segments to target), while decisions about promotional positioning are about deciding how to dominate the mental space of the chosen segments in the market (i.e. which creative tactic to use). Figure 3.4 is a representation of this relationship. Now, since the mental space belongs to consumers, and consumers make up the market, strategic questions about which segments to target must be answered first before we can decide what positioning tactics to use.

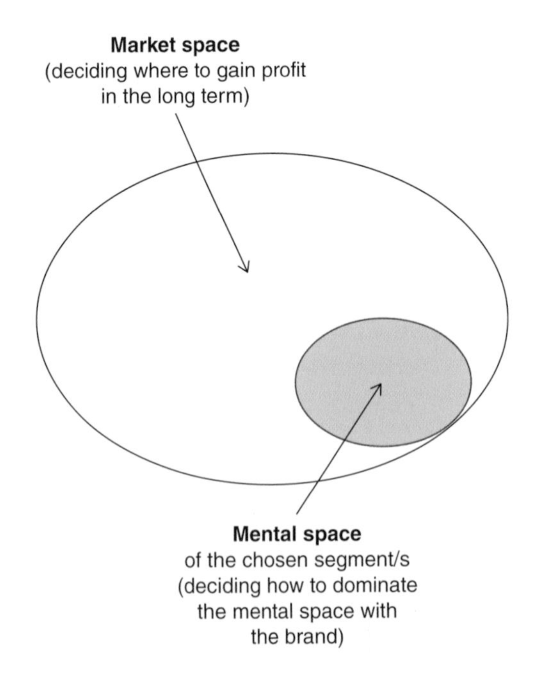

Figure 3.4 Market space versus mental space

POSITIONING FRAMEWORKS AND THE BRAND POSITIONING STATEMENT

Different positioning frameworks have been discussed by various authors. From the perspective of industrial economics, Michael Porter argues that to be competitive, a firm has three positioning strategies to choose from: differentiation, cost leader or niche. He points out that it is better to be strong in one of these positions rather than being 'stuck in the middle'; that is, average in all three.[12] In marketing strategy, the common framework used is that of Kotler, where a firm can be a market leader, challenger, follower or nicher. Thus, depending on whether a firm is a leader or a challenger and so forth, the competitive strategies would vary accordingly.[13]

In the context of marcoms, the emphasis is on the brand. Here, the positioning statement of the brand becomes important. The brand positioning statement is simply a succinct statement articulating what the brand stands for, to whom and why. It helps ensure that the marcoms strategy is on target.

Consider how you would write a positioning statement for a business school like Harvard, which was founded in 1908. If the main motivation for doing an MBA for a young business executive is to help them quickly move up the corporate ladder, and Harvard's competitive advantage is its reputation in delivering state-of-the art business education, then its brand positioning statement could look something like this:

> **For** [young business executives] **who want** [to quickly move up the corporate ladder], **Harvard is the** [business school] **that has a** [reputation of delivering quality business education] **because** [it has been doing so for over 100 years].

Notice that such a statement has several components: target audience, need motivation, product category, key brand benefit and competitive advantage. These are shown in brackets in the hypothetical statement above and figure 3.5 represents a general framework for writing a brand positioning statement.

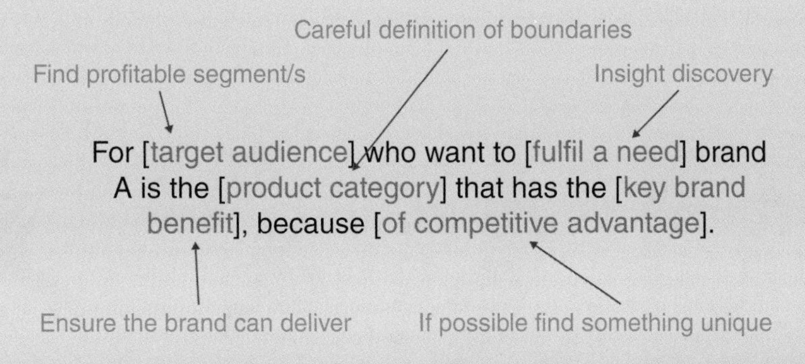

Figure 3.5 A framework for a brand positioning statement

The purple words in brackets represent the components of the brand positioning statement while the red words are the comments, which are fairly straightforward since these have already been discussed. However, a few words need to be said about the difference between a brand positioning statement and a message proposition (discussed in chapter 2). A message proposition may change from campaign to campaign but positioning of the brand generally does not. For instance, the campaign for BMW has changed over the years, but it is still the 'Ultimate Driving Machine', which is the essence of the brand (targeting the well-heeled). As we will see later in chapter 6, the message proposition is to ensure that the advertising is 'on message'. But note that the advertising can still be 'off strategy' even though it is 'on message' (i.e. saying all the right things with a good execution). This is because, for instance, the wrong audience has been targeted, which is why segmentation must come first. Hence the importance of doing one's homework and working out a credible brand positioning statement before thinking of any creative ideas. In chapter 7, we discuss in greater detail the difference between a creative idea and its execution.

Tactics for positioning the brand in the mental space

How does one go about creating dominance in the mind of the chosen segments? There are many ways of doing this, some of which are outlined in this section, but whichever way we choose, it is ultimately about creating strong, favourable, relevant and unique associations for the brand. This means consistently and clearly communicating this message. Therefore, two elements have to work: (i) associating the brand with the right conveyor and (ii) repetition.

A conveyor can be defined as any entity (e.g. a picture, music, celebrity or packaging) that has desirable dominant associations that a brand can appropriate for the purpose of creating its ideal positioning. This means repeatedly pairing the brand with this entity so that the desired associations can be transferred to the brand. In psychology, this is called 'evaluative conditioning'.[14] A good example of a consistent use of a conveyor is that of the Scotch Whisky brand, Johnnie Walker (see figure 3.6). The logo is that of a Striding Man, which was created to bring the brand character to life. It symbolises the spirit of the pioneers who forged the business in the 1800s – restless, ambitious, committed; pursuing quality and flavour above all else … always believing more was possible.

Figure 3.6 Changes in the Johnnie Walker logo over the years

The following information box and subsequent discussion suggest the various positioning tactics one can use.[15]

SOME POSITIONING TACTICS

✓ Suggestive brand name and logo
✓ Packaging, colour and website or brand home page
✓ Attribute, consequences (benefit or emotion) and values (A-C-V)
✓ Competitor comparison
✓ Brand image, brand personality and celebrities
✓ User imagery
✓ Reputation cues
✓ Country of origin, region and cultural icons
✓ Price, quality and status cues
✓ Occasions, usage and applications

Suggestive brand name and logo

The brand is one of the most powerful cues consumers use to quickly gauge the quality of products or services. It simplifies decision-making for the buyer and helps differentiate itself from the competition. It is also an asset the company wholly owns which competitors cannot copy or infringe. As such, it should be as distinctive as possible to stand out in the marketplace. This helps increase its salience and hence encourage purchase.

For a new brand, its name and logo are also the most important elements to use in its positioning because this is the first question a person would ask (i.e. 'What is the brand?'). A good brand name should be easy to remember, simple to pronounce and distinctive and, most importantly, should connote the intended, relevant meaning. Interestingly, if the name is difficult to pronounce, its relevance will be diminished.[16]

The meaning is often the benefit, and one common way of creating brand names is to include a 'semantic embed' in the name; that is, a word that clearly connotes the benefit. For instance, a TV brand called Picture Perfect will produce a higher recall of this benefit than a brand called Emporium, which does not suggest an explicit benefit.[17] In other words, the more explicit the embedded benefit in the brand name, the more likely consumers will recall the benefit of the product. However, there is a downside when the brand is too explicitly entwined with the benefit – it may limit the introduction of a new benefit later on. For instance, if we now want to advertise that our Picture Perfect TV also has a superior sound, the recall for this new benefit will be lower than if the brand name is not that suggestive of the first benefit. A name that is very suggestive, because of its semantic embed, can limit flexibility later on.

One way to avoid this problem is to create a brand name that uses sound symbolism. Sound symbolism relies on the fact that some letters tend to naturally connote certain meanings; words that imitate or suggest the source of the sound they describe are also known as 'onomatopoeic'. For instance, the non-word 'mil' tends to be perceived as smaller than the non-word 'mal', although they differ by only one letter.[18] Generally, vowel sounds such as 'e' and 'i' tend to be perceived as smaller, brighter, lighter, softer, thinner, faster, weaker, softer and more 'feminine' than the vowel sounds of 'o' and 'u'. Similarly, the consonant sounds of 'f', 's', 'v' and 'z' tend to be smaller, lighter, softer and more feminine than those of 'p', 't', 'b', 'g', 'd', 'k' or 'c'. We can use this principle to create non-word brand names. For instance, a shampoo called Silbee will be perceived as softer than Polbee, because it uses the consonant 's' and the vowel 'i'. People also like this brand name more.[19] Sound symbolism may thus be more suitable to use if we need to reposition the brand in future, because the letters have a more varied interpretation than do semantic embeds.

Another consideration is the logo of the brand. The logo is usually an insignia that accompanies the brand name. For instance, Nike has its 'swoosh' logo while Audi's logo uses four interlocking rings. These insignia help consumers recognise a brand name more quickly, since the logo is processed as a unit. Research by Henderson and Cote[20] suggests that if we want consumers to recognise a logo it should contain elements that can be quickly associated in consumers' minds. They suggest the logo should:

- be natural so that it represents the brand and the category clearly (e.g. the apple in Apple Computers or the lemon in Sprite)
- depart from perfect symmetry and balance (e.g. the Volvo arrow)
- use repetition (e.g. Audi's interlocking rings).

Figure 3.7 Good company logos: Sprite (left), Volvo (centre) and Audi (right)

But more than just recognition, a logo can also be crafted to signify a certain meaning. For this reason, major corporations often spend considerable amount of money designing or changing its logo because its meaning can spill over to the firm. For instance, an incomplete type face in a logo is perceived to be *less* trustworthy because of its ambiguity, even though it is perceived to be more interesting and hence more innovative[21] (see figure 3.8).

ELEMENT ELEMENT

Figure 3.8 The typeface logo on the left is perceived to be less trustworthy than the one on the right

On the other hand, an asymmetric logo will make the brand more arousing, and when combined with a brand with an exciting personality will improve brand attitude and make the brand more valuable[22] (see figure 3.9). A circular logo tends to have a softer association, and when used on a pair of sneakers will generate a softer and more comfortable imagery compared to an angular logo[23] (see figure 3.10). Interestingly, when a circular logo of a sneaker is advertised with a supporting headline espousing its comfortableness, people are more likely to pay more for it than if an angular logo is used.

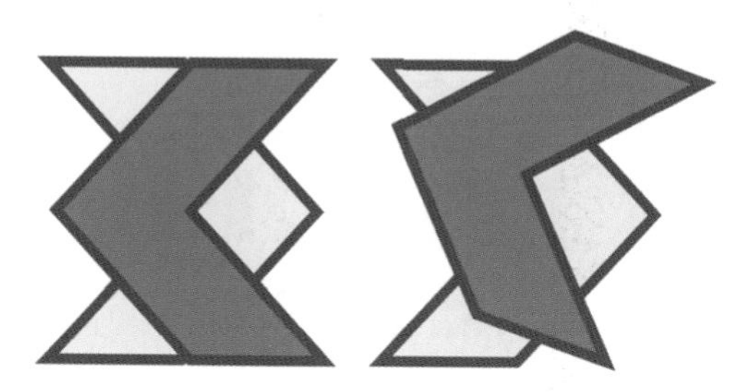

Figure 3.9 The logo on the right is perceived to be more asymmetrical than the one on the left

Figure 3.10 The shoe on the left is perceived to be softer and more comfortable than the one on the right

A logo can also make the brand seem more dynamic, by depicting a movement as if its elements are 'frozen in motion' (see figure 3.11). The more dynamic (or kinetic) the logo, the more likely it is to attract the visual attention of the audience, leading to better evaluation of the company, especially when it is positioned as a forward-looking, modern one.[24]

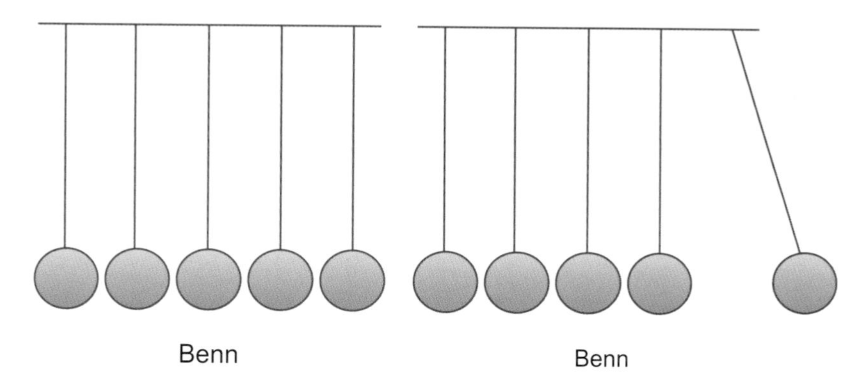

Figure 3.11 The logo on the right is more dynamic than the one on the left

One can also make the brand appear more energetic and this turns out to have strong persuasive effects.[25] Being energetic is more than just giving a sense of movement (or kinetic); it means that some aspect of the logo is working against a resistance, sometimes called 'visual friction'. For instance, the logo on the right in figure 3.12 (for a fictitious brand of jeans) is perceived to be more energetic than the one on the left because the man is depicted to be moving against a gravitational force. Baxter and Ilicic[26] show that energetic logos are very persuasive because they make the brand seem more hardworking – filled with energy. Consumers like this to the extent that they are even predisposed to choose its products. For instance, when people see the energetic logo of Coach on the right in figure 3.13, they are more likely to pick up its combs (74%) than if they were to see the logo on the left (56%).

ASKHAM BRYAN
COLLEGE
LEARNING RESOURCES

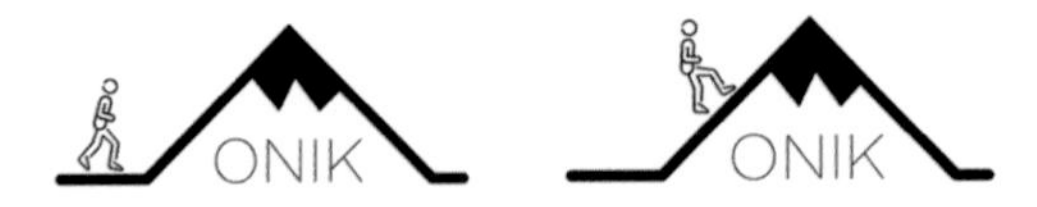

Figure 3.12 A kinetic (left) versus an energetic (right) logo[27]

Figure 3.13 The energetic logo (right) caused more combs to be chosen than the kinetic logo (left)

Research thus shows that a subtle change to a logo can make a significant effect on consumers. This means that a logo should *always* offer some positive information, connotation or visual appeal to the brand name it accompanies[28] or better still effect a real behaviour as we saw with energetic logos. If not, why bother with a logo? But this is not always the case. Look at the examples in figure 3.14. What do you think each logo adds to its brand?

Figure 3.14 What meanings do these logos add?

Finally, it should be noted that sometimes one may be stuck with a brand name or logo which we cannot change. Under such circumstances, one might think of other ways to build the brand (e.g. improve customer service and better brand performance).

REPOSITIONING FOR A HIGHER PURPOSE

During the COVID-19 pandemic, several companies redesigned their logos, albeit temporarily, to publicise social distancing.[29] Below are two illustrations. Can you guess what the brands are? Cute as they may be, they can also trivialise the seriousness of a crisis such as the COVID-19 pandemic. Critics have argued that companies should do much more to make a difference rather than simple logo adjustments.[30] For instance, in Australia, Woolworths, for a limited time, opened its doors earlier exclusively for the elderly and disabled shoppers,[31] while Cambridge University Press provided free online access to all their textbooks for their adopters worldwide. In other words, they did something that can make a material difference to people's lives. Some companies went even further by retooling their manufacturing to produce life-saving products. LVMH, the luxury group, started making and donating sanitisers to French hospitals;[32] Tesla started making medical ventilators;[33] and Apple, medical face shields.[34]

Figure 3.15 Small changes in company logos during the COVID-19 pandemic

In chapter 9, we will discuss the concept of brand purpose advertising, where companies can adopt a position to show the human side. Beyond just earning profits for shareholders and certainly beyond making trivial changes to their logos, more companies should regroup, reassess and realign[35] what their brands really stand for. In times of a crisis like the COVID-19 pandemic, companies that make a material difference will go further by adopting a higher purpose in helping *humanity*.

Packaging, colour and website or brand home page

Packaging is another way to position the brand. While packaging is principally used to protect the goods inside, it can also be leveraged to convey something more about the product. Further, since 70% of our purchases in supermarkets are unplanned, one can think of packaging as the last chance to influence the consumer. It has to stand out.

The L'eggs packaging of women's stockings, which Roger Ferriter developed in 1969 in New York, is a classic example of this. The packaging was shaped like an egg – a novelty at the time (and probably now too). With the L' (French for 'the') followed by eggs, the brand name gave the product a distinctive, French cachet. Since it is also pronounced as 'legs' in English, it reminds women of leg stockings. The advertising slogan was 'Our L'eggs fit your legs'. It became one of the most successful brands in the category.

Colour is also another important component of packaging design, and managers should be sensitive to the theory of colour. Generally, longer wavelength colours like red and orange tend to elicit arousal and excitement, while shorter wavelength colours like blue and green are calmer and more relaxing.[36] However, brands can create their own meaning in the colours they choose. For instance, the generic colour purple can trigger the meaning of excitement,[37] but when primed with the Cadbury brand, it is now perceived to be more sincere. This is because Cadbury's iconic purple (which is slightly different form the generic purple) has over the years been associated with Cadbury's positioning of being family-oriented and cheerful.[38]

Now, there is an added complication if a brand were to be sold in different cultures. Under such circumstances, management must be sensitive to cultural differences. In North America and Western Europe, for instance, blue is generally associated with tranquillity and sincerity, while red suggests warmth and excitement.[39] Black is associated with sophistication (i.e. cool), formality, sexiness, although it is also associated with mourning (i.e. funeral). In the Chinese culture, however, red is associated with good luck and prosperity, but black is associated almost exclusively with death, especially in Singapore and Malaysia.[40] Nothing cool about being 'men in black' there.

Websites now represent the face of a brand (or firm) online. They also help position the brand. If a website is well designed, it can greatly enhance the brand's image. This is an important consideration because consumers often search for information on the internet. A search engine might very well bring the consumer to the website or brand home page. If the website gives the consumer a bad impression, this will detract from its positioning. This logic also extends to brand pages in social media. For instance, the more interactive, entertaining and informative the brand page (e.g. contains videos, polls, pictures), the more likely consumers will like it, and their liking of the brand page is then transferred onto the brand.[41]

Attributes, consequence (benefit or emotions) and values (A-C-V)

Consistently communicating that a brand possesses a special attribute is one of the oldest methods of positioning a brand. However, this tactic will only work if the attribute is superior in some way. The classic example is the unique selling proposition (USP). The concept of the USP was invented by Rosser Reeves of Ted Bates and Company, a 1950s advertising agency.[42] To Rosser Reeves, the three most important rules of advertising were:

1. There must be a proposition.
2. The proposition must be unique, or something that the competition cannot or does not want to offer.
3. The proposition is strong enough to sell to the masses.

The benefit of the USP approach is the emphasis on a single, clear proposition that others do not possess. A famous example is M&M's campaign as the first sugar-coated chocolate in the US, which used the slogan 'Melts in your mouth, not in your hand'. The positioning strategy of USP means creatively looking for that one important, unique attribute that the company can deliver better than others. Since the emphasis is on a single product attribute, it focuses our minds on finding that attribute.

Today, this positioning tactic is often used for innovative electronic goods. For instance, if a computer is the lightest in the market, a firm can position the brand on this uniqueness. However, uniqueness based on innovativeness can be short-lived if competitors can easily copy the innovation. For instance, we may spend a million dollars on a campaign proclaiming how light our computer is, only to be superseded six months later by a lighter model from a competing brand.

Instead of only showing an attribute, the ad can also show or suggest how the attribute is linked to consequence (benefit), as discussed in chapter 2, under the means–end laddering research technique. This can also be accompanied by emotions,[43] which may be particularly important for hedonic–experiential consumer goods or services. Ads for Disneyworld, for instance, often show how happy the patrons are.

For utilitarian goods or services (such as a business-to-business service), portraying the end value of service (e.g. customer satisfaction) may be all that is needed. Note that when consequence or benefit of the claim is exaggerated, it is called 'hyperbole'. For instance, one can claim that a brand of soup is 'the most delicious soup in the world'. This is acceptable because consumers generally understand such claims to be non-factual (and so it is not false advertising).

What happens if the brand does not possess any superior attribute? For instance, many beers are similar to each other. They even taste the same in blind taste tests. What then? One option is to have a great ad so that the creative concept, rather than a unique attribute, acts as the brand positioning. Usually this means the brand is the first to use such a concept, and this makes it difficult for competition to encroach. For instance, Las Vegas owns the positioning of 'naughty fun', with the tagline 'What happens in Vegas stays in Vegas', created in 2005 by R&R Partners for the Las Vegas Convention and Visitors Authority. Now, in reality, New York might be a better place to have 'naughty fun', but that positioning now belongs uniquely to Las Vegas. Therefore, if a brand does not own a superior attribute, then it should aim to at least be the first to own a (mental) position. This is also called 'pre-emptive positioning'. However, be warned, whatever is being promised, the brand *must* deliver.

CASE STUDY 3.1 EDSEL: THE CAR THAT OVER-PROMISES BUT UNDER-DELIVERS

We discussed in chapter 1 that 'nothing kills a bad product faster than a great campaign'. This case study not only illustrates this point succinctly, but also cautions against over-promising.

In 1957, Ford launched a whole line of automobiles named after the son of its founder, Henry Ford, called Edsel. Although the name sounded awkward, it was 10 years in the planning. It was supposed to be Ford's premium line of medium-sized cars, positioned to be so revolutionary that no consumers had ever experienced such a vehicle before. Ford was so confident of its success that it invested US$250 million into its development and campaign (in 1957!).

So, what went wrong? Ford essentially created a 'lemon' and, worse still, went all out to promote how good the car was. When Edsel was first launched, it was plagued with a host of technical problems, like oil leaks, peeling paintwork and missing parts, and bizarrely had booths that could not be opened (even with a hammer!). But worst of all, the car was a petrol guzzler, and to top it off, priced very expensively. Consumers at the time were moving towards more fuel-efficient and smaller cars. And even though Edsel had innovative features (e.g. automatic transmission with a touch of a button), there was not enough service support when breakdowns occurred. The mechanics at the dealership were not trained to handle all the innovative features. Edsel received such bad press that sales tanked.

The campaign however was brilliant. The year-long, pre-launch campaign (starting in the spring of 1957), began with a teaser to get everyone talking. It consisted of the tagline, 'The Edsel is Coming'. But cleverly, no image of the car was used in the campaign, and everyone involved with the campaign was sworn to secrecy until 4 September 1957 when the car was officially unveiled on 'E-day'. This secrecy up to E-day created an enormous amount of suspense. The Ford name was not even mentioned because the corporation wanted to create a new stand-alone division for this range. The strategy was to upsell current Ford car buyers to Edsel so that they did not lose these upgraders to other competing brands like Buick, Pontiac, Oldsmobile, Dodge, Desoto and Chrysler. Ford only had one brand, Mercury, serving the same segment. Bizarrely, on launch day, Ford unveiled 18 different variations of Edsel! Too many choices can be bad because it confuses the buyer.[44]

Furthermore, Ford had overhyped Edsel. For instance, the tag line 'Car of the future' in a related campaign raised such expectation that it could only fail. The campaign created a powerful impression that it was an irresistible car of the future. One wonders if *any* car could live up to such a hype!

By the time corrective actions were taken in subsequent roll outs, it was too late. The damage had already been done. The Edsel range was lumbered with such a bad reputation that repositioning it was useless. American consumers could only think of Edsel as an ugly petrol-guzzler. Ford lost US$350 million (which was no small change in the 1950s).

DISCUSSION QUESTIONS

1. How does this case illustrate the notion that 'nothing kills a bad product faster than a great campaign' discussed in chapter 1? What is the single most important lesson learnt about this case that relates to this notion?
2. Do you think Edsel would have survived had Ford instituted a soft launch? Explain your answer.
3. Do you think given time and with continuous improvement, the Edsel could survive as a car brand? Explain your answer.

Competitor comparison

In marcoms, especially advertising, positioning through competitor comparison can be direct or indirect. In direct comparative advertising, the competitor is named, as in the famous 'Pepsi Challenge' campaign, which invited consumers to taste two glasses of cola and indicate which they preferred. The brands of the two colas were then revealed. The voice-over then announced that Pepsi was preferred by more consumers than 'Coke'. Indirect comparative advertising, on the other hand, does not name the competitor. Instead, the advertising simply shows a generic product. Comparison is then made between the focal brand and this generic product.

Comparative advertising works by encouraging consumers to reflect more on the attributes being compared.[45] Therefore, this tactic only makes sense if the advertised brand is smaller than the referent brand it is compared to, which is usually the leading brand. That way, the smaller brand essentially (i) leverages on the higher brand familiarity of the leading brand, and then (ii) points out it is better than the leading brand on the chosen attribute. For instance, the 'Pepsi Challenge' campaign encouraged consumers to think again about the merits of Pepsi (i.e. it tasted better than 'Coke'). Smaller or unknown brands also benefit from a 'sleeper effect', meaning that consumers become more favourable to the brand over time (say a week after they see an ad). This occurs because while consumers generally do not think highly of unknown brands, comparative advertising encourages them to think more deeply about an unknown brand's benefits. This leads to higher brand attitude as time passes.[46] This does not happen for the leading brand since it is already well regarded.

So, generally, it does not make sense for a leading brand to engage in comparative advertising. It will only draw attention to the smaller brand, which usually has lower brand awareness, and this can only undermine its own position as a leading brand because people will now think that it is similar to the smaller brand.[47]

It is also important that the focal attribute being compared between the two brands be similar as well as important.[48] This makes processing easier. So, in the case of Pepsi versus Coke, the attribute being compared between the two brands is taste, which also happens to be an important attribute. If what is being compared is not the same, like taste for Pepsi and calories for Coke, the ad will end up very confusing because people cannot align the comparison attribute clearly.

Finally, it is important that the tone of the comparison is positive. A derogatory approach to the referent brand will lower the believability and credibility of the ad, which are always an issue with comparative advertising.[49] So, the best approach is to first acknowledge the referent brand as favourable (on the target attribute), but then say that the advertised brand is even better. People are less likely to counterargue against such a format. Thus, it is better to say: 'You are OK. I am *more* OK' than 'You are not OK. I am OK.' The classic Avis 'We try harder' campaign we discussed earlier is a good example of this.

Brand image, brand personality and celebrities

Many years ago, David Ogilvy, the British advertising legend who founded Ogilvy, Benson & Mather in 1948 (now called Ogilvy & Mather and part of the WPP group), suggested positioning should make the brand the hero by emphasising its brand image or brand personality. He suggested that brand advertising is like building a 'kind of indestructible image that makes a brand part of the fabric of life . . . it is almost always the total personality of a brand rather than any trivial product difference which decides its ultimate advertising attribute'.[50]

Many fashion and car brands use this strategy to build their uniqueness. Even a nation may use images in this way: for instance, the image of Australia draws on its ruggedness, size, beautiful beaches, and green and clean produce. Indonesia, our near neighbour, has a different set of salient associations, namely its cuisine, culture, island life, religious festivals, temples and crowdedness. So, although both countries are geographically close, there is distance between them in terms of their mental space.

The image of a brand can also take on a persona. In chapter 2, we learnt that metaphors of a person can be elicited for a brand using projective techniques. In advertising, one way of quickly instituting a brand personality is to use a human symbol (e.g. the 'Michelin man' or 'Ronald McDonald') or a real human representation. The classic example of the latter is the Marlboro cigarette. The visual image is that of a masculine cowboy created in 1960 by the advertising agency Leo Burnett. The power of brand personality is underscored by the fact that the sales of Marlboro cigarettes were abysmal at less than 1%, before the advertising agency created this iconic image. It quickly became the fourth best-selling cigarette brand at that time.

Finally, J. Aaker[51] has controversially suggested that brands can be classified using five personality dimensions:

1. sincere (i.e. down to earth, honest, wholesome and cheerful); for example, Disney
2. exciting (i.e. daring, spirited, imaginative and up to date); for example, Porsche
3. competent (i.e. reliable, intelligent and successful); for example, IBM
4. sophisticated (i.e. upper class, charming); for example, Rolex
5. rugged (i.e. outdoorsy and tough); for example, Hard Yakka.

Note that there is a difference between brand *image* and brand *personality*. Only when the image is that of a person (persona) is it brand personality, so we can think of brand personality as a more specific form of brand image.

One way of giving the brand an instant brand personality is to use celebrities. Celebrities tend to attract our attention and their image is easily transferred to that of the brand. In chapter 7 we will discuss in more detail the pros and cons of using celebrities.

IS THIS THE BEST TOURISM AD FOR AUSTRALIA?

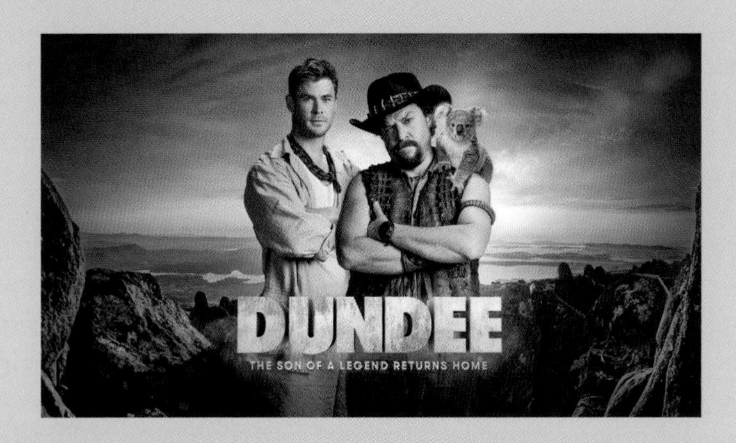

Figure 3.16 Still shots of the supposedly new Dundee movie

When is a movie an ad? Or when is an ad a movie? This deliberate confusion was created by Tourism Australia in 2018 when they launched a campaign in the US to attract visitors. But they did it in such a way that the ad (to be shown during the 2018 Super Bowl) looked like an upcoming movie instead (*Dundee: The Son of Legend Returns Home*), and they managed to hoodwink the American public. The key to their success was that the 'movie' trailer looked so real and exciting that people actually wanted to go to watch it. Part of this realism came from the use of Aussie actors, well-known celebrities in the US (e.g. Chris Hemsworth, Margot Robbie, Hugh Jackman, Russell Crowe, Ruby Rose, Liam Hemsworth, Paul Hogan, Danny McBride, Isla Fischer), who were starring in this movie. This is what happened:

- 16 days prior to Super Bowl, Tourism Australia released the first teaser for the movie (starring Danny McBride); this created so much interest on social media that the traditional media (e.g. TV programs) further amplified it.
- 13 days prior to Super Bowl, Tourism Australia released the full film trailer (starring Chris Hemsworth) and it went viral (see chapter 8 on viral marketing).
- 7 days prior to Super Bowl, Tourism Australia released another trailer showing who else would be starring in it. That trailer created the highest level of pre–Super Bowl digital engagement.
- On Super Bowl day, Tourism Australia let the cat out of the bag. Halfway through the commercial for the 'movie', Chris Hemsworth and Danny McBride admitted on camera that there was no Dundee movie, but rather it was a tourism ad for Australia. It created another media storm.

This campaign became the most successful tourism ad for Australia, seen by more than one billion people worldwide, resulting in a 900% increase in organic bookings to Australia![52]

Figure 3.17 Still shots of the 'movie trailer' featuring Aussie celebrities.

User imagery

User imagery refers to the image of the brand users. For instance, women tend to be consumers of sparkling wine while men tend to drink beer, and certain kinds of consumers tend to shop in certain places or buy certain brands. A simple execution of this tactic is to show a typical user juxtaposed with the brand. For example, one might show a jogger with a pair of running shoes (e.g. Adidas). Ideally, the user depicted should be someone the target audience aspires to become. For instance, in our Adidas example, the jogger could be made to look like a very fit, healthy person.

User imagery can also be used to reposition the competition. A very clever use of this tactic is Apple's 'Get a Mac' campaign.[53] The Apple campaign was launched in 2006 in response to Microsoft's new Windows. It showed two men talking. Apple was represented by a slim, cool 'dude', wearing an open-collar shirt, T-shirt or skivvy, while the other person, representing the PC, was a little, bespectacled, chubby man, wearing a suit and a tie. In a series of humorous vignettes, the two men discussed what they could or could not do, with the 'Apple guy' always coming out on top. Although these characters were used to represent the brands (i.e. they were a personification), they also represented an ideal of what the users of the products were like. In other words, users of Apple were the 'cool' ones, while PC users were behind the times. The campaign was so successful that sales of Apple computers quickly doubled.[54]

Reputation cues

If a brand already has a good reputation, then we should capitalise on it. Reputation is one of the most important drivers of purchase. This is because it serves as a heuristic for quality. In consumer-packaged goods, more people tend to buy strong brands, and they tend to do so more frequently.[55] Further, as the reputation of the firm improves so do its sales.[56] The greater the reputation, the higher the purchase intentions[57] and eventual consumer loyalty.[58]

There are a number of ways of using this strategy. One way is to emphasise the heritage value of the brand. For instance, many established banks do this by making the claim that it has been in business for a long time (e.g. 100 years). Established business schools also do it when they claim to be the top-ranking business school in the country, based on a survey of experts. In an interesting twist to this idea, the watchmaker Patek Philippe's long-running campaign has the slogan 'You never actually own a Patek Philippe. You merely look after it for the next generation' (see figure 3.18). It clearly positions the watch as timeless which befits its very expensive price.

Figure 3.18 A Patek Philippe print ad

Another tactic is the popularity claim. For example, a brand of shampoo can claim that it is the number one brand of shampoo, backed up by sales figures in the small print. Popularity claims can be very effective because they activate the heuristic of social proof (see chapter 10), suggesting that the consumer cannot go wrong since many others are buying it too.

The reputation of the brand can also be inferred by the quality and quantity of advertising. Generally, the more creative the ad, the more likely consumers will think highly of the brand.[59] Similarly, heavily advertised brands are more likely to be perceived as high-quality and financially 'fit', because they can afford expensive advertising.[60] Whether a brand's reputation cue is based on heritage, popularity or the quality and quantity of its advertising, the purpose is to create trust.

However, trust can also be quickly destroyed if the claims are not true. For instance, a shampoo cannot claim to be the number one shampoo if it is not. These are factual claims. But even so, what happens if it is no longer number one next year? This is the danger of the popularity claim. As in the case of making claims based on attribute superiority, it is important that the popularity claims are sustainable. In the case of making a claim based on heritage, there are also dangers. An established business school or bank with heritage can also be perceived to be old-fashioned and staid.

Country of origin, region and cultural icons

Another approach to position a brand is to communicate its country of origin. Some countries tend to be positively associated with certain product categories: for example, watches from Switzerland (such as Rolex), wine from France (such as Moët & Chandon), cars from Germany (such as BMW), and designer clothes from Italy (such as Prada). If the country of origin effect is positive, the cue can also be primed to influence decision-making. This is especially useful if the brand is new or when the buyer is a novice. The country of origin serves as a heuristic for quality.

The country of origin effect can be enhanced further by presenting a competing and more inferior brand side by side.[61] Let's consider an example of how this side-by-side comparison can be subtly applied in the context of real estate. Assume that a sales agent is trying to sell a property with a newly renovated German kitchen. A buyer has expressed interest in this house but is also considering another property (i.e. the next best alternative). The sales agent could subtly ask what the kitchen is like in the other house. If the answer is not as good, then he or she could say that this house has a Gaggenau kitchen. And if this is met with a blank stare, he could follow up with a statement like this: 'This is a German kitchen that has the latest technology. It is the best on the market. Most kitchens tend to be Chinese-made.' By so doing, the sales agent not only triggers the country of origin effect (i.e. the kitchen is German-made), but also accentuates its positive effect with side-by-side comparison with something inferior (Chinese-made), presumably found in the other house. Germans are famous for their technical prowess.

Sometimes, the use of a particular region of a country can be just as effective. We see this in the wine business. Champagne, for example, can legally only be labelled champagne if it is from that region in France, and other sparkling wine cannot use the name although it may be made in the same way as champagne. That is why non-champagne sparkling wines often have the words *méthode traditionnelle* written on their labels, to signify that the mode of production is just as intensive as that of champagne. However, the sparkling wine no longer possesses 'snob' appeal, and so cannot command a premium price. This is a good example of how legislation can create a monopoly on a mind space for a product.

Many products that originate in one country may no longer be made in that country. For instance, Volkswagen may conjure up the German engineering of its parent country, but in fact the make is also manufactured in Brazil and other countries. If the quality is maintained, consumers are unlikely to care. Therefore, what is more important is the culture in which the brand originates, sometimes called 'culture of brand origin'.[62] Since this is where the uniqueness lies, it should be protected.

A related way of doing this is to use a well-known cultural symbol. Many national airlines use this strategy. For instance, Qantas Airways uses the flying kangaroo (see figure 3.19), which has strong symbolic value both inside and outside Australia. For similar reasons, Thai Airways uses the tropical orchid as its logo. Singapore Airlines has taken this strategy a step further, by using images of its flight attendants wearing the distinctive, traditional attire (called a *sarong kebaya*), to evoke associations with the company's reputation for world-class service, a truly unique quality in the marketplace – see the example in figure 3.20. Partly as a result of this sort of advertisement, Singapore Airlines' flight attendants have come to be seen as the epitome of Asian grace and hospitality.

Figure 3.19 Qantas' flying kangaroo liveries over the years

Figure 3.20 Singapore Airlines – an example of a cultural icon
Source: © Singapore Airlines

The use of this positioning tactic has a downside, which is often beyond the control of the firm. What happens if the country falls out of favour? Consider the recent dispute between China and Japan over the ownership of the Diaoyu (or Senkaku) Islands, just off the Japanese coast.

China asserted its ownership of the islands and the ongoing imbroglio whipped up nationalistic fervour on both sides. But it was the Japanese car-makers in China that bore the brunt as Chinese consumers boycotted them. Compared to 2011, Japanese car sales in September 2012 were disastrous, with Toyota plunging by 49.8%, Honda by 40.5%, Suzuki by 42.5%, Nissan by 34.6%,[63] Mitsubishi by 63% and Mazda by 36%.[64]

Price, quality and status cues

A brand can also be positioned by its price point, using the heuristic 'The higher price, the higher the quality'. We often hear this when a sales agent tries to justify a higher price by saying, 'You get what you pay for'. Consumers tend to adopt this heuristic when they do not have any other information to independently verify the intrinsic qualities of the brand.[65] As a result they rely on an extrinsic cue – such as its price – to infer its quality.[66] Research also shows that this heuristic is powerful when there are significant price differences between brands in the category, since this signals real quality differences among the offerings.[67]

Price is also a powerful cue for quality when consumers do not have enough experience[68] of the goods or services before purchase due to lack of opportunity, motivation or ability to search and compare competing offers. This means the brand's utility value becomes difficult to establish. Sometimes, even after searching and comparing, the consumer still cannot establish this reliably for many credence goods or services (e.g. vitamins, plumbing services or a medical check-up). Such goods or services are also susceptible to the above-mentioned heuristic.[69] The classic example is a busy professional who has no time or motivation to compare complex insurance policies.

Price also signifies status. The higher the price, the less people can afford it, which creates a sense of exclusivity. People are more susceptible to price–status heuristics for publicly consumed goods such as luxury brands. Sociologists call this phenomenon 'conspicuous consumption'. For instance, although consumers cannot easily discern the intrinsic attributes of lipsticks, they are still more willing to pay many times more if the brand is well known (e.g. Chanel) as opposed to an unknown one. Therefore, when there is a possibility that consumers regard status as an important attribute, a higher price can be charged.

In short, consumers who are not familiar with the brand, or are too busy or incapable of examining the intrinsic qualities of a product in a category that has wide-varying price differentials, tend to be most susceptible to the price–quality heuristic. And if the goods are also publicly consumed, they would also be susceptible to the price–status heuristic.

Occasions, usage and applications

Certain products tend to be used for certain occasions. For instance, we drink coffee in the morning, less so in the evening; we drink champagne when we want to celebrate special occasions (e.g. marriages and birthdays), but not ordinarily for dinner; and of course only a diamond ring will do for a marriage proposal!

All these examples show that in our minds, certain products tend to be 'locked' into how they are used. However, this does not mean that the brand should necessarily be limited to this usage. For instance, Arm & Hammer baking powder is also advertised as a smell absorber for the refrigerator. Similarly, some champagne producers also market small (200 millilitre) bottles called *piccolos*, positioning the product as a 'small indulgence', to encourage more everyday consumption. This idea of use occasion also extends to fast-food restaurants. McDonald's used to serve only lunch and dinner and only later decided to cater for the breakfast market too. Now, we can go to McDonald's for breakfast, lunch and dinner.

If we are interested in expanding the usage occasions of a brand, it pays to understand how consumers are now using the product in order to address limitations. For instance, WD40, a rust-reducing spray, is principally used for rust prevention by being sprayed on metal surfaces, but it was discovered that consumers would buy the product, use it a few times, and then forget where they put it in the garage. To address this issue, the brand expanded its usage to include not only rust prevention, but also greasing of squeaky hinges and the removal of all dirt and marks from walls, floors and carpets (it is claimed that it has 300 cleaning uses).

CASE STUDY 3.2 THE CHAMPAGNE STORY: THE ART OF POSITIONING A SPARKLING WINE

When we think of champagne, what do we think of? French, expensive, indulgent, celebration, New Year and sparkling wine. And when someone brings a bottle of champagne for your dinner or gives you a bottle as a gift, does it make a statement? Of course, it does!

So, where do the positive associations of champagne originate from? One explanation lies in its heritage value. Historically, Reims, the largest city in France's Champagne region, was where all the monarchs of France were coronated. For hundreds of years, Reims and, by association, its wine (i.e. champagne) was synonymous with French royalty. Philippe II, Duke of Orléans loved sparkling champagne so much that it also became the favourite among the French aristocrats. Napoleon Bonaparte's favourite champagne was said to be Moët & Chandon; he named it the official champagne in his Imperial Court, much to the envy of the other champagne producers. So, champagne has great heritage value, and it is not unusual for some champagne houses to play this card in their marketing. For instance, Ruinart prides itself as being the first established champagne house, since 1729. Heritage positioning implies prestige and quality (and snobbery of course!).

In modern times, champagne is associated more with celebrities rather than royalty, although one would be surprised if royal weddings today are *not* celebrated with champagne. However, in terms of advertising, it is not unusual to use celebrities to endorse their brand. In 2012, Moët & Chandon signed a five-year contract with tennis great Roger Federer for a reported fee of US$30 million, replacing its previous ambassador, Scarlett Johansson. Product placements in films are also used. In many celebratory movie scenes, champagne is almost always depicted. For instance, Dom Pérignon and later Bollinger had long associations with the Bond films.

Champagne is also expensive, and this is probably the single most important determinant of its status. And since not many people can afford to buy champagne, it creates a sense of exclusivity, which is why champagne tends to be drunk only on special occasions. Two main reasons can account for why champagne is expensive. First, it is labour intensive to produce. Second, the wine must be cellared at a constant temperature of 11–12 degrees Celsius for the flavours and complexity to develop. For non-vintage champagne, the cellaring period is 2–3 years; whereas for vintage champagne, it is 4–10 years.

Popular folklore also fuels the notion of champagne being a special treat. The most famous example of this is that a blind French Benedictine monk by the name of Dom Pierre Pérignon (December 1638 – 14 September 1715) invented the secondary fermentation. Legend has it that he exclaimed, 'Come quickly, I am tasting the stars!' when his lips first touched the wine. This is nonsense. History[70] tells us that it was the English physician and scientist Christopher Merrett who first documented (in 1662) that it was the sugar that causes the secondary fermentation in the wine. This technique was already used in producing English cider in 17th-century England, some 30 years before the method was adopted in Champagne (around the mid-19th century in France). Finally, Dom Pierre Pérignon was *not* blind, and the words he supposedly uttered about seeing stars when drinking champagne first appeared in a print ad in the 19th century, some 100 years *after* his death![71] He could not have uttered it (well maybe from his grave).

But historical inaccuracies aside, this did not prevent Moët & Chandon from using the monk as their moniker. There is even a bronze statue of the monk in the courtyard of the champagne house of Moët & Chandon, giving tourists countless photo opportunities. Of course, the statue itself is another myth since no one knew what he looked like. But it makes an interesting back story, which adds to the allure of Moët & Chandon.

Finally, the name 'Champagne' is also protected to prevent dilution of its exclusive cache. Champagne refers to a special region in France, not just its sparkling wine. And only the sparkling wine made to a specification in this region is allowed to be called champagne. So a quality sparkling wine from Tasmania (e.g. Arras) cannot be called champagne even though it is made in the traditional labour-intensive method (or *méthode traditionnelle*). If this is violated, the wine producer will be taken to court by Comité Champagne, which represents the interests of Champagne producers. Their stated objective is to promote and protect the Champagne AOC across the world, with this tagline from its website: 'Champagne only comes from Champagne, France'.

DISCUSSION QUESTIONS

1. Why do you think champagne producers continue to propagate historical inaccuracies? Do you think it is ethical?
2. If consumers know the myths associated with champagne, do you think it will affect the prestige positioning of champagne? Explain your answer.
3. How could quality sparkling wine producers in Australia compete with champagne? Or should they?

THE CHALLENGES OF REPOSITIONING

Repositioning a brand becomes more important during the later stages of a life cycle, when new competitors enter the scene or when consumers' tastes change. What is then required is to reposition the brand in people's minds. For instance, Lucozade was primarily a drink for convalescent children in the 1970s but was repositioned as an energy and sports drink in 2000. Such changes help broaden the appeal.[72] Incidentally, 'Coca-Cola' also started life in 1886 as a health tonic.[73]

Sometimes the need for repositioning can be enforced by law. Consider the case of Intel using ingredient branding as a tactic.[74] In 1991, Intel lost the right to use its existing number '386' as a brand because the court ruled this to be a generic code for different types of microprocessors, not a brand in its own right. Intel had to quickly come up with a new branding strategy. They hit upon the idea of encouraging consumers to look inside the computer and think about the importance of the 'brain' of the computer, the microchip. The result was the 'Intel Inside' campaign. Coupled with a co-op advertising program targeting PC manufacturers, Intel eventually won this market's support. In addition to a mass media campaign, Intel also managed to convince manufacturers to carry the Intel logo on its packaging and computer. The logo helped make the brand more familiar to the consumers. The clever thing about this rebranding was that it repositioned the microchip as the most important component of a computer, implying that nothing else mattered as much. Further, the positioning is reinforced as consumers see the logo on their computer every time they use it. The campaign was so successful in repositioning the Intel brand that, today, Intel is so well known that one is hard-pressed to think of a competing manufacturer of computer chips (Advanced Micro Devices is one).

While positioning of a brand can be hard work, repositioning it can be even harder. It is more difficult if the current brand associations are strong. When this occurs, the new position may not be acceptable. For instance, to reposition McDonald's as a healthy fast-food outlet will not be easy; that position probably belongs to Subway. Kodak filed for bankruptcy in the US because it failed to make the transition into the digital era. We could argue that its film heritage makes this a difficult task. Imprisoned by the mindset that people (actually women) take pictures 'to preserve their memories', Kodak's management hung onto this positioning for too long. The world had moved on to digital and consumer behaviour had changed so that pictures were taken (mostly by men) to be shared.[75] Ironically, it was Kodak that invented the digital camera in 1975.[76]

Repositioning can occur in one of two ways: staged repositioning or complete overhaul. In a staged repositioning, a brand can be repositioned in intermediate steps en route to a new identity, as often happens in mergers and acquisitions. When insurance firm A (e.g. AXA) acquires insurance firm B (National Mutual), the combined entity would be first renamed with a compound name of the two brands; that is, brand A–B (e.g. AXA–National Mutual). Then, after a few years, the name of brand B (e.g. National Mutual) will be quietly dropped, so that only the name of brand A remains (e.g. AXA). This fusion of names at the beginning assists in the transfer of goodwill from the old brands to the newly merged one.

A complete overhaul is more drastic, involving wholesales changes in pricing, advertising, distribution, product range, customer services, store location, shopping experience and so on. The name is the only thing that remains unchanged. This is what happened to apparel brand Abercrombie & Fitch when it changed its positioning from an outdoor brand to a luxury fashion brand. In fact, it is now such a desirable brand that its clothes are counterfeited in the Far East, leading the firm to implement a brand protection program.[77] Similarly, supported by a heavy advertising campaign as well as changes to its planes, lounges, stewards' uniform, and even its airport signage, Virgin Australia managed to successfully shed its image as a low-cost airline to achieve a more upmarket image.[78]

POINT OF DIFFERENCE, POINT OF PARITY AND FRAME OF REFERENCE

In positioning, the emphasis has always been about the point of difference. This means that, as discussed earlier, we search for something uniquely important that can be used as a source of competitive advantage in communications.

However, what is a point of difference today can become standard tomorrow. We see this in most technological innovations. For instance, Apple used to be known for its ease of use, due to a mouse that helped manage the interface between human and machine. This advantage disappeared when Windows came along as it quickly became standard to use a mouse to point and click. Points of parity are qualities that are not unique to the brand and that other brands may share; they are seen in even more mundane service categories like the hotel industry. For instance, late check-out used to incur a small fee, but now, it is almost given away: all you need to do is ask. In a very interesting article, Keller, Sternthal and Tybout[79] pointed out that such points of parity are necessary to compete successfully in a category. For instance, in the fast food industry, good taste is a must: if it is not tasty, a product will probably not succeed, no matter how good the service is. Taste is therefore a necessity to 'break even'.

The question is how to determine what the point of parity is. In some sense, it does not matter as long as our brand possesses the most important qualities needed to be included in the category (and we communicate that it does). But what happens if the category changes? What if consumers do not make their purchase decisions based on categories but on goal fulfilment? For instance, Keller, Sternthal and Tybout pointed out that Federal Express (FedEx) used to compete with other courier companies but now they compete with new technologies such as email and so have had to shift their advertising to emphasise document security and confidentiality, among other things. The company's competitive frame of reference has shifted. To put it another way, our frame of reference (such as our product category) defines who our competitors are, and this definition helps pin down the point of difference we should use to differentiate the brand, and the point of parity we will need to break even.[80]

Consumers as well as companies have a frame of reference: the question is, how do we establish what it is? One way is to understand how product usage substitution occurs. Usage substitution has nothing to do with how a product is classified. It has more to do with consumption behaviour of the target audience in a certain context. For instance, we might ordinarily classify orange juice with other juices – apple, mango, lime and so on – rather than with coffee. Yet if we are competing in the breakfast market, the main competing product is coffee. If we are going for the afternoon timeslot, that product might be tea. In short, the notion of frame of reference that Keller, Sternthal and Tybout developed is more general than a product category because it takes into account dynamic changes in product boundaries as well as subtle and often idiosyncratic aspects of consumer behaviour.

BRAND EQUITY

Brand equity is another important concept to understand. In essence, it means the value that attaches to a brand, and it often forms the basis of the firm's financial health. There are many perspectives on brand equity, but broadly it can be examined from the perspectives of finance, sales growth, price elasticity, revenue premium, consumers, and brand strength and stature (the relationship between brand associations, brand 'building', brand positioning and brand equity will be discussed later in the Managerial Application for this chapter).

Financial perspective

The financial perspective is driven by the need to put a value (i.e. a dollar figure) on a brand in order to account for the goodwill a firm enjoys. In accounting terms, goodwill is essentially all the intangible assets (including the brand name) that allow the firm to earn cashflow beyond its return from tangible assets (such as plant, property and inventory). This is needed in a merger-and-acquisition situation. For instance, in 1998, Nestlé bought confectionery producer Rowntree-Mackintosh (which owned Kit Kat, Aero, Polo, Fruit Pastilles, Smarties and Quality Street) for US$4.5 billion,[81] or six times its net tangible assets and 26 times its annual profit. This begs the obvious question: 'How do you value the financial worth of a brand?'[82]

One assessment is the future growth valuation approach, which requires two steps. The first is to assess the profitability of a brand, above and beyond what a generic product will earn. The second is to adjust this profitability figure by a multiplier based on a series of factors accounting for future growth. For instance, in the case of Interbrand, a leading brand valuation company, the multiplier is determined by a weighted index of the following factors:

1. leadership (weighted at 0.25)
2. stability (0.15)
3. market (0.10)
4. internationality (0.25)
5. trend (0.10)
6. support (0.10)
7. protection (0.05).

Let's look at an example using The Coca-Cola Company, with the two steps of future growth valuation in mind (figures are not real).

STEP 1

Assume that The Coca-Cola Company has earned an average of $10 billion a year in the past three years from its brand 'Coke'. If the operating margin is 30%, then it will have an operating profit of $3 billion (i.e. 0.3 × $10 billion = $3 billion). Now, assume further that the firm has an asset of $5 billion, from which it can generate a 5% return. This means that a generic cola will yield an operating profit of $25 million anyway (i.e. 0.05 × $5 billion = $25 million). If we subtract $25 million from $3 billion, we can see that the 'Coke' label is responsible for a profit of $2.75 billion before tax (i.e. $3 billion – $25 million = $2.75 billion). After adjusting for tax, this figure could be around $2.5 billion.

STEP 2

If we now multiply the figure of $2.5 billion by an index based on the seven factors listed above, say 18, then the final valuation figure of 'Coke' would be $45 billion (i.e. $2.5 billion × 18 = $45 billion). Or, to put it another way, the 'Coke' brand is worth $45 billion.

The advantage of this approach is that it is appealing to an accountant or chief financial officer because it provides a number that signifies a value for the brand. The disadvantage is that the estimation of the multiplier (in this case, 18) based on a weighted index of the seven factors can be subjective. This perspective also assumes that one can separate and evaluate the seven factors independently of each other. Table 3.1 shows the brand value of different brands (in 2018) based on this methodology.

Table 3.1 World's top 10 most valuable brands in 2018 (according to Interbrand)[83]

Ranking	Brands	Brand value in 2018 (US$ million)
1	Apple	214 480
2	Google	155 500
3	Amazon	100 760
4	Microsoft	92 716
5	Coca-Cola	69 733
6	Samsung	59 890
7	Toyota	53 604
8	Mercedes-Benz	48 601
9	Facebook	45 168
10	IBM	43 417

Sales growth perspective

One simple way of assessing brand equity is to examine its sales figures. If a brand is 'healthy', it should be reflected in its sales. While this might seem obvious, the twist is that the sales should be continuous. In other words, a healthy brand should be one in which it is bought continuously by consumers. Mirzaei and colleagues[84] pointed out that one simple way of assessing the long-term health of the brand is to see if it has had continuous sales growth over a period, say 5–10 years, taking into account its variability. If a band is healthy, then it should be reflected in continuous sales growth with very little volatility.

Price elasticity perspective

The price elasticity perspective is another way of thinking about brand equity which is more sophisticated.[85] In a traditional pricing model, when a brand cuts its price the customers are likely to buy more and sales go up. The rate at which sales rise is the price elasticity. Conversely, if the brand increases its price there will be fewer sales. It follows that if a brand has high brand equity, it should be able to maintain its sales even when prices increase (up to a point); that is, it can expect an inelastic response to price increase.[86] It will also be less vulnerable to price-cutting by its competitors, which is equivalent to a price increase (because it means that customers are less likely to switch to that competitor). However, when a high-equity brand has a price cut, its customers will see it as a bargain and rush out and buy it. Sales will go up quickly, in a more elastic response to price decrease. In short, a high-equity brand tends to have greater elasticity with a price cut than a price increase.

This way of conceptualising brand equity is useful because, by examining the extent to which sales change with price, it provides insights into the value of the brand. It also allows us to see which brands customers are switching to and hence provides clues about their competitive set.

Revenue premium perspective

Revenue premium is related to the price elasticity perspective, but is more financially based, taking into account both market volume and price.[87] The formula is as follows:

$$\text{Revenue premium} = (\text{brand volume}) \times (\text{brand price}) - (\text{private label volume}) \times (\text{private label price})$$

The formula states that if a brand has high equity, then the result of multiplying its volume and price should be significantly higher than that of a private (or generic) label brand. On the other hand, if there is no difference then this implies that consumers are not willing to buy more of the brand, nor to pay more. The ideal situation is for a brand to not only sell more but also be able to command a higher price. Therefore, by combining volume and price and comparing the results to those of another brand, it provides a convenient way of conceptualising value.

Although both the price elasticity and revenue premium perspectives provide two ways of conceptualising brand equity, they do not give specific clues about what a manager should do next. The advantage of these two perspectives is that data on sales volume and price is readily available (at least in an area such as consumer-packaged goods).

Consumer perspective

One prominent approach to brand equity that is useful in suggesting what to do is based on that suggested by Kevin Keller, who defines brand equity as 'the differential effect of brand knowledge on consumer response to the marketing of the brand'.[88] This simply means whether knowing the brand – usually the brand identity – will make any difference to how people feel or what they do about the product or service. The notion of a differential effect that comes from knowing the brand compared to an unknown one is powerful because it enables very quick assessment.

Differential effects could be a difference in brand attitude, ad attitude, purchase intention or the amount of money the target audience is willing to pay once the brand is identified, compared to when it is not. Compare a blank coffee cup and one labelled with the Starbucks logo – how much would you pay for a Starbucks coffee?

For instance, in the PC category we could ask, 'What is the incremental dollar value you are willing to pay over a no-name clone computer brand?' The following is the result of a study by Intelliquest, a market research firm,[89] showing the price premium consumers are willing to pay for various brands, compared to a clone:

IBM: +$339; Compaq: +$318; Hewlett Packard: +$260; Dell: +$230

Of course, we usually want the difference to be positive (as shown above). If the difference is negative, we would say that the brand has 'negative equity'.

The concept of brand equity can also be used as a benchmark for the effectiveness of a marcoms campaign. For instance, if before the campaign only 10% of the target audience said that they were willing to pay $25 more for the brand compared to a generic (or competing) brand, then if the campaign is effective, we would expect the percentage to rise significantly above 10% after the campaign. The disadvantage with this perspective, in contrast to the revenue premium approach, is that it requires consumer surveys or experiments (e.g. conjoint analysis, a statistical technique for evaluating consumer choice) to evaluate brand equity. This can be cumbersome and, in contrast to the financial perspective, it produces no final number to signify the financial value of a brand.

Brand strength and brand stature perspective

A final approach discussed here is that of BrandAsset Valuator® or the BAV® model. The model, developed by Young & Rubicam (an advertising agency conglomerate), is based on the world's largest database of brands. We prefer this approach because it is highly relevant to our discussion in this chapter on brand positioning and differentiation. It is also the most succinct way to point out the sources of consumer-based brand equity that a manager can use to plan his or her actions.

This approach suggests that a brand has to be strong on two important dimensions – brand strength and brand stature – to enhance its equity. What is brand strength? It is made up of two factors: brand differentiation and brand relevance. Differentiation, as we saw earlier, means that the brand holds a distinctive and hopefully unique position in the target audience's mind. However, being differentiated is not enough to be competitive. The brand must also be relevant. This means that the brand has to possess qualities that the target audience considers important. What is the point of being unique if the target audience does not care about it? A brand that is clearly differentiated from its competitors and also relevant possesses brand strength.

This model also has another dimension, brand stature, which also consists of two factors: brand esteem and brand knowledge. The former refers to the extent to which consumers view the brand favourably, while the latter means the extent to which the brand is familiar. In our parlance, brand stature measures how well regarded (brand esteem) and well known (brand knowledge) a brand is. The higher it is on these measures, the greater the stature of the brand.

This approach is attractive because these four factors – brand esteem, knowledge, differentiation and relevance – can be used to compare brands across different product categories. For instance, we might compare where Apple stands on the four factors (in the computing market) compared to Mercedes-Benz (in the luxury car market). Since the measures are conceptually similar, the two brands can be meaningfully compared although they belong to two different categories.[90]

Generally, brand leaders tend to be strong on all four factors, while new brands tend to be weak on all four. Niche brands tend to be strong on differentiation and relevance, while commodity (or eroding) brands tend to be weak on these factors. Figure 3.21 illustrates this idea. The BAV® model has been found to correlate with changes in shareholder value over time.[91]

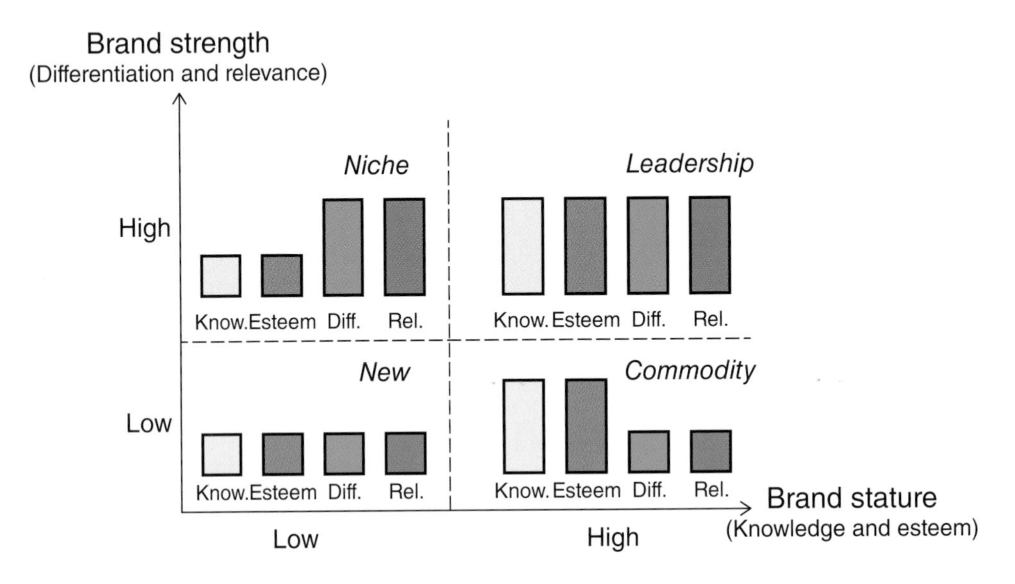

Figure 3.21 The BrandAsset Valuator® Power Grid

BRAND PREFERENCE

To make a better sense of the brand equity concepts discussed above, let's use the BrandAsset Valuator® model (see figures 3.21 and 3.22) as a starting point. The logic of the model is as follows.

First, the brand has to have a certain level of stature. This means it should be well regarded (brand esteem) and well known (brand knowledge). However, because of competition, it also has to be different. This implies that the brand also possesses some unique qualities (brand differentiation) and these qualities must be important (brand relevance). When all these elements come together, the result is a brand that is well known and well regarded, different from its competitors, and relevant to the target audience. This should lead to higher preference for the brand. Then, as more people come to prefer this brand (over the competition) and are willing to pay a premium for it, the brand will become more valuable (brand equity). Figure 3.22 shows how the various concepts are related.

In summary, the thrust of this chapter has been about positioning, the strategic issues it involves and the tactics that can be used. The objective is to build brand equity by increasing brand preference, making the brand more valuable in the long run. But is positioning always necessary? The answer is no. Positioning is most needed when there is competitive pressure (or a desire) to differentiate to be able to charge a premium price. If a firm is happy to play the low-cost game and be a 'me-too' (or commodity) brand, then there is no need to bother with positioning.

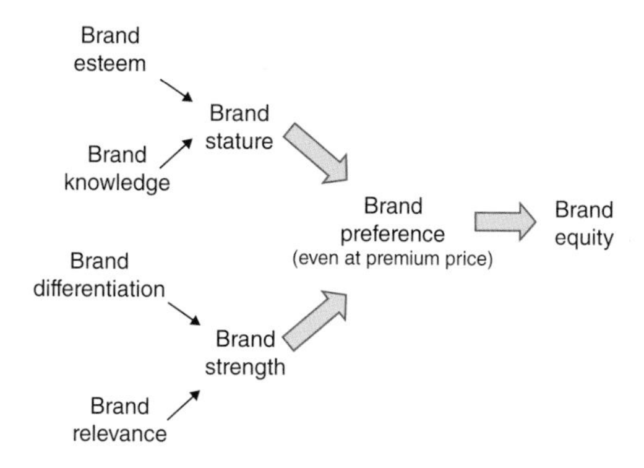

Figure 3.22 An approach to brand equity adapted from the BrandAsset Valuator®

MANAGERIAL APPLICATION: PUTTING IT TOGETHER

Very often we hear the phrase 'we have to build the brand'. But what does this phrase actually mean? And how does this relate to brand positioning and brand equity? To understand this, we first need to ask what exactly is a brand? Basic marketing text will suggest that a brand is a 'name, term, sign symbol (or a combination of these) that identifies the maker or seller of the product'.[92] But such a definition, while important, is limited because a brand (e.g. Qantas) goes *beyond* serving the purpose of identification. It must be able to conjure up desirable thoughts and feelings in our mind (e.g. a safe way to fly) that are powerful enough to win our vote (i.e. preference). Therefore, from a marcoms perspective, it is better to think of a brand as an imprint which conjures up a network of mental associations - ideas, memories and feelings - whenever the brand is identified. Branding then is the process of creating, strengthening and maintaining those associations to the brand so that this knowledge can be easily triggered when we think of the brand.

Positioning, on the other hand, is to ensure that those associations will make the brand competitive, and hence increase people's preference for it. Over time, that preference is translated to real value, where people are even willing to pay more for it. A brand's equity, therefore, lies in the power of the formed associations being unique and meaningfully relevant (i.e. desirable),[93] which can predispose consumers to choose it continuously over other brands. The ultimate kudos, of course, is when consumers are even willing to pay more for it now, and in the future![94]

Of course, these associations do not just come from marcoms alone. They can come from customer usage experience, customer service and word of mouth (and other new and ever-evolving marketing activities). This means the brand must always deliver as promised. Therefore, 'building the brand' means employing various marketing activities (including marcomms) to consistently reinforce those unique and desirable associations so that they are always salient.

However, it should be noted that advertising has one distinct advantage over other brand-building activities. It can efficiently *reach* a large number of potential new customers, building layers upon layers of desirable associations in their minds so that when they are ready to buy, these associations will be activated when they think about the brand. Or to put in another way, advertising helps lay down desirable associations long *before* people are ready to buy. And to be even more radical, some brands (such as Olay) are now creating musicals and full-blown music videos to achieve this purpose.[95]

FURTHER THINKING: UNIQUENESS

In this chapter, we discussed the importance of having a unique selling proposition (USP). But why is uniqueness important?

LEARNING GOALS

After reading this section, you will understand:

- why uniqueness is important
- how the Fishbein–Ajzen theory of attitude structure works in practice.

ASSESSING BRAND UNIQUENESS

Uniqueness is important because it helps brand differentiation, which reduces switching (or substitution). If a brand is seen to be the same as others, it means it can be easily replaced; consumers will then buy on price, since there is no discernible difference between brands. Brand loyalty will suffer, as will market share and profitability. In the longstanding Profit Impact of Market Strategy (PIMS) study, where a large sample of consumer goods (4789 observations) were tracked over time, Boulding, Lee and Staelin[96] found that if the advertising is unique (and positive), say in period t – 1, the brand will be more able to insulate itself from a future competitive price onslaught in period t. This is a robust finding, which highlights the importance of uniqueness.

But how does one actually assess uniqueness and make it operational in a campaign? Let's look at an example. Imagine that you are about to buy a mobile phone and have several brands to consider. Of all the attributes of a mobile phone, the most important is the range of coverage (i.e. network coverage) since you live in the country. Other important attributes of the phone are its ease of use and its screen size, although these are not as important as network coverage. Table 3.2 shows the importance weights of these attributes on a scale of 1–5, where a higher number signifies greater importance.

Table 3.2 The importance weights of three attributes

Attributes	Importance
Network coverage	5
Ease of use	3
Screen size	1

Now assume that there are two brands you are considering buying, which you believe differ on their performance on these attributes. This is shown in table 3.3 rated on scale of 1–5, where a higher number signifies greater performance beliefs. We can quickly see that brand A is strongest in network coverage (rated 5) while B is the weakest (rated 1). Brand B, on the other hand, is strongest in ease of use (rated 5) where A is the weakest (rated 1). The two handsets have the same screen size (both brands rated 5).

Table 3.3 The performance beliefs of two brands on three attributes

	Performance beliefs	
Attributes	***Brand A***	***Brand B***
Network coverage	5	1
Ease of use	1	5
Screen size	5	5

If we multiply each attribute by its importance weight and then sum, we will get the weighted sum for brand A as 33; that is, the sum of $(5 \times 5) + (1 \times 3) + (5 \times 1)$. The weighted sum for brand B is 25; that is, the sum of $(1 \times 5) + (5 \times 3) + (5 \times 1)$. These calculations show that brand A is perceived as overall more positive than brand B, at 33 to 25. See table 3.4.

Table 3.4 How the weighted sum is derived

	Performance beliefs		
Attributes	***Brand A***	***Brand B***	**Importance**
Network coverage	5	1	5
Ease of use	1	5	3
Screen size	5	5	1
Weighted sum	**33**	**25**	

This calculation is one way of assessing the attitudinal structure of a brand based on the Fishbein–Ajzen formula.[97] This formula is derived from the expectancy-value model of human behaviour, meaning we tend to do what rewards us. In chapter 10, we will discuss this theory in more depth. But in the current context, the above formula simply says that how we feel about an object is determined by the importance we attach to its constituents (i.e. to individual attributes) and the extent to which we believe the object owns these constituents. Therefore, the more an object has these desirable constituents (as calculated in the formula), the more we will like it; and the more we like it, the higher our attitude towards it (i.e. the brand attitude for this product will be higher).

What would you do if you are the marcoms manager for brand A? The most obvious option would be to keep emphasising the importance of network coverage, since this plays to the strength of the brand. But what would you do as the marcoms manager for brand B? Brand B is in a more difficult position since it has the worst performance on the most important attribute (i.e. network coverage). Therefore, the most obvious strategy is to raise the performance belief that it has weak network coverage. This can be done quickly if this belief is false – just a perception – in which case an effective creative concept should be able to rectify the problem. But how can we tell if this strategy is working? One way is to track the changes in beliefs for the target segments. If the campaign is effective, we would expect the belief rating of brand B on the attribute of network coverage to improve, preferably showing a big jump from 1 to 5.

But what happens if the belief of this performance is real – that is, the network coverage is really bad – and it is not simply a perception? If so, then other more drastic strategic decisions may have to be made (e.g. switching partnership carriers or making other new technological improvements) if this is the long-term desired positioning for brand B. Another possibility is to target another segment that does not value network coverage as highly or, better still, to pursue segments that value ease of use, since this is brand B's greatest strength. Through this example, we can see that positioning decisions can have wide-ranging implications for the firm: they are by no means a simple matter.

DISCUSSION QUESTIONS

1. What is brand positioning? Do you agree or disagree that brand positioning is in part about playing 'mind games'?
2. What is the difference between brand positioning, brand image, brand personality and user imagery?
3. Why is understanding consumers' competitive frame of reference important in brand positioning? How are the notions of point of difference and point of parity related to this concept?
4. Imagine that you are tasked with creating an image for a new product. What would you do first? Which positioning tactic would you use and why?
5. What are the advantages and disadvantages of having a brand name that suggests the product benefit? How would you develop a brand name that does not suffer from any disadvantage?
6. If you were designing a logo, what characteristics would you want the logo to have?
7. In executing competitive advertising, what should you always bear in mind?
8. What is the difference between positioning based on country of origin, region and culture? In what ways are these approaches different from, or similar to, positioning using reputation cues?
9. There are different perspectives on brand equity. Of all the different perspectives on brand equity, which one do you think is the strongest, and why? Explain the strengths and weaknesses of each perspective.
10. One view of brand equity is that of the BrandAsset Valuator® developed by Young & Rubicam. It is made up of two major dimensions: brand stature and brand strength. What are the factors that form these two dimensions? How would you use this model to compare brands across categories?
11. Do you agree or disagree that brand associations form the basis of assessing how effective one's marcoms activities are? If so, what do you think of brands creating Broadway musicals to sell their products? Please justify your answer.

NOTES

1 E Goffman, *The presentation of self in everyday life*, Doubleday, New York, 1959.

2 See S Moriarty, N Mitchell and W Wells, *Advertising and IMC: principles and practice*, 9th edition, Prentice Hall, New Jersey, 2012, p. 206.

3 SD Levitt and SJ Dubner, *Freakonomics: a rogue economist explores the hidden side of everything*, HarperCollins, New York, 2009, p. 87.

4 A Ries and J Trout, *Positioning: the battle for your mind*, McGraw-Hill, New York, 1980.

5 Kevin Keller is the first to actually articulate the importance of the characteristics of associations very well, and I am grateful for his perceptive articulation. Readers who are interested in dwelling deeper on this issue should read his book, *Strategic brand management: building, measuring and managing brand equity*, Prentice Hall, New Jersey, 1998.

6 See www.grabinerhall.com/press-detail.php?a=17. Accessed September 2012.

7 T Telford, 'McDonald's loses Big Mac trademark. Burger King adds "Like a Big Mac, but actually big"', *The Washington Post*, 11 February 2019. Accessed June 2019 at www.washingtonpost.com/business/2019/02/11/mcdonalds-loses-big-mac-trademark-burger-king-adds-like-big-mac-actually-big-burger/?noredirect=on&utm_term=.1157de1ab27d.

8 V Vishwanath and J Mark, 'Your brand's best strategy', *Harvard Business Review*, 75(3), 1997, pp. 123–9.

9 M Ritson, 'Power of Apple's positioning', 8 July 2019. Accessed September 2019 at www.youtube.com/watch?v=1iAEqKH8ebE.

10 N Liddell, '7 steps to effective brand positioning', World Advertising Research Centre (WARC). Accessed May 2018 at www.warc.com/content/paywall/article/7-steps-to-effective-brand-positioning/108533.

11 J Eyers, 'How the Kardashians helped Nick Molnar launch Afterpay in the US', *Australian Financial Review*, May 31, 2019. Accessed June 2019 at www.afr.com/rich-list/how-the-kardashians-helped-nick-molnar-launch-afterpay-in-the-us-20190530-p51sqa.

12 M E Porter, *Competitive advantage: creating and sustaining superior performance*, Free Press, 1998.

13 G Armstong et al., *Principles of marketing*, 11th edition, Pearson, Englewood Cliffs, NJ, 2015.

14 JD Houwer, S Thomas and F Bayeans, 'Associative learning of likes and dislikes: a review of 25 years of research on human evaluative conditioning', *Psychological Bulletin*, 127(6), 2001, pp. 853–69; S Sweldens et al., 'Evaluative conditioning procedures and resilience of conditioned brand attitudes', *Journal of Consumer Research*, 37, October 2010, pp. 473–89.

15 This list of tactics draws on the work of DA Aaker and JG Shansby, 'Positioning your product', *Business Horizons*, 25, May–June 1982, pp. 56–62.

16 Y Bao, AT Shao and D Rivers, 'Creating new brand names: effects of relevance, connotation and pronunciation', *Journal of Advertising Research*, 48(1), 2008, pp. 148–62.

17 KL Keller, SE Heckler and MJ Houston, 'The effects of brand name suggestiveness on advertising recall', *Journal of Marketing*, 62, January 1998, pp. 48–57.

18 E Sapir, 'A study in phonetic symbolism', *Journal of Experimental Psychology*, 12, June 1929, pp. 225–39.

19 R Klink, 'Creating meaningful new brand names: a study of semantics and sound symbolism', Journal of Marketing Theory and Practice, Spring, 2001, pp. 27–34.

20 PW Henderson and JA Cote, 'Guidelines for selecting or modifying logos', *Journal of Marketing*, 62(2), 1998, pp. 14–30. In a subsequent study, these authors examined what makes a typeface of a brand pleasing, reassuring, engaging and prominent. Interested readers may want to track down this interesting study: PW Henderson, JL Giese and JA Cote, 'Impression management using typeface design', *Journal of Marketing*, 68, October 2004, pp. 60–72.

21 H Hagtvedt, 'The impact of incomplete typeface logos on perceptions of the firm', *Journal of Marketing*, 75(4), 2011, pp. 86–93.

22 J Luffarelli, A Stamatogiannakis and H Yang, 'The visual asymmetry effect: an interplay of logo design and brand personality on brand equity', *Journal of Marketing Research*, 56(1), 2019, pp. 89–103.

23 Y Jiang et al., 'Does your company have the right logo? How and why circular-and angular-logo shapes influence brand attribute judgments', *Journal of Consumer Research*, 42(5), 2016, pp. 709–26.

24 L Cian, A Krishna and RS Elder, 'This logo moves me: dynamic imagery from static images', *Journal of Marketing Research,* 51, 2014, pp. 184–97.

25 In the original conceptualisation, Baxter and Ilicic argued that a dynamic logo gave a sense of energy, and it was this energy that made the brand persuasive. For this reason, I would call such logos energetic rather than dynamic. See SM Baxter and J Ilicic, 'May the force drag your dynamic logo: the brand work-energy effect', *International Journal of Research in Marketing,* 35, 2018, pp. 509–23.

26 I would like to thank Jasmina Ilicic for kindly providing these images.

27 Reprinted from SM Baxter and J Ilicic, 'May the force drag your dynamic logo: the brand work-energy effect', *International Journal of Research in Marketing*, 35, 2018, pp. 509–23, with permission from Elsevier.

28 According to Keller, it is not always the case that a logo will enhance the brand name. It is possible that when a logo is added to the brand name, it actually makes it *less* appealing. In this situation, it is better not to have the logo, or to change it. See Keller (1998), *Strategic brand management*, note 5.

29 H Boland, 'Big brands keep their social distance with revamped logos', *The Telegraph*, 29 March 2020. Accessed April 2020 at www.telegraph.co.uk/business/2020/03/29/big-brands-keep-social-distance-revamped-logos/.

30 J Valinsky, 'McDonald's and other brands are making "social distancing" logos', *CNN*, 26 March 2020. Accessed April 2020 at https://edition.cnn.com/2020/03/26/business/social-distancing-brand-logos-coronavirus/index.html.

31 Woolworths Group, 'Woolworths to introduce a dedicated shopping hour for the elderly and people with disability', 2020. Accessed April 2020 at www.woolworthsgroup.com.au/page/media/Latest_News/woolworths-to-introduce-a-dedicated-shopping-hour-for-the-elderly-and-people-with-disability/.

32 BBC News, 'Coronavirus: Louis Vuitton owner to start making hand sanitiser', 2020. Accessed April 2020 at www.bbc.com/news/business-51868756.

33 You can see Telsa's engineering plan for producing medical ventilators here. Accessed April 2020 at https://youtu.be/zZbDg24dfN0.

34 S Byford, 'Apple is designing and shipping face shields for medical workers', *The Verge*, 5 April 2020. Accessed April 2020 at www.theverge.com/2020/4/5/21209270/apple-face-shields-masks-covid-19-coronavirus?mod=djemCMOToday.

35 D Armano, 'How the pandemic is pressure-testing a brand's purpose', 2020. Accessed April 2020 at www.edelman.com/covid-19/perspectives/testing-brands-purpose.

36 AJ Elliot et al., 'Color and psychological functioning: the effect of red on performance attainment', *Journal of Experimental Psychology: General*, 136(1), 2007, pp. 154–68.

37 N Hynes, 'Color and meaning in corporate logos: an empirical study', *Journal of Brand Management*, 16(8), 2009, pp. 545–55.

38 This is another brilliant study by Baxter and colleagues: SM Baxter, J Ilicic and A Kulczynski, 'Roses are red, violets are blue, sophisticated brands have a Tiffany Hue: the effect of iconic brand color priming on brand personality judgments', *Journal of Brand Management*, 25, 2018, pp. 384–94.

39 LL Labrecque and GR Milne, 'Exciting red and competent blue: the importance of color in marketing', *Journal of the Academy of Marketing Science*, 40(5), 2012, pp. 711–27.

40 M Bortoli and J Maroto, 'Colours across cultures: translating colours in interactive marketing communications', first published with the title 'Translating colours in web site localisation' in 2001 in the Proceedings of the European Languages and the Implementation of Communication and Information Technologies (Elicit) conference. University of Paisley. Accessed June 2019 at www.globalpropaganda.com/articles/TranslatingColours.pdf.

41 M Airs and L Ang, 'Avoiding the ad-avoidance blues?', ANZMAC conference, Adelaide, 2012.

42 R Reeves, *Reality in advertising*, Alfred A Knopf, New York, 1961.

43 JR Rossiter and S Bellman, *Marketing communications: theory and applications*, Pearson Australia, Frenchs Forest, NSW, 2005.

44 B Schwartz, *The paradox of choice: why more is less*, Harper Collins, 2003.

45 D Grewal et al., 'Comparative versus non-comparative advertising: a meta-analysis', *Journal of Marketing*, 36, 1997, pp. 345–55.

46 A Chattopadhyay, 'When does comparative advertising influence brand attitude? The role of delay and market position', *Psychology and Marketing*, 15(5), 1998, pp. 461–75.

47 S Ang and S Leong, 'Comparative advertising: superiority despite interference?', *Asia Pacific Journal of Management*, 11, 1994, pp. 33–46.

48 S Zhang, FR Kardes and ML Cronley, 'Comparative advertising: effects of structural alignability on target brand evaluations', *Journal of Consumer Psychology*, 12(4), 2002, pp. 303–11.

49 SP Jain and SS Posavac, 'Valenced comparisons', *Journal of Marketing Research*, 41, 2004, pp. 46–58.

50 David Ogilvy gave a speech called 'The image and the brand' to the American Association of Advertising Agencies, Chicago, on 14 October 1955.

51 J Aaker, 'Dimensions of brand personality', *Journal of Marketing Research*, 34, 1997, pp. 342–52.

52 This campaign won a major creative award in D&AD in 2019. For more information go to www.dandad.org/awards/professional/2019/digital-marketing/230756/dundee-the-son-of-a-legend-returns-home/. Accessed June 2019.

53 Some of these ads are available online at www.youtube.com/watch?v=VCL5UgxtoLs.

54 D Leonard, 'Hey, PC, who taught you to fight back?', *New York Times*, 29 August 2009. Accessed October 2012 at www.nytimes.com/2009/08/30/business/media/30ad.html?pagewanted=all.

55 ASC Ehrenberg, GG Goodhardt and TP Barwise, 'Double jeopardy revisited', *Journal of Marketing*, 54(3), 1990, pp. 82–91.

56 C Shapiro, 'Consumer information, product quality and seller reputation', *Bell Journal of Economics*, 13, 1982, pp. 20–35.

57 E Yoon, HJ Guffey and V Kijewski, 'The effects of information and company reputation on intentions to buy a business service', *Journal of Business Research*, 27, 1993, pp. 215–28.

58 F Allen, 'Reputation and product quality', *Rand Journal of Economics*, 15, Autumn, 1984, pp. 311–27.

59 M Dahlen, S Rosengren and F Torn, 'Advertising creativity matters', *Journal of Advertising Research*, 48(3), 2003, pp. 392–403.

60 T Ambler and E Hollier, 'The waste in advertising is the part that works', *Journal of Advertising Research*, 44(4), 2004, pp. 375–89.

61 P-Y Chu et al., 'Countering negative country of origin effects: the role of evaluation mode', *European Journal of Marketing*, 44(7/8), 2010, pp. 1065–76.

62 L Kenny and O Aron, 'Consumer brand classifications: an assessment of culture of origin versus country of origin', *Journal of Product and Brand Management*, 10(2), 2001, pp. 120–36.

63 K Rapoza, 'China island dispute whacks Japanese auto sales', *Forbes*, 2012. Accessed October 2012 at www.forbes.com/sites/kenrapoza/2012/10/09/china-island-dispute-whacks-japanese-auto-sales/.

64 Guardian, 'Japanese car sales plunge in China after islands dispute', 2012. Accessed October 2012 at www.guardian.co.uk/business/2012/oct/09/japanese-car-sales-china-islands-dispute.

65 KB Monroe, 'Buyer's subjective perception of price', *Journal of Marketing Research*, 10, February 1973, pp. 70–80.

66 J Olson, 'Price as an informational cue: effects in product evaluation', in AG Woodside, JN Sheth and PD Bennet (eds), *Consumer and industrial buying behavior*, North Holland Publishing Company, New York, 1977, pp. 267–86.

67 RA Peterson and WR Wilson, 'Perceived risk and price-reliance schema and price-perceived-quality mediators', in J Jacoby and J Olson (eds), *Perceived quality*, Lexington Books, Lexington, MA, 1985, pp. 247–68.

68 AR Rao and KB Monroe, 'The moderating effect of prior knowledge on cue utilization in product evaluations', *Journal of Consumer Research*, 15, September 1988, pp. 253–64.

69 V Zeithaml, 'Consumer perceptions of price, quality, and value: a means–end model and synthesis of evidence', *Journal of Marketing*, 52, July 1988, pp. 2–22.

70 Thomas Brennan, *Burgundy to Champagne: the modern wine trade in modern early France*, Johns Hopkins University Press, 1997, pp. 252–3.

71 It seems most of the myths started with Dom Grossard, the last treasury of the abbey motivated perhaps to increase the prestige of the abbey. It seems monks are not averse to telling a little white lie (see R Walters, *Bursting bubbles*, Bibendum Wine & Co., 2016, p. 31).

72 H Davidson, *Offensive marketing*, Penguin, Harmondsworth, 1997, p. 400.

73 M Pendergrast, *For God, country and Coca-Cola*, Basic Books, New York, 2000, p. 32.

74 For a detailed discussion of this case study see Keller (1998), *Strategic brand management*, note 5.

75 K Munir, 'The demise of Kodak: five reasons', *Wall Street Journal* [blog], 2012. Accessed October 2012 at http://blogs.wsj.com/source/2012/02/26/the-demise-of-kodak-five-reasons/.

76 'The last Kodak moment?', *Economist*, 14 January 2012.

77 'Abercrombie & Fitch brand protection: things to know', 2012. Accessed October 2012 at www.abercrombie.com/webapp/wcs/stores/servlet/CustomerService?textKey=HELP_BRANDPROTECTION&catalogId=10901&langId=-1&pageName=brand-protection&storeId=11203.

78 Marketing Mag, 'From Virgin Blue to Virgin Australia – the rebrand', 30 November 2012. Accessed July 2013 at www.marketingmag.com.au/case-studies/from-blue-to-true-blue-virgin-australia-rebrand-28140/#.UfjWMnf4KSo.

79 KL Keller, B Sternthal and A Tybout, 'Three questions you need to ask about our brand', *Harvard Business Review*, September 2002, pp. 80–6.

80 Rossiter and Percy have stated that, in addition to point of difference, points of parity should be included in the positioning statement if it is important to gain entry into the category. See JR Rossiter and L Percy, *Advertising communications and promotion management*, 2nd edition, McGraw-Hill, New York, 1997, p. 151.

81 New York Times, 'Company news; Suchard drops out', 25 June 1988. Accessed 26 August 2007 at www.nytimes.com/1988/06/25/business/company-news-suchard-drops-out.html.

82 M Urde, C Baumgarth and B Merrilees, 'Brand orientation and market orientation: from alternatives to synergy', *Journal of Business Research*, 66, 2013, pp. 13–20.

83 Interbrand, 'Best global brands 2018 rankings', www.interbrand.com/best-brands/best-global-brands/2018/ranking/.

84 A Mizaraei et al., 'A behavioural long-term based measure to monitor the health of a brand', *Journal of Brand Management*, 22(4), 2015, pp. 299–322.

85 S Herman, 'Dynamics of price elasticity and brand life cycles', *Journal of Marketing Research*, 16, November 1979, pp. 439–52.

86 WL Boulding, E Lee and R Staelin, 'Mastering the mix: do advertising, promotion, and sales force activities lead to differentiation?', *Journal of Marketing Research*, 31, May 1994, pp. 159–72.

87 KL Ailawadi, SA Neslin and DR Lehmann, 'Revenue premium as an outcome measure of brand equity', *Journal of Marketing*, 67(4), 2003, pp. 1–17.

88 Keller (1998), *Strategic brand management*, p. 45, note 5.

89 Ibid., p. 60.

90 Our perspective is necessarily simplified. But for a dynamic view of how this model can be used for different brands, see the BAV Consulting website, http://bavconsulting.com/apps/. Accessed October 2012.

91 CP de Mortanges and AV Riel, 'Brand equity and shareholder value', *European Management Journal*, 21(4), 2003, pp. 521–7.

92 P Kotler and G Armstrong, *Principles of marketing*, 17th Global edition, Pearson, 2018.

93 D Poole, 'Measuring long-term ad effects: a meaningfully different approach'. Accessed June 2019 at www.millwardbrown.com/docs/default-source/insight-documents/points-of-view/MillwardBrown_POV_Measuring_Long-Term_Ad_Effects.pdf.

94 I am a big fan of Nigel Hollis, from Kantar, who wrote this wonderful book about creating premium brands. N Hollis, *Brand premium*, Palgrave Macmillan, New York, 2013.

95 K Shipley, 'Beyond the jingle: how brand music videos are born', Think with Google. Accessed April 2019 at www.thinkwithgoogle.com/advertising-channels/video/brand-jingle-for-brand-awareness/.

96 See Boulding, Lee and Staelin (1994), 'Mastering the mix', note 86.

97 M Fishbein and I Ajzen, *Belief, attitude, intention, and behavior: an introduction to theory and research*, Addison-Wesley, Reading, MA, 1975.

CHAPTER 4
MEDIA PLANNING FOR GROWTH

CHAPTER OVERVIEW

This chapter is about media planning and budgeting in advertising. It is also about dollars and 'sense' (not cents), recognising that up to 90% of the advertising budget can be spent on media. Many industries spend as much as one-third of their profit (not revenue) on media and promotions.[1] This means that a media plan that is not well thought out and executed will affect the company's bottom line very quickly.

Although this chapter is principally about media planning and budgeting, it is also about communication objectives and consumer behaviour. This is because unless we first determine what we want to achieve with our communications, we will not be able to know if we have achieved it. And if we do not understand where and when consumers buy our product or service, we will not be able to place and time the exposure frequency of our advertisement to best influence consumers as well. If we understand consumer behaviour, then we can decide on the most cost-effective channel, the best time and the ideal frequency to reach consumers using the right media vehicles. We should also factor into this decision whether the organisation wants to grow. If so, then being able to reach as many consumers as possible becomes important, aided by having distinctive creative assets and excess share of voice. Each of these decisions has implications for the budget and so media planning and budgeting are quite complex. And this complexity is compounded as more online channels and platforms become available, although the advent of programmatic media buying improves the efficiency of ad placements, notwithstanding its weaknesses. In this chapter, you will gain a good appreciation of these issues.

Learning goals

After reading this chapter, you will understand:

- what advertising is supposed to do
- what DAGMAR (Defining Advertising Goals for Measured Advertising Results) is and how to use it
- the theory of weak versus strong advertising
- the importance of assessing communications objectives and sales simultaneously
- the share of voice (SOV) and share of market (SOM) budgeting methods
- the relationship between opportunity to see (OTS), media weight, average frequency and reach
- differences between the s-shape and convex sales-to-advertising response functions and their implications for media planning
- the concept of recent exposure and its implication for recency media planning, frequency and continuous schedules
- the role of experimentation, scale effects and post-buy evaluation in media planning

- what questions to ask when developing a media strategy, and the relationship between media strategy and media neutrality
- the importance of reach, distinctiveness and salience in increasing market share
- how to balance short- and long-term goals in media planning
- the pros and cons of programmatic media buying.

The businessman John Wanamaker was thought to have said in the late 1800s, 'Half the money I spend on advertising is wasted; the trouble is I don't know which half.'[2] This saying epitomises the great uncertainty often associated with media spending – and it is still true today! This is because the relationship between advertising and sales (or another outcome such as purchase intentions) is not clear cut. In fact, the same uncertainty also applies to other marcoms activities as well (e.g. marketing-oriented PR). Unless we know the response function, we cannot link the input to the output. It also complicates the issue that a response function discovered for one campaign may not necessarily apply to the next, simply because the context may be different (e.g. a new creative idea or new competition). And if multiple media vehicles are used, this will further muddle our understanding. The aim of this chapter is to explore issues such as these which plague management and to provide a theoretically sound solution to the major problems.[3]

WHAT IS ADVERTISING SUPPOSED TO DO?

Consider the following. In manufacturing, we know that if we put in 20 hours of labour, plus x number of units, with y units of assembly supervision, we can accurately predict output. And, as we practice, our efficiency increases because we learn how to do our task better. However, in advertising the linkage between input and output is not entirely clear. Unless we carefully document and study the history of effectiveness of various campaigns for the brand there will be no cumulative learning. (Managers also come and go, and often the same mistakes are made by new ones.) A significant part of the uncertainty comes from deciding what we should be measuring in advertising. If we cannot determine that, then the budgeting process becomes guesswork. We can begin to reduce this uncertainty by asking one simple question: what is advertising supposed to do?

The hierarchy of effects model

One perspective is that advertising should increase sales by progressively moving the target audience towards purchase. Called the hierarchy of effects (HOE) model, there are a number of variations. This theory states that advertising should first make the target audience aware of the brand, what it stands for, likes and prefers, and then eventually try it. Although this model has been criticised (see chapter 7), it is one way of thinking how advertising can be linked to sales. It is also useful in estimating the breakeven point of a campaign and, in the process, to stimulate our thinking to improve its efficiency.

ESTIMATING THE BREAKEVEN POINT OF A CAMPAIGN AND IMPROVING EFFICIENCY

Table 4.1 shows the communication attrition rate of a hypothetical brand, with an estimated target audience of 3 million potential customers. The campaign manages to achieve 60% brand awareness, which amounts to 1.8 million potential customers or 'prospects' (i.e. 60% of

ASKHAM BRYAN
COLLEGE
LEARNING RESOURCES

3 million = 1.8 million). But say that only 50% of the 1.8 million potential customers fully comprehend the ad (i.e. what the brand stands for). This means that the market now shrinks to 900 000 (i.e. 50% of 1.8 million = 900 000). Imagine that, from those 900 000 prospects, only 270 000, or 30%, like the brand (i.e. 30% of 900 000 = 270 000). And of those 270 000 people, only 54 000, or 20%, develop a preference (i.e. 20% of 270 000 = 54 000). Finally, if only 5% of that smaller pool of prospects decides to buy the brand, the final number of potential customers is now only 2700 (i.e. 5% of 54 000 = 2700).

Table 4.1 The effects of the communication attrition rate

Hierarchy of effects stages	Attrition rate
60% awareness	0.6 × 3 million = 1.8 million
50% comprehension	0.5 × 1.8 million = 900 000
30% liking	0.3 × 900 000 = 270 000
20% brand preference	0.2 × 270 000 = 54 000
5% trial	0.05 × 54 000 = 2700

Now imagine that the marcoms manager is thinking of investing $1 million in this campaign. Based on the estimates above, it means that each product (or group of products) sold must have a profit margin of $370.37 (i.e. $1 000 000/2700) just to break even.

Besides breakeven estimation, one can also use this model to think of ways to improve efficiency. Much of this comes down to how one can reach more people and reduce the attrition rate. In this cognitive–affective–conative sequence, the pool of potential customers has shrunk from 3 million to 2700 customers as a result of the attrition percentages at each stage. In fact, the awareness-to-trial conversion ratio is only 0.0009 (i.e. 0.6 × 0.5 × 0.3 × 0.2 × 0.05 = 0.0009). Although this exercise is hypothetical, it stimulates thinking about improving efficiency. For instance:

- The marcoms manager may contemplate increasing reach using TV. That way, instead of reaching 60% of the market, one can increase this to 80%. By achieving 80% brand awareness right from the start, a greater percentage of the market may try the brand in the end. The marcoms manager may then ask if this is achievable with a budget of $1 million. And if not, what else can be done to lift this awareness?
- Further, the marcoms manager may think of ways of improving the 5% trial rate given 20% brand preference. Perhaps improving distribution is most likely to do this.

The DAGMAR model

Not everyone agrees that advertising should or can necessarily lead to sales. One prominent opposing perspective was developed in 1961 by Colley and later updated by Solomon Dutka.[4] Defining Advertising Goals for Measured Advertising Results (DAGMAR) is a perspective that makes a number of well-formed arguments that advertising is first and foremost a communication task, and therefore the assessment of its effects should also be communication-related (not sales-related).

But the model proposed by DAGMAR is one version of the traditional hierarchy of effects (HOE) model of advertising. Although there are many versions of HOE (see chapter 7), the DAGMAR version starts with 'awareness' then 'comprehension', 'conviction' and finally 'action'. However, the last step of 'action' in DAGMAR does not mean purchase. Here, 'action' is simply the overt moves consumers make towards the purchase of the product. But purchase may not necessarily occur. For instance: 'They may have visited a dealer's showroom and asked for a demonstration. Or they may have asked for literature or for a salesperson to call. Or they may have asked for or reached for the brand at the retail store.'[5] This is not the same as making a purchase because 'the dealer did not have the model in stock, a trade-in allowance may have been too low, a salesperson may have failed to follow up the lead, a price might be considered too high, or a product may lack appeal when physically examined. Nonetheless, advertising induced action'.[6]

Further, it can be argued that increasing sales is not a legitimate marcoms objective because many factors can affect sales, including:

- changes in environmental, economic and political climate (e.g. recession or war)
- demographic and psychographic changes
- intensive competitive activities
- carry-over effects (effects that are not immediate but that will influence future purchase)
- poor distribution, pricing or selling skills.

Therefore, even though our advertising may get the message across well, sales may still not increase because of these extraneous factors. In other words, since advertising is not the only factor that affects sales, it is not fair for sales to be included as an objective for advertising. According to the DAGMAR perspective, sales is a marketing objective, not an advertising one.

If we agree with this perspective, it also means that these communication objectives (i.e. awareness, comprehension, conviction and action) become the objectives of advertising. Measurement then revolves around these communication objectives, not sales. For instance, an increase in the number of consumers who are aware of the brand after a campaign can be taken as a sign of success, as would be improvements in comprehension, conviction and action. By measuring these changes, advertisers can get a handle on how to assess the effectiveness of the communications without worrying about sales. So, by redefining what advertising should accomplish, DAGMAR does away with sales as the ultimate objective (which a marketing manager may not find satisfactory). The challenge then comes down to agreeing on how advertising communications is supposed to work even if sales is ignored.

The weak versus strong theory of advertising

The controversy does not end there. The DAGMAR perspective also assumes that consumers progressively go through each of these (pre-buying) stages en route to action. Dubbed the 'strong theory of advertising', it says that advertising should be strong enough to ensure that consumers move progressively through each stage. As they go from awareness to action, the number of customers reduces as the probability of their making a purchase rises. We have already discussed this earlier in the form of communication attrition (see table 4.1). Another way of visualising this is to think of the attrition as a 'funnel' (this is shown in figure 4.1). Here we try to target (i.e. reach) as many consumers as we can (at the top of the funnel) so that in the end (at the bottom) we will end up with a small, but viable, number of purchasers.

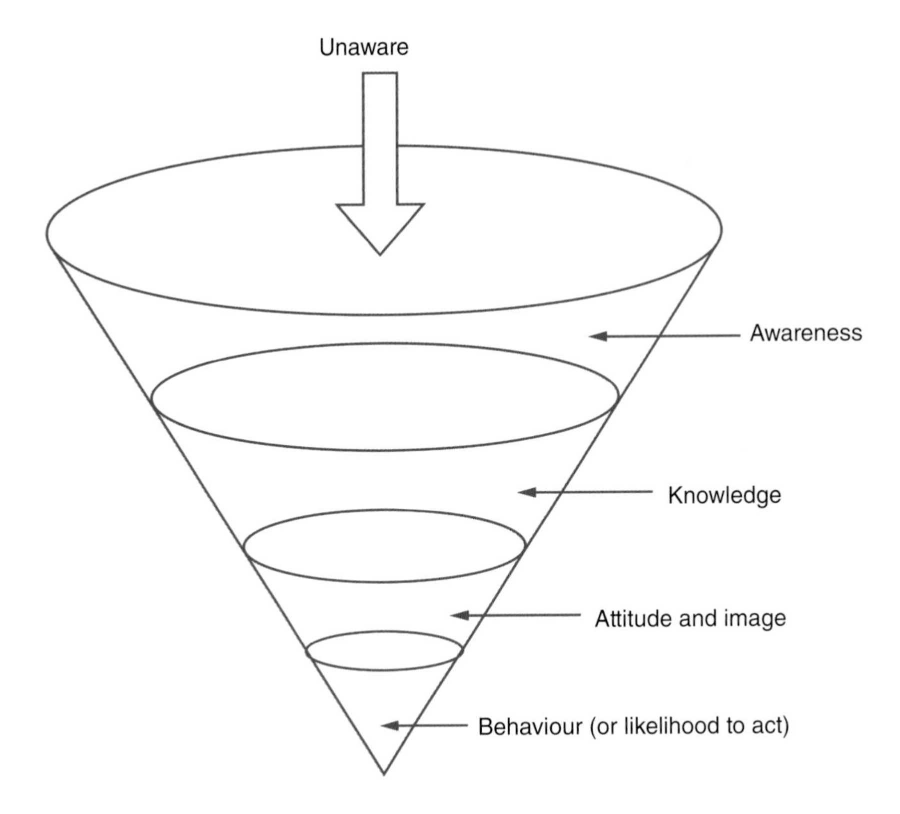

Figure 4.1 The 'funnel' is a way of representing communication attrition

But what happens when the product is low involvement (e.g. a cheap product) or is already well known (e.g. a brand leader in consumer-packaged goods)? Under such circumstances, consumers are not likely to spend much time agonising about the purchase and may be willing to just try it first, since it is cheap. In this case, the metaphor of the funnel is not relevant because in this instance the trial will come first, and from the trial we can learn more about the brand. Subsequent advertising serves to reinforce this and hopefully induce repeat purchase. In other words, for low-involvement products where consumers are willing to risk purchase, advertising does not need to move consumers through the different stages. In this way, it can be argued that most advertising is weak;[7] as Andrew Ehrenberg observed, advertising does not lead to changes in market share.[8] Rather, factors such as penetration and purchase rates influence market share. Advertising is then more about reinforcing existing behaviour, after awareness and trial. One interpretation of the Ehrenbergian view is that advertising is simply about refreshing consumers' brand associations, keeping it uppermost in their minds and thus stopping them from switching. In this perspective, there is no need to evoke mental states such as brand equity or purchase intention. It is all reflected in market share.[9] This is often called the 'weak theory of advertising'. Figure 4.2 illustrates the two different perspectives we have been discussing.

If we accept Ehrenberg's view, we are effectively opening a can of worms. This is because it implies that, theoretically, there may be other variations of the DAGMAR model involving a different sequence.

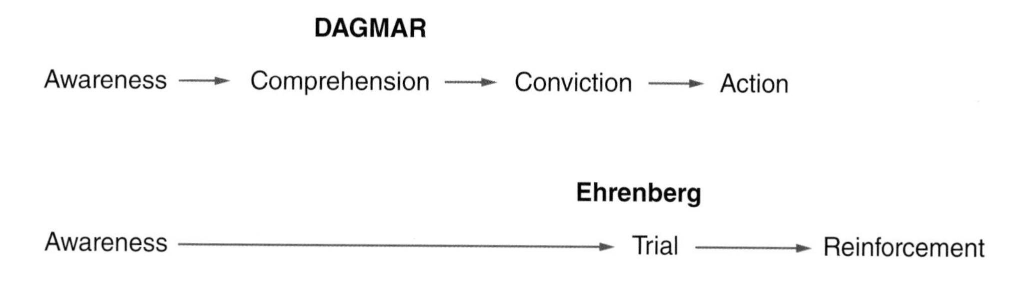

Figure 4.2 The 'strong' and 'weak' models of advertising

According to Dutka, this is not an issue because DAGMAR can easily handle this by adjusting the stages that are most suitable for our brand, even if this means truncating the stages. So, the principle is the same, and only the number and sequence of stages may be different, depending on the brand. As a general rule, the funnel model tends to be apt for high-involvement goods, while the Ehrenbergian perspective applies to low-involvement goods.

In this way, the DAGMAR principle can still be useful although it does not include use of the sales objective. This is because it encourages a manager to think more deeply about whether consumers are ready to buy and, if they are not, how to coordinate various marcoms tools to move them closer to action. It also reinforces the fact that the measurement used must match the objectives selected.

THE IMPORTANCE OF ASSESSING COMMUNICATIONS AND SALES OBJECTIVES SIMULTANEOUSLY

If we do not include sales as an objective, is this satisfactory? We could argue that redefining of the role of advertising as primarily a communication tool is unsatisfactory from the perspective of marketing. This is because hundreds of billions of dollars every year are spent on advertising (about US$558 billion in 2018[10]), and it is hard to justify claiming that our only interest in it is communication effectiveness.

One solution is to assess the communication and sales objectives at the same time. That way, the communication objectives can be used to diagnose why sales are or are not improving. For instance, if sales are not improving but the campaign is delivering on its communication objectives, we can safely eliminate poor advertising as the cause. Even if sales are rising, it still pays to track communication objectives to understand why it is so effective. We will discuss campaign tracking in chapter 12.

OBJECTIVE-AND-TASK BUDGETING METHOD

Another way of rectifying the shortcomings of DAGMAR is to simply incorporate sales outcomes into the calculation during the planning stage. But to do so we need to make some assumptions about the tasks needed to achieve this. Two examples are given in the box below. The first demonstrates the use of a simple click-through rate for internet advertising. The second presents a more complicated example of a new product launch using radio advertising. These examples also illustrate how a campaign budget can be set for one specific task.

EXAMPLE 1

Assume we can make a profit of $20 per customer. However, our analysis of internet traffic found that only 5% of those who clicked on our banner ad end up becoming our customers. This means every click represents an income of $1 (i.e. 0.05 × $20 = $1.00).

Now imagine we paid (bid) 10 cents per click for the desired keyword. This means, for every 10 cents we spend, we make $1.00. Not bad. Or, to put it another way, our return of $1 (or 100 cents) is 10 times our investment of 10 cents (i.e. 100/10 = 10).

To increase profit, we can either increase our margin (say from $20 to $21), try to increase our conversion rate (say from 5% to 10%) or pay less per click (say 5 cents instead of 10 cents).

Now, imagine for our internet campaign we plan to buy 30 key words. We make the same sort of assumption (or run tests) for each word and add up accordingly.

EXAMPLE 2

In this example, let's assume that we are launching a new product where the awareness to purchase conversion ratio is 0.05. That is, for every 100 consumers that come through the funnel every month, only 5% end up being our customers. To be viable, we calculated that we need to sell 200 units per month to these customers. This means we need to have 200/0.05 consumers to be aware (for a start), which is a target of 4000 consumers (i.e. 200/0.05 = 4000).

The next question is how we can reach these 4000 customers. Our research reveals that radio is the best medium given its cost, our target audience's media usage habits and our creative concept (e.g. has a great jingle). Further, to become aware, consumers need to be exposed to our radio ad three times. But since consumers do not pay too much attention to radio advertising, we have to factor this in, which is estimated to elicit attention 30% of the time. This means you will need 3/0.3 (or 10 radio spots) to gain awareness (i.e. 3/0.3 = 10). If it costs $800 for a spot, it means our estimated investment over 12 months will be $96 000 (i.e. $800 × 10 spots × 12 months = $96 000).

To this figure ($96 000), we can add other costs, such as research and creative production. Once the full cost is established, we make sure that the 2400 total units to be sold (i.e. 200 units × 12 = 2400) remain profitable after the total deduction of the cost.[11]

There is often a lot of uncertainty attached to advertising spend. These two examples illustrate how a marcoms manager can try to achieve some certainty by making certain assumptions about what a particular task can accomplish.

In the calculated examples given in the box above, one medium is discussed at a time (internet or radio). For a large campaign, however, other media (or tactics) will be involved, but the principle remains the same. For each task (and there may be many), we estimate how much it will cost to create the desired sales and profit. This is essentially what we call the objective-and-task method of budgeting.

Of course, there are other methods of budgeting. In fact, a pioneering paper by White[12] found that there were at least 15 different methods. But all the methods suffer from an inherent weakness in that they do not inform a manager about what to do, and some are even backward-looking. The objective-and-task method is by far the most logical one. It is also the most consistent with the IMC philosophy of integrating different tools and channels to more effectively accomplish the desired objectives. But, as the examples above show, it is also the most conceptually demanding. Much rests on the assumptions we make about effectiveness of frequency and the ability of our ads to reach and convert our target audience. It is also roughly right because it is logical.

CASE STUDY 4.1 JOHN LEWIS: A CASE OF REACH, DISTINCTIVENESS AND SALIENCE

John Lewis is an upmarket department store in the UK with about 50 outlets. Its first outlet was opened in 1864. This case study is about how it used its Christmas campaigns (2011 and 2015) to grow its market share.

John Lewis' Christmas advertising is famous in the UK. Each year during Christmas, the British people look forward to John Lewis' TV commercial (TVC) which marks the start of the Christmas shopping season (usually in the first week of November). The launch of the campaign was such an event that even the media got behind it. In 2015, for instance, the *Telegraph* set up a count-down clock on its website to show how long before John Lewis launched its Christmas TVC.

Figure 4.3 John Lewis department store

John Lewis' growth strategy centred almost entirely on their Christmas TVCs.[13] Between 2012 and 2015, these were: 'The long wait', 'The journey', 'Monty the penguin' and 'Man on the moon', which won many creative awards. Over the four years, John Lewis' market share grew by nearly 30%, which was phenomenal. Although many lessons can be drawn from this success, this case study will concentrate on two important lessons that are relevant to this chapter: (i) reach if one is to grow; and (ii) being clear on what tasks (guided by the objective) need to be accomplished in order to grow.

LESSON 1: INCREASING REACH FOR GROWTH USING DISTINCTIVE ASSETS

There is no question that to grow market share, the campaign must reach as many people as possible. The more one can reach, the greater the likelihood that some will be converted to become customers.[14] In other words, growth is essentially a numbers game. This implies that one's media plan must include channels that can best achieve this objective in a cost-efficient way. In the case of John Lewis, they discovered that TV was still the most suitable medium because almost every household in Britain (90%) owned at least one TV set, and the British people spent about 3.3 hours a week watching TV.

Of course, if a firm is not interested in growth, then using TV will be a waste of reach (and hence money). Under such circumstances, one can adopt targeting only one's own customers, for instance, by using direct marketing (see chapter 11). Coupled with deep knowledge of customer preference, firms can be very effective in customising offerings to current customers and hence maintain their loyalty. But this non-growth customer retention strategy can be dangerous because loyal customers will eventually die! For some product categories where sales are based on subscription, like insurance or home loans, effective customer acquisition is the only option.

If customer acquisition is a more effective strategy in growing a company than customer retention,[15] then it implies that a mass medium like TV still has a place in the modern digital era because it can reach a high number of consumers, turning them into first time customers (albeit light users). However, this strategy can lead to some wastage of reach since one would still be reaching consumers who are not ready to buy. There are two ways of handling this. First, as we will discuss later, to have a lower but still a cost-efficient reach. For instance, instead of trying to reach 90% of the market, one can opt to reach 50%. Then use other means of non-overlapping media to achieve incremental reach.

Second, to ensure that the branded message is uniquely distinctive and tightly linked to various purchase triggers, so that when activated, the brand easily comes to mind. This is called brand salience, which can be defined as the ease in which the brand is triggered by a variety of purchase-motivating situations. In this sense, no reach is wasted provided positive brand memories can be effectively built in people's minds. But to achieve this, the ad and its other brand elements (e.g. colour, logo) must be distinctive so that it is unique and easily identifiable. It must also be tightly linked to the category and associated with a motivating need or event that can trigger the purchase.

In the case of John Lewis, all the TVCs are so distinctly unique that people have little trouble identifying them correctly. Furthermore, since the product category (i.e. departmental stores) will become an important trigger during Christmas, a brand like John Lewis which is tightly linked to the category (i.e. high brand awareness) with a desirable association (i.e. shoppers are considered thoughtful gift givers) will also become a salient (see figure 4.4).

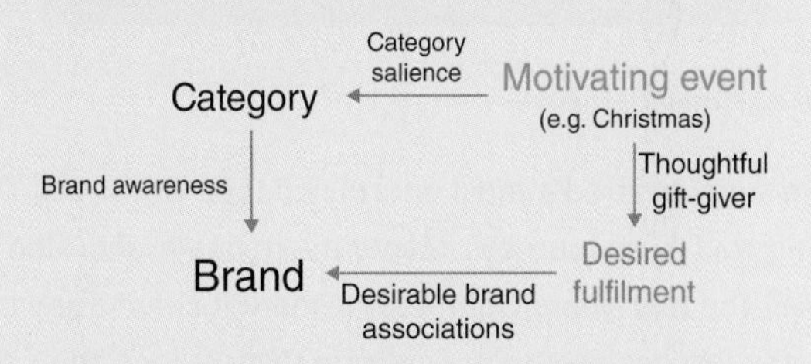

Figure 4.4 Conceptual relationships between brand and motivating event

In time, through evaluative conditioning (see chapter 3), the motivating event alone (i.e. Christmas) will automatically trigger the brand (i.e. John Lewis). That is why over the years, everyone in Britain has looked forward to watching John Lewis' TVC every Christmas (see figure 4.5). As a general rule, the more purchase-triggering situations a brand can be linked to, the greater will be its mental market share because it can be more easily triggered.[16] (In chapter 9, we will return to a related idea called issue salience, important in agenda-setting theory in media.)

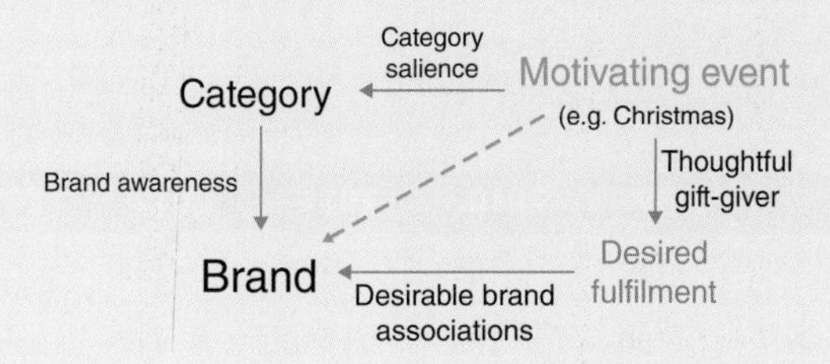

Figure 4.5 Conceptual illustration of how a brand is conditioned to a motivating event

LESSON 2: OBJECTIVE AND TASK

The second lesson is how systematic the objectives were laid out and assessed. This exemplifies clear thinking. The advertising task is to create outstanding TVCs the British people want to watch, love and talk about during the Christmas period. As we saw in chapter 1, these communication objectives are unobservable intermediary effects (but still measurable). They serve as an unseen 'bridge' between observable behavioural outcome like store traffic and sales to the advertising task.

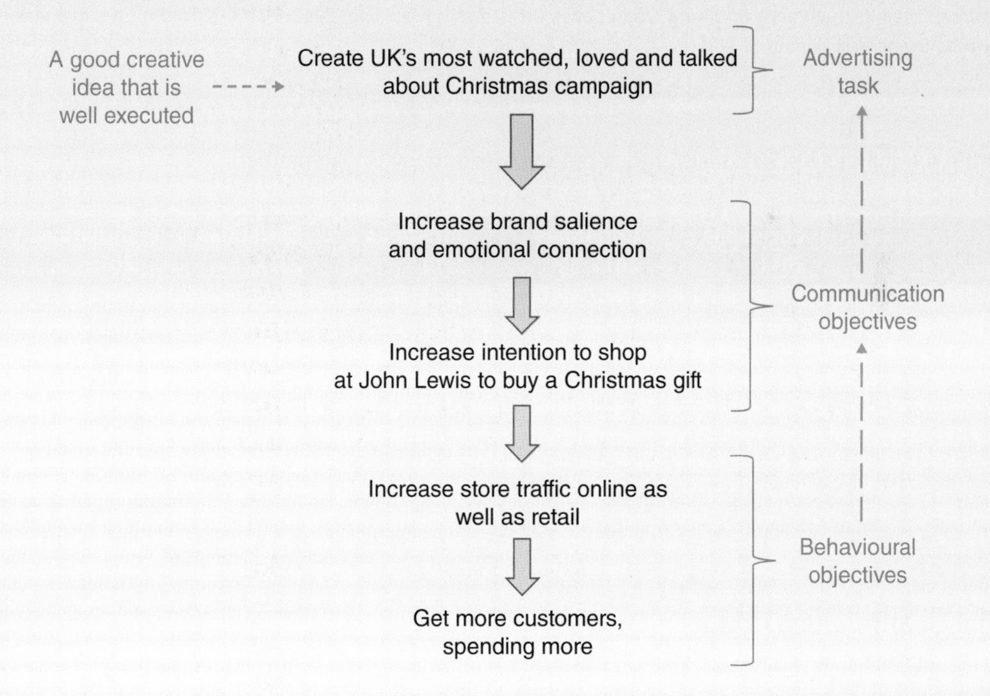

Figure 4.6 Causal effect of an advertising task

One way of evaluating ad effectiveness is to understand the causality of effect. For instance, one can examine the behavioural outcome first and then linking in back up to the causal chain. As an illustration, consider the following results. After the campaign, John Lewis had more customers, spending more (see table 4.2). This is supported by data showing that John Lewis had more visitors both online and offline (see table 4.3). Going further up the causal chain, the TVC is also consistently voted as Britain's favourite Christmas TVC among mothers (see table 4.4), as well as receiving lots of mentions on social media, which spiked at the time of the launch every year (see figure 4.7).[17]

Table 4.2 Number of customers and average spend

	2009	2010	2011	2012	2013	2014	2015
Number of customers	100	105	106	115	118	123	126
Average spend per customer	100	106	110	117	121	125	127
Total sales	100	112	117	134	144	154	160

Source: 'The gift that keeps on giving: John Lewis Christmas advertising, 2012–2015', 2016 IPA Effectiveness Awards Grand Prix Winner

Table 4.3 Foot traffic visiting the physical store (based on camera installed in 2013)

	December 2013	December 2014	December 2015
Footfall	929 429	1 473 425	1 442 603

Source: 'The gift that keeps on giving: John Lewis Christmas advertising, 2012–2015', 2016 IPA Effectiveness Awards Grand Prix Winner

Table 4.4 John Lewis' ad consistently rated the favourite by British mothers

	Christmas 2011	Christmas 2012	Christmas 2013	Christmas 2014	Christmas 2015
Netmums	John Lewis 1st	John Lewis 1st	John Lewis 1st	John Lewis 1st	John Lewis 1st
Marketing Magazine	N/A	N/A	John Lewis 1st	John Lewis 1st	John Lewis 2nd

Source: 'The gift that keeps on giving: John Lewis Christmas advertising, 2012–2015', 2016 IPA Effectiveness Awards Grand Prix Winner

DISCUSSION QUESTIONS

1. TV advertising is often criticised for being too general since it is advertising to the masses. Yet, the case of John Lewis shows that it is possible to grow market share using TV advertising. Why do you think this strategy worked for them?
2. What collaborative evidence shows that it is John Lewis' Christmas TV advertising that is the key to their success and not something else?
3. Instead of using TV advertising, would using direct response, social media advertising or other digital tactics work just as well? Explain your answer.

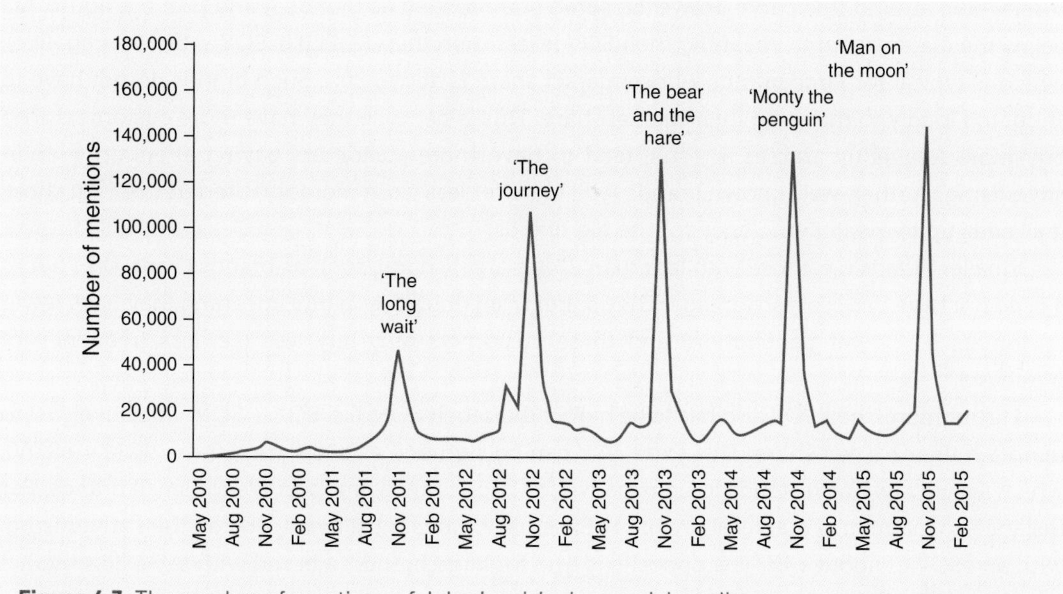

Figure 4.7 The number of mentions of John Lewis' ad on social media

THE SHARE OF VOICE AND SHARE OF MARKET BUDGETING METHODS

Share of voice (SOV) is an important concept in media budgeting. This essentially means assessing whether the brand is 'shouting' enough relative to its competition. There is now ample evidence to show that this is a very important factor in determining the success of one's advertising.[18] SOV of a brand can be determined by dividing its media spend by the total spend for the category. For instance, if brand A spends $2 million on its advertising, and the total category spend is $10 million (e.g. spend of brand A + spend of brand B + spend of brand C + spend of brand D = $10 million), then brand A's SOV is 20% (i.e. $2/10 \times 100 = 20$).

One way of understanding this notion is to compare our SOV with our share of the market (SOM). Figure 4.8, adapted from James C Schroer's model,[19] illustrates this idea. The diagonal curve signifies that SOV is approximately equal to SOM (i.e. SOV = SOM). Most brands fall

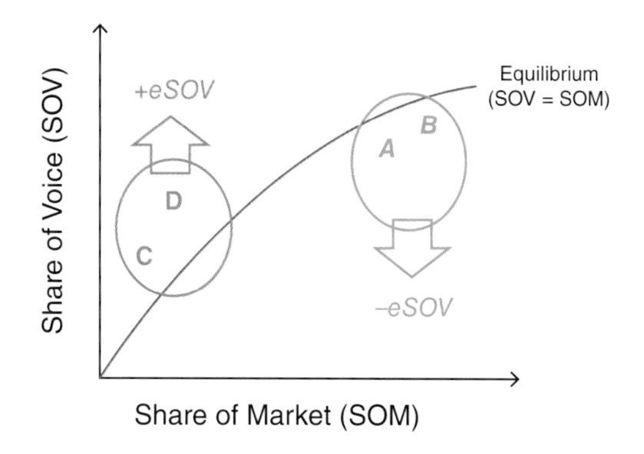

Figure 4.8 The state of equilibrium for different brands[20]

somewhere around this curve. However, some brands, such as brands A and B in the figure, fall below the diagonal curve, meaning their SOV is less than their SOM (i.e. SOV – SOM = negative), which is typical for large brands whose market share is above 20%. Such brands do not have to shout too loudly to maintain their market share. This is because they have more customers who buy more frequently and, as a result, tend to have more customers paying attention to their advertising. Further, well-known brands tend to suffer less from memory interference.[21] In short, it all adds up to greater efficiency for the big brands.

Smaller brands (i.e. those with less than 20% market share), such as brands C and D in figure 4.8, do not have this scale advantage. They suffer from double jeopardy, meaning they have fewer customers (i.e. lower penetration) and these customers also buy less (i.e. less frequency of purchase).[22]

Furthermore, their SOV also has to be higher than their SOM (i.e. SOV – SOM = positive) just to maintain their market share. This extra SOV can be signified as eSOV (i.e. SOV – SOM = eSOV), which, as we saw above, tends to be negative for large brands, but positive for small brands. For instance, to maintain a market share of say 5%, small brands must overspend on their advertising, with an eSOV of about +4%. The opposite is true for large brands; a brand with say a 26% market share has an eSOV of about –5%.[23]

Typically, nothing happens in the market and everyone is happy with this equilibrium shown in figure 4.8. However, if a brand decides to try to out-advertise their competitors by increasing their SOV, it can lead to permanent changes in market share or a 'new equilibrium' since, as we have known for some time, there is a relationship between SOV and SOM. For instance, after examining 117 product categories in 23 countries, John Philip Jones found that brands whose SOV was higher than their SOM tended to have a *rising* market share. Conversely, brands whose SOV was less than their SOM by 4% tended to have a declining market share.[24] As a general rule, the annual growth rate of SOM is proportional to 0.05 of its eSOV. This means to achieve a market share growth of 1 percentage point every year, a sustained eSOV of 20 is needed (i.e. $0.05 \times 20 = 1$). If the eSOV is sustained at 10, then the market share will grow by 0.5% (i.e. $0.05 \times 10 = 0.5$).[25] Market share therefore grows very slowly to communication investments, which is why it is important to measure its long-term effects.

DOUBLE JEOPARDY VERSUS ESOV

The double jeopardy suffered by small brands would imply that it is difficult for small brands to increase their market share. Yet the concept of eSOV also implies that this is possible, provided the brand has a compelling message (or it is new). When this occurs, consumers are more likely to pay attention when accompanied by large eSOV.

This was exactly the case with Lidl, the German discount supermarket chain in the UK. For 20 years, Lidl battled with four major supermarket giants and could only carve up a market share of 3%. The barrier was that British people thought that Lidl's products were of poor quality because they were cheap (being a discount store). However, the shoppers were pleasantly surprised when they accidentally discovered this was not the case. Armed with this insight, Lidl came up with the 'Surprise with Truth' campaign, which candidly captured how surprised British shoppers were when they tried Lidl's products.

The campaign was a hit, but more importantly, they increased their eSOV to +6% (in 2014, from 3% in 2013) and then to a massive +16% (in 2015 and 2016). Lidl's market share doubled from 3% to 6% in 2018, with their advertising responsible for an incremental sale of £2.8 billion.[26]

Competitive dynamics of SOV–SOM budgeting

SOV and SOM can also be used to examine competitive dynamics of established brands in regional markets. Figure 4.9a shows the situation when competitive SOV is high, while figure 4.9b shows the situation when SOV is low. Schroer suggested that if one's brand is the market leader in a region (e.g. Brand A in figure 4.9), and the competitor (usually the largest one) decides to be aggressive by increasing its SOV, then the regional market leader should defend its brand by increasing its spend (see Brand A in figure 4.9a showing an increasing arrow of Brand A). If it does not, its market share will most likely drop, especially if the aggressive competitor is willing to sustain its spending for 18–36 months at twice the leader's current advertising spend. We may ask how it is possible that a regional market leader will let this happen. According to Schroer, it is quite common because the regional market leader may be more interested in using its funds for sales promotion (to buy shelf space) or propping up its profit (see chapter 11 and the Lidl example above).

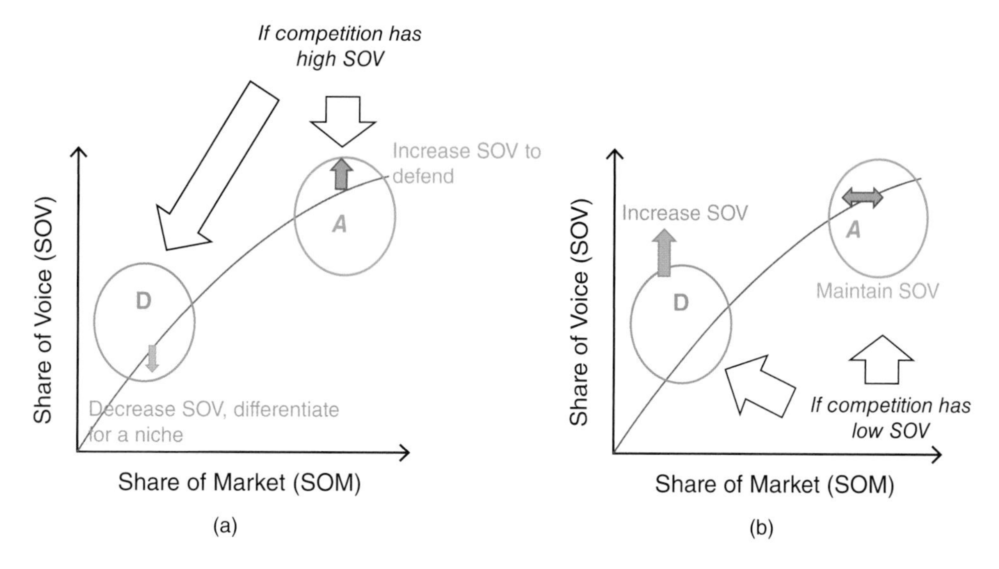

Figure 4.9 The competitive dynamics of SOV and SOM[27]

On the other hand, if the competitor has a low SOV (see figure 4.9b), there is no need for the regional market leader (Brand A) to increase its spend (see flat arrow of Brand A in figure 4.9b). All that is needed is to spend slightly above the equilibrium amount to maintain market share. This is the ideal situation for a regional market leader.

However, the situation is slightly more complicated if a brand is not the regional market leader (Brand D). If a brand has a small market share (i.e. low SOM), it can only realistically compete against those with a low SOV. If a competitor has a high SOV (like a national market leader), Schroer advises against trying to out-spend them. It will not be economically viable to do so, because market leaders usually have a cost advantage. In this situation, it might be more strategically clever to find a niche and differentiate (see figure 4.9a showing a decreasing arrow of Brand D). The media spend should deliver just enough reach and frequency (we will discuss these further below). On the other hand, if the competitor is another small brand with small SOV, then it might pay to attack with large SOV in order to gain market share from this brand (see figure 4.9b showing an increasing arrow of Brand D).

The important lesson is this: we should always be alert and know when to be aggressive and when to 'live and let live', region by region. We should also set advertising budget market by market, which is more logical than doing so nationally. This is not inconsistent with the objective-and-task budgeting philosophy, in which the advertising spend is linked to some tasks to achieve the desired objective, in this case to maintain or increase market share against a competitor.

THE RELATIONSHIP BETWEEN OPPORTUNITY TO SEE, MEDIA WEIGHT, AVERAGE FREQUENCY AND REACH

Deciding how frequently to advertise means deciding how many times, on average, we want to create opportunities for the target audience to see the ad (OTS). This does not mean that they will actually see the ad (i.e. be exposed to the ad every time it appears); it just means increasing the opportunity to do so.[28] It follows that the more frequently we advertise in many different regions, the greater the OTS. The concept of reach captures the idea of width of coverage. It is defined as the percentage of an unduplicated target audience who will have at least one OTS – it is a measure of 'dispersion'. By unduplicated, it means different people (or different households) who have at least one OTS. Therefore, if one is interested in achieving a high reach in a campaign, we have to make it possible for our target audience to encounter our advertising (on average) at least *once* (this is sometimes denoted as +1).

If we multiply average frequency and reach, we obtain the media weight of the campaign. The conceptual formula is:

Media weight = reach × frequency

For example, in order to sell 400 million units of its brands (such as Tide, Crest and Pantene), the manufacturer Procter & Gamble will have to reach more than 90% of American households six or seven times a year.[29]

The concept of media weight can take various forms. If it is in terms of dollars, then it forms the media budget. If it is in terms of rating points, then it forms gross rating points (GRP). GRP can also be understood as reach multiplied by frequency. The conceptual formula is similar, as follows:

Gross Rating Points (GRP) = reach × frequency

One rating point is defined as reaching 1% of the audience (if the rating point is specific to a certain target group – for example, 40–55-year-olds – it is called 'target audience rating points' or TARP). Therefore, when we talk about the GRP of a campaign, which may involve many placements of ads in many different programs of varying ratings, GRP is then the sum of them all. For instance, if in one week we advertise in program A with ratings of 32, program B with ratings of 20 and program C with ratings of 25, then the weekly GRP of this campaign is simply 32 + 20 + 25 = 75.

This represents the media weight. Now, if each rating point costs an average of $10 000, then the weekly expenditure is $750 000 (i.e. 75 × $10 000 = $750 000). This is also the media weight. So, the greater the reach and frequency the more likely OTS becomes.

The formula above also implies there is a trade-off between (average) frequency and reach. For a given budget, if we want to cover more regions, we cannot afford to advertise too frequently. Conversely, if we want to advertise more frequently, we cannot afford too wide a reach. The extreme example of this is the Super Bowl, one of the best-known US sporting events. A 30-second TV ad aired during the event costs $3.8 million and most advertisers can only afford one placement. But that ad reaches 46.4% of American households.[30]

An example of reach and frequency schedules

Let's look at a simple example illustrating how the concepts of reach and frequency can be used when scheduling an ad. Let's assume there are 10 households in our target audience (see figure 4.10). Each symbol (X) represents a program that the household has watched during a week, from a choice of five programs (i.e. program K on Monday, program L on Tuesday, program M on Wednesday and so on). We can see that in the top diagram, six households have watched these programs during the week, but four households (F, H, I and J) have not.

Now, let's assume we place one ad in each of the programs people watch in that week. Since it is only one ad per program, we can also represent this with an X. If X now presents one ad placement, we can see that schedule A (top diagram) is a frequency schedule while B (bottom diagram) is a reach schedule. Notice that in schedule A the ad placements (X) in each program tend to be concentrated in a smaller number of households (only six of the 10 households for a total reach of 60). These are households A, B, C, D, E and G. Then, notice that in schedule B the placements (X) are more dispersed, this time in eight of the 10 households for a total reach of 80. These are households A, B, C, D, E, F, G and H.

Note, too, that both schedules have GRP of 120 and total impressions of 12. The (average) frequency of schedule A is 2 (i.e. frequency = GRP/reach or 120/60 = 2; or 12 impressions/6 households = 2), while in the case of schedule B, the (average) frequency is 1.5 (i.e. frequency = GRP/reach or 120/80 = 1.5; or 12 impressions/8 households = 1.5).

Now, let's group the households together in terms of their number of placements (shown with a tick in the figure). Notice that, in schedule A, three households out of 10 (i.e. 30%) have one placement – these are households A, C and G. In schedule B, five households out of 10 (or 50%) have one placement – these are households A, C, F, G and H. Now, if we compare the two frequency distributions further, we notice that in schedule B only one household (or 10%) has three or more placements. This means schedule B reaches only 10% of the target audience with its 3+ frequency. In the case of schedule A, its 3+ reach is twice as high at 20%. Schedule A reached fewer households but with a higher level of frequency than schedule B.

Why bother drawing this distinction? If we believe that this campaign needs a higher placement frequency of at least 3+ to work, then schedule A will be more effective. In this example, the frequency of 3+ is called the 'effective frequency'; this means only households that received 3 or more ad placements will be influenced. The reach at this level (which is 20%) is called the 'effective reach'. For schedule B, the effective reach (at 3+) is half of schedule A at 10%. If, on the other hand, we think that a frequency of 3+ is not necessary then schedule B is better. Its reach at 1+ is 80% (i.e. 50 + 20 + 10 = 80), while that of schedule A is less at 60% (i.e. 30 + 10 + 10 + 10 = 60).

	Schedule A (or period 1)						Frequency distribution				
	Household	Program K	Program L	Program M	Program N	Program O	1	2	3	4	impression
Household 1	A	x					✓				1
Household 2	B		x	x	x	x				✓	4
Household 3	C		x				✓				1
Household 4	D			x	x	x			✓		3
Household 5	E				x	x		✓			2
Household 6	F										0
Household 7	G					x	✓				1
Household 8	H										0
Household 9	I										0
Household 10	J										0
Rating		10%	20%	20%	20%	40%	30%	10%	10%	10%	12
Gross rating points (GRP)		10	10	30	30	120					
New households reached		A	B.C	O	E	G					
% New households reached		10	20	10	10	10					
Reach		10	30	40	50	40			20%		
Frequency		1.00	1.00	1.25	1.55	2.00					

	Schedule B (or period 2)						Frequency distribution				
	Household	Program K	Program L	Program M	Program N	Program O	1	2	3	4	impression
Household 1	A	x					✓				1
Household 2	B			x	x	x			✓		3
Household 3	C		x				✓				1
Household 4	D			x		x		✓			1
Household 5	E				x	x		✓			2
Household 6	F					x	✓				1
Household 7	G		x				✓				1
Household 8	H				x		✓				1
Household 9	I										0
Household 10	J										0
Rating		10%	20%	20%	10%	40%	50%	30%	10%	0%	12
Gross rating points (GRP)		10	10	50	no	120					
New households reached		A	C,G	B,D	E,H	F					
% New households reached		10	20	20	20	10					
Reach		10	30	50	10	60			10%		
Frequency		1.00	1.00	1.00	1.14	1.50					

Figure 4.10 Reach (bottom diagram) and frequency (top diagram) schedules for two periods in a TV campaign[31]

From this example, we can draw several important points about scheduling of ads.

First, the only way we can deliver the ads is by inserting them in the media vehicles (e.g. programs). This is represented by X in the figure. The aim is to create opportunities for our ads to be seen (or heard) by choosing the right vehicles.

Second, it is far more informative to look at the pattern of ad placements – such as its frequency distribution – rather than rely on simple indices like (average) frequency or GRP. This distribution will tell us what percentage of the target population we can reach at a frequency we think is effective (i.e. effective reach). From this, we can factor in the cost to reach this target audience at the desired frequency (we have not shown the cost in this example).

Third, we can also insert more than one ad per program, in which case OTS will increase. Here, our frequency schedule will capitalise on high *within-vehicle* audience duplication (the proportion of similar audiences who use the same vehicle). This means that we rely on the same audience seeing multiple placements of the ad in the same vehicle.

Fourth, although we have used five TV programs in this example (i.e. programs K to O), the programs may be different in either schedule. In fact, they could even be programs in another medium (e.g. schedule B could include more radio programs). If we want a high-reach schedule, we should use multiple media and choose vehicles that have low *between-vehicle* audience duplication; that is, as little audience overlap as possible between vehicles (between-vehicle audience duplication is the proportion of similar audiences who use different vehicles).

Fifth, the example given above is for two different schedules (A and B). It could also apply to two different periods (1 and 2). For instance, we might start with the high-frequency schedule such as schedule A (in period 1), and then evolve to one that is less frequent but has a greater reach like schedule B (in period 2). Depending on the budget and objective, there can be many more such periods in a campaign. And the duration of each period could vary to be as short as a matter of days or as long as several weeks. There is considerable flexibility and, therefore, complexity in the available scheduling options.

ADVERTISING-TO-SALES RESPONSE FUNCTION

All these media terms represent advertising input and not advertising output (e.g. sales). However, the relationship between input and output is not always clear in advertising, as discussed above. One way of deciding this relationship is to ask how many times the target audience must see the ad (distinct from seeing the media vehicle) before they decide to buy. This is called the 'effective frequency', an important media planning concept popularised by Michael Naples in the late 1970s.[32] We will now discuss this notion in the context of two kinds of sales-to-advertising response functions: the s-shape function and the convex function.

The s-shape curve

The s-shape response function suggests that a minimum amount of advertising is needed before any effect can be seen. The horizontal axis in figure 4.11 represents different 'quantities' of advertising. This can be represented by GRP, media dollars, consumer impressions or placements (consumer impressions being defined as the size of the total audience an ad is reaching). The vertical axis represents incremental sales. In the s-shape function, the threshold needs to be exceeded before any consumers will act. In figure 4.11, this is shown as point (c), also known as the 'point of inflexion'. Any advertising conducted below point (c) is wasted.

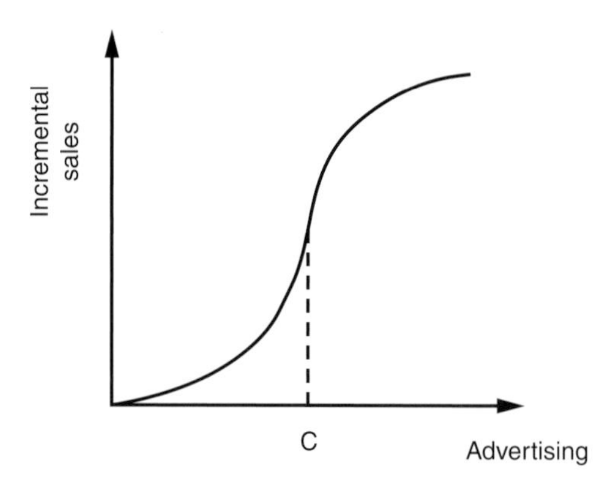

Figure 4.11 The s-shape sales-to-advertising response function

The evidence for the s-shape curve was first supported by Colin McDonald's original study of British ads in the UK.[33] But how much exposure is needed then? McDonald found that responses peaked at two. Herbert Krugman[34] suggested that the target audience must see the ad at least three times before it becomes effective. We can call this the 'three-exposure' or the 'three-hit' theory. Krugman's theory is also consistent with psychological learning theory, which basically states that consumers need repetition to learn. On first exposure, consumers respond to the ad by asking: (1) 'What is it?' The second exposure evokes an evaluative response: (2) 'What of it?' The third exposure is a reminder and evokes a decision: (3) 'I will (or will not) buy it'. Krugman argues that all subsequent exposures are just reminders, similar to the third response.

Over the years, this has evolved into the 3+ rule of thumb in media planning. This means a consumer must be exposed to the ad at least three times (per purchase cycle) before buying. There may be more than three exposures, but this is the minimum for each cycle. But, as Naples reminds us, each brand should experiment to find out what its own effective frequency is and not to rely on any 'magic number'.[35] Nevertheless, the concept of needing a minimum number of exposures has major implications for media planning. One implication is that frequency should always be given a higher priority than reach because unless an ad achieves this minimum, all the exposures will be wasted.

However, the 3+ rule of thumb creates two problems. First, some product categories tend to have longer purchase cycles than others. For instance, a refrigerator lasts a long time (about 10 years) while potato crisps last a very short time (around 7 days once opened). Therefore, 3+ exposures per purchase cycle is too broad a generalisation. Second, not all products or situations are the same. There are different levels of complexity of the advertised product or service, message, competitive clutter and so on, all of which will influence the planning decision.

This theory of effective frequency leads to different ways of scheduling the exposure, or more accurately OTS, when the element of time is taken into consideration. Below are three common frequency schedules. The first schedule is to institute effective frequency evenly spaced over the year (see figure 4.12a). We will want to vary this for a new product launch, which will usually require a blitz during its introduction (see figure 4.12b). This usually means high OTS over several advertising cycles at the start of the campaign followed by a slow tapering-off. For 'soft' launches, the reverse is more likely (see figure 4.12c). This usually occurs when we have not achieved wide distribution, or when we want to maintain exclusivity in the early part of the launch. Later, when the word has spread about the new product, we can then increase its OTS.[36]

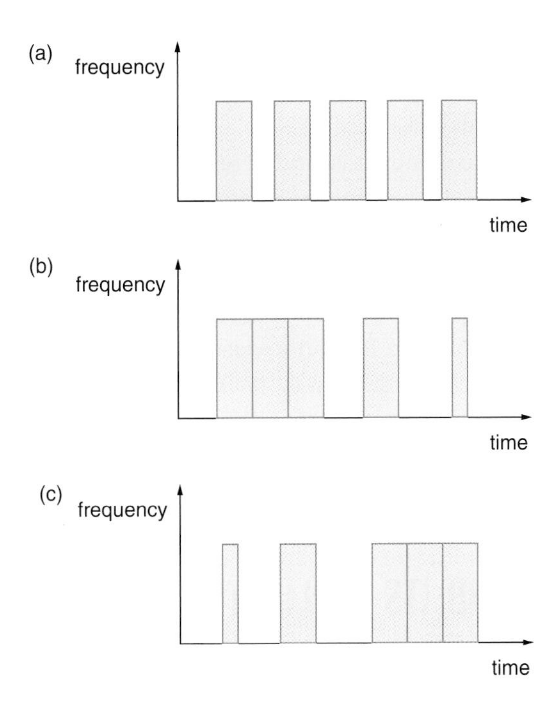

Figure 4.12 Different types of advertising schedules

Finally, when there is clear seasonality in the purchase (e.g. a skiing holiday or products), the pattern of OTS should also coincide with the target audience's purchase propensity. The most likely schedule will be the one resembling the new product launch since we want a blitz before the season starts (again, this is figure 4.12b). In the context of our discussion, the important point to remember is that the frequency must be the minimally effective one, whatever it may be (3+, 4+, 5+, or more).

The convex-shape curve

Th convex-shape curve is an alternative theory to the s-shape curve. It is based on a convex sales-to-advertising response function (shown in figure 4.13). Convex curve theory says that the

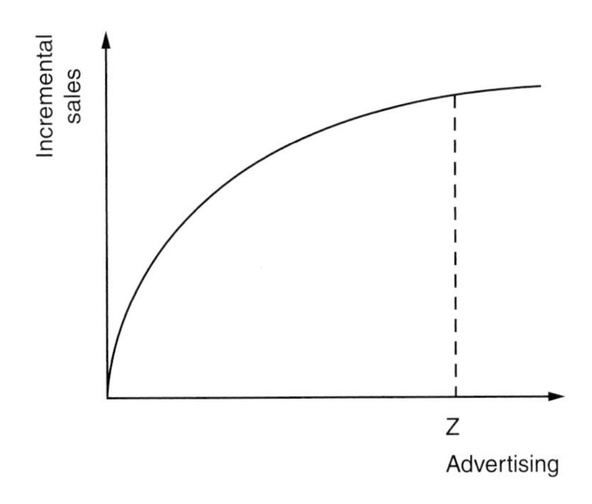

Figure 4.13 The convex-shape sales-to-advertising response function

more one advertises, the more sales are achieved but with ever-decreasing effectiveness, until it reaches an asymptote at point (Z). Beyond this point, no matter how much more one advertises, very few more sales will be achieved.

Most sales panel data tend to exhibit this kind of response function. Jones has claimed that, of the 200 campaigns of brands he documented, only 10 showed an s-shaped curve.[37] Most of these 10 brands were new products that needed to overcome the threshold effect, as depicted in the s-shape. However, most brands tended to show the convex shape in their response function. There is one other important finding in this area, most clearly articulated by Jones: that the most powerful sales effect comes from the first ad exposure. In fact, 73% of purchases came from households after the first exposure, with the rest (27%) from households with multiple exposures, demonstrating that there is a sharp diminishing return after the first exposure.[38] This phenomenon may not be universal; however, Jones found it less drastic in Germany, where there was a 46:54 split in favour of first-exposure purchase.[39]

RECENT EXPOSURE AND ITS IMPLICATIONS FOR RECENCY MEDIA PLANNING

This 'one exposure'[40] effect was discovered by comparing the brand's share of purchase occasions in households which had the opportunity to see the brand's TV advertising at least once in the previous seven days, compared to those who did not have this opportunity. This sort of data is called 'single-source data' because we can now match the purchasing behaviour of households with their viewing behaviour. If TV advertising is effective, we may expect the exposed households to exhibit higher total purchase share of the brand compared to unexposed households. For instance, if the share of the exposed households is 8.4% and that of the unexposed households is 7.8%, then we can say advertising had an effect because 7.8 is the lower number. Figure 4.14 shows the average increase in share across 78 brands as the number of exposures increased and demonstrates that the biggest jump came from just one OTS.

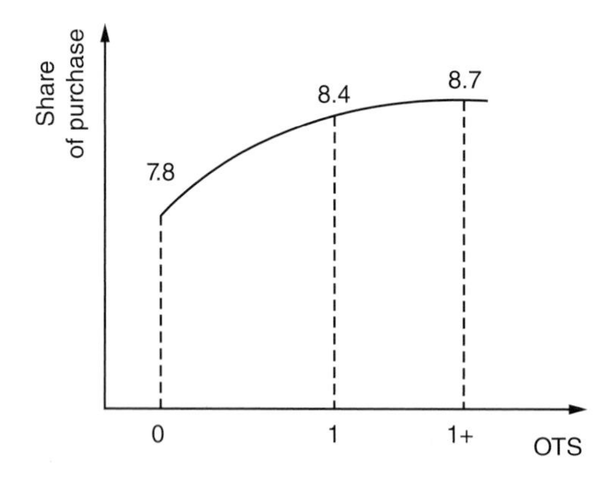

Figure 4.14 Changes in share of purchase as a function of OTS[41]

Since this first study (published in 1997), other studies have found the same effect.[42] But Jones' study had by far the largest number of observations, comprising 110 000 purchasing occasions (or 1400 per brand) for 78 brands over 12 product categories. So, there is strong evidence to support this theory.

How does this result reconcile with the low advertising elasticity often observed? Low elasticity means that sales do not slump when advertising stops and neither does it surge when advertising starts. One study based on 128 separate campaigns found the average elasticity to be 0.22.[43] This means that a 1% increase in advertising will only lead to a 0.22% increase in sales or, to put it another way, a 10% increase in advertising will lead to a 2.2% increase in sales. This low elasticity has been noted by some researchers[44] and is often interpreted to mean that advertising is weak or not effective. Yet single-source data, such as Jones's study, shows otherwise.

This difference can be explained as a methodological one. Advertising elasticity studies are based on aggregate data of sales to advertising. This is less sensitive than single-source data. As an analogy, imagine we are running a direct mail campaign where we send offers to 1000 households. The effectiveness of this campaign can be evaluated by gauging how many of the 1000 households actually respond. We do not evaluate the effectiveness by aggregating the sales of the whole suburb (including the 1000 households we sent an offer to) against the advertising. This, by analogy, is what aggregate advertising elasticity studies do – a very different methodology to single-source studies.

RECENCY MEDIA PLANNING

It should be noted that the 'one exposure' effect does not mean that one exposure is enough. It means that, in the short term, creating more than one exposure leads to dramatically diminishing return. Further, although Jones' study focused on households that had one opportunity to see the advertising in the previous seven days, the same households may have seen the ad many times before. So, the 'one exposure' effect does not mean it is the first opportunity, but rather the most recent in a series of opportunities. Support for this comes from the finding that households that are exposed closer to the time of their purchase are more likely to buy compared to those exposed longer ago.[45] This is called 'propinquity'. In other words, the timing is just as important – we want the exposure to be as close as possible to when consumers are most likely to purchase. It acts as a reminding trigger.

Knowing this, we can now choose to adopt either a continuous media schedule (in which we advertise continuously) or a flighting schedule (which is advertising in a certain period or periods only). But since we do not know for sure when consumers buy – with the exception of seasonal products – it is better to adopt a continuous media schedule[46] (see figure 4.15a). With flighting, there will be no advertising at some periods. Our SOV during those periods will be zero (see figure 4.15b). During this time, our associations of the brand may decay, which makes the brand more vulnerable to competitive activity. There is a third, more expensive compromise: a pulsing schedule, which allows us to continue to have a small SOV throughout and yet significantly increase our spend when we need to (see figure 4.15c).

According to Erwin Ephron,[47] since purchase occurs every week (by someone, somewhere), it is silly not to have a continuing presence. Recency therefore does not eliminate frequency. It just means the frequency is reduced in order to add more weeks. According to this perspective, there is no need to 'burst' or blitz the market. The only time this is needed is when there is clear seasonality in product purchase or when we are introducing a new product. Recency planning also applies to high-involvement goods (e.g. cars) simply because there will always be someone somewhere who is ready to buy the goods. The implication is that there should always be a brand presence in the market for as long as the budget allows, so that there is a greater chance of being

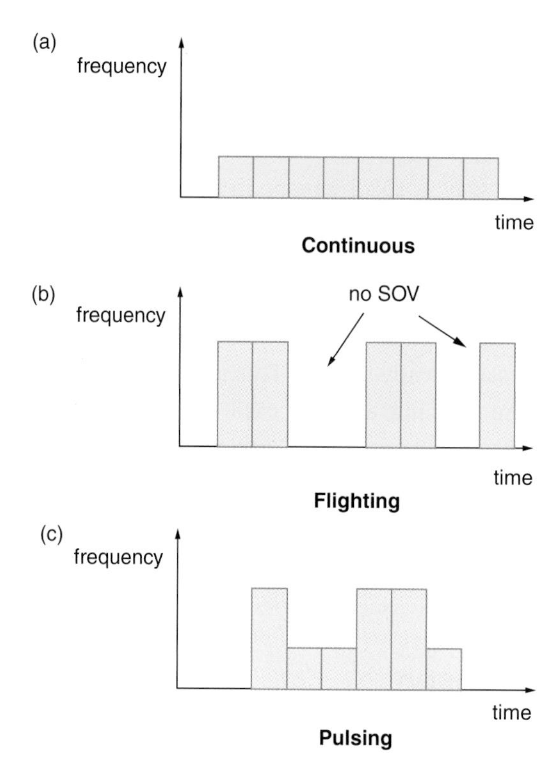

Figure 4.15 Continuous, flighting and pulsing schedules

seen by different consumers at least once, or to achieve greater reach with the same budget. This also means that the pulsing schedule is not cost-effective since it will curtail the brand's presence in the market. In practical terms, recency planning means it is better to:

- buy placements in different types of programs (e.g. day parts and prime-time programs), rather than the same type of programs (e.g. all-day parts) to achieve greater reach
- buy a lower number of placements in highly rated programs to get greater audiences (rather than more placements in low-rated programs)[48]
- shorten the planning horizon to weekly
- aim for a reach of at least 35% per week, 65% per month or 85% per quarter in our target audience.[49]

However, with the rise of technology, one can now improve on recency planning, provided we know with even greater precision when consumers are most likely to buy. For instance, with dynamic advertising, one can ensure that the advertising only occurs at the time when consumers are most accepting. For instance, in chapter 2 (see case study 2.1 Narellan Pools), we saw that two continuous days of exceptional high temperatures triggered people to think about installing a swimming pool in their homes. This then automatically activates an online campaign for the company, marked by great effectiveness and efficiency.

FREQUENCY VERSUS CONTINUOUS SCHEDULES

The debate between the two different advertising-to-sales response functions (discussed above) is essentially about trying to decide which media schedule is best: frequency or continuous. It has been suggested by some that both schedules are correct depending on the context.[50] Since the 'one exposure' effect was found using familiar brands, in the consumer-packaged goods area, this implies that a continuous schedule is better suited to familiar brands, where the message is delivered in a simple way. In fact, if we observe figure 4.14, we can see that even with no exposure (i.e. 0) in the previous seven days, panel respondents were still buying (i.e. registering a share of 7.8). This is only possible with an established brand. So, we should opt for a continuous schedule for such brands and be aware that increasing frequency will only irritate and bore the target audience.

On the other hand, if the product is new, if we are trying to reposition a brand, if the message is complex or if there is much clutter in the category (e.g. fast food),[51] then repetition of the ad (i.e. frequency) should be the priority. In fact, for a new TV campaign, it is generally more effective to begin with a 'big bang' in the first two weeks.[52] In those circumstances, we would recommend three or more placements (expressed as 3+) per cycle.

High frequency, however, creates boredom and irritation. One solution to is to vary the creative executions. The theme can remain the same, but the executions differ. This is called variation of the same theme (chapter 7 discusses creative executions in more detail). Another solution is to model sales effects by keeping good records. For instance, one simulation study found that even with low weekly TARPs of 15, a slightly better sales result will occur than one with weekly TARPs of 55, simply because more weeks were covered.[53]

EXPERIMENTATION, SCALE EFFECTS AND POST-BUY EVALUATION

Whichever schedule we choose, and whatever adjustments we make to estimate the effective frequency, the media plan is largely a theoretical document – essentially a blueprint for what we hope to achieve. As such, it remains theoretical until we are ready to run or test it.

One way of reducing the risk is to run a controlled test in which one region is exposed to one media plan while another is exposed to a different plan. This is usually carried out with consumer panels, where the two (or more) test areas are matched using demographics (and/or consumer-buying habits). Cable TV is often used for controlled exposure in broadcast media.[54] While a creative concept can be tested quickly (see chapter 12), testing a media plan is not easy. However, it is worth testing the plan for a campaign, since the cost of the campaign may run into tens of millions of dollars.

If we have decided to go ahead with such a test, what do we look for? The most important (and clearest) result is a large-scale effect with the new media plan.[55] Figure 4.16 illustrates this. Response curve (b) is what we hope to achieve. For the same quantity of advertising, Q, plan (b) yields a larger incremental sale than that of plan (a). Of course, there can still be a poor outcome, as shown in the response curve of media plan (c).

With online advertising, split testing (or sometimes called A/B testing) is a lot easier. Facebook, for instance, has built a special facility (using drop boxes and check boxes) for advertisers to test if the same piece of creative content is more effective on Instagram or on Facebook (note Facebook owns Instagram).

Finally, it is also important to carry out a post-buy evaluation, especially with traditional media. This ensures that what we paid for in the media plan actually occurred. For instance, if the new media plan (b) targets a GRP of 6000 but achieves only 4800 (because of the sudden drop in the ratings of its TV programs), then we will surely want to get a refund. If we spent $10 000 for

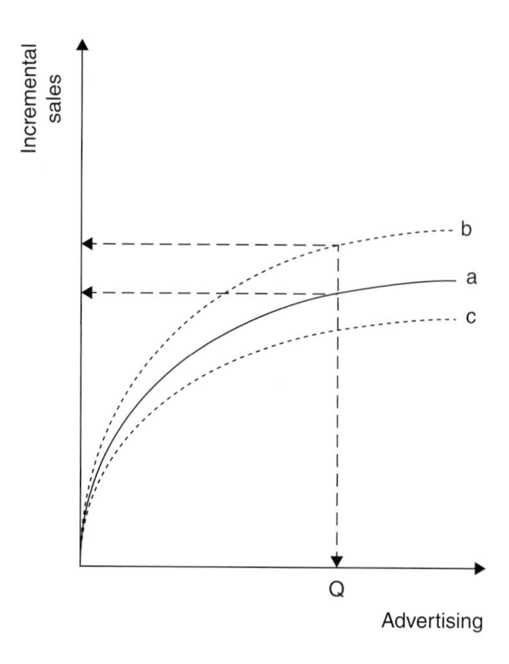

Figure 4.16 Different sales-to-advertising response functions for different media plans

one rating point, then the shortfall amounts to $12 million (i.e. 6000 – 4800 = 1200; 1200 × $10 000 = $12 000 000). A post-buy evaluation also includes checking that the ads have been placed correctly, for example, in the right location at the right frequency.

MEDIA STRATEGY

Now that we understand some of the media concepts, we can now begin to develop a media strategy for the campaign. Media strategy is defined as planning the most efficient way of scheduling the ads in the chosen media vehicles so that the branded message can have the maximum exposure opportunity (i.e. OTS) at a time most conducive to triggering the desired action in the target audience. While this may sound straightforward enough, it is in fact quite complicated to execute because of the countless permutations in the use of different media and, more importantly, the assumptions we have to make about their effectiveness in reach and frequency. The marcoms manager could use the following questions to guide discussions with their media planner.

Who is the target audience and what percentage do we want to reach?

This question basically tries to link the business objective to the most responsive customer segments. In the media context, deciding on customer segments usually means looking at which geographical area to target. This is driven by: (i) where the customer segments reside, (ii) the availability of the brand in the area, and (iii) what budget is available to reach the area. Of course, ideally, we want to reach 100% of our target audience, but this may well be prohibitively expensive, assuming it is even possible.

As an example, if a product is made for the Chinese market in Australia, and most of these people live in Sydney and Melbourne, then it makes no sense to advertise nationally. And if our budget is small, we will need to concentrate on only some cities (e.g. two out of five cities).

Which media should we use to reach the target audience?

Once we know who to advertise to, we can decide which media vehicles to use. This may include specific newspaper titles, magazines, radio or TV programs. Since there are almost an infinite number of options, which should we choose? The most accurate way is to understand the media usage habits of the target customer segments. This is consistent with the philosophy of media neutrality – in other words, we use the media best suited to reach the target audience, without any preconceived bias towards a particular medium.[56] Alternatively, we may not decide to involve any media at all; we could choose to plan events or advergames to achieve the desired outcome. The concept of media neutrality means the choice must be driven by the channels that will be most effective in supporting the creative idea that will trigger the decisive factors for purchase.

It is also important to assess the overlap of media the segments might be using. This will help reduce duplication. For instance, an advertiser may discover that their face cream is especially appealing to mothers. But they also discover that young mothers tend not to watch TV but are instead heavy internet users. Older mothers, on the other hand, tend to be heavy TV watchers only. This means using TV and internet will minimise duplication, and hence maximise reach to all mothers.

If we do not have direct media usage data of our target audience, we have to rely on syndicated data. For instance, if our lapsed customers are men aged between 55 and 65 years, we can use syndicated research to find out the best way to reach this group (e.g. what do they regularly watch, listen to and read). There will be some differences, since not all 55–65-year-olds in the syndicate data are lapsed customers. Note that, as the media options multiply, different audience databases need to be integrated and data extrapolated (this is sometimes called data fusion) to yield a more complete picture of the audience we are targeting.[57] If this is not available, then we have to resort to more coarser medium consumption data. Figure 4.17 shows the weekly reach of different medium in the UK for 2019. It shows that the media of TV and out-of-home (OOH) have enormous reach.

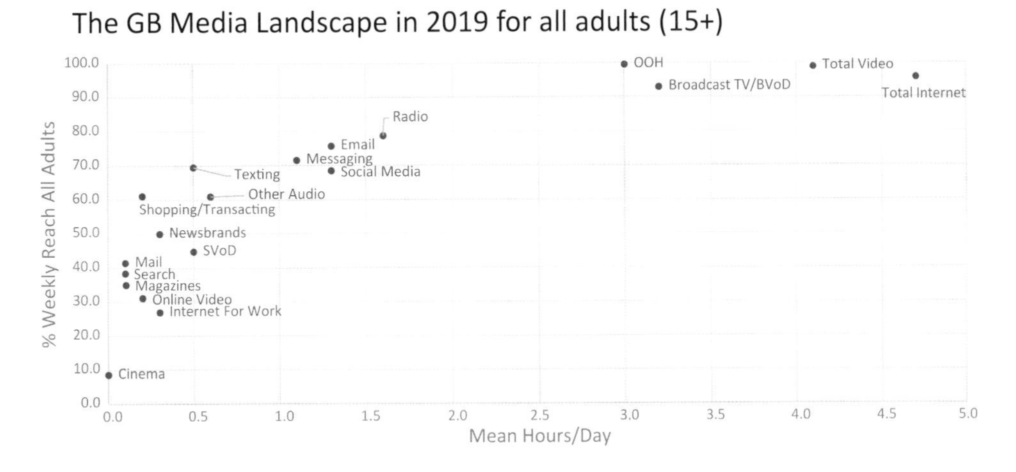

Figure 4.17 Media consumption in UK (2019)[58]

Reach is an important consideration for a campaign if our goal is to increase market share, or to grow a firm's customer base. To grow, new customers need to be continually acquired at a greater rate to replace lapsed customers (i.e. penetration),[59] and therefore reaching as many potential new customers as possible holds the key. This means using media like TV and out-of-home with high reach should be considered. However, there is one caveat, and that is the cost. For a medium like TV, it is prohibitively expensive to be used exclusively to achieve high reach (unless one is a big advertiser, of course). For example, figure 4.18 shows that it will cost $37.5 million to reach 90% of 18–49-year-olds! An alternative is to reach a lower percentage (e.g. 50%) of the target audience, and then add other non-overlapping media to get more reach. This then attests to the importance of having a multi-channel media strategy. But it also means that the first medium or the primary medium one uses is extremely important. If reach is the objective, the primary medium must maximise this because subsequent addition of media will inevitably result in some duplication. For instance, one study into alcoholic beverages found that up to 60% of the reach of the second medium is duplicated.[60] So planning is important.

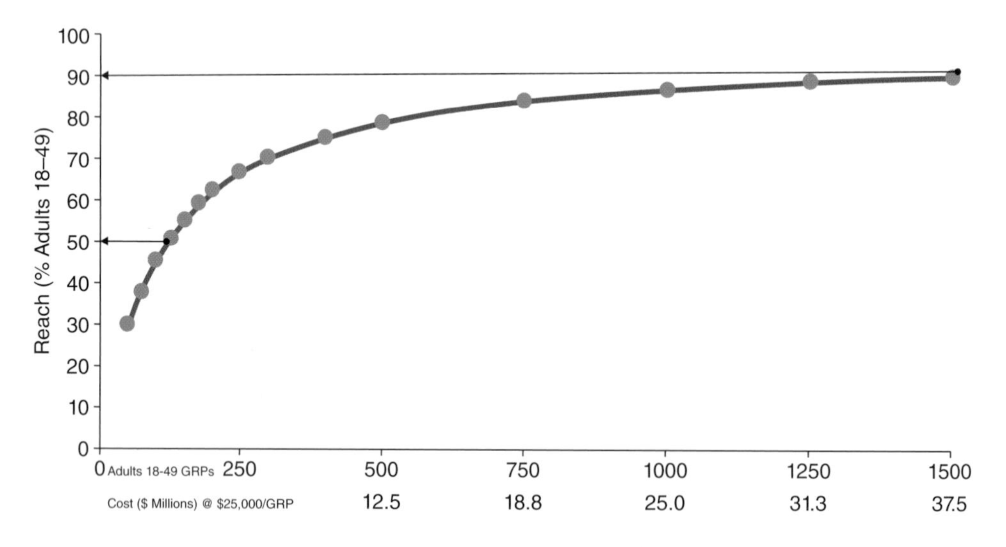

Figure 4.18 Estimated percentage reach based on cost and GRPs[61]

Therefore, as a general principle, if we want to maximise reach, we should select the first medium that will give us the widest reach possible but is still affordable, and then subsequently add more media with as little overlap as possible (see figure 4.19). Then within each medium,

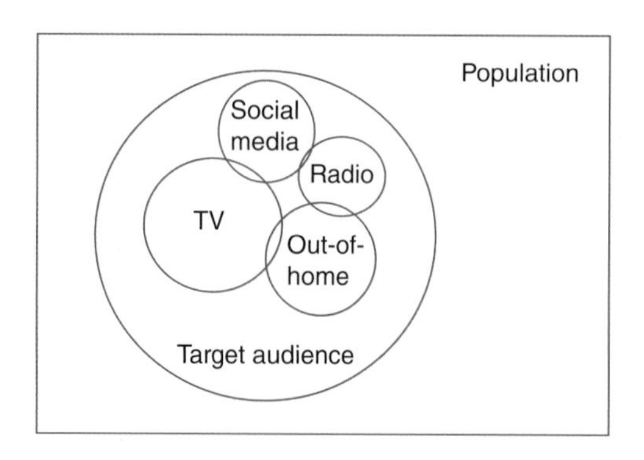

Figure 4.19 Using multiple media with little overlap to maximise reach

choose media vehicles or ad placements that have minimum audience overlap as well. For instance, one would avoid buying two advertising spots in the same vehicle (e.g. two TVCs in one TV program, or two print ads in the same magazine). Conversely, to maximise frequency, one does the opposite.

How well can the creative concept be portrayed using these media?

The media selected must also be able to show off the creative concept, or else all the hard work to get from creative development to execution will be wasted. In other words, the medium chosen must support the creative concept. For instance, if the creative concept requires sound and vision, then both media of print and radio media are eliminated. This point cannot be overstated because, as we will see in chapters 6 and 7, it is important to have high-quality creative ideas, and the chosen creative idea must be well executed.

However, this does not detract from the fact that some concepts tend to work better with some media than others (e.g. a singalong concept will not work in print!). Therefore, the creative concept and the medium are interdependent.

Which media will yield the most impact?

Once we have a rough idea of which media vehicle to use to best reach the target audience (based on a close study of their media usage habits), we can now explore which options are likely to yield the most cost-effective impact per week.

To ascertain this, we can interrogate previous campaigns, or examine other studies. For instance, it has been found that the best combination for TV advertising is digital. Relative to TV alone, if the TV campaign is combined with a digital one, the ROI is 60% higher. With print, it is 19%, and with radio, it is 20%. This suggests that digital adds much more value to TV campaigns than either radio or print.[62] This is because digital channels can provide incremental reach (e.g. the video is now available online) as well as serving as a new activation medium (e.g. online promotions or shopping). This may not be true in all cases. But it is a good place to start.

Such effectiveness information is useful. But what if such indices are not available, which is often true when it comes to the vehicle (not medium) we are thinking of using. One suggestion is to make assumptions about the target audience's attention to various media vehicles and about the penetration of usage of those vehicles.

How should we schedule the exposures?

Once we decide which media and its vehicles to use, we have to decide on the timing and schedule. This will affect how the budget is going to be allocated. Since consumers generally do not buy capriciously, it makes sense to time the advertising just before their purchase. If, on the other hand, we plan to advertise outside the time period in which consumers normally buy (e.g. advertising ice-cream during winter), because of less competitive clutter, then we need to have enough budget left to advertise during the peak buying season (e.g. advertising ice-cream during summer) to avoid being drowned out by competition. This means we often have to consider which part of the day (called day-part) is most conducive in reaching the target audience and on which devices. For instance, smartphones are the device to use when consumers are out and about (e.g. evenings and weekends).

If there is no seasonality, we should adopt a planning horizon that fits our objective. For instance, if consumers buy weekly (as in many consumer-packaged goods), then our planning should also be on a weekly basis. If, on the other hand, our campaign requires a daily burst around lunch time, then the planning period should be daily.

After we have set the planning horizon, we can decide on an ideal exposure pattern of reach and frequency, using the various vehicles selected and constraints of the budget we set for that period. It is often difficult to work this out manually because there are many media vehicles with different levels of audience duplication. However, media-mix optimisation software[63] will help suggest an optimal solution by looking at how many ads can be placed in which media vehicles without blowing the budget.[64] Depending on how much we are prepared to spend in total, we then decide how many cycles we can afford to advertise in continuously. Several iterations are often required before a plan is finalised.

CASE STUDY 4.2 HOW A TV ADVERTISING CAMPAIGN THREW OUT A DICTATOR

For most people, 5 October 1998 is not a well-known date, but it is the day Chile voted its dictator Augusto Pinochet out of power in a landmark referendum. Until then, Pinochet had ruled Chile oppressively for 15 years, using police violence, torture, rape, execution and intimidation on anyone who dared to oppose him. Under international pressure to step down, he nevertheless wanted to continue to rule (for another eight years). Cleverly, he thought calling for a referendum on this issue (and winning it) would legitimise his mandate, and hence shut up his critics.

Pinochet was very confident of winning, given the disarray of the opposition. He thought that he would get the support of his people since he managed to turn the economy around by introducing free market economics. This had improved living standards in Chile, reversing years of economic malaise under the previous Marxist government, where strikes, inflation and food queues were common. Therefore, he was quietly confident that the Chileans would vote 'Yes' to this referendum, since voting 'No' would mean returning to the bad old days of economic chaos, he thought. Besides, many Chileans would be too fearful to vote 'No' anyway given the high-handedness of his junta. Therefore, by all reasoning, it looked like Pinochet was set to win another eight years.

However, what Pinochet did not count on was the brilliance of a group of advertising creatives, including one person by the name of Eugenio Garcia, who were able to galvanise the whole country to vote 'No' with an advertising campaign. Two other creative directors, José Salcedo and Geraldine Walker, were also involved.[65] What makes this case interesting is that it illustrates how TV can change lives. Pinochet's biggest mistake was to grant his opposition (i.e. the No campaigners) 15 minutes of free TV airtime to put their case to the people. They were allowed to do so for 27 days until it was time to vote. This was necessary in order to appear fair and statesman-like. The 'Yes' campaign was given an equal amount of free airtime for next 27 days (from 5 September to 1 October 1988). However, since TV was state controlled, the regime could also pump out propaganda throughout the day. The 15 minutes of free airtime for the opposition was also scheduled only for late night telecast (11 p.m.); the regime was counting that it would be too late for Chileans to watch.

However, the junta did not realise that TV represents high reach, and even though the 'No' campaign was given a late slot, it was still prime time (i.e. 10.30 p.m. to 1.00 a.m.; Chileans sleep late!). Also, by advertising standards, 15 minutes is a very long time – a luxury! It presented Garcia and his collaborators countless opportunities to develop many creative assets to convince the Chilean people to vote 'No'. Curiously, because this was the *only* time given to the opposition, it attracted an enormous audience. Everyone tuned in and ratings went through the roof. The late-night scheduling intended to restrict viewing created the opposite effect! Furthermore, to be able to freely broadcast consecutively over 27 nights was also beneficial – unheard of nowadays. But more importantly, it represented a small window of opportunity, and perhaps the *only* means for the Chilean people to legitimately throw out the regime.

Eugenio Garcia (and his collaborators) seized this golden opportunity and proceeded to work assiduously. But first, they needed a creative concept. This was a challenge because unlike selling a product, there was none here. For instance, there was no single opposition leader (given the state of disarray), while the 'Yes' campaign had Pinochet. Instead Garcia had to sell the idea of democracy, which is quite an ephemeral concept, even by today's standards. Chileans at that time did not understand what democracy meant. It was tempting to go with a creative concept that criticised the military junta, citing their brutality, political killings, and their oppressive rule, and so forth. But Garcia knew such a concept would not work because Chileans already knew this. Using a negative concept to fight an oppressive regime does not constitute a solution. Worse, it may backfire because highlighting the regime's brutality may have created *more* fear, which in turn may have discouraged people from coming out to vote. What was needed instead, was a concept that was dramatically different, something that would give the Chileans hope that things would change for the better after 5 October.

Figure 4.20 The NO emblem

After much research, the team came up with the idea of joy. Like a ray of sunshine, voting 'No' would give the Chileans hope and a chance for democracy. It was a message of optimism for a better future, a future that would be decided in a referendum. But it also represented a real opportunity for Chileans to live happily as a community, without ever having to fear the police or the military again. After much tweaking, the No camp came up with the slogan 'Chile, la alegría ya viene' or Chile, joy is coming. Their emblem was a rainbow which represented the end of a storm, as well as diversity (see figure 4.20).

On the day of the campaign launch, Chileans were glued to their TVs. The ad opened with Patricio Bañados, a well-respected newsreader, prominently announcing: 'Chile, la alegría ya viene'. It also featured many ordinary Chileans (e.g. mothers, doctors, children, singers, dancers, butchers, taxi drivers) saying they will support the 'No' motion, in their own inimitable way, like the taxi driver waving his finger left and right mimicking the movement of his windscreen wipers. It also had music, laughter and dancing, not typical of any political advertising. It was entertaining! The campaign also featured testimonials, where the young, women and poor were interviewed on screen, expressing their dissatisfaction with the government, and some added heart-felt stories of torture of their loved ones under the brutal regime, all of which created a sense of authenticity. It rang true. By contrast, the junta's 'Yes' campaign was drab, old-fashioned and worse still completely out-of-touch. Their strategy was to play on the fear that the country would once again sink into an economic malaise if Pinochet was not at the helm. In short, the 'Yes' campaign was not well conceptualised or executed; the regime was so confident of winning that they did not bother to take opposition seriously, and hence did not put much effort into coming up with a good campaign.

The 'No' campaign sparked a revolution and on 5 October 7.2 million Chileans turned out to vote, the highest on record. The 'No' camp won 54.7% of the vote. Pinochet reluctantly relinquished power to a civilian government.

It is sometimes easy to forget that advertising can create social change. While much has been written about Barack Obama's 2008 'hope and change' campaign,[66] this Chilean campaign was more significant because it involved the removal of a sitting dictator. Furthermore, some cast members of the 'No' campaign were harassed and feared for their lives throughout the campaign.[67] The 'No' campaign also mobilised the best creative minds in the country to collaborate with each other in order to defeat Pinochet,[68] something seldom seen in the industry.

I cannot think of another campaign that even comes close to this with this level of achievement. This real-life story was eventually made into a film, which received a nomination for the best Foreign Language Film in the 2013 Academy Awards.[69]

DISCUSSION QUESTIONS

1. Do you think the regime made a mistake in allowing the 'No' camp to make their case on TV? If the regime had restricted the campaign to print, would they have won? Explain your answer.
2. If the 'Yes' team had an unfair advantage in terms of access to media, why didn't it take better advantage of this; for instance, by developing better creative assets to push their case?
3. Some marketing academics vehemently argue that advertising is a weak force (see earlier discussion on the Ehrengbergian view). After reading this case, do you still think this is the case? Explain your answer.

MANAGERIAL APPLICATION: PUTTING IT TOGETHER

Media planning is challenging but it is also important to get the plan (roughly) right because media spend is one of the largest items in a marketing budget. It is worth reminding ourselves that the ultimate purpose of IMC is to build brand equity in the long term, but in the short term still be capable of achieving some financial returns (see definition of IMC in chapter 1). By short term, Binet suggests six months, which is reasonable.[70]

Long-term building of brand equity should be given priority because its effects are more long-lasting. Advertising using TV, for instance, is a very effective way of building brand associations, and even after it is stopped, it can still generate sales two years later.[71] Its effectiveness can be attributed to its ability to elicit emotions because TV is an immersive medium.[72] Furthermore, emotional ads are generally very memorable.[73] Thus the laying down of strong and favourable brand memories (that are also different, yet relevant) takes time. But once formed, it will serve the brand well in the long run. Furthermore, these memories can be formed in consumers even when they are not ready to buy. But when they are ready, these memories will influence their purchase.[74] This means one should strive for broad reach, to continue to renew one's customer base for the long run. It is difficult to create desirable emotional memories using short-term sales promotion or activation.

Now, if one were to subscribe to this long-term view of building brand associations, it also means that more budget should be allocated to this activity. A balance needs to be found. One recommendation is to devote 60% to this endeavour (and 40% to short-term sales activation).[75] The implication is that brands should not exclusively target certain segments of the market using product-related campaigns (e.g. attribute or benefit). Rather budget should *also* be devoted to creating a brand image but one that will appeal to a broad market in order to convert more customers. And finally, within this mix, strive for synergy as discussed in chapter 1.

PROGRAMMATIC MEDIA BUYING – COST OVER QUALITY?

The availability of multi-channels creates complexity in media buying. This is because as the number of communication channels increases, targeting different consumers across different locations and platforms, it becomes cumbersome, if not impossible to work out how best to allocate the media spend. There is an infinite number of permutations, and this is not counting the added difficulty of tracking the results.

In recent years, the use of programmatic media buying has greatly increased both the efficiency and to some extent the effectiveness of media placements. One can define programmatic media buying as the use of automated technology to optimise the ad buying process in real time across different digital screens (e.g. display, mobile, social, video, internet, TV) for the purpose of serving the ad to one's desired audience. Bidding for the ad space is done automatically and in real time (sometimes called real-time bidding, or RTB) on several websites or ad exchanges simultaneously. All the websites have specific browsing information on their visitors (e.g. men who viewed bodybuilding products) because of cookie or other identification technologies. And if these visitors are your target audience, whose characteristics can be pre-specified, the ad buying system (sometimes called a trading desk or demand side platform) will automatically bid on your behalf (in milliseconds) based on cost of impression (i.e. 'eyeballs'). The program allows a marketer to buy media placements that have the highest number of impressions at the lowest price. Furthermore, as the campaign progresses, the system learns which characteristics (e.g. time, location) perform best as impressions change across the various websites, and adjustments are made to the placements accordingly in real time.

The beauty with this technology is that the marcoms manager knows what he/she is paying for in terms of the quality of reach (i.e. exact number of target audience visiting these platforms). Assuming the optimising is accurate (i.e. the data and algorithm are good, and sampling errors minimised[76]), it means the ad is exposed to only those people who are truly interested (e.g. men who are interested in buying bodybuilding products). This technology therefore removes all the grunt work for the media planner and frees up time for more creative thinking.

However, programmatic buying has become embroiled in several controversies. First, the issue of reputation harm to the brand (sometimes called brand safety). Because of the automaticity of ad placements, a number of leading brands have had their online ads appear alongside unsavoury (e.g. pornography, drugs) or extremist (e.g. jihadist, violence) content.[77] This has led to these brands pulling their online ads from Google and YouTube.[78] Second, the lack of transparency on how the media budget is being divided between website owners (i.e. publishers) and the intermediaries in the media supply chain. Unethical practices take the form of undisclosed rebates, dual rate cards or high mark-ups which advertisers are not aware of.[79] Third, fraudulent impression data. One study estimates that between 9% and 21% of display ads and videos are not seen by humans but bots![80] This is an important lesson to remember. One should never compromise the quality of the audience one seeks. One should always buy the largest amount of high-quality audience at the lowest cost, not the other way around. But with fast, easy technology, quality has taken a back seat to cost.

Due to such issues, programmatic buying has been moving inhouse as firms continue to improve their expertise.[81] What is interesting is that for large well-known corporations (e.g. Qantas), who also have their owned digital assets with lots of online traffic of their own, there is very little need to advertise on other websites (sometimes called third-party websites). This means much of the programmatic buying can be geared towards their own digital properties.[82] But for organisations that do not have this privilege, they will still be dependent on the third-party websites to reach potential customers.

FURTHER THINKING: LINKING CONSUMPTION AND REVENUE

LEARNING GOALS

After reading this section, you will understand:

- how to link consumption behaviour to revenue in order to create a benchmark
- how to increase revenue to improve from this benchmark.

This chapter has demonstrated that much of our media planning rests on our understanding of how consumers behave. Understanding their behaviour helps create opportunities for the message to be seen or heard and for it to change their behaviour as a result. However, to detect that change, we need to know what the current level of behaviour is and how this level is linked to revenue and profit, which will give us a better idea of how much the behaviour needs to change to increase revenue and profit. This, in turn, will guide us in our campaign planning. The following steps are necessary for the analysis.

ESTABLISH THE LINK BETWEEN CONSUMPTION BEHAVIOUR AND REVENUE

A good place to start is to understand how the current consumption rate contributes to revenue (and hence profit) of the brand. Let's take the example of a pharmaceutical business based in the US. Assume that a patient repeats his or her prescription every 55 days. This means that in a year there would be an average of 6.6 repeats a year for each patient (i.e. 365/55 = 6.6).

If each of the 6.6 repeats consists of six pills, then one patient will consume 39.6 pills in a year (i.e. 6.6 × 6 = 39.6).

To derive revenue, we need to consider two more factors – the number of customers and the price they paid – and then factor in (or estimate) the profit. For example, if there are 3 million current users of this brand of pill in the US, this means that the total number of pills sold a year by the firm is 118.8 million (i.e. 3 million × 39.6 = 118.8 million). At $10 a pill, the current revenue for the firm is $1.18 billion (i.e. $10 × 118.8 million = $1188 million or $1.18 billion). Assuming a profit of 20%, the annual profit from this brand is $237.6 million (i.e. 0.2 × $1.18 billion = $237.6 million).

Once we have these numbers, we can now check if the figures are in line with our total revenue (as well as our profit). If they are not in line, then our understanding about the consumers' behaviour (e.g. usage amount or repeat rate) is wrong, and we need to take another look. On the other hand, if they are in line, they set a benchmark from which we can move forward with confidence.

DECIDE ON HOW BEST TO INCREASE SALES

Once we are confident, we can now consider the best way of increasing sales. We can use the conceptual formula outlined in figure 4.21, which may be modified for different situations. Let's consider each of the available options more closely.

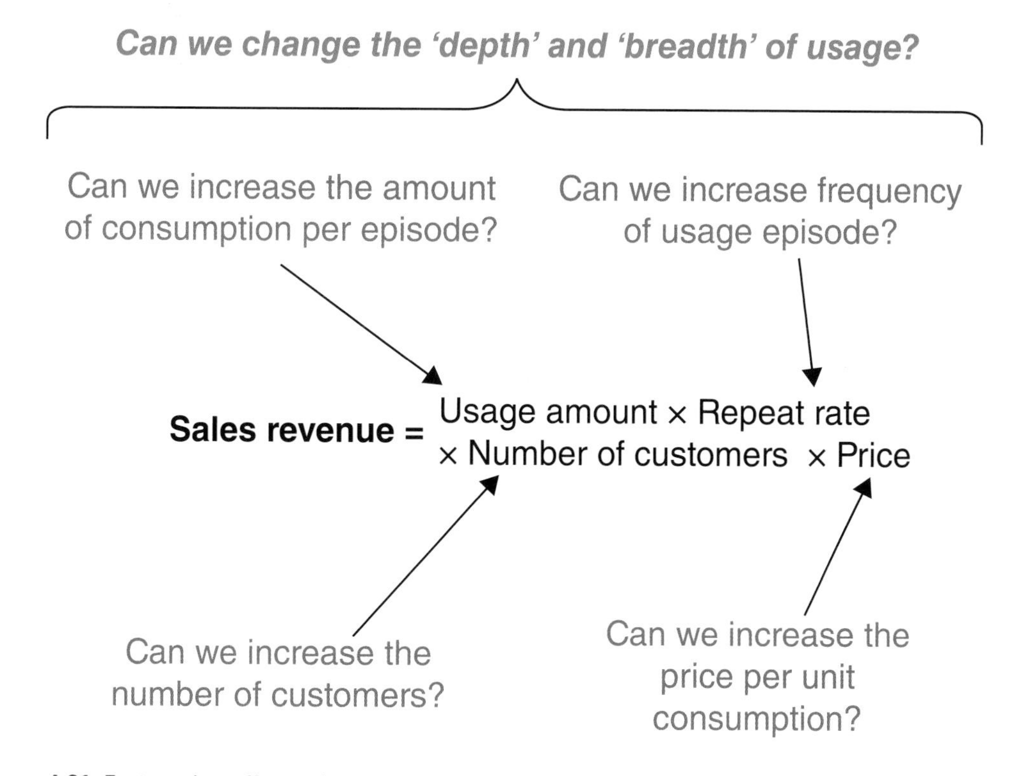

Figure 4.21 Factors that affect sales revenue

COVID-19

A GOLDEN OPPORTUNITY TO INCREASE SALES AND MARKET SHARE

During a global crisis, advertising is often cut.[83] However, this may represent a golden opportunity to steal a march on one's competitors. For example, a study which tracked 250 companies during the Great Depression (1920–1921) found that companies that cut their advertising during the depression saw their sales drop,[84] but companies that increased their advertising grew their sales quickly, even three years after the recession. Another study that examined several recessions from 1920 to 2005 came to the same conclusion: companies that maintained their advertising during recession saw an increase in sales. Furthermore, those that *increased* their advertising actually grew both the sales and market share.[85]

Therefore, by maintaining or even ramping up one's advertising, a significant cut-through can be achieved simply because our competitors are likely to retreat. With less noise, it will give us greater share of voice. We know that with every 10% 'extra share of voice' (or eSOV) sustained over the year, an increase of +0.5% market share is likely to occur (+5.7% if the ad is creative[86]). Furthermore, media cost during this period is also expected to drop because of falling demand[87] (even in social media[88]). This translates to cheaper eSOV.

The COVID-19 pandemic may well have represented a golden opportunity to increase sales and market share.[89]

INCREASE USAGE AMOUNT AND REPEAT RATE AFTER TRIAL

To increase sales revenue, we can try to increase the amount of usage or repeat usage rate of the brand. These are the first two terms in the equation in figure 4.21. Increasing the usage amount means more consumption per episode, while increasing the repeat rate means increasing the frequency of usage. We can think of this strategy as attempting to increase the 'depth' of usage (the use of loading devices in promotion tactics, for example, bonus packs, is a way to do this), but it does not always work because consumers are creatures of habit. Further, in a product category such as medicine, it is not ethical to encourage unnecessary consumption.

FIND NEW USES FOR THE BRAND

A better way to increase both the amount and repeat usage rate is to broaden the occasions of usage or to find new uses for the brand. For instance, champagne sellers tried to broaden its usage beyond special occasions (see chapter 3), while Arm & Hammer baking soda and WD40 lubricant have been repositioned to include many uses. Clorox, a bleaching agent for brightening clothes, long ago broadened its usage to include cleaning of tiles, floors, windows and countertops. Danone yoghurt can be used as a substitute for eggs and oil in baking muffins and brownies, and Campbell's Soup is used as a flavour-enhancer for old recipes. In medicine, aspirin can be used to prevent stroke among the elderly and Botox is now being used to alleviate sinus problems. We can think of this strategy as attempting to increase the 'breadth' of the brand's usage, and all the examples mentioned worked because the new usage is cheap, convenient and effective.[90]

INCREASE THE CUSTOMER BASE

We can also increase our customer base to increase revenue. This by far may be the fastest way to grow revenue. To do this, we need to classify our customer base before deciding who to target. A simple classification would be:

- current users (who may be light or heavy users)
- lapsed users (who have switched to other brands or no longer need the product)
- potential new users (who are new to the category).

The objective is typically to protect our current users from competition and then to target lapsed users or potential new users. For each of these groups, we can also investigate how easy or difficult it is to maintain or shift usage upwards, as discussed above. (The exception is in social marketing, like an anti-smoking campaign where the task is to reduce consumption.) While thinking about shifting behaviour, we can conceptualise two sets of opposing forces – motivating and inhibiting factors (as discussed in chapter 1). The insights we gain about these factors will assist in developing the creative concept (see chapter 2).

But, by far, the fastest (but sometimes the most expensive) way of increasing revenue is to reach as many potential new users (or light users) as possible. So even with a low trial rate (say 5%), if one can reach 90% of the market (say, one million consumers), using TV, our customer number is 45 000 (i.e. $0.05 \times 0.9 \times 1\,000\,000 = 45\,000$). On the other hand, if our reach is halved – that is, 45% (instead of 90%) – then the number of new customers is also halved at 22 500 (i.e. $0.05 \times 0.45 \times 1\,000\,000 = 22\,500$). This can make a huge difference to the bottom line. An alternative is to improve our trial rate. Therefore, if we aim to have 45 000 new customers, and we can only afford a reach of 45%, then we essentially have to double our trial rate to 10% from 5% (i.e. $0.10 \times 0.45 \times 1\,000\,000 = 45\,000$). Therefore, the critical question is how realistic it is to double our trial rate. Or is there a way of reaching 90% of our market with a combination of media which is cheaper in total: for example, 50% reach via TV and 40% reach via internet (with minimum overlap between two segments). One can also explore some other levels of reach and conversion rates, all while asking ourselves if it is realistic.

Ideally, one should be productive all along the consumer decision journey – for example, the ad should work the first time and every time – and the conversion rates all along the consumer decision path should be optimal (see chapter 5). This therefore requires a little bit of thinking, but it is better to be (roughly) right than completely wrong.

INCREASE PRICE

Finally, we can also try to increase price by repositioning the product as a premium brand. This allows higher-than-average pricing, which usually leads to greater profitability. We have discussed using price as a positioning tactic in chapter 3.

DISCUSSION QUESTIONS

1. What is the DAGMAR perspective on advertising? Why do you think it remains influential more than 50 years after it was developed?
2. How would you respond if an advertising agency were to argue that the sales objective is not a legitimate criterion for assessing its performance? What would be your solution if your marketing manager disagreed?

3. Explain the objective-and-task method of budgeting. What is good and bad about this method?
4. Imagine that you are the owner of a brewery that produces a small but profitable regional brand of beer. You have always dreamed of expanding nationwide. Is it a good idea? Under what circumstances will you succeed? In your response, focus on SOV and SOM dynamics.
5. Why is it important to think about the pattern of ad placement, such as its frequency distribution, during media planning? Explain the concepts of effective frequency and effective reach in this context.
6. What are the media planning implications of an s-shaped advertising response function? What are the implications of a convex shape?
7. How has the idea of the 'one exposure' effect influenced the development of recency media planning?
8. Explain the trade-off that exists between frequency and continuous schedules.
9. Why is it important to conduct post-buy evaluation of the media plan?
10. Apart from reach, TV is said to be effective in creating emotional memories. Why is this important? Or is it? Explain your answer.
11. What does striking a balance between a short- and long-term perspective in media planning mean?
12. What are the advantages and disadvantages of programmatic media buying?
13. Do you think it is important to link consumption behaviour to sales revenue? How would knowing this link influence a campaign?

NOTES

1 L Lodish, *The advertising and promotion challenge*, Oxford University Press, New York, 1986.

2 J Wanamaker at Wikipedia, http://en.wikipedia.org/wiki/John_Wanamaker. Accessed October 2012.

3 I am persuaded very much by Len Lodish's argument that very often it is better to be vaguely right than precisely wrong. See Lodish (1986), *The advertising and promotion challenge*, note 1.

4 S Dutka, *DAGMAR: defining advertising goals for measured advertising results*, 2nd edition, Association of National Advertisers, NTC Business Books, Lincolnwood, IL, 1995.

5 Ibid., p. 67.

6 Ibid., p. 68.

7 ASC Ehrenberg, 'Repetitive advertising and the consumer', *Journal of Advertising Research*, 12(2), 1974, pp. 25–34.

8 Ibid.

9 B Sharp, *How brands grow*, Oxford University Press, Melbourne, 2010.

10 Statista, 'Global advertising spending from 2010 to 2018', 2018. Accessed September 2018 at www.statista.com/statistics/236943/global-advertising-spending.

11 For more examples, see JR Rossiter and S Bellman, *Marketing communications: theory and applications*, Pearson Education Australia, Frenchs Forest, NSW, 2005.

12 R White, 'How to use the budget better', *Admap*, December, 1999.

13 This is based on the award-winning IPA case study by Les Binet, 'The gift that keeps on giving: John Lewis Christmas advertising, 2012–2015'. It won the Grand Prix and Gold, IPA (UK) Effectiveness Awards in 2016. World Advertising Research Centre (WARC). Accessed July 2018 at www.warc.com/content/paywall/article/ipa/the_gift_that_keeps_on_giving_john_lewis_christmas_advertising_2012_2015/107992.

14 J Romaniul and B Sharp, *How brands grow*, Oxford University Press, Melbourne, 2016.

15 E Riebe, M Wright, P Stern and B Sharp, 'How to grow a brand: acquisition or retention', *Journal of Business Research*, 67(5), May 2014, pp. 990–9.

16 J Romaniuk, 'Modeling mental market share', *Journal of Business Research*, 66(2), 2013, pp. 188–95.

17 There is a lot more data in the actual case study; here, I have only drawn out the most relevant for our discussion in this chapter.

18 L Binet, 'Toolkit 2017 – effectiveness in the digital age', World Advertising Research Centre (WARC), 2017. Accessed September 2018 at www.warc.com/content/paywall/article/warc-webinar-toolkit-2017—effectiveness-in-the-digital-age/110499.

19 JC Schroer, 'Ad spending: growing market share', *Harvard Business Review*, January/February, 1990, pp. 231–5.

20 Adapted from Schroer (1990), 'Ad spending', note 19.

21 RJ Kent and CT Allen, 'Competitive interference effects in consumer memory for advertising: the role of brand familiarity', *Journal of Marketing*, 58(3), 1994, pp. 97–105.

22 A Ehrenberg, *Repeat buying: theory and application*, American Elsevier, New York, 1972.

23 JP Jones, 'Ad spending: maintaining market share', *Harvard Business Review*, 68, 1990, pp. 38–42.

24 Ibid.

25 L Binet and P Field, *The long and the short of it: balancing short and long-term marketing strategies*. Institute of Practitioners in Advertising, London, 2013.

26 See UK Effie Award, 'How Lidl grew a lot', 2018. Accessed August 2019 at www.effie.org/case_database/case/UK_2018_E-206-125.

27 Adapted from Schroer (1990), 'Ad spending', note 19.

28 HM Cannon and EA Riordan, 'Effective research and frequency: does it really make sense?', *Journal of Advertising Research*, 34, March/April 1994, pp. 19–28.

29 These figures come from Edwin Artz, former chairman of Procter & Gamble. Cited in MJ Naples, 'Effective frequency: then and now', *Journal of Advertising Research*, July/August 1997, pp. 7–12.

30 Newswire, 'Super Bowl XLVII: how we watch and connect across screens'. Accessed March 2013 at www.nielsen.com/us/en/newswire/2013/super-bowl-xlvii-draws-108-7-million-viewers-26-1-tweets.html.

31 The diagram also shows the ratings of each program. Ratings are calculated as a percentage of households that tuned into the program. For example, program K has ratings of 10% because only 1 in 10 households tuned in. Reach is calculated by the summation of percentage of new households tuning in. For example, program M added 10% new audience in schedule A. By this time, the total reach for all three programs (K, L and M) is 40 (i.e. 10 + 20 + 10 = 40).

32 MJ Naples (ed.), *Effective frequency: the relationship between frequency and advertising effectiveness*, Association of National Advertisers, New York, 1979.

33 C McDonald, 'What is the short-term effect of advertising?', in S Broadbent (ed.), *Market researchers look at advertising: a collection of ESOMAR papers 1949–1979*, Sigmatext, Amsterdam, pp. 39–50; see also Naples (1979), *Effective frequency*, note 32 (and chapter 2).

34 HE Krugman, 'Why three exposures may be enough', *Journal of Advertising Research*, 12(6), 1972, pp. 11–14.
35 MJ Naples, 'Effective frequency: then and now', *Journal of Advertising Research*, 37(4), 1997, pp. 7–12.
36 See Rossiter and Bellman (2005), *Marketing communications*, note 11, for a detailed discussion of the different models of reach we can implement.
37 JP Jones, *The ultimate secrets of advertising*, Sage Publications, Thousand Oaks, CA, 2002, p. 82.
38 JP Jones, *When ads work: new proof that advertising triggers sales*, Simon & Schuster/Lexington Books, New York, 1995, p. 145.
39 JP Jones, 'What does effective frequency mean in 1997?', *Journal of Advertising Research*, July/August, 1997, pp. 14–20.
40 Although the word 'exposure' is used, it is strictly an 'opportunity to see' (OTS) or placement.
41 Adapted from Jones (1997), 'What does effective frequency mean in 1997?', note 39.
42 Jones (1997), 'What does effective frequency mean in 1997?', note 39. See also L Gibson, 'What can one exposure do?', *Journal of Advertising Research*, March/April, 1996, pp. 239–48; J Taylor, R Kennedy and B Sharp, 'Making generalizations about advertising's convex sales response function: is once really enough?' *Journal of Advertising Research*, 49(2), 2009, pp. 198–200.
43 G Assmus, JU Farlet and DR Lehman, 'How advertising affects sales: meta-analysis of economic results', *Journal of Marketing Research*, February, 1984, pp. 65–74.
44 GJ Tellis, 'The price elasticity of selective demand: a meta-analysis of econometric models of sales', *Journal of Marketing Research*, 25, November 1988, pp. 331–41.
45 C McDonald, 'From "frequency" to "continuity" – is it a new dawn?', *Journal of Advertising Research*, July/August, 1997, pp. 21–5.
46 E Ephron, 'Recency planning', *Journal of Advertising Research*, July/August, 1997, pp. 61–5.
47 Ibid.
48 K Longman, 'If not effective frequency, then what?', *Journal of Advertising Research*, July/August, 1997, pp. 44–50.
49 Ephron (1997), 'Recency planning', note 46.
50 GJ Tellis, 'Effective frequency: one exposure or three factors?', *Journal of Advertising Research*, July/August, 1997, pp. 75–80.
51 P Gallucci, 'There are no absolutes in media planning', *Admap*, July, 1997.
52 Millward Brown, 'How should you take TV advertising clutter into account?', Millward Brown Knowledge Point, 2011.
53 W Reichel and L Wood, 'Recency in media planning – redefined', *Journal of Advertising Research*, July/August, 1997, pp. 66–74.
54 Y Hu, L Lodish, A Krieger and B Hayati, 'An analysis of real world TV advertising tests: a recent update', *Journal of Advertising Research*, 49, 2009, pp. 201–6.
55 See Lodish (1986), *The advertising and promotion challenge*, pp. 94–5, note 1.
56 See Martin Sorrell's manifesto on what advertising should do. M Sorrell, 'A manifesto for media neutrality'. Accessed March 2013 at www.wpp.com/wpp/marketing/media/a-manifesto-for-media-neutrality.
57 For an example of out-of-home advertisement optimisation, see T Jarvis and P Walsh, 'Reach/frequency and optimization challenges as traditional media go digital: a solution from out-of-home'. *ESOMAR*, WM3, Berlin, October 2010. Accessed January 2020.

58 This is taken from a webinar by L Binet, 'Toolkit 2017 – effectiveness in the digital age', note 18.

59 J Romaniuk and B Sharp, *How brands grow*, part 2, Oxford University Press, Melbourne, 2016.

60 J Romaniuk, V Beal and M Uncles, 'Achieving reach in a multi-media environment: how a marketer's first step provides the direction for the second', *Journal of Advertising Research*, 53(2), 2013, pp. 221–30.

61 Adapted from DraftFCB Reach 2007 in JZ Sissors and RB Baron, *Advertising media planning*, 7th edition, McGraw Hill, p. 128.

62 J Snyder and M Garcia-Garcia, 'Advertising across platforms: conditions for multimedia campaigns – a method for determining optimal media investment and creative strategies across platforms', *Journal of Advertising Research*, 56(4), 2016, pp. 352–67.

63 For example, see E Ephron, 'Media-mix optimisers', *Admap*, March, 2000.

64 S White and C Dawson, 'Frequency and recency: keeping your customer close', *Admap*, 441, July 2003, pp. 41–3. An example is the ADPlus software from Telmar (www.telmar.com/products-for-marketers-agencies/multimedia/adplus).

65 PT Cronovich, 'The "No" campaign in Chile: paving a peaceful transition to democracy', 2013, delivered 22 February 2013 at the Conversation on the Liberal Arts, Westmont College, Santa Barbara, CA.

66 J Quelch, 'How better marketing elected Barack Obama,' *Harvard Business Review*, 5 November 2008. Accessed September 2018 at hbr.org/2008/11/how-better-marketing-elected-b. JS Wenner, 'How Obama won', *Rolling Stone*, 27 November 2008. Accessed September 2018 at www.rollingstone.com/politics/politics-news/how-obama-won-42930/.

67 P Kendall, 'How Chile's ad men ousted Pinochet: the real life story behind new film "No"', *The Telegraph*, 7 February, 2013. Accessed September 2018 at www.telegraph.co.uk/culture/film/9842723/How-Chiles-ad-men-ousted-Pinochet-the-real-life-story-behind-new-film-No.html.

68 Cronovich (2013), 'The "No" campaign in Chile', note 65.

69 You can watch the 2013 *NO* trailer starring Gael García Bernal on YouTube, www.youtube.com/watch?v=lOeiw_BJPas. Accessed September 2018.

70 L Binet, 'Toolkit 2017 – effectiveness in the digital age', note 18.

71 Y Hu, L Lodish, A Krieger and B Hayati, 'An analysis of real world TV advertising tests: a recent update', *Journal of Advertising Research*, 49, 2009, pp. 201–6.

72 A Steele, D Jacobs, C Siefert, R Rule, B Levine and C D Marci, 'Leveraging synergy and emotion in a multi-platform world: a neuroscience-informed model of engagement', *Journal of Advertising Research*, 53(4), 2013, pp. 417–30.

73 T Bakalash and H Riemer, 'Exploring ad-elicited emotional arousal and memory for the ad using fMRI', *Journal of Advertising*, 42, 4, 2013, pp. 275–291.

74 D Poole, 'Measuring long-term ad effects: a meaningfully different approach'. Accessed September 2018 at www.warc.com/content/paywall/article/measuring-long-term-ad-effects-a-meaningfully-different-approach/102521.

75 L Binet and P Field, 'Effectiveness in context', Presentation at Effectiveness Works, 18 October 2017. Accessed September 2018 at www.youtube.com/watch?v=i0OKdtaJ8g0.

76 Let's assume you have four datasets you want to use for the campaign but each contains 15% sampling error. Overall, you might end up with a large sampling error the more databases you employ. So don't assume that being very targeted is good. First you end up with a small audience, and second, your sampling errors are compounded.

77 S Vizard, 'Google faces up to advertiser boycott', *Marketing Week*, 28 March 2017. Accessed July 2018 at www.marketingweek.com/2017/03/28/google-faces-advertiser-boycott/.

78 E Knight, 'Why advertisers are boycotting Google's YouTube', *Sydney Morning Herald*, 28 March 2017. Accessed July 2018 at www.smh.com.au/business/companies/why-advertisers-are-boycotting-googles-youtube-20170327-gv7db6.html.

79 T Hobbs, 'What marketers need to know about the ANA media transparency report', *Marketing Week*, 7 June 2016. Accessed July 2018 at www.marketingweek.com/2016/06/07/ana-media-transparency-report-finds-fundamental-disconnect-between-marketers-and-media-agencies/.

80 D Roberts, 'The problems with programmatic advertising', *Rocket*. Accessed July 2018 at www.rocketagency.com.au/resource/the-problems-with-programmatic-advertising.

81 Interactive Advertising Bureau (IAB) white paper, *Programmatic in-housing: benefits, challenges and key steps to building internal capability*, 2018.

82 N Camerson, 'Qantas CMO: What it's taking to evolve our customer experience'. Accessed July 2018 at www.cmo.com.au/article/619797/qantas-cmo-what-it-taking-evolve-our-customer-experience/.

83 V Mitchell, 'Advertising and marketing spend significantly impacted by COVID-19', *CMO*, 31 March 2020. Accessed April 2020 at www.cmo.com.au/article/672354/advertising-marketing-spend-significantly-impacted-by-covid-19/.

84 RS Vaile, 'The use of advertising during depression', *Harvard Business Review*, 5, 1927, pp. 323–30.

85 GJ Tellis and K Tellis, 'Research on advertising in a recession: a critical review and synthesis', *Journal of Advertising Research*, 49(3), 2009, pp. 304–27.

86 P Field, *The link between creativity and effectiveness*, Institute of Practitioners in Advertising, London, 2011.

87 This is a paradox. As viewers stay at home, ratings across different mediums have soared. Yet advertisers decided to cut spending. Media companies are responding by offering more services to retain them. See, for instance, J Lynch, 'NBCUniversal will permanently reduce linear ads amid COVID-19 crisis', 2020. www.adweek.com/tv-video/nbcuniversal-will-permanently-reduce-linear-ads-amid-covid-19-crisis/amp/?__twitter_impression=true.

88 Social Bakers, 'COVID-19 is changing behavior on social media for both brands and users', 2020. Accessed April 2020 at www.socialbakers.com/blog/covid-19-is-changing-behavior-on-social-media-for-both-brands-and-users.

89 Of course, it may not be uniform. Some sectors will be affected more than others (e.g. restaurants and education). This means realignment is paramount for these industries (e.g. food delivery and online teaching, respectively). However, the same principle applies. Assuming realignment is well executed, then companies with the loudest advertising relative to competitors (i.e. eSOV) will win.

90 B Wansink and JM Gilmore, 'New uses that revitalize old brands', *Journal of Advertising Research*, 39 (2), April/May 1999, pp. 90–8.

CHAPTER 5
INTEGRATING DIGITAL AND NON-DIGITAL CHANNELS

CHAPTER OVERVIEW

In the past decade, the media landscape has changed dramatically, affecting how marcoms are implemented. The media has become fragmented and is increasingly digitised. Consumers can now instantly access brand information from multiple websites using multiple devices, and this is not counting the rise of social media. The job of a marcoms manager has become extremely complex. But here is the good news: it also means greater creative possibilities. The objective of this chapter is to help a marcoms manager negotiate this complexity. To this end, the marcoms manager should understand the strengths and weaknesses of different communication channels and be guided by a set of principles.

Learning goals

After reading this chapter, you will understand:

- the principles of guiding consumers to purchase
- the vast number of media options available
- the difference between a medium and a vehicle
- pros and cons for each of the media options
- the different media terminologies used to measure audiences of programs and the logic behind their usage
- that these measures are often about the media vehicles (programs) and not the ad.

In the past decade, the media has become fragmented and increasingly digitised. Figure 5.1 shows that globally, digital media has been growing and has now surpassed TV in advertising expenditure. Digital and TV are the two biggest media to advertise in and together they account for about 74% of all global media expenditure, with digital being the most popular at 38.5%, followed by TV (35.5%). The print media of newspapers and magazines are at a distant third (13.2%) (see figure 5.1). In the next section, we consider these media in greater detail.

DEVELOPING A STRATEGY TO MELD DIGITAL AND NON-DIGITAL CHANNELS

The rise of digital means a combination of digital and non-digital channels are now needed in any campaign. Gone are the days where one can rely solely on a traditional mass media like TV. Paradoxically, even traditional mediums like TV and even outdoor are also becoming digital (e.g. addressable TV). But here is the challenge. The number of digital channels has also exploded. Furthermore, consumer behaviour has also changed. Shoppers can now instantly gain

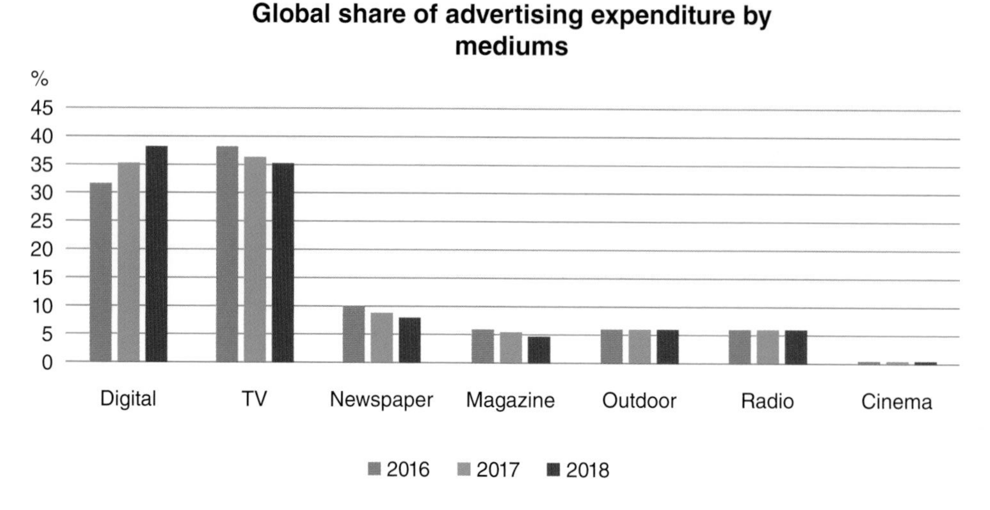

Figure 5.1 Percentage of global expenditure on media between 2016 and 2018[1]

information from several internet sites (e.g. different types of social media, aggregate websites, search engines, product review websites) using different means (e.g. smartphones, watches, voice assistants, QR codes, apps). Being virtually connected to the internet via smartphones, younger consumers, sometimes called digital natives, are expecting faster customer service. So how is a marcoms manager to make sense of these changes? The following principles could serve as a guide in developing a marcoms strategy.

Principle 1: Drive and excite

This principle basically means driving as many people to purchase as possible using an exciting idea. In the digital age, this usually means driving consumers to the firm's own channel – like its website, retail outlets, call centre, affiliate partners or blogsite. That excitement will breed word-of-mouth which will in turn attract more visitors and so on (see case study 5.1 Snickers Hungerithm). The channel can be used to host exciting competitions and games to encourage customer involvement. When this occurs, sales are more likely to occur since the point of purchase is now closer.[2] It also encourages impulse buying if the website offers other buying opportunities. For example, if one were to visit Amazon's website, one would be tempted to buy something. If the visitors can be encouraged to leave their personal details, the website can also become an in-bound portal to capture sales leads.

Furthermore, in the age of omnichannel, a firm provides multiple ways – both online and offline – for consumers to examine, buy or seek a restitution (e.g. refund or return). Having consumers land on one's owned asset (or ecosystem) means better control. For instance, a customer may order a pair of jeans online, but on receipt discover that the fit is not good. The omnichannel facility would enable the customer to return the pair of jeans to the nearest retail outlet to swap for another pair or get a refund. Research has shown that attracting customers to revisit the retail outlet encourages more buying.[3] Consumers now expect seamlessness across the firm's different channels (e.g. website, physical store, call centre, salesperson) to deliver the outcome they desire. But more importantly, once a customer can be identified and tracked within the brand's ecosystem, whether it is online or offline, it will allow the organisation to retarget them (see also chapter 11).

One way of thinking about this principle is to remember the POSE acronym, which stands for Paid, Owned, Shared and Earned media.[4] A firm can pay for the exposure (e.g. banner advertising or radio advertising) or it can hope to earn positive word-of-mouth in the mainstream press (e.g. good review). If the creative asset generates real excitement, it could be shared on social media (e.g. tweets, 'likes') or passed along among friends through emails. All these should increase the probability of consumers visiting the firm's website or other sales channel (i.e. owned assets or channel).[5] Traditionally, the objective is to use paid media to drive earned media (i.e. through path A1 – see figure 5.2) in order to improve media efficiency.[6] But in the age of internet, all channels are connected in some way. For instance, paid media can ask consumers to visit the firm's website and its social media page (i.e. path A2 and path B), but so can the publicity generated from earned media (path C and A3) or the excitement generated from social media (path S).

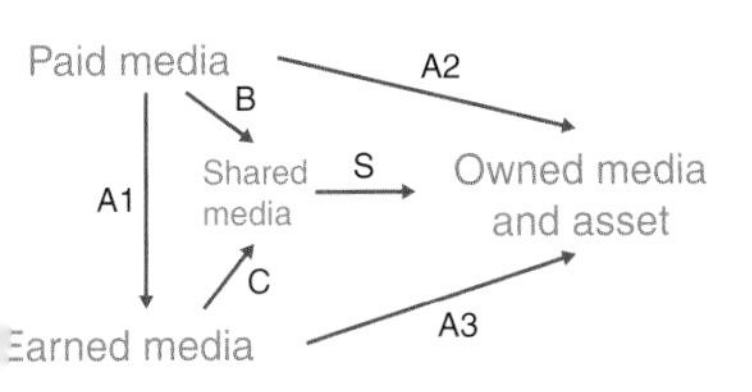

Figure 5.2 The POSE model

Thus, this principle is probably the most important of all principles discussed here for several reasons. First, it reminds us that the traditional demarcation between online and offline media is now meaningless. Often both digital and non-digital channels are intricately linked in all campaigns. Second, it reminds the marcoms manager to optimise for better results. For instance, it pays to make the firm's website sticky and to optimise search outcome. In fact, given the importance of search marketing, the POSE model can be extended to include search media. If so, the picture now becomes a little bit more complicated. We can call this the POSSE model (to include an additional 'S' for search).[7] Figure 5.3 illustrates this model.

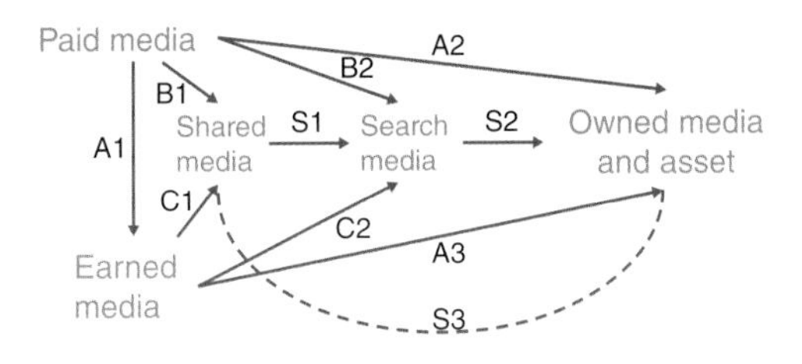

Figure 5.3 The POSSE model

Finally, this principle has another important application: it stimulates thinking about how different creative assets can be developed to best serve the marcoms objective. For instance, the POSSE model may remind a marcoms manager to think of ways of gaining free publicity or better manage the brand's negative reviews (see chapter 8). It may also stimulate managers to think of how the creative assets (e.g. an advertisement, a content story or a #hashtag) that are developed for each channel can create excitement synergistically (see chapter 1).

APPLYING THE POSSE FRAMEWORK

To make the concept of POSSE more concrete, consider the following example. Imagine one is tasked with coming up with an IMC campaign for repositioning an established brand of face cream for the younger demographics. The objective is to give the face cream a personality, one that is fun and irreverent.

One may decide that TV is vital given its repositioning objective. But to create excitement, it is thought the use of social media is the most productive. In this regard three ideas come to mind. First, to enlist the help of influencers to make a series of short videos touting the benefits of the cream, and second, to develop a series of blogs to be released through social media and the content made available on the brand's website. And finally, there will be a snazzy competition where visitors to the website can participate. It involves consumers uploading a three-minute video showing how the cream can be applied in an irreverent way (e.g. different parts of the body, to different family members, and even the pets). The more creative, the better, and to fuel more excitement, these videos will be voted on by members of the public. The winning prize is a trip to Germany where the cream is manufactured. But to participate, consumers have to leave their personal details so that they can collect the prize, should they win. Radio advertising (i.e. paid media) will also be used to fuel excitement for this competition, encouraging consumers to visit the brand's website.

At the same time, there is also a sales promotion where the consumers can get an e-coupon through the brand's app on their smartphones, specifically developed for this campaign. This app can only be downloaded from the website. Once the personal information is captured, an email will be sent to these consumers with new content on the face cream to encourage them to visit the pharmacy for a free trial (and purchase) and to subscribe to an online magazine.

For happy customers, one can solicit them for a testimonial and to recommend a friend. Their testimonials will be listed on the brand's forum website. Throughout the campaign, search engine optimisation (see later) will be implemented to ensure the brand is one of the top three brands listed in the search results. Figure 5.4 is a graphic outline of this strategy, using the POSSE framework.

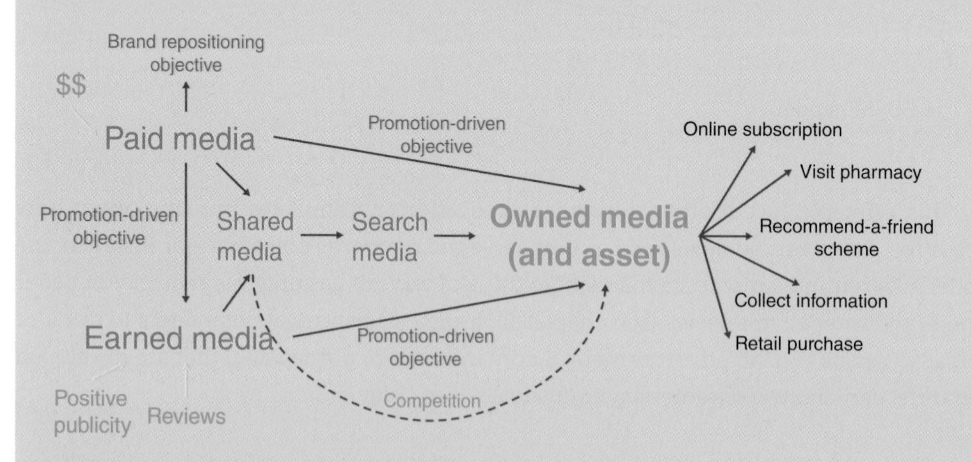

Figure 5.4 How a POSSE framework is applied

Principle 2: Strive for a good idea!

We can see from principle 1 that there are infinite possibilities on how various communications tools can be used to drive sales. But this can create confusion precisely because there are so many possibilities. Therefore, in order to excite and drive, a good idea is essential so that all tactics can coalesce around it to create synergy. Having a creative idea has always been the unique strength of the traditional advertising agency (and it still is). But media agencies are also beginning to hire creative personnel to come up with creative ideas. There is one facet over which media agencies trump traditional advertising agencies, and that is they have access to media data across multiple media platforms that can more precisely reach and track the target audiences. What this suggests is that a marcoms manager can now insist that media agencies come out with a novel idea of increasing effective reach. Or better still, media agencies should proactively suggest such ideas.

Principle 3: Leverage on partnerships for media innovations

One of the characteristics of an increasingly digitised world is the speed in which media technologies are improving. For instance, it is now possible to place video ads selectively based on what a viewer has previously watched. Similarly, with addressable TV advertising, different ads can be shown to different households even though they are all watching the same program. With artificial intelligence, it is now possible to serve content with the right images to the right audience, based on their viewing habits.[8] There will always be innovation, and this should be taken advantage of. If successful, this helps secure a better future for the brand.

CASE STUDY 5.1 SNICKERS HUNGERITHM

In 2018, Snickers Australia, in partnership with 7-Eleven, introduced a media innovation where the mood of the Australian public was constantly gauged from 14 000 social media posts per day.

The mood was then linked to the price of Snickers. The angrier the social media, the lower the price. This then made everyone happy! This was fun for the consumers because the mood on social media could be influenced by a swag of negative events in real time, including the ranting of politicians (e.g. Donald Trump), which in turn encouraged more consumers to jump onto social media to vent their anger. And the more they vented, the lower the price of Snickers, which then motivated the consumers to visit a 7-Eleven store to purchase a Snickers.

This is an example of social media meets dynamic pricing. The prices were updated 144 times a day. All customers needed to do was to download the app, walk into any 7-Eleven store and pay the discounted price using their smartphone.[9] The campaign called Snickers Hungerithm garnered a lot of publicity. It created 30 million impressions, a 1740% rise in social media traffic and a 67% increase in sales for the brand. It was also consistent with the brand's position, 'You're not you if you're hungry'.

DISCUSSION QUESTIONS

1. This piece of media innovation had nothing to do with the consumer decision journey, but still led to greater sales. Does this mean that the concept of decision journey is not universal? Discuss.
2. Will this creative idea work with a traditional medium like TV? Explain your answer.
3. Although the sales of Snickers had gone up during the campaign, its profit probably went down because people were buying Snickers at a discount. If so, can you say the campaign had been a success? Explain your answer.

Partnerships are also important for two other reasons. First, the right partners can bring their own online audience or subscribers. The classic examples are influencers or micro-celebrities[10] (see chapter 8). Some of these online personalities have large followings (fraudulent numbers aside); partnering with them can give the brand instant access to their audience. They are especially effective in reaching the younger demographics. Second, partnerships are needed because of the shortage of digital marketing skills in organisations. And the larger and more complicated the campaign, the more help a marcoms manager needs. As the media ecosystem changes, and with increasing automation (see chapter 13), even more specialised skills are now needed. Partnerships are becoming a necessity.

Now that we understand these three principles, let's discuss the strengths and weaknesses of different mediums, how audience size is calculated, the terminologies used, and where appropriate discuss examples of synergy. We will start with traditional mediums before tackling the non-traditional ones.

TRADITIONAL MEDIA

Television

Despite the explosion in the number of video channels (e.g. video-streaming services and social media), TV is still the king for massive reach. In most developed countries, almost every household has a TV, sometimes more than one. TV is still a major source of entertainment and Australians spend an average of 2 hours and 27 minutes per day watching TV either live or time-shifted.[11] Therefore, one of the key strengths of this medium is its ability to reach a large audience.

The other advantage of TV is its visual nature, its combination of sound, colour and motion. Advertising that uses this medium takes advantage of these qualities. It is also the medium most suited to the portrayal of emotions. When the creative idea relies on strong visual elements to make it work, TV is often the medium of choice. Certain executional styles, such as slice-of-life, demonstrations and problem-solution, are also best portrayed using TV (see chapter 7). In fact, a recent meta-analysis found that creativity works better via a dynamic medium like TV than a static one like print.[12]

The elements of visuals, sound, colour and motion in TV also make it highly attention-getting, which benefits brand awareness[13] (especially if it is creatively well integrated). While this can be an advantage, TV commercials (TVCs) suffer from being 'zapped' (when the viewer changes channels) or 'zipped' (when the viewer fast-forwards over the ad during pre-recorded programs). Since most homes have TV, it is also a good medium to reach a national audience, which makes it extremely convenient for advertisers conducting a national campaign. However, it can lead to wasted reach since non-target audiences can also tune in. Different programs created for different segmental audiences can mitigate this waste. TV is thus a very versatile medium. Finally, compared to social media like Facebook and YouTube across multiple devices, TV is more effective in generating attention, and hence sales. This is because the screen of TVs gives 100% coverage to the ad, resulting in 100% visibility all the time. There is also less visual clutter compared to what you see on social media.[14]

In terms of media terminology, a program (e.g. *60 Minutes*) within a class of medium (e.g. TV) is called a 'media vehicle'. This is because a program carries many ads (e.g. Vegemite and Toyota ads). Figure 5.5 illustrates this nested idea for TV.

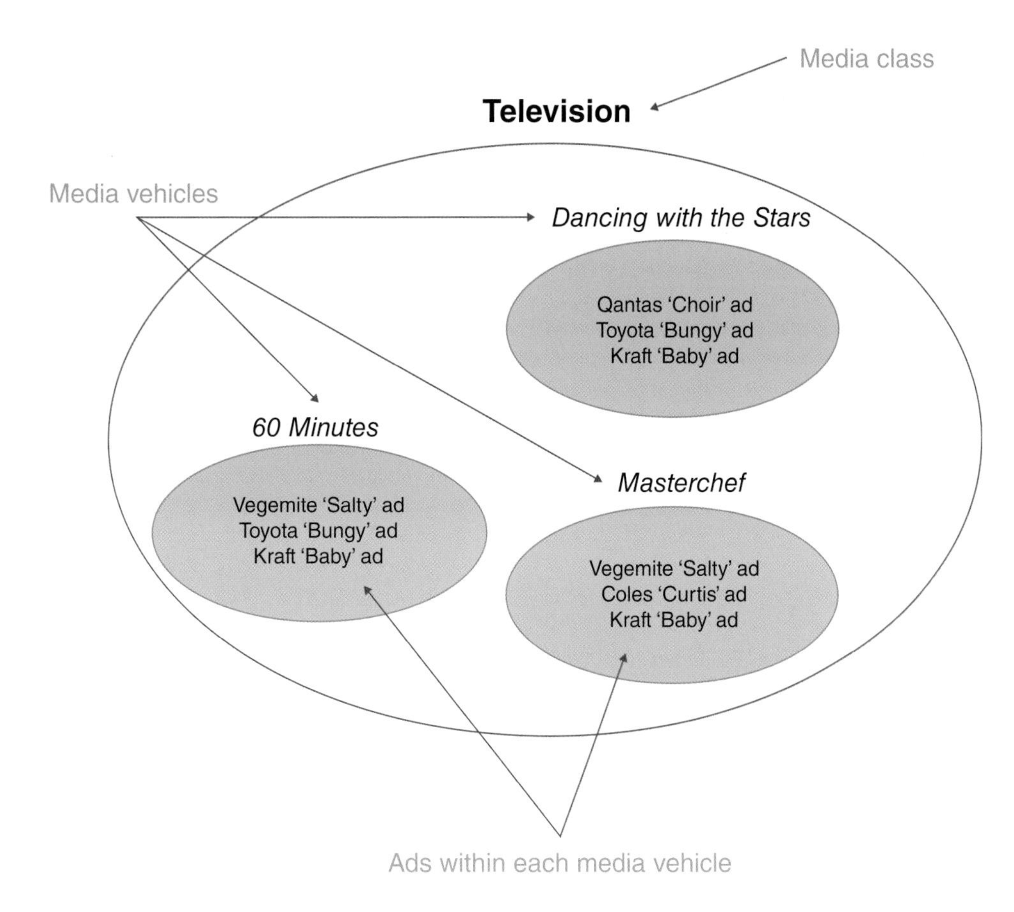

Figure 5.5 The difference between ads, media vehicles and media class (for TV)

While TV is cost-efficient, it is not cheap. In Australia, a 30-second ad in prime time (i.e. 7 p.m. to 10.30 p.m.)[15] costs an average of $25 000.[16] So, if a TVC is not effective, we are wasting $25 000 every 30 seconds! (In the 2019 Super Bowl, a 30-second TVC cost an eye-watering US$5.3 million.) Further, the cost of making a TVC is high: it is more expensive (on average, per second) to make a

TVC than to make a movie. This does not count the use of celebrities, which usually adds a substantial amount to the production cost. Once a TVC is made, it cannot be easily changed (unlike, say, a radio ad). This means it takes longer to research and produce a high-quality TVC.

TV also suffers from clutter because of the large number of ads carried during the commercial break in each program. This is a major issue but, in the face of cost pressures, media organisations continue to carry as many ads as they can. However, in most countries, there is legislation on how long the ad break can be. In the UK, for example, the break can be between 6 and 12 minutes for every 30 minutes.[17] Ads that appear at the start and end of the commercial break are usually more effective in getting attention.[18]

TVCs also have different lengths. Table 5.1 shows the typical number of seconds for each TVC in Australia, US and UK, although 30-second TVCs are the most common. In Finland, 7-second, 10-second and 15-second TVCs are common. A one-second TVC is called a 'blipvert' and a TVC of between one and five seconds is called an 'ident'.[19] Short 6-second ads are also used in the US but, by far, the most popular is still the 30-second format.

Table 5.1 Typical length of TV commercials in Australia, US and UK (in seconds)

Australia	US	UK
15s	15s	10s
30s	30s	20s
60s	45s	30s
	60s	40s
	90s	50s
	120s	60s
		90s
		120s

In terms of synergy, a TVC can also be easily combined with another medium to create a more effective campaign. Note, on average Australians have about 6.6 screens to consume video content (e.g. personal computer, smartphones, tablets) and may be looking at multiple screens at the same time.[20] Binet and Field found that combining the TVC with online videos is especially effective in developing long-term growth effects for the brand, than when using the TVC alone.[21]

About 84% of smartphone and tablet users have these devices as a second screen while watching TV to read social media discussions about the show or search for show-related information. Two-thirds of smartphone users also use their phones to search online for something they saw in a TVC. These may include searching for more information, prices, specifications, nearest retail outlets, and so forth; and there could be many such micro-moments like these if the ad is effective.[22] What this implies is that the brand should have a strong digital presence when the TVC is on by synching its paid search to coincide with the exposure. For instance, when a TVC comes on, one should ensure that the brand comes up on top of the search position, to take advantage of this moment when the consumers are most curious.[23] About a third of sales generated from search marketing (to be discussed later) originate from TV advertising. Search marketing without TV advertising is 46% *less* effective in generating sales.[24]

SOCIAL INTERACTIVITY AND INTERACTIVE TV ADS

Watching TV used to be a passive affair. But with the development of new technology, viewers can now interact with the program or TVC. Interactivity means allowing the viewer to have control, to engage in live, two-way communication with the firm, and to interact socially with others about the interesting content provided.[25] Social viewing is generally more enjoyable,[26] although it can also distract.[27] But fundamentally, people like to talk, especially about TV given its emotional content. Synergistically, combining TV and social media can bring consumers closer to the brand, and hence increase the probability of sales. One British study found that when British people are exposed to both TV and Twitter, the intention to shop at Sainsbury's, a British supermarket chain, jumped 21%.[28]

But there are different levels of interactivity. At the simplest level, a solo viewer can interact with the program by adjusting their viewing angle (e.g. when a viewer wants to see how a goal is scored from another angle). At a more complex level, a viewer can influence the outcome of the program (e.g. voting a participant out of a reality show) but the content remains substantially unchanged. At the most complex level, the viewer can change the content of the program as well (e.g. voting to change the storyline for an alternative ending). Finally, all these changes can also involve large swaths of people on social media (e.g. voting using hashtag) on different devices.

In advertising, however, changes to the ad content never occur since this is sacrosanct. But changes in how the ad is viewed or voted on have been attempted. For instance, in the UK, interactive TV (iTV) has a high household penetration (about 80%). The most effective form of interaction is to take viewers temporarily away from the program they are watching, to view the ad in a fuller and more entertaining way. After this, viewers can come back to the program to pick up where they left off. Compared to regular TVCs, interactive ads tend to better engage viewers, resulting in higher levels of awareness, positive thoughts and purchase intentions for the brand.[29] In Norway, Volkswagen developed an app which allowed readers of a few magazines to undertake a 'test drive' of the car using their smartphone.[30] By hovering the smartphone over a road map in the magazine, the screen of the smartphone showed how the car was travelling under three features (i.e. lane assist, adaptive lights and cruise control). The phone also vibrated during this simulation. Voting of ads by the public is more common. It is an easy way to increase viewer involvement. This is often seen during the Super Bowl.[31]

MEASURING TV AUDIENCE

Several terms have been developed to measure the audience size of TV (and radio) programs. This is an important measure for media companies because the larger the audience, the more they can charge the advertiser. The advertisers, of course, want independent verification to ensure that the audience size delivered is what they expected.

Outside Australia, one research company dominates the measurement of TV audience: AC Nielsen. In Australia, however, the three major TV channels have created their own company, Oztam, to measure their audience. Commonly, audience comparison looks at the number of households that have at least one TV, and this is often the denominator of a rating calculation. It is often called 'households using TV' (HUT). Note that the rating is a measure of the number of households looking at a TV, not of the number of individuals. A program's rating is defined as the percentage of TVs turned on at the time of the program (e.g. the percentage switched on at 7.30 p.m. on a Sunday, when *60 Minutes* airs). For instance, if there are 20 million TV households in Australia, then a rating of 14 means that 14% of 20 million households, or about 2.8 million (i.e. 0.14 × 20 million = 2.8 million households), have tuned into this program. Another way of expressing the rating of a program is the percentage of TV households tuned into the program. The equation (see figure 5.6) is as follows:

$$\frac{\text{Number of households tuned into '60 Minutes'}}{\text{Total number of households using TV}} = \frac{2.8\text{ million}}{20\text{ million}} \times 100 = 14\%$$

Ratings for '60 Minutes' = 14

Figure 5.6 Equation for calculating the rating of a TV program, *60 Minutes*

However, we could argue that rating is not an accurate measure, since we are not comparing the program with other programs at the *same* time. For instance, if *60 Minutes* is shown at 7.30 p.m. on Sunday, then it is more informative to compare its TV household audiences with other programs at the *same* time to measure its share of the audience at that time. In our example, it is 7.30 p.m. on Sunday. Now, assuming that only 40% of Australian households have their TVs turned on at that time on that day, then the denominator would be 40% of 20 million, or 8 million (i.e. 0.40 × 20 million = 8 million households). The denominator is now much smaller at 8 million households instead of 20 million. The audience share of *60 Minutes* is now calculated at 35%. The equation (see figure 5.7) is as follows:

$$\frac{\text{Number of households tuned into '60 Minutes'}}{\text{Total number of households using TV at 7.30 p.m.}} = \frac{2.8\text{ million}}{8\text{ million}} \times 100 = 35\%$$

Audience share of '60 Minutes' at 7.30 p.m. = 35%

Figure 5.7 Equation for calculating the audience share of a TV program, *60 Minutes*

IMPRESSIONS, OPPORTUNITY TO SEE AND TIME-SHIFTING OF THE VEHICLE

Understanding ratings and share is a subtle matter. Share of audience of a program will always be higher than its rating since the denominator will always be smaller. Again, these figures are not of individuals, but in respect of HUT. Further, these figures (whether for rating or share) refer to the program (vehicle) and not the ad that appears in the program.

If we are interested in individuals, then the terminology used is that of exposure, or more accurately of impression. For instance, if 1.4 million individuals watch *60 Minutes*, then this program has a potential of creating 1.4 million impressions with one ad. So, impression is basically one person's opportunity to see an ad once. If an ad appears three times in the program, it means there are three opportunities for a viewer to see this ad. That is, the 'opportunity to see' (OTS) is 3.

To calculate the total audience size that an ad is reaching, we simply multiply the number of viewers by the OTS. In this example, the number of viewers is 1.4 million and the OTS is 3. This means the total impression this ad can make is 4.2 million (i.e. 3 × 1.4 million = 4.2 million). The result of this calculation is called a 'gross impression'. The formula is as follows:

Gross impression = number of opportunities to see the *ad* in the program (OTS)
× number of people watching the *program*

However, gross impression only refers to the total number of audience exposures an advertiser has bought. It does not mean that the individuals actually saw the ad in the program. Further, data using impressions tends to be on the high side, because they refer to the potential number of viewers (not households) exposed to the ad. This makes comparison across programs cumbersome. For this reason, media planners still prefer to use rating and share of programs to make media planning decisions.

PEOPLE-METER TECHNOLOGY

People-meter technology is an advancement of the old media diary method. The old method required a sample of viewers to fill in their media habits in a diary. A people meter, on the other hand, requires viewers to push buttons in a receiver (not unlike a standard remote control) to denote who in the household is watching the program. In the US, the sample household is a random sample of 5000 households in 210 TV markets. In Australia, the sample consists of 5200 homes in Sydney, Melbourne, Brisbane, Adelaide and Perth, as well as 2120 homes for subscription TV (e.g. Foxtel).[32]

Marcoms managers should be mindful that figures of share and rating only refer to that of the program (not the ads broadcast with them). The fact that one advertises in a program does not mean that the ads are being watched. Another issue with TV ratings is that it does not take program viewership on different devices (e.g. smartphone, tablet and PC) into consideration. Even so, combining such data with traditional TV ratings will be a challenge.[33]

ADDRESSABLE TV (AND AD STREAMING)[34]

Watching live TV has been declining by about 23% in the last five years.[35] Furthermore, we are now watching entertaining content on all sorts of devices and platforms. 'Subscription video on demand' (SVOD) services like Stan, Netflix and Amazon Prime Video have grown in popularity. Traditional TV broadcasters also launched their own 'video on demand' (VOD) services, sometimes called 'broadcast video on demand' (BVOD), in order to retain their viewers. This allows viewers to catch up on TV programs at a more suitable time, sometimes dubbed catch-up TV.

In terms of advertising, however, addressable TV will be a game changer. This means showing different TVCs to different households even though they may all be watching the same program. This is because with the technology of using set top boxes, or cable or satellite, one can selectively stream only certain ads to certain households. Interestingly, this also allows the marcoms manager to experiment with different ads and run split testing across different segments (see chapter 4). It also means addressable TV comes close to the precision of direct marketing or the digital precision that Google and Facebook have in targeting their users.

This represents a significant improvement over traditional TV advertising which relies exclusively on the viewership and scheduling of programs. The major issue with this approach (sometimes called linear TV) is the considerable amount of wastage in impressions. This is because the program in which the ad is embedded is assumed to be watched by consumers who are interested in the brand. But this may not be so. For instance, a marcoms manager for an online travel agency may be hard-pressed to find what TV programs avid travellers watch. This is because viewership of traditional TV programs is segmented by demographics, not category interest. The marcoms manager then tries to match demographic details of the program with product usage choosing the programs that come closest. For instance, research may show that women aged between 18 and 29 years old are the most avid travellers. If so, then all TV programs being watched by this demographic group can be earmarked as potential media vehicles for the ads of this online travel firm. Now, the problem is that not all 18–29-year-old women are avid travellers, hence the wastage.

One way of solving this problem is to employ backward matching. This means only buying media placements for TV programs that one's customers watch, assuming we know their media habits. This is called first party data. Now, if we don't know this, then one can try to partner with firms whose customers share somewhat similar needs. For instance, one might partner with a credit card company that is interested in targeting customers who travel to certain destinations. This is second party data (or someone else's first party data). Finally, one can also use data from a third party. This data usually comes from a number of sources where the media habits of different product category users are collected (e.g. syndicate research). Thus, by combining different data sources (sometimes called data fusion), the best media usage profile of a customer segment can be built up.

However, for addressable advertising to work, the streaming technology must be precise. The use of set top boxes, for instance, where the right ads within the embedded program can be streamed to the right households is critical. So, instead of 'spray and pray', seen in traditional TV advertising, advertisers will know they are serving the right ads to households who are interested in the product category or brand.[36] But to evaluate if addressable advertising is effective, the purchase behaviour of the households being served the target ads must be compared to a control group not served the ads.

An initial study with three product categories of online travel, credit cards and amusement parks suggests that addressable TV holds promise. Compared to the control group, households that were exposed to addressable ads exhibited higher advertisement recognition and recall, purchase consideration and applications to purchase.[37] Another study more notable with automobile and retail shows that households exposed to the targeted ads show 20.9% and 60.6% higher sales, respectively, compared to the control group.[38]

Radio

Radio, unlike TV, does not have the benefit of visuals or motion. From a creative point of view, this means that most ads on radio are of the 'announcement' type. Like TV, radio suffers from clutter during the program breaks. Therefore, to achieve cut-through, radio ads should try to create visual imagery in people's minds. This can take the form of a drama, a conversation, humour or any sound effect that creates a 'theatre of the mind'. One way of achieving this is to creatively integrate the brand's TVC into its radio ad. For instance, the audio track of the TVC can be used in the radio ad. Then, when the listener hears a radio ad, it automatically triggers images of the TVC. However, to achieve this, viewers must first be familiar with the TVC through its repeated exposure. A TV-then-radio sequence is effective in raising both brand and ad awareness. In the same vein, advertisers should create ads with mnemonic qualities. This can include repetition of phrases, brands and any important information. The use of a jingle is a classic example of this tactic. See chapter 7 for more details of executional tactics.

Radio is also less intrusive than TV, which means that it lacks TV's cut-through power. We pay less attention to anything on radio. In fact, most of the time, people use radio as background. This in turn means that once a radio station is set on the dial, it is less likely to be changed even during a commercial break, unlike TV where people tend to zap during the ad break. The production cost of a radio ad is also significantly less than that of TV (especially if it is in the form of announcements). This makes it easy and more cost effective to create and make last-minute changes. But it also means that advertisers are less likely to invest in developing a big creative idea for this medium. As a medium, radio also has the advantage of reaching niche audiences, as there are different types of radio stations, ranging from talkback to reggae music programs. The rise of internet radio (with different music genres) and live music streaming services (e.g. Spotify[39]) also makes this easier.

This segmentation capability gives advertisers some flexibility. Further, because the media cost of radio is cheaper than TV, radio is a better medium for local tie-ins. The lower cost allows a higher-frequency schedule, which can be a very effective reminder to buy at the appropriate time. For instance, McDonald's can run their radio promotions around lunchtime to lure patrons into their restaurants. The following are various day parts that are commonly used to decide when to advertise. Drive times are usually the most expensive because this is when the audience is the largest; these are the times in which the greatest number of listeners are likely to travel to and from work, hence the name.

- Morning drive time: 6–10 a.m.
- Midday: 10 a.m. to 3 p.m.
- Evening drive time: 3–7 p.m.
- Evening: 7 p.m. to midnight
- Late night: midnight to 6 a.m.

Unlike TVCs, radio also has the advantage of developing an intimacy with its listeners when the host of the program is likeable. When such programs have a strong following, the host can exert considerable influence in setting or changing the public agenda (see chapter 9). Since the advertisers have no control over what a radio host says, this level of intimacy can be an advantage or disadvantage to the advertiser. If what is said during the program is consistent with the brand image, then it is an advantage. However, if what is said is controversial or not in good taste (assuming the brand does not want to pursue controversy), then the advertised brand can be tainted with the ensuing controversy.

MEASURING RADIO AUDIENCES

The calculation of audience ratings and share used to describe a TV program can also be used with a radio program.

In broadcast media, it is common to compare the cost of reaching 1% of the program's audience (i.e. its ratings, as discussed earlier). This index is called the 'cost per rating point' (CPRP), and it refers to the cost for purchase of one rating point.

Let's take TV as an example. CPRP is calculated by dividing the cost to place an ad in that program with its rating. In program A (see table 5.2), the cost to place a 30-second TVC is $40 300. With a rating of 16.3, the CPRP is $2472 (i.e. $40 300/16.3 = $2472). In other words, it costs $2472 to reach 1% of the audience of this particular program. CPRP allows us to compare the cost-efficiency across different programs.

Table 5.2 How CPRP is calculated

	Cost of 30-second ad	Rating	CPRP
Program A	$40 300	16.3	$2472
Program B	$25 020	17.1	$1463
Program C	$39 280	6.3	$6235
Program D	$20 220	8.5	$2379
Program E	$620	3.1	$200
Program F	$30 140	18.8	$1603
Program G	$60 022	10.2	$5885
Program H	$12 016	1.3	$9243

Of course, not every viewer of each of these programs is your target audience. Assuming that your target audience is people between 18 and 25 years old, they may make up between 30% and 50% of the broadcast audience. (We know this through the people-meter technology.) If we take this into consideration, the ratings, after adjustment, are called the 'target audience rating point' (TARP). We merely multiply the percentage of one's target audience with the existing ratings. For instance, for program A, although the rating is 16.3, the TARP is only 4.89 ($0.3 \times 16.3 = 4.89$) (see column E, table 5.3).

Once we have the TARP figures, we can recompute the cost to reach the target audience for each program. This is called the 'cost per target audience rating point' (CPTARP). Table 5.3 shows the new figures, with CPTARP in column F (the result of dividing column A by column E).

Table 5.3 How cost per TARP (CTARP) is calculated

	Cost of a 30-second ad [A]	Rating [B]	CPRP [C]	Percentage of target audience [D]	TARP [E]	CTARP [F]
Program A	$40 300	16.3	$2472	0.3	4.89	$8241
Program B	$25 020	17.1	$1463	0.4	6.84	$3658
Program C	$39 280	6.3	$6235	0.35	2.21	$17 773
Program D	$20 220	8.5	$2379	0.34	2.89	$6997
Program E	$620	3.1	$200	0.32	0.99	$626
Program F	$30 140	18.8	$1603	0.39	7.33	$4112
Program G	$60 022	10.2	$5885	0.5	5.10	$11 769
Program H	$12 016	1.3	$9243	0.48	0.62	$19 256

A comparison of columns C and F in table 5.3 shows that the cost to reach 1% of our target audience (18 to 25-year-olds) has risen considerably. This is not surprising since our target audience is always smaller than the general number of households that have a TV.

Cinema

This is another common broadcast media although not as large as TV or radio. But this medium has been suffering because of the rise of on-demand TV. This has led to a decline in the number of movie-goers due to the growth of in-home entertainment. However, this is changing. Cinema seems to be on the comeback with younger audiences increasingly fuelled by recent hits like *The Lion King*, *Toy Story 4* and, of course, *Avengers Endgame*. This is supported by the rise of theatre screens in recent years.[40] Movies also have distinct advantages. Unlike TV or radio, a cinema has a captive audience. In the movies, the viewing environment is dark, except for the screen. This helps increase the focal attention of the audience and therefore reduces distraction. In contrast, the small screens of smartphones where videos are viewed in a hurried and unfocussed manner cannot compete with the cinemas in building emotional layers of branded associations. In fact, 'big visuals' generally perform better in evoking emotional response than 'small visuals'.[41]

The cinema medium also has segmentation qualities, since advertisers can target the audience depending on the kind of movie being shown. It is also more effective than radio for local tie-ins, since movie-goers tend to live in the same vicinity as the cinema. However, like TVCs, the cost to produce a movie ad can be expensive if the campaign calls for brand image advertising. In this case, the production cost for the ad will be about the same as that of TV. Also, like TV programs, the more popular the movie, the higher the advertising rate.

Advertisers should not forget that the movies also offer special creative opportunities that the TVC does not, and therefore the movie ad should not be simply a TVC. For instance, one advertiser, BMW, has used the lights in the theatre to great effect. The theatre is dark as patrons wait for the movie to start. The BMW ad opens with a car driving in the distance on a long, winding country road. We cannot see the car, but we can hear it. Then, on the screen and in the darkness, we see two headlights approaching. As it gets nearer, the theatre lights also increase until they flood the theatre with light. Then, just as suddenly, the headlights on the screen and the theatre lights are turned off simultaneously, darkening the whole theatre once again. This creative execution demonstrates the power of BMW's Bi-Xenon headlights. It is also an example of how an execution can be customised for the medium in order to achieve a greater effect (see also chapter 7).

In recent years, movies (and some TV programs) have adopted product placement to help defray production costs. Some movies, such as the James Bond franchise, are notorious for product placement, which is the planned and often undisclosed use of brands (or logos and symbols) in a show in exchange for monetary or commercial considerations. In an important study, Dutch researchers found that if the image of a brand (e.g. Slim-Fast, a meal-replacement product) is consistent with the image of a program (e.g. *Your Real Age*, a health entertainment program), then product placement can move the image of the brand in the direction of the program (i.e. towards a more healthy image) with just one exposure, even if viewers cannot remember seeing the brand in the program![42] This is a powerful demonstration that memory is not necessary to change brand image when we use product placement as a tactic.

On the other hand, if increasing brand awareness is our objective, then research has shown that for a brand placement to be successfully recalled it has to be integrated into the storyline, prominent and centrally placed.[43] One way of achieving this is to show the character of the movie using the brand,[44] as in the case of James Bond (who drives an Aston Martin and famously now drinks Heineken beer as well as his usual vodka martini). Similarly, if there are competing brands (e.g. Porsche versus Ferrari) in a scene, the marcoms manager should negotiate for his or her brand to come up on top (e.g. a winner in a chase scene).

In short, if product placement is an option, the marcoms manager should strive for the brand to be immersed in a naturalistic, credible setting and preferably portrayed in a prominent and advantageous way, so that it is integrated into the storyline (or editorial).

Print

Unlike broadcast media, print suffers from a lack of dynamic elements. There is no sound or movement in print, which makes it extremely challenging to capture the attention of the reader: on average, people spend about two seconds on a print ad. This means that if the message and brand (i.e. the branded message) are not clearly communicated within this short period of time, the money of the advertiser is wasted.

Although print lacks dynamic elements, other structural elements such as size, colour and positioning of the ad can be used to try to get the attention of the reader (see chapter 7). These are important considerations because print – including newspapers, magazines and directories – still constitutes a large share of media spending. Globally, in terms of expenditure, print is the third-largest medium, after digital and TV, as we saw in figure 5.1 earlier.

NEWSPAPER

One major advantage of newspaper is its wide coverage, especially in the case of titles that have national circulation. Yet regional or local newspapers also have potential to reach the local audience. This gives this medium geographic flexibility. Since the aim of newspaper is to report 'news of the day', which can be daily, weekly or even monthly, it also gives advertisers the flexibility of different scheduling possibilities with different titles. The speed of turnover for each issue also makes it a good medium for making announcements. For example, if there is a need for a product recall due to a defect, the organisation can quickly advertise this in the daily papers. Only a short lead time is needed (a few days). This means each issue has a short lifespan. As a result, ads in newspapers generally tend to have poor production values and are almost always in black and white. However, as a medium, newspapers have a high level of credibility and tend to be favoured by educated audiences.

There are different kinds of newspaper ads, of which the most dominant is the display ad. Display ads hold the greatest creative possibilities and can be placed anywhere in the newspaper except in the editorial pages. Advertisers usually take advantage of this type of ad for its ability to carry detailed information. The cost of a display ad varies depending on its size, position and colour.

Classified ads, on the other hand, are small ads that advertisers can use to sell personal goods or services. Classifieds are usually black and white and found at the back of the newspapers in different sections. Such ads used to be a reliable source of revenue for newspapers (up to as much as 40%) – indeed, in the 1980s the Australian media tycoon Kerry Packer dubbed them 'rivers of gold'. However, in the digital era, this is no longer true. Many internet-based trading or exchange websites (e.g. eBay, Gumtree and Craigslist) have taken market share away from the classifieds.

The last kind of newspaper ads are freestanding inserts and supplements. These are advertisements printed by a third party and inserted into newspapers in the form of single or multiple sheets (called a 'freestanding insert' [FSI] in a newspaper and a 'supplement' in a weekend edition or a magazine). Retailers like FSIs because they can choose to insert these ads in newspapers destined for certain areas. Since FSIs tend to drop out of a newspaper, they are an excellent way to attract consumers' attention.

Supplements are magazine-like publications, often inserted in the Sunday edition of newspapers, which allow advertisers to target readers. Like specialised magazines, these supplements can be on topics ranging from travel to food, fashion and health. But unlike specialised magazines, these supplements are of lower editorial quality. They still provide media companies with another source of advertising revenue, however. Both FSIs and supplements can give retailers better control in the quality of the production. Marcoms managers should consider advertising on Sundays since research has found that readers are generally more receptive to advertising because they are more relaxed.[45]

Measuring newspaper audience

Several terms have been developed to measure the audience size of newspapers, of which the most commonly used is 'circulation'. This means the number of copies sold either at the news stand or through home delivery. This is equivalent to the concept of 'impression' in TV, which we discussed earlier. Newspapers that enjoy a large circulation will charge more for their advertising. This means that it is important for circulation figures to be independently verified. In the US, the Audit Bureau of Circulations has this auditing function.

'Circulation' is different from 'readership'. The latter refers to the number of people reading the newspaper. Normally, readership figures are higher than circulation numbers because readers usually pass a newspaper along to others to read. For instance, although only one copy of a newspaper is delivered to a cafe, many customers may read it. Readership is determined by surveys.

MAGAZINES

There are two major categories of magazine – those that appeal to consumers and those that appeal to businesses. Consumer magazines, in turn, can be of the general kind (e.g. *Time* magazine) or of special interest (e.g. *Gourmet Traveller*).

Business magazines can be classified as trade magazines (aimed at distributors), industrial (aimed at manufacturers), professional (aimed at professionals such as doctors and lawyers), agricultural (aimed at farmers and others working in the sector) and corporate (published by the organisation and aimed at its own customers).

Magazines are less topical than newspapers. But one major advantage of magazines is that they offer many more creative possibilities than newspapers. For instance, colour production allows the portrayal of emotional qualities (more similar to TVCs). This also means that a longer lead time is needed. This is not necessarily bad because it means more thought has to be devoted to producing an ad. The greater creative possibilities of this medium also mean it is better than newspapers in building brand image. As a medium, it is generally more expensive than newspapers.

The other major advantage of magazines is the plethora of titles available to appeal to different segmented interests, ranging from wine appreciation to fly fishing. Although some niche magazines have limited circulation, each has a strong appeal among those who buy or subscribe to it. Also, consumers are less likely to throw out their copies and, in fact, often buy these specialist magazines for the information contained in the ads. For an advertiser, this is a major advantage because not only is this segment self-selecting (thus saving on trying to reach them), but also the target audience is probably very receptive to the advertised message.

Measuring cost-per-thousand impressions[46]

Table 5.4 shows how advertisers can compare the cost of reaching 1000 members of its target audience across different magazine titles. (The same metric applies here as to newspapers.) This table shows that magazine A has a circulation of 3.1 million; in other words, 3.1 million copies of the magazine are sold. However, as discussed above, readership figures are always higher than circulation figures because of pass-along readers. In table 5.4, we assume that three times as many people read the magazine. Thus, although magazine A has a circulation of 3.1 million, the number of readers is 9.3 million (i.e. 3 × 3.1 million = 9.3 million).

Table 5.4 How CPM is calculated

	Cost per full-page ad [A]	Circulation [B]	Readership [C]	CPM [D]
Magazine A	$400 300	3 106 667	9 320 000	$42.95
Magazine B	$250 020	2 100 000	6 300 000	$39.69
Magazine C	$390 280	2 744 667	8 234 000	$47.40
Magazine D	$205 220	3 308 000	9 924 000	$20.68
Magazine E	$6220	1 444 667	4 334 000	$1.44
Magazine F	$301 140	4 276 667	12 830 000	$23.47
Magazine G	$602 022	3 422 667	10 268 000	$58.63
Magazine H	$124 016	433 467	1 300 400	$95.37

Note: Column D = A/C × 1000

What is the cost of reaching 1000 of these readers? This index is called cost-per-thousand impressions (CPM). In this example, CPM is calculated by dividing the cost of the ad by the readership figures and then multiplying this number by 1000. For example, the CPM for magazine A is $42.95 (i.e. [$400 300/9.32 million] × 1000 = $42.95; see column D in table 5.4). With CPM, we can now compare the efficiency of reaching 1000 of the readers. In this example, we see that the most efficient is magazine E, with a CPM of $1.44. However, efficiency is not an indicator of effectiveness. For instance, our target audience may not read magazine E, although it is the cheapest. See chapter 4 on media planning.

Effective cost-per-thousand impressions

The concept of CPM may be numbered as marketers gain precision in serving ads to their target audience. The main problem is that the CPM calculation includes viewers who may *not* be interested in one's brand. Imagine we pay $10 to reach 1000 of our target audience (i.e. CPM = $10). But if only

10% of the target audience are interested, we would have overpaid. In fact, we are actually paying $100 for every 1000 viewers (i.e. $10/0.10 = $100) instead of $10; this is 10 times *less* efficient. Or to put in another way, our effective cost-per-thousand impressions (eCPM) is actually $100.[47] The eCPM measure is thus more accurate because it takes into account those who are genuinely interested.

In search engine marketing (SEM), the concept of eCPM has another application. It is used to evaluate a campaign's effectiveness in increasing traffic. For instance, in Google's campaign management system, eCPM can be listed as a separate column based on how much a publisher has *earned* from hosting Google ads on its site. It is calculated based on how many people have visited the website daily, indexed on one thousand ('000) impressions. For instance, in table 5.5, we can see that on Monday, August 20, this advertiser earned $2.40 in advertising fees from this landing page, which attracted 824 viewers. This equates to $2.91 per 1000 viewers (i.e. $2.40/824 × 1000 = $2.91, or column E/column A × 1000).

Table 5.5 How eCPM is calculated

Date	[A] Page impressions	[B] Clicks	[C] Page CTR	[D] Page eCPM	[E] Your earnings
Monday, August 20	824	8	1.0%	$2.91	$2.40
Tuesday, August 21	560	11	2.0%	$3.57	$2.00
Wednesday, August 22	479	4	0.8%	$1.25	$0.60
Thursday, August 23	780	9	1.2%	$0.90	$0.70
Friday, August 24	650	4	0.6%	$0.62	$0.40
Saturday, August 25	945	14	1.5%	$1.90	$1.80
Sunday, August 26	710	15	2.1%	$1.41	$1.00
Total	4948	65	9.0%	$12.56	$8.90

Out-of-home

Out-of-home (OOH) media can take many forms, including billboards, posters on street furniture or transit (e.g. buses). These media will be the main focus of this discussion, although out-of-home can also be classified under the more general heading of ambient ads, a much broader category that includes the following (according to the Cannes International Advertising Festival):

- floor media
- washrooms
- 3D
- petrol pumps
- ticket barriers
- special or one-off buildings
- miscellaneous (e.g. napkins, coasters).

In Australia, out-of-home media has been growing, with revenue predicted to hit $1.98 billion by 2018 (see figure 5.8).[48] This is because of the rise of digital outdoor marketing. Digital out-of-home (DOOH) media is attractive to service providers because each location can carry multiple ads and hence generate more revenue. But this is not necessarily good for the advertiser because the brand will be competing for attention. However, OOH continue to be attractive for advertisers because of population growth in cities.

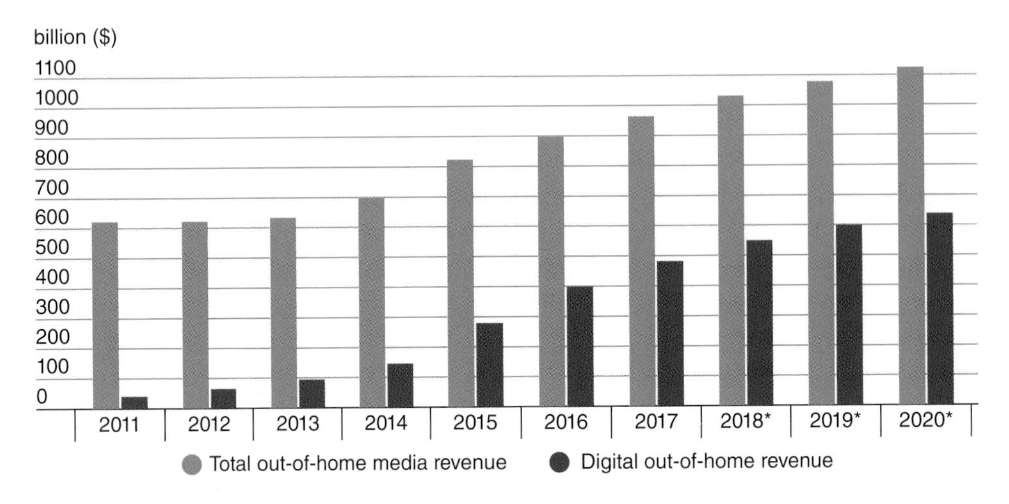

Figure 5.8 Revenue growth of out-of-home media in Australia

BILLBOARDS

Billboard advertising has by far had the largest share of all outdoor advertising – about 60%. One characteristic of this medium is its large-size format. This is needed to attract the attention of passers-by or drivers. The larger the size, the more likely are consumers to recognise it.[49] Larger billboards receive longer viewing times averaging 1.08 seconds compared to 0.53 seconds for smaller billboards,[50] as well as receiving more glances.[51] On highways, billboards serve a directional purpose by telling drivers how to get to the advertised location (e.g. restaurants, parks or hotels). Such billboard ads typically use pre-printed laminated sheets that can be quickly glued onto the signage structure for the duration of the exposure (usually 30 days).

Billboards can also serve a frequency function. Since people often use the same route to travel to and from home, they pass the same billboard every day. This means that the medium has a natural built-in frequency of exposure, which helps build brand awareness and image.[52] However, the frequency of exposure can be good or bad: good if the advertising is interesting and passers-by do not mind looking at it; bad if the ad is poor or boring, when it quickly becomes an eyesore.

Advertisers can use billboards to build brand awareness. When this is the communication objective, the visual elements of a brand and its logo must be prominent. If words are to be used, they should be as few as possible since passers-by are unlikely to stop and read complex messages. This is not necessarily bad because it forces the creative personnel to distil the essence of the communication.

Billboard ads can also be used to deliver a short-branded message. Given the limitation of words in this regard, this is usually done with the clever use of visuals. Sometimes, a series of visuals is more powerful in saying something about the brand than the use of words. For example, in a billboard for Kraft strawberry jam, the image showed a series of strawberries being slowly transformed into a jar of Kraft strawberry jam, which cleverly emphasised the purity of the product without saying too much.

The size of the billboard facilitates the advertiser's creativity.[53] Creative personnel love billboards because they can use the space as a canvas to show off their creativity – to think outside the box. The billboard's prominence also makes it ideal for creating controversy for the brand so that people talk about it (if this is the objective). In this regard, the medium is ideal for generating publicity for the product (see chapter 9).

One common publicity tactic is to use controversial pictures (or headlines). In Paris in 1981, the advertising legend David Ogilvy showed a series of billboards of a woman slowly stripping away her bathing suit. The client was Avenir, a billboard and signage firm. It was used to demonstrate that billboards can be very effective. Needless to say, it generated much publicity, even in usually permissive France!

In recent years, improving electronic technology has created electronic billboards that consist of many screens. This technology allows us to create giant moving images or many dazzling, coordinated images (with sound), something traditional static billboards could not achieve. A giant electronic screen is often used at big venues during special festivals or functions. The Coca-Cola Company took the electronic technology one step further by unveiling the first three-dimensional billboard in Times Square New York (see figure 5.9). Consisting of 1750 LED screens, the giant billboard includes screen panels which are able to move independently and are choreographed using robotics. In unison, the billboard comes alive with wave-like motion, while at the same time exhibiting changing images of different 'Coca-Cola' beverages. Such a tactic increases visual saliency which is memorable for consumers.[54] What's more, the message can change depending on the time of the day. During lunch time, the message might become that of 'Coke' with meals.[55]

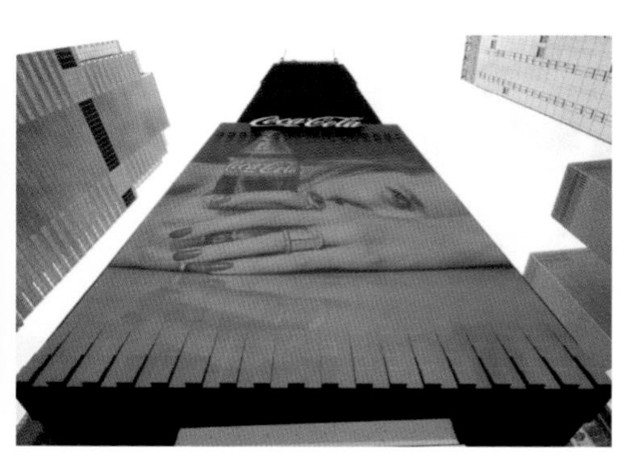

Figure 5.9 The 'Coca-Cola' 3D billboard

Electronic billboards also have one other important capability, that of allowing one to build in some sort of real-time interactivity that consumers can relate to. For instance, in a campaign for men's underwear, Bonds (in conjunction with Clemenger BBDO) erected a seven-storey, interactive billboard in Melbourne showing how weather impacts men's testicles or 'boys' (see figure 5.10). When the temperature is cold, the two boys shrink to the top of the billboard, and when it is warm, they hang lower, and when it is windy, they swing from side to side. The billboard garnered a lot of publicity for the brand.[56] Needless to say, care should always be taken whenever we wish to attempt brand controversy. There is always a danger that it will backfire if it is not appropriate, is in bad taste or risks causing a traffic hazard.

One limitation of billboards is their reach if only a limited number of locations are bought. On the other hand, with a national buy, billboards can potentially reach wide sections of the population. But what happens if one cannot afford a national buy? One way of overcoming reach limitation is to combine the medium with an event which can then be streamed over the internet. This will increase reach, provided it is exciting enough. In other words, if the creative content is well executed, the billboard is a good platform for an exciting integrated campaign, even if only a single billboard is used. A good example is when Xbox launched the game 'Rise of the Tomb Raider'.[57] It challenged eight fans of the game to stand for 24 hours

Figure 5.10 Bond's 'Boys' billboard

outdoors, on a windy autumn day in London, perched at the edge of the billboard as part of the artwork. The headline 'Survival of the Grittiest' was written across their bodies. The winner was the last person standing, and the prize was a free trip around the world to various locations inspired by the game. But what makes this billboard memorable is that the endurance of the participants over the 24 hours was streamed live through the website survivalbillboard.com. And to add to the drama, other fans could vote on what other artificial weather could be inflicted on these participants (e.g. wind, snowstorm, intense heat and cold). The winner lasted 22 hours.

The campaign was a roaring success, generating 22 000 public votes with 3.5 million views in a single day, plus 56 000 hours of streamed content. The website became a 'destination' website with an average of eight minutes dwell time, compared to an average of eight seconds typical of out-of-home execution websites. The stunt won the top prize for the Event Awards in 2016 as well as the awards for the Best Integrated Marketing Campaign, The Game Changer and Outstanding Creative Idea.[58]

POSTERS ON STREET FURNITURE AND TRANSIT

Posters are like little billboards and are either stationary (on street furniture) or transit ads (on moving vehicles). Street furniture is an outside structure, often found where people are likely to walk or wait, such as bus stops, benches, subways, train stations and standalone street signage or kiosks. Transit ads can be found behind, on the sides or inside buses, taxis and trains.

Like billboards, posters have only a short time to communicate since they are subject to many environmental distractions. The exceptions are posters on the inside of buses and taxis, where longer copy is fine since the attention of viewers is likely to be captive. An interesting twist to the notion of the captive audience is posters on the back of public bathroom doors.[59] Where else can the person look?

One distinct advantage that posters have over newspapers is that they can be geographically targeted on the ground. For instance, if we are targeting office workers in a central business district (CBD), one logical option is to place our ads in all the street furniture such as bus stops, subways or kiosks in the CBD. This can be supported by billboard advertising in the area as well as transit advertising on all bus routes in the CBD.

Posters on some street furniture will face competitive clutter if more than one brand is being advertised. For example, some street kiosks have rotating ads, which may attract our attention (because of the movement) but are also likely to create competitive interference.

NON-TRADITIONAL MEDIA

Websites, microsites and mobile websites

The website can be considered the digital home of the advertiser. At the most basic level, a website can be simply an online brochure, with only one webpage connected to the World Wide Web. This is the homepage which is the main page of the website, and it is also the first page a visitor sees. At a more complex level, a website can contain a collection of webpages, having different forms (e.g. text, images, videos) and different functionalities (e.g. email, news, online sales, applications, online games, FAQ and social forums).

Generally, a website encourages a certain level of interactivity to help visitors 'stick' around. Such interactivity is commonplace, and it is crucial in increasing a brand's click-through rate.[60] The longer a visitor stays on the website, the greater the probability they will be influenced. However, interactivity can have a downside – the focus of the online brand campaign may be lost in the milieu. For instance, the website ends up too interactive and the consumer is distracted from their purchase decision. There are a number of design solutions. One solution is to create a microsite for each online campaign run (i.e. a subpage), so that only interested consumers can be quickly directed on its page.

In terms of organisation, the website should be easy to navigate, and the most interesting content should be clearly visible to the viewer without requiring them to scroll down. Generally, ads that appear at the bottom of the homepage tend to be ignored.[61] All the important information should be above the 'fold', that is, the visible line that separates what is first seen on the screen, and what cannot be seen unless the user scrolls down. All common applications should be located in the typically familiar areas. For instance, the section on comments and feedback are typically found at the end, while display advertisements are typically found at the top, although they are increasingly embedded within the text. Also, typically, websites use a grid format where different information is organised in digital tiles which allow a user to click through (see chapter 7).

Many websites now have e-commerce functionality to allow the target audience to buy goods (e.g. Amazon.com), buy services (e.g. Freelancer.com), customise their purchase (e.g. Nike's iD shoes), track progress (e.g. FedEx), check room availability and book a hotel room (e.g. Expedia.com). E-commerce can be very versatile, but if not well designed can become clumsy.

Websites can be used to disseminate important information about new products or services. This can take the form of a microsite that appears at the parent website. For instance, when Volkswagen launched its Jetta TDI model, it created a microsite within its corporate site. Microsites allow the parent organisation to be more flexible since they can easily take the site down when no longer needed. Very often such sites serve as a PR platform from which to publicise the latest news about the organisation. Since the website is so versatile, it pays to drive traffic to the website. This means publicising the URL address as widely as possible, which can be done in a number of ways:

- Create a URL that is memorable, unique, short and (preferably) branded.
- Display the URL on all print ads, email campaigns and blogs.
- Remind your target audience to bookmark the URL or make it their home page.
- Share links with other related websites, a micro-celebrity or a digital influencer (sometimes called back links).
- Optimise search engine advertising, so that the URL link appears at the top of consumer internet searches (see below).

The effectiveness of one's website can now be easily assessed using various forms of research. One form often carried out at the design stage is useability research. The user is told to interact with the website, as researchers follow what they do as the user navigates the website. More sophisticated versions involve eye-tracking. After the behaviour is evaluated, the researcher typically asks the user what happened at various points during the navigation. Typically, they are double-checking if certain key creative elements (e.g. certain links or buttons) are well executed or can be improved. This form of research where the interface between the user and website is evaluated is called CI (or Customer–Interface) research.

Another form of website research relies on analytics. One can adopt an A/B testing regime to see which variant of the website is more effective. This will be discussed in greater detail in chapter 11 (direct marketing). One can also evaluate the website against industry benchmarks across several metrics. For instance, if not enough consumers are clicking on the pay button, or scrolling down, then it may imply that the way it is designed (e.g. colour or positioning) is problematic. One useful analytic is the bounce rate, which should be as small as possible; a high bounce rate (e.g. more than 50%) means a high number of users are leaving the website. This signals wastage because many resources may have been devoted to drive these consumers to the website, and yet one cannot retain them. Another useful metric is click-through rate as discussed earlier. One should note that each page of one's website can be evaluated on several such metrics. Studying such metrics would give us some ideas on how to improve.

Finally, special care must be taken when designing websites for smartphones because the interface is so different. For instance, the screens are smaller which means the design has to be narrower and the format longer. In other words, a thinner format.

Search engine optimisation, paid social and paid search

In the last decade or more, digital marketing has grown in sophistication and popularity. This is because we can now reach consumers directly, and our increased knowledge of their preference allows us to be more persuasive in communicating our offers. This in turn allows us to know very quickly if our digital campaign is working. A medium like the traditional TV, which relies on 'spray and pray', does not possess this level of precision. As a result, it is now mandatory for a campaign to include some aspects of digital marketing where the target audience can be precisely reached. At the *minimum*, consumers should be able to find the brand's website quickly, and SEO is a technique to do this. Beyond this minimum, the marcoms manager can choose to use social media (i.e. paid social) to arouse the interest of the target audience about the brand, or to anticipate key words consumers might use in their search (i.e. paid search). Regardless, the destination should be the brand's website (or an online affiliate) in order to get a sales conversion. Thus, paid search, paid social and search engine optimisation are all connected, as shown in figure 5.11. We will now discuss each of these in more detail.

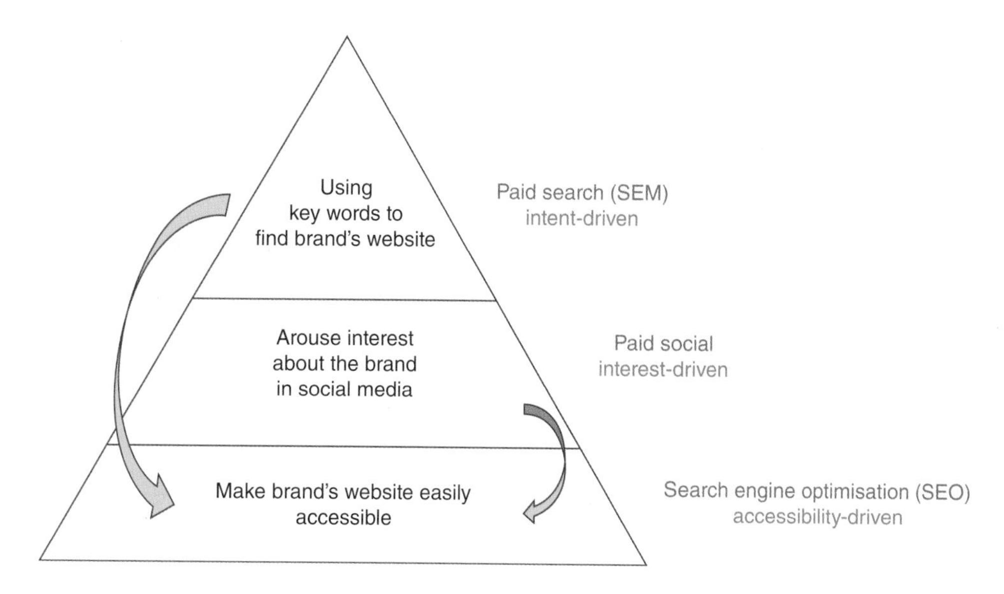

Figure 5.11 The relationship between paid search, paid social and search engine optimisation

SEARCH ENGINE OPTIMISATION

Search engine optimisation is the art and science of ensuring that the brand's URL emerges naturally (or organically) at the top of the search result page. This page is sometimes called Serp or search engine result page. The reason it is an 'art' is because the quality of the brand's landing page (associated with the listed URL) can be 'tweaked' to improve its quality (see later). This will in turn improve a visitor's experience at the website and grow its popularity. However, search engines such as Google, which has by far the largest share of internet search, do not publish their algorithms on how the position is decided. Furthermore, the ranking algorithms change with new developments (and without warning).

Generally, the more people visit our website the more likely its link will be listed high on the Serp. And the higher the URL position (preferably in the top three results) the higher the click-through rate (CTR).[62] Of all traffic 92% goes to the first page of Serp, with the top position taking 32.5% of the traffic (the second position, 17.6% and the third, 11.4%).[63] One can liken this position hierarchy as the set of brands that come to mind when we think about a product category. In other words, SEO is like an accessibility device. Thus, one should always make one's website popular so that its URL will be among the top 10 of organic searches listed on the first page. This increases the probability that it will be clicked.

Organic listings are generally more trusted than paid listings (discussed later in this chapter).[64] Of course if a website is new, there is little chance that it will be top listed in the search result since no one knows about it. This is where the quality of the content found on the website becomes important. Note, Google itself, unlike most websites, does not publish any content, but rather directs searchers to those websites that it thinks provide good content. By good, it means that the landing page of the website has a clear purpose (e.g. clear simple title) and its main content exudes expertise, authority and trustworthiness (or e-a-t). Thus, having reputation links attached to one's website can help raise its quality rating. Furthermore, if the website possesses e-commerce functionality (e.g. online shopping and financial transaction), it should also have satisfying customer service information. These are important characteristics Google looks for in landing pages of websites.[65] Visitors to such websites are more likely to stick around longer, and less likely to bounce (see earlier discussion on websites, microsites and mobile websites).

Google's business fundamentally requires users to trust its results, otherwise user experience will be compromised, which will in turn affect its search business. Its strength lies in its capability of finding quality content for its users in a split second. In the interests of providing better search results, Google recently introduced a new feature on its Serp. It shows what other people are also searching, providing additional links one can click on. This appears in a separate box (see figure 5.12) but only after you have clicked the original link and come back, presumably because the initial information provided was not satisfactory.

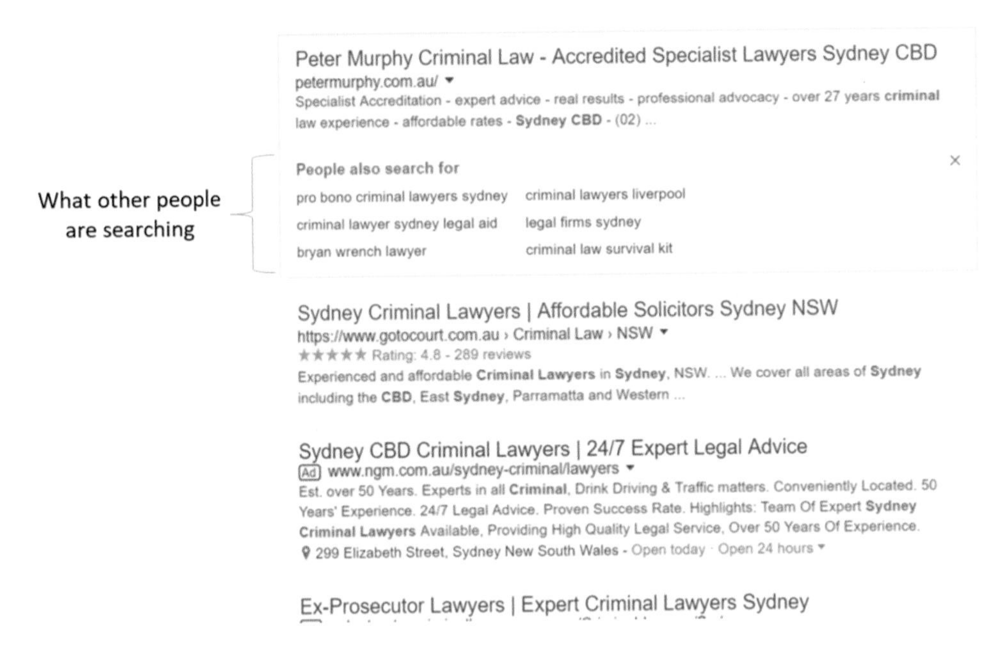

Figure 5.12 A page of search results showing what other people are searching

PAID SOCIAL

Social media platforms are now considered to be an important channel in an IMC campaign. Of all the platforms (e.g. Facebook, Twitter, Instagram, Snapchat), the biggest and by far the most important is Facebook. Facebook now has over 2 billion users worldwide. This is bigger than the population of China! But unlike the Chinese government, Facebook knows the buying predispositions of its users. Through users social musings, online preference-revealing activities, and their initial profile, Facebook can build a database of its users' profiles. This includes their first name, demographics, interest, behaviour, income level, address and, of course, their social connections. To make it easy for advertisers to select their target audience right down to this granular level (e.g. high-income earners who live within a certain distance from a retail outlet), Facebook built an easy-to-use interface, often consisting of nothing more than ticking of check-boxes from drop-down menus.

Barring privacy concerns, this has allowed organisations to insert even more relevant ads on the home pages of users. For instance, advertisers can decide which country, demographic age group, gender and interest to target, based on the profile they provided. As a form of 'behavioural targeting', Facebook ads will only appear to these selected users. This platform also allows advertisers to create their ads (e.g. writing a headline and text) and upload images, videos, links or offers, to be shown to the target audience one has selected, and the placement location within their Facebook page (e.g. right-hand column, News Feed). This is a good example of precision targeting where an advertiser knows exactly who the ad is exposed to and who has reacted to it (e.g. clicked, liked). This allows an advertiser to test different versions of their ads to different subgroups and to track its effectiveness. Advertisers can choose to pay for impressions or clicks, with a pre-set daily budget (e.g. $1000 per day), which allows them to work out their ROI for various possible executions. Facebook also has an inbuilt campaign management system that helps advertisers track its effectiveness.

One major advantage with social media advertising is its popularity with younger consumers who tend to be perpetually connected to their favourite social network via their smartphones. Consequently, social media ads are very effective in creating interest among this demographic, provided it is well executed.

PAID SEARCH

This is an important tool (sometimes called Search Engine Marketing or SEM) because a search engine is the first step a consumer takes when they search for information using key words. It is therefore an intent-driven behaviour; when a user searches for a product, it usually signals that the person is considering buying the brand. Paid search is more expensive to implement than paid social, but if well implemented, its ROI is higher simply because we are capturing users who are closer to making a purchase decision. In paid social, on the other hand, users are merely interacting with their social content, but happen to see a sponsored post.

Google dominates the search engine market with about 93% market share in Australia.[66] A consumer will type in a search term, and then a list of links will come up. There are two kinds: the first is called 'organic listing' and is based on natural (or organic) search; the second is the 'paid listing', or 'sponsored link', which is basically a text-based ad. The top 10 organic listings will appear on the first page of the search result (or Serp, as discussed earlier), with paid listings interspersed between these. A paid listing has the word 'Ad' in a box written next to the URL (see figure 5.13). Paid search constitutes the largest chunk of media spend on the internet.

For a brand's URL to be prominently listed in Serp, the quality of the brand's landing page must be high (see earlier discussion on SEO). The advertiser must also pay for key words to get on Serp. These are words consumers are likely to use while using the search engine. For instance, a

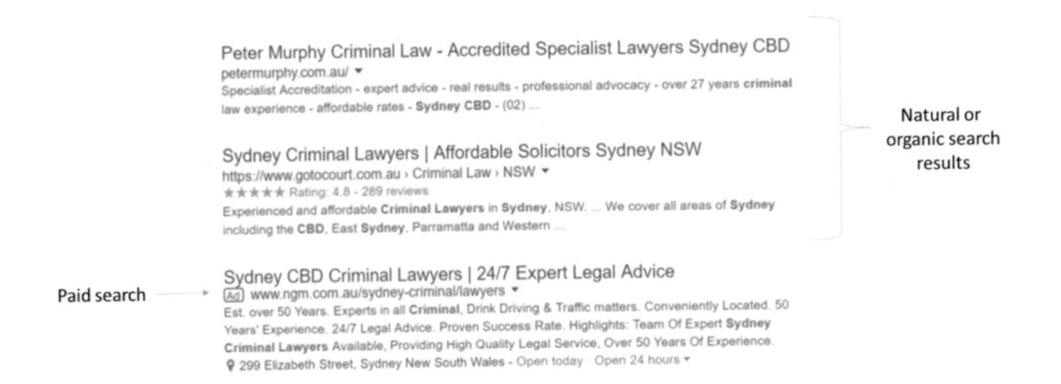

Figure 5.13 A page of search results showing the difference between natural (organic) and paid search results

criminal law practice in Sydney may pay $1.20 for key words like 'Est. over 50 years; Experts in Criminal, Drink Driving & Traffic matters.' Now, other law firms may also want to own these key words, and the greater the demand, the higher will be the suggested bid for these key words (from Google). If the law practice makes the winning bid for these key words, then whenever users search using these words, the URL of the law firm will appear since it is connected with these key words. And every time the URL of the law firm is clicked, it will cost the firm $1.20. This is called 'pay per click' (PPC). The total daily cost to the law firm will be the total number of clicks made per day. The firm can set a daily maximum budget they are willing to pay for these key words, or how these words are phrased (e.g. broadly or exactly). These key words therefore act like an entry ticket to get the brand's URL on the Serp. Its position on the Serp is essentially this: winning bid × page quality.

Note, these key words should be chosen carefully. Competitive analyses should be undertaken to choose the best set of key words without paying too much. This means one should always calculate how much it would cost to acquire a customer. Toolkits are now available (e.g. SEMRush) which allow one to more easily conduct key word research and track the key words used by competitors.

Google's AdWords system can then help advertisers put their paid listing ad together. The most important is to cleverly craft the key words into the headline and description of the ad. This is because these are the very words the searcher uses in their research. Therefore, seeing the same key words appear in the ad increases its relevance to the searcher and will encourage the searcher to click on the link. It is also important to include a benefit or a call-to-action or simply to arouse curiosity (e.g. using the words 'Learn more' or 'WATCH' if it is a video) to the ad. Since the ad is so short, every line should be crafted to sell. The advertiser can also include a link to product reviews, and even a phone number so that there is greater credibility. This will also allow the advertiser to capture more of the real-estate space on the Serp.

Search engines such as Google, Bing and Yahoo! also provide advertisers with detailed information about the performance of each sponsored ad via its own campaign management system. Table 5.6 is an example for a hotel chain, where Rutz and Bucklin investigate the effectiveness of two kinds of key words – generic and branded.

So, how do we interpret the numbers shown in table 5.6? The hotel chain pays Google $182.14 per day for the use of certain generic key words (e.g. 'hotels in Los Angeles'). This gives the chain

Table 5.6 Generic and branded key words (adapted from Rutz and Bucklin[67])

	Cost	Impressions	Clicks	No. of reservations	Click-through rate (CTR) (%)	Conversion rate (%)	Cost per click (CPC)	Cost per reservation
Generic key words	$182.14	126 051	334	4	0.26	1.20	$0.55	$45.54
Branded key words	$406.46	16 753	2292	138	13.68	6.02	$0.18	$2.95
Total	$588.60	142 804	2626	142	13.95	7.22	$0.72	$48.48

126 051 impressions, which result in 334 clicks. This means the CTR is only 0.26% (i.e. 334/126 051 × 100 = 0.26) for those generic key words. Out of 334 clicks, only four are converted into bookings. This means a conversion rate of only 1.2% (i.e. 4/334 × 100 = 1.2%). We can also work out the cost per click (CPC), which is $0.55 (i.e. $182.14/334 = $0.55) as well as cost per reservation, which is $45.54 (i.e. $182.14/4 = $45.54).

What about the performance of branded key words (e.g. 'Hilton in Los Angeles')? If we conduct a similar analysis, we find that it is much more cost-effective. For instance, instead of four reservations, these branded key words yield 138 conversions, with a conversion rate of 6.02%. Why is this so?

We know that consumers tend to use generic key words to search broadly first before settling on specific branded key words to conduct further research as they get closer to making a purchase. This does not mean that an organisation should abandon buying generic key words, because a search for these generic key words still points consumers to the relevant brand during the search. But how many generic key words should we buy? One automobile study found that 50% of key words generate no clicks at all, and that only 38% of generic key words generated 10 clicks or more (i.e. clicks through to the website).[68] If this study is any guide, it means that 60% of generic key words a firm buys are a waste of money.

Banner and display ads

These are small ads on other websites, used to lure target audiences to the home page. The objective here is to tempt viewers to switch from the host site for the ad to the brand page, by making these ads as interesting as possible. The key to success is the ability to capture consumers' attention. Therefore, banner ads should take advantage of the web's interactivity qualities, rather than being just a simple translation of the print ad, although, as we will see in chapter 7, there is no guarantee that interactivity is universally effective.

In recent years, however, the average CTR of such ads has dropped to below 1%. One study found that it is about 0.01%,[69] which is abysmal, yet this form of advertising constitutes the second-largest income, after search advertising. Banner ads can take many formats including the following:

- Pop-ups (or pop-behinds): ads that burst onto the screen when the user lands on or leaves the page. Pop-ups are intrusive and irritating for consumers.
- Skyscrapers: thin-format ads that run on the right- or left-hand side of a website. This kind of ad is generally more effective than horizontal ads.[70]

- Superstitials: animations that appear in a window when you go from one page of the website to another.[71] (These are interstitial ads that use different technology.)

Online classified ads

Classified ads still exist on the internet, albeit in a different way from their print format. Gumtree, for instance, is a community-based exchange service that allows people to buy or sell their goods or services. It does not charge advertising fees, except for real estate or job postings.

Figure 5.14 'The Best Job in the World' campaign

Although classified ads may appear old-fashioned, if cleverly used with another medium, the format can still be very powerful. A good example is the 2009 'Best Job in the World' campaign for Queensland Tourism (see figure 5.14). With the objective of raising brand awareness of the Great Barrier Reef, the advertising agency (Cummins Nitro) placed classified ads all over the world looking for a person to look after Hamilton Island. This person would be paid $8800 per month for six months, living rent-free in a luxurious villa. In return, the winner had to blog about their experience of feeding the fish, collecting mail and exploring the islands of the reef. A 'destination' website (www.IslandReefJob.com) was created for the campaign, allowing contestants to send in their application, a 60-second video explaining why they were the right person for the job. To whip up a frenzy, the public was encouraged to vote for their favourite applicant. The campaign, budgeted on a minuscule $1.2 million, garnered publicity worth $350 million around the world, and no doubt raised the profile of the island. Ben Southall, a 34-year-old from the UK, won the job.

Online ads and viral campaigns

Just as banner ads are not merely online versions of print ads, online ads are not the same as TVCs. Many marcoms managers think that all a digital strategy needs is to transfer TVCs into online formats, but nothing could be further from the truth. With such an approach, online ads (as in the case of banner display ads) would not take advantage of the interactive qualities of the internet, and neither would the viral potential of such ads be considered.

'Viral ads' are those that are passed along from one person to another, spreading quickly, almost like a disease. Figure 5.15 shows that, while in traditional media we 'spray' many in order to get at one buyer (see the picture on the left of the figure), in a viral campaign we target one influencer (or a few influencers) in order to help reach many (see the picture on the right). The logic is the reverse of that of traditional media (see chapter 8 for a more in-depth discussion of social influence).

Blogs and podcasts

Blogs, podcasts and tweets are user-generated content (UGC) found on social networking sites. Blogs are simply online musings written by a person, while podcasts are the audio version of a blog. One famous example of a blog is that of the cooking enthusiast Julie Powell, which later

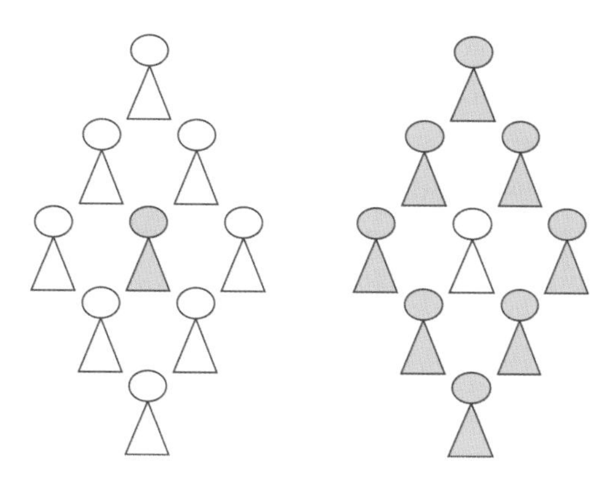

Figure 5.15 The conceptual difference between a traditional mass media campaign (left) and a viral campaign (right)

became a movie, *Julie & Julia*. In that blog, Powell wrote about her experience of cooking for a year from Julia Child's cookbook of French recipes. The blog had a huge following and became a book and then a movie.

Because of the personal nature of blogs, they generally have much higher credibility than advertising. However, not all blogs are that successful – in fact, most are not. Technocratic, an online research outfit, found that, out of 10 million active blogs, only 100 000 generate page views.[72] Blogging is time-consuming, and most bloggers eventually run out of steam.

While most personal blogs tend to offer one-way communication (i.e. from blogger to reader), blogs emanating from corporations are expected to field enquiries and address issues. Further, the person charged with blogging on behalf of the organisation has to clearly understand the firm's policies so that they do not inadvertently communicate the wrong message.

Organisations can also put out a series of podcasts to advise consumers on a whole series of issues, ranging from new products (e.g. General Motor cars) to advice on animal welfare (e.g. Purina Pet Food). Therefore, unlike blogs, podcasts tend to be better produced, sometimes with high-level production values, similar to a radio program. A number of blog platforms now exist on the internet including WordPress, Blogger, Tumblr, Medium, Svbtle and Quora. For professional bloggers, Google offers an advertising system, called Adsense, which allows one's blog site to be automatically populated with related PPC ads, so that every time a reader clicks on these ads, the blogger earns some income.

In recent years, podcasts have grown in popularity. This is because people are getting busier and mobility has increased. Listening to new content on the move (through the smartphone) is less taxing than trying to read a blog. We are also living in the age of assistance, where consumers are using voice-activate technology to do their chores (e.g. make a phone call, online shopping, play music or listen to an e-book). Listening to a podcast fits nicely into this new behaviour. However, the podcast suffers from one major weakness. It cannot easily redirect listeners to the brand's website, unlike a blog where the reader can click on a link. Nevertheless, one can consider both podcasts and blogs as 'ninja' tools in the sense that they can be used to arouse the interest of users without being too overtly sales-like. If the content is good, they will also be widely distributed among friends. This is one of the principles of content marketing strategy (see chapter 8).

Online videos

YouTube is another important social media website in terms of video UGC. In fact, it is the world's largest online video community, with a user base of more than 1.5 billion.[73] About 400 hours of videos are uploaded every minute, and more than 1 billion hours of YouTube videos are watched a day, which is more than Netflix and Facebook video combined. In online videos, YouTube dominates. With so much online content, it is not surprising that 90% of people say they discover new products through YouTube.[74]

There are many options one can choose to target one's ad to YouTube audiences (sometimes called pre-rolls) including their demographics, interests, specific YouTube topics, past interactions with our videos (called video retargeting). Finally, one can also choose the format in which to place one's ads. There are essentially three different formats to choose from:

- In-stream video advertisement: the ad appears on-screen before, during or at the end of video content. Users can skip the ad after five seconds. If the user does not skip but watches the full ad, it is called a 'TrueView'. And you pay only for those who watched the video ad.
- Overlay in-video advertisement: the ad appears on the lower 20% half of the video.
- Display advertisement: a banner ad of 300 × 250 pixels, which appears on the right-hand side of the screen (but not in the video).

Generally, YouTube users do not like advertisements, especially in-stream ads, which may cause them to leave the YouTube site altogether. However, if viewers are allowed to skip the ads after five seconds, they are about eight times more likely to stick around.[75]

Email

Email campaigns are one of the most cost-efficient forms of direct marketing and can be very effective if well implemented (see chapter 11). There is no need to print brochures or letters and no postage is required. Email is also effective in directing customers to the brand website. In some countries, including Australia, there is a requirement for prospects to 'double opt-in'. This means the potential customer must give his or her approval twice to be included in future correspondence with the organisation. For instance, when a prospect logs on to a firm's website, the firm can ask them to provide their email address if they consent to be contacted. The organisation then sends an email to the prospect confirming that they do indeed want to be contacted and, if so, the prospect clicks the 'yes' button provided. It is only after the second confirmation that the organisation can correspond with the prospect. The double opt-in requirement is not necessarily bad because only interested prospects will bother to make the effort. It also reduces spam.

In the wake of numerous scandals where the privacy of consumers has been violated, the European Union has instituted a new law called General Data Protection Regulation (GDPR), where data collection and processing are based on a set of principles designed to protect the individual's privacy. For instance, the permission of consumers must be granted before user-identification technology can be used to track how they behave when they visit a website. Furthermore, all consumer data collected must be anonymised. Breaches by an enterprise can incur a fine of €20 million or up to 4% of its annual turnover of the preceding financial year, whichever is greater.[76]

E-zines or zines

Electronic magazines are usually free and are known as 'e-zines' or simply 'zines'. Once a user has subscribed (again using the opt-in model), they will receive regular updates about the brand. This helps keep subscribers informed. Some organisations choose to keep their employees informed of the latest developments in the form of a 'staff news' e-zine. While the subscription may be free, the key is to provide interesting content so that the target audience will continue to be engaged.

Promotions, emails and e-zines can be used in combination to build a mailing list. Imagine that you are in the business of selling luxury boats and have just paid a handsome fee to exhibit in a boat show (such as the Sydney Boat Show). In that exhibition, many prospective customers will come and admire what you have to sell on the exhibition pier. One way of capturing the names of these prospects is to run a concurrent competition or promotion: to enter the competition, prospects have to sign up. Part of the prize can be a subscription to an e-zine about boats, which boat enthusiasts will value.

Mobile telephony, applications and location-based advertising

Of all the electronic devices we own, nothing is more personal than our smartphones. This is because we carry them with us everywhere, so that others can contact us immediately. Among adults, especially teenagers (12–17-year-olds), a smartphone is an especially valuable way for them to keep in contact with their peers. A study conducted by CISCO among 1800 generation-Y consumers (18 to 30-year-olds)[77] found the following:

- Nine out of 10 reported using their smartphones for texting, emailing and updating social media before starting their day as part of their morning ritual.
- One in five checked for email, text and social media updates every 10 minutes.
- Twenty-nine per cent said that they checked their phone so constantly that they lost count of the number of times.
- Three out of four used a smartphone in bed.
- More than one-third used a smartphone in the bathroom.
- More than 40 per cent reported that they would experience a 'withdrawal' effect and 'feel anxious, like part of me was missing' if they could not check their smartphone constantly.

In recent times, the smartphone is the device consumers turn to when they are idling. For instance, consumers are increasingly more likely to use their smartphones to watch videos. In the US, this is up to 42%. Without a doubt, it is the top device for video streaming or downloadable video content.[78] Although the screen is small, and the viewing experience not as good as a normal TV, millennials do not seem to mind. Perhaps, having grown up with their smartphone in their pockets, instant access may be more important. This separation from the TV (with its appointment-oriented programming, albeit some with time-shifting facility) is dubbed 'cord-cutting'.

However, the personal nature of mobile devices makes mobile advertising intrusive, especially when a user receives irrelevant solicitations.[79] The screens are also too small to be truly useful for effective advertising. Downloading of advertising images also takes time and drains the user's account balance. Complicating the creation of a mobile ad is the fact that screen sizes, capabilities and touch pads are different for each brand of smartphone. For this reason, a creative strategy based on textual information is more suited to this technology.

The growing popularity of tablets, however, overcomes many of the creative limitations of smartphones. Advertisers see tablets as equivalent to a desktop computer, and they do not need to radically change their creative designs. Further, as shown in table 5.7, the CTR (especially that of Apple's iPad) is much higher (at 2.2%) than any other wireless device, to the extent that advertisers are willing to pay a bit more for 1000 impressions.[80]

Table 5.7 CTR and CPM for a range of wireless devices

	Android smartphone	Android tablet	iPhone smartphone	iPad tablet
Click-through rate (CTR) (%)	1.10%	0.90%	1.50%	2.20%
Cost-per-thousand impressions (CPM) ($)	$0.80	$0.99	$1.04	$1.40

Smartphones open up new opportunities. Rather than trying to disrupt to gain attention with ads, a better way of using this technology is to empower consumers. One way is to build useful, fun branded apps for consumers to download. For example, Kraft created a menu app called 'iFood Assistant powered by Kraft', which has easy recipes, how-to videos, and even a built-in shopping list to help consumers save time.[81] Another way is to use technology to facilitate the distribution of incentives, for instance, by electronically offering coupons to shoppers to encourage purchase.[82] Technology entrepreneurs have also taken advantage of the GPS facility of smartphones to offer location-based services. For example, ShopSavvy informs users of where to buy a similar product most cheaply[83] and eHound enables users to find a store in their local area.[84] Yet another way is to enhance service experience. For instance, in the US, users can now pay for coffee at one of 7000 Starbucks outlets using their credit card app.[85] There are also apps that allow us to give gifts to our friends using our smartphones called social gifting.[86] Recently, cosmetic giant L'Oréal has developed a high-tech smartphone app that can help consumers see what they look like with different makeup. It was a stunning success.

CASE STUDY 5.2 L'ORÉAL'S *MAKEUP GENIUS* APP: WHEN AUGMENTED REALITY CHANGES CONSUMER BEHAVIOUR

Millennials are perhaps the most tech-savvy of consumers we have ever seen. Brought up with the smartphone as appendages, they are almost and always connected to the internet. They are also plugged into their social media, monitoring what their friends are doing. Now, imagine you are running a large company selling more than 2000 beauty and personal care products in over 130 countries. How do you ensure that the new generations of consumers (i.e. millennials) will continue to buy your products? Surely, a digital strategy must be on the cards. This is precisely the challenge the French cosmetic and health care giant L'Oréal faced. But to do this well, L'Oréal needed to understand the digital ecosystem within which millennials' consumer behaviour operated, and then devise a way in which a competitive advantage could be built around it.

Part of the solution was a number of creative assets L'Oréal used to enhance the millennials' shopping experience; in particular, to increase the trial of its products among new consumers. This should have increased market penetration, as more consumers became regular users. But the problem was this: trying new cosmetic products was a slow process and if carried out in retail cosmetic counters it was limited to a few products at a time. One digital solution was to use augmented reality (or AR). AR can be defined as using technology to superimpose a computer-generated image, in real time, onto a user's view of the real world, thus providing a composite view.[87] It is thus different from virtual reality (VR), which creates a totally artificial environment for the viewer (e.g. the experience of swimming with virtual sharks in a virtual ocean). In the case of AR, the existing environment is adopted, and new information is overlayed on top of it. For instance, in 2013, Ikea used AR technology to allow consumers to see 3D-animated furniture images in their catalogue when viewed through their smartphones.

L'Oréal's first experimentation with AR technology was a lipstick-only app. The objective was to see if it helped sales. It did, which then prompted L'Oréal to develop a new makeup AR smartphone app. L'Oréal partnered with Perfect Corp., which used its cosmetic editor technology called YouCam to incorporate all of L'Oréal's products.[88]

So how does this technology work? As we probably know, a smartphone can also act as a mirror by reversing the camera function, so that we take an image of our face – a selfie. Now, through AR technology, the image of our face can be overlayed with the makeup of our own choosing. So, as we smile or grimace, so does our cosmeticised mirror image we see, made possible with the smartphone's camera, facial recognition and motion tracking technology. It took 18 months, but the result was a ground-breaking app that allowed a consumer to scan their face and then overlap their image of their face with any of L'Oréal's cosmetic products. The app was launched in 2014 to a stunning success. It has been downloaded by 10 million people worldwide experimenting with 25 million different looks using 65 million products (and counting).[89]

The app is considered ground-breaking. For a start, it takes the guesswork out of buying makeup by making evaluation instantaneous. This reduces confusion. It also reduces the hassle of trying different cosmetic products quickly. It is also fun which in turn encourages even more trials. In terms of offline behaviour, consumers no longer need to visit cosmetic counters, which is traditionally where new product trials are carried out. For some countries like China where there is no culture of mothers teaching young girls how to apply makeup, the app is a godsend for the modern Chinese girl. These Chinese girls are also conservative, and unlikely to visit a cosmetic counter to try different makeup in public. The app also allows them to experiment with un-Asian colours like black eye shadows and lipsticks out of the glare of the public.[90] Consumers can also post their images on social media or send them to their friends which encourages conversation. Finally, the app also creates opportunities for interlinking of L'Oréal's different creative assets. For instance, visitors to L'Oréal stores and cosmetic counters can test the app, which in turn increases learning of the products and encourages online purchase through the company's website. This creates synergy right across the different assets. In short, hundreds of millions of consumers can test L'Oréal's cosmetic products, learn about them, and shop online because of cross-publicising.

The success of this app has a number of important lessons. The most important is that it enhances the pre-purchase shopping experience of millennials. Since the smartphone is never far away for this segment, it is a device that can assist their information search. In the US, 80% of consumers use their smartphone to find out more about the product before visiting a store. Up to 40 contact points can be consulted before a purchase is made,[91] and the more one is interested in a product, the more intensive is the information search.[92] In this regard, a smartphone app increases convenience.

The app also makes product evaluation fun. While the evaluation stage of the consumer decision journey is well known, very little is discussed in what form the actual experience should take. One theoretical framework we can apply is the IEI principle. This means the evaluation process should be **I**nteractive, **E**ntertaining and **I**nformative. The more a creative asset (i.e. app) possesses such qualities, the more it will be used. This is consistent with the findings that the app should be benevolent in nature, in that they do not possess an explicit selling function, but rather provide a worthwhile service so as to build up trust.[93]

This app also taps into the zeitgeist of the social media culture where seeking of social approval is so important. For females, physical attractiveness is increasingly important. It has been noted that the sales of cosmetic products have shot up as more and more females are taking selfies.[94] As this trend continues, and as positive words spread about this app, it will become a power creative asset for L'Oréal to use to acquire more customers. However, in the short term, this app is unlikely to significantly increase online sales. Worldwide, e-commerce sales of L'Oréal's products are less than 5%. L'Oréal still needs the support of retailers to push its numerous products.[95]

DISCUSSION QUESTIONS

1. In 2013, Ikea also had an AR-enhanced catalogue. Why do you think it is not as ground-breaking as L'Oreal's *Makeup Genius*?
2. Which technology do you think is more useful for marketing? Virtual reality (VR) or augmented reality (AR)? Why?
3. It is often said that changing consumer behaviour is difficult because consumers are creatures of habit. But L'Oreal's AR app shows that consumer behaviour can be changed to a profitable end. How does the app change consumer behaviour and why do you think there is very little resistance?

LOCATION-BASED ADVERTISING

The ubiquitous nature of smartphone usage combined with real-time tracking technology has enabled the development of location-based advertising (or LBA). This is an attractive option because now the message can take into account the specific location the consumer is in. For instance, if a consumer is in the vicinity of a product that has an offer (e.g. supermarket aisle), a notification can be sent to the consumer's smartphone. This not only raises the attention of the consumer (by being intrusive), but also encourages consumers to think that the products are more valuable and relevant.[96] As technology improves together with better knowledge of our customers, our ability to customise promotional offers will also improve. But one must be careful not to violate consumers' privacy and only implement this tool with their permission; for instance, agreeing to the condition when they download the app on their smartphone.

Quick response codes

One creative device that can bridge the online/offline divide using the smartphone is the quick response (QR) code.

Figure 5.16 A QR code

QR code evolved from the older barcode, which was invented by Denso Wave (a Toyota subsidiary)[97] to help track vehicles during manufacturing. Unlike barcodes, QR code is two-dimensional (see figure 5.16), which allows it to store several hundred times more digital information. A smartphone with a QR reader app can scan a QR code to reveal information and, more importantly, direct the phone's browser to a brand's website. The code is extremely versatile, as it can be attached to a product, packaging, print ad, flyers, store signage, outdoor poster, business cards, and even on the side of a bus. For instance, the QR code shown in figure 5.17 is found on a cookie, but in principle it can be used on any object.

Figure 5.17 A QR code used in an ad for Qkies[98]

The versatility of QR codes offers consumers a deeper brand experience, helping to bridge the offline/online divide. In department stores, for instance, shoppers can scan a QR code on a product or even at window signage to get more information. They can even connect to the store's website for online purchase. An even more innovative use of QR code was trialed by Australia Post in the Christmas of 2014 when they transformed the humble stamp into a QR code (see figure 5.18).

Through this, a sender can record a personal message to accompany the package. Upon receipt, the receiver can simply scan the QR stamp with their smartphone to retrieve the message (see figure 5.19). Using this technology, Australia Post essentially created a 'video stamp' which helps connect the sender and receiver digitally.[99]

Figure 5.18 A stamp being transformed into a QR code

Figure 5.19 Retrieving the message by scanning the QR code

THE VERSATILITY OF QR CODES

- They can contain and hence provide lots of information – such as product information, map links, URLs, read site summary (RSS) feed links and short message service (SMS) messages, as well as contact details. This is useful for time-poor consumers.
- They are convenient – consumers do not have to type complex and long URLs. This is useful in reducing attrition.
- They can direct consumers to the appropriate page, a specific video or a microsite created especially for the campaign. This is useful in overcoming clutter.
- They can be used to track consumer behaviour in real time. This is useful for evaluating the effectiveness of the campaign.

Advergames

In-game advertising can be used to reach teenagers, who are otherwise difficult to reach with traditional media. As with movies, advertisers can now use brand placement to reach this target audience in order to help subsidise the development cost. Gamers generally do not mind seeing brands while playing; in fact, they like the realism.[100] However, to achieve brand recall, the brand must be an integral part of the game.[101] For instance, in a racing-car game, sponsored by a car manufacturer, instead of just seeing the name of the car in the game setting (e.g. on a billboard on the race track), the gamer can actually interact with it (e.g. driving or customising the particular make and model). This increases their immersion in the game, and the brand attitude of the car increases among those who drive the car in the game.[102] It is as if games allow new users to trial the product, albeit virtually. It is interesting to note that the US Army has created game centres filled with computers and Xbox 360 controllers pre-loaded with military video games to assist their recruitment of soldiers.[103]

As clever as the US Army's strategy may be, The Coca-Cola Company has taken branded app gamification to another level. In Hong Kong, they came up with an idea of combining a smartphone app with a TV promotion. This is how it works: at 10 p.m. during the campaign period, a 'Coke' ad will appear on TV. In the ad, viewers will see 'Coke' bottle caps flying everywhere. Then, by shaking a smartphone rapidly at the ad ('choking'), viewers can 'catch' these caps, which can be used as tokens to earn discounts, buy mobile games and virtual collectibles. (Note that the word 'chok' is the latest Hong Kong teenage slang for rapid movement.) However, viewers can only play this game if they have this app, which was downloaded 380 000 times in the month of its release. People viewed the ad on TV, YouTube and Weibo 9 million times. Sales of 'Coke' have increased 11% year on year, while teen consumption of 'Coke' has increased from 78% to 83%. This is the most successful promotion campaign yet in Hong Kong.[104] According to Yau, it is a good example of the 'fluid integration of a traditional and modern medium, an innovative combination of the old and the new that successfully transformed a 30-second TV commercial into 30 seconds of fun'.[105]

Finally, from an ethical standpoint, advergames should *not* be used to target young children (aged between 8 and 9 years old). They are especially vulnerable to the persuasive effects of advergames compared to traditional advertising.[106]

MANAGERIAL APPLICATION: PUTTING IT TOGETHER

With so many different media options, how do we make coherent sense of it all? One approach is to strive for digital integration. Figure 5.20 demonstrates this notion. Since the internet has many online 'destinations', the objective is to always drive prospects to visit one's digital asset (e.g. the firm's landing page). Once there, various tactics can be used to encourage purchase (using e-commerce facilities). In the offline world, this is analogous to getting people to the point of purchase (e.g. retail point of sale or showroom). In other words, these 'destinations' become the sites of conversion.

This figure also shows that both online and offline activities (triggered by a high-quality creative idea) are now so closely linked that the marcoms manager should think of the two media in parallel during planning. Consumers no longer follow a single, uniform path to purchase but instead use multiple, overlapping channels to obtain information, whether online or offline. For instance, a consumer may first see a new product (e.g. a Dyson handheld vacuum cleaner) on TV, then jump on the internet to find out more, make a visit to a retail shop to see a live demonstration, use the internet again to compare prices (e.g. visit product review websites) or to get more personal recommendations (e.g. social media websites), before deciding whether to buy and, if so, from whom (either online of offline). In fact, the more excited a consumer is about a purchase, the more sources he or she will consult before deciding.[107] All this illustrates that a consumer's path to consumption is non-linear and hence one should cater for this possibility. About 25% of shoppers change their choice of brand after active search.[108]

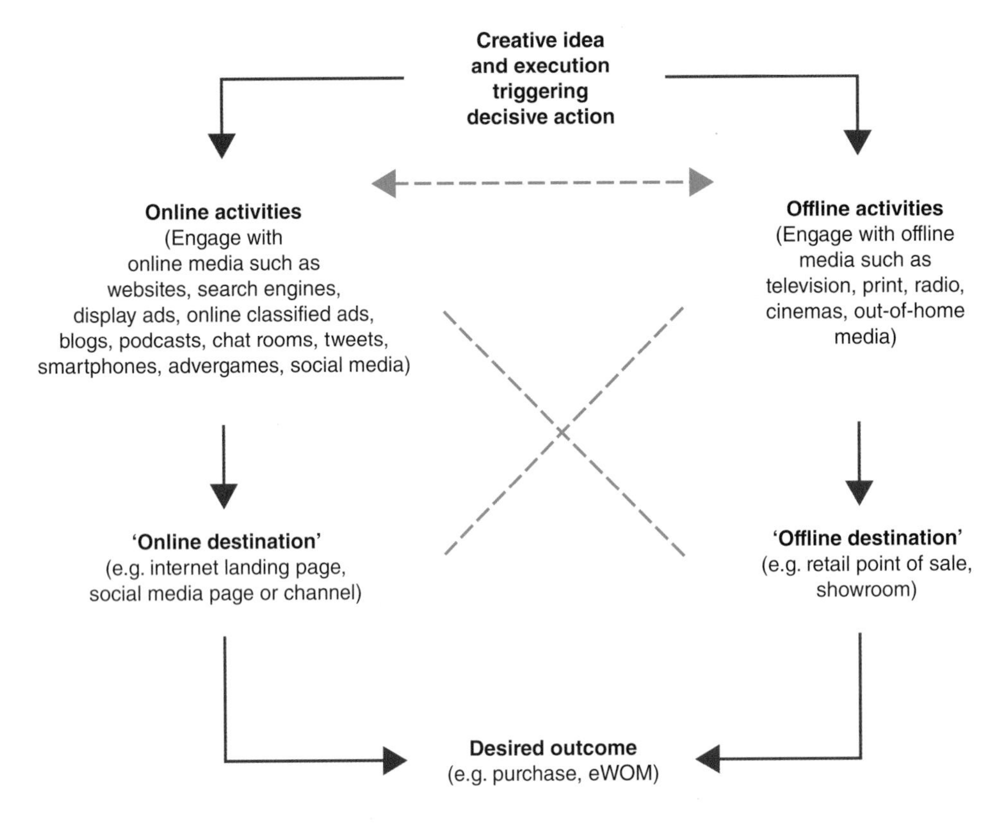

Figure 5.20 Towards digital coherence

FURTHER THINKING: HOW TO USE THE CONSUMER DECISION JOURNEY

LEARNING GOALS

After reading this section, you will understand:

- how to use the consumer decision journey as a guide for adapting one's communications
- the logic of measuring productive efficiencies along the decision journey.

Although the previous discussion in this chapter goes into considerable detail about the strength and weaknesses of different channels, what is missing is their relationship to the consumer decision journey. It is important to understand this since some mediums may be more suited to different parts of the decision journey.

Typically, mass media advertising is more efficient in need activation at the start of the decision journey because of its reach. One way of achieving need activation in the digital age is to arouse curiosity with the use of content marketing. Reading or viewing something interesting in a blog or post, for instance, will spark subsequent search and evaluation. This makes search engine optimisation important in order to facilitate ease of consumer search and evaluation. Similarly, print media with heavy information content is especially useful for consumer evaluation needs, as are product review websites. Further down the journey, purchase becomes the main objective. To facilitate this, e-commerce facility is almost mandatory. Communication channels (like a website) can also act like sales channels. This is consistent with the trend towards omnichannelling. For reactivation of purchase and building brand loyalty even further down the decision path, use tools that can precisely reach the target audience leveraging on their past purchase preferences. In this regard, email campaigns are especially cost effective. The best way to remember this principle is as follows (see figure 5.21):

(1) Use high-reach channels at the beginning of the decision journey for the big activation needs.
(2) Use precise and addressable channels to facilitate purchase or reactivate purchase at the latter part of the decision journey.
(3) In between these two extremes, ensure all positive branded information is readily accessible on as many platforms as possible for potential customers to find and evaluate. These micro-moments of search and evaluation can occur at any time[109] and on any device or app.

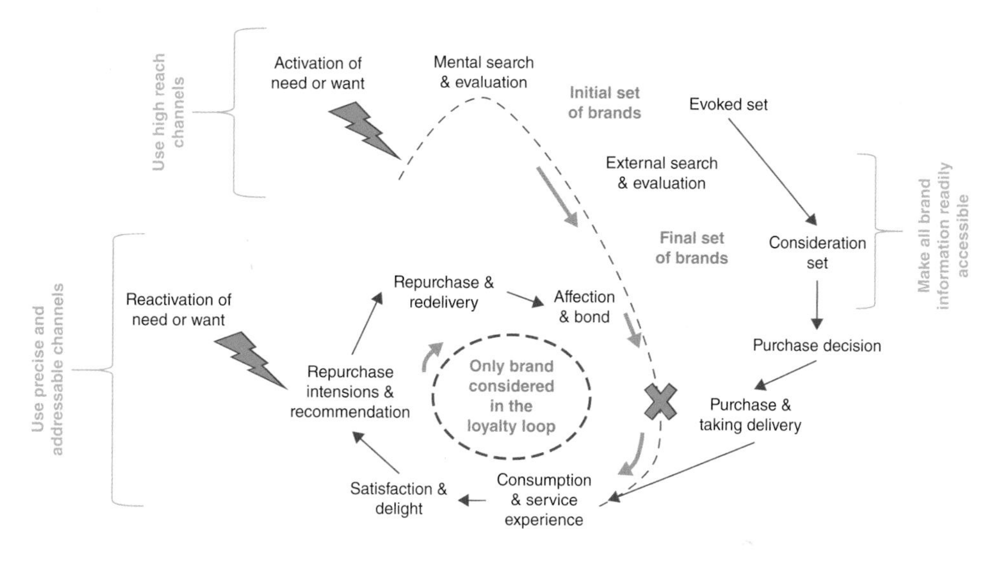

Figure 5.21 Adapt communication needs accordingly along the journey

DISCUSSION QUESTIONS

1. What is the difference between media, media vehicles and advertisements? Why is it important to draw a distinction between these terms?
2. How does the concept of opportunity to see (OTS) in respect of an ad relate to its gross impression? Give an example of the relationship in practice.
3. In measuring the audience size of a TV (or radio) program, what does its rating mean? How is this different from its share? Give a numerical example to illustrate the difference.
4. Billboard advertising tends to have limited reach because of its geographical limitations. How would you overcome this limitation if you were to design a campaign using billboards as one of your marcoms tools?
5. What is the difference between SEO, paid social and paid search? How are they related to each other?
6. What is the difference between cost per rating point (CPRP) versus cost per target audience rating point (CTARP) versus effective cost per impression (eCPM)? Is it important to know the difference? Please justify your answer.

7. Product placement can influence viewers in subtle ways. Why do you think that this can sometimes be effective?
8. In measuring the print media audience, what is the difference between circulation and readership?
9. Imagine that you are in the perfume business. Which print medium would you use in your advertising? Explain your reasons.
10. Do you think location-based advertising is the future of consumer engagement? Explain your opinion.
11. Explain how the versatility of a QR code can bridge the online/offline divide.
12. If consumers adopt both online and offline research activities before making a purchase, what does this mean for a marcoms manager in terms of planning?
13. Do you think the consumer decision journey is important in planning a marcoms strategy? Explain your answer.

NOTES

1 Dentsu Aegis Network, 'Global ad spend forecasts', 2018. Accessed October 2020 at www.carat.com/caratcdn/media/9388/jan-2018-executive-summary-final.pdf.

2 Srivinasan et al. were able to show that even for low-involvement, large-packaged consumer goods getting consumers to the firm's website is twice more effective than earned media (i.e. Facebook likes) and TV in driving its sales. See S Srinivasan, OJ Rutz and K Pauwels, 'Paths to and off purchase: quantifying the impact of traditional marketing and online consumer activity', *Journal of the Academy of Marketing Science*, 44, 2016, pp. 440–53.

3 R Zomok, 'Omnichannel returns are no longer optional', *Retail Touchpoints*, August 2019. Accessed January 2010 at www.retailtouchpoints.com/features/executive-viewpoints/omnichannel-returns-are-no-longer-optional.

4 Traditionally, the acronym is just POE to stand for the three forms of media, Paid, Owned and Earned. However, with the rise of social media, the POE acronym is incomplete. Some researchers differentiate between Earned Traditional and Earned Social, but this is confusing. To more clearly delineate the difference, Earned Social should be termed Shared Media because fundamentally the content is generated by consumers for the purpose of sharing with their friends. Earned Media should be reserved for professionals of traditional media who write about the firm or issue.

5 I prefer the term Owned Asset rather than Owned Media because the main objective of this principle is to drive sales, and not simply to impart information.

6 A Green, 'Paid, owned and earned media: Integration's Holy Grail', *Admap*, June, 2011. Accessed February 2018 at www.warc.com/content/paywall/article/admap/paid_owned_and_earned_media_integrations_holy_grail/94566.

7 The POSSE model is somewhat stylised since there are many situations where a media can possess more than one characteristic. For instance, a company's website can also encourage social sharing through the forum section of the website, and similarly, a social media tool like Facebook

also carries paid advertising. But predominantly the POSSE model signals its main characteristics.

8 I thank Shalini Parthiban, digital optimisation specialist at Commonwealth Bank, for sharing this piece of information.

9 'Hungerithm (Snickers Campaign)', Clemenger Proximity, 28 June 2018. Accessed July 2020 at https://vimeo.com/277569972.

10 S Khamis, L Ang and R Welling, 'Self-branding, "micro-celebrity" and the rise of social media influencers', *Celebrity Studies*, 8(2), 2017, pp. 191–208.

11 *Australian video viewing report*, quarter 4, 2017, Regional TAM, OzTAM, Nielsen, 2018. Accessed August 2018 at www.nielsen.com/au/en/insights/reports/2018/screen-time-still-an-australian-pastime.html.

12 See S Rosengren, M Eisend, M Dahlen and S Koslow, 'A meta-analysis of when and how advertising creativity works', *Journal of Marketing*, 2020, forthcoming.

13 J Lafayette, 'Study shows TV's impact on consumer purchasing behaviour', *TV Week*, 16 April 2009. Accessed January 2013 at www.tvweek.com.

14 B Hemphill, 'Research proves the power and effectiveness of TV across devices', *Future of TV Advertising Forum*, February, 2018. Accessed September 2019 at www.warc.com/content/paywall/article/research-proves-the-power-and-effectiveness-of-tv-across-devices/121514.

15 OzTAM, 'Frequently asked questions'. Accessed August 2018 at www.oztam.com.au/FAQs.aspx.

16 P Kohr, 'How much does TV advertising cost?' *Savvy SME*. Accessed August 2018 at www.savvysme.com.au/question/9-how-much-does-tv-advertising-cost.

17 P Revior, 'Ready for the six-minute advert break? Ofcom relaxes rules on commercials (... so you won't need to rush to put the kettle on)', *Daily Mail*, 23 February 2011. Accessed January 2013 at www.dailymail.co.uk/news/article-1359637/6-minute-advert-break-Ofcom-relaxes-rules-commercials.htm.

18 S White and C Dawson, 'TV's ad position. It's make or break', *Admap*, 496, July/August 2008, pp. 34–6.

19 P Barry, *The advertising concept book*, Thames & Hudson, London, 2008; 'TV advertisement', *Wikipedia*. Accessed July 2013 at en.wikipedia.org/wiki/TV_advertisement.

20 *Australian video viewing report*, quarter 4, 2017, (2018), note 11.

21 J Clift, 'Marketing in the digital age: Binet and Field on how media choices impact effectiveness', *WARC*. Accessed September 2019 at www.warc.com/content/paywall/article/marketing-in-the-digital-age-binet-and-field-on-how-media-choices-impact-effectiveness/109330.

22 L Gevelber, 'Second-screen searches: crucial I-want-to-know moments for brands', *Think with Google*, 2015. Accessed August 2018 at www.thinkwithgoogle.com/advertising-channels/mobile-marketing/second-screen-searches-crucial-i-want-to-know-moments-for-brands/.

23 M Joo, KC Wilbur, B Cowgill and Y Zhu, 'TV advertising and online search,' *Management Science*, 60(1), 2014, pp. 56–73.

24 'How to use TV effectively in the media mix', *Warc Best Practice*, September 2017. Accessed September 2019 at www.warc.com/content/paywall/article/how-to-use-tv-effectively-in-the-media-mix/112320.

25 S Bellman, A Schweda and D Varan, 'The importance of social motives for watching and interacting with digital TV', *International Journal of Market Research*, 52(1), 2010 pp. 2–15.

26 R Bhargave and NV Montgomery, 'The social context of temporal sequences: why first impressions shape shared experiences', *Journal of Consumer Research*, 40(3), 2013, pp. 501–17.

27 People's liking of the advertised brand plus their ability to remember the name of the brand decreases with more social viewing. See S Bellman, JA Robinson, B Wooley and D Varan, 'The effects of social TV on TV advertising effectiveness', *Journal of Marketing Communications*, 23(1), 2017, pp. 73–91.

28 'How to use TV effectively in the media mix', (2017), note 24.

29 S Bellman, A Schweda and D Varan, 'A comparison of three interactive TV ad formats', *Journal of Interactive Advertising*, 10(1), 2009, pp. 14–34.

30 T Nudd, 'Test drive a Volkswagen . . . inside a print ad', *Creativity*, 9 March 2011. Accessed August 2018 at www.adweek.com/creativity/test-drive-volkswagen-inside-print-ad-126972/.

31 S Sadowski, 'Vote for your favorite Super Bowl 2018 ad through noon today', *Pennsylvania Entertainment*, 6 February 2018. Accessed August 2018 at www.pennlive.com/entertainment/index.ssf/2018/02/super_bowl_2018_ad_vote_here.html.

32 'About OzTam ratings', https://oztam.com.au/AboutOzTAMRatings.aspx. Accessed September 2019.

33 N Cameron, 'Explainer: What VOZ is and what it isn't', *CMO*, 27 February 2020. Accessed July 2020 at www.cmo.com.au/article/671096/explainer-what-voz-what-it-isn-t/.

34 A Hickman, 'Australia to roll out "world leading" addressable TV solutions this year', *AdNews.com*, 7 May 2018. Accessed August 2018 at www.adnews.com.au/news/australia-to-roll-out-world-leading-addressable-tv-solutions-this-year#J1IMFmC0uwBQbFSx.99.

35 A Murray, L Chiarella and M Fox, 'The impact of SVOD on the media landscape', *Media Federation Australia Conference*, UM Media Agency, 21 February 2020.

36 J Myers, 'The near- and far-term future of addressable TV advertising', *Tomorrow Today*, 11 July 2018. Accessed August 2018 at www.mediavillage.com/article/the-near-and-far-term-future-of-addressable-tv-advertising.

37 R Welday, 'Addressable advertising: an upgrade for travel brands', *Adage*, 11 December 2017. Accessed August 2018 at http://adage.com/article/att-adworks/addressable-advertising-upgrade-travel-brands/311556/.

38 Experian, 'Addressable TV' White paper', Experian Information Solutions, Inc., 2018. Accessed August 2018 at www.experian.com/marketing-services/addressable-tv-advertising-whitepaper.html.

39 The rise of this medium can be seen by the large number of Australians now listening to Spotify, about 8.7 million monthly.

40 Screen Australia, 'Cinema industry trends screens and theatres'. Accessed September 2019 at www.screenaustralia.gov.au/fact-finders/cinema/industry-trends/screens-and-theatres.

41 G Page of Millward Brown, found that mediums with 'big' visuals like cinema generally tend to create better emotional bonding with consumers (+3.62%), followed by outdoors (+1.89%) and then magazines (+1.53%). See 'Millward Brown on why salience isn't everything – and magazines still matter'. Accessed September 2019 at www.warc.com/content/paywall/article/event-reports/millward-brown-on-why-salience-isnt-everything—and-magazines-still-matter/107898.

42 EA van Reijmersdal, PC Neijens and EG Smit, 'Effects of TV brand placement on brand image', *Psychology and Marketing*, 24(5), 2007, pp. 403–20.

43 P Gupta and K Lord, 'Product placement in movies: the effect of prominence and mode on audience recall', *Journal of Current Issues and Research in Advertising*, 20(1), 1998, pp. 47–59.

44 D Delorme and L Reid, 'Moviegoers' experiences and interpretations of brand in films revisited', *Journal of Advertising*, 28(20), 1999, pp. 71–95.

45 F Bronner, 'In the mood for advertising', *International Journal of Advertising*, 26(3), 2007 pp. 333–55.

46 The 'M' in CPM represents the Roman numeral for 1000 (or milli), although it makes more sense in modern days to call this CPT.

47 M Kubin, 'eCPMs: you only get one chance to make an effective impression', *Invidi*, 8 January 2018. Accessed August 2018 at www.invidi.com/blog/ecpms-you-only-get-one-chance-to-make-an-effective-impression/.

48 J Duke, 'Out-of-home advertising market tipped to hit $1 billion in 2018', *Sydney Morning Herald*, 19 December 2017. Accessed August 2018 at www.smh.com.au/business/companies/out-of-home-advertising-market-tipped-to-hit-1-billion-in-2018-20171215-p4yxra.html.

49 RT Wilson, DW Baack and BD Till, 'Creativity, attention and the memory for brands: an outdoor advertising field study', *International Journal of Advertising*, 34(2), 2015, pp. 232–61.

50 DD Beijer, 'Driver distraction due to roadside advertising', Masters thesis, Graduate Department of Mechanical and Industrial Engineering, University of Toronto, 2002. Cited in Wilson, Baack and Till (2015), 'Creativity, attention and the memory for brands', note 49.

51 C Thomas-Smith, and G Barnett, 'Seeing is believing: viewing engagement in place-based Media', in *Your audience D media consumer C generator*, DS Fellows (ed.), ESOMAR, Amsterdam, 2010, pp. 247–62. Cited in Wilson, Baack and Till (2015), 'Creativity, attention and the memory for brands', note 49.

52 H Graf, 'Outdoor as the segue between mass and class', *Brandweek*, 20 July 1999, p. 19.

53 Wilson, Baack and Till (2015), 'Creativity, attention and the memory for brands', note 49.

54 See Wilson, Baack and Till (2015), 'Creativity, attention and memory for brands', note 49.

55 EJ Schultz, 'By the numbers: Coca-Cola's Times Square billboard', *Adage*, 12 September 2017. Accessed August 2018 at http://adage.com/article/media/numbers-coca-cola-s-times-square-billboard/310406/.

56 R Micaleff, 'Giant Bonds balls hit Melbourne billboard', *AdNews*, 18 April 2016. Accessed August 2018 at www.adnews.com.au/news/giant-bonds-balls-hit-melbourne-billboard#dclBmhDVG5FduWpI.99.

57 A Jardin, '"Tomb Raider" fans spend 24 hours enduring the harsh outdoors on a billboard', *AdAge*, 12 November 2015. Accessed August 2018 at http://creativity-online.com/work/xbox-tomb-raider-survival-billboard/44250.

58 A Ledger, 'Event Awards 2016: Why Microsoft Xbox Survival Billboard took the Grand Prix', *Campaign*, 7 November 2016. Accessed August 2018 at www.campaignlive.co.uk/event-awards-2016-why-microsoft-xbox-survival-billboard-took-grand-prix/%7Bsubjects%7D/article/1414703.

59 Although such posters are strictly not street furniture but more of an ambient ad, they are used to illustrate the idea of a captive audience.

60 G Rosenkrans, 'The creativeness and effectiveness of online interactive rich media advertising', *Journal of Advertising Research*, 9(2), 2009. Accessed January 2013 at www.jiad.org/article114.html.

61 Eyetrack III, 'Online news consumer behavior in the age of multimedia', 2004. Accessed January 2013 at www.poynter.org/extra/eyetrack2004/advertising.htm.

62 S Buresh, 'Organic SEO or pay-per-click advertising – which should you choose?', *AJ 2000 Internet Marketing website*, 2012. Accessed April 2012 at www.aj2000.com/articles/seo-vs-ppc.htm.

63 J Lee, 'No. 1 position in Google gets 33% of search traffic', *SEO*, 20 June 2013. Accessed August 2018 at https://searchenginewatch.com/sew/study/2276184/no-1-position-in-google-gets-33-of-search-traffic-study.

64 Ibid.

65 'Search quality evaluation guidelines', *Google Inc*, 2018, pp. 18–21.

66 Statscounter, GlobalStats. Accessed August 2018 at http://gs.statcounter.com/search-engine-market-share/all/australia/#monthly-201801-201808.

67 See OJ Rutz and RE Bucklin, 'From generic to branded: a model of spillover in paid search advertising', *Journal of Marketing Research*, 48, 2011, pp. 87–102.

68 O Rutz, M Trusov and RE Bucklin, 'Modeling indirect effects of paid search advertising: which keywords lead to more future visits?', *Marketing Science*, 30(4), 2011, pp. 646–65.

69 E Sherman, 'Ad campaign smackdown: Facebook vs Google', *Inc.*, 24 May 2012. Accessed April 2013 at www.inc.com/erik-sherman/ad-campaign-smackdown-facebook-v-google.html.

70 S Outing and L Ruel, 'The best of Eyetrack III: what we saw when we looked through their eyes', *Poynter*, 2004. Accessed July 2020 at www.math.unipd.it/~massimo/corsi/tecweb2/Eyetrack-III.pdf.

71 P Barry, *The advertising concept book*, Thames & Hudson, London, 2008.

72 D Quenqua, 'Blogs falling in an empty forest', *New York Times*, 7 June 2009. Accessed January 2013 at www.nytimes.com.

73 Statista, 'YouTube – statistics & facts', 2018. Accessed August 2018 at www.statista.com/topics/2019/youtube/.

74 Google/Magid Advisors, Global (US, CA, BR, UK, DE, FR, JP, IN, KR, AU), 'The role of digital video in people's lives', August 2018.

75 M Pashkevich et al., 'Empowering online advertisements by empowering viewers with the right to choose', *Journal of Advertising Research*, December 2012, pp. 451–7.

76 'What is General Data Protection Regulation?', *Forbes*, 14 February 2018, Consumer Tech. Accessed September 2019 at www.forbes.com/sites/quora/2018/02/14/what-is-general-data-protection-regulation/#646c1f7b62dd.

77 This is based on the *Cisco Connected World Technology Report*, 2012. See also 'Toothpaste, toilet paper and texting – say good morning to Gen Y', press release, 12 December 2012. Accessed February 2013 at http://newsroom.cisco.com/release/1114955.

78 Experian, 'Addressable TV', white paper, Experian Information Solutions, Inc., 2018. Accessed August 2018 at www.experian.com/marketing-services/addressable-tv-advertising-whitepaper.html.

79 Y Truonga and G Simmons, 'Perceived intrusiveness in digital advertising: strategic marketing implications', *Journal of Strategic Marketing*, 18(3), 2012, pp. 239–56.

80 These figures are based on 1–7 January 2013. See J Constine, 'iPad becomes advertisers' best friend', *TechCrunch*, 16 January 2013. Accessed March 2013 at http://techcrunch.com/2013/01/16/ipad-becomes-advertisers-best-friend.

81 You can check out the iFood Assistant here: www.kraftrecipes.com/media/ifood.aspx. Accessed January 2013.

82 There is even an app for coupons that you can download from Apple iTunes, at https://itunes.apple.com/au/app/the-coupons-app/id461062822?mt=8. Accessed January 2013.

83 Visit this innovative website: http://shopsavvy.mobi/. Accessed January 2013.

84 Visit this website: www.ehoundplatform.com/mobile-store-locator. Accessed January 2013.

85 H McCracken, 'Pay with Square at Starbucks: the biggest moment yet for mobile-phone wallets', *Time*, 8 August 2012. Accessed January 2013 at http://techland.time.com/2012/08/08/pay-with-square-at-starbucks-the-biggest-moment-yet-for-mobile-phone-wallets/#ixzz2Iy4kYTbS.

86 A US company called Karma, which has been acquired by Facebook, specialises in this. See R Needleman, 'You'll be using this soon: Karma social gift-giving', *CNET*, 27 February 2012.

Accessed January 2013 at http://news.cnet.com/8301-19882_3-57386261-250/youll-be-using-this-soon-karma-social-gift-giving.

87 Google dictionary: www.google.com.au/search?q=What+is+augmented+reality%3F&ie=utf-8&oe=utf-8&client=firefox-b&gfe_rd=cr&dcr=0&ei=pPyRWsbjEczr8Af25qnwBg. Accessed February 2018.

88 Business wire, 'L'Oréal joins YouCam Makeup, Perfect Corp.'s Augmented Reality Makeover app', 2017. Accessed February 2018 at www.businesswire.com/news/home/20170710005692/en/L'Oréal-Joins-YouCam-Makeup-Perfect-Corp.'s-Augmented.

89 Makep Genius, McCann: www.mccann.com/work/makeup-genius. Accessed February 2018.

90 A Doland, 'Why millions in China downloaded L'Oreal's Makeup Genius app', *Adage*, 25 August 2015. Accessed February 2018 at http://adage.com/article/special-report-women-to-watch-china-2015/4-7-million-chinese-women-downloaded-l-oreal-s-makeup-app/299878/.

91 A Borde, 'Online beauty: L'Oréal's e-commerce strategy', *L'Oréal Monthly Digest*, 2018. Accessed February 2018 at www.monthly-digest-loreal.com/en/article/english-online-beauty-loreals-e-commerce-strategy/.

92 Ibid.

93 G Urban and F Sultan, 'The case of benevolent mobile apps', *MIT Sloan Management Review*, 56(2), 2015, pp. 31–7.

94 C Sorrell, 'L'Oreal makeup sales jumped because people want to look good in selfies' *FastCompany*, 18 February 2016. Accessed July 2020 at www.fastcompany.com/3056798/loreal-makeup-sales-jumped-because-people-want-to-look-good-in-selfies.

95 Borde (2018), 'Online beauty', note 91.

96 AE Hühn et al., 'Does location congruence matter? A field study on the effects of location-based advertising on perceived ad intrusiveness, relevance & value', *Computers in Human Behavior*, 73, 2017, pp. 659–68.

97 See 'Will the new iQR Code take the spotlight?', *Mobile Commerce News*, 28 February 2011. Accessed January 2013 at www.qrcodepress.com/tag/toyota-denso-wave.

98 Image from J Schöning, Y Rogers and A Krüger, 'Digitally enhanced food: pervasive computing', *IEEE*, 11(3), 2012, pp. 4–6.

99 Australia Post Video Stamp: www.dandad.org/awards/professional/2014/integrated-earned-media/23071/australia-post-video-stamp/?subscribe_user. Accessed September 2019.

100 M Nelson, H Keum and R Yaros, 'Advertainment or adcreep? Game players' attitudes toward advertising and product placements in computer games', *Journal of Interactive Advertising*, 5(1), 2004, pp. 3–30.

101 FE Dardis, M Schmierbach and AM Limperos, 'The impact of game customization and control mechanisms on recall of integral and peripheral brand placements in videogames', *Journal of Interactive Advertising*, 12(2), Spring 2012, pp. 1–12.

102 T Mackay et al., 'The effect of product placement in computer games on brand attitude and recall', *International Journal of Advertising*, 28(3), 2009, pp. 423–38.

103 D Resinger, 'Would video games get you to join the Army?', *CNET*, 9 January 2009. Accessed January 2013 at http://news.cnet.com/8301-13506_3-10138411-17.html.

104 J Kirby, 'A unique approach to marketing Coca-Cola in Hong Kong', *Harvard Business Review*, 14 February 2013. Accessed March 2013 at http://blogs.hbr.org/hbr/hbreditors/2013/02/a_unique_approach_to_marketing_coca_cola_in_hong_kong.html?utm_source=feedburner&utm_medium=feed&utm_campaign=Feed%3A+harvardbusiness+%28HBR.org%29.

ASKHAM BRYAN
COLLEGE
LEARNING RESOURCES

105 P Yau, 'Coca-Cola: Chok! Chok! Chok!', Warc Prize for Asian Strategy, Runner-up, Low Budget, 2012. Accessed March 2013 at www.warc.com.

106 L Hudders, V Cauberghe and K Panic, 'How advertising literacy training affect children's responses to TV commercials versus advergames', *International Journal of Advertising*, 2016, 35(6), pp. 909–31.

107 E Keller and B Fay, 'Word-of-mouth advocacy', *Journal of Advertising Research*, December, 2012, pp. 459–64.

108 T Powers, et al., 'Digital and social media in the purchase decision process', *Journal of Advertising Research*, December, 2012, pp. 479–89.

109 J Lecinski, *Winning the Zero Moment of Truth*, Google, 2011.

CHAPTER 6
ADVERTISING CREATIVITY

CHAPTER OVERVIEW

This chapter and chapter 7 are about advertising, which is a paid form of communication by a sponsor. The aim of this chapter is to give the reader a better understanding of creativity and its importance to advertising. Although advertising is only one marcoms tool, it is the most important tool for brand (re)positioning. However, for advertising to be effective, it must possess the creative power to cut through the noise and clutter.

This chapter explores the importance of advertising creativity and sets out how to get it right. This is a complex area because our processing of a creative ad can be completely hijacked by unintended associations, which commonly occurs when we attempt anything original. To minimise this, a marcoms manager needs to understand the theory of advertising creativity, as well as how to nurture the emergence of the creative idea, which must be guided by a creative strategy summarised in a creative brief.

Learning goals

After reading this chapter, you will understand:

- a theoretical framework of communication
- why creativity is important
- a range of theoretical perspectives of creativity
- theories of remote associate thinking (RAT) and remote associative matching (RAM)
- how processing can go wrong with creative advertising
- what a creative idea is, and how it can be creatively integrated
- the importance of developing a sound creative strategy first (using convergent thinking) before coming up with a creative idea (using divergent thinking)
- why a creative brief is important, and the characteristics of a good one
- the role of ideation principles in the development of a creative idea.

Imagine that you are asking someone out for a date. How would you approach him or her? No doubt, you would spend some time thinking of an effective approach, perhaps an interesting opening line to arouse their interest, or maybe try to catch their eye with a smile across the room. Well, advertising is not unlike trying to get a date – you need something interesting to stand a chance. This chapter is about making an ad interesting through creativity in order to overcome a host of communication barriers (see chapter 1).

DO ALL ADS HAVE TO BE CREATIVE?

Before we discuss creativity in advertising, we might ask whether all ads need to be creative. The answer is no. Many promotional ads that rely on price discounts can be just as effective. The cost of media placements of such ads is usually low, and the ad is a one-off and not part of a major campaign. A price discount, especially a large one, is usually enough to motivate consumers to buy. The downside, as we will see in chapter 11, is that it does not necessarily enhance brand equity. Having said that, we may wonder whether, even with discount ads, a little creativity is still useful; at least people will find it interesting to read. They may also come to like the ad – not just the discount – and, in turn, the brand. Therefore, all things being equal, a clever discount ad will probably be more effective than an ordinary one. Figure 6.1 is an example of a clever discount ad from Avis.

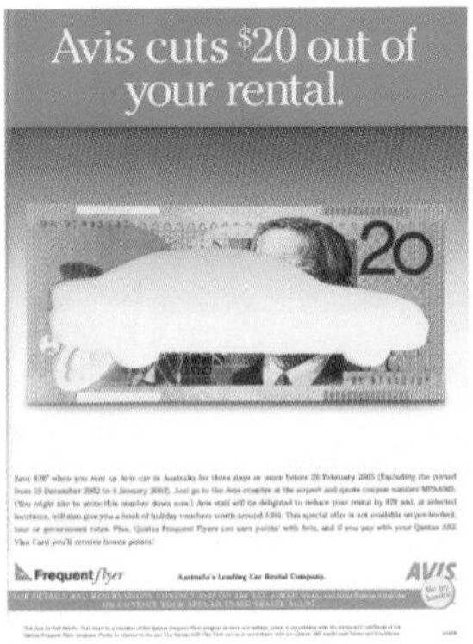

Figure 6.1 A discount ad that is also creative

WHY CREATIVITY IS IMPORTANT

There is no doubt that creativity is a critical component for the success of an advertising campaign. Given the communication barriers we discussed in chapter 1, a big idea is necessary to break through the noise and clutter to engage the audience. 'Creative' means that the ad is original yet relevant. Such ads are good predictors of advertising success. They tend to attract a greater level of attention,[1] create more consumer enjoyment, and have a positive association with purchase intent ($r = 0.55$).[2] In fact, after market share, creative execution is the most important driver of advertising profitability.[3]

But what do 'original' and 'relevant' mean? 'Original' means that the execution is unique, which will make the ad distinctive from other ads and help cut through the noise and clutter. 'Relevant' means that the message is well branded and compelling to the target audience. A high-quality creative idea is one that encapsulates all these qualities in a coherent manner that can solve (or at least help to solve) a business problem.

Of all the traditional media (i.e. print, radio and TV), creativity is the most important for TV advertising because of the large cost in media placement. For instance, a 30-second TV commercial in a popular TV program in the US costs at least US$200 000. So, if a TV ad is not effective, a marcoms manager is wasting US$200 000 every 30 seconds! For this reason, this chapter and chapter 12 (on advertising pre-testing and campaign evaluation) concentrate on TV advertising.

One early study based on a survey of experts (with a sample of 114 advertisers and agencies) found that, for the same budget, the selling power of a great creative idea can exceed that of an ordinary budget by 10 times, and that this is far more profitable than cutting costs.[4] Another early study found that highly persuasive ads are seven times more important than media investment in predicting market share in the next four months.[5] Blair[6] has illustrated this dramatically for TV ads introducing new products. Poor-quality ads cannot significantly increase the trial rate beyond 2%, even if they are backed up with huge media investment (e.g. at 7000 gross rating points). Figure 6.2 illustrates this idea, showing the difference between a high-quality and low-quality creative ad.

This study has a few implications. First, it implies that once you have a low-quality ad, no amount of media spend will help lift its effectiveness. Second, it goes against the (still) prevailing notion that ads need time to 'wear in'. So, just like a new pair of jeans, which need repeated wearing before they become comfortable, a new ad is said to need more media spend before its effects come through. And if the effects are not observed, then this suggests that more spend is needed. We can quickly see how self-serving this circular argument is, since more repetition means more commission for the agency (if the reward is structured as such). Research has shown

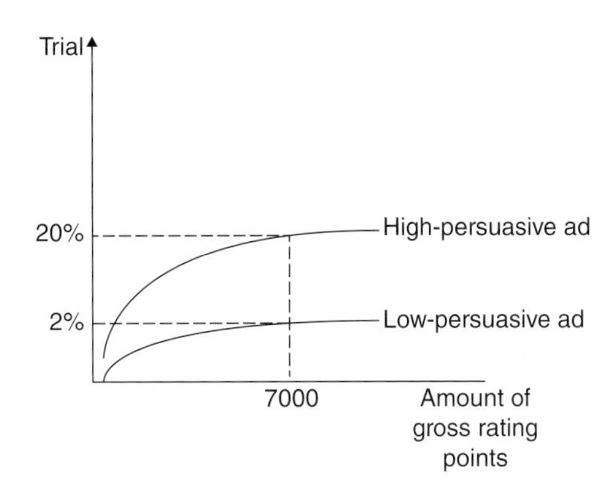

Figure 6.2 The relationship between trial and media spend for different levels of persuasive ads[7]

that if an ad is effective it works quickly,[8] and we are likely to see results in the first burst. So, it is more prudent to drop poorly performing ads quickly than to hope that more media spend will improve the situation.[9]

However, there is another side to this argument. If a low-quality creative ad cannot be saved with a higher media spend, then does a high-quality creative ad become even more effective the more that is spent on it? The answer is yes. But how can we decide what counts as a higher media spend? One way of thinking about it is to use an index called 'extra share of voice' (eSOV). This is defined as SOV (or share of voice) of the brand minus its market share (i.e. SOV – SOM). If the difference is positive, it means the brand is spending more than its market share.

In his landmark study, Donald Gunn found that 86% of creative award-winning ads in 28 countries between 1992 and 1995 increased sales.[10] In a subsequent study between 2000 and 2008, he further confirmed that creative award-winning ads in the UK were about 11 times more successful in growing market share than non-awarded creative campaigns.[11]

Further, when the winning creative ads were compared with non-winning ones, it was also found that non-creative ads in fact had a higher eSOV, and yet this only generated 0.5% growth in market share. On the other hand, for creative award-winning ads, spending the extra equivalent of eSOV generated an average market share gain of 5.7%.[12] What is even more interesting is that the award-winning ads also generated more WOM and as such tended to increase the brand's status.[13] Gunn's study suggests that if your ad wins an award, it is wise to fully exploit it by increasing its media spend, because it will probably lead to a gain in market share. In other words, the extra media spend can ratchet up the sales effects for a high-quality creative ad but will not do so for one of low quality. A recent study by McKinsey confirmed the relationship between creativity and financial performance. Companies that consistently win creative awards tend to have better financial performance.[14]

There are also other benefits for having high-quality creative ads. A creative ad sends positive signals to the marketplace about the 'fitness' of the brand.[15] This means that consumers can perceive the brand to be successful and wealthy. Further, the higher the creativity level of the ad, the higher the brand's perceived ability to deal with future problems and develop valuable products. This, in turn, signals that the brand is of a high quality.[16]

Creative ads also improve the image of the advertising industry. Such ads have been compiled to create entertaining programs along the lines of *The world's greatest commercials* or *The world's funniest commercials*. In the US, Super Bowl ads create buzz before the actual showing (often only once). In the UK, people have been known to go to movies early just to watch the commercials.[17] In Australia, there is a popular TV program called *Gruen*, in which a panel of advertising personnel poke fun about brands, advertising, consumers and the like. It continues to be a very popular program more than 10 years after it first aired.[18] YouTube also allows people to enjoy all these commercials.

Creativity is also important for the advertising agency. If an effective creative idea can be created for the client, the agency is more likely to retain their account longer, which means greater long-term profitability for the agency since the creative idea is likely to have longevity and so can run for years if not decades to come. Winning an award may also attract new clients and talent because it raises the agency's profile.

Finally, in the age of the internet, creative ads get extra mileage. Globally, the online audience is huge. For instance, five billion YouTube videos are watched in a single day.[19] An ad is more likely to 'go viral' among this huge audience if the ad is creative.[20] Viral viewing can be considered free advertising and constitutes extra exposures for the brand worldwide.

In summary, it pays to invest in a high-quality creative ad for several reasons:

- It is more likely to attract attention, be enjoyed more, create higher purchase intentions and increase market share for the brand.
- It is an extreme waste of money not to have one in some media, such as TV.
- It is seven times more important than media investment in predicting short-term market share.
- It can ratchet up market share by as much as 5–6 % (the same cannot be said for low-quality creative ads).
- It signals a high-quality brand.
- It gives the advertising industry a better image.
- It is more profitable for an advertising agency.
- It is likely to lead to viral viewing and so extra free exposures.

CASE STUDY 6.1 VOLVO'S INTERCEPT AT THE SUPER BOWL[21]

In the US, the Super Bowl is the most watched football match, with 70% of the population tuning in. It is therefore not surprising that it is very expensive to advertise during this program. A 30-second TV ad will cost the brand US$4.5 million. But there is no shortage of takers. For instance, in the 2015 Super Bowl, a number of automobile brands like Kia, Nissan, Fiat, Toyota, Mercedes-Benz and Lexus had all chosen to advertise during the commercial break. This event is often used to showcase new products or to make a statement. For instance, the aforementioned automobile brands spent a total of US$60 million on their latest models during the ad break. The ads are often creatively brilliant in order to generate excitement. But what happens if you do not have the budget to compete with other major brands in this big event? Well, you may give up or think of something clever. Perhaps a competition?

Question: Would you like to win a new car for your mum, or someone you love? Of course you would, provided it does not take too much effort to enter the competition. What if it is really simple; all it takes is to type in the name of your loved ones. Such a competition should work. But creating a competition is not an end to itself. The objective is to help build the brand's stature and esteem so that sales can be continually generated long after the competition is over. But the first challenge is still to make the competition a success, and that means publicising it widely and getting as many people as possible excited about it and hence the brand. This may require some resources, but if you are clever enough, you may be able to do this without spending too much publicising the competition, and yet succeed, as in the case of Volvo.

In 2015, Volvo and their ad agency Grey, New York, devised a cunning plan to do just that during the Super Bowl without buying a spot. This is what they did. Using social media, Volvo let the word out that you can win a brand new Volvo (model XC60) for someone you love by simply tweeting their name and #VolvoContest every time a car ad appeared during the Super Bowl. The idea was to divert the attention away from any of the car commercials to tweeting about Volvo instead, and it worked! Up to 2000 #VolvoContest-tweets were recorded (per minute) every time a car ad came on. In total, over 55 000 tweets were sent by the end of the game. But more importantly, the tactic created excitement in the Volvo brand throughout the game. It rendered the other car brands irrelevant despite them paying dearly for a 30-second spot. Volvo 'stole' their attention, beat the clutter of competing ads, and achieved top of mind throughout the entire game.

RESULTS

The campaign generated US$200 million of earned media. Sales of the Volvo XC60 model shot up 70% in the month following the Super Bowl. This is unbelievable considering the fact that Volvo did not spend a single cent on paid media. Volvo simply gave away the car. They also did not need to make any ads to generate excitement for the brand, which is typically the case with Super Bowl advertising. Most of the excitement was generated by the consumers themselves talking to each other. How clever is that?

DISCUSSION QUESTIONS

1. Why do you think other car manufacturers did not think of the same idea as Volvo, even though they had more resources?
2. What lessons could you learn from this case about beating clutter?
3. This case illustrates that watching TV is a social event. Yet advertisers have traditionally ignored this facet. Why do you think this is so? Do you think this is changing now?

THEORETICAL PERSPECTIVES ON CREATIVITY

Creativity has been studied in a wide range of disciplines – in religion, art, abnormal and cognitive psychology, neurobiology, linguistics, technology, education, sociology and, of course, advertising.

Creativity and its many faces

As a process, the word 'creative' simply means *to create* or *to produce*. It is derived from the Latin word *creare*, meaning 'to make'. In the advertising profession, 'a creative' is usually someone who works in the artistic department in an advertising agency (e.g. copywriters, art directors, graphic designers, broadcast specialists).

An ad can also be described as creative. This usually means the ad is perceived to be original, novel, unique, ingenious, clever or imaginative, to the extent that it can enrich, entertain and connect with the target audience. However, this view of creative advertising also has negative connotations, because, by virtue of being original, the ad also risks being weird and bizarre to the point that comprehension of the selling point suffers.[22] It is now generally accepted that for an ad to be creative, it has to be relevant, by which we mean that it is appropriate, meaningful, valuable and on message. In sum, we can simply think of an effective creative ad as one that is original and on message.[23]

Remote associate thinking and remote associative matching

Creativity has been studied from different perspectives, from fine arts to engineering. But in advertising, the main challenge is to overcome the various barriers in marketing communications (discussed in chapter 1). It is the job of creative personnel to artfully present the brand in such a way that it will arouse the interest of the target audience. Indeed, good advertising agencies often encourage their own creative personnel to fulfil these dual functions – being able to sell the brand in an exciting and imaginative way.

But how can we include the brand in the scheme of things? To do this, we first need to understand the theory of remote associate thinking (RAT). Conceived in the early 1960s by a psychologist called Sarnoff Mednick,[24] this theory refers to the time-honoured idea that creative thinking is the ability to combine elements using existing knowledge from distant domains.[25]

For instance, if you were to be given two words, 'rock' and 'ware', then one word that could link these two words together is the word 'hard'. This is because the word 'hard' can be combined with 'rock' to form *hard rock* but can also be combined with 'ware' to form *hardware*. So, by using the word 'hard', a new combination is found for these two words. Figure 6.3 illustrates this idea structurally. According to Mednick, it is this ability to link seemingly unrelated words that constitutes creative thinking. The telling sign is that the person will have an 'Aha' experience, characteristic of a creative insight.

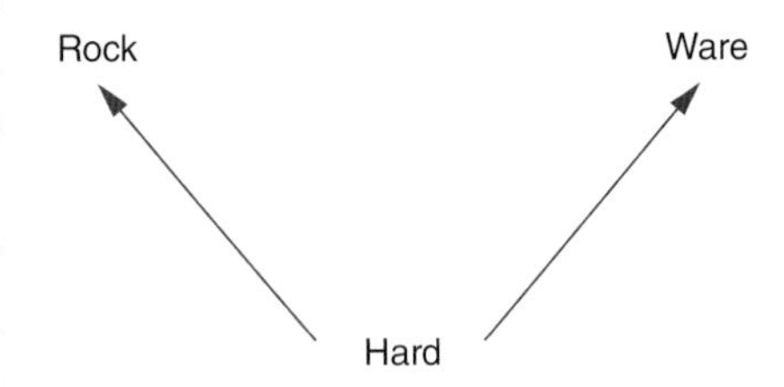

Figure 6.3 A structural representation of remote associate thinking (RAT)

We can easily modify this theory for advertising by substituting each word for one element of an ad. For instance, we can substitute the word 'ware' for the brand; replace the word 'rock' with a picture; and include a headline instead of the word 'hard'. Let's take an example of a print ad to illustrate this. Figure 6.4 shows a rhinoceros. On its own, it is pretty eye-catching. The logo shows the product, a fishing rod make called Zebco, and a fishing rod is also clearly visible in the ad. The viewer will first ask what a rhinoceros has got to do with a fishing rod, until they read the headline. The headline joins the picture and the brand together with the key benefit 'tough'. The ad suddenly makes sense.

The structure of this ad bears a resemblance to Mednick's theory because the ad uses a picture that we would not naturally associate with this brand, and it is only after reading the headline that we can see the connection. The picture (i.e. rhinoceros) is 'remote' in the sense that the probability of it being associated with the brand (Zebco) is low. Yet the picture is powerful because it contains the right association that can be linked to the brand's benefit (i.e. the product is tough).

Figure 6.4 A structural representation of a remote conveyor

The picture is called the 'conveyor', the headline is the 'benefit prompt'. This theory is known as the remote associative matching (RAM) theory of creativity.[26] The structural element of the theory is shown in figure 6.5.

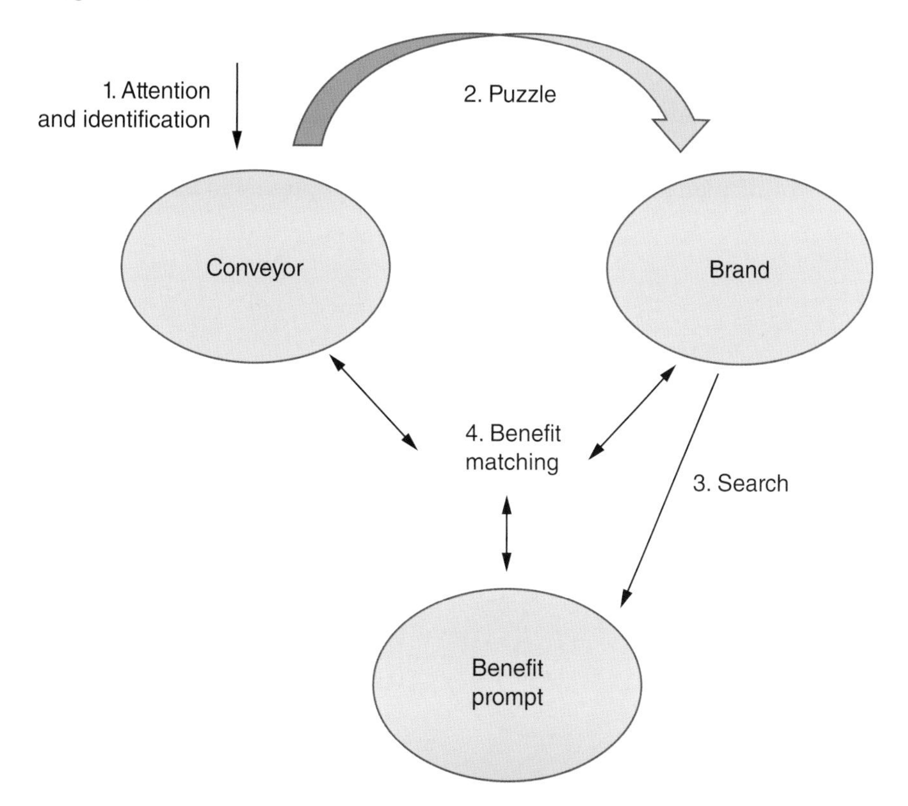

Figure 6.5 A structural representation of the remote benefit matching model

The RAM model consists of four processing steps:

1. The function of the conveyor is primarily to attract attention. It should also be easily identified. This is step 1. There are many ways this can be achieved, such as by using eye-catching pictures.
2. However, the link to the brand must not be too obvious, in order to arouse some curiosity[27] in the reader. This is step 2. By not making the link too obvious, the advertiser implies that they assume a certain level of intelligence in the reader who wants to know more.
3. Since the meaning is not immediately obvious, the reader is then motivated to search for it in the ad, which is the selling point. This is step 3. This increases the dwell time of the ad, and therefore increases the probability the message will be processed. However, this step also implies that the target audience has the time (i.e. opportunity) to search for the headline. Sometimes, the benefit prompt is found in the copy instead. The more difficult it is to find the prompt, the less likely the target audience will 'get' the ad.
4. The last step is the most crucial. It requires the target audience to find a match between the associations of the domain of the conveyor and the brand (guided by the benefit prompt). When a match is found, the target audience experiences an 'Aha' insight accompanied by a sense of satisfaction and positive feelings.[28] This is the sudden realisation of how the conveyor has amplified the benefit of the brand. If a match is not found, new (i.e. secondary) associations will be activated. This means the consumer will again search the product and conveyor space for a link between the two domains. That is why this step is drawn with double-headed arrows in the diagram.

Although the RAM theory was developed for creative print advertising, it is in fact quite broadly generalisable to other mediums. This is because the theory can be used to account for different levels of creativity across any medium. For instance, an ad does not have to use a remote conveyor but one that is common for the product category. Car ads are a good example. Almost all car ads show the car snaking along a road; there may be variations, but it is almost always the same idea. A car snaking along a road is not a remote conveyor, and therefore it is unlikely to arouse any curiosity (unless other unusual elements are added). Sometimes, no conveyor is included in the ad, in the case of a straight ad that simply shows the product. The structural model of such an ad, which is much simpler, is represented in figure 6.6.

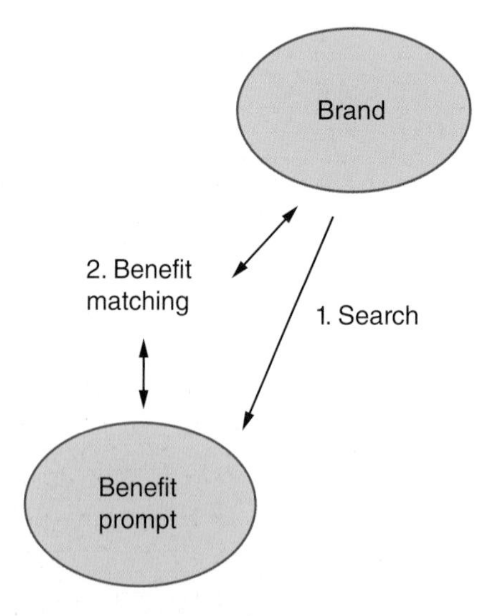

Figure 6.6 A structural representation of a straight ad

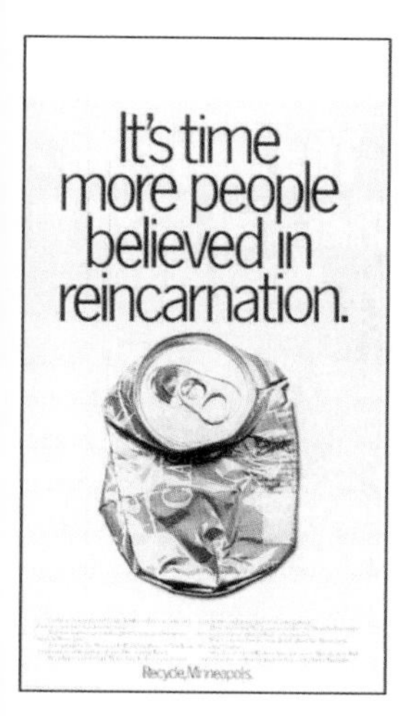

Figure 6.7 Use of a remote verbal conveyor in the headline

However, this does not mean that straight ads are not useful. If the objective is to simply inform the target audience, then a structurally simple ad is all that is needed. For instance, if a person is in the market to buy a product (e.g. a BMW car), or already has an interest in the category (e.g. cars in general), they are likely to seek out such ads anyway. For this group of customers, a simple, straightforward ad will suffice.

If this appears too boring, another option is to create a deviant headline. The remote conveyor now moves to the headline (a remote verbal conveyor), and the benefit prompt is now in the picture or the copy. Figure 6.7 is an example showing an ad promoting recycling in the city of Minneapolis, where the headline is 'deviant' (due to the word 'reincarnation') but the picture is 'straight' (because the picture of a crushed can directly supports the idea of recycling).[29]

The RAM model has managerial uses too: it is quite useful in preventing creative personnel from becoming too zany and delivering an ad that is too bizarre. Things can go wrong in the different processing steps as shown in the box below.

PROBLEMS IN PROCESSING STEPS

WHEN THE TARGET AUDIENCE DOES NOT HAVE ENOUGH TIME (OR IS NOT MOTIVATED) TO SEARCH FOR THE BENEFIT PROMPT

For instance, transit ads found on the outside of buses and taxis should be straight. Drivers normally do not have time to ponder. This becomes even more difficult when an ad does not have a headline (i.e. a benefit prompt). We fail at step 3 of the RAM model.

WHEN THE CONVEYOR (OR A CRITICAL PART OF IT) CANNOT BE EASILY IDENTIFIED

This is important because in order for the target audience to match the associations (step 4), it must know the identity of the conveyor. This means that it must be easily labelled. In the example of the Zebco ad (see figure 6.4), the right associations will not be activated if the target audience cannot recognise the image as a rhinoceros. Similarly, in the recycling ad (see figure 6.7), if the target audience does not know what reincarnation means (a remote verbal conveyor), no matching of associations will occur.

WHEN THE DOMINANT ASSOCIATIONS OF THE CHOSEN CONVEYOR DO NOT AMPLIFY THE BENEFIT OF THE BRAND

For instance, the ad for a fictitious brand of projector shows a picture of a snail (see figure 6.8). The very small headline touts the key benefit of the projector, 'WideVision'. If the dominant association of a snail is its slowness (or maybe its sliminess), then these associations cannot amplify the benefit of a data projector. Step 4 fails.

WHEN SECONDARY ASSOCIATIONS ALSO FAIL TO AMPLIFY THE BENEFIT

In the WideVision example, if we realise that the two outspread feelers are in fact the eye stalks of the snail, then the benefit of WideVision suddenly makes sense. On the other hand, if we are ignorant of this fact or cannot see the eyes at the end of the stalks (so, failing at step 1), then the ad will not make sense. No matching will occur at step 4.

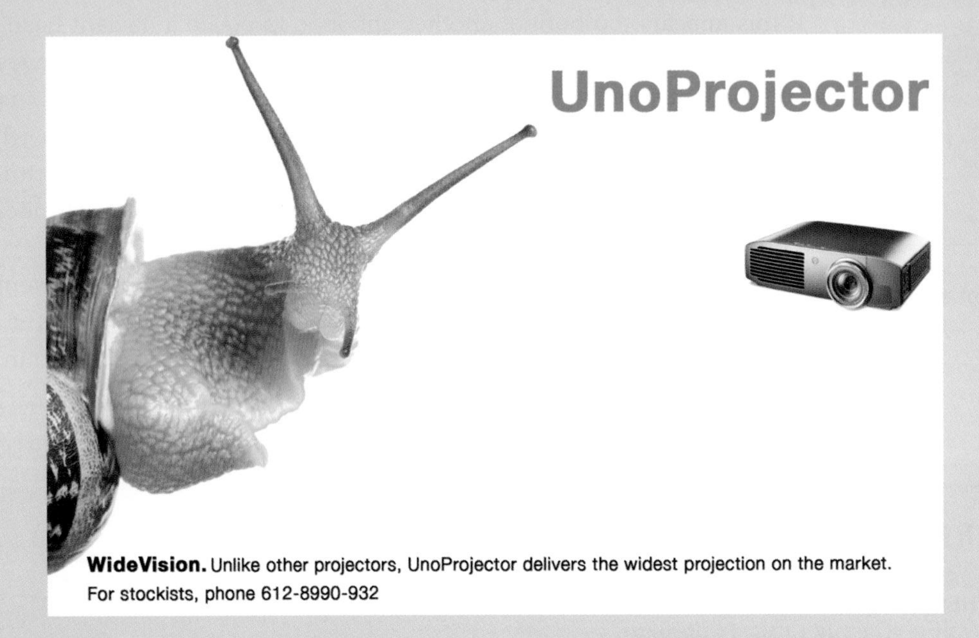

Figure 6.8 An ad that illustrates the *what?*

From the above discussion, we can quickly realise how risky a creative ad can be if it is not well thought out and executed, and we can appreciate the importance of pre-testing the ad. As the RAM theory specifies quite clearly the various pitfalls, it becomes managerially useful.

Using secondary activations to find a match

Now, let's discuss an example in which the conveyor is remote and does not possess a benefit prompt (e.g. a headline) and yet still works. Look carefully at the following ad for Fabulon (see figure 6.9), a starch-based ironing aid that helps remove creases fast, and then consider – did you understand it?

The picture shows an elephant, which is a remote conveyor (i.e. what has an elephant got to do with ironing?). This puzzle attracts our attention and arouses our curiosity. But there is no headline, which means we must infer the message. In our minds, we are asking how an elephant helps to convey the benefit of an ironing aid, and we begin to activate some associations.

We might first attempt to match the dominant associations of the elephant (e.g. strength, intelligence, African) with the benefit of using an ironing aid (e.g. helps remove creases fast). This fails because these associations do not make sense in selling an ironing aid. Then we notice that, in the image, the rear half of the elephant has no creases. This provides the first clue. Suddenly it

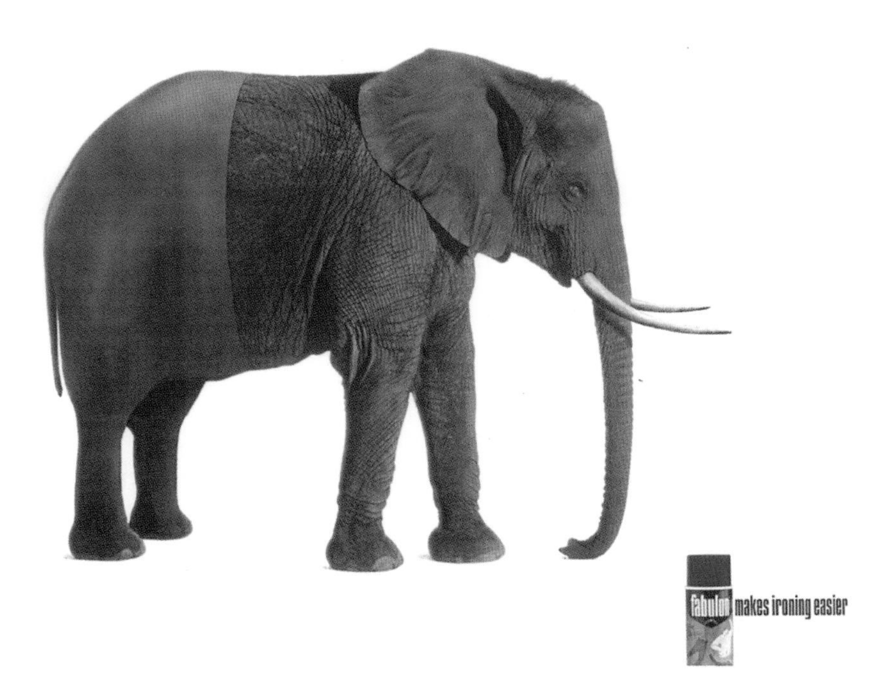

Figure 6.9 An ad without a benefit prompt

dawns on us that the message is about how good Fabulon is in removing creases, to the extent that even an elephant's tough and rough skin can be easily smoothed with the product.

This is an example in which the dominant associations of the conveyor (the first to be activated) are completely irrelevant and yet the ad still works by using secondary activations to amplify the benefit. Notice that, even without a prompt, this ad can still work provided there is an opportunity and motivation for the audience to 'solve' it. Naturally, such an ad is risky since the prompt (i.e. the headline) is especially important for consumers' comprehension – it also helps a reader learn about the benefit.[30] Ads without a benefit prompt are not recommended for new products or situations where consumers are not motivated to search for a match.

Matching elements

We may ask what else can be matched since, although the RAM model emphasises the importance of benefit matching, many other elements can also theoretically be matched. Which brand elements we choose to match will depend on the desired positioning of the brand. Theoretically, the more elements we can match, the more creatively integrated the brand and so the easier the learning.

Figure 6.10 shows there are many possibilities for matching to occur between the dominant characteristics of the conveyor and the brand. The creative idea of the Zebco fishing rod ad seen earlier (see figure 6.4) uses a rhinoceros to amplify toughness, a benefit.

Now, consider the ad in figure 6.11. It is a Heineken beer ad, which visually amplifies how our reaction time slows down when we drink alcohol, and how therefore we should not drink and drive. What is being amplified is our (slowed) behaviour, an action. Finally, consider the ad in

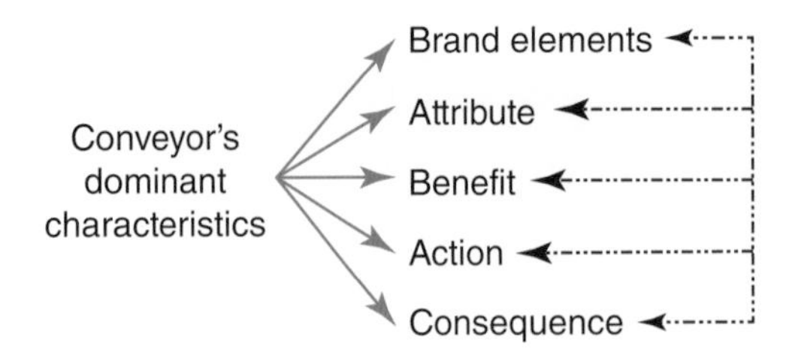

Figure 6.10 The many ways in which a conveyor can be linked to a brand

figure 6.12. It is an ad for an undertaker but uses the idea of smoking to convey the idea of death, a negative consequence – indeed, a deadly one! So, there are many ways in which a conveyor can amplify the selling point of a message, and it is not always about product benefits.

Figure 6.11 An ad conveying the idea of action

Figure 6.12 An ad conveying the idea of consequences

In summary, when all the right elements come together, a creative ad can be very powerful. Not only will such an ad get more attention, arouse more curiosity, encourage consumers to look for longer and process more deeply, but it will also be liked more if it is understood. A well-integrated brand will lead to greater liking and memory of awareness for the brand, as well as to higher purchasing intentions. However, a badly conceived or executed ad will be misinterpreted and ineffective.

WHAT IS A CREATIVE IDEA?

Now that we have seen how a creative idea can amplify a selling point, it paves a way for the business objective to be realised. In this regard, three requirements are necessary. First, the message containing the benefit must be linked to the brand, or else the ad will be misattributed to another brand, essentially ending up advertising for that brand. This requirement may seem obvious, but in fact up to 50% of TV ads are misidentified.[31] The second requirement is that the branded message must be delivered in a compelling way (e.g. a heart-wrenching storyline) to cut through the clutter and involve the target audience.[32] Third, the creative idea must be 'own-able'. This means that the creative idea is unique – the way it is configured has not been used by a competing brand. This is especially important if the brand does not possess a superior attribute or benefit, which many brands do not. Then by at least owning a unique creative idea, the brand will become distinctive. With consistent use, this becomes its identifiable selling style, which in turn becomes a distinctive asset for the brand.

If we take this functional view, it means that a creative idea serves two purposes. At the strategic level, it assists the firm to solve its business problem (or capitalise on an opportunity), and at the individual level, it breaks through the clutter and hopefully encourages the target audience to accept and act on the brand's message. With this in mind, we can now define an effective creative idea as:

> A unique and compelling way of amplifying the selling point in a branded message so that it will trigger the desired outcome in the target audience and help fulfil the firm's business objectives.
>
> It should have the magical ability to capture and hold the attention of the target audience while we give them some information, or a demonstration, or a storyline, or an experience that changes the way they think, feel and do.[33]

CREATIVE INTEGRATION

This definition of an effective creative idea suggests what is required for creative integration. Figure 6.13 shows the necessary components in a Venn diagram. Here, D is the ideal ad as it is not only compelling but also contains a well-branded message. But an ad can also have a compelling storyline without the target audience knowing what the brand or message is, as shown in A. This is the familiar situation when, after watching a TV ad, we scratch our heads and ask, 'What was that about?' Although the ad got our attention, we do not know what it means. Such an ad can be referred to as entertainingly 'empty'. Sometimes, an ad can be less 'empty', as shown in E, where we know the brand but not the message; or as shown in F, where we know the message but not the brand. Finally, it is also possible for an ad to deliver the message in a boring way, even though the message is well branded, as shown in G.

So, one can think of this Venn diagram as representing all the elements of an effective creative idea. The more the elements come together in an integrated manner, the easier it is for consumers to process. In short, we aim to achieve the ideal where the ad has amplified the branded message in a compelling way, as in D. We call this 'full creative integration', and if these three elements are configured in a novel way, then the creative idea is considered *unique*. A unique creative idea is considered *effective* when it can be communicated in a simple, coherent manner (ideally lending itself to several different but related executions) to fulfil the firm's business objectives. In practice, this usually means one main selling point, delivered in single-minded focus. Otherwise, the ad would be too confusing.[34]

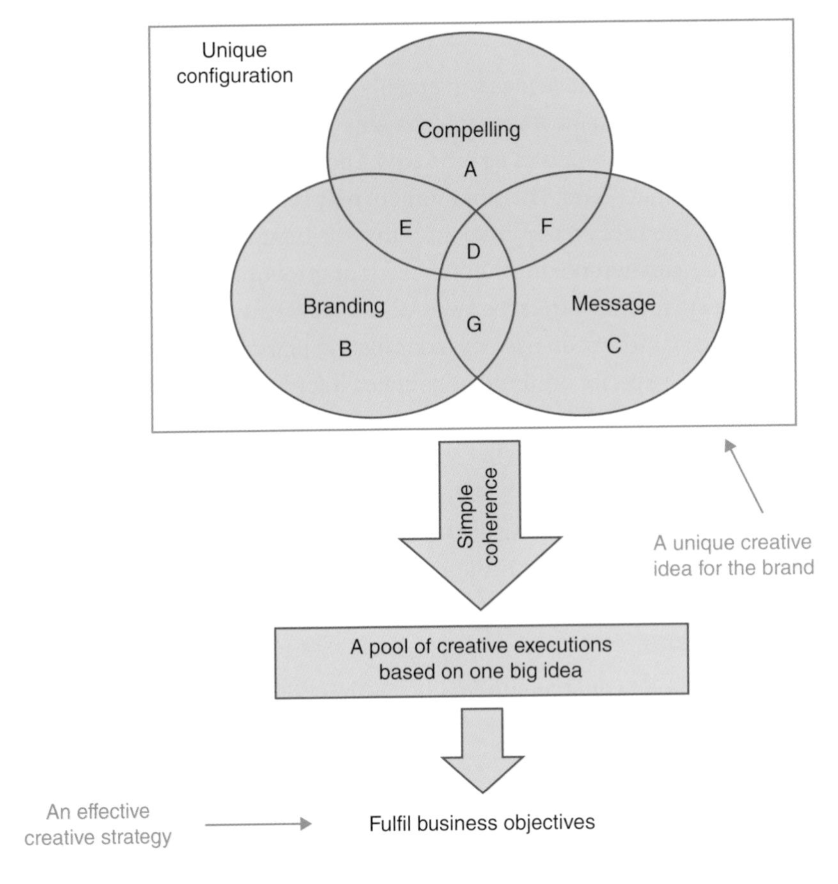

Figure 6.13 An illustration of creative integration

A good example of the power of simple coherence is the TV ad for the Manix brand of condom (see figure 6.14). The TV ad begins with someone putting a condom over a finger. The finger then presses onto an ink pad before transferring the mark onto a piece of paper. Surprisingly, the pattern of the fingerprint can be seen on the paper, demonstrating how thin the condom is. The last scene shows the brand name, Manix 002.

Figure 6.14 An example of simplicity in a creative idea

Although this TV ad demonstrates the power of simplicity, it has one weakness. The brand is not prominent except for the last scene. For instance, we could easily substitute another brand of condom and the ad will still work. Generally, we want the brand to be so tightly woven into the ad that no other brand can be substituted without destroying it. For example, a typical Qantas TV ad, which features all the iconic symbols of Australia (e.g. the outback, the kangaroo, Uluru, the Great Barrier Reef), would not work if another airline were substituted, say, United Airlines.

Ideally, we also want the most dramatic aspect of the ad to feature the brand as well.[35] That way, when our attention is arrested by the drama, we also see the brand. Finally, if neither of these creative integration tactics can be achieved in the concept, then the brand name should be simply repeated (see chapter 7).

An ad campaign by Yalumba wine demonstrates how a brand can be creatively integrated into an ad. These ads are for the Y-series, a mid-range wine (around $15) aimed squarely at a customer segment that buys at this price point or lower. The communication objective is 'about encouraging people to confidently pick up their favourites, or try something new, any day of the week'.[36]

The creative concept playfully revolves around key words with the letter 'Y' missing. The screw cap of the wine then conveniently replaces it to complete the message. These key words also happen to be the message to convey the benefits of the wine (e.g. zesty, spicy, yum) or a reminder to buy (e.g. on Friday), all missing the letter 'Y' (i.e. zest_, spic_, _um and Frida_).

The letter 'Y', of course, stands for the brand Yalumba and its Y-series. Therefore, by using the screw cap to complete the message, the brand (and product) is creatively integrated into the message. This ad would not work for another brand of wine, unless of course its brand name also started with 'Y'.

Figure 6.15 Yalumba web banner, point-of-sale and cinema ads

THE CREATIVE BRIEF

The creative brief is one of the most important documents a marcoms manager has to give the advertising agency. It summarises the important elements of the campaign. A large part of the brief revolves around articulating the creative strategy, the process of setting a direction for the brand's positioning in the campaign – or, to put it colloquially, how the brand is to be sold to the target audience that will unlock growth.

The key elements that should be in the creative brief according to best practice[37] are shown in the box below.

WHAT IS IN THE CREATIVE BRIEF?

- Business issues: What are the firm's current problems and obstacles?
- Business objectives: What do you want to accomplish? Why is it important?
- About the firm: What is the nature of the firm's business? What is the firm's organisational structure?
- About the brand: its current positioning, reputation, history, attributes and usage benefits.
- Consumer benefits and insight: in-depth understanding of the motivation driving consumers' usage (or lack of usage) and the resulting emotional rewards of their experience.
- Current market structure: competition, SWOT, distribution and pricing issues (if any).
- Brand positioning: preferably encompassing a unique point of difference that can be exploited, such as an amazing fact about the brand or firm.
- Message proposition: preferably a unique selling proposition based on some human truth that can help spark the birth of a big idea.
- Campaign task and desired target audiences' response: marcoms objectives, target audience, possible new positioning for the brand/firm, mandatories, timetable.
- Budget: a fixed amount or a range.
- Advertising pre-testing and campaign evaluation: methodology and criteria for success.

Figure 6.16 shows that the marcoms manager must drive the creative brief, informed by insightful research (as discussed in chapter 2). It also shows that even before the creative brief goes to the creative personnel, the account planner must thoroughly vet it (this role is sometimes called a 'brand planner' or 'strategic planner').

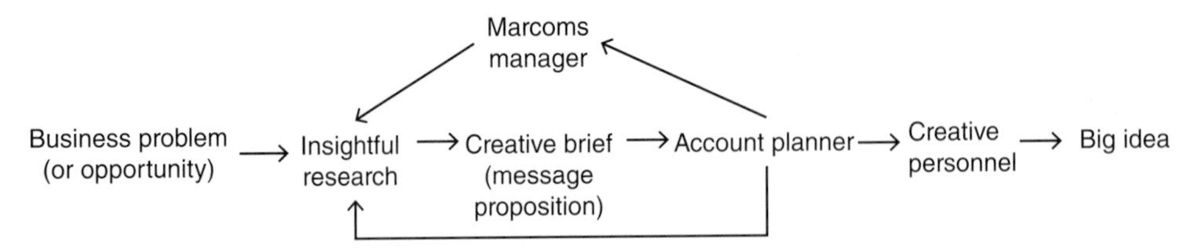

Figure 6.16 The position of the creative brief in the creative development process

However, very often the marcoms manager does not have the time to write the creative brief, and the task falls on the account planner. Account planning is a British invention created in the 1950s to improve strategic planning and achieve the desired consumer response in order to address a business issue[38] (see also chapter 2). Account planning therefore embraces three perspectives: that of the client's business, that of the creative personnel, and finally that of the target audience, when responding to the proposed creative solution.[39] Of the three perspectives, account planners have come to be responsible for the last (i.e. the response of target audiences). Account planners are said to represent the voice of the consumer in the advertising agency and finding the human truth, which is then summarised in the message proposition found in the creative brief. This is then used to assist the creative personnel to develop the 'big idea'. Although in practice the account planner often writes the creative brief, the responsibility should rest on the shoulders of the marcoms manager. In chapter 2, we discussed the role account planners play in their search for insight.

Show clearly what is required

It is not unusual for the advertising agency to disagree with the suggested positioning or what is required to solve the problem as specified in the brief. This can create friction. For this reason, it is important for a marcoms manager to work closely with the account planner. In fact, it is vital that a verbal briefing is carried out first (before anything is written) because the problems faced may be multifaceted. Discussion opens opportunities for both parties to brainstorm possible solutions (under certain preconditions), in particular around how the brand or certain features of the product or service can be uniquely exploited, and how this should be communicated to the right audience in order to induce the desired response. Further research and thinking may be necessary. Therefore, in many ways, the creative brief is co-written or revised with the account planner at the agency.

There is also a practical reason why clarity is important. The clearer the requirements, the more focused the creative personnel will be in working on the creative solution. We want the creative personnel to devote 100% of their time to finding the 'big idea' for our brand, without second-guessing what is required. It is a real problem: currently, a third of creative time is wasted because of poor briefing.[40] This in turn saps creatives' energy and motivation, which affects the quality of their work.

Communicate the vision with a sense of excitement

The brief should be inspiring. By communicating a vision of what is possible for the brand, the marcoms manager raises the expectations of what the creative idea can achieve. This vision also suggests the right tone for the campaign, which in turn guides the creative work.

There is another, more selfish, reason why a marcoms manager needs to show such excitement. For a medium to large agency, the creative personnel are usually working on more than one campaign at once. Therefore, the more inspiring your brief is, the more likely the creative team will work for you (even on their day off!). This is especially important when no key insight is found during research (see chapter 2), in which case we really need to inspire the creative personnel to deliver.

Ideation principles

Since having a high-quality creative idea is important, we next ask how this can be accomplished. There is no fixed formula, but below are some principles that can increase the probability of success. But before we look at these, we need to nail down the business problem (or opportunity) facing the organisation. This requires convergent thinking, which means using knowledge and critical thinking to achieve an in-depth understanding of the business issues that are motivating the campaign.

Once we understand this, we can engage in divergent thinking to search for a creative solution. In this context, this means searching for the creative frame that we can use as a starting point in the development of the creative idea. Once we have found the initial creative frame, that becomes the driving force for the pursuit of various artful deviations that can cleverly amplify the brand benefit. From this, several creative ideas will emerge, and from these a few will be chosen for further evaluation.

CASE STUDY 6.2 WALKERS CRISPS

Let's take an example. In 2011, Walkers, a British brand of potato chip, wanted to increase the sales of their single-pack products. 'Out-of-home' sales were declining, both in terms of volume and value. This was a massive challenge because the brand was already top of its category. Further, there was really nothing new to say about the product and nor was there a clear benefit (e.g. tastier or crunchier than other chips). But the business problem was clearly defined for the advertising agency, AMV/BBDO.

After some research, the planners, Tom White and Bridget Angear, realised that the greatest potential of increasing sales lay in stimulating impulse purchase during lunchtime, targeting their core market of men between the ages of 25 and 34.[41] This idea fits with single-pack purchasing behaviour. Further, since only 10% of British people buy potato chips with their lunch, this represented great potential. For instance, if the campaign could double the purchase rate to 20%, it could well arrest the decline.

Tom and Bridget researched the category and found that British people believed that potato chips would make their lunchtime sandwich more exciting. As British people normally have sandwiches for lunch, perhaps there could be a way to link the brand to sandwiches. This was the key insight. According to Steve Coll, the creative director on the Walkers campaign at that time, the two product categories of a sandwich and potato chips were 'miles apart and nobody [had] connected it as a potential opportunity. So, what we [were] really looking to do [was] to remind people that they went together ... specifically that Walkers could make any sandwich more exciting.'[42]

In our terms, Tom and Bridget found the creative frame 'to make the sandwich more exciting with Walkers'. We can therefore define the creative frame as the domain in which initial ideas are to be generated or sampled from, in this example, the domain of Walkers' crisps and sandwiches. But this was not the final creative solution. They still needed a creative idea, one that could also gain trade support, since they also wanted to make it easier for consumers to buy both sandwiches and Walkers' chips at retail.

So what was the creative twist? It so happens – no kidding – that there is a sleepy country town in Kent, England, called Sandwich. So, why not make this town exciting again for three days, by creating and filming a series of memorable events (linked to Walkers) that the local residents would never forget?[43] The program included:

- Pamela Anderson (an American actress) pouring beer and giving away Walkers' chips as a barmaid at the local pub.

- Al Murray (a British comedian) hosting a quiz night at the same pub.
- Marco Pierre White (a three-Michelin-starred chef) making and giving away sandwiches with Walkers' chips.
- Gary Lineker (a British ex-soccer star and celebrity ambassador for Walkers) dressing up as a sandwich and giving away Walkers' chips.
- Frank Lampard (a British soccer star) playing with the local soccer team.
- Jenson Button (a British Formula 1 driver) driving around town delivering parcels and picking up retirees in a taxi.
- The British boyband JLS performing at a local college.

When I asked Steve Coll where the idea of using this country town came from, he said:

> We had very little time to crack this brief, so I sat down with my fellow Creative Director, Colin Jones, and the Board Account Director, Justin Pahl, to talk it through. We liked the starting point that Walkers could make any sandwich more exciting. We came up with five or six ideas before the conversation turned to Sandwich, Kent and from there we had a really unique idea that would work in advertising, PR and social media. Making the sleeping town of Sandwich more exciting also made the lunchtime sandwich more exciting, by analogy, if it was bought with Walkers.

Cleverly, the campaign was also amplified many times with a social media strategy. Locals posted hundreds of photographs and videos of the events; online destinations such as the Walkers YouTube channel and homepage were created for the event; celebrities tweeted about the event and invited fans to visit the online destinations; a staged release of 26 pieces of separate content (with lots of behind-the-scenes footage) was used to extend the campaign and yet keep it fresh. To fuel more reach, journalists were also planted in the town of Sandwich for the event to help write and spread the event in the mainstream media. This was supplemented by celebrities giving separate interviews on TV. The campaign was a huge success, as proven by the following statistics (among others):

- Walkers sold 10 million extra units.
- The campaign received media coverage worth £3.2 million.
- The campaign won the Grand Prix award for creative effectiveness at Cannes.
- Major UK supermarkets now place Walkers next to sandwiches.

This campaign shows that a well-conceived creative concept can engage a nation and influence trade.

DISCUSSION QUESTIONS

1. What was the insight about the buying behaviour of chips that allowed the agency to come up with a winning idea that unlocked growth?
2. Do you think luck played a role here in finding the creative idea? Explain your answer.
3. How does the use of social media and celebrity further amplify the message? Do you think this is a cost-effective campaign? Explain your answer.

Figure 6.17 shows the sequence of using convergent thinking to define the business issue clearly, followed by divergent thinking to find different creative solutions, and finally convergent thinking again for the ultimate selection of the creative idea.

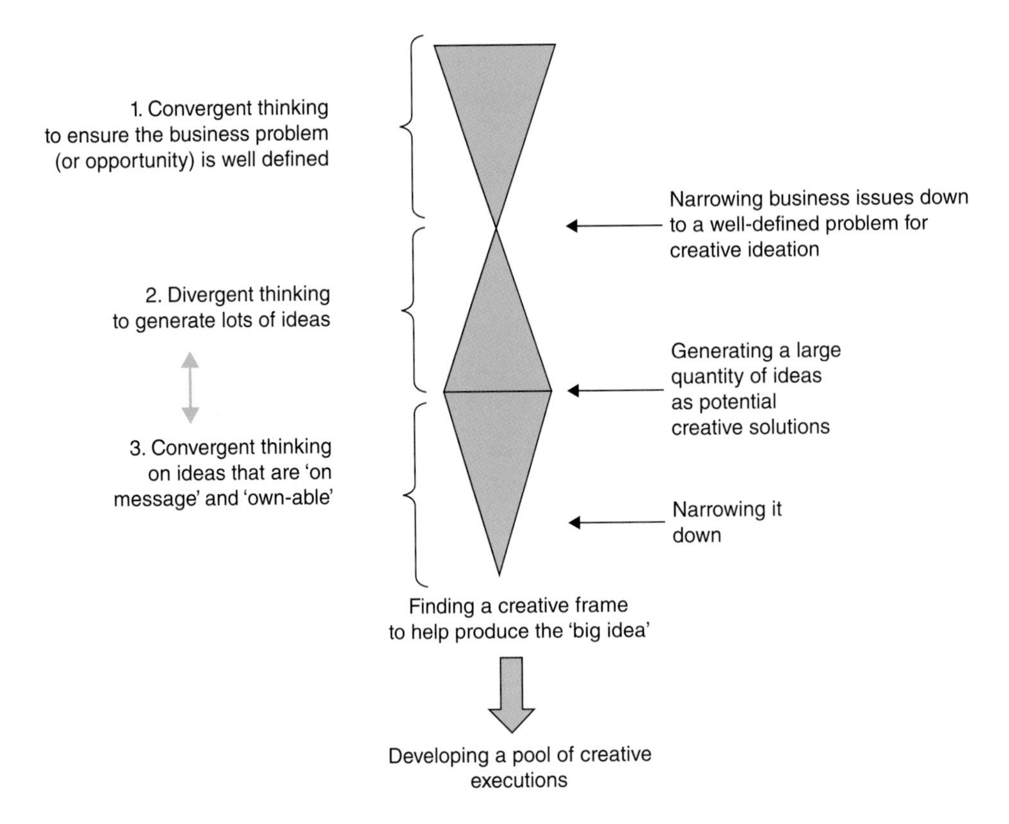

Figure 6.17 How convergent and divergent thinking combine during concept development

Note that the initial convergent thinking is needed to ensure that the business problem is well defined. This is usually the job of the account planner, who distils all the business issues into a coherent creative strategy. With a well-defined problem, the resulting creative idea is more likely to be 'on message' and 'own-able'.

Once the problem has been well defined, the creative team then takes over, engaging in divergent thinking in search of the 'big idea'. They will generate many ideas. This is followed by convergent thinking, through which they will discard many unsuitable ideas. For experienced creative personnel, the cycle between divergent and convergent thinking (i.e. from step 2 and 3 in figure 6.17) occurs very quickly and can last for hours.[44] This is indicated by the double-headed arrow in figure 6.17.

Now that we understand how convergent and divergent thinking occur in the development of creative concepts, let's concentrate on a few creative principles that can help us to find a big idea that is also 'on message'.[45]

PRINCIPLE 1: SEEK ACCURATE INPUT

This principle means the information must be accurate, to ensure that the ad is 'on message'. This is because accuracy forms the foundation of subsequent principles. If a creative idea is the result of a combination of two or more existing ideas, then input towards its formation must be accurate. If the information is wrong to start with, then the subsequent combinations will be completely 'off message' no matter how novel the combination. For this reason, it is important for the creative brief to be accurate.

PRINCIPLE 2: LOOK FOR AMAZING FACTS ABOUT THE BRAND OR ORGANISATION

Related to the idea of accurate input is unearthing an amazing fact about the brand that the creative personnel can exploit. Amazing facts will naturally arouse the curiosity of the target audience because they are inherently interesting. They are also something against which the target audience cannot easily argue.

Creative personnel love amazing facts because there is a unique truism that they are unbeatable – an easy USP. The classic example is David Ogilvy's 1957 'Clock' ad for Rolls Royce. When Ogilvy got the Rolls account, he spent three weeks reading all the material about the car and came across this amazing fact: 'At 60 miles an hour, the loudest noise comes from the electric clock.' This became the headline for a winning campaign.[46] Another example is that of Saab (i.e. Svenska Aeroplan AB), which incidentally means 'Swedish Aeroplane Company'. The amazing fact is that this car started life at an aeroplane company. But according to David Barker of Humphreys Bull & Barker, this fact was buried in the creative brief, which, once unearthed, paved the way for the 'Aircraft Inspired' winning campaign. It led to Saab's sales doubling in only a few years.[47]

Another good example of this principle is the ad for the Australian beer company Coopers. The ad (see figure 6.18) appears on Australia Day with copy that emphasises the amazing fact that Coopers remains successfully family-owned, 150 years after its creation in 1862. The headline

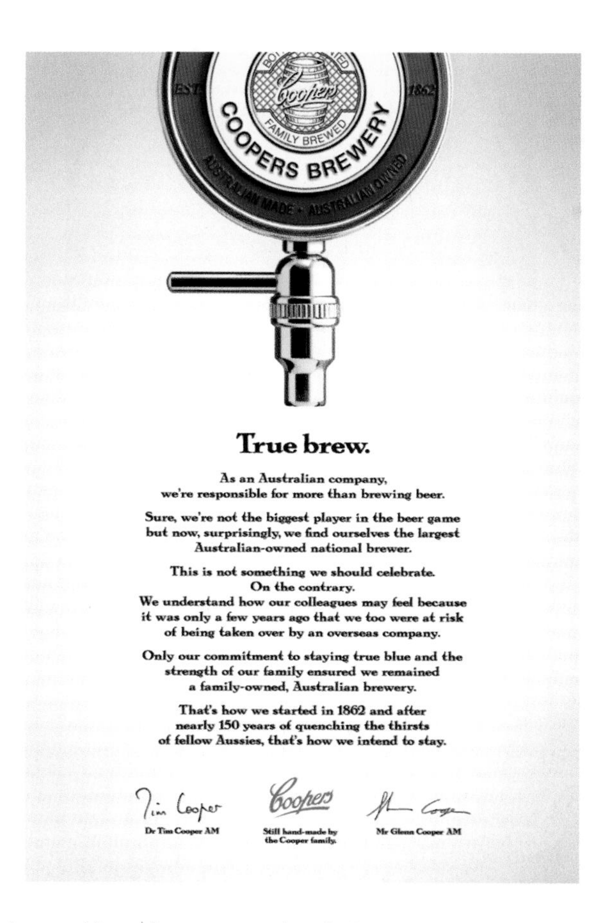

Figure 6.18 A Coopers beer ad based on an amazing fact

'True brew' plays on the phrase 'True blue' (meaning authentic Australian), popularised by the Australian folk singer John Williamson – a very fitting sentiment for a national day.

And what about this as an amazing fact to sell Burger King: founded in 1954, Burger King has prided itself as the burger that is flamed grilled (i.e. barbequed), not fried (like McDonald's). But cooking with fire can be dangerous and Burger King has the greatest number of restaurants burnt down since its inception. This amazing fact has been cleverly used to position its burger as 'flame grilled'.

PRINCIPLE 3: GO FOR QUANTITY

Would you settle for the first idea that comes to mind? Probably not, because the first idea is rarely a good one. This principle rests on two assumptions: sampling distribution and randomness of solutions. Sampling distribution means that, in any given pool of ideas, some will be good and some will be bad, but most (within two standard deviations) will be average. Therefore, to get to the extremely good ideas, you need to generate lots of them. In other words, the more ideas we generate, the greater the probability that a good idea will emerge (hitting top 5% of the distribution). In other words, it is simply the law of averages,[48] as represented in a normal distribution curve (shown in figure 6.19). But to get to this normal distribution, we need to generate at least 25 different ideas.

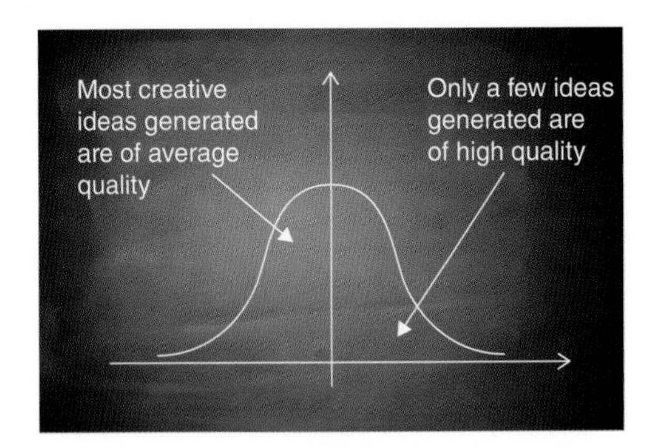

Figure 6.19 An illustration of normal distribution of the quality of creative ideas

Studies of creative achievements show a high correlation between quantity and quality ($r = 0.8$ and 0.9 for females and males, respectively).[49] If the ideas come from different sources, even better, because this maximises differences between viewpoints. However, to produce lots of ideas, the creative personnel must have a passion for their work and must be persistent. Another important requirement is to separate the creative phase from that of the evaluation, in order to minimise disruption to the creative flow (see the Further Thinking section of this chapter on brainstorming). So, generate lots of ideas *first* before evaluating them. This includes coming up with different variations of the same idea as well (e.g. by rejigging, modifying, re-doodling, or rewriting the initial idea). Evaluation can come later, even days later.

PRINCIPLE 4: LOOK FOR HUMAN TRUTH AND LINK IT TO THE BRAND'S BENEFIT

Related to the idea of looking for an amazing fact is to look for truisms about consumers' lives. These are sayings that are so self-evident that on their own they are banal. However, when linked to a brand's benefit, such sayings suddenly become interesting. This tends to disarm the viewers and lessens counterarguments. Comedians have long understood that human truths can be mined for their comic value. Jerry Seinfeld's keen observations about human behaviour (typically of the New York kind) are a prime example of this. Below are some examples in the form of slogans.

- Life is too short to drink lousy coffee (Dunkin' Donuts)
- Take a break (Kit Kat)
- An apple a day keeps the doctor away (US apple growers)
- Don't make the same mistake *once* (*The Economist* magazine)

Human truths sometimes take the form of storytelling but have a twist which makes the amplification of the brand benefit compelling. For instance, getting people to donate for a charitable cause often involves telling a heart-warming story (see A Minute of Silence below).

But what happens if we cannot find a simple human truth in a product? Then a simple wordplay, linked to a visual that exaggerates a benefit, is another viable option (see figure 6.20).

Figure 6.20 An example of wordplay with visual exaggeration of the benefit

Of course, if neither human truths nor visual exaggeration can be achieved, then stick to a straightforward linkage of the brand to the benefit as in these examples.

- Designed for driving pleasure (BMW – Germany)
- The ultimate driving machine (BMW – US)
- Connecting people (Nokia)
- Breakfast of champions (Wheaties)
- Raid kills bugs dead (Raid)

A MINUTE OF SILENCE

One truism in life is we want to feel connected. One way to feel connected is to be part of something important. Technology can also help facilitate this. A good example is the 'minute of silence' campaign by the RSL (or Returned and Services League), a body set up to support veterans of war and their families.

Every year during Anzac Day (25 April), commemorations will begin by observing a minute of silence. It is meant to remind all of us of the atrocities of war (lest we forget). During this time, we feel charitable and want to donate to the RSL by buying an ANZAC badge. But few do because we do not carry cash. RSL came up with an ingenious idea where we can donate using our smartphone. All we need to do is to ring a telephone number and observe silence for one minute. There is no need for credit cards or apps, just listen silently for a minute. When you hang up, the donation goes straight onto your phone bill, accompanied by a thank you text message, as well as a link to a video showing a veteran thanking you for your donation. It is heart-warming, and you can electronically send the appeal to your friends via your smartphone. This campaign is supported by print, radio, outdoor, and social media, as well as a series of short films of veterans recalling memories and telling of stories. They serve to remind donors that their donation is not ephemeral, but real.

This is an ingenious way of using technology because the donor does not have to do (or say) anything, just ring and observe a minute of silence before hanging up. Fundamentally, we all want to do good, and sometimes, the clever use of technology makes this easier. The campaign has raised over $3 million.[50]

PRINCIPLE 5: COMPARATIVE JUXTAPOSITION

The classic example of this tactic is the 'pre–post difference in weight loss' ad. The 'before' picture is one of a person pre-weight loss and the 'after' picture is that of the same person, but this time, magically transformed into a slim, highly attractive person. This tactic is highly effective because it triggers our curiosity as we try to understand the differences in the juxtapositions. But the juxtaposition does not always have to be this obvious. It can also take on a more subtle form, as shown in the ad for WWF (see figure 6.21). The risk is viewers may not 'get it'. Fundamentally, however, it is still about comparing the juxtapositions and understanding the differences.

Figure 6.21 An example of the comparative juxtaposition tactic

PRINCIPLE 6: BLEND, COMBINE AND OPPOSE

While quantity breeds quality, combining two earlier ordinary ideas can lead to more ideas. If these two ideas come from different domains, the resulting idea will be even more interesting. This, as we know, is the basis of RAT in creativity. It also means that there is never a bad idea, because when an idea is blended and combined with another, a new and better one will emerge. One simple tactic is to blend the brand name with its benefit, as seen in the Heineken ad

Figure 6.22 An example of 'blending' the brand name with its benefit

(see figure 6.22). Another tactic is to combine two benefits. When Apple launched its MacBook Air campaign in 2008, one of its print campaigns had a simple one-word headline: 'Thinnovation'. MacBook Air was the thinnest personal computer at that time.

Modern technology has greatly increased the versatility of the blending tactic. In January 2020, Uber Eats, the food delivery conglomerate, enlisted the help of tennis superstars and hijacked the Australian Open in a series of clever TV ads. The Australian Open is a grand slam event attracting top-class players from around the world. In one ad, the players interrupt their play mid-stream, look to camera and say, 'Tonight, I will be eating [Thai Chicken]'; an Uber Eats package is then handed to the player. In another TV ad, Rafael Nadal has an argument with the referee not over a point but over what dish to order from Uber Eats. The ads were executed in such a way that they looked as if they were happening during a live match. Viewers would think they were returning to the match after a commercial break, only to realise that it was actually an ad for Uber Eats. The ads were so well blended (i.e. shot, edited and placed) and seamlessly integrated into the live program that some viewers began to wonder if at any time the game would suddenly become an Uber Eats ad.

Figure 6.23 The Roman god Janus – a god with two faces

Sometimes we can choose to deliberately think of opposing ideas, which can also lead to novel combination. This is called 'bisociation' or 'Janusian thinking', after the Roman god Janus, who faces and looks into the past and future simultaneously (see figure 6.23).

EXAMPLES OF 'JANUSIAN' (OPPOSING) HEADLINES

- Tough on dirt. Gentle on fabrics (Whirlpool washing machines)
- Alive with bugs, dead with Raid (Raid)
- Devilishly good taste, 90 saintly calories (Baskin-Robbins ice-cream)
- Life's short, play more (Xbox 360)
- Apocalypse: beauty and horror in contemporary art (Royal Academy, London)
- Dress like a model, shop like an accountant (eBay)

PRINCIPLE 7: CONSIDER ANALOGIES, METAPHOR, PERSONIFICATION AND PUNS

This section is all about exploiting multiple or similar-sounding meanings of words or visuals, for an intended creative effect. When such tactics fail, it is because the ambiguities are not understood. So, there is always a danger in using them.

Great storytellers have long understood the power of using analogies, metaphors and parables to tell stories. The fame of the Ancient Greek figure Aesop (660–560 BCE) survived because of his stories such as 'The hare and the tortoise' or 'The goose that laid the golden egg'. Analogies make the message interesting by drawing out similarities from another domain.[51] In the case of

Aesop's fables, the domain is often that of animals, but the point being made is about human nature.

An example of this principle is an ad for a chiropractor, Orlando Prado (see figure 6.24). By using two different shaped pretzels to represent the human backbone before and after seeing Prado, the ad cleverly conveys his expertise. This form of visual metaphor is called 'personification', the attribution of human qualities to inanimate objects.

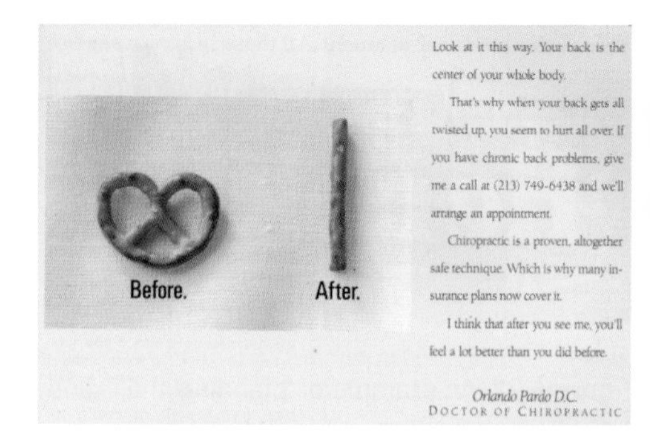

Figure 6.24 An ad that illustrates a visual analogy

Another good example of this tactic is the Bonds ad for men's underwear we saw in chapter 5. Instead of showing real testicles, the ad shows two boys sitting in a basket (see figure 5.10).

The use of the pun is another tactic. Puns are words that have more than one meaning. We often see this tactic used in news headlines. For example, when Margaret Thatcher ('the Iron Lady') died, one newspaper had the following headline: 'May she rust in peace'. The headline of an article about the shoemaker extraordinaire Jimmy Choo was 'If the Choo fits'.

What about the headline of print ads? Early research found that the use of such rhetorical devices, including that of pun, is indeed quite common. And it can also be effective if it is properly executed. For instance, in one study the headline of a flashlight ad reads, 'The gift idea that leaves everyone beaming'. The control ad had the word 'happy' instead of 'beaming'. It was found that ads like those of the flashlight resulted in better recall than the control ad.[52] This is because such ads invite the reader to elaborate on the message, so creating multiple pathways in memory. They are also interesting for the reader and may in fact be more efficient, since fewer words are needed to deliver the same message. In Australia, the Remedy company that sells a kombucha drink (without sugar) came up with a clever pun for its headline (see figure 6.25).

Figure 6.25 An ad's headline that illustrates pun

PRINCIPLE 8: ENTERTAIN EXAGGERATIONS

To understand this principle, please complete this sentence:

This superglue is so sticky that ________________.

Completing such a sentence[53] will trigger all sorts of ideas that can amplify the benefits, as in these examples:

- sticking a person upside down on the ceiling (Superglue 3)
- sticking a car on a billboard (Araldite)
- gluing two safety bolts together before the bungy jump[54] (Krazy Glue)
- using it on a mousetrap[55] (Pattex glue – see figure 6.26).

Figure 6.26 An ad that uses exaggeration

Figure 6.27 Another ad that uses exaggeration

This principle is a good place to start when we try to think divergently about the benefit. The outcome can be quite bizarre and humorous, but it tends to be very effective because it is clearly linked to the benefit (see chapter 7 on the dangers of using humour). Figure 6.27 is a good example of this, illustrating the idea of spiciness (an attribute) for Heinz Spicy Pepper sauce, which makes the food more delicious (a benefit).

Exaggerations are easy to execute with animation, and if accompanied with a catchy tune, the whole ad can be truly entertaining. A good example is the 'Dumb ways to die' campaign for the Metro Melbourne train system (see figure 6.28). The objective of the campaign is to reduce accidents around stations which had at one point been on the rise. However, it seems young people, being rebellious, don't listen to public safety messages, and often behave foolishly around trains (e.g. dashing across tracks, slipping off platforms). The key message is to be safe around trains, and the strategy is to use humour and music to highlight this message. The campaign, which is one of the most successful in history, shows animated characters being humorously stabbed, cut, bitten, eaten, electrocuted, exploded, run over, while doing foolish things. The music is catchy, and its simplicity is almost hypnotic, which makes it easy and enjoyable to sing along.

Figure 6.28 Image of 'Dumb ways to die' campaign

PRINCIPLE 9: USE INSTINCTIVE CUES

We tend to be inherently attracted to certain cues. The most basic of these are sexual cues and cues from babies, which instinctively create approach tendencies in us. We can call these 'instinctive-approach' cues. Sexual cues are common in advertising and are often seen in ads for jeans, perfume and lingerie. Figure 6.29 shows how such cues can also be cleverly used by a law firm, and this example also plays on a human truth, discussed in the previous section, while figure 6.30 shows how such cues can also be used to sell luxury lingerie in retail in upmarket shopping centres in Australia.

Figure 6.29 An ad that uses instinctive cues

Figure 6.30 A retail use of instinctive cues

Sometimes, images of gore, blood and other taboos are used in advertising (e.g. Benetton ads). This is called 'shock advertising' and the cues they create are called 'instinctive-avoidance' cues. Although such cues attract our attention, they also create avoidance tendencies in consumers, so we must apply them carefully or risk them backfiring. We often see such cues in social marketing ads (e.g. anti-smoking or anti-speeding ads).

Australia in fact leads the world in legislating what images may be placed on cigarette packaging. The objective is to minimise branding, so that consumers cannot differentiate between brands, sometimes called plain packaging. However, as the plain packaging guideline shows (see figure 6.31), it is far from plain! The attention-grabbing graphic image is designed to make cigarettes unattractive, and presumably to create fear. In chapter 7, we will discuss in greater detail how to effectively use a fear appeal in TV advertising.

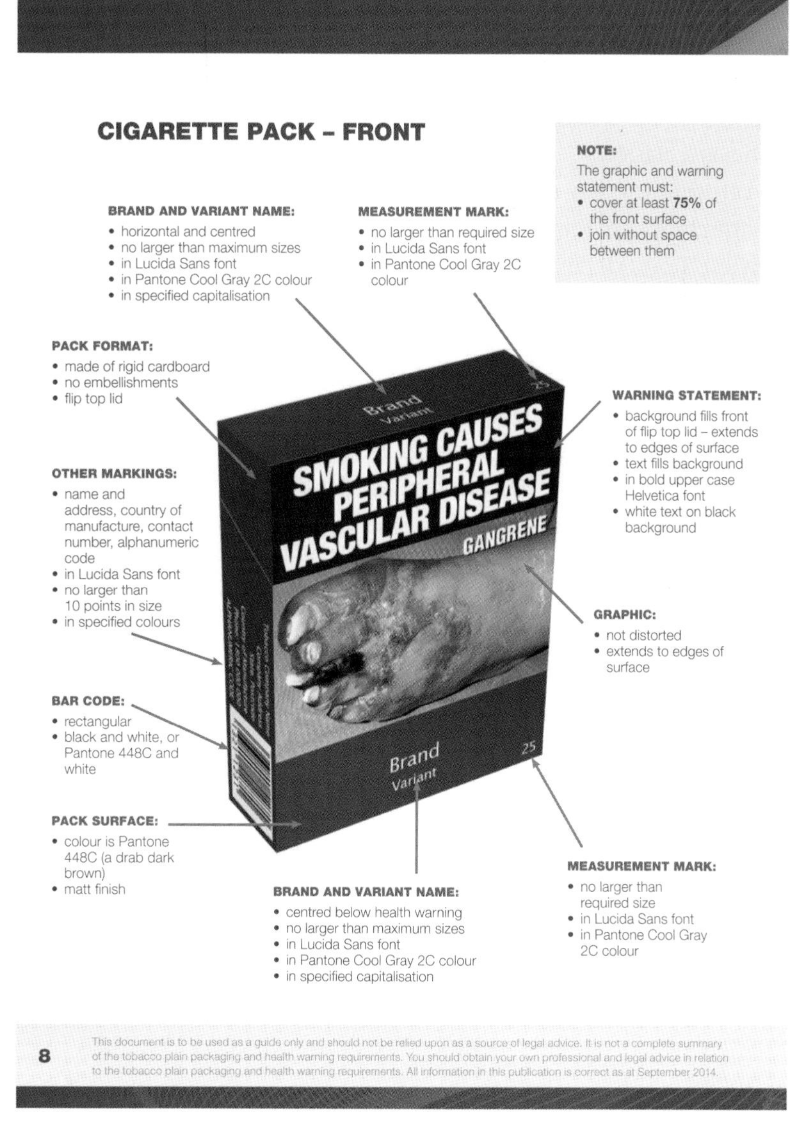

Figure 6.31 Plain packaging guideline of cigarette packs in Australia[57]

PRINCIPLE 10: TRY A DEVIANT VISUAL TWIST[56]

Look at the ad for SPSS data-collection software, now an IBM product (see figure 6.32). The ad shows an 11-pronged fork, unusual because it has many more prongs than usual. The fork instantly arouses readers' curiosity, but only by reading the headline – 'Data collection software that picks up more data' – can they make the link between the image and the software being promoted. In this example, the unusual feature of the fork is used to amplify the characteristics of the SPSS-branded software: the fork's distinctive picking-up qualities mirror the benefits of the SPSS-branded software, namely its superior data-collection capacity. Using an image of an ordinary fork would not have generated the same effect, because the associative match between the benefit of the conveyor (the ordinary fork) and the benefit of the product would not have been as strong or memorable.

Figure 6.32 A deviant ad that amplifies the brand benefit[58]

An ad by Kodak (see figure 6.33) is another example. This time the deviancy (a two-eyed dog) is used to amplify the attributes of the brand (i.e. dual lens). This is a classic.

This notion of deviancy can also be extended to a three-dimensional image as seen in the campaign for Victoria Transport Accident Commission. Instead of showing gory details of road accidents, the agency came up with the character Graham. While not exactly an ad, Graham is a grotesque sculpture (see figure 6.34) showing how the human form will need to change in order to survive a low-impact road accident. Developed in collaboration with a surgeon and a road safety engineer, using accident and medical data, a renowned sculptor reimagined how such a human would look. Through interactivity, Graham became an educational tool and ultimately a conversation starter about accidents and road safety throughout Australia. It is confronting and, certainly, a deviant human form.

Figure 6.33 A deviant ad that amplifies the brand attribute

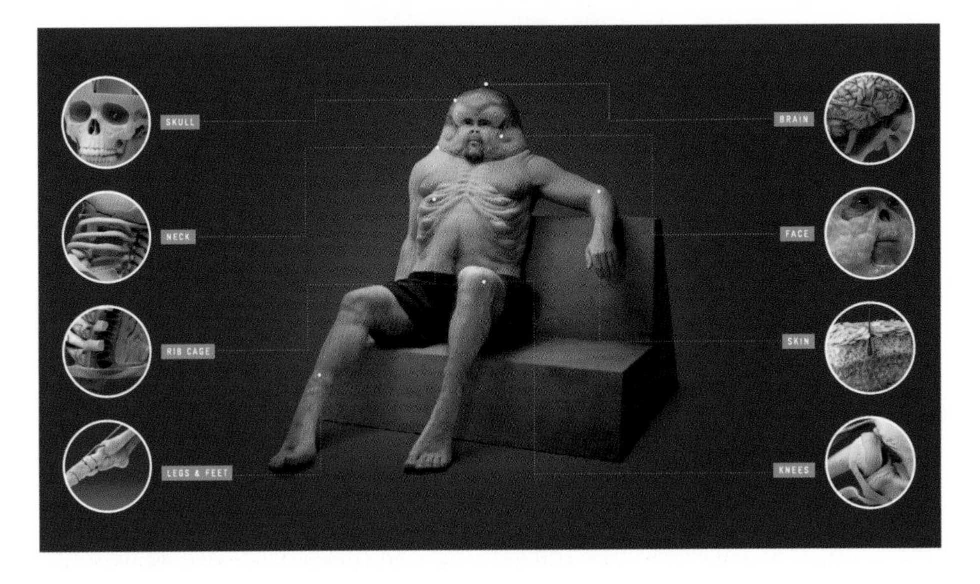

Figure 6.34 A deviant human form to drive home the message

PRINCIPLE 11: CREATE INSTINCTIVELY DEVIANT CUES

Finally, we can also combine principles 8 and 9 by making the instinctive cues deviant. The brand name FCUK is an example of this. It actually stands for French Connection United Kingdom but is also a deliberate misspelling of a well-known swearword. When this principle is applied visually, the result can be even more evocative. A good example is an Evian ad that featured babies wearing roller-skates. The TV ad showed babies still in their nappies roller-skating and doing impossible stunts. Instinctively we are drawn to babies and when they perform dramatic stunts, they become even more evocative.

Figure 6.35 An ad that is instinctively deviant

This principle can also be applied to print ads. The deviancy of such ads will increase our looking time, as we try to understand the relevance of the deviancy. Figure 6.35 is an example. It shows the classic Gillette ad that depicted a baby shaving. The creative idea of the ad was to demonstrate how safe it is to use a Gillette shaver. Since we like babies and know that babies do not shave, the ad combines both instinctive and deviant cues to startling effect. In another similar ad, which showed a baby smoking (not shown here), we found that the visual fixation time was about 4.2 seconds, more than twice that of an ordinary print ad.[59]

A note of caution

Although there are many ways to create deviancy,[60] it should be cautioned that whenever a deviant picture is to be used, the headline must solve the deviancy by prompting what the brand benefit is, or else comprehension will suffer. Or to put it in another way, if the picture is deviant, then the headline must be straightforward (and vice versa). If both the picture and the headline are deviant, then it is unlikely people will comprehend it.

Many of the principles above are illustrated with print ads or posters, for the simple reason that a good creative idea should be able to be summarised succinctly in this form. But as illustrated, the principles are also applicable to other digital forms. Testing a creative idea in a print ad is also a quick way to check whether the creative idea is 'on message'. If a creative idea cannot be succinctly summarised in this format, it is probably not crystal clear.

DIGITAL INNOVATION TO DRIVE BEHAVIOUR

As technology develops, there will be new ways to drive behaviour, as we saw in chapter 5 with Snickers Hungerithm (see case study 5.1). As another example, Burger King US developed an app where you can find a voucher to purchase a Burger King Whopper for just US$0.01. In other words, for just 1 cent, you can get a Burger King Whopper, but only if you have the Burger King app. The catch is that the app can only be downloaded if you are at McDonald's. In other words, Burger King is trying to steal McDonald's customers. It was an enormous success – another example of a clever use of technology to drive behaviour, which is great with promotions (see chapter 11). However, the downside is that it may not be profitable (at 1 cent a burger?), unless the change is permanent. Ideally, however, any innovative technological idea should be employed in a profitable way right from the beginning, as seen with Volvo's Intercept campaign (discussed in case study 6.1).

MANAGERIAL APPLICATION: PUTTING IT TOGETHER

Given the many diverse issues of advertising creativity discussed in this chapter, how can we make sense of it all? Figure 6.36 summarises the key ideas. First, it is important to understand the business problem (or opportunity) right from the start. A good creative brief is more likely to emerge if the marcoms manager has a clear understanding of the business issue. From this understanding, a new vision will emerge for the brand if it needs a new positioning, or if not, we can assume that the objective is to simply find new ideas to 'refresh' the brand. This sets the direction or creative strategy as summarised in the creative brief. The creative personnel are thoroughly briefed on this.

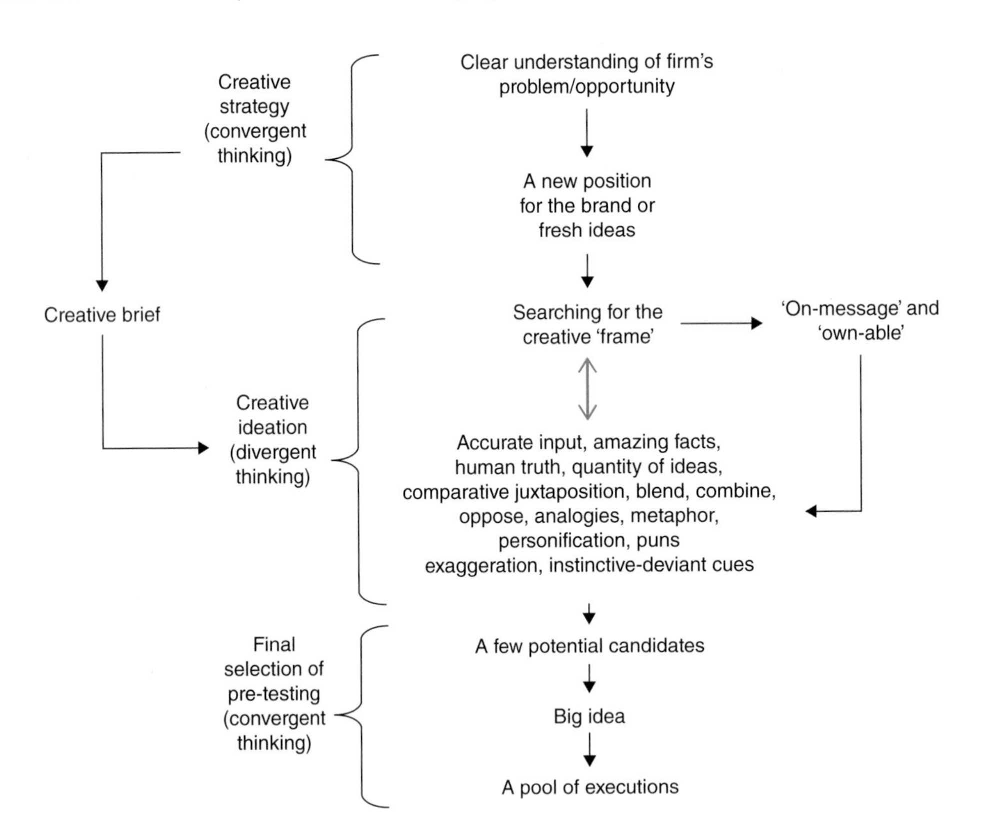

Figure 6.36 How key concepts in this chapter are connected

Once the creative personnel are briefed, they will begin to search for a creative 'frame' from which the final creative idea will emerge. As part of the ideation process, they will explore many ideas. The initial ideas may be off the mark, but eventually a pool of good ideas will emerge. Some may still lack the 'spark', but by further pushing the creative envelope, with divergent thinking (such as blending, combining exaggerating, and artful deviation), a prime candidate or two will edge towards finality.[61] Since this divergent thinking is rooted in solving the firm's problem, dictated right at the beginning, this final round of emergent ideas is likely to be 'on message' and 'own-able'.

The last stage is to select through a convergent thinking process the most promising of the ideas for evaluation or pre-testing. Note with the internet, pre-testing has become considerably cheaper, so it pays to test multiple potential good ideas, not just one (see chapter 12). The objective is to find the 'big idea' to enable a pool of creative executions to be derived from it. Finally, it should also be noted that even if the campaign were to be successful, the marcoms manager should not rest on his or her laurels. From time to time, a new idea should be commissioned and pre-tested to see if it can beat the incumbent idea.

FURTHER THINKING: BARRIERS TO CREATIVITY

So far we've discussed many aspects of advertising creativity. However, effective creative ideas still have to be generated, which is not easy. This section will briefly discuss barriers to creative advertising at the individual, group and organisation levels.

LEARNING GOALS

After reading this section, you will understand:

- how our cognitive associative network prevents us from thinking divergently
- what brainstorming is, why it is not necessarily the most productive way of generating ideas and how to overcome its shortcomings
- barriers to creativity at group and organisational levels (between clients and the agency), and how to overcome them.

CREATIVITY BARRIER AT THE INDIVIDUAL LEVEL

One reason why it is difficult to come up with creative ideas is the way our knowledge is structured. Human knowledge is said to be represented in the form of semantic networks.[62] Concepts and ideas are stored in interconnected memory nodes, so that semantically related concepts are strongly connected to each other. The activation of one concept induces the activation of other closely related concepts. This is called 'spreading activation'.[63] As a result, we tend to generate ideas that are similar to each other, sometimes called fluency.[64] But what is required in creative advertising is cognitive flexibility or divergent thinking, in which different concepts or ideas from another domain are generated instead – this is the basis of RAT.

Try this word-association test. What word comes to mind if you hear the word 'dog'? You might quickly say 'cat'. This is because these two words are most closely associated to each other in our semantic network. However, when a creative person is asked the same question, they might answer 'Miu Miu', the fashion brand, in which case we scratch our heads and ask why. The creative person explains that for him or her, the word 'dog' triggers 'cat', which triggers 'meow', which in turn triggers 'Miu Miu' because of the sound similarity. This example illustrates the notion that creative people might be quicker (i.e. more fluent) in accessing uncommon associations.[65] They are more likely to jump from one remote idea to another, displaying cognitive flexibility. A classic example is the late comedian Robin Williams, who could effortlessly spin jokes from one topic to another. For this reason, creative personnel are valued because they can come up with 'weird' ideas, but their energies need to be properly channelled so that the ideas will work.

This does not mean that creative personnel do not need help in coming up with workable solutions. They get tired, ideas dry up and there is the constant pressure to deliver a winning idea for the next client. To overcome such issues, books and even software have been written to assist them.[66] One leading advertising agency even developed a proprietary database of winning ads from around the world to assist their creative personnel.[67] All of these ads share one common element. They stimulate divergent thinking by using words or phrases or pictures from different semantic categories to trigger new solutions. They act as 'primes'. For instance, in an advertising task for a brand of chocolate, we can ask participants to think about ideas that relate to celebrities, countries or flowers. Each semantic category acts as a search cue to trigger a new train of thought[68] – that is, it primes trigger thoughts in semantic categories – that would otherwise not be easily accessible, and so overcomes cognitive fixation. Or to put it another way, the use of such primes can jolt a person out of a 'mental rut'. In fact, the more primes you give a person, the more productive they become,[69] and if the primes are unusual[70] or diverse,[71] they are also more likely to generate more useful ideas than common primes.

Although such divergent thinking tools exist, creative professionals tend to look at them unfavourably. This is because the creatives are already very good at thinking divergently, having internalised their own methods of doing so. Rather, what they need is a clear strategy.[72] That is why we emphasised the importance of having a well-defined problem right from the start, supported by a good brief (see figure 6.36).

Finally, all the techniques of divergent thinking in the world will not help if creative personnel have no passion for their work. Without an intrinsic motivation to want to produce outstanding work, they are less likely to produce good ads.[73]

CREATIVITY BARRIER AT THE GROUP LEVEL

Creativity at the individual level may not be sufficient because we work in teams (including virtual teams),[74] especially when multimedia integration across different platforms is called for. Being able to work effectively as a team to produce the best ideas becomes critical, and this is another potential barrier to creative work.

Brainstorming is the best known method for creative problem-solving. It involves a group of people sitting around discussing how to solve a problem. In the case of advertising, the objective is to come up with the big idea. Celebrated advertising executive Alex Osborn of BBDO (the 'O' in the BBDO) popularised brainstorming 60 years ago,[75] suggesting that to achieve the best results brainstorming has to follow four rules during the interaction:

1. generate lots of ideas
2. refrain from criticisms
3. encourage 'freewheeling' (going for the outrageous)
4. learn to combine and improve on existing ideas.

Early research confirmed the importance of Osborn's suggestions: groups that subscribe to these rules tend to be more productive than groups that do not.[76] However, subsequent research showed that although Osborn was correct when comparing across different *group* conditions, he was not correct when *individuals* are compared with groups.[77] Interactive group brainstorming in fact results in fewer ideas, sometimes as little as 50% of the equivalent number of individuals who first brainstormed individually and then had their ideas totalled.[78] Over the next 50 years, a huge amount of research effort was devoted by organisational psychologists (but not advertising researchers) towards understanding this seemingly counterintuitive, but robust, finding. Essentially, four major causes can explain why interactive group brainstorming is suboptimal:

1. *Production blocking*. Interactive group members have to wait their turn to speak, which not only leads members to self-censor or forget what they were about to say, but also interferes with their own idea-generation process.[79] This is especially true when delays are long and unpredictable.[80]
2. *Evaluation anxiety*. Interactive group members are afraid that others in the group may criticise their ideas. This may cause them to withdraw from the group or increase cognitive interference and so production blocking.[81] Research has shown that positive emotions, such as happiness and joy, tend to open up a person's mind and allow more information to flow in and be used for creative association. It also helps de-focus attention, so that a person becomes less fixated on old ideas. This increases the probability that diverse cognitive elements can be enlisted for associative work.[82] This theory is generally supported in a recent meta-analytical study.[83]
3. *Social loafing*. Interactive group members may let others in the group generate the bulk of the ideas and choose to simply 'loaf' or 'free-ride'. This is especially so when they think their contributions are unmonitored or irrelevant.[84] On the other hand, free-riding is diminished when each member's contribution is identified or when individuals are made accountable.[85]
4. *Downward social matching*. Interactive group members may adopt a low benchmark set early in the brainstorming session (due to the above three factors), leading to continually low output. In other words, once a low benchmark is established early in the brainstorming session, it becomes the norm. This then serves as a brake on productivity throughout the brainstorming period. This downward bias will continue because interactive group members may not want to create any tension or look foolish within the group.[86]

Given these major inhibitive factors cause loss of productivity, what can we do to counter them? Table 6.1 shows some suggested solutions.

Table 6.1 Sources of inhibition and some potential solutions

Inhibitive sources	Potential solutions and suggestions
Production blocking	*The solution is to independently generate new ideas before the meeting and to manage the combinatory process systematically so that there is no loss of productivity.* • Ask group members to independently generate a large number of ideas before coming to the meeting. • Say that the ideas should be different and that it is all right to be outrageous. • Collect all the written ideas at the beginning of the meeting and systematically discuss them one by one in no particular order so that no ideas are missed. • For each idea discussed, spend time thinking how it can be combined with others.
Evaluation anxiety	*The solution is to have fun during brainstorming so that there is no evaluation anxiety.* • Create a fun atmosphere before the meeting starts, perhaps showing a short, humorous clip.

Table 6.1 *(cont.)*

Inhibitive sources	Potential solutions and suggestions
	• Stress that there are no bad ideas but only ideas that can be improved. • Since there are no right or wrong answers, group members are encouraged to explore without pre-judgement. • Ban criticism of ideas until the evaluation stage. • Leave evaluation to the end of the meeting.
Social loafing	*The solution is to ensure that all respondents work hard before and during brainstorming so that no one will be allowed to be slack.* • Tell members before the meeting that all ideas will be taken seriously. • Inform them that at the start of the meeting that all ideas will be put on the table as evidence that members have done their homework. • The owner of each idea will be clearly identified during the meeting to increase accountability.
Downward social matching	*The solution is to set high expectations that respondents will generate a large number of ideas and to strive for this ideal right from the start.* • Tell members that a large quantity of ideas are expected, and that it is better to be known as a person who has ideas rather than a person who has none. • Create a fast momentum at the beginning by generating new ideas quickly in order to establish a higher norm. • Ensure that all ideas are fully explored so that the momentum is not lost.

CREATIVITY BARRIER AT THE ORGANISATIONAL LEVEL

Finally, creativity can also be chocked at the organisational level, simply because it is risky.[87] The key to fixing this problem is the relationship between the client (i.e. the marketer) and the agency. While the advertising agency's role is to create the ad, the client who commissions the campaign is just as responsible for its success. For instance, if the client is not open to new ideas, does not support the agency with insightful research, does not give the agency sufficient time to ruminate, and is too dictatorially evaluative or even too sophisticated, the creative quality of the ad will suffer.[88]

Sometimes, a creativity barrier can occur within the advertising agency itself. One study found that the more support the advertising agency gives its creative personnel the more likely they are to produce high-quality creative ads.[89] This effect is twice as powerful if the creative personnel are also passionate about their work. Therefore, the key lesson is to ensure that the creative personnel feel that passion and support them in their work. When this occurs, they are more likely to produce outstanding work and win awards.[90]

But ultimately, great campaigns can only come about when there is true and trusting partnership between the client and its advertising agency. The partnership between Apple and TBWA/Chiat/Day is a good example; together, they created one of the most iconic campaigns in the history of modern advertising, that of 'Think Different'.[91]

DISCUSSION QUESTIONS

1. What is the theory of remote associate thinking (RAT) developed by Sarnoff Mednick? How is RAT related to the remote associative matching (RAM) model of advertising creativity?
2. Using the RAM model, explain how a creative ad can go wrong in terms of how people process it.
3. What is the difference between a creative idea and a creative strategy?
4. How does a good creative brief relate to the creative idea and the creative strategy? Do you think is it important to have one? Explain your answer.
5. Why do you think it is important to have accurate input before thinking of a creative idea for a brand?
6. Why is it important to generate lots of ideas while thinking of a creative idea (the 'go for quantity' principle)? How does this relate to convergent and divergent thinking?
7. How is it possible to tell whether the execution of a creative idea is creatively integrated?
8. Choose one example from today's media to illustrate each of the divergent thinking advertising principles. Discuss each in terms of whether it is creatively integrated.
9. Explain what falling into a 'mental rut' means in the creative thinking process. What is a potential solution to this issue?
10. What four basic principles of brainstorming did Alex Osborn suggest 60 years ago? What are the four inhibitive factors that hamper the productivity level of group brainstorming, and how can we counter them?
11. High-quality creative output can be dampened at the organisational level. What would you do if you were a marcoms manager in charge of a yet-to-be developed campaign?

NOTES

1 M Wedel and R Pieters, 'Eye fixations on advertisements and memory for brands: a model and findings', *Marketing Science*, 19(4), 2000, pp. 297–312.

2 S Cramphorn, 'Does originality contribute to ad effectiveness?', *Admap*, 465, 2005, pp. 16–17.

3 P Dyson, 'Top 10 drivers of advertising profitability', *Admap*, September, 2014. Accessed September 2019 at www.warc.com/content/paywall/article/top-10-drivers-of-advertising-profitability/102715.

4 Booz Allen & Hamilton, *Management and advertising problems in the advertiser–agency relationship*, Association of National Advertisers, New York, 1965.

5 RD Buzzell, 'Predicting short-term changes in market share as a function of advertising strategy', *Journal of Marketing Research*, 1(3), 1964, pp. 27–31.

6 MH Blair, 'An empirical investigation of advertising wearin and wearout', *Journal of Advertising Research*, 40(6), 2000, pp. 95–100.

7 Adapted from Blair (2000), 'An empirical investigation', note 6.

8 L Lodish and CF Mela, 'If brands are built over years, why are they managed over quarters?', *Harvard Business Review*, July–August, 2007, pp. 104–12.
9 D McCrudden, '10 lessons for media planning', *Warc Trends*, 18–19 December, 2011, pp. 18–19.
10 D Gunn, 1966, 'Do award winning commercials sell?'. Accessed April 2013 at www.youtube.com/watch?v=I9KNh9fb9r8.
11 P Field, 'Creativity and effectiveness', *Institute of Practitioners in Advertising from Advertising Works*, 19, 2010, pp. 3–6.
12 P Field, 'The value of creativity', *Market Leader*, Quarter 2, 2011, pp. 42–5.
13 This is based on Les Binet and Peter Field's IPA case studies, reported in Cila Warncke, 'Advertising effectiveness: the long and short of it', *Event Reports*, 2012.
14 M Brodherson, J Heller, J Perrey and D Remley, 'Creativity's bottom line: How winning companies turn creativity into business value and growth', 16 June 2017. Accessed July 2018 on McKinsey.com at: www.mckinsey.com/business-functions/digital-mckinsey/our-insights/creativitys-bottom-line-how-winning-companies-turn-creativity-into-business-value-and-growth.
15 T Ambler and EA Hollier, 'The waste in advertising is the part that works', *Journal of Advertising Research*, 44(4), 2004, pp. 375–89.
16 M Dahlen, F Torn and S Rosengren, 'Advertising creativity matters', *Journal of Advertising* Research, 48(3), September 2008, pp. 392–403. A recent meta-analysis on creative-induced advertising affects, it is this signaling that causes consumers to like the brand most. See S Rosengren, M Eisend, M Dahlen and S Koslow, 'A meta-analysis of when and how advertising creativity works', *Journal of Marketing*, 2020, forthcoming.
17 J Steel, *Truth, lies and advertising: the art of account planning*, John Wiley & Sons, New York, 1998.
18 J Samios, 'ABC's Gruen the most watched non-news show of Wednesday night', 2018. Accessed June 2019 at https://mumbrella.com.au/abcs-gruen-the-most-watched-non-news-show-of-wednesday-night-518174.
19 Merchdope, '37 Mind Blowing YouTube Facts, Figures and Statistics – 2019', January 2019. Accessed June 2019 at https://merchdope.com/youtube-stats/.
20 D Southgate, N Westoby and G Page, 'Creative determinants of viral video viewing', *International Journal of Advertising*, 29(3), 2010, pp. 349–68.
21 WARC, 'Volvo US: the greatest interception', Cannes Creative Lions, Creative Effectiveness Lions, 2016. Accessed October 2020 at www.carat.com/caratcdn/media/9388/jan-2018-executive-summary-final.pdf.
22 A Politz, 'The dilemma of creative advertising', *Journal of Marketing*, 25(2), 1960, pp. 1–6.
23 S Koslow, SL Sasser and EA Riordan, 'Do marketers get the advertising they need or the advertising they deserve? Agency views of how clients impact creativity', *Journal of Advertising Research*, 35 (3), 2006, pp. 81–101. In this book, we prefer the term 'on message' rather than 'on strategy' because the latter is much more difficult to assess in terms of communication objectives.
24 S Mednick, 'The associative basis of creative thinking', *Psychological Review*, 69, 1962, pp. 220–32.
25 Although there are many ways of looking at creativity in advertising, the fundamental thing is its ability to bring together elements from different domains.
26 See L Ang, 'The incongruity-resolution theory of advertising creativity', PhD dissertation, Australian Graduate School of Management, University of New South Wales, 1995, for my original conceptualisation of this theory. For a subsequent test, see L Ang, 'Towards a structural theory of creativity in print advertising: the remote associate matching theory model', *Australasian Marketing Journal*, 8(1), 2000, pp. 31–44. For further elaboration see JR Rossiter and L Percy,

Advertising communications and promotion management, McGraw-Hill, New York, 1997. I am grateful to John Rossiter for his input in our collaborative effort. My theory was recently confirmed by Niek Althuizen; see 'Communicating a key benefit claim ceatively and effectively through five conveyor properties', *Psychology & Marketing*, 34(1), 2017, pp. 5–18.

27 The importance of creativity triggering curiosity (or the postponement of closure) is supported by X Yang and RE Smith, 'Beyond attention effects: modeling the persuasive emotional effects of advertising creativity', *Marketing Science*, September/October 2009, pp. 935–49.

28 BJ Philips, 'The impact of verbal anchoring on consumer response to image ads', *Journal of Advertising*, 29, Spring, 2000, pp. 15–24.

29 This ad is inspired by a somewhat similar ad for the city of Minneapolis. We were not able to obtain permission to show the original ad.

30 L Bergkvist, D Eiderback and M Palimbo, 'The brand communication effects of using a headline to prompt the key benefit in ads with pictorial metaphors', *Journal of Advertising*, 41(2), 2012, pp. 67–75.

31 J Romaniuk, 'Lifting the productivity of TV advertising', *Journal of Advertising Research*, 2, 2012, pp. 146–8.

32 In interviewing copywriters, Kover found that breaking through and delivering the message are their uppermost concerns. See J Arthur, 'Copywriters' implicit theories of communication: an exploration', *Journal of Consumer Research*, 21(4), 1995, pp. 596–611.

33 The second part of this definition is modified from Andrew Robertson, President and CEO of BBDO Worldwide. See Gunn 100, 'Why creativity is king in an age of personalization', *100 – Lessons from the world's best creative campaign*, p. 6.

34 Creative ads are generally more complex which affects processing. See S Rosengren, M Eisend, M Dahlen and S Koslow, 'A meta-analysis of when and how advertising creativity works', *Journal of Marketing*, 2020, forthcoming. That is why it is important that a creative ad should also be single-minded. Case study 6.1 is a good example of this.

35 This is based on the idea of the creative magnifier by Millward Brown. See A Farr and S Gardiner, 'Creative enough for the financial director?', *Admap*, 36(3), March 2001, pp. 25–8.

36 Campaign Brief, 'Yalumba wine points to "Y" in new campaign and spot for its "Y Series" via Adelaide agency kwp!', 1 November 2012. Accessed April 2013 at www.campaignbrief.com/2012/11/yalumba-wine-points-to-y-in-ne.html.

37 R White, 'Best practice: briefing creative agencies', *Admap*, 440, 2003, pp. 12–13. I included the additional item of a message proposition, separating it from brand positioning because of its importance in sparking a creative idea.

38 J Best, 'A history of planning: planning through the decades', *Admap*, February 2010, pp. 30–1.

39 See Steel (1998), *Truth, lies and advertising*, note 17.

40 JM Dru, *Disruption: overturning conventions and shaking up the marketplace*, John Wiley & Sons, New York, 1997.

41 T White and G Roberts, 'PepsiCo Walkers: Sandwich', Institute of Practitioners in Advertising, Bronze, IPA Effectiveness Awards, 2011.

42 Interview with Steve Coll. Accessed July 2013 at www.bestadsontv.com/ad/37809/Campaign-Brief-Creative-Effectiveness-Grand-Prix-winner-Steve-Coll.

43 You can see the explanation here: www.youtube.com/watch?v=DClOTJyVQzc.

44 SL Sasser and S Koslow, 'Desperately seeking advertising creativity', *Journal of Advertising*, 37(4), 2008, pp. 5–19.

45 Another template one can use is that of Goldenberg et al., but it is a little more abstract. See J Goldenberg, D Mazursky and S Solomon, 'The fundamental templates of quality ads', *Marketing Science*, 18(3), 1999, pp. 333–51.

46 D Ogilvy, *Ogilvy on advertising*, Prion Books, London, 2000.

47 D Barker, 'How to write an inspiring creative brief', *Admap*, 419, July 2001.

48 Many years ago, Irwin Gross suggested a mathematical formula to work this out more precisely, taking into consideration the number of ideas generated and the validity and reliability of the pre-testing methodology. I Gross, 'The creative aspects of advertising', *Sloan Management Review*, 14(1), 1967, pp. 83–109.

49 KH Kim, 'Can we trust creativity tests? A review of the Torrance Tests of Creative Thinking (TTCT)', *Creativity Research Journal*, 18(1), 2006, pp. 3–14.

50 This campaign won a major creativity award, which you can watch here www.dandad.org/awards/professional/2015/white-pencil-creativity-for-good/24222/minute-of-silence/. Accessed June 2019.

51 Picture analogy is by far the largest class of tactic used among creative award-winning ads at 38%. J Goldenberg, D Mazursky and S Solomon, 'The fundamental templates of quality ads', *Marketing Science*, 18(3), 1999, pp. 333–51.

52 EF McQuarrie and GD Mick, 'Visual and verbal rhetorical figures under directed processing versus incidental exposure to advertising', *Journal of Consumer Research*, 29, 2003, pp. 579–87.

53 Pete Barry has suggested this technique. See P Barry, *The advertising concept book*, Thames & Hudson, London, 2008, p. 136.

54 You can see this on this Facebook site: www.facebook.com/krazyglue?sk=app_163102550429279

55 This is also an analogy where the glue is used as a replacement for the tapping mechanism. Exaggeration can lead to this outcome.

56 This is similar to the suggestion (by Goldenberg, Mazursky and Solomon (1999), 'The fundamental templates of quality ads', note 51) of using an extreme attribute or worth for this class of extreme situation. This class makes up 13% of all creative ads in their study.

57 Australian Government, Department of Health, 'Tobacco plain packaging – your guide'. Accessed June 2019.

58 SPSS Inc. was acquired by IBM in October 2009.

59 L Ang and S Hutton, 'Achieving visual attention in print: a preliminary study of visual fixations to deviant and evocative ads', *International Conference of Research in Advertising*, Lisbon, Portugal, June, 2007.

60 For example, see Ang (1995), 'The incongruity-resolution theory of advertising creativity', note 26.

61 Sometimes, having guidance on what makes an ad original can help produce a consistent result – see J Goldenberg and D Mazursky, 'When deep structures surface', *Journal of Advertising*, 37(4), 2008, pp. 21–34.

62 JR Anderson, *Cognitive psychology and its implications*, 5th edition, Worth Publishers, New York, 2000.

63 AM Collins and EF Loftus, 'A spreading-activation theory of semantic processing', *Psychological Review*, 82, 1975, pp. 407–28.

64 JP Guildford, 'Creativity', *American Psychologist*, 5, 1950, pp. 444–54.

65 M Benedek and AC Neubauer, 'Revisiting Mednick's Model on Creativity-Related Differences in Associative Hierarchies. Evidence for a common path to uncommon thought', *The Journal of Creative Behaviour*, 47(4), 2013, pp. 273–89.

66 R Von Oech, *A whack on the side of the head: how to unlock your mind for innovation*, Warner Books, New York, 1983. ThoughtOffice™ is one of the many brainstorming software products in the market.

67 See Dru (1997), *Disruption*, note 40.

68 BA Nijstad, W Stroebe and HFM Lodewijkx, 'Cognitive stimulation and interference in groups: exposure effects in an idea-generating task', *Journal of Experimental Social Psychology*, 38, 2002, pp. 535–44.

69 H Coskun et al., 'Cognitive stimulation and problem presentation in idea-generation groups', *Group Dynamics: Theory, Research and Practice*, 4, 2000, pp. 307–29.

70 KL Leggett, 'The effectiveness of categorical priming in brainstorming', unpublished Masters' thesis, University of Texas, Arlington, 1997.

71 Nijstad, Stroebe and Lodewijkx (2002), 'Cognitive stimulation and interference in groups', note 68.

72 M Kilgour and S Koslow, 'Why and how do creative thinking techniques work? Trading off originality and appropriateness to make more creative advertising', *Journal of Academy of Marketing Science*, 37(3), 2009, pp. 298–309.

73 S Sasser and S Koslow, 'Passion, expertise, politics and support', *Journal of Advertising*, 41(3), 2012, pp. 5–17.

74 In the modern digital era, there is far more collaboration and teamwork in developing a concept. The pairing of an art director with a copywriter may be passing. See N Southgate, 'Three key steps to briefing creative', *Warc Best Practices*, 506, 2009, pp. 12–13.

75 AF Osborn, *Applied imagination: principles and procedures of creative problem-solving*, Charles Scribner's Sons, New York, 1953.

76 SJ Parnes and A Meadow, 'Effects of "brainstorming" instructions on creative problem solving by trained and untrained subjects', *Journal of Educational Psychology*, 50, 1959, pp. 171–6.

77 DW Taylor, PC Berry and CH Block, 'Does group participation when brainstorming facilitate or inhibit creative thinking?', *Administrative Science Quarterly*, 3, 1958, pp. 23–47.

78 For a review see NL Kerr and RS Tindale, 'Group performance and decision making', *Annual Review of Psychology*, 55, 2004, pp. 623–55.

79 W Stroebe and M Diehl, 'Why groups are less effective than their members: on productivity losses in idea-generating groups', in W Stroebe and M Hewstone (eds), *European review of social psychology*, vol. 5, Wiley, London, 1994, pp. 271–303.

80 BA Nijstad, W Stroebe and HFM Lodewijkx, 'Production blocking and idea generation: does blocking interfere with cognitive processes?', *Journal of Experimental Social Psychology*, 39, 2003, pp. 531–48.

81 ML Camacho and PB Paulus, 'The role of anxiousness in group brainstorming', *Journal of Personality and Social Psychology*, 68, 1995, pp. 1071–80.

82 AM Isen, KA Daubman and GP Nowicki, 'Positive affect facilitates creative problem solving', *Journal of Personality and Social Psychology*, 52(6), 1987, pp. 1122–31; BL Fredrickson, 'The role of positive emotions in positive psychology: the broaden-and-build theory of positive emotions', *American Psychologist*, 56(3), 2001, pp. 218–26.

83 M Baas, CKW De Dreu and BA Nijstad, 'A meta-analysis of 25 years of mood-creativity research: hedonic tone, activation, or regulatory focus?', *Psychological Bulletin*, 134(6), November 2008, pp. 779–806.

84 JA Sheppard, 'Productivity loss in performance groups: a motivation analysis', *Psychological Bulletin*, 113, 1993, pp. 67–81.

85 SG Harkins and RE Petty, 'Effects of task difficulty and task uniqueness on social loafing', *Journal of Personality and Social Psychology*, 43(6), 1982, pp. 1214–29.

86 P Paulus and MT Dzindolet, 'Social influence process in group brainstorming', *Journal of Personality and Social Psychology*, 64, 1993, pp. 575–86.

87 J El-Murad and DC West, 'Risk and Creativity in Advertising', *Journal of Marketing Management*, 19, 2003, pp. 657–673.

88 S Koslow, S Sasser and EA Riordan, 'Do marketers get the advertising they need or the advertising they deserve?', *Journal of Advertising*, 35(3), 2006, pp. 81–101.

89 Sasser and Koslow (2012), 'Passion, expertise, politics and support', note 73.

90 A Dutch study also found that with organisational encouragement, agencies are more likely to win awards. See W Verbeke et al., 'Finding the keys to creativity in ad agencies', *Journal of Advertising*, 37(4), 2008, pp. 121–30.

91 'TBWA\Chiat\Day talks on making of Apple's Think Different campaign'. Accessed January 2019 at www.youtube.com/watch?v=p6djV0dX5AE.

CHAPTER 7
PLANNING AND EXECUTING THE CREATIVE APPEAL

CHAPTER OVERVIEW

In chapter 6 we discussed what an advertising creative idea is and how to increase the probability of finding the big idea. But what happens after that? Ideally, we should pre-test the idea (see chapter 12). But to do so, we need to first create the ad, sometimes called 'execution'. Things can still go wrong if the creative idea is not well executed, no matter how good it is; for instance, if the copy is difficult to comprehend, the humour is irrelevant, or the celebrity chosen does not fit the brand and so on. The aim of this chapter is to discuss how executional tactics can be used effectively. The discussion centres on what creative execution means and explains the difference between creative execution and the creative idea, stressing that executions must be guided by the creative idea. Under some circumstances, the creative execution is also the creative idea. We will also discuss different types of executional tactics and how to use them effectively.

Learning goals

After reading this chapter, you will understand:

- the difference between an advertising creative idea and its executions
- when to use a single ('one-off') execution and when to use multiple executions
- what 'wear-out' is, and how multiple executions can prevent it
- the strengths and weaknesses of different executional tactics
- the need to customise online videos
- the two important considerations in deciding which executional tactics to use
- three different theoretical perspectives of celebrity endorsement
- the decision model for selecting a celebrity endorser.

In the previous chapter we discussed at length creative theories and convergent and divergent thinking, all of which have the ultimate objective of finding the 'big idea'. However, consumers are not interested in the creative idea. They are more interested in the actual ad – what they can see – the execution itself. Further, if we are pre-testing, the creative idea also needs to be executed at least to a level that is testable. Finally, although a creative idea may be of high quality, its execution may still be defective, in which case all the effort of searching for a high-quality creative idea (discussed in the last chapter) is wasted.

Having said that, there is nowadays a greater tendency for ads to be heavily executed with special effects because of the advent of new (and cheap) digital technology. The temptation is to jump into the execution stage without first thinking through the creative strategy. The danger with this is that the ad may get attention but it may not be 'on message', resulting in more style than substance. Therefore, the execution must flow from the creative idea, which in turn should be guided by the creative strategy. If not, then any executional tactics will do, which is plainly absurd.

WHAT IS THE DIFFERENCE BETWEEN A CREATIVE IDEA AND ITS EXECUTION?

Have you ever noticed that your favourite song disappoints you when a mediocre singer performs it, while in the hands of a good singer it makes your emotions soar? It is still the same song, yet how it is sung (or executed) can make a significant difference to the outcome. The same logic applies to advertising.

There is a big difference between creative idea and creative execution. As we saw in chapter 6, a creative idea is defined as a unique and compelling way of amplifying the branded message that can help fulfil the firm's business objectives. On the other hand, the creative execution is the ad itself, or the craft needed to turn the creative idea into a reality – to make it come to fruition.[1] It is important to draw this distinction because a creative idea can typically be executed in many ways; we opt for the most effective way to enhance the idea. For example, although we may decide to use a specific demonstration to highlight the benefit of a new product, there are still many ways of doing that, such as the use of different angle shots or even music to enhance the effect. Similarly, we may plan for an actor in our ad to smile at this point as he delivers that line. But there are many ways of smiling, and how that is executed can make a huge difference to the quality of the ad. As Binet and Carter so aptly pointed out, 'people share kitten videos not because cute kittens are a new idea, but because of the *precise* way those kittens are being cute' [italics added].[2]

A good example is the Old Spice ad 'The man your man could smell like', featuring the actor Isaiah Mustafa (see figure 7.1). Part of the appeal of this ad comes from Mustafa's ability to deliver the lines in a tongue-in-cheek manner, with the right intonation and facial expression. A lesser actor would not have been able to pull this off. The aim of creative execution then is to craft the ad in such a way that it can best enhance the creative idea.

Figure 7.1 Old Spice advertisement, when Isaiah Mustafa first appeared in the advertisement (left) and reprising his role in early 2020 (right)

Ideally, the creative idea must be capable of generating numerous executions that are equally compelling. But this is not always necessary. Sometimes the execution itself is the idea. A good example is the classic Honda 'Cog' ad (see figure 7.2). This is an ad that shows how the parts from

Figure 7.2 A frame of the Honda 'Cog' TV ad

a disassembled car can be cleverly used to convey the idea of sophisticated engineering. It should be noted that, in this 120-second TV ad, not a single word was said about Honda. All the benefits are implied. The ad shows how a disembodied car, with its parts strewn across the floor, can still mysteriously come alive as one part triggers another to move. It is a mesmerising sequence of action executed without the use of digital trickery. The campaign changed the perception that Honda had inferior engineering compared to its European competition.

This TV ad also demonstrates the importance of planning the execution. Developed by Weiden +Kennedy, a US advertising agency based in Portland, Oregon, it took two months of planning (with lots of sketches and storyboards of interacting car parts) and another four months of testing. During the testing phase, some sequences (such as the airbag explosion) were rejected because they were found to be too difficult or expensive to execute. It took four days and nights to shoot the ad, and not until the 606th take did they get it right! The ad cost Honda US$1 million to produce.

A good example of a print ad where the creative execution is also the creative idea is the classic Volvo safety pin car ad. It shows a safety pin in the shape of a car with the brand 'Volvo' embossed at the top of it. It is also a brilliant remote conveyor whose dominant association (safety) fits the image of the brand. Figure 7.3 is another example – a job ad for a copywriter. This is less straightforward

Figure 7.3 Example of a 'one-off' execution

because the conveyor shows a mangled pen lid, which implies nervousness. But the headline also plays on the word 'Hungry' to connote someone who is hardworking (see puns in chapter 6).

Another difference between the creative idea and its execution is that the latter requires a different set of skills in order to make the idea come alive. While the big creative idea may come from one person, its execution usually requires the skills of a number of people to make it happen.

It is also important to realise that some executions are illegal in certain countries. For instance, in the US it is illegal to show people drinking a beer (but it is all right to show them cheering each other). Similarly, in Saudi Arabia it is illegal to show images of women whose skin is not covered.

The final difference is that many executions can flow from one creative idea. Figure 7.4 shows some examples of Absolut Vodka that revolve around the same creative idea. This is called 'variation of the theme', where the executions share the same idea yet are different enough to be interesting. Research has shown that such variations tend to result in better liking of the ad and the brand, as well as less decay, with repeated exposure.[3] Note that the Absolut campaign has been running for decades using the same concept. Therefore, a truly good creative idea also has longevity, with little risk of 'wear-out' – when the creative idea (or campaign) is no longer able to deliver the desired effects.

Figure 7.4 A campaign showing variation of the same theme
(© Absolut Company AB)

The strategic question to ask is when to use single versus multiple executions. Generally, if there is a need to build a brand over the long term, then it is imperative to have a consistent image so that the target audience will learn faster. To prevent the creative idea from 'wearing out', it is better to come up with a high-quality creative idea that: (a) is 'on message', (b) can spawn different but related executions, and (c) can be used across different media platforms including digital and social media. In this regard, it pays to ensure that the creative idea has digital and interactive potential (including mobile technologies). This is because, with the increasing prevalence of digital media (in all its varied forms), the marcoms manager should try to maximise this potential right from the start. It is most important to think of how the creative idea and its executions can be customised across the different platforms.

In summary, it is important to draw this distinction between a creative idea and its execution for a number of reasons (figure 7.5 also summarises these strategic ideas).

- It is easy to get distracted by the brilliance of the execution and miss the strategic intent behind the executional idea. Ideally, they should match. If not, it is better to go back to the drawing board and come up with a better creative idea than to proceed with a poor selling idea that is well executed.
- A good creative idea also has longevity – preferably many variations of the same theme can flow from it. An ad, no matter how brilliant its execution, will eventually 'wear out'. Therefore, if the purpose is to build a brand, it is better to take a long-term perspective, in which case it is better to choose a creative idea that allows a consistent theme to emerge with the use of different, but related executions.

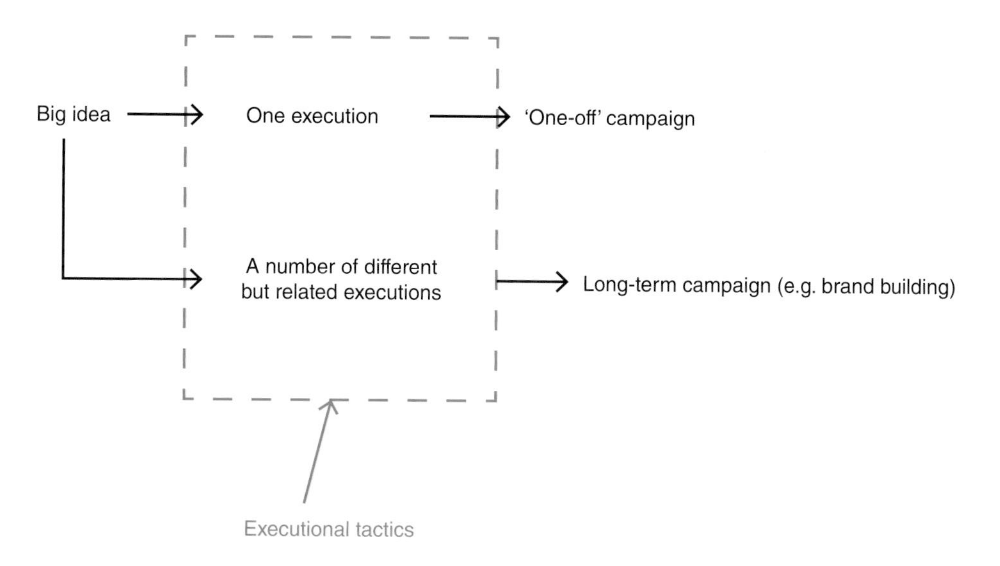

Figure 7.5 The relationship between the big idea, types of campaigns and executional tactics

EXECUTIONAL TACTICS

As we saw earlier, skills, knowledge and planning are needed for the execution of the ad. However, it should be noted that there is already a body of knowledge to suggest that some executional tactics tend to be more effective than others under certain circumstances. Let's look at some of the considerations.

Attention

Attention is the single most difficult task in advertising and indeed in any marcoms activity. With increasing competitive clutter, consumer apathy and media fragmentation, it is getting harder and harder to capture and sustain the attention of our target audience.[4]

Attention to a stimulus can be defined broadly as the allocation of a resource to its processing, while ignoring others.[5] We do this because we cannot attend to everything simultaneously and, as such, we exhibit selective attention. We can describe attention as driven by two processes:

1. a bottom-up process, in which a feature in the ad captures our attention
2. a top-down process in which our goal directs attention to the stimulus (i.e. the ad).

Attention-capture is a bottom-up process because it originates from the feature of the stimulus, a low-level property. It is also involuntary or automatic in nature. A good example is when we come across a sexually evocative ad. Directed-attention, on the other hand, is a top-down, voluntary process because it is driven by high-level goals. For instance, we deliberately seek out ads of apartments when we are in the market to buy one. Although our attention is influenced by these two modes at any one time, it is the involuntary attention-capture that is emphasised in marcoms. There are several ways of achieving this.

USE EVOCATIVE CUES

One way of achieving automatic attention-capture is to use emotionally arousing cues. These may include cues that hold biological, social or economic significance or that are deviant or unexpected in some way. For instance, the use of sexual images and of celebrities in ads are examples of biological and socially significant cues, respectively. The word 'free' is often seen in promotional ads and is an example of an economically significant cue,[6] while an incongruous picture is an example of a deviant cue. Such cues tend to arouse our emotions,[7] and emotional cues are powerful because we quickly become oriented to them even though they may initially appear in our peripheral vision.[8]

With TV, one can take advantage of its dynamic format to develop a storyline for a brand that pulls at the heartstrings of viewers. Emotional ads are generally very memorable,[9] because we tend to get more involved with the narrative, which is easy to follow and relatable. But the emotions have to be positive (i.e. the feel-good factor must be high) in order for such ads to be also persuasive.[10] In other words, one should try to avoid creating emotionally negative ads. Such ads tend not to be enjoyable. One approach is to create an ad with an affectionate storyline that can resonate deeply. A Spanish TV ad for their Christmas lottery is a good example (i.e. Loterias y Apuestas del Estado: 'December 21st'). It tells the story of an elderly retired schoolteacher who mistakenly thought that she won the lottery. But her loved ones could not bear to tell her the truth and soon the whole village got into the spirit of celebrating in order to help keep the illusion alive. In the last scene, she said she could not keep the winning ticket and instead gave it to her son with a big hug.[11]

For the campaign, social media groups were also created to further encourage viewers to be engaged with the story. Viewership figures were impressive: 3 million people watched the ad; it earned free media worth €5.5 million, with 3.5 billion impressions to boost, all within 24 hours. Lottery sales also increased by a modest 3.5%.

MAKE THE AD LARGE AND STIMULUS-RICH

Another bottom-up method of attention-capture is to imbue the ad with a high level of stimulus intensity, for instance, in terms of size, brightness, colour, contrast, volume and movement. Generally, the bigger and more colourful the print ad, the more likely people will notice it.[12,13] So, instead of worrying about which specific creative cues to use, we simply change the physical characteristics of the ad so that it becomes large and vivid.

DEVELOP A DIS-HABITUATION STRATEGY

All new ads, regardless of how evocative or intensive they are, will eventually lose their power to attract. This is because we become accustomed to them, a process called 'habituation'. In order to dis-habituate, some novelty needs to injected back into the stimulus (i.e. advertising) so that interest in the branded message can be maintained. One option is to change the execution but maintain the same theme, as we saw earlier.

CHANGE THE AD PLACEMENT OR ITS SURROUNDING CONTEXT

Sometimes instead of changing the ad itself, we can change the placement or context surrounding the ad. For instance, a print ad that faces another ad (or picture) in a magazine tends to result in lower recognition, but recognition is higher when the ad is placed either facing text or on the inside cover.[14] There is less interference.

In TV advertising, consumers often turn away during the commercial break, and therefore it is generally better to be the first ad during the commercial break than in any other position. Such ads are more likely to be seen. This is especially true if the commercial break is short.[15] Further, since consumers are more likely to remember the first thing they see (called the 'primacy effect'), such ads tend to be better recalled too.[16]

In internet advertising, up to 80% of subjects fail to notice any banner ads at the top of the website. This is called 'banner blindness'. But still worse, the more intrusive the banner ad, the more adept consumers are at ignoring it because now it looks even more *like* an ad.[17] In fact, it is often better to embed the advertisement in the website so that it blends with the content.[18] This could explain why animation in banner ads is not always effective.[19] In this situation, there is no point trying to improve the banner ad itself. Rather, it might be more effective to change the content of the website (if this is possible). Web pages that are based on videos or pictures (rather than text-based) generally tend to attract more attention for its banner ads. This is because readers find image-based web pages easier to process and so have more resource left to examine banner ads on such web pages.[20]

Websites have grown longer over the years, allowing the publisher greater opportunity to embed advertisements. Websites are also now using more visual-based 'tiles' in a grid format. This allows the publisher to hold a greater amount of content, but one that is organised systematically. For instance, the New York City website (i.e. www.nycgo.com), which is an extremely popular tourism website in the US, consists of many visual tiles, each signifying different areas of interest (e.g. museums, attractions, restaurants and Broadway). These tiles are attractive, tempting viewers to click on them, thereby improving the 'stickiness' of the website.[21] (see figure 7.6).

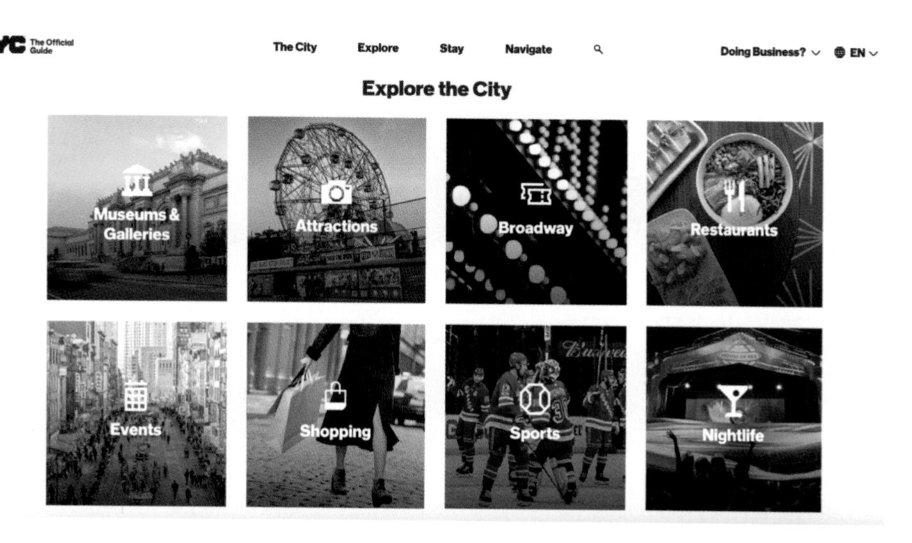

Figure 7.6 New York City website showing the visual tiles in a grid format

Hence it is important to plan the development of the website using a screen blueprint as a visual guide to represent the skeletal framework of a website (also called wireframe). This is a good principle to remember and should be applied to all advertising execution. For instance, in TV advertising the director often sketches out the different frames of the advertisement (called storyboards) to guide filming.

USE HUMOUR

Research has generally shown that humour increases our attention towards the ad and improves brand attitude.[22] It works principally by creating a positive, playful mood in the target audience. When this occurs, we are less likely to be judgemental and to counterargue against the ad. It also makes us like the ad more and, in turn, the brand.

Humour is more useful when there is little worthwhile information to communicate, or when what is being communicated constitutes a simple argument. Thus, many low-involvement product categories (e.g. consumer-packaged goods) fit this bill.[23] Humorous ads also tend to work better when the target audience already has a favourable attitude towards the brand.[24] It is easier to be persuasive under such circumstances. If the existing attitude is not favourable, humour is less likely to work. The ad, however, must become increasingly funny so that viewers are more likely to be continuously hooked, smiling all the way to the end.[25]

However, humour is not easy to get right for several reasons. First, the view of one person (e.g. the copywriter) on what is humorous may not be shared by another (e.g. the target audience). For the same reason, humour in one country does not always work in another, which limits its use in international campaigns. Part of the problem is that there are different kinds of humour, such as sarcasm, slapstick and even subtle, dry wit (like the 'British sense of humour'). Not all are appropriate for the brand or category. There is always a danger that the humour will misfire and end up insulting (instead of entertaining) the target audience. As a rule, it is best to steer clear of humour that pokes fun at socially sensitive issues, such as those involving religion and minority groups.

Second, it may be difficult to integrate the humour with the brand (not just the product category). How can we tell? As in chapter 6, we can mentally test for creative integration by asking whether the ad will be destroyed if another brand is used in its place. There is no creative integration if another brand will work just as well. When this occurs, there is a danger that the target audience will remember the joke but not the brand. One way to minimise this risk in a TV ad is to make sure the punchline reinforces the branded message, sometimes called 'klitchniks'.[26]

CASE STUDY 7.1 BEST APOLOGY AD EVER? HOW AN ADVERTISING AGENCY TURNED A CRISIS INTO AN AWARD-WINNING EXECUTION

In February 2018, about 600 Kentucky Fried Chicken outlets in the UK had to be closed temporarily for more than a week. This is because not enough chickens were being delivered to these outlets due to delivery issues. The closure created bad publicity for the brand – the British people were also angry that they even complained to the police and local members of parliament. Social media went wild and of course the mainstream media (e.g. TV and newspaper) continued to stir the pot. KFC staff were also abused and berated by the public (unfairly). Problems started on 14 February when DHL and QSL took over the delivery business from Bidvest Logistics who was KFC's old contractor. DHL did not seem to know what they were doing, with poor communications about the delivery task and drivers being stuck in traffic, resulting in massive delays in picking up fresh chickens for delivery.[27]

Although DHL apologised for the debacle, they seemed to do it grudgingly, citing the fact that they were not the only contractor involved: 'Whilst we are not the only party responsible for the supply chain to KFC, we do apologize for the inconvenience and disappointment caused to KFC and their customers by this incident', a DHL spokesperson said.[28]

KFC, on the other hand, took the bold step of being honest and open, apologising undeservedly, but with a witty twist as well. The ad switched the KFC letters to 'FCK' with copy below apologising (i.e. we're sorry) and explaining the situation. 'A chicken shop without any chicken. It's not ideal. Huge apologies to our customers, especially those who travelled out of their way to find we were closed.' This print ad won a silver and three gold Lions at the Cannes festival as well as three Pencils at the D&AD Awards.

Figure 7.7 KFC's print ad during its UK chicken crisis

Figure 7.8 KFC's website during its UK chicken crisis

Consumers were encouraged to go to KFC's website to check for updates. The website used the same humour as seen in the headline (i.e. 'some chickens have now crossed the road'). And when the debacle was over, the website message changed to one of 'thank you'.

Figure 7.9 KFC's website after its UK chicken crisis

DISCUSSION QUESTIONS

1. The apology ad was celebrated for its creativity and won major awards. But do you think the apology campaign was also well integrated? Explain your answer.
2. Early in this chapter, the point was made that it is difficult to build a brand with a one-off execution. Since KFC's 'We're Sorry' ad was a one-off execution developed for the crisis, does this thesis still hold? Explain your answer.

USE SEXUAL IMAGERY

Like humour, sexual imagery is very effective in attracting our attention. But the product category must be relevant (e.g. body oil). If it is not related (e.g. a tool set), the use of sexual imagery will not only lead to lower levels of purchase intention compared to the use of non-sexual imagery,[29] it will also harm brand recall, especially among consumers who reject the use of such imagery.[30] Also like humour, if sexual content is not relevant it distracts and interferes with the processing of the ad. One recent study found that the use of moderate-level sexual content on a website can significantly increase traffic (on eBay), although it does not necessarily translate to winning bids.[31] It is even worse with ads using taboo themes around sex or death. This not only decreases brand attitude for new products but also triggers social pressure not to buy it.[32]

SOLVE A PROBLEM

The executional tactic of problem solution involves showing the target audience a problem and identifying how the brand can solve it. It is one of the most persuasive tools.[33] 'Solving' can involve removing the problem. The classic example of this tactic is what you typically see in a laundry detergent ad, where the dirt in a piece of clothing is expediently removed with the detergent. Sometimes the problem can be solved by preventing the problem from occurring in the first place. For instance, a campaign to reduce vehicle crime in the UK led to a 37% decline between 1999 and 2005, simply by reminding drivers to lock their cars and remove their valuables from sight.[34]

DEMONSTRATE THE PRODUCT IN USE

Demonstrating the product in use in an ad clearly shows how your product performs in use, and in so doing irrevocably impresses its benefit on people's minds. One important benefit is convenience of use.[35] Demonstrations need not be dull (as we saw in chapter 6, when we discussed how benefits can be exaggerated). If done cleverly, this will get the attention of the audience. Recall of the benefit will also be higher,[36] as will persuasion.[37] Demonstration and convenience of use are two important executions for TV advertising. Instagram is effective in demonstrating the benefits of new products because its videos are often short and thus have to be on point.

PROVIDE REAL NEWS

This is one of the most powerful methods of persuading the audience. People are genuinely interested in anything new. This might be a new product, new features, new ways of doing things, new forms of customer service and so forth. The words 'new' and 'improved' are among the most powerful words in advertising because they signal new benefits.

One study found that with new products, a 10% increase in advertising expenditure leads to a 2.6% increase in sales compared to 0.5% for established products[38] (i.e. advertising elasticity for a new product is 0.26 and for established products is 0.05, a fivefold increase). In interactive advertising, the word 'new' can lift the response rate in financial services by 450%.[39] It is therefore not surprising that advertising agencies love this tactic. Unfortunately, it is expensive (and impractical) to come up with new products all the time.

COMPARE THE BRAND

This means comparing the focal brand with another on an attribute or benefit where the focal brand excels. It is generally more effective if the focal brand is a smaller brand, is new or has a clear comparative advantage on the chosen attribute or benefit.[40] When the comparison is credibly made (preferably with objective data or factual evidence) against the market leader, it is even better. The comparison style should be positive; that is, aimed not to denigrate the competition (at least to minimise legal actions), but more to portray the product's own benefits more positively. Negative comparison generally does not work – it leads to more counterarguments because the target audience thinks the ad is biased.[41]

A good example of a positive comparison is a cheeky BMW ad positioning itself against Mercedes. When the CEO of Daimler and Mercedes, Dieter Zetsche, retired, there was much fanfare in the German press. BMW took advantage of this. The ads show him leaving the office, saying goodbye to everyone, handing over the office access card, and then finally being chauffeured home in a Mercedes S class. Now retired, he is free to drive whatever car he likes. There is freedom. And here's the twist. In the ad the actor playing Dieter is seen driving off in a BMW i8roadster (not a Mercedes!). The tagline is 'Thank you, Dieter Zetsche, for so many years of inspiring competition'.

This is an example of a comparison where no specific product attribute is mentioned. One can also make an indirect comparison, where no specific competitor is named. Here, the claimed superiority is against all the other brands in the category in general. It is an effective way of positioning a brand against the entire market[42] (see also chapter 3 on competitor comparison).

TELL A STORY OR SHOW AN (EMOTIONAL) SLICE OF LIFE

This means showing a snippet or an episode of everyday life that the target audience can relate to. It may involve a short storyline or dramatic interaction between characters. This tactic has generally been found to be very persuasive.[43] If the target audience also identifies with the characters and can relate to the events depicted in the ad, it may begin to lose self-awareness and experience what is called 'emotional resonance', meaning that they feel what the characters are feeling, like an echo. The most celebrated example of this is Taster's Choice coffee where a series of commercials (like a 'soap opera') was created, teasing the target audience to tune in for each episode in order to follow the blossoming romance between a woman and her male neighbour. Sales were said to have jumped by 10%.[44]

Generally, storytelling is an effective way of drawing a viewer in because as humans, we have been telling stories since time immemorial, long before the written word was invented. A story is also easy to follow and having gripping opening scenes and ensuing suspense will also help attract and sustain attention. However, the story must be told in such a way that reflects the experiences, values and aspirations of the target audience, and is especially effective if the target audience can identify with the characters in the ad.[45] That way, the viewers will be less defensive, and more open to accepting its message,[46] even when difficult scientific facts are used.[47] The story itself may have dramatic highs and lows as the plot unfolds, but the brand must always play a positive emotional role in the story for associative learning (i.e. evaluative conditioning) to occur. So, with this tactic the brand is part of the narrative, and the claim can often be implicit.

With technology, storytelling can also be transplanted onto the packaging. One Australian start-up called Third Aurora uses augmented-reality technology to tell the story of a winery. By simply scanning the label on the bottle, consumers will be able to access the story behind the winery, right in front of them (see figure 7.10). But if the consumer is in the winery itself, scanning will yield a different story. This gives the buyer a more personalised experience.[48]

Figure 7.10 The story behind a winery using augmented-reality technology

PUBLICISE ENDORSEMENTS

These are testimonials given by people about the wonders of the brand. Sometimes called a 'talking head', creative personnel generally do not like this tactic because it is uncreative.[49] Target audiences also tend to be sceptical since such endorsers are obviously paid. If the endorser is a customer, then it is best to portray a real customer (and not an actor unless disclosed). Using real customers is generally more effective.[50] The hidden-camera technique, showing a typical customer buying or using a product, generally leads to better brand attitude and preference.[51,52]

If we cannot find a customer to endorse the brand, we can use a spokesperson. This person should look similar to the target audience in terms of gender, trait and appearance. This is called the 'similarity principle' and has long been used by effective salespeople[53] (see also chapter 10). If you want an endorser to look trustworthy, select one with a baby face;[54] if you want them to look honest, diligent and authoritative, have them wear glasses.[55]

We can also use experts to endorse our brand. This is especially useful if it is a high-involvement product or a new product, in which case their expertise can quickly establish the product's credibility. An expert's view of products and services has long been valued by naive consumers. We see this in a whole range of products and services, from restaurants to movies, computers and cars. For instance, a good review of a Broadway play will generally lead to a greater number of ticket sales.[56]

In some product categories, where quality is difficult to judge, the views of experts can wield enormous influence. A prime example is the US wine critic Robert Parker, whose rating of a wine label can affect its pricing and distribution or even destroy it overnight. For instance, if a wine scores 95 points or more out of 100, the value of the vintage can increase by 15%.[57] But to be even more effective, the expert's score should appear at the price label. That way, the sales of that wine can shoot up by as much as 25%![58] But inserting a critic's score at retail is not practical. In Australia, where buying wine online is common, the critic's score is often publicised next to the wine's image (see figure 7.11).

Figure 7.11 Publicising a critic's score next to the wine can be very effective

CREATE FEAR

This tactic is useful for social messages, such as anti-speeding or anti-smoking messages. For such a message to work, the ad has to have two parts. The first part shows the severity of the health threat (or the strength of social disapproval), while the second shows what (protective) actions can be taken. This two-stage model is most effective if the quality of the argument for the second stage is strong. Interestingly, arguments about the risk level of the person (i.e. their vulnerability) or whether the person has the ability to take the recommended actions (i.e. their self-efficacy) make little difference to the persuasiveness of the message.[59]

One common mistake that advertisers make with using the fear tactic is eliciting too high a fear level. The target audience avert their eyes from the scene, feeling fearful. The key is to elicit a 'moderate' level of fear. The problem is that we do not know what 'moderate' means to this specific audience, unless we pre-test the ads. A better approach is to measure the tension of the ad continuously in the target audience while they are watching the ad. Fear ads that show a 'relief' at the end are generally more effective than those that do not.[60] As in the two-stage model discussed above, the second stage is very important in making the fear-arousing ads effective. In this case, the fear–relief pattern is crucial – the rising fear in stage 1 must be accompanied by a reduction in stage 2 (see figure 7.12a), or else the viewer remains fearful (see figure 7.12b).

USE MUSIC, SOUND EFFECTS AND JINGLES

Music accompanying spoken words generally tends to interfere with processing. This is especially detrimental for high-involvement products.[61] As a rule, avoid unusual sound effects that

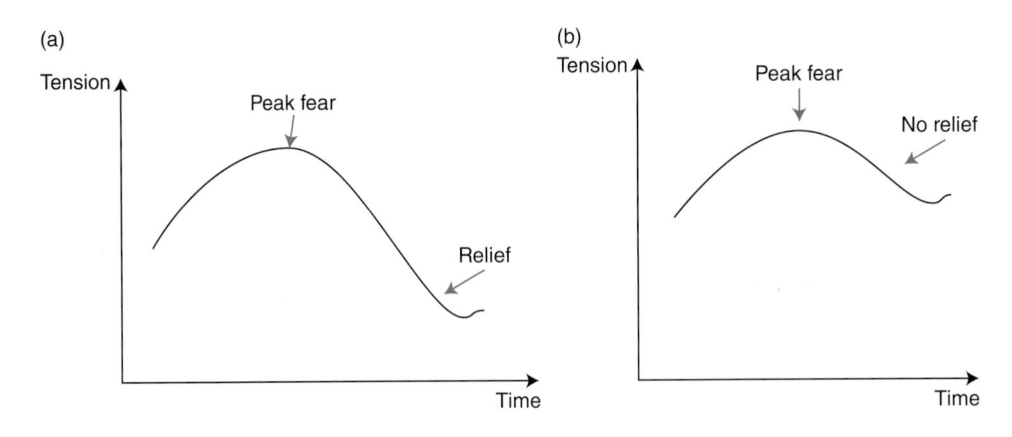

Figure 7.12 A subject may feel relief towards the end of an ad (a) or not (b)

the target audience is not familiar with because it will distract them. Music and sound effects are good for arousing emotions and imagery, but they must match the brand. For instance, playing French music leads to higher sales for French wine (in a supermarket) and likewise German music for German wine.[62] Ads with jingles are generally more persuasive than ads without jingles.[63] Of course, jingles have to be used appropriately.

USE SHORT ADS TO MINIMISE DECAY

One observation is that short TV ads, around 15 seconds or less, are *not* generally good in establishing new associations or changing people's minds. This is because their extremely short duration does not allow a brand to tell an emotional story. Instead, use 15-second TV ads only *after* the initial associations have been formed through longer duration ads, to re-establish brand associations (or brand awareness). In other words, the shorter ad needs only to hold mental territory that has already been created.[64] With a shorter ad, we can then afford to stay longer in the field and hence minimise decay.[65] Short ads are generally more suitable for brands that are already established, where the message can be short, as for a sales promotion.[66]

ROTATE EXECUTIONS IN TURN

When we expose multiple ads of the same brand simultaneously (e.g. all in one week), the media weight for each will be reduced, since it has to be split among all the executions. This results in lower exposure strength, resulting in 'execution anorexia',[67] and makes the overall campaign less effective.[68] If there are multiple executions, each version should be exposed in turn (i.e. rotated) rather than simultaneously.

USE TWO-SIDED ARGUMENTS

This tactic means putting two sides of the argument together in a message, one opposing and one refuting the opposition. For this to work, the opposing argument should not be more important than the subsequent refutation. The nature of the refutation should be about an important benefit of the brand. This tactic is effective for audiences who hold strong opposing views about the brand, in which case they will perceive the message to be more trustworthy. It would also work better for high-involvement buying situations where the target audience are more likely to engage in deliberation.[69]

USE PAUSES AND SILENCES

For important visual information, it is important to hold the scene for about 1.5 seconds or more. For instance, pack shots or brand logos found at the end of the commercial should not be interrupted.[70] Similarly, just before an important point is to be made there should be silence before and after the presentation (about two seconds each). The silence before the verbal presentation increases tension while the silence after the presentation helps processing.[71]

CREATE THE RIGHT NUMBER OF CUTS AND SCENES

If the delivery of information is important, the ads should not have too many scenes. Fast-cut ads (e.g. 11 or more 'cuts' for a 30-second ad) are too overwhelming for the target audience to process the claims properly.[72]

CHOOSE AN ONSCREEN SPOKESPERSON, NOT A VOICE-OVER

Evidence from tracking research generally shows that the voice-over tactic is not as effective in holding our attention as an onscreen spokesperson, who speaks directly at you.[73] This is because we are naturally attracted to faces and eyes.

USE SUPER (SUBTITLES) AND AUDIOVISUAL SYNCHRONISATION

To aid comprehension, we can use super (subtitles) to reinforce the audio.[74] In the same vein, if a voice-over is used, the audio must synchronise with the visual scenes. If we use a presenter, the movement of their lips must be in synch with the spoken words.[75]

CONSIDER BRAND PROMINENCE, ESPECIALLY IN OPENING AND ENDING

When products and the brand are shown in ads, the audience quickly understands what is being sold.[76] Therefore, as a rule, we want the brand to be prominent throughout the ad. However, most TV ads begin too softly. Since 'noise' and competitive clutter are a big issue, it pays to open with fire.[77] Further, if this dramatic opening is related to the brand (and its benefit) it will be even more persuasive.[78] The first 5 seconds is crucial in capturing attention. This becomes especially important for online videos where viewership dies off quickly (see digital customisation of online videos later in this chapter).

To take advantage of the fact that we tend to remember items at the beginning (the 'primacy effect') and at the end of a list (the 'recency effect'), the brand and its benefit should ideally appear in the opening 5 to 8 seconds of a TV ad,[79] and end with a brand signoff. One study found that 61% of US prime-time TV ads do not even show the brand until one-third through the ad.[80] Creative personnel do not like putting the brand up-front because it may detract from the storyline and compromise the ability to sustain viewers' attention. However, we should insist on a brand signoff at the end of the ad. For a TV ad, the signoff scene containing the brand should last at least 1.5 seconds,[81] since neuroscience research shows that visual scenes of this duration are more likely to result in better encoding and hence recognition.[82]

In radio advertising, one study found that a two-second 'blip' ad at the start of the commercial break followed by a 60-second ad towards the end of the break will result in significantly more people recalling the ad (44%), rather than only one or other of a two-second ad (3%) or 60-second ad.[83]

Interestingly, people tend to notice banner ads that appear on the first page of a website (i.e. the home page) more than ads that appear on subsequent pages. In fact, outside the home page, the attention-holding of banner ads drops dramatically.[84]

CREATE IMAGERY IN THE MIND

Since imagery tends to increase our memory, radio ads are wise to use this tactic. It increases the vividness of the ad in consumers' minds. So instead of just making announcements about the brand, we can create a scene (together with sound effects) so that a mental picture is formed in the mind, to elicit more attention.[85] In short, create a 'theatre of the mind' when it comes to radio ads. If properly executed, this tactic will benefit both the ad and brand awareness in a cost-efficient way.[86]

The power of imagery can be explained by the phenomenon called the 'picture superiority effect', which means that we tend to remember visual images better than text. One explanation for this is that pictures tend to be dually encoded in both our verbal and non-verbal (or pictorial) memory systems. Text, on the other hand, tends to be encoded only in our verbal system. Dual-coding[87] makes the memory trace of the object stronger. Mental imagery can also be created with print ads. For instance, Pitt shows that an exposure to a print ad of a food product depicting people sharing the food makes consumers immerse themselves in the picture, and imagine the tastes and stories about eating with others. These narrative immersions subsequently heighten their purchase intentions.[88]

LEVERAGE ON WHAT'S TOPICAL OR UNPREDICTABLE (QUICKLY)

Related to the idea of imagery is to take advantage of what is topical in the public's mind and cleverly associate this with the brand (without necessarily harming it). To be effective, this tactic relies on the agility of the advertiser, but the event must be unpredictable.[89] Consider the following: during the 2013 Super Bowl game in the US, the lights suddenly went out. There was a sudden power outage and the whole stadium sunk into total darkness. But Oreo was quick with a tweet: 'Power out? No problem. You can still dunk in the dark', (see figure 7.13). The tweet quickly went viral, accumulating thousands of likes and retweets. This tactic is sometimes called topical advertising or real-time marketing. One Dutch study found that the more responsive the advertiser, the more retweets and likes a brand will accumulate in social media.[90]

One can also see the same nimbleness applied to out-of-home advertising. A recent example is a billboard for Vegemite. The billboard (see figure 7.14) compares the taste of Vegemite to a recent surfing competition that saw Australian surfer Mick Fanning punch a shark in the face when it got a little too close for comfort: 'Tastes like Australia'.

Figure 7.13 Oreo's tweet during the 2013 Super Bowl blackout

This tactic can also be applied to a planned event provided it is salient in people's minds. In the historic meeting between US President Trump and North Korean leader Kim Jong-un, held in Singapore (12 June 2018), many enterprising restaurateurs and bar owners in the island state developed a special menu and drinks hoping to cash in on this historical event (e.g. kimchee burgers; rocket man taco; Trump and Kim cocktails). Some of these have proven to be a hit with patrons, resulting in higher revenue.[91] Even the Singapore Mint cashed in on the mania by issuing commemorative gold and silver medallions after an overwhelming response.[92]

Figure 7.14 Vegemite's cheeky comparison to Australian surfer Mick Fanning

The Coca-Cola Company launched limited-edition cans, displaying a hopeful message, both in English and Korean: 'Here's to peace, hope and understanding' (see figure 7.15). The Coca-Cola Company also created an animation showing Trump and Kim approaching each other from opposite sides and ending with them shaking hands when they meet in the middle (see figure 7.16). No words were spoken, and the branding relied on the familiar red and white swirl of 'Coca Cola'. This creative asset was shown in outdoor advertising and social media in Singapore.

Figure 7.15 Limited edition 'Coca-Cola' cans

Figure 7.16 An animation of the historic meeting between Trump and Kim in Singapore

This tactic can also be applied to a cause. For instance, on the eve of the International Women's Day (2017), State Street Global Advisors, a New York investment firm, unveiled a bronze statue of a small girl facing off the Wall Street' Charging Bull, dubbed 'Fearless Girl' (see figure 7.17). The firm wanted to make a statement that companies with strong female leadership tend to perform better than companies with male-led leadership. Supported by social media, it represents a rallying cry for women and girls to assert themselves – a new symbol of feminism. It made such a huge impact that women around the world began to adopt the stance. The small statue now stands as a permanent fixture opposite the bull in New York.[93] The message of gender equality is so powerful that it resonated around the world, and now there are replicas of the fearless girl in Oslo, Melbourne and Cape Town.[94]

Figure 7.17 The Fearless Girl has come to symbolise the new feminism (New York)

MAKE THE HEADLINE ENTICING

If the objective is to get people to read the copy of the print ad (or brochure), it makes sense for the headline to arouse some curiosity and invite the reader into the copy. So use words such as 'why', 'how to',[95] 'amazing' or 'introducing'. Do not use full stops (or in fact any punctuation) in the headline, since this is likely to stop the reader from continuing into the copy.[96] In short, create an inviting headline with a relevant first paragraph.

LINK THE HEADLINE TO THE PICTURE

Generally, ads that make a clear link between the headline and the picture tend to be recalled better.[97] This is especially important if the picture is incongruous, in which case (as discussed in chapter 6) the headline must point out the relevance of the picture. If we use a curious headline, then the reverse must occur; the picture must resolve the incongruous headline. In other words, if you have a 'crooked' picture, the headline must be 'straight'; but if you have a 'crooked' headline, then the picture must be 'straight'.[98]

USE SIMPLE, CONCRETE WORDS IN THE HEADLINE AND IN COPY

The more abstract the headline or copy, the less it is able to sell; it is important to use simple, concrete words in the ad. Avoid ambiguous or complicated words that are likely to lead the reader astray. The general principle that can apply to all ads is to make it easy for readers to follow.[99]

A simple way to remember this is to remind ourselves to always use consumer language – the language that the target audience uses every day.

USE HIGH-TECH TO CREATE A MULTI-SENSORY EXPERIENCE

Figure 7.18 Ikea's AR app

The use of sensory marketing is common in retailing, the classic example being that of taste-test. But with the advent of increasing sophisticated technology, multi-sensory campaigns are becoming more common in marcoms. For instance, we can take a virtual tour of Ikea's store on the internet, learn about the products and buy, all from the comfort of home. With an app making use of augmented reality (AR), shoppers can more easily imagine what a piece of furniture will look like in their living room.[100]

Another example is the Virtual Crash Billboard where it captured the reaction of a pedestrian involved in a crash, except that the crash was not real. The Paris traffic authorities had set up a smart billboard with a secret camera, a loudspeaker and motion detector at a designated crossing. When a pedestrian was caught crossing on a red light, a high brake-screeching sound was suddenly blared, sending the jaywalker jumping to avoid a supposedly approaching vehicle (see figure 7.19).

Figure 7.19 A pedestrian shocked by an impending vehicle

Of course, there was no vehicle, just the sound effects. The whole incident was recorded on a camera and was immediately transferred onto an interactive digital billboard across the road. The bewildered jay-walker approached the billboard, which showed their face in a state of shock and the headline 'Don't take the risk to face death' (see figure 7.20).

The billboard also had a QR code that allowed the jaywalker to hear messages of other crash survivors.

Figure 7.20 The billboard capturing her reaction

They were also asked to pledge not to cross red lights again. The pictures were displayed on other billboards and online to raise awareness about pedestrian accidents. The campaign had 80 million views and 3 million interactions.[101]

Choosing an executional tactic

With so many executional tactics to choose from, how does one make sense of them? The following three considerations will help.

1. IS INTENSIVE INFORMATION PROCESSING REQUIRED?

If the buying decision requires a lot of deliberation (e.g. an expensive product) then the message of the ad must *not* be distracting. Under such circumstances, avoid entertaining tactics. Tactics such as sex, humour, music, jingles or songs will probably not work because they will interfere with the processing of important information. The slice-of-life tactic may work if it is simple, and the tactic of using pauses and silences should not be overlooked. Similarly, where it is appropriate, the use of demonstration, showing the product in use, or comparison can also be considered. If there is resistance to the message, then you can consider a two-sided argument. It would be difficult to execute all these in a 15-second TV ad, so avoid this.

2. DO THE EXECUTIONAL TACTICS COHERENTLY ENHANCE THE CREATIVE IDEA?

The second consideration is that executional tactics must coherently support the creative idea. For instance, if the creative idea does not involve a jingle, then it makes no sense to employ one, or if the creative idea involves the use of fear, then the use of a jingle is not compatible. The creative idea must guide the use of executional tactics and the executional tactics must coherently enhance the creative idea.

3. HOW CAN THE EXECUTIONS BE BEST CUSTOMISED FOR THE MEDIA?

While thinking about the first two questions, the marcoms manager should simultaneously think about the customisation of the execution. This is because consumers now have different devices and view the ads across different platforms. Below are some points to remember. [102]

DIGITAL CUSTOMISATION OF ONLINE VIDEOS

As we discussed in chapter 1, one should always tailor the execution to fit the medium. For instance, one should not just put a 30-second TV ad onto the internet without modification. Even with a cut-down version, one should think carefully. This is because in the digital world, viewers are more in control and are less forgiving if the content is boring. So, if the ad is click-and-play, which is often seen on Facebook, then it is important that the initial visual frame and the promise described in the introductory text are compelling. People generally do not like to click on such ads; the viewing penetration is low, about 10%.

If the video is a skippable, say a YouTube ad, then the challenge is sustaining the viewing right to the end. Viewership for such ads drops away very quickly. On average, you lose about 50% of the viewers 10 seconds into the YouTube ad. This means that the first 5 seconds is gold. The impact must come early, and the brand integrated quickly. Further, if the video ad were to be consumed on smartphones, then the image size of the brand or product should be prominent. If it is not prominent, it will be lost when viewed through the smaller screens of these phones. As a principle, customisation will vary across platforms, so it is important to understand the nature of the different viewing experiences. It pays to think of such differences during creative development.

CELEBRITY ENDORSEMENTS

This section is devoted to the use of celebrities, a common – yet expensive – execution tactic. Globally, about $50 billion is spent on sponsorships and endorsements, and in the US, celebrity endorsement is estimated to be between 20% and 25% of ads,[103] with Asian countries being more prevalent (e.g. Japan, 70%; Taiwan, 45%, South Korea, 61%).[104,105] The reason for its universal popularity is the belief that celebrities are attention-getting and likeable, and that they can transfer positive associations to the endorsed brand. However, the use of celebrities is also fraught with problems (which we will discuss later in the chapter). In fact, one study of 263 TV ads that used celebrities found that they were generally not effective compared to a control group of ads that did not use celebrities, and in many cases the celebrity ad even hurt the brand.[106]

Theories of celebrity endorsement

To minimise mistakes in celebrity endorsement, it pays to understand three essential theoretical perspectives.

1. SOURCE EFFECTIVENESS THEORY

The first perspective is based on the effectiveness of the source of the communication. This is partly based on the attractiveness of the source, which, in its most simplistic form, says to the consumer 'anything beautiful is good'. So, if a celebrity is attractive, then he or she must also be 'good' in other ways too[107] (e.g. outgoing, kind, warm or sensitive), spreading to the brand he or she endorses. This is called the 'halo effect', meaning that a person who is perceived to excel in one domain is assumed to excel on another, perhaps driven by the need to be consistent. This also makes the celebrity more likeable. Physically attractive celebrities are generally more effective in changing consumers' beliefs[108] as well as increasing brand attitude and purchase intentions than unattractive ones.[109]

However, the fact that a celebrity is attractive does not necessarily mean that they are effective in selling the product. They also need to be trusted (i.e. honest, sincere and reliable) and perceived as knowing something about the product (called 'expertise') – a perceived source of valid assertions. We can say that the celebrity is credible if the celebrity has a combination of trustworthiness and expertise.[110] The more credible the endorser, the more persuasive is the endorser.[111] A credible endorser also increases the credibility of the brand and hence its equity.[112] However, of the two factors of credibility (i.e. trustworthiness and expertise), expertise is more powerful in increasing brand evaluations.[113] Trustworthiness is discounted by knowing that the celebrities are being paid. For this reason, it is better for the celebrity *not* to make an explicit claim about how good the brand is. This will turn people off. Instead show how the celebrity might be happy using the brand,[114] motivated by product quality rather than money.[115] Or to put it in another way, an implicit claim by a celebrity is far more effective than an explicit one.[116]

However, some researchers have found that other source characteristics are also powerful in persuading people. One such factor is being able to identify with the celebrity. By 'identification' we mean that the target audience takes on the identity, goals and perspective of the celebrity.[117, 118] Identification helps explain why some fans display so strong an attachment (sometimes called 'affinity') that they lose their own self-identity, imitate the behaviour of the celebrity and buy the products they endorse.[119, 120] Fans aspire to be like them, and therefore celebrities should be portrayed in an idealistic, aspirational manner in the ads. Generally, the more fans identify with the celebrity, the more resistant they are to any transgressions the celebrity might commit.[121] In their eyes, their favourite celebrity can do no wrong! We see this in India, for instance, where the phenomenon of celebrity worship is widely observed – argued by Sahgal to be influenced by the prevalence of spirituality in the Indian culture.[122]

Some researchers also theorise that power is an important characteristic, especially for social messages that make use of fear to change behaviour.[123] Other researchers also postulate that a celebrity needs to command a sense of respect and esteem to be effective.[124] We can simply call this characteristic 'authority', since it has long been known to be an important principle in persuasion[125] (see chapter 10 for more discussion of persuasion).

The final characteristic is how recognisable or well known the celebrity is. Celebrities have inherent news value (good or bad). The more famous (or infamous) the celebrity, the more attention he or she can elicit.[126] In other words, the celebrity helps the ad to cut through the 'noise' and clutter and by so doing is able to give the brand an instant brand personality. This becomes especially useful if the celebrity is globally recognised and the campaign is a global one. This is very efficient. Furthermore, in the age of social media, celebrities also have social media followers, which gives advertisers a more solid assessment of the celebrity's reach (fraudulent reach estimates aside). Figure 7.21 summarises the various source characteristics.

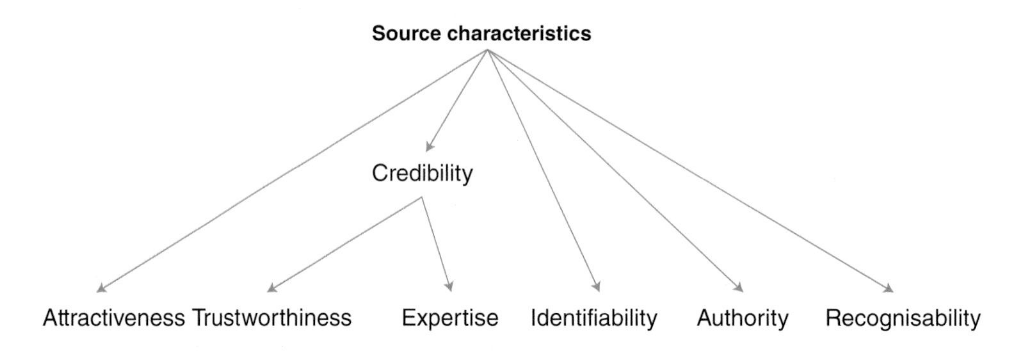

Figure 7.21 Various types of source characteristics

2. TRANSFER OF SYMBOLIC MEANING THEORY

Source theories, whether based on attractiveness or credibility, have been criticised for being too simplistic. Consumers do not just buy products, but rather symbols that add meaning to their lives, and it is this meaning that helps enhance their self-image.[127] McCracken extended this idea of symbolic meaning to that of celebrities,[128] arguing that a celebrity comes with a whole constellation of meaning (e.g. lifestyle, status, gender, age, trendiness) and when a marcoms manager selects a celebrity endorser, he or she is taking advantage of this. McCracken proposed that when a celebrity endorses a brand, a transfer process occurs in which the meaning of celebrity and all its cultural symbolism is being transferred first to the product,[129] and then from the product to the target audience when they buy it. We can extend this model to include identification where the target audience also adopts the identity and goals of the celebrity when they identify with him or her (see figure 7.22).

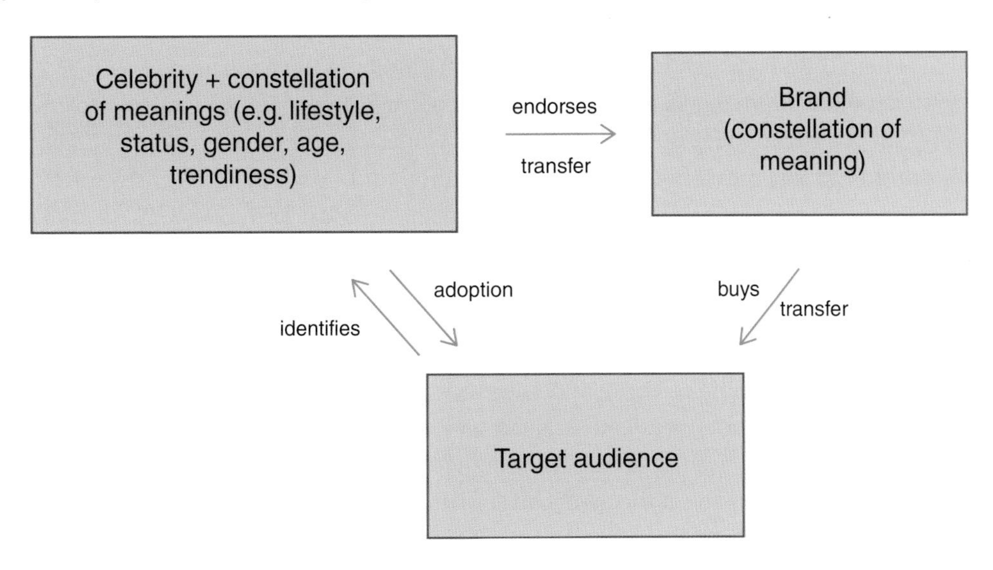

Figure 7.22 How transfer of meaning can occur

One of the intriguing research questions in this topic area is how does the transfer process occur when a celebrity endorses a brand?[130] The latest neuroscience study found that when a person sees a well-known celebrity this spontaneously activates positive memories of the celebrity.[131] These memories then become associated with the brand through evaluative conditioning.

3. MATCH-UP HYPOTHESIS OR CONGRUENCY

Yet another theoretical perspective is that of endorser match, sometimes called the match-up hypothesis.[132] This hypothesis arose from the observation that the use of an attractive model is not universally effective for all products but tends to be effective for beauty-related ones.[133] Or imagine this: which Chinese restaurant would you patronise? The one that has a Chinese chef or the one with an Indian chef? Most respondents would opt for the Chinese one, even if they can only tell from the chef's accent in a radio ad. A Chinese-accented chef is far more persuasive than an Indian-accented chef because it goes to the credibility of the Chinese restaurant.[134]

This theoretical perspective of congruency turns out to be very powerful in explaining a celebrity's positive effect on brand attitude.[135] Its effect is very robust, to the extent that consumers are even willing to overlook a celebrity's transgression provided the 'fit' between the celebrity and the brand is good (e.g. Tiger Woods and Nike). If, on the other hand, the fit is bad (e.g. Tiger Woods and Accenture), then the celebrity's transgression will affect brand attitude and purchase intentions.[136] So, it is important to ensure that the celebrity selected fits the brand and, better still, fits closely on the most important characteristic that will persuade the target audience.[137] However, this theory suffers from a number of problems, not least how to assess that fit.[138]

Pitfalls of celebrity endorsement

Although these approaches give us some insights, it is not sufficient to help a marcoms manager navigate the many pitfalls that come with the use of celebrity endorsement. Let's look at some of the many challenges.

CELEBRITY ENDORSEMENT IS VERY EXPENSIVE

Almost three decades ago, Michael Jackson was paid $10 million to endorse Pepsi,[139] while in 2005, Nike paid golfer Tiger Woods $100 million to endorse its new Golf Division over five years. Australian actress Cate Blanchett was reportedly paid $10 million to be the ambassador of Armani fragrance.[140] In the modern digital era, a celebrity, like pop star Taylor Swift, who has a following of 83 million, can charge up to $10 000 per tweet, which works out at more than $70 per character.[141]

One solution to this problem is not to use a celebrity (or to use a less expensive one), but to create a memorable spokesperson[142] (e.g. Sam Kevovich for Meat and Livestock Australia's 'Eat Lamb' campaigns)[143] or a spokescharacter[144] (e.g. Louie the fly for Mortein Australia), or to simply use an ordinary presenter.

THE CHOSEN CELEBRITY MAY NOT 'FIT' THE BRAND

Research shows that when the celebrity and brand are incongruent consumers quickly reject the whole ad, which leads to poor recall.[145] One simple way of assessing 'fit' is to ask whether the celebrity is likely to own or use the brand. For instance, if Tom Cruise were to endorse a Mazda 3 car, consumers would likely reject the ad because it would be difficult to imagine him owning or driving such a car. Perhaps that is why Chanel's 2012 campaign featuring Brad Pitt was widely lampooned. Although Chanel has a range of men's fragrance, it is primarily known as a woman's fragrance. The campaign made history because he was the first (and only) man to be featured in a Chanel ad. Brad Pitt was paid $7 million for his troubles![146]

CELEBRITIES LOSE CREDIBILITY WHEN THEY ENDORSE TOO MANY BRANDS

The more brands a celebrity endorses, the worse their credibility[147] and the less distinctive will be the celebrity–brand link.[148] Further, some consumers may come to feel that the celebrity caused the price of the endorsed brand to increase, therefore becoming less likely to buy it.[149] One solution is to only use celebrities who have not endorsed any brands (or have done so very minimally over the years).

CELEBRITIES MISBEHAVE

Sometimes, celebrities misbehave – as in the case of Tiger Woods – and the negative associations they create are rubbed onto the endorsed brand.[150] In this situation, the power of celebrities to elicit attention becomes a severe disadvantage – a double-edged sword. In fact, this is the biggest drawback of using celebrities. A meta-analysis of 32 studies, spanning more than 30 years, found that negative information about the celebrity had the biggest negative impact on the brand.[151] This is especially the case if the transgressions are considered immoral (e.g. drug and alcohol abuse) rather than incompetent (e.g. bad actor),[152] and if responsible, the celebrity should readily admit to the transgressions rather than denying them, in order to maintain their trustworthiness. When there is an admittance of wrongdoing, the transgression is not likely to affect the brand.[153]

Unfortunately, we cannot control how celebrities behave, and in the age of paparazzi, it is easy for celebrities to get caught misbehaving, and for the news or scandal to go viral. One solution is to choose an appropriate deceased celebrity, such as Albert Einstein or Marilyn Monroe, and pay a fee to their estate. They cannot misbehave! One variation of this tactic is to create a configuration that looks like the dead celebrity. Figure 7.23 is an example of this for Lindt chocolates. It cleverly uses chocolates to create an image of (the deceased comic film star) Groucho Marx with a fitting headline that integrates the benefit.

Figure 7.23 A product configuration of a dead celebrity

CELEBRITIES DISTRACT VIEWERS

Viewers tend to concentrate on the celebrity rather than the brand,[154] and this often leads to lower persuasion[155] and lower product preference.[156] One study in print advertising found that although celebrities attract readers' attention to the ad, it does not necessarily increase their recognition of the brand nor motivate them to read further.[157] Using eye tracking, one recent study with print advertising found that although celebrity ads tend to be viewed longer compared to non-celebrity ads, the faces of celebrities still captured more of the dwell time rather than the brand.[158] Another study found that only 41% of celebrity commercials created above-average brand awareness.[159] Most studies show that using celebrities in ads tended to result in lower persuasion scores, to the extent that even decades ago the advertising guru David Ogilvy discouraged the use of celebrity.[160] Finally, a recent meta-analysis of 46 experimental studies found that although using celebrities did lead to better brand evaluations, it had a *zero* effect on purchase intentions.[161] Table 7.1 summarises the major issues and suggests some things to consider when using celebrities as endorsers.

Table 7.1 Issues and considerations when using celebrities

Issues	Considerations
Celebrity endorsement is very expensive	• Do not use a celebrity • Use a less expensive celebrity (there is a trade-off as they will be less recognisable) • Use an ordinary presenter who comes across as trustworthy • Create a spokesperson who comes across as an expert and is trustworthy
The chosen celebrity may not 'fit' the brand	• Choose a celebrity who is perceived to own or use the brand • Ensure a good 'fit' – this should be high on the source characteristic that is perceived to be the most important in selling the brand
Celebrities lose credibility when they endorse too many brands	• Select a celebrity who has perceived expertise about the product • Select a celebrity who has not (or has only minimally) endorsed another brand or brands • For sports celebrities, bet on winners (see below)
Celebrities misbehave	• Choose a deceased celebrity
Celebrities distract viewers	• Do not use a celebrity • Creatively integrate the celebrity (or presenter) with the brand in the execution • Ensure prominence of the brand in the execution • Conduct careful pre-testing (see also chapter 12)

Benefits of using celebrities

Given the number of issues involved in using celebrity, we may well ask: why bother? The use of celebrities can accord the brand some advantages (at a price); for example, giving it an instant personality, increasing prestige, bringing media attention to it, and (as one German study showed) benefiting from the expertise of the celebrity in a delayed, but positive effect on the brand.[162] If we are willing to take a risk, then the recommendation is to bet on a 'winner' because the payoff could be huge. One recent study of celebrity athletes who achieved success in their sports found that on average this group of star athletes helped increase weekly sales by 4% for brands they endorsed, with the biggest increase occurring immediately after they won a big tournament.[163] However, there is no guarantee that this will occur for every star athlete,[164] nor with other kinds of celebrities (e.g. actors, TV hosts, fashion models).

CASE STUDY 7.2 HOW TO GENERATE EXCITEMENT USING AN OLYMPIC ATHLETE TO LAUNCH AN ONLINE STORE

Although its sales are confidential, the Australian technology company Acer probably scored a significant increase when the athlete who endorsed them, Sally Pearson, won gold at the London Olympics. Interestingly, Acer was already an official sponsor of the Olympics. Their advertising agency, First Impressions,[165] suggested that Acer should take advantage of their sponsorship by making Sally Pearson their brand ambassador. What is clever with this suggestion is that Sally Pearson was already World Champion at the 100-metre hurdles, and she was likely to win the Olympic gold.

To build further excitement throughout the Olympic period (six weeks), the advertising agency (i) leveraged on its relationship with Sally Pearson on social media, (ii) created an online racing game, called Acer Racer, and (iii) developed an interactive facility so that fans could send and receive messages to and from Sally Pearson. All these activities generated 45 000 social media interactions, with not a single negative comment!

Of special note is the online game Acer Racer. This game allowed fans to enter a digital race with an avatar of themselves. But to gain speed, power and performance for their avatar, fans had to interact with the Acer brand (e.g. visiting its website, watching its product videos, liking the brand and tweeting). The more a fan engaged in such activities, the more powerful his or her avatar became. Then, each Thursday, a digital race was staged, when all the avatars competed with each other for a chance to win Acer computers in the final race. Tens of thousands logged on to watch their avatar race, and Sally Pearson offered words of encouragement to losers. The winners were posted on Facebook, which fuelled more social conversations.

The campaign was so successful that it helped Acer launch their online store and grew its fan base from 5000 to 50 000 fans within the space of six weeks! Strategically, having direct access to customers means better control of the brand's image. According to David Sunton, Acer's general manager of marketing and communications, the 'Acer Racer is a great social engagement model that hugely drives the success of Acer's online store in Australia'.[166]

This is a good example of betting on a winner and cleverly leveraging the bet for maximum social effect.

DISCUSSION QUESTIONS

1. How is it different using a celebrity to sell a computer versus using an Olympic athlete in this way? In what way is it better or worse compared to a normal straight endorsement?
2. What is the single most important benefit the campaign has achieved in helping Acer launch its online store?

MANAGERIAL APPLICATION: PUTTING IT TOGETHER

CHOOSING A CELEBRITY OR PRESENTER

Since there are so many potential endorsers, how do we choose which endorser to use? Below is a suggested decision-making process that can assist a marcoms manager in his or her deliberation (see figure 7.24). The most critical part of the process is the prior research (steps 4 to 6) into the source characteristics of the selected celebrity that will benefit the brand. In the modern digital era, we can even go one step further to quickly test the effectiveness of the endorsement using Twitter. Since celebrities themselves have a following (some more than others), they can be paid to 'test-tweet' on behalf of the brand (e.g. tweeting how wonderful the brand is). If the response from the celebrity's following is poor (e.g. poor sales, likes, retweets, comments), there is probably no point going any further. It is a cheap way of testing step 5. For instance, a marcoms manager may pay $10 000 to Kristen Bell to tweet about the brand. If there is no response from her 2.5 million followers, then it implies that Kristen may not be the right creative asset to use. Of course, some celebrities who have a large social media following can charge an astronomical amount even for a single tweet or a post, in which case, it may not be worth using this method as a pre-test. For instance, Kim Kardashian charges between US$300 000 and US$500 000 for an Instagram post! Her justification is that she is one of the few celebrities on the planet that has a large

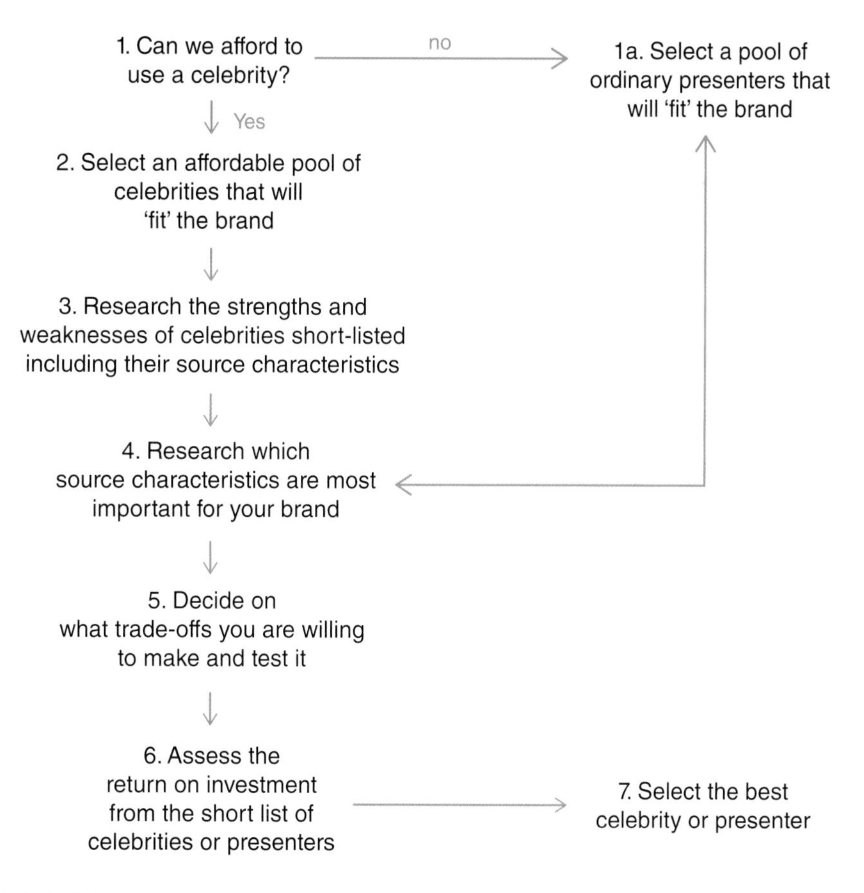

Figure 7.24 A decision-making process for selecting a celebrity or presenter

following: 120 million on Instagram and about 60 million on Twitter.[167] In Australia, the cost is lower; for an influencer with 3000–20 000 followers, the fee is $75–$300 per post; for 100 000–250 000 followers, the fee is $550–$800; and for those with 500 000+ followers, the fee is $1200.[168]

Once a few celebrities are shortlisted, each of them should be tested again with the endorsed brand. The control should be the endorsed brand alone. Juxtaposing the brand with the celebrity should increase purchase intentions, which will help ascertain which celebrity should be included. Note that if we cannot afford to hire a celebrity at stage 1, we can also hire ordinary presenters at stage 1(a), and the research principles remain the same.

FURTHER THINKING: EXPLORING THE MODELS

In this chapter, we have looked at a host of executions we can use, and under some circumstances one tactic may be more effective than another. In other words, the effectiveness of an execution tactic is contingent on circumstances (or conditions). This raises the question: what are these contingent circumstances? How can we make sense of the range of circumstances that can arise? In this section, we explore various grand frameworks of advertising, which try to make sense of the various circumstances.

LEARNING GOALS

After reading this section, you will understand:

- the hierarchy of effect (HOE) model
- the Foote, Cone & Belding (FCB) and Rossiter–Percy (RP) planning models
- the cognitive processing (CP) model
- how the CP model can guide the use of executional tactics in advertising.

HIERARCHY OF EFFECTS MODEL

One of the earliest models of advertising, the hierarchy of effects (HOE) model, by St Elmo Lewis, dates back to 1898.[169] This model states that although advertising does not immediately create a purchase, it creates intermediate stages in the target audience. The earliest model proposed stages called 'Attention, Interest, Desire and Action' (AIDA). This model was originally developed for selling but has been used for advertising. There are different versions of this basic model but perhaps the most detailed model is the one with this sequence: Awareness, Knowledge, Liking, Preference, Conviction and Purchase. Whichever model we choose, they all share two characteristics:

1. The target audience will go through different stages (or hierarchy) before purchase is made.
2. These stages can be divided into Cognitive, Affective and Conative stages.

Figure 7.25 summarises the commonality between different variants of the HOE model.

The HOE model and its many variants have been criticised on a number of grounds. The most problematic is that there are many circumstances in which the Cognitive–Affective–Conative sequence does not hold. For instance, when we buy sweets (or other low-involvement goods) we are likely to just make the purchase first (i.e. conative) instead of spending too much time thinking or feeling (i.e. cognitive or affective) about it. We have already encountered this criticism in chapter 4 in the context of media planning.

Cognitive stage →	Affective stage →	Conative stage
Attention →	Interest → Desire →	Action
Attention →	Interest → Desire → Conviction →	Action
Attention →	Interest → Evaluation →	Trial → Action
Attention → Knowledge →	Liking → Preference → Conviction →	Purchase

Figure 7.25 Various versions of the HOE model

FOOTE, CONE & BELDING[170] MODEL

The Foote, Cone & Belding (FCB)[171] model improved on the HOE models by postulating that the sequence of Cognitive–Affective–Conative is not invariable but rather changes with different buying circumstances. The key is to understand what those circumstances are. The advertising agency that developed it, Foote, Cone & Belding (or FCB), aimed to create a planning model that could assist their clients in their advertising. They changed the terminology from Cognitive, Affective and Conative to Think, Feel and Do.

The model postulates that in advertising the most important circumstances are the buying situation, which can be low- or high-involvement, and whether the target audience will devote more to thinking or feeling about the purchase. By putting these two dimensions together, we end up with four quadrants. Depending on which quadrant the product falls into, the sequence of Think, Feel and Do will differ. Figure 7.26 illustrates this idea. Note that the HOE model only fits

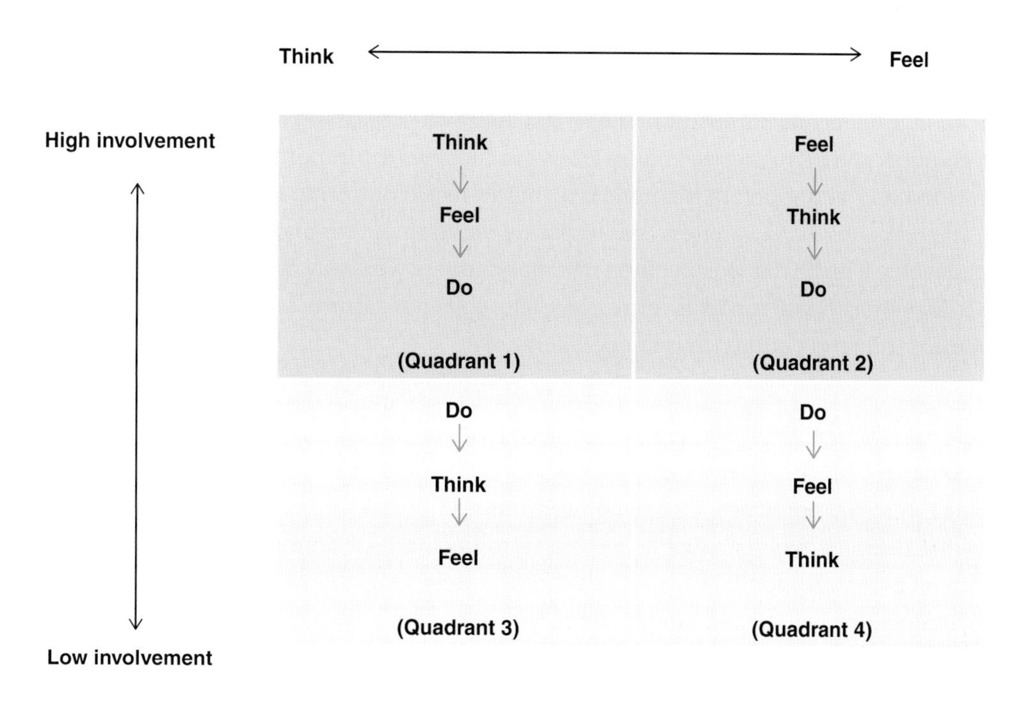

Figure 7.26 The Foote, Cone & Belding (FCB) model[171]

into one quadrant of the FCB model, when the product is high-involvement and when people spend a lot of time thinking about the purchase. This is quadrant 1 in figure 7.26.

The FCB model represents an improvement over HOE because it recognises the contingency that drives different purchase situations. For instance, in the low-involvement buying situations of quadrants 3 and 4, the target audience can simply Do first (i.e. buy the product), before they Think and Feel (quadrant 3) or Feel and Think (quadrant 4) about the purchase. Products in quadrant 3 are household products such as detergents and toilet paper, for which thinking about the purchase is more dominant than feeling. Products in quadrant 4 are snacks and soft drinks, where feeling about the purchase is more dominant than thinking.

Conversely, in the high-involvement buying situations of quadrants 1 and 2, the target audience can only Do last (i.e. purchase as the last stage) because they must Think or Feel (quadrant 1) or Feel and Think (quadrant 2) before they make the purchase. Again, what distinguishes quadrants 1 and 2 are the products. Products in quadrant 1 are those that are high-risk, such as getting a loan or buying a house, where rational performance is important, and so thinking comes before feeling. Products in quadrant 2, on the other hand, like perfume and jewellery, are more feeling-based and therefore feeling comes before thinking.

As we can quickly see, the FCB model suffers from a number of conceptual problems. For instance, is it really possible to separate thinking from feeling during a purchase?

ROSSITER–PERCY MODEL

First introduced in 1987 by Rossiter and Percy (RP),[172] this model represents an improvement over the FCB model by specifying in greater detail the four quadrants. The key difference is that the RP model does away with the three stages of Think–Do–Feel. While the purchase involvement is largely the same, it replaces Think–Do–Feel with two kinds of purchase motivation. According to RP, purchase motive can be negatively originated or positive ending. The negative motivation is also labelled 'informational' and includes problem removal, problem avoidance and normal depletion. The positive motivation is also labelled as 'transformational' and includes sensory gratification, intellectual stimulation and social approval.

In addition, the RP model (see figure 7.27) also specifies the importance of brand awareness in decision-making either before the purchase (brand recall) or during the purchase (brand recognition). It postulates that awareness is a necessary requirement for brand preference[173]; that is, we cannot develop a positive predisposition to a brand unless we are aware of it. Thus, in comparison to the FCB model, the RP model is more complete, does not assume any sequence and takes both the product and target audience into consideration.

COGNITIVE PROCESSING MODEL

One of the most influential models in persuasion is the cognitive processing (CP) model, which originated in social cognition. The major contribution of this approach is that it tries to understand what happens when a person is exposed to persuasive communication (e.g. advertising). How does a person respond? What causes them to yield to its arguments?

This form of research has a long tradition but stems from the recurrent observation that there is no relationship between the recall of a message and attitude change (i.e. persuasion) even though the person has processed the message thoroughly. Logic would suggest that if someone is persuaded by a message, surely they should be able to remember that message. But the

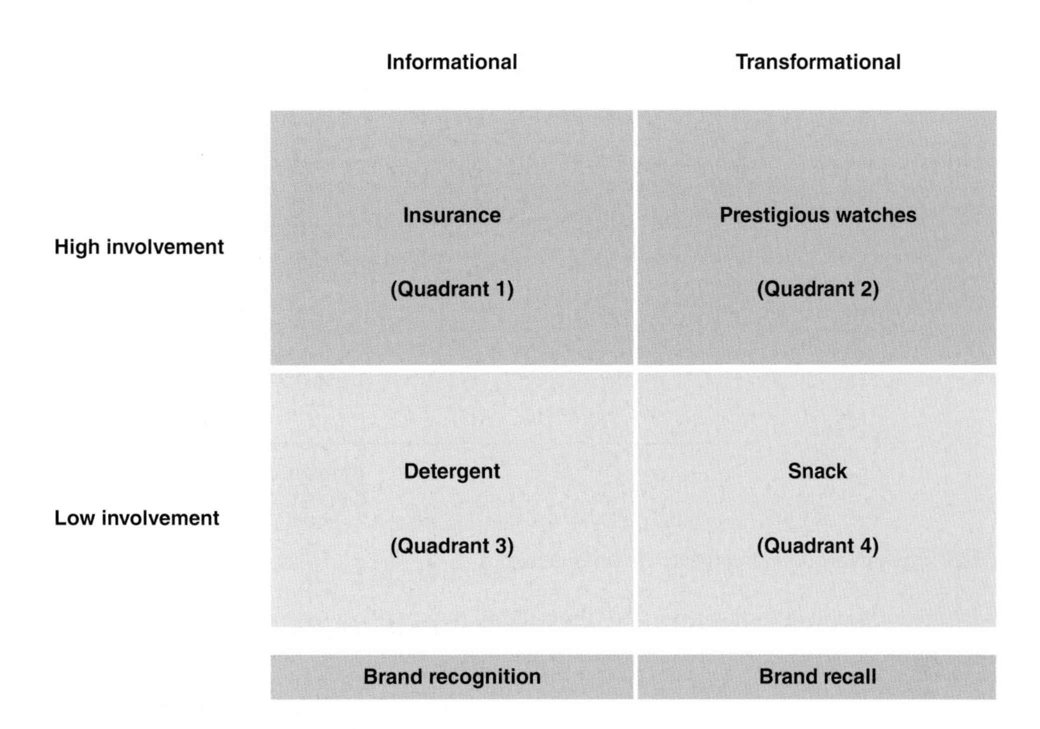

Figure 7.27 The Rossiter-Percy (RP) model[174]

correlation is low. It turns out that a more important factor than message memory is what people think about the message, called 'cognitive response'.[175] The thoughts that the message generates more accurately predict persuasion than the memory of the message. What is interesting about this perspective is that it does not assume that a person passively absorbs the information, but instead posits that they actively process the ad.

How does the CP model work? The idea is actually quite basic, yet ingenious. If a message generates positive thoughts, then it will be more persuasive. On the other hand, if the message generates negative thoughts (sometimes called 'counterarguments'), then there will be no attitude change. While there is nothing clever about this notion, the theory has expanded to specify the conditions in which this simple process will occur (or not occur). Consider the following.

When a person is exposed to a strong message argument, they are likely to generate positive thoughts, thus leading to attitude change. On the other hand, when a person is exposed to a weak message, the converse occurs. Negative thoughts will be generated, and the message will not be persuasive. However, we can reverse this effect by introducing distraction.

If someone is exposed to a strong message argument (e.g. listening to an argument), but at the same time creates distraction, so that they cannot process the message properly (e.g. by a flashing light), then what was previously a persuasive message is suddenly no longer so. We have disrupted the generation of positive thoughts. In fact, the more distraction there is, the less persuasion occurs.

But what is even more interesting is that, with a weak message, the reverse occurs. That is, a weak message suddenly becomes *more* persuasive with distraction, simply because we now disrupt the production of negative thoughts! And as distraction increases so does persuasion, even though the argument is supposed to be a weak one to start with (see figure 7.28).

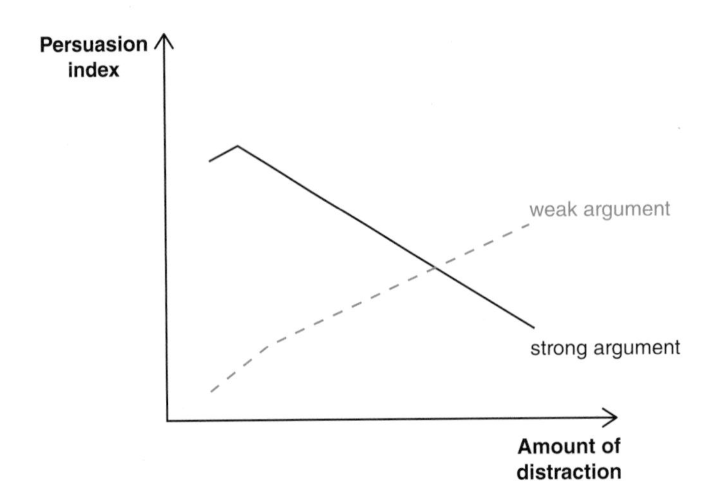

Figure 7.28 A weak argument can also be persuasive[176]

These are powerful demonstrations for the validity of the theory, and much research has shown that the CP approach can explain many persuasion effects. Indeed, the idea of distraction became the impetus for further development of the theory into what are now known as the Elaboration Likelihood Model (ELM)[177] and Heuristic–Systematic Model (HSM)[178] of CP. Both models are very similar. Very simply, they postulate that there are two routes to persuasion. In one route, we choose to process the message very carefully and systematically, in which case we are persuaded by the strength of the argument. This is also called the 'central processing route'. (This intensive–systematic processing also helps explain why strong arguments create positive thoughts and weak arguments negative thoughts.) When we do this, the resultant attitude towards the object tends to be long-lasting.

However, we do not always have the motivation, ability or opportunity to process a given message.[179] For instance, we may be rushing to get somewhere. This does not mean the message is not persuasive, since we use heuristics or 'rules of thumb' to make a judgement. For instance, if the ad shows an attractive model, it might trigger an 'attractive = good' heuristic, and we then assume that the advertised brand must also be good. In other words, as consumers we take short cuts. Or, to put it another way, the peripheral cues influence our thinking. However, attitudes formed this way tend to be short-lived compared to when we use intensive–systematic processing (i.e. taking the central processing route).

This peripheral route to persuasion using heuristic cues is an important theoretical plank for advertising because consumers' attention span is getting shorter and shorter.[180] We may be using more easy-heuristic processing nowadays. However, the two routes of persuasion are not mutually exclusive. For instance, if a person is still uncertain after examining the arguments carefully (i.e. using intensive–systematic processing), he or she could use the peripheral cues to assist. Since not all heuristic cues are equally persuasive, this means that it is important to use those that are.

In short, the CP model and its later forms have many implications for how executional tactics should be applied in advertising.

- If there is something important to say, say it clearly and convincingly. That is, make a strong argument in order to generate positive thoughts. Under these circumstances, do not use executional tactics that might distract the person from processing the message properly (e.g. music).
- If there is nothing important to say, or the argument is weak, then use executional tactics to entertain or distract, so that people will not generate too many negative thoughts as a result.

- Always use heuristic cues that have strong and relevant associations, just in case the target audience does not have the motivation, ability or opportunity to process the ad systematically.

In chapter 12, we will discuss another model, the Dual-Motive Dual-Processing (DMDP) model, which can help a marcoms manager evaluate the persuasiveness of an ad.

DISCUSSION QUESTIONS

1. What is the difference between a creative idea and creative execution? Which should take precedence, and why?
2. What are the similarities between the use of humour and sex in advertising?
3. What is the difference between a 'slice-of-life' and 'problem solution' format such as might be used in TV advertising?
4. Give an example of advertising based on fear. What are the major considerations to ensure that such advertising will be effective?
5. Under what circumstances should you use two-sided arguments in an ad? How might you combine this with comparison advertising?
6. Explain the radio advertising tactic of creating a 'theatre of the mind'. How is this different from an announcement? Give an example of how you would create such an ad for Starbucks coffee.
7. In the age of social media, topical advertising may become more important. Do you agree or disagree? Explain your answer.
8. With so many executional tactics available, what considerations should guide your selection? Discuss why they are important.
9. If using celebrities are fraught with problems, speculate about why this is such a popular tactic. Choose one weakness in using celebrity and discuss how you would mitigate this risk.
10. Imagine that you are running a company that sells a brand of coffee. Which celebrity would you enlist to help, and why? Assume now that your company cannot afford to use a celebrity. What kind of presenter would you use and why? Describe your decision-making process in both scenarios.
11. There are many variants of the hierarchy of effects (HOE) model. What do they all have in common? How would you apply HOE to the purchase of a car and a packet of potato chips?
12. What is the difference between the Foote, Cone & Belding (FCB) and Rossiter–Percy (RP) models of advertising? How are each related to the notion of HOE?
13. Explain the cognitive processing (CP) model and discuss in what ways it is important for advertising, if any. What are the implications of CP for executional tactics in advertising?

NOTES

1 Very often, the advertisement itself is also called the execution. But I like to think of execution as a craft, as in the execution was well carried out.

2 L Binet and S Carter, 'Mythbuster: creativity is about ideas', *Admap*, November, 2012, p. 9.

3 DW Schumann, RE Petty and DS Clemons, 'Predicting the effectiveness of different strategies of advertising variation: a test of the repetition-variation hypotheses', *Journal of Consumer Research*, 17(2), 1990, pp. 192–202.

4 TH Davenport and JC Beck, *The attention economy: understanding the new currency of business*, Harvard Business Press, n.p., 2002.

5 B Goldstein, *Encyclopaedia of perception*, vol. 1, Sage Publications, Thousand Oaks, CA, 2010, p. 71.

6 In interactive TV advertising, the word 'free' is powerful enough to lift its response rate of by 250%. See S Bellman, A Schweda and D Varan, 'Interactive TV advertising: iTV and executional factors', *Journal of Business Research*, 65(6), 2012, pp. 831–9.

7 PJ Lang et al., 'Looking at pictures: affective, facial, visceral and behavioural reactions', *Psychophysiology*, 30(3), 1993, pp. 261–73.

8 JH Nielsen, SA Shapiro and CH Mason, 'Emotionality and semantic onsets: exploring orienting attention responses in advertising', *Journal of Marketing Research*, 47(6), December 2010, pp. 1138–50.

9 T Bakalash and H Riemer, 'Exploring ad-elicited emotional arousal and memory for the ad using fMRI', *Journal of Advertising*, 42(4), 2013, pp. 275–91.

10 Millward Brown, 'Should my advertising stimulate an emotional response?' Knowledge Point, 2009. Accessed July 2018 at https://s3.amazonaws.com/academia.edu.documents/34249953/MillwardBrown_KnowledgePoint_EmotionalResponse.pdf.

11 Loterias y Apuestas del Estado, 'December 21st', Spain, Warc, 2018. Accessed at www.warc.com/content/paywall/article/loterias-y-apuestas-del-estado-december-21st-spain/119944.

12 R Pieters and M Wedel, 'Attention capture and transfer in advertising: brand, pictorial, and text-size effects', *Journal of Marketing*, 68, April 2004, pp. 36–50.

13 BA Huhmann, GR Franke and DL Mothersbaugh, 'Print advertising: executional factors and the RPB grid', *Journal of Business Research*, 65(6), 2012, pp. 849–54.

14 Ibid.

15 If the commercial break is long, consumers will continue to tune in to check whether the program has restarted, in which case even ads late in the commercial break will benefit from a surge in audience numbers. There are other conditions, like the popularity of the programs, that also affects audience exposure. See S Srinivasan and R Kent, 'Second-by-second analysis of advertising exposure in TV pods', *Journal of Advertising Research*, 53(1), 2013, pp. 91–100.

16 S Terry, 'Serial position effects in recall of television commercials', *Journal of General Psychology*, 132(2), 2005, pp. 151–63. See also Srinivasan and Kent (2013), 'Second-by-second analysis of advertising exposure in TV pods', note 15.

17 See review by YC Hsieh, KH Chen and MY Ma, 'Retain viewers' attention on banner ad by manipulating information type of the content', *Computers in Human Behavior*, 20, 2012, pp. 1692–9.

18 Eyetrack III, 'Online news consumer behavior in the age of multimedia', 2004. Accessed January 2013 at www.poynter.org/extra/eyetrack2004/advertising.htm.

19 G Baltas, 'Determinants of internet advertising effectiveness: an empirical study', *International Journal of Market Research*, 45(4), 2003, pp. 505–13.

20 YC Hsieh and KH Chen, 'How different information types affect viewers' attention on internet advertising', *Computers in Human Behavior*, 27, 2011, pp. 935–45.

21 G Nissim, Indago Digital, personal communication, 2018 (i.e. https://indagodigital.com.au) made this important observation.

22 M Eisend, 'A meta-analysis of humor in advertising', *Journal of the Academy of Marketing Science*, 37, 2009, pp. 191–203.

23 TW Cline and JJ Kellaris, 'The influence of humour strength and humour-message relatedness on ad memorability: a dual process model', *Journal of Advertising*, 36(10), 2007, pp. 55–67.

24 A Chattopadhyay and K Basu, 'Humor in advertising: the moderating role of prior brand evaluation', *Journal of Marketing Research*, 27, November 1990, pp. 466–76.

25 S Bellman et al., 'What makes a television commercial sell? Using biometrics to identify successful ads', *Journal of Advertising Research*, 2017, 57(1), pp 53–66.

26 J Rossiter and L Percy, *Advertising and promotions management*, 2nd edition, McGraw-Hill, New York, 1997. For an updated edition, see JR Rossiter, L Percy and L Bergkvist, *Marketing communications*, Sage, 2018.

27 H Borland, 'It could be up to a month before KFC opens again', *News.com*. Accessed July 2018 at www.news.com.au/lifestyle/food/restaurants-bars/it-could-be-up-to-a-month-before-kfc-opens-again/news-story/ee54e9c6819d49758853c1f8feb83191.

28 S Meredith, 'Hundreds of KFC branches in the UK to remain closed amid ongoing chicken shortage', *Europe New*, 21 February 2018. Accessed July 2018 at www.cnbc.com/2018/02/21/kfc-branches-in-britain-to-remain-closed-amid-ongoing-chicken-shortage.html.

29 PM Simpson, S Horton and G Brown, 'Male nudity and advertisements: a modified replication and extension of gender and product effects', *Journal of the Academy of Marketing Science*, 24(3), 1996, pp. 257–62.

30 M Steadman, 'How sexy illustrations affect brand recall', *Journal of Advertising Research*, 9(1), 1969, pp. 15–19.

31 M Giebelhausen and TP Novak, 'Web advertising: sexual content on eBay', *Journal of Business Research*, 65(6), 2012, pp. 840–2.

32 O Sabri and C Obermiller, 'Consumer perception of taboo in ads', *Journal of Business Research*, 65(6), 2012, pp. 869–73.

33 DW Stewart and S Koslow, 'Executional factors and advertising effectiveness: a replication', *Journal of Advertising*, 18(3), 1988, pp. 21–32.

34 S Armstrong, *Persuasive advertising: evidence-based principles*, Palgrave Macmillan, New York, 2010.

35 DW Stewart and DH Furse, *Effective advertising: a study of 1000 commercials*, Lexington Books, Lexington, MA, 1986.

36 Armstrong (2010), *Persuasive advertising*, note 34.

37 Stewart and Furse (1986), *Effective advertising*, note 35.

38 L Lodish et al., 'How TV advertising works: a meta-analysis of 289 real world split cable TV advertising experiments', *Journal of Marketing Research*, 32, May 1995, pp. 123–39.

39 Bellman, Schweda and Varan (2012), 'Interactive TV advertising: iTV and executional factors', note 6.

40 D Grewal et al., 'Comparative versus noncomparative advertising: a meta-analysis', *Journal of Marketing*, 61, October 1997, pp. 1–15.

41 SP Jain and SS Posavac, 'Valenced comparisons', *Journal of Marketing Research*, 41(1), 2004, pp. 46–58.

42 M Kacha, C Dianoux and T Hsu, 'Effectiveness of indirect versus direct comparative advertising: the role of comparison brand usage', *Creating Marketing Magic and Innovative Future Marketing Trends*, 2016, pp 63–4.

43 J Deighton, D Romer and J McQueen, 'Using drama to persuade', *Journal of Consumer Research*, 16, 1989, pp. 335–43.

44 You can see one of the ads here: www.youtube.com/watch?v=hpOBFELO0Qc. The original creative idea was for the instant coffee Nescafé Gold Blend in the UK. The same two main actors (Anthony Head and Susan Maugham) also played the roles there. For an inside peek go to: www .youtube.com/watch?feature=endscreen&NR=1&v=jLRJu-dS704. Accessed July 2013.

45 L. Dessart, 'Do ads that tell a story always perform better? The role of character identification and character type in storytelling ads', *International Journal of Research in Marketing*, 35, 2018, pp. 289–304.

46 JR Deighton, D Romer and J McQueen, 'Using drama to persuade', *Journal of Consumer Research*, 16, 1989, pp. 335–43.

47 A Sundin, K Andersson and R Watt, 'Rethinking communication: integrating storytelling for increased stakeholder engagement in environmental evidence synthesis', *Environmental Evidence*, 2018, pp. 7. Accessed June 2019.

48 '"Location-Aware" wine labels to drive new sales says Third Aurora', *PR News Wire*, 4 September 2019. Accessed September 2019 at https://finance.yahoo.com/news/location-aware-wine-labels-drive-123600146.html.

49 D Ogilvy, *Ogilvy on advertising*, Prior Books, London, 2000.

50 J Stanton and J Burke, 'Comparative effectiveness of executional elements in TV advertising: 15- versus 30-second commercials', *Journal of Advertising Research*, November/December, 1998, pp. 7–15.

51 JM Hunt, YJ Domzal and JB Kernan, 'Causal attribution and persuasion: the case of disconfirmed expectancies', *Advances in Consumer Research*, 9, 1982, pp. 287–92.

52 Ogilvy (2000), *Ogilvy on advertising*, note 49.

53 AG Woodside and JW Davenport, 'Effect of salesman similarity and expertise on consumer purchasing behaviour', *Journal of Marketing Research*, 11, May 1974, pp. 198–202.

54 D O'Keefe, *Persuasion: theory and research*, 2nd edition, Sage, London, 2002.

55 GR Thorton, 'The effect of wearing glasses upon judgement of personality traits of persons seen briefly', *Journal of Applied Psychology*, 28, May 1944, pp. 203–7.

56 S Reddy, V Swaminathan and CM Motley, 'Exploring the determinants of Broadway show success', *Journal of Marketing Research*, 35, August 1998, pp. 305–20.

57 C Stewart, 'Less bold, just as beautiful', *Australian Financial Review*, 28 March–1 April 2013, p. 30.

58 J Hilger, G Rafert and S Villas-Boas 'Expert opinion and the demand for experience goods: an experimental approach in the retail wine market', *The Review of Economics and Statistics*, 93(4), 2011, pp. 1289–96.

59 N De Hoog, W Stroebe and J DeWitt, 'The impact of vulnerability to and severity of a health risk on processing acceptance of fear-arousing communications: a meta-analysis', *Review of General Psychology*, 11, 2007, pp. 258–85.

60 JR Rossiter and J Stanton, 'Fear-pattern analysis supports the fear-drive model for antispeeding road-safety TV ads', *Psychology and Marketing*, 21(11), 2004, pp. 945–60.

61 CW Park and M Young, 'Consumer response to television commercials: the impact of involvement and background music on brand attitude formation', *Journal of Marketing Research*, 23, February 1986, pp. 11–24.

62 AC North, DJ Hargreaves and J McKendrick, 'The influence of in-store music on wine selections', *Journal of Applied Psychology*, 84, 1999, pp. 271–6.

63 Armstrong (2010), *Persuasive advertising*, note 34.

64 M Sutherland, *Advertising and the mind of the consumer*, Allen & Unwin, St Leonards, NSW, 2008.

65 D McCrudden, '10 lessons for media planning', *Warc Trends*, December 2011, pp. 18–19.

66 'What we know about TV and video ad length', *Warc Best Practice*. Accessed September 2019 at www.warc.com/content/paywall/article/what-we-know-about-tv-and-video-ad-length/107157.

67 M Sutherland and A Sylvester, *Advertising and the mind of the consumer*, 2nd edition, Allen & Unwin, Crows Nest, NSW, 2000, chapter 18.

68 McCrudden (2011), '10 lessons for media planning', note 65.

69 Armstrong (2010), *Persuasive advertising*, p. 124, note 34.

70 Rossiter and Percy (1997), *Advertising and promotions management*, note 26.

71 Armstrong (2010), *Persuasive advertising*, note 34.

72 PD Bolls, DD Muehling and K Yoon, 'The effects of television commercial pacing on viewers' attention and memory', *Journal of Marketing Communications*, 9(1), 2003, pp. 17–28.

73 Sutherland and Sylvester (2000), *Advertising and the mind of the consumer*, note 67.

74 WD Hoyer, RK Srivastava and J Jacoby, 'Sources of miscomprehension in television advertising', *Journal of Advertising*, 13(2), 1984, pp. 17–26.

75 Sutherland and Sylvester (2000), *Advertising and the mind of the consumer*, note 67.

76 D Ogilvy and J Raphelson, 'Research on advertising techniques that work – and don't work', *Harvard Business Review*, 60, July–August 1982, pp. 14–15.

77 Ogilvy (2000), *Ogilvy on advertising*, note 49.

78 Ogilvy and Raphelson (1982), 'Research on advertising techniques', note 76.

79 D Walker and MF von Goten, 'Explaining related recall outcomes: new answers from a better model', *Journal of Advertising Research*, 29(3), 1989, pp. 11–21. See also Stanton and Burke (1998), 'Comparative effectiveness of executional elements in TV advertising', note 50.

80 J Romaniuk, 'Lifting the productivity of TV advertising', *Journal of Advertising Research*, 2, 2012, pp. 146–8.

81 J Rossiter and S Bellman, *Marketing communications: theory and applications*, Pearson Education Australia, Frenchs Forest, NSW, 2005.

82 J Rossiter et al., 'Brain-imaging detection of visual scene encoding in long-term memory for TV commercials', *Journal of Advertising*, 41(2), 2001, pp. 13–21.

83 D Allan, 'Radio advertising: blip commercials', *Journal of Business Research*, 65, 2012, pp. 880–1.

84 Hsieh and Chen (2011), 'How different information types affect viewer's attention on internet advertising', note 20.

85 Rossiter and Percy (1997), *Advertising and promotions management*, note 26.

86 JA Edell and KL Keller, 'The information processing coordinated media campaigns', *Journal of Marketing Research*, 26(2), 1989, pp. 149–63.

87 A Paivio, *Mental representations: a dual-coding approach*, Oxford University Press, New York, 1986.

88 JN Pitt, 2015, *Multi-modal food story immersion: a persuasion mechanism and theory of photographic depiction of food products in advertising and marketing*, Macquarie University, Sydney, Australia, 2015.

89 LM Willemsen, K Mazerant, AL Kamphuis and G van der Veen, 'Let's get real (time)! The potential of real-time marketing to catalyze the sharing of brand messages', *International Journal of Advertising*, 37(5), 2018, pp. 828–48.

90 K Mazerant and LM Willemsen, 'Now and wow! How temporal characteristics affect the word of mouth of topical advertising' in V Cauberghe, L Hudders and M Eisend (eds), *Advances in*

advertising research IX, power to consumers, European Advertising Academy, Springer-Gabler, 2018.

91 'Singapore hits the jackpot with Trump-Kim summit', *CNBC Reports*, 11 June 2018. Accessed July 2018 at www.youtube.com/watch?v=leiuWrvZprs.

92 'Singapore businesses cash in on Trump-Kim mania', *SBS News*, 9 June 2018. Accessed July 2018 at www.sbs.com.au/news/singapore-businesses-cash-in-on-trump-kim-mania.

93 'Fearless Girl: How a small statue mad a big impact', Gunn 100 – Lessons from the world's best creative campaigns, *Warc*, 2018, p. 12. Accessed July 2020 at www.warc.com/content/paywall/article/gunn-100-lessons-from-the-worlds-best-creative-campaigns/121714.

94 G Bath, 'The controversial story of how "Fearless Girl" became a global symbol for gender equality', *MamaMia*, 27 February 2019. Accessed May 2019 at www.mamamia.com.au/fearless-girl-melbourne/.

95 J Caples and FE Hahn, *Tested advertising methods*, 5th edition, Prentice Hall, Englewood Cliffs, NJ, 1998.

96 Ogilvy (2000), *Ogilvy on advertising*, note 49.

97 Armstrong (2010), *Persuasive advertising*, p. 249, note 34.

98 J Aitchinson, *Cutting edge advertising*, Prentice Hall, Singapore, 1999, p. 187.

99 Ogilvy (2000), *Ogilvy on advertising*, note 49.

100 K Richards, 'Ikea and 72andSunny Amsterdam share how they worked together to launch AR app Ikea Place', *Adweek*, 19 September 2017. Accessed July 2018 at www.adweek.com/brand-marketing/ikea-and-72andsunny-amsterdam-share-how-they-worked-together-to-launch-ar-app-ikea-place/.

101 Virtual Crash Billboard, Eurobest, 2017. Accessed July 2018 at www2.eurobest.com/winners/2017/promoactivation/entry.cfm?entryid=1097&award=4.

102 There is a large-scale 2014 study by Millward Brown into how video content ads effective in different mediums. See Millward Brown, 'AdReaction: video creative in a digital world', Global Report. Accessed May 2019 at www.ert.gr/wp-content/uploads/2015/11/Millward_Brown_AdReaction_Video_Global_reduced.pdf.

103 J Motavalli, 'Advertising blunders of the rich and famous', *Adweek's Marketing Week*, 11, January 1988, pp. 18–19.

104 C Praet, 'The influence of national culture on the use of celebrity endorsement in television advertising: a multi-country study', *Paper presented at the International Conference on Research in Advertising (ICORIA)*, Antwerp, Belgium, 2008.

105 D Crutchfield, 'Celebrity endorsements still push product: why in the era of social media, the rewards continue to outweigh the risks', *Ad Age*, 22 September 2010. Accessed July 2013 at http://adage.com/article/cmo-strategy/marketing-celebrity-endorsements-push-product/146023.

106 'Celebrity advertisements – exposing a myth of advertising effectiveness', Ace metrix website, 2012. Accessed April 2013 at http://mktg.acemetrix.com/acton/attachment/563/563:f-0d9b/0/p-001d/-/%7B%7BEnv.SrcId%7D%7D/%7B%7BEnv.RecId%7D%7D.

107 W McGuire, 'Attitudes and attitude change', in L Garner and E Aronson (eds), *Handbook of social psychology*, vol. 3, Random House, New York, 1969, pp. 223–346. This chapter also emphasised the importance of familiarity, likeability and similarity (as well as attractiveness).

108 S Chaiken, 'Communicator physical attractiveness and persuasion', *Journal of Personality and Social Psychology*, 137, August 1979, pp. 1387–97.

109 LR Kahle and PM Homer, 'Physical attractiveness of celebrity endorser: a social adaptation perspective', *Journal of Consumer Research*, 11(4), 1985, pp. 954–61.

110 Some researchers, such as Ohanian, have classified all three factors of attractiveness, trustworthiness and expertise as being credible. However, I find little face validity in this conceptualisation, simply because one can be attractive and yet not credible – imagine Paris Hilton selling computers! R Ohanian, 'The impact of celebrity spokesperson's perceived image on consumers' intention to purchase', *Journal of Advertising Research*, 31(1), 1991, pp. 46–52.

111 R Goldsmith, B Lafferty, B and S Newell, 'The impact of corporate credibility and celebrity credibility on consumer reaction to advertisements and brands', *Journal of Advertising*, 29(3), 2000, pp. 43–54.

112 A Spry, R Pappu and TB Cornwell, 'celebrity endorsement, brand credibility and brand equity', *European Journal of Marketing*, 45(6), 2011, pp. 882–909.

113 JR Rossiter and A Smidts, 'Print advertising: celebrity presenters', *Journal of Business* Research, 65, 2012, pp. 874–9.

114 C Pornpitakpan, 'The persuasiveness of source credibility: a critical review of five decades' evidence', *Journal of Applied Social Psychology*, 34(2), 2004, pp. 243–81.

115 L Bergkvist, H Hjalmarson, and A Magi, 'A new model of how celebrity endorsements work: attitude toward the endorsement as a mediator of celebrity source and endorsement effects', *International Journal of Advertising*, 35(2), 2016, pp. 171–84.

116 J Knoll and J Matthes, 'The effectiveness of celebrity endorsements: a meta-analysis', *Journal of the Academy of Marketing Science*, 45, 2017, pp. 55–75.

117 J Cohen, 'Defining identification: a theoretical look at the identification of audiences with media characters', *Mass Communication and Society*, 4(3), 2001, pp. 245–64.

118 BP Fraser and WJ Brown, 'Media, celebrities, and social influence: identification with Elvis Presley', *Mass Communication and Society*, 5(2), 2002, pp. 183–206.

119 MD Basil, 'Identification as a mediator of celebrity effects', *Journal of Broadcasting and Electronic Media*, 40, 1996, pp. 478–95.

120 J Zhao, 'An experimental comparison of celebrity spokespersons' credibility, attractiveness, expertise, and identification on attitudes toward the ads and future interest', unpublished Masters' thesis, University of Lethbridge, Alberta, Canada, 2004.

121 NH Um, 'Celebrity scandal fallout: how attribution style can protect the sponsor', *Psychology and Marketing*, 30(6), 2013, pp. 529–41.

122 A Sahgal, 'Towards an understanding of celebrity worship among Indian consumers: an ethnoconsumerist approach', PhD thesis, Macquarie University, 2019.

123 Rossiter and Percy (1997), *Advertising and promotions management*, note 26.

124 T Shimp, *Advertising promotion and other aspects of integrated marketing communications*, 8th edition, South-Western College Publication, Mason, OH, 2010.

125 RB Cialdini, *Influence: science and practice*, Allyn & Bacon, Boston, MA, 2009.

126 Huhmann, Franke and Mothersbaugh (2012), 'Print advertising', note 13.

127 S Levy, 'Symbols for sale', *Harvard Business Review*, 37, July/August 1959, pp. 117–24.

128 G McCracken, 'Who is the celebrity endorser? Cultural foundations of the endorser process', *Journal of Consumer Research*, 16(3), 1989, pp. 310–21.

129 Langmeyer and Walker successfully tested this theory – see L Langmeyer and M Walker, 'A first step to identify the meaning in celebrity endorsers', in RR Holman and MR Solomon (eds), *Advances*

ASKHAM BRYAN
COLLEGE
LEARNING RESOURCES

in consumer research, 18, 1991, pp. 364–71; also L Langmeyer and M Walker, 'Assessing the effects of celebrity endorsers: preliminary findings', in RR Holman (ed.), *American Academy of Advertising Proceedings*, 1991, pp. 32–42.

130 The whole area is understudied. For a good critique, see L Bergkvist and K Qiang Zhou, 'Celebrity endorsements: a literature review and research agenda', *International Journal of Advertising*, 35 (4), 2016, pp. 642–63.

131 M Stallen et al., 'Celebrities and shoes on the female brain: the neural correlates of product evaluation in the context of fame', *Journal of Economic Psychology*, 31, 2010, pp. 802–11.

132 M Kamins, 'An investigation into the "match-up" hypothesis in celebrity advertising: when beauty is only skin deep', *Journal of Advertising*, 19(1), 1990, pp. 4–13.

133 A Eagly et al., 'What is beautiful is good, but . . . A meta-analytic review of research on physical attractiveness stereotype', *Psychological Bulletin*, 110(10), 1991, pp. 109–28.

134 M Dubey, J Farrell and L Ang, 'How accent and pitch affect persuasiveness in radio advertising', *Advances in Advertising Research*, IX, Springer, 2018, pp. 117–30.

135 Knoll and Matthes (2017), 'The effectiveness of celebrity endorsements', pp. 55–75, note 116.

136 FA Carrillat, A d'Astous, and J Lazure, 'For better, for worse? What to do when celebrity endorsements go bad', *Journal of Advertising Research*, 53, 2013, pp. 15–30.

137 J Rossiter and A Smidts, 'Print advertising: celebrity presenters', *Journal of Business Research*, 65, 2012, pp. 874–9.

138 L Ang and C Dubelaar, 'Explaining celebrity match-up: co-activation theory of dominant support', in M Craig-Lees, G Gregory and T Davis (eds), *Advances in Consumer Research – Asia Pacific*, 7, 2007, pp. 377–83.

139 J Freiden, 'Advertising spokesperson effects: an examination of endorser type and gender on two audiences', *Journal of Advertising Research*, 24, October–November 1984, pp. 33–43.

140 B London, 'The sweet smell of success for Cate Blanchett: actress lands Armani fragrance campaign worth a reported $10 MILLION', *MailOnline*, 30 March 2013. Accessed May 2019 at www.dailymail.co.uk/femail/article-2301002/Cate-Blanchett-lands-Armani-fragrance-campaign-worth-reported-10-MILLION.html.

141 Game of Glam, 'See how much these celebrities earn on twitter and instagram', *Buzz*, 20 May 2019. Accessed May 2019 at http://gameofglam.com/see-much-celebrities-earn-twitter-instagram/.

142 G Tom et al., 'The use of created versus celebrity spokesperson in advertisements', *Journal of Consumer Marketing*, 9(4), 1992, pp. 45–51.

143 Sam Kekovich, an Australia sports announcer, has been the spokesperson character for the Australian meat and livestock association since 2006. He appears every Australia Day extolling consumers to eat lamb: https://mumbrella.com.au/original-lambassador-sam-kekovich-ditches-lamb-in-australian-made-ad-targeting-tradies-561582. Accessed May 2019.

144 JA Folse, RG Netemeyer and S Burton, 'Spokescharacters', *Journal of Advertising*, 41(1), 2012, pp. 17–32.

145 S Misra and S Beatty, 'Celebrity spokesperson and brand congruence', *Journal of Business Research*, 21, 1990, pp. 159–73.

146 A Lisa, 'Celebrity endorsement deals with insane payouts', GO Banking Rates, 14 March 2019. Accessed May 2019 at www.gobankingrates.com/net-worth/celebrities/celebrity-endorsement-deals-paid-how-much/?utm_campaign=490665&utm_source=yahoo.com&utm_content=1#10.

147 C Tripp, TD Jenson and L Carlson, 'The effects of multiple product endorsements by celebrities on consumers' attitudes and intentions', *Journal of Consumer Research*, 20, March 1994, pp. 535–47.

148 JC Mowen and SW Brown, 'On explaining and predicting the effectiveness of celebrity endorsers', in KB Monroe (ed.), *Advances in Consumer Research*, 8, 1981, pp. 437–41.

149 M Cooper, 'Can celebrities really sell products?', *Marketing and Media Decisions*, 120, September 1984, pp. 64–5.

150 BD Till and T Shimp, 'Endorsers in advertising: the case of negative celebrity information', *Journal of Advertising*, 27(1), 1998, pp. 67–81.

151 C Amos, G Holmes and D Strutton, 'Exploring the relationship between celebrity endorser effects and advertising effectiveness', *International Journal of Advertising*, 27(2), 2008, pp. 209–34.

152 NL Votolato and HR Unnava, 'Spillover of negative information on brand alliances', *Journal of Consumer Psychology*, 16(2), 2006, pp. 196–202.

153 Carrillat, d'Astous and Lazure (2013), 'For better, for worse?' note 136.

154 A Mehta, 'How advertising response modelling (ARM) can increase ad effectiveness', *Journal of Advertising Research*, 34(3), 1994, pp. 62–74.

155 Stewart and Furse (1986), *Effective advertising*, note 35.

156 Ogilvy and Raphelson (1982), 'Research on advertising techniques', note 76.

157 Huhmann, Franke and Mothersbaugh (2012), 'Print advertising', note 13.

158 D Bruns, T Langner and L Bergkvist, 'When your celebrity endorser turns into Dracula: the vampire effect revisited', *International Congress of Research in Advertising*, Valencia, 2018.

159 'The mood/image appeal: giving the product good vibrations!', *Topline*, 4, 1985; reprinted in *Marketing News,* 19(1), 1 March 1986, p. 36.

160 Ogilvy (2000), *Ogilvy on advertising*, note 49.

161 Knoll and Matthes (2017), 'The effectiveness of celebrity endorsements', pp. 55–75, note 116.

162 M Eisend and T Langer, 'Immediate and delayed advertising effects of celebrity endorsers attractiveness and expertise', *International Journal of Advertising*, 29(4), 2010, pp. 527–46.

163 A Elberse and J Verleun, 'The economic value of celebrity endorsers', *Journal of Advertising Research*, 2(2), 2012, pp. 149–65.

164 KYC Chung, TP Derdenger and K Srinivasan, 'Economic value of celebrity endorsements: Tiger Woods' impact on sales of Nike golf balls', *Marketing Science* 32, 2013, pp. 271–93.

165 I would like to thank Paul Blanket, Principal of First Impressions, for providing this information. For more information, visit the First Impressions website at www.firstimpressions.net.au. Accessed May 2013.

166 P Blanket, First Impressions, personal communications.

167 E Livni, 'What it costs to hire Kim Kardashian', *Quartzy*, 10 May 2019. Accessed May 2019.

168 H Tattersall, 'Social media's rock stars of wealth', *Financial Review*, 25 July 2019. Accessed September 2019 at www.afr.com/wealth/people/social-media-s-rock-stars-of-wealth-20190723-p529wa.

169 EK Strong, *The psychology of selling*, McGraw-Hill, New York, 1925.

170 R Vaughn, 'How advertising works: a planning model', *Journal of Advertising Research*, 20(5), 1980, pp. 27–33.

171 Adapted from Vaughn (1980), 'How advertising works', note 170.

172 JR Rossiter and L Percy, *Advertising and promotion management*, McGraw-Hill, New York, 1987.

173 In the 2005 edition of Rossiter and Bellman *Marketing communications*, brand preference has now been replaced by brand attitude.

174 Adapted from Rossiter and Bellman (2005), *Marketing communications*, p. 152, note 81.

175 RE Petty, TM Ostrom and TC Brock (eds), *Cognitive responses in persuasion*, Erlbaum, Hillsdale, NJ, 1981.

176 Adapted from RE Petty, GL Wells and TC Brock, 'Distraction can enhance or reduce yielding to propaganda: thought disruption versus effort justification', *Journal of Personality and Social Psychology*, 34, 1976, pp. 874–84.

177 RE Petty and DT Wegner, 'The elaboration likelihood model: current status and controversies', in S Chaiken and T Trope (eds), *Dual-process theories in social psychology*, Guilford Press, New York, 1999, pp. 37–72.

178 S Chaiken, 'Heuristic versus systematic information processing and the use of source versus message cues in persuasion', *Journal of Personality and Social Psychology*, 41, 1980, pp. 1–12.

179 DJ MacInnis, C Moorman and BJ Jaworski, 'Enhancing and measuring consumers' motivation, opportunity, and ability to process brand information from ads', *Journal of Marketing*, 55, October 1991, pp. 32–53.

180 Davenport and Beck (2002), *Attention economy*, note 4.

CHAPTER 8
SOCIAL INFLUENCE AND SOCIAL MEDIA

CHAPTER OVERVIEW

Humans are social animals: we influence and are influenced by each other. Traditional models of marketing communications do not place much weight on social influence, but with the rise of social media and social commerce, companies are beginning to take this form of communication seriously. This chapter presents a way of thinking about IMC that incorporates these modern communication methods and the broader principle of social influence.

The chapter starts by providing some context: it outlines how information flows and introduces some basic principles that govern behaviour in social networks. It then delves into the more substantial issues: what social media is, what its four core characteristics are, and how organisations have exploited these. This is followed by a close examination of certain types of social communication, such as WOM, buzz and viral marketing. The emphasis throughout the chapter is on understanding the preconditions necessary for what we call 'viral contagion' to occur. This leads to a discussion of social commerce.

Learning goals

After reading this chapter, you will understand:

- how information flows in marketing
- what social ties are, and why they are influential
- what social media is, its contingent usage and integration
- the principles of social influence, including six degrees of separation, three degrees of influence and the strength of weak ties
- differences between opinion leaders, market mavens, brand loyalists and brand communities
- distinctions between WOM, recommendations, buzz marketing and viral marketing
- the concept of a branded conversation
- the rise of social movements and #hashtag
- what viral contagion is, what its preconditions are, and why it is so difficult to create a viral campaign
- what social commerce is.

People are social animals: witness the way we gossip, spread rumours and generally hang out with people who are similar to us. It is a basic, primal human instinct to congregate and interact with people we like. In fact, one of the most severe forms of imprisonment is solitary confinement; simply depriving prisoners of social companionship is enough to break their will and perhaps send them insane.[1] It can cause serious psychiatric harm (e.g. agitated confusion and paranoia, delirium, impulsive and self-directed violence), even for prisoners who have no history of mental illness. About 50% of prison suicides occur in solitary confinement.[2]

Being social animals, we are embedded in a rich network of social ties. Within this network, we tend to copy and influence each other. How central we are in the network and the number of social ties we have shapes our emotions, health, happiness, political persuasions and even our IQ. For instance, an obese person is on average more likely to have friends who are also obese. Further, happy people tend to cluster with other happy people and, likewise, unhappy people tend to find other unhappy people. This turns out to be a better predictor of a person's happiness than earning more money.[3] Network effects are powerful.

The advertising industry is now beginning to factor social ties into its communication strategies. This is because, historically, the disciplines of marketing and advertising were based on the paradigm of individual-based processing. We only have to look at the grand frameworks of advertising to see how entrenched this paradigm is (see chapter 7). Social ties and network relationships were also ignored in the past because they are complex and require new ways of thinking and a new vocabulary. However, with the rise of social media, the effects of social ties can no longer be ignored. For instance, there are about 2.49 billion monthly active users on Facebook (1.59 billion *daily*), the most popular social media platform on the planet.[4] Contrast this figure with the following *monthly* figures of active users from other social media platforms: YouTube: 2.0 billion; WeChat: 2 billion; Facebook Messenger: 1.3 billion; WeChat: 1.2 billion; Instagram: 1 billion; TikTok: 800 million; Reddit: 430 million; Snapchat: 398 million; Twitter: 386 million.[5]

If Facebook were a country, it would be the largest. The reasons why consumers use Facebook is because they enjoy it (i.e. interesting and fun), their friends are on it, and they find it useful (e.g. increased efficiency in connecting and sharing with friends).[6] Facebook also knows its users intimately, based on the data it collects about their profile and online activities. Even governments do not have the same level of information about their citizens. This makes Facebook a powerful tool for targeting.[7] It is predicted that social media advertising worldwide will grow from US$32 billion in 2014 to US$48 billion by 2021.[8] This revenue comes from ad placements on users' home pages, as advertisers pay for impressions or clicks of their ads.

However, before we discuss social media and its implications for IMC, let's first try to understand how information flows in social networks, and then consider the principles of social ties and influence.

HOW INFORMATION FLOWS

In the 1940 US presidential elections, Paul Lazarsfeld and his colleagues[9] wanted to find out how information from an election campaign influenced voting behaviour. The prevailing theory was that information from the mass media influenced each person directly, and that to be efficient all that was needed was to vary the channels to ensure you reached all the different audience segments. This view assumed a 'one-step' flow of information, as shown in figure 8.1. However, by assuming that each person gets the message directly from those channels, we ignore the fact that people influence and convey information to each other.

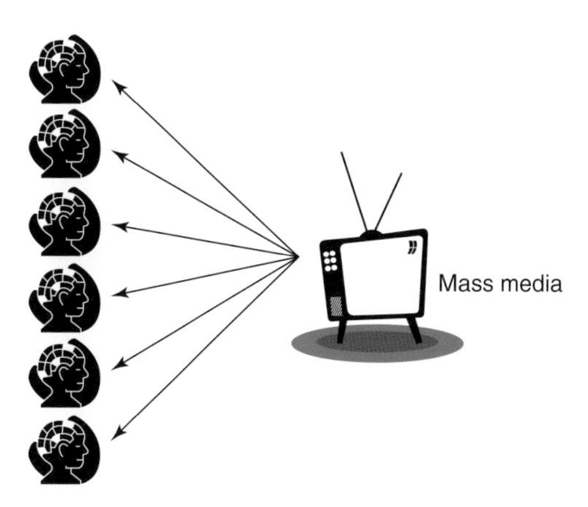

Figure 8.1 A 'one-step' information flow

To Lazarsfeld and his colleagues' surprise, they found that mass media did not have any significant effect on voting behaviour. Instead they found that a much more powerful factor was the social group a person belonged to and, in particular, the one influential member of that group who seemed better informed than others in the group (because this person is more attuned to the media). This influential person is called the 'opinion leader'.

This discovery led Lazarsfeld and his colleagues to develop their idea of a 'two-step' model of information flow. There are various versions of the model, but figure 8.2 essentially shows it at its simplest: in step 1, information is passed to the opinion leader and in step 2 it is then transmitted to the rest of the group.

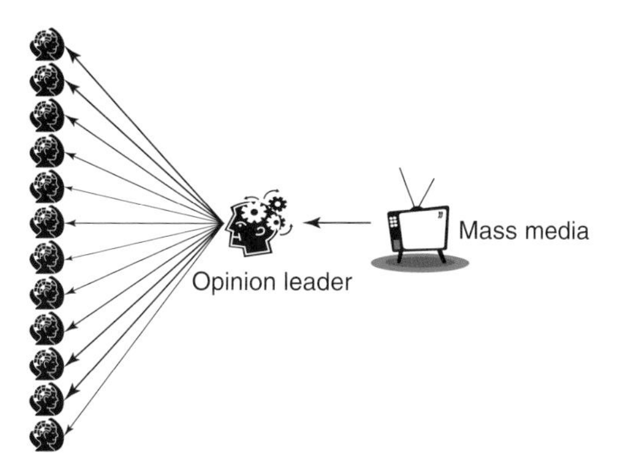

Figure 8.2 A 'two-step' information flow

No doubt, this model is too simplistic. In today's world, where most people have access to many channels of communication, including social media networks, it is inaccurate to base a model on linear transmissions of information. These days, a multi-step approach (see figure 8.3) is the generally accepted view. This means that a person receives information from multiple sources, not just from the opinion leader. However, this does not mean that information travels randomly: we are still more likely to engage in WOM with people whom we have close social ties, as discussed above. So, the multi-step model of information flow highlights the importance of social networks. Let's expand on this point with a hypothetical example of a social network.

Figure 8.3 shows the multi-step flow of information in a social network. As you can see, it is much more complicated than the two-step model. The influential opinion leader at point A is still important because he or she remains widely respected. However, unlike in the two-step model, other people in the network are also directly exposed to messages from the mass media, not just from the opinion leader. They also interact directly with each other, as symbolised by the double-headed arrows. The model also recognises that some people, like B and H in this example, may ignore the message from the media even though they are directly exposed to it (for instance, because they find the ad boring).

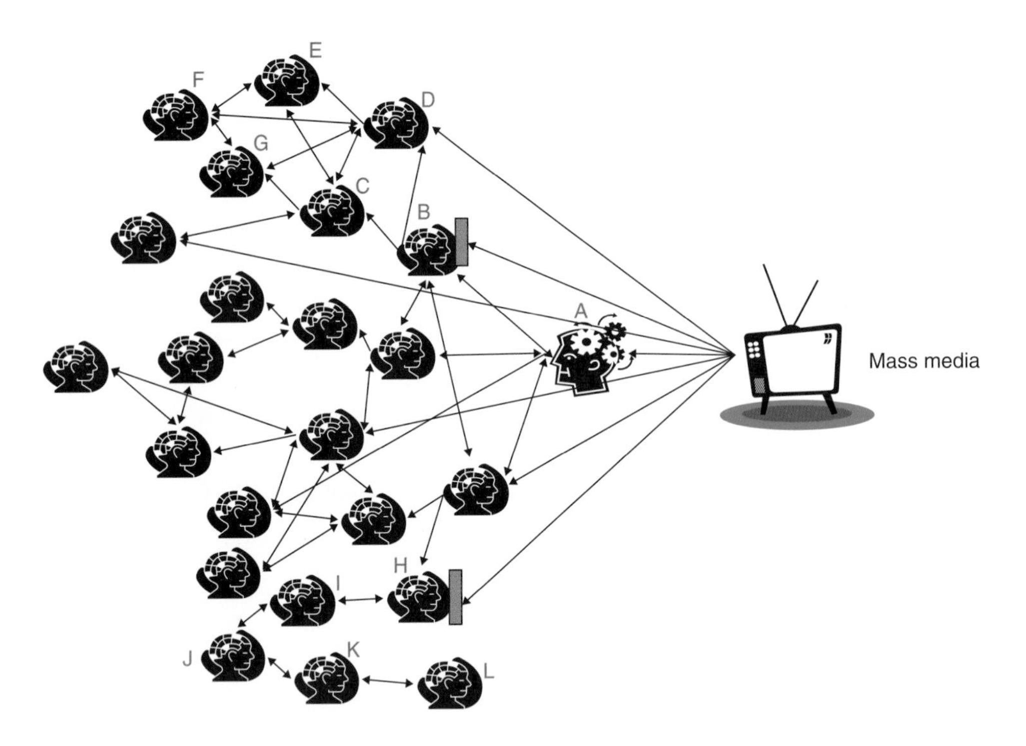

Figure 8.3 A multi-step information flow

Figure 8.3 also illustrates other important points if we depict information flow and social ties in the same way.[10] Note that some people are more tightly connected with each other, such as people C, D, E, F and G in the diagram. These five people seem to know each other. Compare this with people H, I, J, K and L, who seem more loosely connected. It stands to reason that clusters with high connectivity are more likely to share information, and hence more likely to influence each other, than those with low connectivity.

Generally, the central person in the network is the most influential, because of his or her connectedness. Therefore, initially targeting this person with the information we want to spread seems logical. But identifying this central person is not easy because collecting network data is expensive. However, Banerjee and colleagues discovered one simple way, the 'gossip' method.[11] This involves asking a sample of people in the network who they would go to if they wanted to spread some information about a certain topic. For example, to find out who is central in your network, we simply ask: 'If I want to spread information about a topic to everyone in my network, who should I speak to?' If a person is consistently nominated, then chances are that person is central to that network. And that is the person one should initially approach.

SOCIAL TIES AND THEIR INFLUENCE

Let's now examine some basic principles about social networks and how they influence our behaviour. These are essential concepts, and if we understand these, we will better appreciate social media and its implications for marketing communications.

Principle 1: We are socially embedded in a small world

As the saying goes, 'No man is an island'. Since humans are social animals, it is not surprising that we all live in a socially embedded world characterised by social ties. We also hear people say, 'It is a small world'. How would we prove this?

Travers and Milgram[12] took up this challenge and asked how many steps we need to get a piece of information to an unknown person if indeed we live in a small world. To test this, they devised an ingenious study: they wrote a letter addressed to a stockbroker living in Boston, and gave copies of the letter to a few hundred people in Nebraska, asking each of them to send it to someone who might have a better chance of knowing this particular stockbroker. Travers and Milgram found that on average it took only six steps for the letter to reach the correct stockbroker in Boston. This result is quite incredible, and it illustrates that no matter how big the physical world is, in socio-metric terms it is actually quite small, because of the social ties we have with each other. This phenomenon is sometimes called 'six degrees of separation' (a friend is separated from you by one degree, your friend's friend is separated by two degrees, your friend's friend's friend by three degrees, and so on).

Although Travers and Milgram's original study was published in 1969, the findings were replicated about 34 years later by Dodds, Muhamad and Watts.[13] This time in a study involving the forwarding of an email (instead of a letter) to reach 18 different targets in 13 different countries (e.g. a professor in the US, a technology consultant in India, a policeman in Australia and a veterinarian in the Norwegian army) instead of just one person (i.e. the Boston stockbroker) in one country (i.e. the US). In total, about 61 000 people were recruited to participate in the study. Amazingly, the same basic result was found; it took between four and seven forwarded emails to reach the targets. However, among Facebook users, their degree of separation from each other is about 3.57.[14] This means news spreads faster within social networks. This is good because if a company can excel, the good news will spread faster; but the reverse is also true.

However, there was one important finding that differs from the Travers and Milgram study. The earlier study found that not all six degrees of separation were the same. A large number of letters reached the stockbroker via the same three people, who seemed to be very well connected. These 'super-connectors', or 'hubs', seemed to play an important role in the diffusion of information. But in the Dodd and colleagues' study, they found that the super-connectors were only responsible for 5% of the information flow and therefore did not play a significant role in the transmission of the information. They found that it is more important to reach a certain critical mass of easily influenced people,[15] and that once this occurs viral transmission will happen naturally. In this sense, viral diffusion is similar to a forest fire: a small spark can cause a huge fire if the prevailing environmental conditions are correct. There is nothing special about the spark. Or, to put it another way, there is no need for the super-connectors to create viral diffusion.

All this should be good news to the marcoms manager because it means that any marketing message can theoretically be transmitted around the world from person to person within six steps. Or, to put it another way, because of our social connections, marketing messages can diffuse very quickly around the world. A good example is that of a 'viral' message, where information quickly spreads from one end of the world to another via the internet. The diffusion seems to be quite an egalitarian process without the need for any super-connectors (such as celebrities or mainstream media).

However, this does not mean that *all* marketing messages will 'go viral'. It only means that there is the potential for this to happen. We should not be surprised that most messages are not retransmitted. Even in the Travers and Milgram study, only 18 out of 96 letter chains (or 19%) were connected. Likewise, in the Dodd and colleagues' replication, only 386 out of 24 163 email chains were completed, which is an even smaller percentage (1.6%). Why do people not pass on the emails? When this question was asked as part of these studies, only 0.3% of participants responded that it was because they did not know anyone to forward it to, which suggests that the failure to pass a message has more to do with the lack of incentive than lack of connectivity.

Thus, while the phenomenon of six degrees of separation clearly shows that the potential for viral marketing campaigns exists, this is not enough. As we will discuss later, several preconditions are necessary before a marketing message will be passed along; for instance, it helps if incentives can be given to encourage forwarding.

Principle 2: The strength of weak ties

Forty years ago, Mark Granovetter[16] suggested that it is people at the periphery of the network (such as K or L in figure 8.3[17]) who helped spread information in society. Since we interact with those close to us, we tend already to know what they know – there is no new information. On the other hand, people at the periphery of our network are likely to have new information, because they are also connected to other networks: they act like bridges to the next group. In other words, the individuals who connect these network clusters are influential because they have control over the transmission of information that originates from other groups.

To test this theory, Granovetter cleverly surveyed technical, professional and managerial respondents by asking them how often they interacted with the person who helped them obtain their present job. Interestingly, a large majority (83%) reported interacting either rarely or occasionally. This means that socially distant acquaintances are more likely to contain new information that we might find useful, including leads about new jobs. Dodd and colleagues' recent study[18] also supports this theory, finding that when people want to forward an email to an unknown target (as described above), they tend to choose as recipients those friends who are not extremely close to them.

This implies that more so than super-connectors, it is the consumers at the peripherals of a cluster that help diffuse the marketing information. However, since we do not know who the peripherals are, it may pay to simply embark on a large seeding program for a viral campaign.

Principle 3: We influence and are influenced by each other (some more so than others)

Being socially embedded in a network has profound implications. We influence and are influenced by those who are close to us. However, not everyone in our network is equally influential. Generally, the more interconnected we are, the more we will influence each other.[19] The most influential are those closest to us, our family members and our closest five friends, with whom we spend 60% of our social time.[20] Outside this close circle, the influence people have on us is smaller and decreases with increasing distance.

The most dramatic example is this: a husband's risk of death rises dramatically (about 30–100%) in the first 12 months after his wife passes away. This is due not only to the loss of emotional support he experiences, but also to the sudden drop in his social networks. Women are generally more social than men, having more friends, spending more time and talking longer with their friends over the phone than men.[21] Wives tend to rope their husbands into their social circles (rather than the other way around). Over time men increasingly come to depend on their wives for access to social networks. Therefore, when a man's wife passes away, he is often left socially isolated with little support. This effect is compounded by the fact that many men rely on their wives to prepare their meals, perform household chores and maintain the general upkeep of their home – after a wife's death, a man has to take responsibility for these tasks himself. Often, men sink into a depression due to loneliness and domestic disrepair.

Interestingly, the social connectedness of women is also borne out by their greater usage of some social media websites. In a US survey,[22] more women than men tend to use Facebook (women: 74%, men: 62%); Instagram (women: 39%, men: 30%); and Pinterest (women: 41%, men: 16%) and women turn out to be more influential in encouraging others to join a social media network.[23] Not surprisingly, women post more on Facebook than men (especially about nutrition and health).[24]

Research also shows that our influence with our friends does not extend infinitely but only to the third degree of separation.[25] This means we influence our immediate friends (one degree of separation), friends of friends (two degrees of separation), and those friends' friends (three degrees of separation). After that, our influence dissipates. This is known as the 'three degrees of influence'. For instance, in a US study of the health of the community in Framingham, Massachusetts, where two-thirds of the residents are examined by their doctors every two years, and where the records have been meticulously kept for 20 years, Fowler and Christakis[26] were able to map how happy each resident was and their influence on others. They found that a person is likely to be 15% happier if he or she is directly connected to a person who is happy. This drops to 10% if the connection is at two degrees of separation, 6% at three degrees of separation and then to null effect at the fourth degree.

In another US study, Brown and Reingen[27] carefully traced the WOM recommendations for three piano teachers in Tempe, Arizona, none of whom advertised their services. They wanted to find out how those teachers obtained their customers. As expected, the study found that the highest proportion of the customers came via referrals from their close friends (i.e. the first degree of separation). Interestingly, the study also found that 38% of the recommendations came from friends of friends of friends (three degrees of separation). After that, the effects dissipated – less than 1% of recommendations came from the sixth degree of separation. That is why having more friends online does not necessarily mean more influence. It is the closeness of friends, not the quantity of friends, that is more important.[28]

In marketing, we often talk about opinion leaders, market mavens and brand advocates (sometimes called 'evangelists'). We will call these people 'influentials', because this is what they do – they influence others. The term 'opinion leader' is a hangover from the early work of diffusion research, which looked at how some people influence others (as we saw in Lazarsfeld's study of election messages). Generally, it has been found that people who are knowledgeable in a certain domain tend to be able to influence others, especially if the seeker of advice is a novice in that domain. Opinion leaders like to give information for a variety of reasons: they are seeking status enhancement, they like to help others, or they are simply very involved in the product category. Some opinion leaders are influential by virtue of their profession (e.g. doctors and lawyers), in which case it is their expertise that people seek out. Even within networks of similar professionals – such as a referral network of physicians – the opinion leaders within the networks can influence and alter the behaviour of others in the networks.[29]

Market mavens are like opinion leaders, but they serve a different function. Whereas an opinion leader tends to be an expert in one product category, market mavens possess lots of information about different products and services (multi-categories) that they themselves do not necessarily own or use. They seem attuned to what is happening in the market environment (e.g. what new products are being launched), and more importantly they also like to share their knowledge with others.[30]

Brand loyalists make natural influencers because they like the brands. They are willing to queue up for hours to buy the latest model, as we often see with Apple smartphone (see figure 8.4). Some brand loyalists are so committed that their self-concept becomes intricately bound to the brand, and they are even willing to have the brand name or logo tattooed on their body.[31] This enthusiasm makes them ideal brand advocates. Sometimes brand loyalists get together to form brand communities, because they want to feel connected to each other, bonded by their shared love of the brand. Such communities often have three characteristics: first, they share a certain sense of identity (called shared consciousness); second, they practise certain rituals (e.g. Saab drivers honk at each other on the road); and third, they have a moral responsibility to other members (e.g. Saab drivers will pull over and help another Saab driver in need).[32]

Figure 8.4 Apple loyalists lining up to buy the latest model

Marketers love these influentials because of what they can do. Further, since marketers often need to segment and target, the influentials seem like a good place to start. This is especially true if a marketer needs to seed the market with a product, in which case it makes sense to give it to people who are more likely to talk about it. A growing area in marketing is the use of social media influencers who might have a large following on social media (to be discussed later in this chapter).

SOCIAL MEDIA, ITS CONTINGENT USAGE AND INTEGRATION

What is social media? One definition is this: A group of internet-based applications that allow the creation and exchange of user-generated as well as firm-generated content. This simple definition suggests that many applications can be included, from internet forums to social networks, and from social blogs and micro-blogging to wikis, podcasts, image and video-sharing sites and consumer rating sites. Some of the most popular social networking websites are:

- Facebook
- YouTube
- WhatsApp

- WeChat
- Instagram
- TikTok
- Reddit
- Snapchat
- Twitter
- LinkedIn
- Pinterest.

However, not all social media are built equal. Instagram, for instance is a visual-oriented platform, usually of the celebratory kind, more suitable for businesses that rely on visual images to sell (e.g. fashion and food), while Twitter is limited to 140 characters, and the content of Snapchat lasts only for a short period of time as specified by the sender (e.g. 10 seconds). Some platforms are also more suitable for different target audiences. For instance, Facebook is a broad-based popular platform, while Snapchat is especially popular among the younger age group (18–24 year olds).[33] LinkedIn, on the other hand, is more suitable for business-to-business enterprises, while WeChat, predominantly a smartphone app (from Tencent, China), dominates the Chinese market with about 1.2 billion users! It has all the functionality of Facebook and Twitter, but includes the all-important mobile e-payment, where virtually any transaction in China can be made. WeChat is said to have permeated the lives of most Chinese people in China.[34]

THE RISE OF TIKTOK

TikTok started life as a Chinese app in 2016 (previously called Douyin), where teenagers[35] post videos of themselves lip-synching and dancing to a 15-second music track, although it can also encompass other non-musical activities like their hobbies, fashion, fitness, travel or photography. Although TikTok has been growing, its popularity soared during the COVID-19 pandemic.[36] This could be because people were seeking more micro-entertainment to relieve their boredom, and/or with more time on their hands, people were also channelling their creative energies onto this easy-to-use platform. Furthermore, since TikTok videos are generally short and humorous, it was a welcome relief from the relentless news cycle about COVID-19, and hence had virality potential. Instagram influencers are also using TikTok, and hence broadening its demographic appeal. The surge in popularity allowed TikTok to rake in record advertising revenue[37] (in the form of pre-roll advertising, like that of YouTube) and steal a march on some of its social media rivals.

Thus, depending on the target audience and the communications objectives, the marcoms manager should carefully select the right platforms and deploy them in an integrated fashion for the developed creative assets of the campaign. For instance, Facebook and Twitter are more suitable for creating conversations with consumers than YouTube,[38] but the latter trumps in its video capability. Facebook, which is a more hedonic platform than LinkedIn, is more suitable for distributing fun games, products or apps than utilitarian ones.[39] Furthermore, one should not just use social media alone in any campaign since they are generally ineffective on their *own*. One study concerning low-involvement, consumer-packaged goods found that customer online activities (e.g. paid search clicks, website visits, 'likes' or 'unlikes') explained only 7% of the variance in sales; but when other marketing mix elements were added to the modelling (e.g. price, distribution and TV advertising), the explanatory power jumped dramatically to 33%.[40]

To further demonstrate the impact of the relationship between paid, shared, search, earned and owned media (see chapter 5) on sales, the authors showed (among other things) that an increase of one weekly TV GRP (i.e. paid media) not only led to 137 more units sold, but also resulted in 9 additional paid search clicks (i.e. search media), with 5.2 times additional visits to the brand's website (i.e. owned media or asset), as well a small increase of 0.5 Facebook likes (i.e. earned media). Ultimately, all were modelled to see their effects on sales. Figure 8.5 shows a very small and simplified part of their model. Finally, with the proliferation of data, it is often easy to be seduced by various trendy 'engagement' metrics (e.g. clicks or likes), but choose those that matter to the marcoms objectives,[41] and they should be modelled to see their effects on some sort of business outcome (e.g. sales or partnerships).

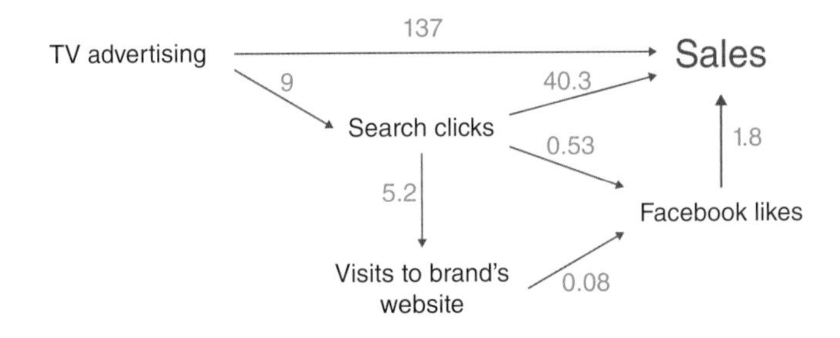

Figure 8.5 Long-term effects of various activities on the sales of low-involvement, consumer-packaged goods, simplified from Srinivasan et al. (2016)

FOUR ASPECTS OF SOCIAL MEDIA: CONNECTIVITY, CONVERSATIONS, CONTENT CREATION AND COLLABORATION

Enabled by social-mediated technologies, all the social media platforms have some aspects of these four elements: connectivity, conversations, content creation and collaboration.

Connectivity

For social networking to grow and prosper, it must first try to create a large community of users. Value is thus created if there are network externalities;[42] that is, social media has no value if you are the only person using it. Connectivity is therefore paramount. This is achieved by having a platform (e.g. Facebook, Twitter, LinkedIn) that makes it easy for users to connect with each other. The prime example of this facilitating technology is the 'friending' application in Facebook: with a push of a button, you can invite people to join your network and once they join you have access to their network of friends and they to yours. Further, if Facebook discovers that you have mutual friends who are not connected directly to you, it will automatically send you an email asking whether you would like them to join your network, and if you do not respond it will send you a reminder. In this way, through the clever use of technologies, a social media platform helps a person build his or her social networks. It also tries to connect you with people who share similar interests (e.g. cycling) and to more cleverly harness the knowledge your network might possess (e.g. search for restaurants your friends have been to in London).[43] The average number of 'friends' an individual has on Facebook is 130.[44]

Conversations

With connectivity comes conversations. While email remains the basic form of online communication, Facebook has evolved the technology to a much more sophisticated level with its News Feed. This allows all the latest information about a person to be simultaneously posted onto the Facebook 'walls' of their friends. Unlike emails, which can be long, 'wall' messages are more like snippets, which allow you quick glimpses into the lives of your friends. For instance, you can read who has 'friended' whom, who has updated their marital status, who has changed their lists of favourite movies as well as commenting on a news article from a source they 'like'. These snippets in turn encourage people to respond, which fuels more exchanges, and so on. Such devices are very powerful because changes are interesting.[45]

Content creation

Human beings also like to create and share. When this occurs on the internet, it is dubbed 'user-generated content' (UGC), the defining characteristic of Web 2.0. Different publishing formats – such as blogs, diaries, forums and picture and video uploads – give users an opportunity to show off and share their content. Indeed, the success of YouTube relies on this basic human motivation. The creators of videos are often motivated by fame: 'I seek fame. I want the world to see my videos.'[46] To stimulate conversations, users are invited to comment on the video, thus fuelling more conversations within the community. When creations are good, they will attract a big buzz. However, it should be noted only a small percentage (about 5–10%) of online users contribute.[47]

Collaboration

With the ease of content creation and sharing comes collaboration. Collaboration means that multiple users can contribute cooperatively to the completion of a project (called a 'wiki'). This often requires a specific online destination where users can come and work together. The classic example is Wikipedia, the free online encyclopedia. It is the multi-person contributions that add value to such projects.

CASE STUDY 8.1 LOADED: WRITTEN AND DIRECTED BY YOU[48]

McDonald's fries are probably one of their best products. They are almost always crunchy and consistently tasty. But what if we can up the taste by letting customers add a special topping (e.g. guacamole and salsa or bacon and cheese sauce) and at the same time customise their meal?

This initiative was going to be launched in the middle of the Australian summer of 2015 (December). In order to stand out from other competing summer distractions, the launch aimed to excite the 18–35-year-old loyal McDonald's customers. The advertising agency came up with the idea of making a short, branded film, featuring McDonald's fries as animated characters. The movie was called *Loaded*. It followed the story of a private detective called Joe Fry who was engaged to find the missing husband of Fryana Spudly. But what is innovative is that the McDonald's Facebook community was encouraged to get involved in shaping the outcome of the story. This was how it worked.

Figure 8.6 McDonald's loaded fries

The movie was presented on Facebook over five episodes. At the end of each episode, the community was asked for suggestions to direct the next episode. They were prompted to contribute (e.g. describe the scene between two characters), and all suggestions were written in the comment box under each video. Everyone in the community could follow each other's contribution. The most creative of these suggestions were rewarded with a storyboard and were posted back to the community in a few hours. But the very best suggestions were shot and made into a short clip and released the next day. These contributors were credited as 'guest writers and directors' at the end of the reel. This process continued until all the episodes were completed. They were then edited together to form a final 8-minute short film. The completed movie was released on Facebook on Boxing Day, which was also the traditional day in which hit movies opened in cinemas. It was also shown in the short-film festival Tropfest with an audience of 90 000 and broadcast around the world, which added to the reach. Tropfest is the world's biggest short-film festival, which consistently attracts Hollywood stars as judges. All this added to the allure of the movie and increased the bonding of the community to the brand.[49]

Figure 8.7 A scene from the movie *Loaded*

RESULTS

The campaign was a great success; 3.48 million McDonald's Facebook fans were involved. The paid reach was 6.4 million people, while the earned reach was 5.2 million. Awareness of the new product reached 79% by the third week (target was 40%), and trial was 20% (target was 10%). It was one of McDonald's most successful new product launches, resulting in record sales (60% above target) in December.

DISCUSSION QUESTIONS

1. After reading this case and watching the film, discuss how well the McDonald's product and brand were integrated into the film.
2. Involving social media can be unpredictable. Many things could go wrong (e.g. the brand becomes parodied). How do you think that McDonald's mitigated the film from becoming a disaster?
3. What lessons of integration can you learn from this case study?

SOCIAL INFLUENCE

The four characteristics of social media dovetail nicely with the idea of social influence. It stands to reason that the more active users in these activities, the more likely they are to influence others in their network. This is because such activities create 'news' within the social network, which in turn encourages more interactions. Social influence is said to occur when a person adapts his or her behaviour, attitude or belief in response to those of others in a social system.[50] Interestingly, Sing and Ang found that simply observing someone using a product on social media can arouse envy[51], and if this is of the inspirational kind (i.e. not malicious), it will positively influence purchase intentions.

However, since only a small percentage of users are active in these activities, it means that only a small percentage of users are influential. In fact, by using frequency of login as a proxy for social influence, it turns out that only 20% of users are influential. Thus, we are not influenced by everyone in our network but only by one-fifth of our friends, enough to influence us to login and interact with them. This, of course, is consistent with what we know about social influence offline (see principle 3, above).

THIS TIME, OUR SOCIALNESS WILL KILL US!

The COVID-19 pandemic suddenly made us understand how our social nature can be deadly. While social distancing was found to be an effective countermeasure to the spread of disease, our social connectedness also revealed how unintentional misinformation[52] can be spread. For instance, one video which went viral suggests that breathing hot air from a hair dryer can fight the disease[53] while others speculate that 5G transmission towers spread COVID-19.[54]

Our motivation to share on social media is rarely driven by accuracy; rather, we long to entertain and gain the approval of others. This makes sensational information, especially those being perpetuated by celebrities,[55] more attractive, which in turn makes it easier to find and perpetuate stories on the internet.[56] Unfortunately, misleading information also crowds out truthful information that can save lives (e.g. medical facts). With more people in lockdown, glued to their social media,[57] such misinformation spread even more.[58] One solution was to actively debunk them. In Australia, ABC Radio, for instance, developed a *daily* podcast called the Coronacast which updated the public and answered listeners' questions about COVID-19, verifying proven claims and debunking the false ones.[59] Independent fact-checking organisations should be endorsed and supported.[60] Prominent celebrities ought to be forced to retract misleading posts, and governments should impose fines and jail term on those who spread misinformation.[61] During the COVID-19 pandemic, tech giants like Google, Mozilla, Facebook, Twitter and Microsoft were criticised for profiteering by hosting disinformative online ads about COVID-19.[62] While social media giants themselves should be held more accountable, ultimately all of us, including our leaders, should be more educated in science and mathematics.

Communities versus customers

It is important to distinguish between a community of users and customers. People generally perceive social media as belonging to them – a community of like-minded people – and do not want anything commercial to intrude (see the Further Thinking section below).

However, from the perspective of a firm, the objective is to convert these people into customers. These conflicting demands must be clearly understood.[63] When this is confused, a marcoms manager may suddenly think that social media advertising is the panacea. But as cautioned above, social media should *not* be used in isolation in a campaign because its effectiveness is often overclaimed in the popular press (see the Further Thinking section below). If social media were to be used, then it is best to leverage on the social relations of the community users (not customers), as in the case of #VolvoContest (see case study 6.1), or develop new creative assets so that the community can collaborate, as in the case of

McDonald's (see case study 8.1). However, given the community nature of social media, it is often useful in social campaigns, as in the case of Singapore's Quit Smoking campaign (see case study 8.2).

CASE STUDY 8.2 SINGAPORE'S QUIT SMOKING HEALTH MOVEMENT

Smoking rates had been declining in Singapore (from 20% in the 1980s to 12.6% in 2004) because of a comprehensive, multi-pronged approach including high taxes on cigarettes, fines, graphic imagery on cigarette packaging, and a fear-based advertising campaign. However, in 2005 the rate of smoking was inching up again at about 2.3% a year and was projected to rise to about 14.7% by 2013. This was a worrying trend because the health cost associated with smoking was estimated to be US$1.4 billion per annum.

The causes for this increase were traced to a number of factors: (1) smoking was now more socially acceptable, fueled by popular culture; (2) the fear-based advertising campaign was no longer effective because of increased habituation to scare tactics caused by (3) the prevalence of health-related campaigns (about 50 a year). In addition, (4) younger age youths (less than 17 years old) were now experimenting with smoking because of their rebelliousness to authority figures and (5) belief that they could quit anytime.

It was against this backdrop that Ogilvy Singapore had to tackle the problem of the rising smoking rate. One challenge was deciding which approach to take. This was an important consideration because Singaporeans are well educated, and already knew that smoking was harmful. Preaching about the harmful effects of smoking in a campaign would probably not work. It was considered it might even backfire because it would be viewed to be top-down government communication, which might have further marginalised the smokers in Singapore.

To meet such challenges, the agency developed two main prongs of attack; first: to prevent non-smokers from taking up smoking and second: to encourage smokers to quit. Prevention was aimed at the youths (under 17 years old) in order to disrupt the start of any consumption lifecycle. Quitting was aimed at smokers of all ages.

PREVENTION OF SMOKING AMONG YOUTHS (2009, 2012)[64]

The idea Ogilvy Singapore came up with was to make non-smoking 'cool'. They did this by trumpeting the idea that 'life is better without smoking'. The campaign was called, 'Live it up, without lighting up'. In phase 1, the agency used print (i.e. press and posters), PR, digital and social media, T-shirts, badges, bags and the taboo motif to create the message that a smoke-free life is cool.

In phase 2, the agency employed radio DJs and artists to blog and ad-lib about the benefits of a smoke-free life. Apps were used to engage youths to make pledges and extensive social media groups were formed to encourage the formation of a community around the idea of a smoke-free life. Once the community was formed, the third phase was activated. Here, live events like fashion shows and concerts were created to give the idea more cultural texture. There was also a Great Audio Experience, held on World No Tobacco Day (29 May), demonstrating the benefit of experiencing a smoke-free day. Benchmarked against a previous campaign in 2009, the result of this campaign over two years was a success:

- overall awareness of the campaign was high among the youths at 75% and message comprehension at 80%

- the appeal of the campaign had increased from 55% (2009) to 70% (2010)
- the youth's intention to remain smoke-free increased from 72% (2009) to 81% (2010)
- intention to quit among youth smokers went up from 33% (2009) to 50% (2010).

ENCOURAGING SMOKERS TO QUIT (2011)[65]

For smokers, Ogilvy Singapore took a slightly different approach. Research showed that up to 60% of them tried quitting but failed. This was because they lacked the knowledge and confidence to do so. Past clinical research had shown that if intenders could be coaxed to take one concrete step towards quitting, it doubled the probability that they would succeed six months later. Therefore, instead of targeting all smokers, the agency decided to target smokers who intended to quit (i.e. would-be quitters) and to provide concrete steps in helping them quit.

Qualitative research revealed that smokers who successfully quit tended to be those who experienced a turning point in their lives (e.g. the discovery of a lump in the lungs).[66] These watershed moments could be turned into poignant stories. Furthermore, when smokers successfully quit, they experienced a sense of accomplishment. This insight (or human truth) prompted the agency to develop a message around the personal value of quitting. So instead of creating an anti-smoking strategy, they decided to develop a pro-quitting strategy. The creative idea was to elevate the lives of would-be quitters to heroes by letting them tell their personal stories and using them as role models to involve the community in supporting them to quit. Social media was used to create a nationwide discourse around quitting. The following is what the agency did.

First, they developed a new visual symbol to signify success in quitting. This was the picture of the smokers' grasp of two fingers (see figure 8.8). It represented the movement from cigarette to lips to that of victory. It became a beloved symbol of success.

Figure 8.8 A visual symbol representing success in quitting

Second, using radio and the press, would-be quitters were recruited and encouraged to make a pledge saying, 'I quit because...'. These mini-pledges were filmed in mobile studios erected around the country. The pledges were written in participants' own writing on a T-shirt, which they wore during the filming. Thousands of these video clips were then put together to form a film montage for a TV ad. Each would-be quitter had a powerful story to tell, which was publicised using different media (print, out-of-home, radio and social media) creating a groundswell of support. It also encouraged more would-be quitters to come forward.

Third, virtual and physical 'I Quit Clubs' were set up throughout Singapore. The Facebook page of the club served as the centrepoint of support for the community where smokers could sign up and ask for help. This included information about smoking cessation programs, as well as counselling services in pharmacies and hospitals. A smartphone app was also developed to provide ease of access to these resources, as well as to track progress. All would-be quitters were contacted by Quitline consultants and ex-smokers were recruited to be the ambassadors of the 'I Quit' movement.

RESULTS

The campaign generated a total of 67 919 interactions and 87% of non-smokers said they now had a greater regard for people who quit. Requests for help at Quitline shot up 313% after the campaign. The number of calls continued to increase even after media spend ceased. More than 70% of would-be quitters now know one new way to quit, and they are now five times more likely to quit. Out of 100 who signed up with the I Quit Club's cessation program, 31.5 of them remained smoke-free, which was three times higher than the success rate of other similar programs. Overall, the upward smoking trend in Singapore was arrested and represented a savings of US$64 billion in health costs.[67] In summary, what started out as a government campaign became a self-sustaining health movement that did not ostracise smokers.

DISCUSSION QUESTIONS

1. Do you agree or disagree with Ogilvy's strategy of separately targeting Singaporean youths and smokers who intend to quit (i.e. would-be quitters)? Explain your answer.
2. An education-style anti-smoking campaign would not work in Singapore, but would it work in Australia? Explain your answer.
3. In the light of #MeToo and success of the Singaporean campaign, what did you learn about developing a social movement for a brand? How different is this from a typical advertising ad campaign?

WORD-OF-MOUTH AND RECOMMENDATION

Word-of-mouth (WOM) can be defined as 'the act of a consumer providing information to another consumer'.[68] When this is carried out on the internet, it is called 'electronic WOM' (eWOM) or sometimes 'word of mouse'. This information can be positive (PWOM) or negative (NWOW), relating to products, services, ideas or organisations.

While monitoring of WOM has always been a challenge offline, it is easier online because of the availability of tracking technologies (e.g. Social Studio, Radian6, BuzzMetrics and Brandwatch) and panels (e.g. comScore, NGage Social Corporation). Organisations can now obtain a sentiment score for their brand by analysing the number of good or bad conversations that occur online. A summary score called the 'Social Influence Marketing' (SIM) score for a brand can be derived by adding all positive and neutral conversations, subtracting any negative ones, and dividing the result by the total number of conversations about the brand. That number is further divided by the net sentiment score for the category. In the US car industry, for example, Ford has the highest SIM score of 31, while GM has the lowest of 5. In between these two extremes are the Japanese makes of Honda at 30, Toyota at 18 and Nissan at 15.[69]

There is strong evidence that PWOM is generally more persuasive than advertising,[70] especially the form that involves direct recommendation of the product. One way of assessing the prevalence of this in the marketplace is to simply ask a person this question: 'In the last six months, how many times have you recommended brand X?'[71] But why should personal recommendations be so powerful? It is because they are based on the personal experience of the recommender. There is strong veracity, leading to a greater level of trustworthiness of the information, especially if the recommender has a high level of expertise. Not all PWOM involves a recommendation, of course. In fact, one study found that most WOM is about mundane day-to-day living. People engage in about 56 WOM social conversations per week, and of these only 15% are about products or services.[72] Most conversations about brands (75%) still occur face-to-face, 15% take place over the phone and only 10% happen online.[73]

What gets marketers excited is that such conversations about products and services can be propagated quickly and widely through the social network for minimal cost. For instance, brands such as Starbucks, 'Coca-Cola' and Disney through their brand pages on Facebook have 20 million fans (remembering that someone becomes a fan when they 'like' your page). But there are even more friends of these fans: for every fan of the top 100 brand pages on Facebook, we can reach an average of an additional 34 friends of fans. This means that an advertiser will be able to reach more people through their fan networks, as demonstrated in table 8.1 for Starbucks. While Starbucks' Facebook page can reach 2.1% of the total US population, the friends of its fans add 3.5% to that number. And the best way to reach this substantial base of friends of fans is through their Facebook news feed. Therefore, the real value of fans is the incremental value they can provide. Fans might be initially important for the business (especially for a small-to-medium enterprises), but their friends are even more important later on.

Table 8.1 Starbucks' total reach and frequency of its Facebook brand page in the US in May 2011[74]

	Total reach	Average frequency	Total Gross Rating Point (GRP)
Starbucks' fans	2.1%	2.7	5.67
Starbucks' friends of fans	3.5%	3.3	11.55

In other words, targeting the friends of fans is also more likely to lead to growth. These friends are likely to be light or non-users of the brand, and research also shows that positive word of mouth is more effective among light users than heavy users.[75] This means that if a fan can influence their friends to be customers, there is a greater chance to grow the brand. Note, the fans themselves are already heavy users and unlikely to increase their purchase rate. However, one major drawback with this approach is that the reach is very low. Fans of major brands usually comprise less than 5% of the customer base.[76]

Product reviews is another way of harnessing word of mouth. It is also very effective. People are 65% more likely to buy a product after engaging with the community of customers and experts.[77] One in three internet users say that product reviews influence their purchase decision,[78] while online reviews of movies have been found to be predictive of box office sales.[79] The more positive the reviews, the greater the box office sales.[80] We see the same phenomenon in books; when online reviews are good, sales go up, and specifically for the site that hosts the positive reviews.[81] Reviews are effective because they are trustworthy[82] and assumed to be written by unbiased experienced users. These users are often intrinsically motivated to write helpful reviews without expectations of any monetary reward. Rewarding reviewers may in fact be counterproductive.[83]

In recent years, however, several fraud cases have been uncovered in product reviews. The most common form is that the reviews were not written by unbiased users, but by 'friendly acquaintances' who often give glowing reviews. Interestingly, research has shown that the more glowing the review, the less trustworthy it is![84] Yet another form of fraud is to subvert negative reviews from appearing. For instance, if staff of a hotel suspect that a customer is unlikely to write a negative review, their email address will be tampered with to prevent the reviews from being shared with the popular travel review websites like Tripadvisor. One service apartment company in Australia was caught doing this and fined $3 million.[85] The ensuing negative publicity damages the reputation of the review industry (e.g. Tripadvisor, Expedia, Opentable, Urbanspoon, and Yelp), where trust is the main currency.[86]

Consumers value attributes differently, and in some product categories certain attributes may be more valuable than others. One large-scale study of restaurant reviews[87] (involving 1.27 million US restaurant reviews) found that patrons value authenticity. Using consumers' star ratings, and the actual words consumers used in the reviews (e.g. authentic, genuine, real), they were able to show that consumers value authenticity *above* price and quality. In other words, the more authentic the restaurant, the higher the rating, even after controlling for price and quality. Furthermore, family-owned restaurants that specialise in a niche cuisine are perceived to be more authentic than chain restaurants (e.g. McDonald's). Proprietors of family-owned restaurants should encourage their patrons to verbalise the business' authenticity in their reviews.

WOM referral was also found to be more effective than PR and event marketing in signing up new customers for a social media website. Modelling shows that WOM referral elasticity is about 0.53[88] (much higher than the advertising elasticity of about 0.22[89]). Positive sentiment on average has been modelled to increase flat-screen TV sales by 7%, while negative sentiments decrease sales by about the same amount (–6.9%). However, because there tend to be more positive than negative sentiments, it means that the power of negative sentiment to decrease sales is in fact greater – in fact, by 4.42 times – than the power of positive sentiments to increase sales.[90]

WOM is difficult to study because it is not directly observable. But one of the most convincing studies to show the influence of information flow on purchase among friends is the study by Guo, Wang and Leskovec.[91] They examined one million users who made at least one transaction between 1 September and 28 October 2009 on a Chinese ecommerce website called Taobao. Their research question was whether the transactions were influenced by what their friends had said. The unique feature of Taobao is that it offers an instant messaging service that allows a shopper to send messages to their friends. They found that there is indeed a correlation between the number of SMS and the transaction amount (shown by a dotted line in figure 8.9). This correlation

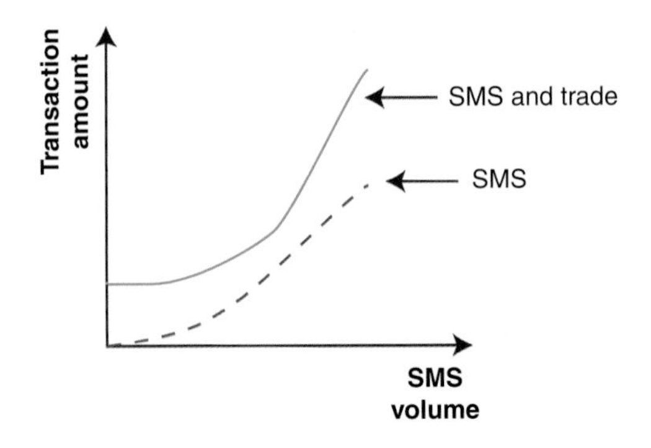

Figure 8.9 The relationship between transaction amount and SMS message volume

becomes stronger if we select only those instances where a transaction is also made (shown by a complete line in the figure).

Further, as price of the goods increases (*x*-axis), so does the amount of messages on the day of the trade (*y*-axis), suggesting that people are more likely to seek recommendations from other people for high-value purchases (see figure 8.10a). This reaches a peak on the day of the transaction (signified by '0' on the *x*-axis) and then declines (see figure 8.10b).

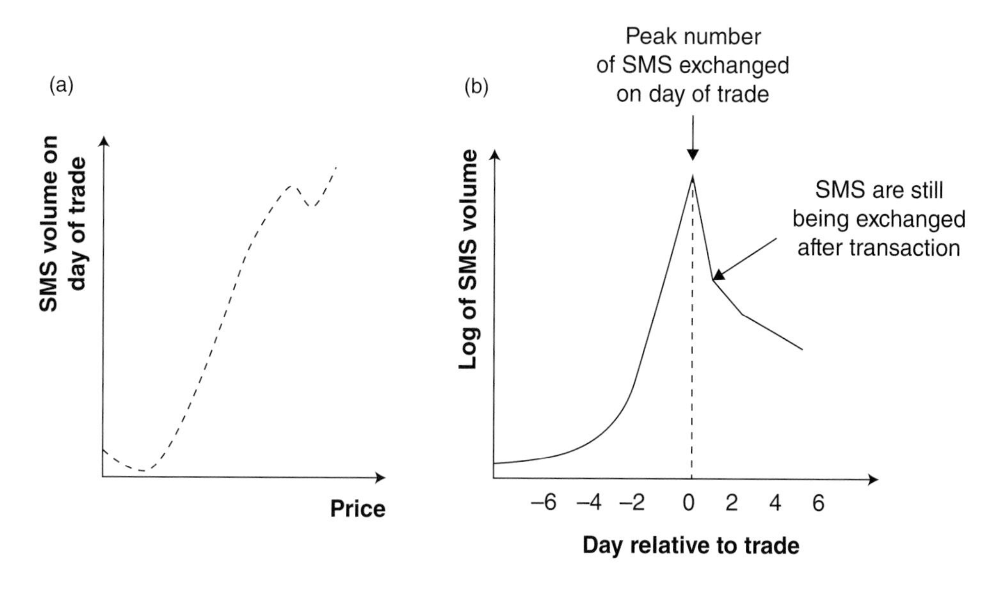

Figure 8.10 How message volume changes with price of purchase (a) and days before and after purchase (b)

TWITTER, #HASHTAG, AND THE #METOO MOVEMENT

In addition to Instagram and Facebook, small to mid-size enterprises (or SMEs) can use Twitter to regularly post content or their latest offerings (e.g. a new product launch or an event) to their followers. Since it is limited to 140 characters (and up to four images and one video),[92] Twitter is often classified as a microblog, in order to encourage micro-word-of-mouth (or MWOM), which is 'any *brief* statement made by a consumer about a commercial entity or offering that is broadcast in real time to some or all members of the sender's social network through a specific web-based service'.[93]

Because tweets are short, they allow consumers to make quick statements on any issues in real time. A Twitter user, on average, has about 45 followers, although celebrities like Katy Perry and Justine Bieber have followers in the tens of millions (@katyperry has 106.8 million; @justinebieber has 104.3 million). Research into new movies has shown that tweets can have a significant effect on box office revenue, dubbed the Twitter effect. Negative tweets are especially devastating in depressing box office sales.[94]

However, with so many people tweeting on countless topics at any one time to their followers, it may be difficult to keep track. One way of aggregating all the tweets into one common stream is to use the hashtag symbol (i.e. #) followed by the focal topic or a keyword. This method was invented in 2007 by Chris Messina at Google.[95] When one clicks on the symbol, one is taken to a webpage that shows all the tweets on the focal topic. Importantly, the hashtag is indexed, which means it is searchable. Thus, anyone who is interested in the focal topic can learn what others have been saying; and if the focal topic is popular, it will be reported as 'trending'. Sometimes, a hashtag can spark such a groundswell that it evolves into a social movement. For example, when the Hollywood mogul Harvey Weinstein was accused of sexual harassment and rape of a number of Hollywood actresses, it sparked a worldwide #MeToo movement, where aggrieved women shared their experience in their tweets.

Thus, by studying these trends and sentiments of tweets, marketers get a sense of what the public is feeling about a focal topic. But marketers can also use the hashtag cleverly in a campaign, as we saw in chapter 6 with the #VolvoContest (see case study 6.1). Any topic can be the focal topic to be used in a campaign, not just contest, like:

- events or festivals (e.g. #vividsydney)
- holidays or celebrations (e.g. #christmas)
- popular culture (e.g. #cominccon)
- media (e.g. #disneychannel)
- movies (e.g. #richcrazyasians)
- interests (e.g. #wineoclock)
- new product launches (e.g. #samsunggalaxynote9).

Although it is not necessary to include the brand in the focal topic, it is theoretically better to do so in order to increase or maintain its brand awareness either for the brand itself (e.g. #apple) or its sub-brand (e.g. #applewatch).

The problem with Net Promoter Score

One popular way of measuring WOM among companies is the Net Promoter Score (or NPS). This metric is based on a simple recommendation question, 'How likely is it that you would recommend [brand x/company x] to a friend?', measured on an 11-point scale, ranging from 0 (not at all likely) to 10 (extremely likely). Those scored between 0 and 6 are called detractors, while those between 9 and 10 are called promoters. NPS is calculated by the difference in the percentages between these two groups. This is a popular measure, because it is easy to compute and changes in percentages can be easily tracked. For instance, in time period 1, a company's NPS may be 20% (i.e. 60% promoters minus 40% detractors), but if by period 2 the NPS has dropped to 0% (e.g. 50% promoters minus 50% detractors), companies may have cause to be worried. NPS is thus designed to measure the net positive effect of WOM by counting the percentage of people who are likely to make a recommendation minus those who are not likely to make a positive one. Note, it does *not* measure whether people are likely to give a *negative* recommendation.

When this metric was first developed, it was reported to be able to predict company performance.[96] But this was subsequently proven to be wrong.[97] Company performance is determined by a whole host of factors, and a simple measure of recommendation like NPS has poor predictability. Furthermore, this measure does not measure WOM properly. Consumers also give negative recommendation, which is just as powerful if not more. But negative recommendation is not captured in NPS.[98] Further, if one were interested in the impact of recommendation on brand choice, then it is more logical to measure the number of people *receiving* recommendation – *both* positive as well as negative.[99] Instead, NPS only measures the number of people *giving positive* recommendation about the brand. Finally, measuring whether people are willing to give positive recommendation does not mean they do. One survey found that only one-third does.[100]

BUZZ MARKETING

Buzz is essentially WOM, measured at the aggregate level; that is, what the whole market is saying about a brand at a particular moment.[101] For instance, if everyone is talking about the London 2012 Olympics then the buzz for this event is high. However, since we are only interested in the brand, for instance, the sponsoring brand, we want to evaluate if people are also talking about the brand. One way of assessing this is called 'share of conversation' (SOC).[102] Let's take an example. Adidas (not Nike) was the official sponsor of the London Olympics. To assess Adidas' SOC, we apply the formula shown in figure 8.11.

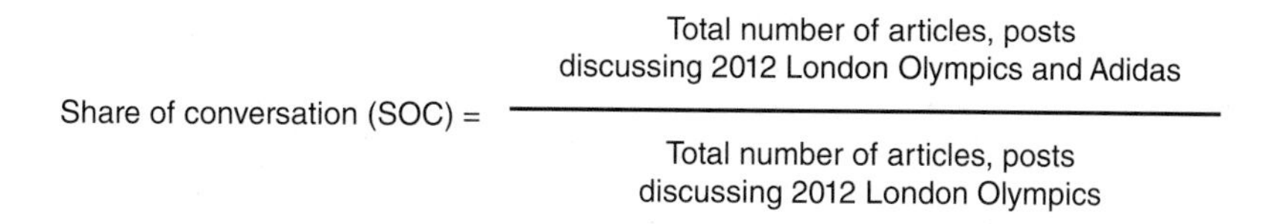

Figure 8.11 Conceptual equation for SOC

Since the numerator is likely to be smaller than the denominator, by virtue of the fact that we are only interested in the conversations linked to the brand, we can assess the percentage of what we can call 'branded conversations'. (Recall that in chapter 6 we discussed the importance of the branded message in creativity, analogous to branded conversation in the social media context.) Or, to put it another way, buzz of a brand is simply the percentage of branded conversations discussed in a particular context at that moment, compared to total conversations in the same context. In our example, the context is the London Olympics. We can examine and compare similar indices for competing brands. For instance, if Nike turned out to have an equal or higher share of conversation during the London Olympics, even though they were not the official sponsor of the event, then we would conclude that their ambush marketing tactics have been effective (ambush marketing is discussed in more detail in chapter 9).

VIRAL MARKETING

We saw earlier that consumers naturally engage in WOM communications with each other. Viral marketing or 'viral contagion' occurs when the WOM suddenly explodes or, in other words, the speed in which WOM spreads increases exponentially. Since spreading WOM is easiest through the internet (i.e. through eWOM), it is taken to be synonymous with online transmission.[103] Thus, we can define marketing viral contagion as the rapid spread of online brand-related conversations because of enhanced interest in the subject matter. When marketers try to start this contagion process for the benefit of their brands, it is called 'viral marketing'. In a survey, most marketers adopt viral marketing to increase brand awareness (71%), followed by online sales (50%) and offline sales (44%).[104]

Although many marcoms managers aspire to create a viral campaign for their brands, it is easier said than done. It is difficult because first, the viral effect is unpredictable, and second, the outcome is not always positive. It is unpredictable because a number of preconditions are necessary before it can take off (discussed below), and those preconditions may not be converging at the same time. One recent Dutch study showed that only 25% of ads can be passed on in social media.[105] Just as viral effects are unpredictable, they are also often beyond the control of the marketer; for example, branded conversations can be hijacked for other purposes. If that happens, the marketer has the unenviable job of trying to stop the message spreading.

If viral viewings of an ad occur, this essentially means 'free' advertising for the brand, representing rapid reach among non-users and an increase in brand awareness (provided the brand is creatively well integrated). Further, it is also likely to forge greater involvement, since viewers are likely to replay and comment on the ad before passing it on. Viewers are generally more likely to view an ad when they receive it from someone they know. This means greater credibility for such ads, which, in turn, improves brand attitude. In short, viral viewings can quickly raise brand awareness and brand attitude for free.

Viral preconditions

Several preconditions may be necessary before viral contagion occurs. These can be product-related, environmental triggers, communication assets and facilitating factors.

PRODUCT-RELATED FACTORS

It has long been known that an innovation (e.g. a new product) will diffuse faster if it possesses these characteristics:[106]

- *Relative advantage*. If we want people to talk about the innovation, it must be worthy of being talked about (or 'talk-worthy'). This means the product must be superior in some ways to the next best alternative. This can be in the form of better economic value or status enhancement.
- *Simplicity*. The innovation must also be easy to use (or easy to understand). This is related to the first point. The relative advantage of the product (over the next best alternative) will be eroded if the product is too complex, making it difficult for consumers to communicate the relative advantage to others.
- *Trialability*. Letting consumers try the product before they buy helps the diffusion process. Marketers have long known about this, the basis of product sampling or trial usage.
- *Observability*. This means the degree to which the product is clearly visible to others. The more consumers can see the relative advantage of the innovation, the faster the news will spread. This is an extremely important attribute in our digital world because of the visual nature of the internet. When it is observable, it also makes it more mentally accessible to trigger on going WOM.[107]
- *Compatibility*. If the innovation is consistent with consumers' needs, values, beliefs and usage behaviour, it will be easier for them to adopt it, since not too much change is needed. Consumers are creatures of habit – the innovation must be compatible with their existing needs before its relative advantage can be realised.

One way of taking advantage of the four qualities of innovative products is to demonstrate these values with a video, for instance, by showing how the product or service is used (ideally in an outrageous way). The most successful example is the series of 'Will it blend?' videos created by Blendtec, a manufacturer of food blenders. Instead of showing the machine blending food, the videos showed it blending mobile phones, golf balls, diamonds, glow sticks, and other items. Sales shot up 43% in the first year of the campaign.[108] All these product-related qualities can form the basis of storytelling for the brand.[109]

ENVIRONMENTAL TRIGGERS

But what if the product we are selling does not have any of those qualities listed above? One solution is to link our brand to a more salient cue that can trigger conversation about our brand. One US study show that just prior to Halloween, people are more likely to recall orange drinks (e.g. Sunkist) and Reese's chocolates (i.e. an orange-packaged chocolate), than a week later.[110] Or consider the case of Rebecca Black, an American YouTube pop singer, who shot to fame in 2011 with her single 'Friday'. Now, the lyrics do not change, but come Friday, the search for her name goes up (see figure 8.12).

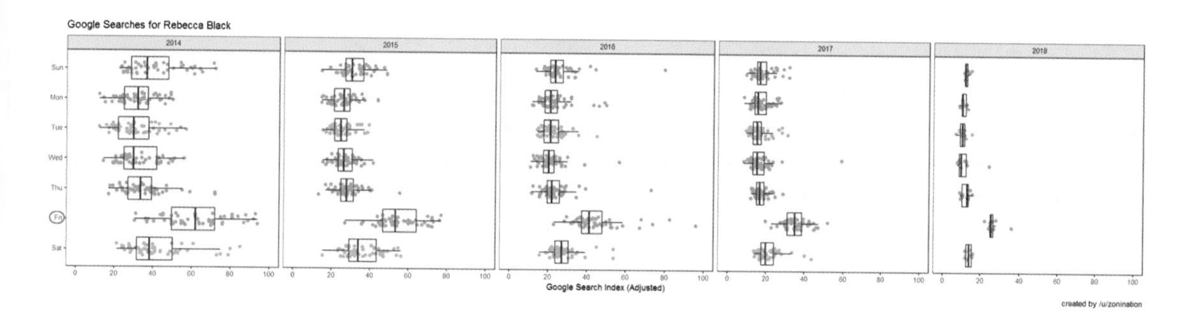

Figure 8.12 The amount of Google search for Rebecca Black by day of the week between 2014 and 2018[112]

Thus, one way of taking advantage of this phenomenon is to link our brand with a salient environmental cue. For instance, in the US the beer Michelob has the tagline 'Weekends were made for Michelob'. As a result, when weekend rolls around, conversations about the brand spike (and presumably its sales too).[111]

COMMUNICATION ASSETS

Besides environmental triggering cues, the creative assets used for the communications should also contain potentially viral qualities. This includes advertising, video ads, blogs, articles, twitter feeds and so on. Of all these, watching and searching for videos are now the most prevalent. About 25% of consumer conversations about brands are about their advertising, of which TV is still by far the main trigger.[113] Therefore, the higher the quality of the ad, the more likely people are to pass it on.[114] The following qualities have been found to be important.

Surprise and joy

Dobele and colleagues[115] examined nine successful viral campaigns to try to understand why they went viral. Their key finding was that all these campaigns tended to be surprising and well targeted. Teixeira and colleagues[116] supported the importance of surprise but found that the reasons why this is so is because surprise concentrates our attention to the ad, especially at the beginning. But surprise by itself is not enough. Teixeira and colleagues found that joy as an emotion is more important than surprise to sustain our attention right to the end. So it seems that surprise and joy work in different ways. Further, they found that there are two ideal emotional trajectories of joy and surprise that best predict success. To grab attention, we want the emotions of surprise and joy to rise quickly and then remain stable. This is called the 'peak-and-stable' pattern (shown in figure 8.13a). To retain the attention of the viewer, the ideal emotional trajectory is a 'peak-valley-peak' pattern (shown in figure 8.13b).

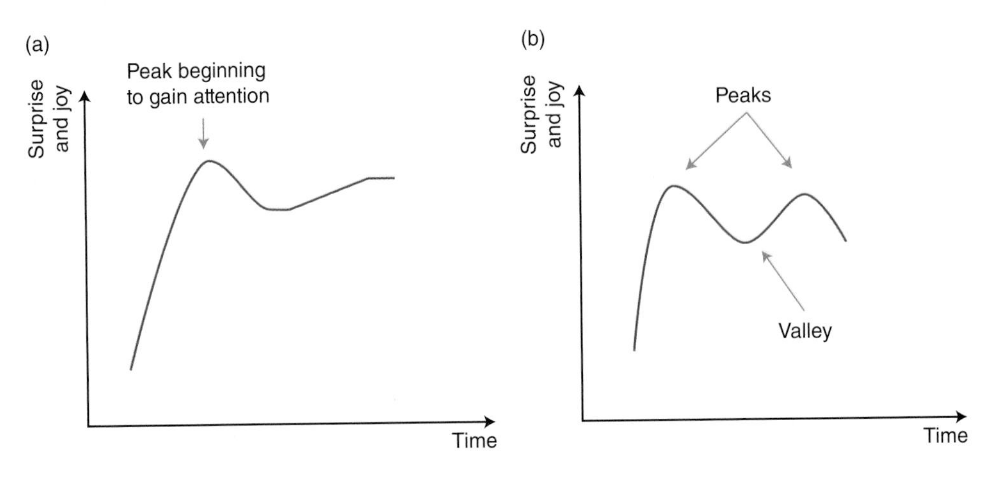

Figure 8.13 Different emotional profiles to gain (a) and sustain (b) attention

Arousal

However, surprise and joy are not the only emotions. If they were, then how do you explain people spreading NWOM when they are angry? For instance, an airline might damage a person's guitar and then refuse to compensate for it.[117] If this story were to appear on an internet news site, you can probably imagine some people would get angry and possibly pass the news item along to their friends.

In a series of studies using both newspaper archival data and experiments, Berger and Milliken[118] found that this is indeed the case: people are likely to pass on articles that arouse negative responses like anger, as well as those that arouse positive responses such as surprise and joy. Berger and Milliken contended that this is because such articles energise people. In other words, the more physiological arousal a news item evokes – regardless of whether it is positive or negative, or whether it is of interest or surprise – the more likely it is that people will email the story to others. In fact, Berger and Milliken found that one standard deviation increase in arousal of awe and anger is likely to increase the 'virality' of the article by 30–34%. This is a massive increase in (free) exposure, and clearly highlights the dangers of angering consumers.

Positivity

What about a good news story? Does it get passed along and, if so, why? In the same study, Berger and Milliken found that people are also more likely to pass along information that is positive rather than negative. In their study, they exposed people to either a high-sadness story (e.g. how someone was maimed in the 9/11 attack) or a low-sadness story (e.g. how someone sustained an injury falling down the stairs). They found that the high-sadness story was less likely to be passed along than the low-sadness story. This finding is also consistent with other WOM studies that found that PWOM tends to be more prevalent than NWOM,[119] contrary to popular opinion. Passing along good news makes the receiver feel good and enhances the sender's self-image.

Enjoyment, involvement, distinctiveness, branding

We might now ask what specific creative qualities we want in our communication, besides a positive tone. To test this, a group of researchers[120] wanted to find out if video ads that are successful offline would also be successful online. The success of online ads would be determined by the number of viewings. The creative quality of the ads had already been evaluated (i.e. on levels of enjoyment, involvement, distinctiveness and branding), and the research question was whether these qualities would affect people's viewing online. Using 102 ads from the UK and US, they found that they do. When the researchers tracked the video ads on YouTube, they were able to correlate the number of weekly viewings for the ads with their offline rated qualities. The correlations they found were enjoyment ($r = 0.40$), involvement ($r = 0.33$) and distinctiveness ($r = 0.46$). Branding on the other hand was not significant ($r = 0.19$, $p = 0.056$).

In addition, they also found that the presence of celebrities in videos helped viewing ($r = 0.31$). But what was even more interesting, and perhaps more to the point, was that they found a significant positive correlation between the number of weekly viewings and people's willingness to pass along the ad ($r = 0.38$).

In a study into more than 800 online video ads that were actually being shared on four social media platforms (i.e. Facebook, Twitter, Google+ and LinkedIn) for 300 brands, Tellis and colleagues[121] essentially came to the same conclusion. Online dramatic video ads that arouse the positive emotions of amusement, excitement, inspiration and warmth in consumers tend to be passed along. Typically, such ads tend to contain babies, animals or celebrities embedded in a surprising plot line. Such emotional online ads tend to fare better on being passed along than information-based, factual ads. The only exceptions are when the informational ads are for new products or are high-priced.

Interest and usefulness

What if our communication collateral does not have the qualities we have mentioned so far? Then ensure that they are at least interesting and useful. Earlier, we saw that one of the main reasons why people pass along information is that they perceive the information as useful and want to help others by sharing it; in other words, it has practical value.[122] In chapter 9, we will see that people tend to report stories that they perceive as newsworthy. Berger and Milliken's study also confirmed this, finding that people tended to pass along articles that they rated as interesting and useful.

In summary, to create a viral campaign, our communications collateral should be arousing and positive in nature. For videos, the emotions aroused should be surprise and joy – surprise to gain attention and joy to sustain it. The emotional trajectory we aim for should be like a rollercoaster. If this can be achieved in a distinctive and amusing way, including through the use of celebrities, there is a good chance that people will enjoy and become involved in the ad. If the use of celebrities is expensive, then consider the use of animals or babies, or create dramatic plot lines that can arouse amusement, excitement, inspiration and warmth. If we cannot achieve this then, at the minimum, the communications should be interesting and useful. This is especially important for a new product or if the product is expensive.

FACILITATING FACTORS

There is no doubt that passing along can be assisted by incentivising people in different ways or by taking advantage of the network structure. Let's look at some common tactics.

Free gifts

Anything that is free tends to attract attention. If what we are giving away is also valuable, word will spread. The use of free samples, T-shirts, hats, sneak previews, latest inside information (or gossip) and beta-test versions of products with opinion leaders will help incentivise WOM. However, the most effective trigger is the product itself. It can boost WOM by 20%. This is because this invites a full experience of its usage and hence is most likely to trigger WOM. The downside is that it will increase the cost of the campaign. The cheaper alternative is to give away non-product extras (e.g. T-shirts and hats). This will boost WOM by 15%.[123]

Product seeding

If what we are giving away is a new product, this is called 'product seeding'. It is essentially systematic sampling that targets opinion leaders. A good example of successful seeding is PowerBar, a high-protein snack bar for runners, launched in 1983 by Brian Maxwell. Maxwell first surveyed more than 1000 runners in the San Francisco Bay area about their diets and exercise regimes. Having obtained their addresses, he then sent each a pack of five PowerBar products, together with a follow-up survey and an order form. The seeding program worked. News spread, and PowerBar sales topped $140 million by the year 2000. The company was eventually sold to Nestlé.[124]

In Australia, The Coca Cola Company carried out a very effective product-seeding 'Share a Coke' campaign where they printed 150 of the most popular names of people on their packaging (e.g. Kylie, Jason, Mates, Bestie, Nan – see figure 8.14). The objective was to encourage people to connect with each other online and offline. These 'personalised' cans were distributed in supermarkets, which sparked enormous interest and generated media attention. The campaign was supported by advertisements and celebrity endorsements and soon requests began pouring in for more names to be printed. Coke obliged. In the end, 378 000 custom cans were printed in shopping centres around the country and social media traffic chatter went off the charts, but more importantly consumption in the 18–25 age group increased 7%, not an easy feat.[125]

Figure 8.14 Putting names of people on packaging to stimulate conversation

In the age of the internet, product seeding often involves the use of micro-celebrities to tell their followers about how good the product is. This can be done in several ways, but one way is to simply send them the product as a gift, and then request that they publicise it, for instance, to their Instagram followers, tagging with the brand handle.[126] For this to be effective, companies must choose micro-celebrities who will appeal to as many people in their target audience as possible. Since these are likely to be niche markets, companies should reward these online micro-celebrities accordingly; often free gifts are all that is needed.[127] But to ensure positive authentic posts, the gifts should be attractive to them.

Referral or affiliate program

Referral programs have been around for a long time. The classic offline examples are the members-get-members schemes often seen in club membership drives (e.g. at a gym). The incentive is that the person who brings in the new customer will get a discount or some sort of financial reward. With the growth of the internet, referrals have migrated online in the form of email marketing. For instance, one might get an email notification about an offer. But at the same time, one is also incentivised to refer to a friend. If the friend were to make their first purchase, one would receive credit, as in the case of Australia's Winesquare (see figure 8.15). This referral system can also be carried out via social media.

Arnaud Baillot A Rising Star Of Burgundy

Arnaud Baillot is located in Beaune, heart of the Cote d'Or. Passonate about the diversity Budgundy offers, Arnaud is producing spectacular range of village and Cru wines as well as being hands-on along the way, selecting the grapes, micromanaging the winemaking process, choosing the type of barrels and aging time for each individual wine.
Respecting the tradition Arnaud Baillot exceptional wines are presented in the authentic heavy glass bottles used by high end Burgundy wines in the 19th century.

2017 Arnaud Baillot Bourgogne Chardonnay $40

Traditional fermentation for 15 days in temperature-controlled stainless steel tanks. The wine is then matured for 12 months in 2-3 year-old French oak barrels.

Figure 8.15 An email referral with incentive

Another variation is affiliate programs. An affiliate program is an online referral system in which a purchase on a website will earn financial rewards for the website's owner if that owner is an affiliate member of the program. For example, a person may own a website or a blog teaching people about yoga. On his or her site are links to suppliers of yoga products (e.g. T-shirts, mats and meditation books). If all these suppliers are part of the affiliate program, then every time someone clicks on one of these links and buys a product, the owner of the website or blog will get a cut of the proceeds. As social media platforms become more sophisticated, much of the referral and affiliate programs discussed will become automated in its implementation.

Brand evangelists, micro-influencers and buzz agents

As we saw earlier, there are some customers who are so devoted to the brand that they are even prepared to tattoo the logo on their bodies. These are the kind of customer the company would want to use to spread WOM. These people will be willing to act as brand evangelists for even a minor incentive, such as a gift. For these brand evangelists, the social recognition they earn for their role is often more important than any material reward.

Another tactic is for brand evangelists to blog about their experience (good or bad). These must be genuine and not fake blogs (sometimes called 'flogs', a ghost blogger usually writes a fake blog). In this age of transparency, any organisation that 'flogs' will surely be found out.[128] The popularity of YouTube has given rise to a class of micro-celebrities[129] (sometimes called micro influencers, with less than 10 000 followers) who exclusively use this medium to vlog their experience, as in travel vlogs. They serve as a source of inspiration for would-be travellers. Vlogs can also take the form of video mini lessons on a whole range of topics and can be enormously popular because they are educational. Some of these online influencers are in fact 'mega' internet stars. For instance, Nikkie de Jager, the beauty vlogger, has 7.8 million subscribers to her makeup channel called Nikkie Tutorials.[130] To create a viral effect, these mega stars could simply encourage their millions of followers to retweet their latest post or video. No incentives need to be involved.

Sometimes you don't even need to have much perceived expertise like the Kardashians. They are, however, famous for having infamous scandals and lifestyle. Regardless, because of their large following, they are able to command 'endorsement' fees when they cleverly weave these brands into their lifestyle. Interestingly, this notion of being famous with little expertise has been recently adopted in the assessment of scientists called the Kardashian index (or the K-index). Here, one compares a scientist's Twitter following against their citations.[131] If a scientist has five times more Twitter followings than his or her citations, then one can cheekily conclude that he or she is not a serious scientist.

One major ethical issue is whether micro-influencers (as well as bloggers and vloggers) should disclose that they are being paid by their sponsors. If they are not paid, they are almost always given some benefits (e.g. free merchandise or trips). Authorities are now closely scrutinising such practices.[132] Generally, disclosure reduces brand attitude because consumers' persuasive knowledge has been activated, resulting in greater scrutiny. This tends to occur if the disclosure is stated upfront. If it comes later in their presentation, it is too late.[133] However, this does not necessarily detract consumers from liking these micro-influencers because consumers often form a virtual (and one-sided) bond with them. Of course, it is just an illusion, sometimes called a parasocial relationship.[134] The prefix 'para', from Greek, means 'beside, abnormal, incorrect, beyond, contrary'.[135] We see a clear demonstration of this phenomenon when fans stalk celebrities thinking they have a relationship with them, or when fans grieve when their favourite TV character dies or leaves the show.[136]

But before employing micro-celebrities, their credentials should be thoroughly checked since there have been several fraudulent cases. This includes micro-influencers claiming to a have more followers than they do because of fake audiences, generating fake comments[137] or they may not fulfil their obligations (e.g. not posting as contracted).[138] It is a shady world (see also native advertising in chapter 9).

Brands are also discovering that they cannot generate enough high-quality branded content to be timely distributed across various platforms. It is also expensive to get creative agencies to do this work. One Australian start up, Tribe, solves this problem on behalf of their clients by enlisting the help of micro-influencers to contribute to their creative content. A brand's brief will be posted on its online platform and micro-influencers are invited to respond. If the resulting creative content is appealing, the brand can buy it and reuse it in any way they want (e.g. repost on the brand's website or social media post). Since these micro-influencers own and presumably like the brand, they would already have authentic branded creative content stored on their smartphones. This platform makes it easy for them to share and get rewarded. At the same time, brands can get access to high-quality content quickly from genuine users.[139]

Besides micro-influencers, a marcoms manager can also hire buzz agents to proselytise the brand. Often this requires engaging a WOM agency (e.g. Bzzagent[140]) to propagate PWOM. This usually means hiring people in different localities to talk to acquaintances about the sponsored brand. In the case of Bzzagent, agents simply record when and where they share WOM about the sponsored brand. Interestingly, they are not required to say anything positive about the sponsored brand. This tactic has been found to be effective,[141] perhaps because using agents makes the sponsored brand appear more authentic,[142] although it can still be criticised for exploiting human relationships.

Passive broadcast

Sometimes just having a clickable URL is all that is needed to spread the word – no active promotion is used, and unintentional promoters are recruited to the cause. The classic example of this tactic is how Hotmail was launched. When Hotmail first started in July 1996, each email a person received through the service contained a line at the bottom of the email saying, 'Get your private, free email at www.hotmail.com'. The user thus served as an unintentional promoter of the service, a role we can call 'passive co-promoters'. Within two years, 12 million users had signed up for Hotmail. The marketing budget was said to be only US$500 000 for that period.[143] Hotmail, which was started by Sabeer Bhatia and Jack Smith, was later acquired by Microsoft for a reported US$400 million. The effectiveness of this tactic is also confirmed in a study by Aral and Walker.[144]

Figure 8.16 summarises the various forms of viral marketing promoter discussed above. The types include passive co-promoters and active co-promoters. There are two types of active co-promoters: those who are explicitly incentivised (e.g. with free gifts, referrals) and those who are not.

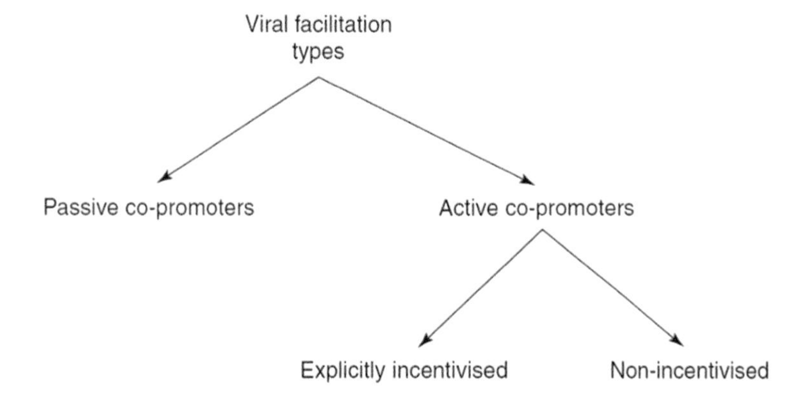

Figure 8.16 Different forms of viral promoter

Non-incentivised WOM

We may well ask why a co-promoter would choose to spread WOM (or even online videos) if they are given no explicit incentive. There are many possible reasons:

- The information is useful (e.g. information about an excellent, newly opened cafe).
- We want to help others (i.e. we are altruistic).[145]
- We want to appear knowledgeable to others.[146]
- We want to signal uniqueness.[147]
- We want to enhance our status.[148]
- We want to create a sense of indebtedness in others (e.g. to encourage more information exchange in the future).
- We are extremely satisfied or unsatisfied.[149]
- We want to reduce cognitive dissonance (e.g. to help justify our own decision).
- We want to deepen social connections with others.[150]
- We want to entertain others because it is enjoyable.[151]

One should not underestimate non-incentivised co-promoters, because they can generate a viral effect that seems organic in nature and therefore has more credibility. Aral and Walker (cited above) found that although the number of people who adopted the Facebook application after receiving an active recommendation was small, they tended to use the application more intensively than those who adopted the application based on passive notifications.

SOCIAL COMMERCE

Social commerce can be defined as:

> a form of e-commerce enabled by social technologies that capitalises on social-based information or relationships to assist in the purchase of goods and services online.

To date, the most obvious method is for social media platforms to directly sell the advertised products from its website. So instead of advertisers trying to drive social media users to the company's own website, users can buy directly from the social media itself (e.g. using Pinterest's Buyable Pins (see figure 8.17) or Twitter's or Facebook's Buy button or Instagram's Shoppable Posts). The beautiful photography and accompanying stories found on such platforms encourage instant purchase and discourage ROPO behaviour, where consumers research online but purchase offline.

Another way of leveraging social commerce is by harnessing recommendations and reviews from friends. Studies have shown that consumer ratings significantly influence both online book sales and movie box office.[152] The social feature of reading another person's review makes the consumer feel more humanly connected and hence develops a greater emotional bond with the merchant.[153] Social gifting is another way of creating warmth. A US company called Karma can update all important events in your social network (e.g. a friend has just given birth to a baby girl), and then allow you to send gifts (and congratulatory e-cards) to your friends from your smartphone. The gifts are selected from a curated catalogue designed to match the receivers' interest. This company was later acquired by Facebook to enhance its mobile monetisation prowess.[154]

Online shopping platforms have also experimented with social commerce. For instance, with eBay's 'Help Me Shop' we can invite our Facebook friends to assist in a purchase decision by commenting or voting on selected products.[155] Tripadvisor has unveiled a beta-version of its

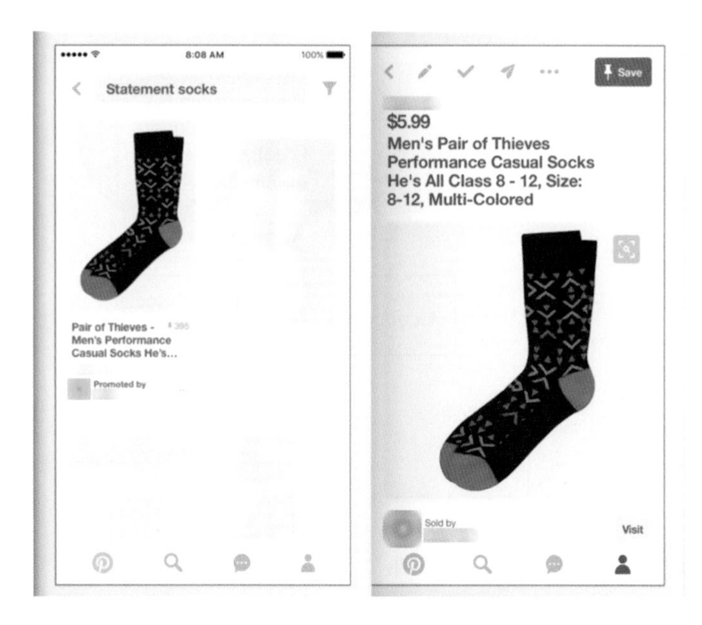

Figure 8.17 Buyable Pin on Pinterest

revamped website to get more enmeshed into the social lives of its users by harnessing their friend's travel recommendations. This is how it works. Imagine before travelling to a new destination we can quickly consult the recommendations of friends through a personalised homepage. It will allow us to view hotels, restaurants and places of interests our friends have visited and recommended. Furthermore, during the trip, when we inadvertently pass a place of interest that our friends have recommended, our smartphone app will automatically alert us. If this place piques our fancy, we can take the next step immediately (e.g. booking). With these new 'social-assistive tools' Tripadvisor hopes to be the 'Facebook' of travel.[156]

MANAGERIAL APPLICATION: PUTTING IT TOGETHER

With so many different ways of looking at the social aspects of marketing, how can we make sense of it all? How can it all come together in a way that is useful to a marcoms manager? Figure 8.18 outlines one approach. Although it may look complicated at first glance, we have in fact already discussed all the key ideas. We will now highlight some of the more important points.

The most interesting point to note is that social contagion is more likely to occur if certain viral preconditions are met (indicated by point [a] in figure 8.18). If these conditions are not met, then social contagion is less likely to occur. This means PWOM will simply be transmitted as normal along path (b) and there will be no explosion in the rate of transmission. Of course, the aim of every marcoms manager is to hope for a viral explosion with all the campaigns implemented.

At point (c), we also see that there are two main target audiences - our own customers and non-customers in a larger community. The aim is to convert the non-customers in the community into customers, or at the minimum to obtain their contact details for future direct marketing opportunities (see chapter 11).

Figure 8.18 also draws a distinction between two important forms of internet behaviour - online search (point [d]) and social interactions (point [e]). Note that online search also includes video-sharing

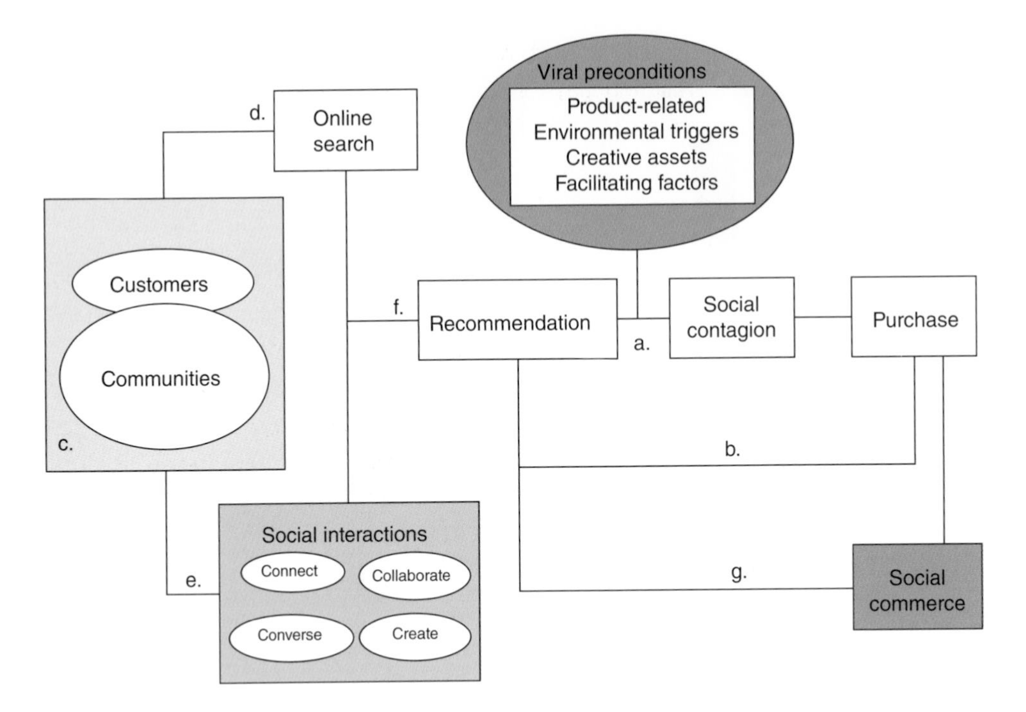

Figure 8.18 How to use social elements to influence purchase

sites (e.g. YouTube), not just search engines (e.g. Google); the target audience is likely to carry out both kinds of activity on the topic of interest, which should be included in any online campaign. This means these two activities must support each other, implying that a certain level of creative integration is necessary. Social interactions and search interact to evoke recommendations at point (f). Of the two activities, however, the marcoms manager can only control online search by ensuring that there is SEO (see chapter 5 on SEO). This should all be well planned at the start of the campaign.

Finally, it is also possible to achieve purchase using social commerce without a viral element. Social commerce is a special form of ecommerce where the social relationships or network information are deliberately harnessed to influence purchase, as depicted in path (g) of figure 8.18.

FURTHER THINKING: LOSING CONTROL OF SOCIAL MEDIA

This section explores some of the issues surrounding social media as a form of communication. The main issue is the lack of control, especially over brand image. We also discuss ways for the marcoms manager to try to seize back some control.

LEARNING GOALS

After reading this section, you will understand:

- why firms may lose control of their brand image online
- what a marcoms manager can do to protect a firm's online reputation.

At the beginning of this chapter, we discussed the idea that humans are social animals, and that the instinct to be social results in the sort of network effects we observed in the marketplace. This instinct has also spurred the popularity of social media. The internet allows us to foster that sociability so that much more information can now be transmitted more quickly within social networks. Further, with technology becoming ever more sophisticated, we can also display our tastes and preferences to members of our social networks, influencing and being influenced by them in turn.

However, using social media is not a free lunch, and just as much care is needed in using social media as in traditional media. First, consumers continue to ignore ads[157] on Facebook pages and, even worse, may come to resent them. To users, social media is not just another channel for commerce, but a personal space in which they share interests and information with others in their network, without the intrusion of brands. In other words, to consumers social media is community-centric, not brand-centric (the exception being brand community). Hence, social media may not be as effective a medium for advertising as search engine portals such as Google or Bing, where people go often to search for information about products. In fact, Google enjoys a higher click-through rate for display ads than does Facebook, although both are higher than average for banner ads in the US (as shown in table 8.2).[158] Furthermore, customers' engagement with a brand's social media webpage is low (between 1% and 6%), even if the social media platform itself may be very popular. Finally, only a tiny percentage of online purchase comes via social media links (about 0.9%).[159] There is a difference between a community of users and customers. Do not rely on social media alone to lead the campaign targeting customers unless there is no choice, which is often the case for small businesses.

Table 8.2 Click-through rates (CTR) for display ads on Google and Facebook

Website	Click-through rate (CTR)
Google	0.4%
Facebook	0.05%
Average for banner ads (US)	0.01%

Second, it is impossible for anyone to control social media. For instance, no one knows who is watching what on YouTube, and how often. As it stands, we can only tell how many people are watching, not who is watching or how often. So, the concepts of reach and frequency do not apply in this context. This also applies to search engines like Google, which the company is trying to rectify by asking users to confirm their identity before they start their search, which in turn raises privacy concerns.

Third, loss of control becomes serious if the image of the brand is hijacked. Using digital technology, any brand logo, image or advertising can be altered or re-created. Coupled with the use of social technologies such as blogging, video sharing and collaborative creation, it is now easy for consumers to hijack and parody brands, using them as a source of entertainment and creative pride. In other words, instead of brands targeting consumers, consumers are now targeting brands[160] and the bigger the brand, the more likely it is to be targeted. It is therefore important that the online image of the brand is closely monitored and, if necessary, protected. Digital memory, unlike human memory, is long-lasting, and misinformation can linger in cyberspace permanently if it is not removed. So, if bad comments (justified or not) are permitted to accumulate on social media or some other website, eventually users will find them. In chapter 4, under programmatic media buying, we have discussed the issue of reputational harm to brands (sometimes called brand safety) if its online ads are placed next to unsavoury or extremist internet content (e.g. pornography, jihadist violence).

Given these issues, organisations should actively engage with consumers, who are now more empowered than ever before and expect more from their brands. Here are three strategies to consider. Start by setting up a system to monitor what consumers are saying about the brand. Once the monitoring of consumers' conversation is set up, then look for opportunities to provide clarifying information and to intervene, if necessary, to protect the reputation of the brand, ensuring that one is always fast and flexible in solving problems and never to offer an inane platitude.[161] Finally, take every opportunity to create and propagate positive buzz for the brand, as we often see in the film industry.

DISCUSSION QUESTIONS

1. Explain 'six degrees of separation', 'three degrees of influence' and 'the strength of weak ties'. What are the implications of these concepts for marketing communications?
2. According to Facebook, its users are now separated from each other by 3.57 degrees of separation. Do you think this is good or bad for a marketer? Explain your answer.
3. There are many forms of social media. What elements do they all have in common?
4. Do you think it is important to draw a distinction between customers and a community of users? Could this explain why social media is not as effective a channel for marketing as first thought? Explain your answer.
5. What is a branded conversation and how is it related to a brand's share of conversation (SOC)? How are these similar or dissimilar to branded messages in advertising?
6. What is the difference between 'buzz' and 'viral contagion'? Should a marcoms manager capitalise on good buzz when it occurs, or should he or she create the buzz?
7. Describe the five product-related characteristics that will aid the diffusion of a viral marketing campaign.
8. What characteristics cause an internet video to have high viral content? How easy or difficult is it to create these characteristics?
9. What is product seeding and how is it different from normal sampling of the sort seen in supermarkets?
10. Why do people engage in WOM even when there is no financial incentive to do so?
11. In the current digital age, the image of a brand can be hijacked or parodied on the internet. What can a marcoms manager do about these issues?

NOTES

1 S Grassian, 'Psychiatric effects of solitary confinement', *Journal of Law and Policy*, 22, 2006, pp. 325–83.

2 J Goldberg, 'Solitary confinement "is driving men insane", exonerated convict testifies', *Los Angeles Times*, 2012. Accessed August 2012 at www.latimes.com/news/nationworld/nation/la-na-solitary-confinement-20120620,0,933674.story.

3 NA Christakis and JH Fowler, *Connected*, Little, Brown & Company, New York, 2011. I recommend you read this book – it is absolutely fascinating.

4 Statista, 'Number of active Facebook users worldwide as of 1st quarter', 2020. Accessed May 2020 at www.statista.com/statistics/346167/facebook-global-dau/.

5 Most popular social networks worldwide as of April 2020, ranked by number of active users (in millions). Accessed May 2020 at www.statista.com/statistics/272014/global-social-networks-ranked-by-number-of-users/.

6 KY Lin and HS Lu, 'Why people use social networking sites: an empirical study integrating network externalities and motivation theory', *Computers in Human Behavior* 27, 2011, pp. 1152–61.

7 The availability of this information also means that it can be easily abused, as seen in the recent Cambridge Analytica scandal where the firm harnessed Facebook information for the political gains of their clients. See S Meredith, 'Here's everything you need to know about the Cambridge Analytica scandal', *CNBC Tech*, 21 March 2018. Accessed September 2018 at www.cnbc.com/2018/03/21/facebook-cambridge-analytica-scandal-everything-you-need-to-know.html.

8 Statista, 'Social media marketing – statistics & facts'. Accessed September 2018 at www.statista.com/topics/1538/social-media-marketing/.

9 P Lazarsfeld, B Berelson and H Gaudent, *The people's choice*, Columbia University Press, New York, 1944.

10 Although information flow about a specific event – such as a referral for a doctor – is not the same as social ties, it is highly correlated since most WOM information is exchanged through social ties. For the sake of simplicity, I have depicted the two the same way in this example.

11 A Banerjee, AG Chandrasekhar, E Duflo and MO Jackson, 'Gossip: identifying central individuals in a social network', National Bureau of Economic Research, Working Paper 20422, 2014. Accessed October 2020 at www.nber.org/papers/w20422.

12 J Travers and S Milgram, 'An experimental study in the small world problem', *Sociometry*, 35(4), 1969, pp. 425–43.

13 PS Dodds, R Muhamad and D Watts, 'An experimental study of search in global social networks', *Science*, 301, 2003, pp. 827–9.

14 S Bhagat, M Burke, C Diuk, I Onur Filiz and S Edunov, 'Three and a half degrees of separation', Facebook Research, 4 February 2016. Accessed September 2018 at https://research.fb.com/three-and-a-half-degrees-of-separation/.

15 DJ Watts and PS Dodds, 'Influentials, networks, and public opinion formation', *Journal of Consumer Research*, 34, 2007, pp. 441–58.

16 M Granovetter, 'The strength of weak ties', *American Journal of Sociology*, 78, 1973, pp. 1360–80.

17 Although not shown in the diagram, persons K and L are also connected to a different network, which forms the basis of their accessibility to new information.

18 Dodds, Muhamad and Watts (2003), 'An experimental study of search in global social networks', note 13.

19 Z Katona, PP Zubcsek and M Sarvary, 'Network effects and personal influences: the diffusion of an online social network', *Journal of Marketing Research*, 48(3), June 2011, pp. 425–43.

20 R Dunbar, 'Social networks: human social networks', *New Scientist*, 2859, 12 April 2012. Accessed August 2012 at www.newscientist.com/article/mg21428590.400-social-networks-human-social-networks.html.

21 Christakis and Fowler (2011), *Connected*, p. 88, note 3.

22 Pew Research Centre, 'Social media use – 2018', 1 March 2018. Accessed September 2018 at www.pewinternet.org/2018/03/01/social-media-use-in-2018/.

23 Katona, Zubcsek and Sarvary (2011), 'Network effects and personal influences', note 19.

24 Facebook IQ, Industry Research, 'Creative strategies with topic data', October 2015. Accessed September 2018 at www.facebook.com/iq/articles/creative-strategies-with-topic-data?ref=wpinsights_rd.

25 Christakis and Fowler (2011), *Connected*, note 3.

26 JH Fowler and NA Christakis, 'Dynamic spread of happiness in large social networks: longitudinal analysis over 20 years in Framingham Heart Study', *British Medical Journal*, 337, 2008, pp. 1–9.

27 JJ Brown and PH Reingen, 'Social ties and word of mouth referral behaviour', *Journal of Consumer Research*, 14, 1987, pp. 350–62.

28 Y Liu-Thompson, 'Seeding viral content – the role of message and network factors', *Journal of Advertising Research*, 52(4), December 2012, pp. 465–78.

29 H Nair, P Mancnanda and T Bhatia, 'Asymmetric peer effects in physician prescription behaviour: the role of opinion leaders', *Journal of Marketing Research*, 47, October 2010, pp. 883–95.

30 L Feick and LL Price, 'The market maven: a diffuser of marketplace information', *Journal of Marketing*, 51, 1987 pp. 83–97.

31 Global coffee review, 'Branded: the psychology behind corporate tattoos', 2011. Accessed April 2013 at http://globalcoffeereview.com/marketing/view/branded-the-psychology-behind-corporate-tattoos.

32 AM Muniz Jr and TC O'Guinn, 'Brand community', *Journal of Consumer Research*, 27, 2001, pp. 412–31.

33 Pew Research Centre, 'Social media use – 2018', 1 March 2018. Accessed September 2018 at www.pewinternet.org/2018/03/01/social-media-use-in-2018/.

34 M Scott, 'WeChat is a way of life for 900 million daily users', *InTheBlack*, 1 May 2018. Accessed September 2018 at www.intheblack.com/articles/2018/05/01/wechat-super-app.

35 Tik Tok is popular among generation Z, that is those born after 1990; see https://brandastic.com/blog/what-is-tiktok-and-why-is-it-so-popular/.

36 DA Williamson, 'US consumers are flocking to TikTok', *eMarketer*, 27 April 2020. Accessed May 2020 at www.emarketer.com/content/us-consumers-are-flocking-to-tiktok.

37 S Pham, 'TikTok is winning over millennials and Instagram stars as its popularity explodes', *CNN Business*, 5 May 2020. Accessed May 2020 at https://edition.cnn.com/2020/05/05/tech/tiktok-bytedance-coronavirus-intl-hnk/index.html.

38 A Smith, E Fischer and C Yongjian (2012), 'How does brand-related user-generated content differ across YouTube, Facebook, and Twitter?', *Journal of Interactive Marketing*, 26(2), 2012, pp. 102–13.

39 C Schulze, L Schöler and B Skiera, 'Not all fun and games: viral marketing for utilitarian products', *Journal of Marketing*, 78, 2014, pp. 1–19.

40 S Srinivasan, OJ Rutz and K Pauwels, 'Paths to and off purchase: quantifying the impact of traditional marketing and online consumer activity', *Journal of the Academy of Marketing Science*, 44, 2016, pp. 440–53.

41 B Smallwood, 'Resisting the siren call of popular digital media measures: Facebook research shows no link between trendy online measures and ad effectiveness', *Journal of Advertising Research*, 56(2) 2016, pp. 126–31.

42 ML Katz and C Shapiro, 'Network externalities, competition and compatibility', *American Economic Review*, 75, 1985, pp. 424–40.

43 Facebook recently (re)launched Facebook Graph Search, which has this built-in intelligent function to allow us to tap into our network. You can see it at www.facebook.com/about/graphsearch.

44 Facebook Statistics. Accessed July 2013 at www.statisticbrain.com/facebook-statistics.
45 DE Berlyne, *Conflict, arousal and curiosity*, McGraw-Hill, New York, 1960.
46 JR Bughin, 'How companies can make the most of user-generated content', *McKinsey Quarterly*, August 2007. Accessed November 2010 at www.mckinseyquarterly.com/How_companies_can_make_the_most_of_user-generated_content_2041.
47 Ibid.
48 You can read more at iabaustralia.com.au/news/vml-takes-first-place-in-creative-showcase-for-mcdonald-s-loaded-campaign/.
49 You can watch the completed film here: https://vimeo.com/162457596/d735e5d8cf.
50 R Leenders, 'Modeling social influence through network autocorrelation: constructing the weight matrix', *Social Networks*, 24(1), 2002, pp. 21–48.
51 C Singh and L Ang, 'Persuasive effects in social media: the case of envy', *International Journal of Advertising*, in press.
52 Conceptually, there is a difference between misinformation and disinformation. Misinformation is false information *not* meant to deliberately cause harm. Disinformation, on the other hand, is false information that is deliberately used to harm individuals, social groups, organisations or countries. See C Wardle and H Derakhshan, 'Information disorder: toward an interdisciplinary framework for research and policy making', *Council of Europe*, October 2017.
53 'Florida commissioner finds cure for coronavirus ... blow dryers to your face', 2020. Accessed on April 2020 on www.youtube.com/watch?v=dBgM_yAkbQk.
54 J Horwitz, 'U.K. debunks 5G-coronavirus link after conspiracy theorists burn cell tower', 3 April 2020. Accessed April 2020 on https://venturebeat.com/2020/04/03/uk-debunks-5g-coronavirus-link-after-conspiracy-theorists-burn-cell-tower/.
55 JS Brennen, FM Simon, PN Howard and RK Nielsen, 'Types, sources, and claims of COVID-19 misinformation', *Reuters Institute*, 2020.
56 This is because popular information has been programmed to be algorithmically ranked higher in search and recommendations engines.
57 S Perez, 'Report: WhatsApp has seen a 40% increase in usage due to COVID-19 pandemic', *TechCrunch*, 27 March 2020. Accessed April 2020 at https://techcrunch.com/2020/03/26/report-whatsapp-has-seen-a-40-increase-in-usage-due-to-covid-19-pandemic/.
58 BBC documented how a Facebook post originating from a person's uncle working in Shenzhen hospital in China, and giving tips on dealing with COVID-19 (e.g. not drinking cold water) went viral around the world. O Robinson and M Spring, 'Coronavirus: how bad information goes viral', 2020. Accessed April 2020 at www.bbc.com/news/blogs-trending-51931394.
59 Australia Broadcasting Corporation Radio, Coronacast, 2020. Accessed April 2020 at www.abc.net.au/radio/programs/coronacast/latest-segments/12025304.
60 One example is UK's Fullfact. Accessed April 2020 at https://fullfact.org/about/.
61 Some countries are quicker than others in this regard. See D Funke and D Flamini, 'A guide to anti-misinformation actions around the world', *Poynter Institute*, 2020. Accessed April 2020 at www.poynter.org/ifcn/anti-misinformation-actions/.
62 FY Chee and G Baczynska, 'EU justice chief urges U.S. tech giants to halt virus clickbaits', *Reuters Technology News*, 3 April 2020. Accessed April 2020 at www.reuters.com/article/us-health-coronavirus-eu-tech/eu-justice-chief-urges-u-s-tech-giants-to-halt-virus-clickbaits-idUSKBN21K2BY.

63 L Ang, 'Community relationship management and social media', *Journal of Database Marketing and Customer Strategy Management*, 18(1), 2011, pp. 31–9.

64 S Narain, 'Health Promotion Board: National Smoking Control campaign', World Advertising Research Centre, 2011. Accessed September 2018 at www.warc.com/content/article/warc-prize-asia/health_promotion_board_national_smoking_control_campaign/94095.

65 S Narain, H Tow and T Chan, 'Smoking Control: I Quit – from anti-smoking to proquitting', World Advertising Research Centre, 2012. Accessed April 2018 at www.warc.com/content/paywall/article/smoking-control-i-quit—from-anti-smoking-to-pro-quitting/97637.

66 S Narain and J Loke, 'Health Promotion Board Singapore: I QUIT – from anti-smoking to pro-quitting', World Advertising Research Centre, 2012. Accessed April 2018 at www.warc.com/content/paywall/article/health-promotion-board-singapore-i-quit—from-anti-smoking-to-pro-quitting/97380.

67 S Narain and T Chan, 'Health Promotion Board of Singapore: creating a proquitting culture', World Advertising Research Centre, 2014. Accessed April 2018 at www.warc.com/content/paywall/article/health-promotion-board-of-singapore-creating-a-pro-quitting-culture/102476.

68 This definition appears on the Word-of-Mouth Marketing Association (WOMMA) website. Accessed August 2012 at http://womma.org/wom101/wom101.pdf.

69 *Razorfish Social Marketing Influence Report 2009*. Accessed April 2019 at http://faculty.cbpp.uaa.alaska.edu/afef/SIM-Razorfish.pdf.

70 S Rustcus, 'Creating brand advocates', in J Kirby and P Marsden (eds), *Connected marketing: the viral, buzz and word-of-mouth revolution*, Butterworth-Heinemann, Oxford, 2006, pp. 47–58.

71 R East, RK Hammond and M Wright, 'The relative incidence of positive and negative word of mouth: a multi-category study', *International Journal of Research in Marketing*, 24(2), 2007, pp. 175–84.

72 Keller Faye Group, cited in AJ Kimmel, *Connecting with consumers*, Oxford University Press, Oxford, 2010, p. 101.

73 E Kellert and B Fay, 'Word-of-mouth advocacy', *Journal of Advertising Research*, 52(4), December 2012, pp. 459–64.

74 Adapted from A Lipsman et al., 'The power of "like"', *Journal of Advertising Research*, 52(1), March 2012, pp. 40–52.

75 J Romaniuk and R East, 'Word-of-mouth facts worth talking about', in J Romaniuk and B Sharp, *How brands grow part 2*, Oxford University Press, Melbourne Australia, pp. 125–44.

76 A Kumar et al., 'From social to sale: the effects of firm-generated content in social media on customer behavior', *Journal of Marketing*, 80 (January 2016), pp. 7–25.

77 J Tsai, 'Everyone's social (already)', *CRM Magazine*, 13(6), 2009, pp. 34–8.

78 T Wasserman, 'Survey gives good reviews to online product reviews', *Brandweek*, 48 (15), 2007, p. 12.

79 C Dellarocas, X Zhang and N Awad, 'Exploring the value of online product reviews in forecasting sales: the case of motion pictures', *Journal of Interactive Marketing*, 21(4), 2007, pp. 23–45.

80 PK Chintagunta, S Gopinath and S Venkataraman, 'The effects of online user reviews on movie box office performance: accounting for sequential rollout and aggregation across local markets,' *Marketing Science*, 29(5), pp. 944–57.

81 JA Chevalier and D Mayzlin, 'The effect of word of mouth on sales: online book reviews', *Journal of Marketing Research*, 43(3), 2006, pp. 345–54.

82 R Liu and W Zhang, 'Informational influence of online customer feedback: an empirical study', *Database Marketing and Customer Strategy Management*, 17(2), 2010, pp. 120–31.

83 Y Sun, X Dong and S McIntyre, 'Motivation of user-generated content: social connectedness moderates the effects of monetary rewards', *Marketing Science*, 36(3), 2017, pp. 329–37.

84 D Kupor and Z Tormala, 'When moderation fosters persuasion: the persuasive power of deviatory reviews', *Journal of Consumer Research*, 45(3), 2018, pp. 490–510.

85 S Johnson, 'Triguboff's Meriton fined $3m over TripAdvisor tampering', *Sydney Morning Herald*, 31 July 2018. Accessed September 2018 at www.smh.com.au/business/companies/triguboff-s-meriton-fined-3m-over-tripadvisor-tampering-20180731-p4zulm.html.

86 U Matzat and C Syijders, 'Rebuilding trust in online shops on consumer review sites: sellers' responses to user-generated complaints', *Journal of Computer-Mediated Communication*, 18, 2012, pp 62–79.

87 B Kovács, GR Carroll and DW Lehman, 'Authenticity and consumer value ratings: empirical tests from the restaurant domain', *Organization Science*, 25(2), 2014, pp 458–78.

88 M Trusov, R Bucklin and K Pauwels, 'Effects of word-of-mouth versus traditional marketing: findings from an internet social networking site', *Journal of Marketing*, 73, September 2009, pp. 90–102.

89 For example, G Assmus, JU Farlet and DR Lehman, 'How advertising affects sales: meta-analysis of economic results', *Journal of Marketing Research*, 21(1), February 1984, pp. 65–74.

90 M Corstjens and A Umblus, 'The power of evil – the damage of negative social media strongly outweigh positive contributions', *Journal of Advertising Research*, 52(4), 2012, pp. 433–49.

91 S Guo, M Wang and J Leskovec, 'The role of social networks in online shopping: information passing, price of trust and consumer choice', *ACM Conference on Electronic Commerce*, 2011, pp. 157–66.

92 Twitter Help Centre, 'How to post photos or GIFs on Twitter'. Accessed September 2018 at https://help.twitter.com/en/using-twitter/tweeting-gifs-and-pictures.

93 T Hennig-Thurau, C Wiertz and F Feldhaus, 'Does Twitter matter? The impact of microblogging word of mouth on consumers' adoption of new movies', *Journal of the Academy of Marketing Science*, 43, 2015, pp. 375–94.

94 Ibid.

95 M Osman, 'How to use hashtags on every social media network', *SproutSocial*. Accessed September 2018 at https://sproutsocial.com/insights/how-to-use-hashtags/.

96 FF Reichheld, 'The one number you need to grow', *Harvard Business Review*, 81(12), 2003, pp. 46–54.

97 TL Keiningham, B Cooil, TW Andreasson and L Aksoy, 'A longitudinal examination of "net promoter" and firm revenue growth', *Journal of Marketing*, 71(3), 2007, pp. 39–51.

98 One simple approach to measure both positive and negative recommendations is to ask the question twice. That is, we ask respondents whether they 'have recommended this brand to somebody'. A 'Yes' response is scored +1 and 'No' scored 0. At the same time, we also ask the negative version of this question: 'Have you recommended *not* to buy this brand to somebody?' This time 'Yes' is scored −1 and 'No' scored 0. For each respondent, we then sum the scores across the two questions. This means that recommenders would be individuals who have a net score of +1 across the two questions. We then simply count the percentages of recommenders for each brand. Using this simple approach, one German study (consisting of about 290 students)

found that the more a person loves a brand, the more likely the person would have recommended the brand to others. This is especially true in the fashion clothing category, where up to 75% have recommended the brand they love to others. See JR Rossiter, 'A new C-OAR-SE-based content-valid and predictively valid measure that distinguishes brand love from brand liking', *Marketing Letters*, 23(2), 2012, pp. 905–16.

99 R East, K Hammond and W Lomax, 'Measuring the impact of positive and negative word of mouth on brand purchase probability', *International Journal of Research in Marketing*, 25, 2008, pp. 215–24.

100 A Parameswaran, cited in N Hollis, 'Word of mouth is powerful but lacks some important qualities', *Kantar Straight Talk*. Accessed June 2019 at www.millwardbrown.com/global-navigation/blogs/post/mb-blog/2019/05/27/word-of-mouth-is-powerful-but-lacks-some-important-qualities?utm_source=Email.

101 E Rosen, *Anatomy of buzz: how to create word-of-mouth marketing*, Doubleday/ Currency, New York, 2002.

102 M LeBrun, 'A social media best practice: the value of growing your share of conversation', *Media Philosopher*, 5 February 2009. Accessed August 2012 at www.mediaphilosopher.com.

103 L Porter and GJ Golan, 'From subservient chickens to brawny men: a comparison of viral advertising to TV advertising', *Journal of Interactive Advertising*, 6(2), 2006, pp. 30–8.

104 See Kimmel (2010), *Connecting with consumers*, p. 272, note 72, who cites the Jupiter study.

105 P Ketelaar, L Janssen, M Vergeer, E Reijmersdal, R Crutzen and J Riet, 'The success of viral ads: social and attitudinal predictors of consumer pass-on behavior on social network sites', *Journal of Business Research*, 69, 2016, pp. 2603–13.

106 EM Rogers, *Diffusion of innovations*, Free Press, New York, 1983.

107 J Berger and EM Schwartz, 'What drives immediate and ongoing word of mouth?', *Journal of Marketing Research*, XLVIII, 2011, pp. 869–80.

108 L Lorber, 'Small business link: how online marketing videos became a hit in their own right', *Wall Street Journal*, 2 July 2007, p. B4. You can see one of the videos here: www.youtube.com/user/Blendtec. Accessed August 2012.

109 J Berger, *Contagious: why things catch on*, Simon and Schuster, New York, 2016.

110 J Berger and G Fitzsimons, 'Dogs on the street, Pumas on your feet: how cues in the environment influence product evaluation and choice', *Journal of Marketing Research*, XLV, 2008, pp. 1–14.

111 Berger (2016), *Contagious*, note 109.

112 This graph is taken from the website Reddit. Accessed September 2018 at www.reddit.com/r/dataisbeautiful/comments/86jqp6/google_searches_for_rebecca_black_peak_on_fridays/.

113 Kellert and Fay (2012), 'Word-of-mouth advertising', note 73.

114 Liu-Thompson (2012), 'Seeding viral content', note 28.

115 A Doebele et al., 'Why pass on viral messages? Because they connect emotionally', *Business Horizons*, 50, 2007, pp. 291–304.

116 T Teixeira, M Wedel and R Pieters, 'Emotion-induced engagement in internet video advertisements', *Journal of Marketing Research*, 49(2), 2012, pp. 144–59.

117 This is based on a true story of a Canadian singer, Dave Carroll. His song 'United breaks guitars' was an instant hit on YouTube. You can watch his music clip here: www.youtube.com/watch?v=5YGc4zOqozo [accessed April 2013].

118 J Berger and KL Milliken, 'What makes online content viral?', *Journal of Marketing Research*, 49(2), 2011, pp. 192–205.

119 East, Hammond and Wright (2007), 'The relative incidence of positive and negative word of mouth', note 71.

120 D Southgate, N Westoby and G Page, 'Creative determinants of viral video viewing', *International Journal of Advertising*, 29(3), 2010, pp. 349–68.

121 GJ Tellis, DJ MacInnis, S Tirunillai and Y Zhang, 'What drives virality (sharing) of online digital content? The critical role of information, emotion, and brand prominence', *Journal of Marketing*, 83(4), 2019, pp. 1–20.

122 Berger (2016), *Contagious*, note 109.

123 J Berger and EM Schwartz, 'What drives immediate and ongoing word of mouth?', *Journal of Marketing Research*, XLVIII, 2011, pp. 869–80.

124 Rosen (2002), *Anatomy of buzz*, note 101.

125 'Share a Coke campaign'. Accessed May 2019 at https://shareacoke-casestudy.tumblr.com/.

126 Shopping Links Blog, February 2018. Accessed May 2019 at https://shoppinglinks.com/blog/blog_detail/product-seding-101.

127 Some would-be online influencers will solicit free gifts from companies, which can be a nuisance as well as cutting into their already thin profits.

128 This was the notorious case of two Walmart 'enthusiasts' (Laura and Jim) who decided to travel across the US, visiting Walmart along the way, and blogging about it. It turns out that their plan was somewhat orchestrated. Although they did travel across the country, the blog, the recreational vehicle and flights of these two people were paid for by Walmart. See P Gogoi, 'Wal-Mart's Jim and Laura: the real story', *Bloomberg Businessweek*, 2006. Accessed April 2013 at www.businessweek.com/stories/2006-10-09/wal-marts-jim-and-laura-the-real-storybusinessweek-business-news-stock-market-and-financial-advice.

129 S Khamis, L Ang and R Welling, 'Self-branding, "micro-celebrity" and the rise of social media influencers', *Celebrity Studies*, 8(2), 2017, pp. 191–208.

130 A Eksouzian-Cavadas, 'Forbes reveal their top 10 beauty influencers for 2017', *Harpers Bazaar*, 4 October 2017. Accessed September 2018 at www.harpersbazaar.com.au/beauty/forbes-top-ten-beauty-influencers-2017-14545.

131 N Hall, 'The Kardashian index: a measure of discrepant social media profile for scientists', *Genome Biology*, 15(7), 2014, p. 424. doi:10.1186/s13059-014-0424-0. PMC 4165362 Freely accessible. PMID 25315513. Accessed 15 August 2014.

132 D Peltier, 'Growing pains for influencer marketing raise questions for travel brands', *Skift*, 17 September 2018. Accessed September 2018 at https://skift.com/2018/09/17/growing-pains-for-influencer-marketing-raise-questions-for-travel-brands/.

133 SC Boerman, EA van Reijmersdal and PC Neijens, 'Effects of sponsorship disclosure timing on the processing of sponsored content: a study on the effectiveness of European Disclosure Regulations', *Psychology and Marketing*, 31(3), 2014, pp. 214–24.

134 L Rasmussen, 'Parasocial interaction in the digital age: an examination of relationship building and the effectiveness of YouTube celebrities', *The Journal of Social Media in Society*, 7(1), 2018, pp. 280–94.

135 Dictionary.com. Accessed September 2018 at www.dictionary.com/browse/para-.

136 J Cohen, 'Parasocial break-up from favorite TV characters: the role of attachment styles and relationship intensity', *Journal of Social and Personal Relationships*, 21(2), 2004, pp. 187–202.

137 A Grant, 'Don't let your business fall for social media influencer fraud', *Forbes*, 20 February 2019. Accessed May 2019 at www.forbes.com/sites/theyec/2019/02/20/dont-let-your-business-fall-for-social-media-influencer-fraud/#1bc31cf05852.

138 J Constine, 'Snapchat's PR firm sues influencer for not promoting Spectacles on Instagram', *Techcrunch*, October 2018. Accessed May 2019 at https://techcrunch.com/2018/10/31/influencer-marketing-lawsuit/.

139 A Ha, 'Australian influencer marketing startup Tribe raises $7.5M as it eyes US expansion', *Techcrunch*, March 2019. Accessed May 2019 at https://techcrunch.com/2019/03/26/tribe-series-a/.

140 The Bzzagent website can be found at www.bzzagent.com. Accessed August 2012.

141 WJ Carl, 'What's all the buzz about?', *Management Communication Quarterly*, 19(4), 2006, pp. 601–34.

142 IRI press release, 'BzzAgent and IRI find everyday influencer marketing programs drive the highest return on ad spend', 3 October 2017. Accessed September 2018 at www.iriworldwide.com/en-US/insights/news/BzzAgent-and-IRI-Find-Everyday-Influencer-Marketing-Programs-Drive-the-Highest-Return-on-Ad-Spend.

143 Cited in A Bruyn and GL Lilien, 'A multi-state model of word-of-mouth influence through agent effectiveness', *International Journal of Research in Marketing*, 25 September 2008, pp. 151–63.

144 S Aral and D Walker, 'Creating social contagion through viral product design: a randomised trial of peer influence in networks', *Management Science*, 57(9), 2011, pp. 1623–39.

145 MJ Lovett, R Peres and R Shachar, 'On brands and word of mouth', *Journal of Marketing Research*, 50(4), 2013, pp. 427–44.

146 CS Lee and L Ma, 'News sharing in social media: the effect of gratifications and prior experience', *Computers in Human Behavior*, 28(2), 2012, pp. 331–9.

147 JYC Ho and M Dempsey, 'Viral marketing: motivations to forward online content', *Journal of Business Research*, 63(9/10), 2010, pp. 1000–6.

148 Berger (2016), *Contagious*, note 109.

149 This is the classic U-shape function. Extreme satisfaction or dissatisfaction will cause people to talk. See EW Anderson, 'Customer satisfaction and word of mouth', *Journal of Service Research*, 1(1), 1998, pp. 5–17.

150 Berger and Milliken (2011), 'What makes online content viral?', note 118.

151 SY Syn and S Oh, 'Why do social network site users share information on Facebook and Twitter?', *Journal of Information Science*, 41(5), 2015, pp. 553–69.

152 JA Chevalier and D Mayzlin, 'The effect of word of mouth on sales: online book reviews', *Journal of Marketing Research*, 43(3), 2006, pp. 345–54; C Dellarocas and XM Zhang, 'The lord of the ratings: is a movie's fate influenced by reviews?', *Proceedings of the 27th International Conference on Information Systems* (ICIS), Milwaukee, Wisconsin, 2006.

153 LC Wang et al., 'Can a retail web site be social?', *Journal of Marketing*, 71(3), 2007, pp. 143–57.

154 TechCrunch, 'Facebook's acquisition of Karma brings mobile commerce, app monetization prowess', 2012. Accessed September 2018 at https://techcrunch.com/2012/05/18/facebook-acquires-karma/.

155 eBay, 'Help Me Shop Buy with a little help from your friend'. Accessed September 2018 at www.ebay.com/helpmeshop/.

156 D Schaal, 'Into social travel with a personalized recommendation feed', *Skift*, 17 September 2018. Accessed September 2018 at https://skift.com/2018/09/17/tripadvisor-digs-deeper-into-social-travel-with-a-personalized-recommendation-feed/.

157 M Airs, 'Avoiding the ad-avoidance blues? An empirical study into the effects of Facebook brand page content and homophily on young adults in Australia', Honours thesis submitted to Macquarie University, Department of Marketing and Management, 2012.

158 This is based on 11 000 display ads between 2009 and 2010, monitored by Wordstream. See E Sherman, 'Ad campaign smackdown: Facebook vs Google', *Inc.,* 2012. Accessed April 2013 at www.inc.com/erik-sherman/ad-campaign-smackdown-facebook-v-google.html.

159 M Ritson made a similar point not to confuse users of social media with customers. Even for online purchase, consumers tend to buy directly from the brand's website (about 40%). This is followed by search engine recommendation (e.g. about 32%), then through the links of other recommended websites (about 20%). See 'Why social media is mostly a waste of time for marketers', *World Marketing and Sales Forum*, Melbourne, 2015. Accessed at www.youtube.com/watch?v=S2NUayn2vPO.

160 S Fournier and J Avery, 'The uninvited brand', *Business Horizons*, 54(3), May/June 2011, pp. 193–207.

161 JR Coyle, T Smith and G Platt, '"I'm here to help": how companies' microblog responses to consumer problems influence brand perceptions', *Journal of Research in Interactive Marketing,* 6(1), 2012, pp. 27–41.

CHAPTER 9

PUBLIC RELATIONS, CORPORATE REPUTATION, SPONSORSHIP, NATIVE ADVERTISING AND CONTENT MARKETING

CHAPTER OVERVIEW

It is sometimes easy to forget that many brands are also the names of the companies, like banks or airlines and even departmental stores. This means very often when things go wrong – like an aeroplane crash or a product recall – the reputation of the whole company takes a trashing. This chapter is all about building and protecting a reputation. In the age of social media, one's reputation can be quickly destroyed, and advertising may not be effective in combating this. It is therefore important for a marcoms manager to learn other communication tools that may be more effective. The first part of this chapter will discuss public relations, corporate and advocacy advertising, sponsorship, corporate social responsibility, brand purpose advertising, native advertising and content marketing. We conclude with a model suggesting how integration can be achieved to enhance a firm's reputation.

Learning goals

After reading this chapter, you will understand:

- the usefulness of public relations (PR) and its advantages and disadvantages
- the symbiotic relationship between media organisations and firms
- what makes a story newsworthy
- Richard Branson's and Donald Trump's strategy of gaining free publicity
- what constitutes corporate reputation, and the advantages of having a good reputation
- when corporate advertising should take precedence over product or service advertising
- how corporate social responsibility (CSR) initiatives and brand purpose campaigns can enhance corporate reputation
- what sponsorship is, its advantages, and how to use it effectively
- what crisis communication is, and how to respond effectively to a crisis
- what native advertising and content marketing are, and the ethics of their usage
- how to use brand architecture to understand the relationship between corporate advertising and product or service advertising
- how to plan and use PR, corporate advertising, sponsorship and content marketing in a coherent way.

Although this chapter contains what seems like unrelated topics, they all serve to build the brand's equity and/or the firm's reputation. It takes a long time to build a good reputation but, unfortunately, it can be destroyed in an instant. Our reputation is fragile and therefore efforts should be expended to protect it.

In developing a firm's reputation, we can use tactics like public relations, corporate and advocacy advertising, sponsorship, corporate social responsibility initiatives and content marketing to build strong, favourable associations that are meaningfully different. Sometimes, unexpected opportunities arise; for instance, when we encounter a piece of good news for the brand, we should try to propagate it so that it reaches as many consumers as possible. This will help build a buffer of goodwill that can help insulate the brand against future reputational crisis. Conversely, when we encounter bad news, we quickly curtail its spread with decisive action. What all this implies is that a marcoms manager should take an ongoing, 'marathon' (i.e. long-term) perspective in managing the reputation. This is not confined to a single campaign (e.g. in advertising) or a short-term sales activation (e.g. during the sales promotion period), but involves a constant lookout for opportunities to propagate good news or curtail bad ones. Or, to summarise, a marcoms manager should be always be thinking of ways to amplify the upside and minimise the downside.

PUBLIC RELATIONS

We might well ask why we would want to mess around with PR when we could simply engage in a massive corporate advertising campaign to improve the image of the firm. In this part, we will explore this question. Consider the following scenario.

> A university's 100th birthday is approaching – a milestone to be celebrated. The university is planning a series of events to mark the occasion, hoping to use the celebration to enhance its reputation among students, staff and the general public. However, the university's PR manager fears that the planned events may be hijacked by the disgruntled students' union, which has been protesting about a recent rise in university fees. If the centenary events are marred by student demonstrations, the positive image the university hopes to project in this once-in-a-lifetime event will be compromised. Worse still, if the media supports the students' cause, bad publicity (instead of goodwill) will ensue. The university therefore needs a contingency plan.

This scenario illustrates the importance of having PR in our communication arsenal. Given the fluid, changing nature of events, traditional communications tools such as mass media advertising may not be enough. As Hutton perceptively pointed out,[1] PR serves very different functions across a range of activities, including:

- conveying information through press conferences or press releases
- conducting media interviews to explain government policies
- developing guidelines on what to say, or not say, in a crisis
- sponsoring sporting events
- handling criticisms of price increases

- dealing with workers' strikes
- creating a positive image to aid a donation drive
- explaining away a politician's gaffe
- neutralising bad publicity arising from the recall of products
- repairing reputational damage due to scandal
- gaining free publicity for a new product launch or a new advertising campaign.

Thus, PR is relevant to a wide range of stakeholders – both internal (e.g. company employees) and external (e.g. customers, shareholders, the media, the government, the financial community, special-interest groups, channel members and unions). In marketing, our main focus is almost always consumers or customers; that is, the external stakeholders. For instance, of all the activities listed above, only the last would qualify as being directly marketing-related, even though all the other activities are just as important to a firm. The use of PR activities to assist marcoms objectives is sometimes called 'marketing-oriented public relations'. Scholars of PR are uncomfortable with this concept because it limits the discipline and subsumes PR under marketing. But from a pragmatic point of view, a marcoms manager should work closely with the PR manager because his or her skill set may be badly needed.

WHAT IS PR?

Although there are many definitions of PR,[2] the definition used here emphasises the importance of establishing and maintaining good relations with different public stakeholders in order to facilitate the marketing function. This is because PR is fundamentally about understanding public opinion of various groups and then managing those relationships in order to advance the interests of the organisation. We define PR as:

> the management process of engaging productively with all relevant internal and external publics, so that a firm's improved relationship with these groups enhances its reputation and generates positive publicity.

Our definition unashamedly sees PR as an IMC tool; although, as we acknowledged above, PR covers more ground than its marketing functions. From this marketing-oriented definition, we can determine that there are two areas a marcoms manager should concentrate on: first, acquiring free publicity and, second, managing corporate reputation. The former is important because it makes marcoms more cost-efficient, while the latter affects brand equity. Its importance will become clearer later in the chapter. Now, let's consider some of advantages and disadvantages of using PR as an IMC tool.

Advantages of PR

PR has enormous advantages over advertising, five of which we will touch on here. First, free publicity means obtaining free media coverage (i.e. editorial space), which is exposure that the organisation would normally have to pay for. This can amount to millions of dollars' worth of free exposure. If a large amount of good publicity is generated, it will be picked up by other publications, potentially triggering a viral effect (see chapter 8 for discussion of viral contagion and its preconditions).

The second advantage is credibility. When an organisation advertises its goods or services, consumers generally discount these advertisements because they are seen as self-serving. On the other hand, if someone else (e.g. the media) reports positively about a brand, it is likely to be more believable because that person has nothing to be gained. This is sometimes called the 'third-party endorsement effect'.[3] A meta-analysis has found that publicity is about three times more credible than a firm's own advertising. This is especially true if the consumers have low prior knowledge of the product.[4]

The third advantage of PR is that publicity can affect sales. With good publicity, sales will increase. It is well known that a film that wins an Oscar is likely to increase its box office numbers by at least 10% after the announcement.[5] It is reported that sales of vibrators shot up for Dr Laura Berman, a prominent sex therapist who also sold sex toys, after just one appearance on Oprah Winfrey's TV channel, the Oprah Winfrey Network.[6] Similarly, sales of pinot noir wine shot up by 16% in the western states of the US after the movie *Sideways* came out; in the movie, the main character is enthusiastic about that grape varietal.[7]

The fourth advantage is that free (positive) publicity, when coupled with greater credibility and sales increase, is more likely to yield greater ROI than advertising. This can be considered the Holy Grail of publicity. In Australia, every time Halliday's (a prominent wine critic) annual wine review comes up, the wine that scored the highest ratings will almost be sold out. The winning wineries or their distribution agents can also take advantage of their good fortune by advertising on Halliday's website.[8]

The fifth advantage is that free publicity gives firms an option in certain, otherwise restrictive circumstances. For instance, PR can help when:

- the firm is small and cannot afford mass media advertising
- the organisation is only allowed to advertise at certain times (e.g. political advertising, only allowed during the election period)
- a profession is barred from using any form of advertising (e.g. doctors)
- there is a crisis that needs to be immediately addressed by someone important (e.g. the CEO needs to publicly give a press conference to explain a mining accident in one of the company's mines).

Disadvantages of PR

There are also disadvantages to free publicity, when compared to advertising. First and most obvious, a PR manager does not have any control over what is reported. As a result, the publicity may not necessarily be good. Bad publicity can hurt sales. For example, when McDonald's burgers were rumoured to contain worm meat, sales dropped by 25%.[9] Restaurants have been known to go bankrupt after bad reviews.[10]

Second, what is reported also may not be accurate. One study found that out of 62 headlines about a medical story, only two were correct, and the rest were either partially correct or completely wrong![11] Sensational headlines can cause public panic, create false expectations and ultimately reduce confidence in the firm and damage its reputation.

Finally, unlike in advertising (where the marcoms manager can control the timing, reach and frequency of the ad exposures), exposure gained through publicity is dependent on media organisations. The PR manager can only hope that they consider a story newsworthy and decide to report it.

CASE STUDY 9.1 CAPTAIN'S PICK?

One of the favourite things to do in Sydney is to take a ferry ride. It is world-class, up there with the Star Ferry ride across Victoria Harbour in Hong Kong, the Bosphorus ferries in Istanbul and the Staten Island Ferry in New York.[12] Whenever my overseas friends visit Sydney, I encourage them to enjoy the ferries. They never fail to show off the beauty of our harbour city.

In 2016, the NSW state government decided to hold a competition to name six new ferries which were to be added to the fleet. Such an exercise can be tricky though. For instance, in 2016, Britain's Natural Environment Research Council invited the British public to suggest as many names as they liked for a £200 million hi-tech polar research vessel. The campaign was called #NameOurShip campaign.[13] It sounded like a good idea to crowdsource the vessel's name, except that the most popular name turned out to be gimmicky, called the RRS[14] *Boaty McBoatface*, suggested by James Hand as a joke. But it garnered 18 000 votes.[15] The main problem was that it did not fit the image of a serious scientific research ship. It sounded more like a kid's boat sponsored by McDonald's. Other silly names included:

- Its Bloody Cold Here!
- What Iceberg?
- Ice, Ice Baby
- Thanks For All The Fish
- Big Metal Floating Thingy Thing.

However, the campaign did engage the British public, with the website crashing when the competition was first launched. In the end, some sense prevailed, and the panel settled on the name RRS *Sir David Attenborough*, which was the fourth most popular choice. Critics cheekily suggested that not choosing *Boaty McBoatface* was tantamount to a 'blow to democracy.'

Now, it was against this backdrop that the Department of Transport and Infrastructure (NSW) decided to adopt a similar undertaking; that is, to hold a naming competition for its six new ferries. Sydneysiders were encouraged to get involved. But to mitigate the PR disaster seen with the *Boaty McBoatface* affair, the department decided to take a few precautions without alienating the public. The idea was to first solicit suggestions from the public. The names had to fall into the categories of Arts and Culture; Connections to Sydney Harbour; or Science, Environment and Innovation. In anticipating that a slew of inappropriate and silly names would emerge, a hand-picked four person panel was set up to advise the Minister, Andrew Constance. The four panel members[16] were:

- Australian National Maritime Museum director, Kevin Sumption
- Australian Museum director, Kim McKay
- NSW Young Australian of the Year, Melissa Abu-Gazaleh
- NSW Volunteer of the Year, Patrick Dodd.

In the second stage, Sydneysiders were asked to vote on the names recommended by the panel, using the Name Your Ferry website and the social media hashtag #yourferry. The sample size was 15 000 people, and the whole multi-stage exercise cost taxpayers $100 000.

In the first open call for public nominations, the name Ferry McFerryFace was the most popular, receiving 229 nominations. But in the second stage, it only garnered 182 votes. Ian Kiernan, the founder of Clean Up Australia, had 2025 votes. That name was the fifth most popular choice in the winning category (see table 9.1).[17]

Table 9.1 Highest votes in each category

First place category	Second place category	Third place category
Science, Environment and Innovation	**Arts and Culture**	**Sydney Harbour Connection**
Fred Hollows	Eternity	Bennelong
Catherine Hamin	May Gibbs	Gadigal
Victor Chang	Jorn Utzon	Kuttabul
Pemulwuy	Dame Marie Bashir	Warayama
Ian Kiernan	Ken Done	Cammeraygal
Bungaree	Dorothea Mackellar	Tottenham
Jack Mundey	Brett Whitley	Memel
Billy Blue	Margaret Preston	Bayingawuwa
Elizabeth Macarthur	Arthur Streeton	Waran
Valerie Taylor	Olive Cotton	Be-lang-le-wool
Ben Lexcen	Roy David Page	Bo-a-millie
Mary Reibey	Esme Timbery	Mat-te-wan-ye

The names for the Sydney ferries were then announced in November 2017: Fred Hollows, Catherine Hamlin, Victor Chang, Pemulwuy, and Bungaree. But one name was missing: Ian Kiernan.

Instead, the Minister chose to go with the Ferry McFerryFace name, saying in a statement, 'Ferry McFerryface will be the harbour's newest icon, and I hope it brings a smile to the faces of visitors and locals alike.'[18] But it became a farce, and soon the Minister found himself caught up in a media circus. This was because Channel 9 obtained the survey results under the freedom of information legislation and found that the Ferry McFerryFace name had only garnered 182 votes, implying that the Minister acted on his own accord, presumably ignoring the recommendation of his department. However, he defended his choice, saying he wanted to create 'only a bit of fun with the kids'.

But the pressure soon mounted, and it was announced that May Gibbs, the Australian children's author, was to replace Ferry McFerryFace. However, this too may be deemed ineligible because she was in the 'Arts and Culture' category, and not in the winning category of 'Science, Innovation and Environment'. Furthermore, as a children's author, her association with Sydney Harbour is probably less salient than that of Ian Keirnan.

What is curious about this case is that the whole crisis could have been avoided. In fact, the idea of creating the multi-stage competition-cum-survey was to avoid the PR disaster that engulfed the *Boaty McBoatface* affair in the UK. But it seems the Minister decided to make a captain's pick[19] in choosing the Ferry McFerryface name. What makes it worse is that he may have also misled the public because in a tweet in November 2017, he said, 'It's not everyone's cup of tea, but the people *voted* for it so we listened (italics added).' Of course, this was not true and, in fact, the results of the survey were kept secret until it was exposed by Channel 9.[20] What was even more curious was that Ian Kiernan had earlier been told by the Minister's department that his name (i.e. Ian Kiernan) would soon grace the ferry. Then to have it overturned and replaced with a gimmicky name like Ferry McFerryface was an insult. He was angry, and he made it clear in a TV interview.[21] This episode became so scandalous that it even made it to the *Washington Post*.[22] With a captain's pick, the Minister may have kicked an own goal!

DISCUSSION QUESTIONS

1. Soliciting names from the public is not an uncommon practice. What are the pros and cons of using this method?
2. Speculate why you think the Minister decided to make a captain's pick, after having spent $100 000 on the survey.
3. What lessons can be learned from this case study for a marcoms manager?

MANAGING PR

Sources of information for PR editorials

To take advantage of PR, we need to know from where journalists source their information when writing editorials. This knowledge will help the PR manager target the right sources. Such sources of information include:

- Press releases and official announcements. These are a major source of information for journalists.
- Visits to press conferences; annual meetings; business or academic conferences; special ceremonies; and sporting occasions. These are usually big events where the journalists can personally witness events unfold.
- Papers in academic journals or databases. In some sectors, for example, medical science, the latest reporting in medical breakthroughs appears in prestigious journals such as *Nature*, *Science* and *The Lancet*.
- Special websites that collate the latest information. For example, in Australia, beauty writers and editors can go to a special directory, called the *Beauty Directory*, which hosts the latest information about new products being launched nationwide.
- Personal visits by journalists to organisations (e.g. factories, warehouses, laboratories) to watch demonstrations. Sometimes an organisation needs to show physically how things are done (e.g. demonstrating robotic equipment in action).
- Follow up on an existing story from another publication. If a story is groundbreaking, then a follow-up confirmation is usually necessary before the journalist republishes the story.

The symbiotic relationship between firms and media organisations

People will always be looking for news, and this will never change. The way they get their news may change (e.g. through iPads and other technology), but the basic thirst for up-to-date news will never be quenched. For this simple reason, media organisations will always be looking for stories to tell.

Figure 9.1 illustrates the symbiotic relationship between the media organisation and the firm. By 'symbiotic', we mean that both parties need each other. Media organisations (e.g. newspaper and TV stations) create news in order to increase or maintain their readership or viewership. The larger the audience, the more the media can charge for their advertising. Since consumers avoid advertising,[23] it is imperative that media publications have good content. But where does content come from? The answer is that it can come from the firms! Media organisations need firms to provide a staple of newsworthy stories for their publications. These stories are the 'raw materials' that media organisations can turn into news, which people buy to read. One 1970s study found that about 48.7% of newspaper articles originated from press releases;[24] a more recent study yielded a similar figure of 52.2%.[25]

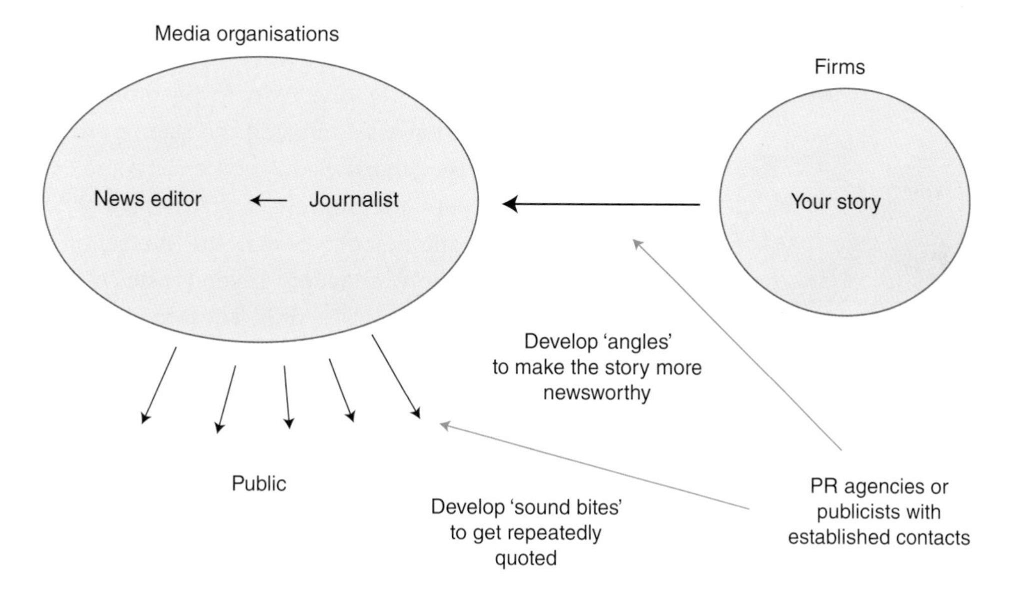

Figure 9.1 The symbiotic relationship between firms and media organisations

Firms, on the other hand, rely on media organisations to help publicise their stories. The first and most important advantage of this is that the firm does not have to pay for the media exposure. The second advantage is that through the reach of the media organisation more people will come to know about the firm (or its brands). If the story of the firm (or its brands) is newsworthy, it will be repeated in other publications, which increases the reach still further. Although there are other ways to disseminate news to the public – for example, through the firm's own website – the most important route is still through established media organisations.

Figure 9.1 shows the firm as the originator (or story source), but the same model can be applied at the industry level. Here, instead of just one firm, it would be the whole industry (e.g. automobile industry or the teacher's union). Similarly, the model can apply to political organisations. The government is especially reliant on the media to get its message out to the public and help win elections. (See the Further Thinking section later in this chapter for more discussion of political marketing.)

In summary, the firm and the news organisation need each other – they are symbiotic. Once we understand this principle, we can easily see why it is always important to craft the firm's (or brand) story in as interesting a way as possible: to maximise the probability of getting a free editorial placement. This is called publicity.

THE FATHER OF MARKETING-ORIENTED PR: DANIEL EDELMAN

The father of marketing-oriented PR is Daniel Edelman (see figure 9.2), who founded the conglomerate PR agency Edelman in 1952, leaving an enormous legacy when he passed away.[26] Edelman conceived PR (not advertising) as the overarching communication function for the firm. He demonstrated his insight and prowess when harnessing PR for his first client, Toni & Co., using twins to promote at-home permanent-wave products. His key idea was for one twin to be professionally coiffed at a salon using the salon's products, and the other styled at home using the Toni & Co. perm. He then challenged the public to tell the difference between the hairstyles. The campaign engaged several sets of twins around the US, and adopted the slogan 'Which twin has the Toni?' It was a great success and marked the beginning of what we now call 'marketing-oriented PR'.

Figure 9.2 Daniel Edelman

Modern-day IMC sees PR as one of many communication tools, but Edelman originally had a larger vision for PR as a discipline – namely, to serve all the communications functions of a firm (of which advertising was a subset). So, he may be considered one of the fathers of IMC, with PR taking the front seat.

Making the story newsworthy and quotable

Figure 9.1 also shows that news organisations act as gatekeepers of public information. Getting a story published is a two-step process. First, the journalist has to select your story (among many) to write about and, second, he or she then needs to convince the news editor that it is newsworthy. One 1970s study found that 67% of press releases were rejected outright because they were deemed to be unworthy of reporting.[27] For a story to be newsworthy it must contain elements that are deviant, and it must also have some social significance for the public.[28] 'Deviant', in this context, refers to people, ideas and events (known as 'PIE') that are unexpected, novel or unusual. They might be political, economic, cultural in nature, or in fact anything that can affect the wellbeing of the public.

Research shows that news releases that are deviant are 60 times more likely to be reported than those that are not. Similarly, news releases that are socially significant are eight times more likely to be reported.[29] Further, news that is both deviant and socially significant accounts for 62% of the variance of prominence in reporting on radio and 43% for TV.[30] Thus it is important for a marcoms manager to craft a press release that is newsworthy. If not, it is best to enlist the help of a PR professional to find the right 'angle'.

Beside newsworthiness, press releases should contain 'sound bites'. These are quotes that are witty, relevant and likely to be repeated by the public. The sound bite is especially pertinent in politics, where very often news organisations will reduce the political message into an eight-second saying.[31] One of the most famous political sound bites is 'It's the economy, stupid', coined by James Carville, the campaign strategist of Bill Clinton when he ran against President George HW Bush in the 1992 US election. It tapped into the zeitgeist at that time because the country was in recession. The phrase has been repeated and recycled countless times over the years. Short of a good sound bite, a catchy headline can also serve the same purpose. In media terms, a newsworthy story increases exposure (i.e. its reach) while a good sound bite increases the probability of the story being repeated (i.e. its frequency).

Of course, the critical question is whether it is possible to continually interest the media (and get free publicity) if a brand is already well established, as, for such a brand, there is nothing deviant or significant to arouse media interest. Indeed, meta-analysis of previous studies shows that for established brands, advertising is more effective than publicity.[32] Customers of established brands also prefer advertising, which is invariably positive, to reinforce their beliefs about the brands. However, this does not mean there is no room for positive publicity about established brands. For instance, every time there is a new campaign, game, app or promotion, we should exploit marketing-oriented PR first, simply because it is three times more credible – and cheaper – than advertising. Someone who understands this is the British entrepreneur Richard Branson.

Richard Branson's publicity strategy

Imagine that you are an entrepreneur who has just started an airline. You have no money to advertise, so what do you do to raise the awareness of your new airline? You could try to generate your own publicity by engaging in publicity stunts. That is precisely what Richard Branson did. When he started Virgin Airlines, he could not compete with the other airlines such as British Airways, but Sir Freddie Laker, a founder of another low-cost airline (Laker Airways), gave him some important advice:

> ... you got to use yourself and get out there and realise that if you dress up in a captain's outfit when you launch your airline, you will get on the front page. If you turn up in ordinary business clothes, you'll be lucky to get a mention. Remember photographers got a job to do ... If you don't give them a photograph that will get them on the front page, they won't turn up to your next event.[33]

Richard Branson has never forgotten that advice and clearly understands the symbiotic relationship between media and firms – as a result, he is perhaps the best exponent of marketing-oriented press relations today. Certainly, no other CEOs have matched Mr Branson's proficiency in this field. He has stated:

> Using yourself ... and talk about [the brand] is a lot cheaper and more effective than a lot of advertising. In fact, if you do it correctly, it can beat advertising hands down and save tens of millions of dollars.[34]

Indeed, according to a 1995 study, Virgin Atlantic spent only 2% of its turnover on advertising, well below the industry average of 5–7 %.[35] So, we can learn from how Richard Branson has done it. Figure 9.3 shows some examples of his attention-seeking activities, and figure 9.4 summarises his publicity tactics. These pictures are a testament to his media skills.

Figure 9.3 Richard Branson's ability to draw attention

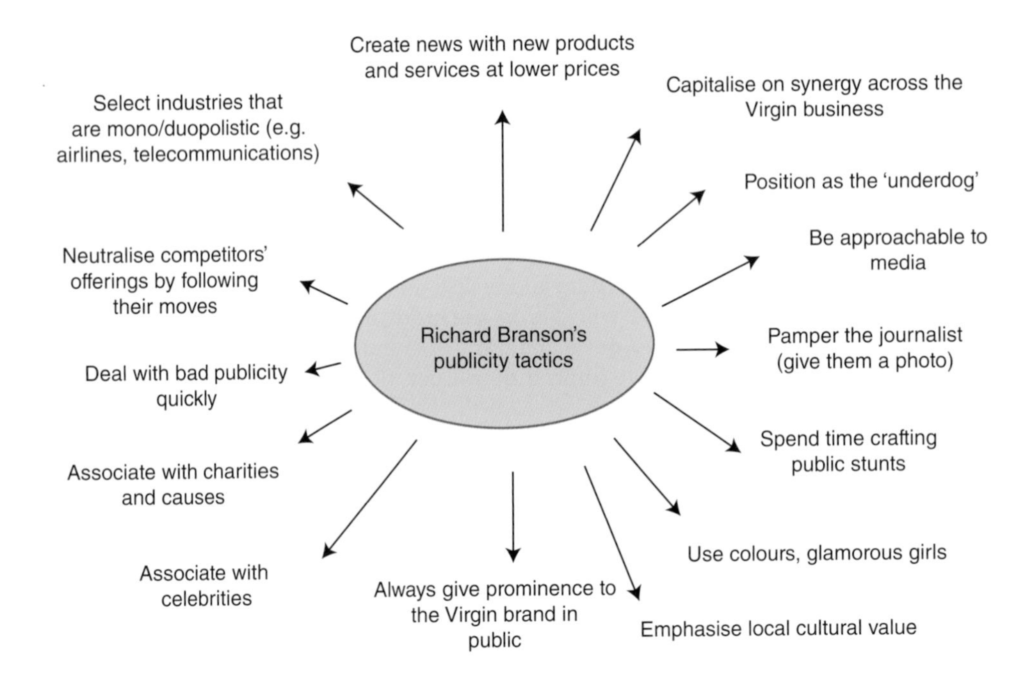

Figure 9.4 The many publicity tactics of Richard Branson

Since taking on the establishment is likely to incur the wrath of major players, Branson is acutely aware of always maintaining good relations with the media so that they will be more reticent in attacking him or the Virgin brand. To this end, he is always approachable to the media and makes it a point to always pamper the journalists. Further, if there is a hint of bad publicity, Virgin is quick to deal with it. This is what Branson said about his communications director and the importance of PR in this regard:

> I suspect in most companies, the PR person is down [at] number 20 in the pecking order . . . But here, he is fighting incredibly important battles. If a negative story . . . in the press is not dealt with fast, it can damage the brand. And so we put enormous weight on our public relations people.[36]

Virgin's contribution to various charities and causes also helps create a reservoir of goodwill that helps buffer the brand against attack (see the discussion of cause-related marketing and corporate social responsibility in the next section).

CASE STUDY 9.2 TRUMP AND THE ART OF OBTAINING FREE MEDIA

Figure 9.5 Donald Trump at a rally

Donald Trump is probably the shrewdest of all US politicians in terms of generating free publicity for himself. One could even argue that he is probably the greatest exponent of this art ever(!), even more so than Richard Branson of Virgin, discussed earlier. When Trump first announced that he was running for the presidency on 16 June 2015, many dismissed this as a publicity stunt, a ploy to enhance the Trump brand, which through licensing generates large revenue. Yet he stunned his critic by not only winning the nomination for the Republican Party, but also defeating Hillary Clinton for the presidency. And he is the first US president to win office without any prior political experience; his claim to fame is hosting two top-rating shows in the US called *The Apprentice* and *The Celebrity Apprentice* between 2004 and 2015.

So how did Trump win the US presidency? While there has been much debate about this,[37] one undeniable factor was Trump's ability to generate free publicity using Twitter. This social media tool allowed him to instantly communicate directly with his followers, bypassing the gatekeepers of traditional media like the network TV channels. And since his comments were often bombastic and controversial, they were retweeted, generating more publicity, which then compelled traditional media channels to report them. Since news networks were also looking to report controversial stories to increase their ratings, Trump was a godsend. Or to put it differently, Trump was able to use social media (i.e. Twitter) to generate earned media from traditional channels, which has greater reach! (see discussion later on memes). Interestingly, because of Trump's ability to continually generate controversy, the sales of *New York Times* and *Washington Post* actually went up[38] at a time when the circulation of most newspapers actually declined – controversy sells newspapers!

However, to win the US presidency required money. A lot of money. Hillary Clinton was able to raise US$1.2 billion compared to Trump's US$280 million. Clinton had 5138 staffers in 15 states, while Trump only had 1409 staffers in 16 states. Clinton also spent US$29.6 million on advertising compared to Trump's US$14.9 million. Therefore, on paper, Hillary Clinton had a much higher marketing firepower with better organised groundtroops. Yet, Trump won a stunning victory on 8 November 2016 with 304 Electoral College votes compared to Clinton's 227.

There is little doubt that Trump's ability to use Twitter made it possible to surpass Clinton's decidedly larger advantage in marketing budget. Table 9.2 compares Trump's ability to generate free media exposure to that of other politicians.[39] Trump's free media value exceeded Clinton's and even that of Obama, who was the first candidate to embrace social media in his bid for presidency back in 2012. And Trump held to his advantage over Clinton right to the end before Election Day.

Table 9.2 Amount of free media generated in two US presidential elections in 2012 and 2016 by various candidates

2012 election	
Barack Obama	US$1.15 billion
Mitt Romney	US$0.70 billion
2016 election	
Donald Trump	US$4.96 billion
Hillary Clinton	US$3.24 billion

Furthermore, Trump was able to steadily grow his Twitter following from 5.7 million in January 2016 to 13 million by Election Day (November). Clinton's equivalent growth on Twitter was 5 million to 10.3 million. In terms of free media from the use of Twitter alone, Trump was able to generate US$402 million of free media compared to Clinton's US$166 million.[40]

To summarise, it is safe to conclude that Donald Trump is an exponent of obtaining free publicity. Although one cannot conclude that this alone was enough for him to clinch the win over Hillary Clinton, it is an important factor.

DISCUSSION QUESTIONS

1. Why do you think Twitter was so effective for Donald Trump compared to say other social media?
2. Why do you think Hillary Clinton was not able to obtain as much free media as Donald Trump, even though she also used Twitter and had a far greater marketing budget and volunteers?
3. Richard Branson was clever in using events (but not Twitter) to generate free publicity for the Virgin brand. Can you name a business owner who is well-versed in using Twitter to publicise his or her company? Give a recent example.

CORPORATE REPUTATION

This section tackles corporate reputation and sponsorship together because they are closely related to each other.

Corporate image advertising

One direct way of improving the corporate reputation of the firm is to advertise its image. But what constitutes a good corporate reputation? Table 9.3 lists and defines a set of possible corporate attributes.[41] The first six are the most commonly discussed in the literature. The seventh, called 'familiarity' (i.e. the familiarity of the corporate name), is important because it provides an identity to which all the positive aspects of attributes 1 to 6 must be linked.

Table 9.3 What is corporate reputation?

Corporate attribute	Definition
1. Social and environmental responsibility	Ethical, environmentally responsible, cares for employees, a desirable place to work
2. Financial performance	Financially sound, with a proven track record
3. Management and corporate strategy	Competent top management, a clear vision for the future, groundbreaking
4. Emotional appeal	Liked by stakeholders and the public
5. Innovative capability	A leader in research and development, exploring cutting-edge technologies, with promising products in the pipeline
6. Product and services	High-quality products and services, reliable, value for money
7. Familiarity	A well-known company (or brand name)

However, there is an exception. If a firm is in what can be considered a distasteful industry, such as tobacco, pornography or the weapons industry, it will lack some of the attributes listed above. For instance, BAE Systems, one of the major global producers of arms, can hardly be deemed ethical. For corporations like these, it can be beneficial to keep a low profile with the general public and avoid raising familiarity through activities such as corporate advertising.[42]

Corporate advertising can take many forms. The most straightforward is that of image corporate advertising. Here, the focus of the advertising is on the firm's characteristics, and not solely on its product or service.

LOOKING AFTER CORPORATE REPUTATION

Looking after the corporate name is important because there are many advantages to having a good corporate reputation. For instance, a firm that enjoys good corporate reputation will:[43]

- be perceived to be more trustworthy
- be able to sell more goods or services
- have more bargaining power in channels
- more easily make appointments for its sales personnel
- be able to access better suppliers or service providers
- achieve greater credibility in advertising
- attract more and better job applicants
- find it easier to convince investors to raise capital
- create more effective CSR initiatives
- be able to access better joint venture partners
- ensure that consumers and journalists are reluctant to accept negative information about the firm.

When we have both brands and corporate reputation to advertise, how do we decide which should take precedence? Corporate advertising is more important when:[44]

- stakeholders do not see much of the product's advertising
- the corporate name is an important attribute in the purchase decision
- the product cycle is long (e.g. more than 12 months), in which case corporate advertising helps reinforce the brand
- issue management is important
- employees need to be thanked (it is better to do this publicly).

WILL YOUR REPUTATION SURVIVE A PANDEMIC?

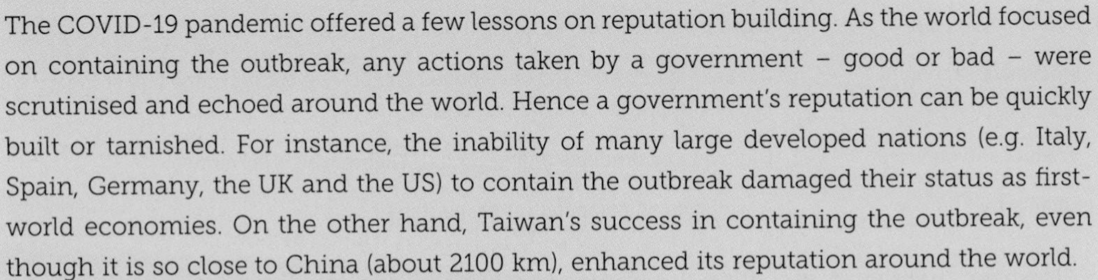

The COVID-19 pandemic offered a few lessons on reputation building. As the world focused on containing the outbreak, any actions taken by a government – good or bad – were scrutinised and echoed around the world. Hence a government's reputation can be quickly built or tarnished. For instance, the inability of many large developed nations (e.g. Italy, Spain, Germany, the UK and the US) to contain the outbreak damaged their status as first-world economies. On the other hand, Taiwan's success in containing the outbreak, even though it is so close to China (about 2100 km), enhanced its reputation around the world.

The pandemic also created unlikely celebrities. In Australia, for instance, Dr Norman Swan, a paediatrician by training, became a household name with his daily broadcasts and tweets[45] on COVID-19. Some believed that it was his sharp critique of the Australian government that prompted an early lockdown, which saved lives.[46] Similarly, the Taiwanese digital minister, Audrey Tang (Tang Feng), became a cult figure when she devised an application that allowed Taiwanese people to monitor the availability of masks in pharmacies nationwide.[47] This knowledge reduced people's anxiety.

In summary, a pandemic crisis will swamp other news. This can sometimes have a perverse effect. For instance, prior to the outbreak, Australia's Morrison government was reeling from the criticism of its sports funding scandal.[48] But once the outbreak occurred, the scandal was forgotten. The reputation of the Australian government rested entirely on its handling of the outbreak, rather than its earlier scandal.

Cause-related marketing and corporate social responsibility

One of the problems with corporate image advertising is that it may appear to be self-serving, and it is usually quite dull and boring. Consumers, who gain nothing by watching such ads, may also think that the firm is simply boasting. However, there are other ways to build reputation without resorting to image-based advertising, one of which is to publicise the good things the firm is doing.

Many firms choose to support a worthwhile cause, often a charitable cause (e.g. a literacy program, a cancer research program or an art event), so that the organisation is perceived as a good corporate citizen and/or socially responsible. This can take the form of sponsorship (which we will discuss below) or a simple philanthropic donation. If this is communicated in an altruistic way, consumers are less likely to be sceptical about the firm's motives.

Such initiatives form a domain known as 'corporate social responsibility' (CSR), and examples of CSR include:[49]

- community services (e.g. support for health programs and education)
- social inclusion programs (e.g. support of people with disabilities)
- employee help (e.g. support for the personal development of employees)
- environmental responsibility (e.g. enforcing pollution controls)
- quality-enhancement activities (e.g. ensuring safety in products)
- ethical overseas operations (e.g. support for fair labour practices).

A socially responsible firm should be 'achieving commercial success in ways that honour ethical values and respect people, communities and the natural environment'.[50] Thus, CSR encompasses more than pushing a cause. It is a set of values that signals a firm's 'status and activities with respect to its perceived societal obligations'.[51] It is thus a way of doing business in which the firm delivers economic, social and environmental benefits for all stakeholders in a sustainable and responsible way. Investors are also increasingly evaluating a company's long-term financial performance through the lens of environmental, social and governance (or ESG) principles.[52]

Interestingly, consumers are generally not aware of a firm's CSR activities, but those who are, usually support it. This leads to a higher level of brand attitude and purchase intentions, which leads to better financial performance.[53] However, this does not mean that consumers are willing to pay a premium for the products or services of firms that have an active CSR profile. In fact, they are quite intolerant if the quality of the product or service drops because of the firm's effort in CSR.[54] So, such initiatives can only act as a tiebreaker if the quality of the products or services is as good as those of the competitors. Since most products and services are on parity, firms that engage in CSR initiatives are likely to gain the upper hand, provided the target audience is made aware of them. One recent study, for instance, found that millennials are willing to pay more for a piece of clothing if they know that the manufacturer follows ethical business practices, donates money to charities, takes care of the environment and adopts fair labour practices.[55]

Research shows that other factors also help facilitate the increase in corporate reputation through CSR initiatives. Let's look at them now.

TIGHT FIT BETWEEN THE CSR INITIATIVE AND THE IMAGE OF THE FIRM

By 'fit' we mean that there is a natural association between the firm and the cause. For example, the firm Johnson & Johnson has a better fit with the Red Cross than with Greenpeace. The Red Cross is about saving human lives, while Greenpeace is about saving whales.

Research suggests that the tighter the fit, the more consumers will like the firm and be more willing to donate to the cause.[56] On the other hand, if the fit is loose or non-existent, the association will lead not only to a blurring of the firm's positioning but also to consumers questioning the basis of the initiative. Their counterarguments will lead to a more negative attitude towards the firm.[57] With a good partnership fit, CSR is even more effective in raising brand attitude than sales promotion or sponsorship because it is considered to be less manipulative.[58]

ALTRUISTIC ATTRIBUTIONS

Fit by itself, however, is not enough. Consumers must perceive the contribution to be altruistic or the firm's motives are sincere.[59] The more altruistic the perceived link, the more likely the firm will benefit from the association.[60] But consider the following association: Drinkwise, a non-profit organisation, was set up to try to encourage the responsible consumption of alcohol in Australia. However, when the public realised that most of the Drinkwise board members came from the alcohol industry (e.g. manufacturers of wine and spirits), there was a backlash because of a perceived conflict of interest and lack of altruism.[61] In this instance, although there was a tight fit between Drinkwise and its anti-alcohol initiatives in the sense that both had a connection to alcohol, the public viewed the situation with great suspicion. Thus, more than fit, we also want consumers to evoke altruistic attributions.

A GOOD REPUTATION

One important but underrated benefit of having a good reputation is that it makes consumers, especially brand loyalists, more reluctant to accept negative information about the sponsor. To achieve this, a firm needs to build up a good track record in their CSR initiatives. Further, these activities should be carried out proactively and genuinely, not as a short-term defensive action in response to bad publicity. Only then can a firm build up a reservoir of goodwill to help to buffer the firm in times of crisis (we will discuss this below). The greater the reputation of the firm, the more it will benefit from CSR initiatives.[62]

STRONG PERSONAL IDENTIFICATION

Finally, it helps if there is a personal connection between the target audience and the nature of the CSR initiative. For instance, a person whose mother died of cancer is more likely to view a firm's support of cancer research more favourably than a person who has no personal connection with the disease. Thus, the more the target audience can identify with the cause, the more likely the person will view the firm's association more favourably.[63] The target audience is also more willing to donate to the cause.[64]

Brand purpose advertising

A closely related idea to CSR, but newer, is the notion of brand purpose. In the search for differentiation, firms are now considering a new communication approach in which they convey a higher purpose other than profit. These higher purpose-led strategies allow a brand to show its humane side. For instance, when there was an outbreak of hepatitis in 2017 caused by imported frozen berries, Australia's largest fruit processor and cannery, SPC, seized the opportunity to start a new initiative called #MyFamilyCan.[65] Since 70% of Australians say they value the provenance of their food, what better way to demonstrate the provenance than to tell the heart-warming stories of SPC farmers and their families on its packaging, all four million items (see figure 9.6). Supported by TV advertising during a football match on Anzac Day, pre-roll videos on social media, point-of-sale support and PR initiatives, it sparked a nation-wide conversation. Market share reached 24% (from 20%), and weekly sales volumes grew 26% above the objective. Purpose-led campaigns thus allowed a firm to show their ambition and beliefs in how they can change the world for the better.[66]

Figure 9.6 Farmers and their families on packaging

While there are several case studies to demonstrate this new way of positioning a brand is promising, these case studies are biased because only the successful ones are publicised. We do not know how many firms have attempted purpose-led campaigns and failed. There are currently no studies to systematically study this new approach, although we suspect the boundary conditions are very similar to that of CSR.

Figure 9.7 Jess Gallagher, global ambassador for Vision Australia

Advocacy advertising

This form of advertising encourages the public to adopt a certain position on an issue. For instance, Vision Australia wants to help Australians who are blind or have low vision to have a strong voice so that they have equal rights as citizens. They enlisted the help of Jess Gallagher, an Australian Paralympian medallist, to help publicise the cause. She is now their global ambassador who happens to be legally blind due to a rare eye disease.

Advocacy advertising can be controversial because the position being advocated by the firm can be self-serving. For instance, in 1974, Mobil created a campaign based on the need for offshore drilling in order to alleviate the energy crisis. Advocacy advertising can also be used by interest groups to influence political outcomes. For example, the American Association of Retired Persons created a campaign to emphasise the importance of social security entitlement, aimed at influencing the public and hence the US Congress in an election year.[67]

Sponsorship

Sponsorship is another way to build corporate reputation (and brands). It can be defined as the payment a firm makes to a property, object or party (e.g. a sports team, a cultural or social event, or a cause-related program) in exchange for the right to commercially exploit the association.

Many things can be sponsored, from an event or team to an organisation or even a non-profit program. Sponsorship has been steadily growing and in 2018, the global spend was US$65.8 billion.[68] In North America the majority of sponsor dollars (about 69%) went to sporting events, mainly because of increasing media coverage of such events. Other reasons for this growth include higher advertising costs, zapping and increasing restrictions of what can be advertised.[69] Sponsoring global sporting events (e.g. Olympics) is also another way of building global brands quickly.[70] But this is not cheap. The cost to The Coca Cola Company, McDonald's and Adidas of their official association with the London Olympics (2012) was more than £700 million.[71] In the Rio Olympics (2016), each of the global sponsors paid US$120 million and with 11 partners, the Olympics collected a cool US$1.32 billion![72]

Sponsorship is popular for both the sponsor and the sponsored party (or the sponsored individual) because of the benefits that can be accrued by being linked to each other – it is a 'win–win' situation. The sponsored group or individual benefits from the financial support (whether cash or in kind) from the sponsor, while the sponsor enjoys the promotional value that comes with the partnership. Some of the benefits to the sponsor are shown in the box below.

BENEFITS OF SPONSORSHIP

- Exposure – some sporting events like the Olympics offer massive audiences worldwide, increasing the reach significantly.

- Lack of clutter – unlike advertising, sponsorship allows the brand to 'shine through', with much less clutter.
- Opportunity to build image – through evaluative conditioning, the sponsor (e.g. Steggles chicken) will benefit from the positive associations of the sponsored group or individual (e.g. Sydney Roosters football team).
- Differentiation – the sponsor is able to differentiate itself from its competition.
- Exclusion of competition – exclusive sponsorship allows the sponsor to prevent competitive access to the same promotional opportunities.
- Opportunity to sell goods or services – exclusivity can extend to goods or services sold; for instance, if The Coca Cola Company is the official sponsor of a sporting event (e.g. the Olympics), it may demand exclusive rights to serve patrons, so that they can only buy the products of The Coca Cola Company.
- Opportunity to transcend cultural borders – major sporting events, such as World Cup soccer and the Olympics, allow global brands to build brand stature without having to worry about local cultural issues (e.g. language differences).
- CSR – the sponsoring firm is able to demonstrate its corporate citizenship if the property of sponsorship is cause-related.
- Access to contact details of patrons – with some event sponsorships, the firms access the contact details of the patrons and follow up after the event with an offering (e.g. through direct mail).

One sporting celebrity who is very proficient in the use of social media to help his sponsors is the soccer star Cristiano Ronaldo (see figure 9.8). Not only is he the most expensive soccer player on the planet, he has a total of 277 million fans(!) across the three social media platforms of Facebook, Instagram and Twitter. He has the single biggest number of fans compared to anyone on the planet, which he has parlayed to lucrative sponsorship deals (e.g. Nike, Herbalife, Tag Heaur and Abbott Labs). In 2017, he generated 580 posts on behalf of his brand partners. At the end of 2016, Nike signed a lifetime sponsorship deal with him reported to be worth US$1 billion.[73]

Figure 9.8 Cristiano Ronaldo holds the record for the highest number of fans on social media

THE RISK OF AMBUSH MARKETING

Although there are many benefits for sponsors, they do not automatically accrue. One of the biggest issues is that non-official sponsors will also try to capitalise on an event, which is sometimes called 'ambush' marketing. For instance, during the 1996 Atlanta Olympics, Nike (not the sponsor for the event) bought a significant amount of billboard space around sporting venues to display its logo. It is no wonder then that, for the 2012 London Olympics, a new law was passed in the UK to allow firms or businesses to be fined for such ambush practices.

'Brand police' were dispatched around London to ensure that the word 'Olympics', the Olympics symbol and logo, and even the words 'London Games' were not used without official sanction.

In order to protect their investment, it is imperative that the official sponsors put in additional resources to publicise their sponsorship. This includes additional advertising, PR exercises, product sampling, and other activities, which can add up to two or three times the cost of the original sponsorship fees.

None of this stops a competitor from increasing its advertising during an event or, indeed, from cleverly engaging in publicity stunts to associate itself with the event. And if they do a better job, they will win the hearts and minds of the viewers. For instance, Nike, which was not the principal London Olympics sponsor, launched a campaign called 'Find Your Greatness' in 25 countries, timed to coincide with the opening ceremony. The ad showed ordinary people in towns around the world striving to do their best, exercising, jogging and slogging away, but still persevering to achieve personal greatness. Adidas' ad, called 'Take the stage', on the other hand, featured short clips of elite British athletes and a voice-over emphasising the importance of the mental concentration needed to compete on the world stage. Cleverly, Nike also developed bright neon yellow-green shoes, which 400 Nike-sponsored athletes wore throughout the event.

In the end, Nike did a better job. Among those who identified the two brands as sponsors in the US, more people said Nike (37%) was the Olympic sponsor than Adidas (24%). Nike also had more social media activities during the Olympics with more than 16 020 tweets associated with the words, 'Nike' and 'Olympics' compared to Adidas with 9300 tweets. Nike's #findgreatness hashtag had 7000 more Tweets than Adidas' #takethestage. Nike also added twice as many Facebook fans as Adidas.[74] No prize for guessing how Adidas, the principal Olympic sponsor, felt about Nike's tactics and success.

EVALUATION OF THE SPONSOR (NOT THE PROPERTY)

A sponsor needs to evaluate the effectiveness of their sponsorship, given the level of their investment. The assessment of its brand awareness, image, sales, number of website hits, social media buzz and even the number of job applications or investors' sentiments should be tracked continuously (see chapter 12 for more discussion of campaign tracking). We might expect these sponsor-related indicators to increase during the sponsorship, and we would also expect this increase to be more for the sponsoring brand (e.g. Adidas) than the non-sponsored, competing brand (e.g. Nike). In this way, we can check whether ambush marketing has affected us.

It should be noted that the tracking should be about the focal brand (e.g. 'Coca-Cola') – that is, about the sponsor – and that it is not muddled up with the sponsored event (e.g. the Olympics) or individual or group (e.g. Manchester United FC). It is irrelevant whether the awareness (or the image) of the property increases. As such, the property should not even be mentioned when assessing the focal brand. We simply track those brand indicators in the normal way; that is, as if no sponsorship has occurred. If the sponsorship is effective, the indicators should go up during the period of sponsorship, and hopefully remain up afterwards as well.

WHEN DOES SPONSORSHIP WORK?

Research shows that the conditions under which sports sponsorship is effective tend to be very similar to sponsorship of causes already discussed in this chapter. That is, there must be:

- a tight fit between the sponsor and the property
- a perception that the sponsor is altruistic
- a good sponsor reputation
- good identification between the target audience and the sponsored event, individual or group.

Under such circumstances, positive effects will flow through to the sponsoring brand or firm.

Of all these conditions, fit is the most important. When there is a good fit, the associations of the sponsored event will 'rub off' onto the sponsor.[75] In other words, the image of the sponsoring brand (e.g. 'Coca-Cola') will take on some of the associations of the sponsored event (e.g. the Olympics). Another point to remember is it can be tempting for an organisation to sponsor events that appeal to the upper management (e.g. the firm's CEO), instead of those to which the target audience relates.

In the case of team sponsorship (e.g. a soccer club), an additional requirement is desirable, which is that the sponsoring team should be a winning side, and preferably have a key star player who can feature.[76] It does not help the image of the sponsor if the team consistently loses in competition. Fans bask in the glory of their winning team, which then spills over to the sponsor (such as a brewery) when the team wins. The fans are also more likely to buy the sponsor's products (such as beer) when their team wins. The flipside is that fans of the rival team will not![77]

But it is unusual for any sports team, even the good ones, to win continuously – they have to lose some time. However, if the sports team has many die-hard fans, they will still buy the brand despite the team's poor performance. One recent study into soccer by Almaiman found precisely that.[78] Using an innovative choice-modelling technique, he discovered that team identification has a slightly stronger effect in influencing brand choice than team performance (about 13% stronger). And this is true even if the brand is not a prominent one. The lesson is this: it pays for management to always find ways of building relationships with fans so that more will come to identify with the team, and hence choose the sponsored brands.

CRISIS COMMUNICATION

Occasionally, organisations get into trouble, including product failures, appalling customer service, sexual harassment in the workplace, abuse of financial or market power, manipulation of stock prices and interest rates, or just plain incompetence. The most memorable is when a passenger was dragged off United Airlines.[79] It went viral on social media and made headlines in traditional media.

If bad publicity is spiralling out of control, the firm often experiences great uncertainty about what to do next. Therefore, always assume that a crisis is going to happen, and hence be prepared for it. This means one should always monitor the social media to see if there is a negative trending in the firm's reputation. If there is an increased activity, then be proactively ready to respond with prepared material, following policy guidelines.

Complicating this issue is the brand architecture of the firm. There are two main ways of branding the portfolio of products or services. When all the products or services use the same brand, usually that of the corporate name, it is called 'branded-house' architecture. For instance, Hewlett-Packard brands all its products in the same way, from a printer to a computer. One major advantage of this architecture is that the cost of advertising can be amortised across many product categories, since there is no need to advertise separate brands. However, the downside is that, should one product become defective or fail badly (leading to harm or death), the negative effects may spill over to the other products, since they all share the same brand (i.e. a single corporate name). The corporate name itself will also be severely tarnished, as in the case of Toyota when it had to recall eight million cars worldwide in 2009–10 due to a faulty acceleration mechanism. Many service organisations, such as banks and airlines, that have this type of brand architecture suffer from the same weakness. Sometimes the whole service sector can suffer, as in the recent banking royal commission which uncovered stories of malfeasance and scandals. The reputation of the entire financial industry is tarnished.[80] It will take years for the industry's reputation to recover.

For this reason, it is sometimes better for a firm to own many individual brands – as in the case of Procter & Gamble where each product has its own distinctive brand name and personality – this is sometimes called the 'house-of-brands' architecture. Any failure or disappointment in one brand is less likely to spill over to the others.

During a crisis, the usefulness of PR comes into focus, more so than any other IMC tool. The firm must respond immediately, often through interviews and press conferences, the forte of PR. The reputation of a firm, which takes years to build, can quickly dissipate if it does not respond appropriately. So, how can we handle a crisis through PR?

Refute and deny

If the transgression is not serious (or the allegation of wrongdoing is unsubstantiated or not credible), then having a good pre-crisis corporate reputation can buffer the firm from further reputational decline. Under such circumstances, the firm can get away with denying the wrongdoing with its expertise (but not its trustworthiness) intact. Of course, if the firm is innocent, then it should *always* refute and defend itself. Remaining silent or refusing to comment (i.e. neither confirming nor denying guilt) implies a reflection of guilt.[81] This is the worst thing for an organisation to do to protect its reputation. So respond immediately, with no more than a 24-hour delay.

Apologise and promise not to reoffend

On the other hand, if the transgression is serious (or the allegations of wrongdoing are substantiated or credible), as when a product is recalled due to its harmfulness, then even a good pre-crisis reputation will not protect the firm from negative perceptions. A firm that has a high corporate reputation may be able to avert some of the blame from its management, but this will not reduce the severity of the problem and the subsequent fallout.

Under such circumstances, it is better for a firm to take responsibility and admit to any transgressions. To repair reputational damage, it should sincerely apologise and accept responsibility, express regret for the wrongdoing and, most importantly, make a commitment that the transgression will not occur again. These actions signal honesty and redemption and will help rebuild trust. Legally, though, admission of guilt implies culpability, and this may leave the firm open to lawsuits.

Respond quickly and compassionately; offer compensation if necessary

The firm should always respond quickly, preferably within 24 hours of the transgression. Research shows that the more severe the product harm crisis, the greater will be the decline in the equity of the brand. Further, the better known the brand, the greater its decline.[82] This is because consumers have come to expect more from brands they know well and are therefore disappointed in a transgression. That is why it is important to respond quickly, before any worse publicity ensues. In the response, do not just say, 'we'll look into it'. Rather express regret and sadness about what has transpired, and then share how the firm's policies will be changed so that such transgressions will not happen again.[83]

Compensation or refunds should always be given to affected customers. Such restitution helps lessen dissatisfaction and prevent further damage to the brand. This is especially important in the era of social media, since negative buzz can quickly spread online (see chapter 8).

NATIVE ADVERTISING AND CONTENT MARKETING

We now live in an increasingly complex world and our lives invariably get busier and busier. When we are on the internet, for instance, we become increasingly impatient in trying to find the relevant information we need. As a result, we tend to avoid ads. This has led to the increasing popularity of ad blockers. Gaining consumers' attention has never been harder. At the same time, the growth of the internet and social media has created many newer channels for firms to reach out to consumers; they do not have to rely solely on traditional media. Conversely, consumers can also look for the firm's posted material on the internet. As a result, the internet has now become a depository of information for consumers to search, and this has changed the way they shop. The confluence of these changes has led to the development of two new ways of attracting consumers, native advertising and content marketing.

Native advertising

Native advertising can be defined as a form of un-branded advertorial in which the format is similar to its surrounding editorial so as to ostensibly give the impression that it is created unbiasedly by the publisher for its audience. This often takes the form of an article[84] such that it is not easily distinguishable from the normal editorial and therefore does not ostensibly disrupt the viewing experience of the readers. For this reason, we can say that the advertorial has gone 'native' such that it looks like its editorial environment. In the age of the digital media, this is easy to manipulate. But this form of advertising is also potentially deceptive.

A good example of this occurred in 2013, when the venerable US news organisation The Atlantic Monthly (which was founded in 1857) ran a lead article on its website (theatlantic.com) about the leader of Scientology, David Miscavige. The article praised his vision in expanding Scientology. The only problem was that it was not a genuine editorial but rather a paid advertorial made to look like a normal editorial. The fact that it was the lead article on the website also gave the impression that it was a genuine editorial. It created such a furore that The Atlantic Monthly had to take it down the next day (about 12 hours later) and issue an apology.

One question raised was whether The Atlantic Monthly should have entered into an advertorial agreement with Scientology. Earlier we argued that companies in undesirable industries like weaponry and smoking should minimise their publicity. But if they dared to do so, then it is better that they use a high-credibility news organisation like The Atlantic Monthly to tell their story, rather than low-credibility ones like BuzzFeed. This will give an entity's story more credibility and its message more persuasiveness.[85] So, in that sense Scientology was correct in partnering with The Atlantic Monthly (rather than BuzzFeed). Its image was not likely to be damaged any further, given the fact that it was already negative. However, it is a different story for an established media organisation, as we saw with the furore. What is often forgotten in the debate is that a news organisation is also a brand, with its own loyal readers (i.e. customers), whose trust can be easily lost if its relationships are mismanaged. However, with news becoming digitised, there is always a temptation to engage in native advertising since it is so easy to manipulate.

What was also interesting in this incident is that the words 'sponsor content' were written at the top left-hand side of the article. Research has shown that nobody understands what this means. Furthermore, it is also too small to be noticed; in fact, only 7–18% of consumers could recognise this to be an ad. Using eye-tracking methodology, Wojdynski and Evans found that disclosure statements found above the headline of an advertorial are not noticed. To be noticed, they have to be placed next to the article itself.[86] The American Society of Magazine Editors in 1989 already recommended that all advertorials be labeled as an advertisement (not sponsored content), using text of equal weight and size (not smaller) as the copy. The copy type should also look *different* from that of the surrounding editorial so that readers can differentiate.[87] Research has shown that native advertising works best when consumers are *not* aware that it is advertising.[88] This makes native advertising potentially dangerous. What was also unethical in this case is that all the negative comments found below the article were removed, giving further false impression that the readers approved of its content.[89]

THE PERSUASION KNOWLEDGE MODEL

One may now ask, why are we so susceptible to ads that do not appear as ads? One theory that can account for our vulnerability is our knowledge of persuasion. The basis of this theory is very simple. All of us through socialisation learn that we are always being influenced. Young children are less cognisant of this, but by the age of 12, they clue up. This knowledge, when activated, makes us more vigilant about advertisements. We become more defensive and critical of the selling message and scrutinise it more closely. This results in higher levels of counterarguments which lowers the persuasiveness of the ad.

This model, called the Persuasion Knowledge Model (PKM), was developed by Friestad and Wright.[90] It is a very influential model and has been successfully applied in several areas. For instance, in TV sponsorship studies we find that brand attitude suffers when the sponsorship is disclosed at the start of the ad compared to when there is no disclosure or when the disclosure comes at the end.[91] Disclosure at the beginning activates our persuasion knowledge which then buffers against any subsequent persuasive attempts. In the same way, when an ad is entertaining it distracts viewers from activating their persuasion knowledge, and hence prevents counterargument from occurring. This makes it an effective tactic for low-involvement goods since these are less risky (see chapter 7).

However, the problem with native advertising is that consumers may not know that they were being advertised to. Very often consumers do not even recognise that the article they are reading is indeed an ad. This means that their persuasion knowledge will not be activated, and hence they become more susceptible to being (unethically) influenced. Or to put it in another way, consumers will not be able to detect the perceived deceptiveness of the article, and hence will consider it credible, developing a positive attitude towards the sponsor. This also makes them more willing to tell others (i.e. eWOM) about the article even though it is actually an ad (see figure 9.9).[92]

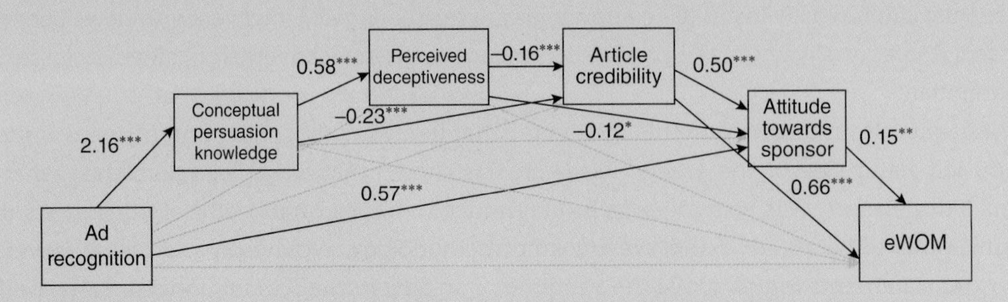

Figure 9.9 A model explaining how recognising a native ad can trigger our persuasion knowledge, leading to a chain of cognition in our minds

Native advertising is here to stay,[93] and the solution to its deceptiveness may lie in consumer education. The more consumers are aware of native advertising, the less effective they become.[94] Alternatively, governments can enforce strict labelling guidelines on native advertising. If these guidelines are violated, heavy financial penalties should be imposed.

Content marketing

If the core principle of marcoms is to build brand equity, then using potentially deceptive tactics like native advertising does not make good business sense. It cannot lay the foundation for a trusting relationship. A better alternative is to provide customers with quality content that they might find educational (e.g. webinars, newsletters, ebooks), entertaining (e.g. videos, movies, podcasts) or something they can interact with (e.g. quizzes, games, apps), and in so doing, come to regard the brand more highly. Content marketing is therefore *not* secretive nor is it promotional, but rather a form of communication that helps fuel the interest of the consumers. It can thus be defined as a form of communication which provides non-promotional content that is educational, entertaining and interactive which consumers find valuable and hence come to regard the brand more highly. This approach is therefore customer-centric where the focus is on the customers themselves and the activities they enjoy. It is *not* about the firm's goods or services per se.

A good practitioner of content marketing is Red Bull. If you were to visit its website (www .redbull.com), it shows very little of the product. Instead it is filled with high-quality images and videos of athletes doing amazing sports, appealing to hard-core sports fans. Red Bull owns its own publishing house which produces this high-quality content. It also publicises various sports events and even has its own TV channel. Finally, Red Bull also collaborates actively with athletes and partners to contribute back to its community of customers. The most celebrated example of this is when Felix Baumgartner made a supersonic freefall from space (see figure 9.10). Red Bull filmed the entire amazing event, as well as all his test jumps and preparations. To date, the video has been watched more than 44 million times, and there is even a website documenting the events and preparations leading up to the feat. In short, it is all about the audience and what makes them passionate. This approach also happens to be consistent with the brand's positioning, 'Red Bull gives you wings'. The implicit message being that you too can become an amazing athlete (i.e. have wings to fly!) *after* you drink Red Bull.

Figure 9.10 Felix Baumgartner about to make the supersonic freefall back to Earth (notice the Red Bull logo on his helmet and jacket)

Another good example is that of River Pools. This is a small-to-medium enterprise in Virginia and Southern Maryland, US, not a giant corporation like Red Bull. During the GFC (in 2008) nobody was buying pools and business was dying. The owner, Marcus Sheridan, saved the business by launching a blog to answer questions about pools.[95] The blog attracted the attention of potential buyers. The blog then expanded to other content (e.g. videos, e-book, guides and articles). Today, it is the most visited pool site in the world, with 20+ million views. It even has a learning centre consisting of 100+ videos and 700+ articles (www.riverpoolsandspas.com). By slowly becoming the 'Wikipedia' of pools, River Pools' business recovered and then prospered. Today it is the leader of fibre-glass pools in the area. So instead of trying to sell pools in its promotions, River Pools became the acknowledged experts of pools and also happened to install them. Like Red Bull, the product was secondary to the promotion activities. In this case, it was all about educating the consumers.

Besides these resources, River Pools also makes it a point to interact with consumers directly through its Facebook page, promising to answer their questions within a day. These questions also give River Pools new insights about customer needs. Finally, River Pools also practises integration by combining old and new content delivered in different formats (see chapter 1 on how cross-publicising of products and complements can create synergy). This is what Marcus Sheridan said:

> I see all content as intricately connected. I may write a blog post today. Tomorrow, I may take that blog post, combine it with five others, and call it an ebook. The next day I might take that ebook and send it to my email list (a list that was built by giving away another free ebook). I might also talk about the thoughts from that blog post through video or during my podcast.

Content marketing is thus totally transparent, providing non-promotional branded material that will fuel the passion of the consumers. While a potentially deceptive tactic like native advertising may work in the short term, it is not a good long-term sustainable strategy because sooner or later it will be found out. Besides, in this digital age consumers expect transparency and security in their dealings with organisations. Generally, being straightforward and honest is a far more sensible strategy.[96]

Finally, the practice of content marketing may not be suitable for everyone because it requires the firm to act more like publishers which require investment and organisational cultural change.

And this must be done correctly because now we are dealing with one's own customers and not simply the audience of another publisher (e.g. The Atlantic Monthly). The firm should view content marketing as a long-term investment and be committed to publishing high-quality material.

However, it should be noted that some organisations use blogs as part of their content strategy. This can be ineffective because disclosure of any financial relationship between the blogger and the sponsored brand generally reduces its persuasiveness.[97] Moreover, bloggers are often driven by their own self-interest in not disclosing this. In a recent Dutch study by Boerman and colleagues (2018)[98] into blogging practices in the Netherlands and the US, it was found that only 15% of the 200 blogs they investigated had a disclosure, and, of these, 64% had the *same* font as the original text which can be potentially deceptive (as discussed above). But the irony is that the study also noted that if a blogger were to acknowledge that their blog was sponsored, but still declared that their opinion was theirs, their credibility would not be affected,[99] and hence they would avoid the risk of being fined. The European Union tends to be stricter than the US on issues of compliance with disclosure, with heavy fines imposed if bloggers fail to declare their financial interest, when and if they are caught.[100]

MANAGERIAL APPLICATION: PUTTING IT TOGETHER

How can we make sense of the different ways of building reputation? Figure 9.11 is a suggested model. It is a 'road-map' to help a marcoms manager systematically plan and integrate the different IMC tools in a coordinated fashion. There are several important points to consider while creating such a plan.

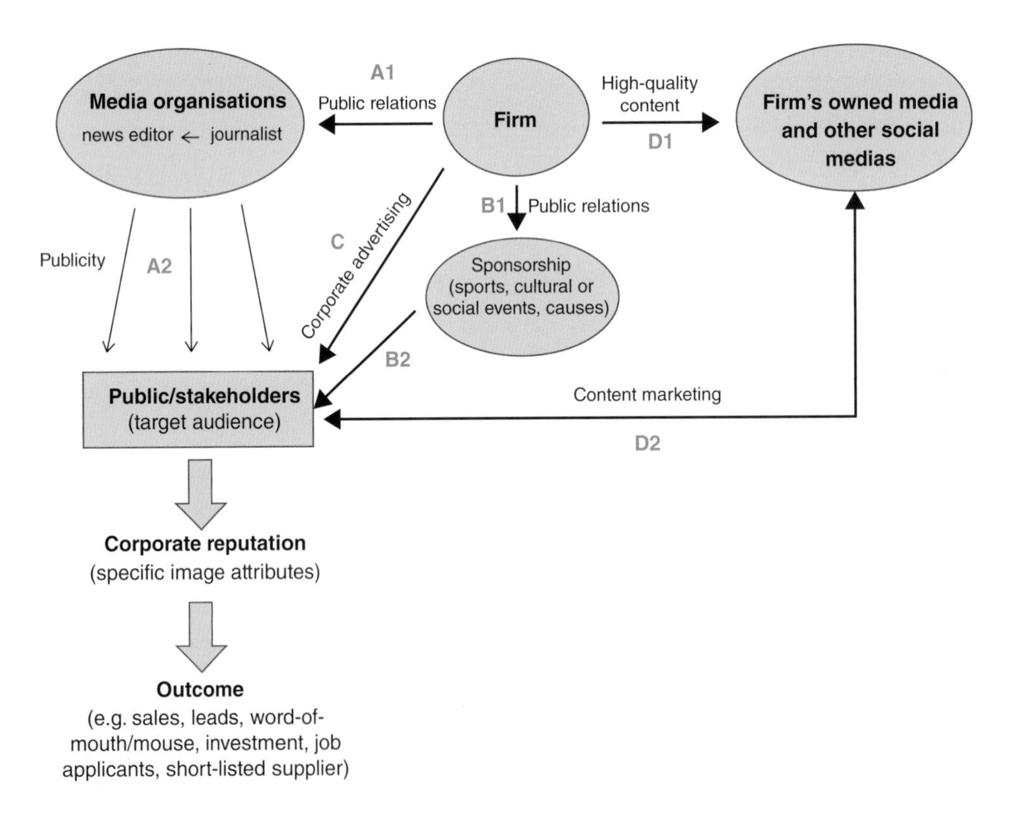

Figure 9.11 How PR, corporate advertising, sponsorship and content marketing affect corporate reputation and outcome

FOCUS ON OUTCOMES

First, we should start with the end in mind – what outcomes do we want to achieve and in which segment of the public? This could be sales, leads, more job applicants or simply being shortlisted as a supplier. Before we start, we have to decide what sort of corporate image can best achieve the desired outcome. This often involves understanding which specific image attribute will be most critical to our success. We have already discussed how to do this in chapter 2, in relation to positioning research.

MONITOR CORPORATE REPUTATION

Further, since the reputation of a corporation is never constant and is a valuable resource, we should constantly monitor it. This involves continuously tracking the opinions of the targeted public offline. In addition, all online conversations on social media sites should be monitored and managed. This is often not done properly; for instance, one study found that only 2% of hotels bothered to respond to criticisms levelled at them on the travel review site Tripadvisor.[101]

PLAN A PATH AND MEASURE ITS EFFECTIVENESS

After we have implemented a way to track corporate reputation offline and online, our next task is to decide which path is the most efficient in achieving the desired outcome. This requires planning. Figure 9.11 shows a number of ways to accomplish this. However, what is effective for one firm may not be so for another. Much depends on the competence of the firm. For instance, in the case of Richard Branson, who has expertise in leveraging marketing-oriented press relations to attain millions of dollars' worth of free publicity, the most efficient route is via paths A1 and A2. We recommend a firm should attempt these paths first because, as the example of Branson clearly demonstrates, if well executed it can be extremely cost-effective. While a firm may not be able to copy all of Branson's tactics, some of them may be worth emulating, for reasons that we discussed earlier.

If we choose paths A1 and A2, then the measure of success often used is the amount of free media publicity, which usually links to the total impressions, frequency and prominence of stories. In print, we can carry out further analysis to assess whether the stories are positive or negative, as well as which publications and/or journalists are responsible for the stories. In summary, the common measures used are:

- total number of impressions across all media
- frequency of mentions across all media
- prominence of mentions
- percentage of positive articles about the firm or brand
- percentage of negative articles about the firm or brand
- ratio of positive to negative articles
- percentage of positive and negative articles by subject
- percentage of positive and negative articles by publication or by journalist.

A firm can also choose to take paths B1 and B2 when seeking to influence the public. Sponsorship is less demanding to execute than paths A1 and A2, and typically involves a multi-year contract with options for renewal. This path provides more stability, although it is not necessarily cheap, but if it is well executed in a consistent manner can build significant goodwill between the firm and the public.

Emirates Airlines is a good example of an organisation that effectively uses sponsorship to build its corporate name. For more than 20 years, the airline has consistently supported major sporting events around the world, including events in soccer (FIFA World Cup), rugby (USA Rugby), tennis (the US Open series), golf (the Australian Open), horse-racing (Melbourne Cup Carnival) and cricket (Cricket World Cup).

A firm can also choose to take path C in influencing the public. This is the least time-consuming path, but can be expensive given the cost of TV advertising during prime time, which is when most corporate advertising occurs. However, in terms of time management, it is the least taxing because much is under the control of the firm.

Interestingly, with the decline of print media readership and the rise of free or low-cost digital hosting platforms (such as YouTube, websites and blogs), many corporations have set up their own media production units in-house to produce content (not just ads) that can be communicated directly to the target public audience.[102] Very often they host the content on their own website or on the brand page of social media (see path D1). By using email, social media posts and blogs,[103] the firms can communicate with their audience directly (e.g. Trump using Twitter), or they can inform the target audience of updates and encourage them to revisit the firm's asset (e.g. website or outlet) to learn more. Consumers obviously can also find the new content through the use of a search engine (hence the double-headed path of D2).

Finally, the marcoms manager should choose the paths (either solely or in combination) that best cater to the strengths of the firm, at minimal cost. Planning is required to ensure all activities are well timed, coordinated, properly sequenced and competently executed, and so forth, to gain maximum impact. Many of the principles of integration discussed in chapter 1 can be applied here. And do not forget these IMC tools can be exploited to quickly build the reputation of a company.

FURTHER THINKING: AGENDA-SETTING

In this section we explore the theory of agenda-setting and how this can be applied in both marketing and political environments.

LEARNING GOALS

After reading this section, you will understand:

- the theory of agenda-setting
- how this can be applied to both marketing and politics.

AGENDA-SETTING AND SALIENCE

Agenda-setting is an important theory in media that is relevant to both marketing and politics. Let's take a marketing example first. Imagine that you are contemplating what to have for lunch. Several options quickly come to mind. You might think about going to McDonald's, Hungry Jack's or Pizza Hut, before opting for Pizza Hut. However, if you thought further about it, other (and perhaps more delicious) options may arise. For instance, you could go to Kentucky Fried Chicken, Subway or even your neighbourhood cafe. But if you stopped thinking after Pizza Hut then you would not consider any of the other options after that. In other words, we never *physically* got to Kentucky Fried Chicken (or Subway or the neighbourhood cafe), because *mentally* we never got there. Sutherland and Galloway have made precisely this point in their discussion of agenda-setting for marketing.[104] Therefore, as the marcoms manager for Kentucky Fried Chicken (or Subway or the neighbourhood cafe), we would want to move the brand up the mental agenda of people's lunch options, preferably right to the top (see chapter 12 on top-of-mind brand awareness).

This is not simply brand awareness, but rather something called 'brand salience' which we discussed in chapter 4. Brand awareness is traditionally defined as the brand that comes to mind when it is cued by the category. Any situation, on the other hand, can cue brand salience. In this example, 'lunch' is the cue, which can cut across many product categories (and hence many category needs).[105] Table 9.4 illustrates the mental agenda of brands cued by our example of 'lunch'. And in chapter 4, we gave an example of how John Lewis built brand salience around 'Christmas time' (see case study 4.1).

Table 9.4 A mental agenda of brands activated by 'lunch'

McDonald's
Hungry Jack's
Pizza Hut
Kentucky Fried Chicken
Subway
Neighbourhood café

We can also see the notion of brand salience at work in the movie business. With the rise of social media, movie studios are deliberately creating buzz in the media by drip-feeding news before a movie is launched. Fuelled by publicity, sometimes with the possibility of an Oscar nomination, the name of the movie is all-pervasive during this time. But the fundamental point is this: as consumers become more empowered and with information widely available, there is no choice but for brands to adapt to this new environment. In other words, the brand becomes mentally accessible and hence salient to consumers.[106] This is sometimes called '360-degree marketing', describing how the brand can have many touch points for the target audience.

In politics, the same thing happens, but around issues facing the country rather than brands. This is much harder to manage because issues change, triggered by what is happening day-to-day in the socio-political environment. Table 9.5 illustrates this. At time 1, the prime minister was preoccupied with illegal immigrants, unemployment and health insurance. But at time 2, the global financial crisis hit, and this was the only salient issue. This then morphed into banking failure and corporate greed in time 3. Finally, in time 4, the salient issues changed to a more positive tone about the booming economy, the Olympics and education. Since, as in these examples, issues are constantly changing, politicians must be nimble in deciding how to deal with them. This is where PR is an effective instrument. Advertising in this context will be too slow to be effective (even if it is allowed). The speed at which issues change is now exacerbated by the internet and a 24-hour news cycle, seven days a week. For this reason, the media will continue to hold, if not increase, its considerable power in influencing the agenda of what people think about in relation to politics. This is where the theory of agenda-setting becomes important.

Table 9.5 Issues change over time

Time 1	Time 2	Time 3	Time 4
illegal immigrants	global financial crisis	banking failure	booming economy
unemployment		corporate greed	Olympics
health insurance			education

ASKHAM BRYAN
COLLEGE
LEARNING RESOURCES

AGENDA-SETTING, ISSUE SALIENCE AND POLITICS

The idea of agenda-setting was first mentioned in 1922 by Lipmann[107] in his book *Public opinion*, but it was McCombs and Shaw's[108] seminal study that really showed the power of agenda-setting. The basic idea behind this theory is that the salience of issues (i.e. 'issue salience') in the news influences their salience to the public. So, whatever that is prominently discussed in the media becomes prominent in the public's mind. Agenda-setting can be defined as the overall process of creating agendas in mass media.

There is now considerable evidence to support this theory; that is, the public uses the salience of the issues in the media to organise their own agenda as to which issues are important.[109, 110, 111] All these studies pick up on what Cohen highlighted back in 1963 when he said that the press 'may not be successful much of the time in telling people what to think, but [it] is stunningly successful in telling readers what to think about'.[112] That is why politicians always try to influence the media to report on issues where the politician has a strong record. For instance, if the economy is going well, the prime minister would want the media to report glowingly on this. The government can then take credit for it even though, objectively speaking, it may not be directly responsible for the success (e.g. the mining boom says nothing about good economic management). In the age of social media, politicians can now communicate directly with the public, without necessarily having to rely on traditional media, as we saw with Trump. Agenda-setting effects observed with traditional media are also observed in social media like Facebook.[113] The influence comes through our network of friends on social media because our friends can incidentally expose the news to us (e.g. posting of stories, comments, likes).

DISCUSSION QUESTIONS

1. What is public relations (PR)? How is this different from marketing-oriented public relations and publicity?
2. What are the advantages and disadvantages of trying to get free publicity?
3. In what ways is publicity more credible than advertising?
4. Why do you think Virgin's Richard Branson is able to garner consistent, free publicity for his company's brand? Why might other CEOs be unwilling or unable to do this?
5. Why was Donald Trump more capable of garnering free media than Hilary Clinton in the 2016 US presidential election, even though Clinton was more credible?
6. What are the benefits of having a good corporate reputation?
7. What is a firm's main objective when it seeks to engage in corporate social responsibility (CSR) initiatives?
8. Under what conditions are CSR initiatives and sponsorship more likely to enhance a firm's reputation?
9. Your firm is sponsoring an event. How would you evaluate whether ambush marketing has had any effect on your brand?
10. Explain the concept of 'fit' between CSR initiatives and the image of the firm. Why is fit not enough in itself to enhance corporate reputation when it comes to CSR initiatives?
11. In crisis communication, when should a firm refute and deny responsibility? When should it apologise and accept responsibility?
12. What is the difference between native advertising and content marketing? In your opinion which of these two tactics is potentially unethical, and why?

13. Imagine you are running a small business and cannot afford TV advertising, what tools would you use to build your reputation? Choose a business and say how the various tools you use can be integrated in an ongoing reputation-building strategy.
14. What is agenda-setting, and how does this concept apply to marketing and political issues?
15. How is brand awareness different from brand salience and issue salience?

NOTES

1 JG Hutton, 'Defining the relationship between public relations and marketing', in RL Heath (ed.), *Handbook of public relations*, Sage Publications, Thousand Oaks, CA, 2001, pp. 205–14.

2 O Baskin, C Aronoff and D Lattimore, *Public relations: the profession and the practice*, McGraw-Hill, Boston, MA, 1997.

3 GT Cameron, 'Does publicity outperform advertising? An ad experimental test of the third-party endorsement', *Journal of Public Relations Research*, 6, 1994, pp. 185–207.

4 M Eisend and F Kuster, 'The effectiveness of publicity versus advertising: a meta-analytical investigation of its moderators', *Journal of Academy of Marketing Science*, 39, 2011, pp. 906–21.

5 M Bebby, 'Oscar a cert for film goers', *Australian Financial Review*, 1–2 April 2000, p. 6.

6 H Howard, 'Vibrators carry the conversation', *New York Times*, 2012. Accessed July 2012 at www.nytimes.com/2011/04/21/fashion/21VIBRATORS.html?pagewanted=all.

7 J Harlow, 'Oscar winner knocks sales of merlot wine sideways', *Sunday Times*, 6 March 2005. Accessed July 2013 at www.thesundaytimes.co.uk/sto/news/world_news/article101655.ece.

8 This is an example of how winning wines can be parlayed on a wine critic's website. It may be profitable for the wine critic, but it can also be perceived as harming the critic's independence because he is also profiteering from his ratings. www.winecompanion.com.au/resources/awards/2020-winners?.

9 B Greene, 'Worms? McDonald's isn't laughing', *Chicago Tribune*, 20 November 1978, A1.

10 M Scheikowski, 'Restaurateurs lose defamation case', *NineMSN*, 2009. Accessed July 2012 at http://news.ninemsn.com.au/national/985341/restaurant-owners-lose-defamation-case.

11 C Bartlett, J Sterne and M Egger, 'What is newsworthy? Longitudinal study of the reporting of medical research in two British newspapers', *British Medical Journal*, 325(7355), 13 July 2002, pp. 81–4.

12 J Borthwick, 'Top 10 best ferry rides worldwide', 2016. Accessed at www.traveller.com.au/the-traveller-10-worlds-best-ferry-rides-gqzq8j.

13 Name Our Ship at https://nameourship.nerc.ac.uk/.

14 RRS means Royal Research Ship.

15 P Walker, 'RRS Boaty McBoatface leads in poll to name polar research vessel'. Accessed July 2020 at www.theguardian.com/environment/2016/mar/20/eccentric-choices-surface-in-quest-to-name-polar-research-vessel.

16 L Vasentine, 'Ferry McFerryface? NSW government launches naming competition for new ferries', 22 July 2016. Accessed July 2020 at www.smh.com.au/national/nsw/ferry-mcferryface-nsw-government-launches-naming-competition-for-new-ferries-20160722-gqb93p.html.

17 C O'Keffe, 'Ferry McFerryface replacement name also ineligible under contest criteria', Channel 9 news, 31 January 2018. Accessed October 2018 at www.9news.com.au/national/2018/01/31/16/15/ferry-mcferryface-replacement-also-ineligible.

18 A Taylor, 'Australian attempt to avoid "Boaty McBoatface" boat-naming debacle results in far worse "Ferry McFerryface" scandal', *Washington Post*, 31 January 2018. Accessed October 2018 at www.washingtonpost.com/news/worldviews/wp/2018/01/31/australian-attempt-to-avoid-boaty-mcboatface-boat-naming-debacle-results-in-far-worse-ferry-mcferryface-scandal/?utm_term=.386a9613d747.

19 The term 'captain's pick' became popular when the Australian Prime Minister Tony Abbott began making selections of personnel unilaterally (i.e. without consultation). The term has now become part of the Australian vernacular.

20 C O'Keffe (2018), 'Ferry McFerryface replacement name also ineligible under contest criteria', note 17.

21 ABC News, 'Ferry McFerryface: Clean up Australia founder Ian Kiernan questions May Gibbs name change', 28 January 2018. Accessed October 2018 at www.abc.net.au/news/2018-01-31/clean-up-australias-ian-kiernan-not-happy-about-may-gibbs-ferry/9377672.

22 A Taylor (2018), 'Australian attempt to avoid "Boaty McBoatface" boat-naming debacle results in far worse "Ferry McFerryface" scandal', note 18.

23 PS Speck and MT Elliott, 'Predictors of advertising avoidance in print and broadcast media', *Journal of Advertising*, 26(3), 1997, pp. 61–76.

24 C Aronoff, 'Predictors of success in placing releases in newspapers', *Public Relations Review*, 2(4), 1976, pp. 43–57.

25 YH Soo, 'The relationship between newsworthiness and publication of news releases in the media', *Public Relations Review*, 34, 2008, pp. 297–9.

26 S Miller, 'Public-relations pioneer began with "Toni Twins" stunt', *Wall Street Journal*, 15 January 2013.

27 Aronoff (1976), 'Predictors of success', note 24.

28 PJ Shoemaker and AA Cohen, *News around the world: content, practitioners, and the public*, Routledge, New York, 2006.

29 Soo (2008), 'The relationship between newsworthiness and publication of news releases in the media', note 25.

30 Shoemaker and Cohen (2006), *News around the world*, note 28.

31 KH Jameison, *Dirty politics: deception, distraction and democracy*, Oxford University Press, London, 1992.

32 Eisend and Kuster (2011), 'Effectiveness of publicity versus advertising', note 4.

33 G Rifkin, 'How Richard Branson works magic', *Strategy and Business*, Booz Hamilton, 4th quarter, 1998. Accessed July 2013 at www.hrh.ch/whoiswho/bransonr/br_page1.html.

34 Ibid.

35 C Larreche, 'Virgin Atlantic Airways – ten years after', *INSEAD Case Study*, INSEAD, Fontainebleau, France, 1995.

36 Rifkin (1998), 'How Richard Branson works magic', note 33.

37 G Sargent, 'Why did Trump win? New research by Democrats offers a worrisome answer', *Washington Post*, 7 May 2017. Accessed October 2918 at www.washingtonpost.com/blogs/plum-line/wp/2017/05/01/why-did-trump-win-new-research-by-democrats-offers-a-worrisome-answer/?utm_term=.430d2fd4d351.

38 K Doctor, 'Trump bump grows into subscription surge – and not just for the New York Times', *The Street*, 3 March 2017. Accessed October 2018 at www.thestreet.com/story/14024114/1/trump-bump-grows-into-subscription-surge.html.

39 PL Francia, 'Free media and Twitter in the 2016 presidential election: the unconventional campaign of Donald Trump', *Social Science Computer Review*, 2017, pp. 1–16.

40 To read more of the excellent analysis see Francia (2017), 'Free media and Twitter in the 2016 presidential election, note 39.

41 Adapted from CJ Fombrun, NA Gardberg and JM Sever, 'The reputation quotient: a multi-stakeholder measure of corporate reputation', *Journal of Brand Management*, 7(4), 2000, pp. 241–55.

42 G Dowling, 'Corporate reputations: should you compete on yours?', working paper, Australian Graduate School of Management, University of New South Wales, June 2003.

43 Most of the ideas are from G Dowling, *Creating corporate reputations*, Oxford University Press, Oxford, 2001, pp. 12–13.

44 Ibid.

45 Dr Norman Swan, a medical journalist for the Australian Broadcasting Corporation, had a Twitter following of 76 000 followers as of February 2020.

46 M Bailey, 'The moment Norman Swan's world stopped', *Australian Financial Review*, 25–26 April 2020. Accessed April 2020 at www.afr.com/life-and-luxury/health-and-wellness/the-moment-norman-swan-s-world-stopped-20200421-p54lp6.

47 I Chiu, 'Digital Minister Audrey Tang: Taiwan's "Genius" and her unique past', Nippon.com, 10 April 2020. Accessed at www.nippon.com/en/japan-topics/g00837/digital-minister-audrey-tang-taiwan%E2%80%99s-genius-and-her-unique-past.html.

48 S Borys and E Coulter, 'Government added projects to "sports rorts" funding list just hours after Scott Morrison called election', *ABC News*, 3 March 2020. Accessed April 2020 at www.abc.net.au/news/2020-03-03/govt-added-projects-to-sports-rorts-list-after-calling-election/12019326.

49 CB Bhattacharya and S Sen, 'Doing good at doing better: when, why and how consumers respond to corporate social initiatives', *California Management Review*, 47(1), Fall 2004, pp. 9–24.

50 See www.bsr.org [accessed July 2012].

51 TJ Brown and PA Pacin, 'The company and the product: corporate associations and consumer product responses', *Journal of Marketing*, 16(1), January 1997, pp. 68–84.

52 T Featherstone, 'Ethical Investing comes of age', *The Australian*, May 2019. Accessed May 2019 at www.afr.com/personal-finance/shares/ethical-investing-comes-of-age-20170518-gw7kuc.

53 P van Beurden and T Gössling, 'The worth of values: a literature review on the relation between corporate social and financial performance', *Journal of Business Ethics*, 2, 2008, pp. 407–24.

54 Bhattacharya and Sen (2004), 'Doing good at doing better', note 49.

55 RL Anderson, SH Dahlquist and MS Garver, 'Millennials' purchasing response to firms' CSR behavior', *Marketing Management Journal*, 28(1), 2018, pp. 14–29.

56 JW Pracejus and D Olsen, 'The role of brand/cause fit in the effectiveness of cause-related marketing campaigns', *Journal of Business Research*, 57, 2004, pp. 635–40.

57 CJ Simmons and KL Becker-Olsen, 'Achieving marketing objectives through social sponsorships', *Journal of Marketing*, 70(4), 2006, pp. 154–69.

58 K Westberg and N Pope, 'Building brand equity with cause related marketing: a comparison with sponsorship and sales promotion', *Journal of Marketing Communications*, 20(6), 2014, pp. 419–37.

59 Y Yoon, Z Giirhan-Canli and N Schwarz, 'The effect of corporate social responsibility (CSR) activities on companies with bad reputations', *Journal of Consumer Psychology*, 16(4), 2006, pp. 377–90.

60 E Olson, 'Does sponsorship work in the same way in different sponsorship contexts?', *European Journal of Marketing*, 44(1), 2010, pp. 180–99.

61 See criticism by Professor Simon Chapman on http://sydney.edu.au/news/84.html?newsstoryid=3776. Accessed July 2012.

62 Bhattacharya and Sen (2004), 'Doing good at doing better', note 49.

63 Ibid.

64 N Koschate-Fischer, VS Isabel and D Hoyer Wayne, 'Willingness to pay for cause-related marketing: the impact of donation amount and moderating effects', *Journal of Marketing Research*, 49(6), December 2012, pp. 910–27.

65 J Williams et al., 'SPC Goulburn Valley: #MyFamilyCan – How a humble can empowered millions of Australians', World Advertising Research (WARC) Awards, Gold, Best Use of Brand Purpose, 2017. Accessed October 2018 at www.warc.com/content/paywall/article/warc-awards/spc-goulburn-valley-myfamilycan–how-a-humble-can-empowered-millions-of-australians/111011.

66 L Aitken, 'What brand purpose is… and what it isn't', World Advertising Research Centre (WARC), 13 June 2017. Accessed October 2018 at www.warc.com/newsandopinion/opinion/what_brand_purpose_is_and_what_it_isnt/2447.

67 You can see the ad here: http://cmagadfacts.tumblr.com/. Accessed July 2012.

68 Statista Global sponsorship spending from 2007 to 2018 (in billion US dollars): www.statista.com/statistics/196864/global-sponsorship-spending-since-2007/. Accessed May 2019.

69 R Speed and P Thompson, 'Determinants of sports sponsorship response', *Journal of the Academy of Marketing Science*, 28(2), 2000, pp. 226–38.

70 J Verity, 'Maximising the marketing potential of sponsorship for global brands', *European Business Journal*, 14(4), 2002, pp. 161–73.

71 'Olympics 2012: Nike plots ambush ad campaign', *Guardian*, 25 July 2012. Accessed February 2013 at www.guardian.co.uk/media/2012/jul/25/olympics-2012-nike-ambush-ad.

72 B Chapman, 'Rio 2016: The richest Games in 120 years of Olympic history', *Independent*, 4 August 2016. Accessed May 2019 at www.independent.co.uk/news/business/analysis-and-features/rio-2016-olympic-games-richest-ever-usain-bolt-mo-farah-a7171811.html.

73 K Badenhausen, 'Cristiano Ronaldo produced nearly $1 billion in value for sponsors on social media', *Forbes*, June 2015. Accessed September 2018 at www.forbes.com/sites/kurtbadenhausen/2017/06/15/cristiano-ronaldo-produces-nearly-1-billion-in-value-for-sponsors-on-social-media-this-year/#285a0d7157df.

74 DE Yohn, 'Olympics advertisers are wasting their sponsorship dollars, *Forbes*, 3 August 2016. Accessed at www.forbes.com/sites/deniselyohn/2016/08/03/olympics-advertisers-are-wasting-their-sponsorship-dollars/#267649192070.

75 KP Gwinner and J Eaton, 'Building brand image through event sponsorship: the role of image transfer', *Journal of Advertising*, XXVIII(4), 1999, pp. 47–57.

76 HMK Ngan, GP Pendergast and ASL Tsang, 'Linking sports sponsorship with purchase intentions', *European Journal of Marketing*, 45(4), 2011, pp. 551–66.

77 L Bergkvist, 'The flipside of the sponsorship coin: do you still buy the beer when the brewer underwrites a rival team?', *Journal of Advertising Research*, 52(1), 2012, pp. 65–73.

78 K Almaiman, 'The effects of sport sponsorship on brand equity: a best–worst scaling approach', PhD thesis, Macquarie University, 2020.

79 This video compiled by Business Insider shows the passenger being forcibly removed, and United Airlines' response: www.youtube.com/watch?v=VrDWY6C1178.

80 C Pash, 'The reputation of Australia's financial industry has collapsed, and now ranks last in a major survey', *Business Insider*, August 2018. Accessed May 2019 at www.businessinsider.com.au/ethics-trust-governance-institute-australia-2018-8.

81 WH Decker, 'A firm's image following alleged wrongdoing: effects of the firm's prior reputation and response to the allegation', *Corporate Reputation Review*, 15(1), 2012, pp. 20–34.

82 C Korkofingas and L Ang, 'Product recall, brand equity, and future choice', *Journal of Marketing Management*, 27(9–10), 2011, pp. 959–75.

83 Forbes, '13 golden rules of PR crisis management', 20 June 2017. Accessed October 2018 at www.forbes.com/sites/forbesagencycouncil/2017/06/20/13-golden-rules-of-pr-crisis-management/#7cd662c21bcf.

84 Wojdynski also perceptively pointed out that off-site hyperlinks found on the publisher's website may also look similar to the publisher's own links! See BW Wojdynski, 'Native advertising: engagement, deception, and implications for theory', in R Brown, V Jones, and BM Wang (eds), *The New Advertising: Branding, Content and Consumer Relationships in the Data-Driven Social Media Era,* Praeger/ABC Clio, Santa Barbara, CA, 2016, pp. 203–36.

85 M Wu, et al., 'A tale of two sources in native advertising: examining the effects of source credibility and priming on content, organizations, and media evaluations', *American Behavioral Scientist*, 60(12), 2016, pp. 1492–1509.

86 BW Wojdynski and NJ Evans, 'Going native: effects of disclosure position and language on the recognition and evaluation of online native advertising', *Journal of Advertising,* 45(2), 2016, pp. 157–68.

87 Wojdynski (2016), 'Native advertising: engagement, deception, and implications for theory', note 84.

88 Wu et al. (2016), 'A tale of two sources in native advertising', note 85.

89 J Bocovici, 'The Atlantic on that Scientology advertorial: "We screwed up"', Forbes, 15 January 2013. Accessed October 2018 at www.forbes.com/sites/jeffbercovici/2013/01/15/the-atlantic-on-that-scientology-advertorial-we-screwed-up/#6a50b0404ef7.

90 M Friestad, and P Wright, 'The persuasion knowledge model: how people cope with persuasion attempts', *Journal of Consumer Research*, 21(1), 1994, pp. 1–31.

91 SC Boerman, EA van Reijmersdal and PC Neijens, 'Effects of sponsorship disclosure timing on the processing of sponsored content: a study on the effectiveness of European Disclosure Regulations', *Psychology and Marketing*, 31(3), 2014, pp. 214–24.

92 BW Wojdynski, 'The deceptiveness of sponsored news articles: how readers recognize and perceive native advertising', *American Behavioral Scientist*, 60(12), 2016, pp. 1475–91.

93 The revenue from print advertising has been devastated by the digital revolution, sending traditional news organisations broke. As a result, there is a constant search for new sources of revenue, including native advertising. Even *Wall Street Journal* has a whole division, called WSJ Custom Studio, devoted to native advertising: see http://view.ceros.com/wall-street-journal/wsjcustomstudios/p/1. Accessed September 2018.

94 Wu et al. (2016), 'A tale of two sources in native advertising', pp. 1492–1509, note 85.

95 B Hayden, 'Case study: How content marketing saved this brick-and-mortar business', *CopyBlogger*, 6 May 2013. Accessed October 2018 at www.copyblogger.com/brick-and-mortar-content-marketing/.

96 C Campbell and LJ Marks, 'Good native advertising isn't a secret', *Business Horizons*, 58(6), 2015, pp. 599–606.

97 V Liljander, J Gummerus and M Söderlund, 'Young consumers' responses to suspected covert and overt blog marketing', *Internet Research*, 25(4), 2015, pp. 610–32.

98 SC Boerman, N Helberger, G van Noort and CJ Hoofnagle, 'Sponsored blog content: What do the regulations say? And what do bloggers say?' *JIPITEC*, 9, 2018, pp. 146–59.

99 Y Hwang and SH Jeong, '"This is a sponsored blog post, but all opinions are my own": The effects of sponsorship disclosure on responses to sponsored blog posts', *Computer and Human Behavior*, 62, 2016, pp. 528–35.

100 It is often difficult for authorities to police and monitor blogging practices since there are so many. And even if this were to be possible, there are many ways and formats in which disclosures can be made, some more effective than others.

101 P O'Connor, 'Managing a hotel's image on TripAdvisor', *Journal of Hospitality and Management*, 19 (7), 2010, pp. 754–72.

102 C Scalon, 'Why study journalism? Because web audiences want quality too?', *Sydney Morning Herald*, 18 July 2012, p. 11.

103 In a recent benchmark study of Australian companies doing content marketing, emails, social media posts and blogs were found to be the top three most common methods of distributing content. See LM Beets and J Sangster, 'Content marketing in Australia: Benchmarks, budgets and trends', report, Content Marketing Institute and ADMA, 2018.

104 M Sutherland and J Galloway, 'Role of advertising: persuasion or agenda-setting?', *Journal of Advertising Research*, 21(5), 1989, pp. 25–9.

105 Of course, it can be argued that in any buying situation, the product category is always activated first, in which case there is no need for the concept of brand salience. However, there are many buying situations. Some brands may be relevant in more buying situations than others. For instance, we might consider going to McDonald's for breakfast, lunch and dinner, but not to KFC.

106 T Powers et al., 'Digital and social media in the purchase decision process', *Journal of Advertising Research*, 52(4), December 2012, pp. 479–89.

107 W Lippmann, *Public opinion*, Harcourt, Brace & Co., New York, 1922.

108 ME McCombs and DL Shaw, 'The agenda-setting function of mass media', *Public Opinion Quarterly*, 36, Summer 1972, pp. 176–87.

109 JP Winter and CH Eyal, 'Agenda-setting for the civil rights issue', *Public Opinion Quarterly*, 45(3), Autumn 1981, pp. 376–83.

110 S Iyengar and DR Kinder, *News that matters: TV and American opinion*, University of Chicago Press, Chicago, 1987.

111 M McCombs and A Reynolds, 'News influence on our pictures of the world', in J Bryant and D Zillmann (eds), *Media effects*, 2nd edition, Lawrence Erlbaum Associates, Mahwah, NJ, 2002, pp. 1–16.

112 B Cohen, *The press and foreign policy*, Princeton University Press, Princeton, NJ, 1963, p. 13.

113 JT Feezell, 'Agenda setting through social media: the importance of incidental news exposure and social filtering in the digital era', *Political Research Quarterly*, 71(2), 2018, pp. 482–94.

CHAPTER 10
INFLUENCE, TACTICS AND INTEGRATION IN PERSONAL SELLING

CHAPTER OVERVIEW

The aim of this chapter is to give the reader a better understanding of the principles of influence in personal selling. Personal selling is especially important for high-involvement purchases. The chapter outlines the steps involved, with special emphasis paid to effective presentation and handling of objections, including multi-attribute reframing, selling the 'improved value' and selling the 'vision'. Also discussed in this chapter are the subtle, yet powerful principles of compliance-seeking tactics. For long-term success, though, a sales agent needs to be trustworthy, and we discuss the factors that give a sales agent this characteristic. We then present a model that summarises the many paths that lead to effective persuasion.

Learning goals

After this chapter, you will understand:

- the important functions of a salesperson (or sales agent)
- the advantages and disadvantages of personal selling
- the eight steps of high-involvement selling
- how to create an effective sales presentation
- the four common ways of handling objections, and their disadvantages
- the expectancy-value model of human behaviour
- how to use the multi-attribute framing technique in a sales presentation or in handling objections
- how to sell 'improved value' and the 'vision'
- how to use selling influence tactics (SITs) contingently
- how artificial intelligence assists in personal selling
- the principles of compliance-seeking tactics
- the four common ways of increasing liking
- why trust and trustworthiness are important
- the different persuasion paths to influence, and ethical considerations in using compliance-seeking tactics.

Imagine you are selling your home after living in it for 10 years. It is a well-appointed house in a good location and has many appealing features: three large bedrooms, two bathrooms, a garage, an alfresco dining area, and a state-of-the-art, built-in sound system that pipes music into every room (see figure 10.1). So it should fetch a good price – but can you sell it? Do you know where to start? Where will you find the right buyers? And, more importantly, do you possess enough persuasive charm to attract potential buyers, negotiate and close the sale at your desired price?

Figure 10.1 A house advertised for sale

Faced with this situation, most people may decide to pay a professional real estate sales agent to sell their home. There are good reasons for doing so. A typical real estate agency has access to a database of prospective buyers, which means it can generate promising leads very quickly, and sales agents are usually experienced in influencing and negotiating with prospective buyers – essential skills for high-involvement buying situations such as this.

The above scenario illustrates some of the issues that arise in high-involvement selling for a new product or service. It also highlights three important attributes of a salesperson: (i) identifying and contacting prospective buyers, (ii) presenting the benefits of the product or service to them convincingly and (iii) persuading them and closing the sale. These attributes are especially important when the product or service offered for sale is expensive, because in that situation most prospective buyers will carefully consider and analyse the offer.

ADVANTAGES AND DISADVANTAGES OF PERSONAL SELLING

Personal selling can be defined as a dyadic (two-way) communication between the sales agent and the prospective buyer, in which the sales agent tries to influence the buyer to buy the product or service. This communication can be face-to-face or over the telephone.

One main advantage of personal selling is that the attention of the buyer is virtually guaranteed once he or she has chosen to interact with the sales agent. Another advantage is that, unlike with other IMC tools, the feedback (good or bad) from the buyer takes place during the sales presentation, without any delay. This allows the sales agent to adapt his or her style, customise the offer and, if necessary, provide additional information immediately to respond to any queries and allay any concerns the buyer might have. This is called 'adaptive selling'.[1] An extension of this dynamic, adaptive selling concept also occurs in industrial selling, when the sales agent also acts as consultant to solve the client's technical problems, which is called 'consultative selling'. The key is to adapt the sales message and update the arguments in real time in response to the buyer's reaction. It is therefore an inherently dynamic influence process,[2] which has been associated with higher sales performance.[3] Personal selling is essentially a very effective communication tool, especially when it comes to showcasing new products. It has an elasticity of 0.31,[4] which is higher than that of advertising (0.22),[5] though less than that of price promotion (–2.62).[6]

Personal selling also has disadvantages, however. First, it is an expensive tool, and so it is generally suitable only for high-involvement products or services. Second, its reach is extremely poor, since the travelling time between contacts can be lengthy. Even if phone contact is the mode of communication, it still takes time to contact each prospective buyer personally. These limitations mean that you should follow three basic rules when using personal selling:

1. use other IMC tools (e.g. general advertising, PR, direct mail or even tradeshows) to create product, brand or corporate awareness before deploying the sales force
2. maximise the success of the sales agents by
   - contacting only promising buyers (through qualification)
   - ensuring the sales presentation or demonstration is convincing
   - allowing them to showcase new products
3. go after large prospects for potentially larger revenues.

THE EIGHT STEPS OF HIGH-INVOLVEMENT SELLING

Since a major limitation of personal selling is its high cost, every opportunity should be maximised in order to make a profitable sale. Figure 10.2 outlines the eight steps that should be followed for high-involvement selling to new customers (a 'new buy'). This model does not apply to situations where existing customers are simply reordering a product or service they have bought before (a 'rebuy'). However, if an existing customer seeks to change a previous order (a 'modified rebuy'), then steps 5 to 8 are necessary.

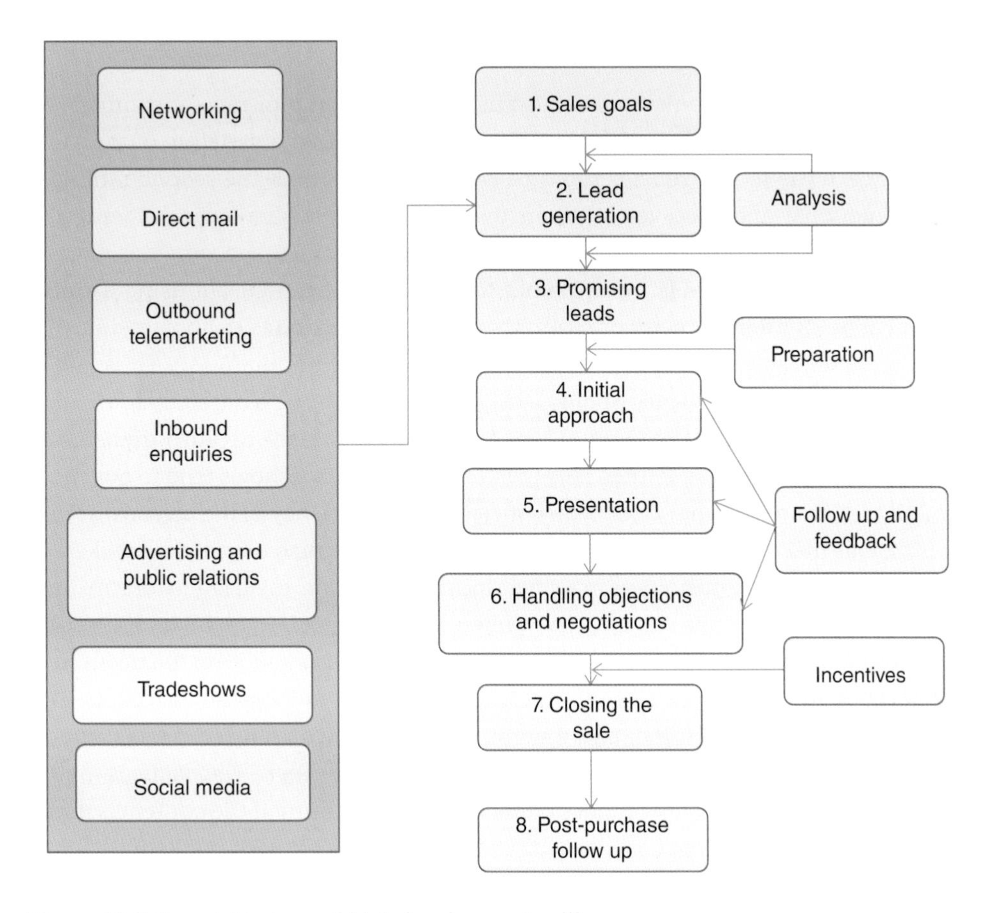

Figure 10.2 The eight steps of high-involvement selling

Step 1: Setting a goal

All sales processes start with a goal. The goal can be expressed in terms of the number of units to be sold or the revenue to be earned. Usually set by senior managers, these goals should be realistic and achievable within a defined time frame and territory. Often the goals are linked to the bonuses and other rewards available to the sales agent to motivate their achievement of the goal. A balance needs to be struck between the agent's base salary and bonuses: usually, for products or services that have a short purchase cycle, the salesperson's remuneration is tied more closely to a bonus (with a lower base salary), while the reverse is true for products or services that have a longer purchase cycle (i.e. there is a higher base salary, but lower bonus).

Step 2: Generating leads

Next comes lead generation (sometimes called 'prospecting'), which involves finding a set of prospective buyers to contact. This is the most important step in the personal selling process because without new customers there is no business. For this reason, it can be argued that an effective salesperson never stops prospecting.

Networking is an important prospecting skill. It involves creating opportunities to get to know one or more people in an informal setting (usually face-to-face), with the intention of gaining new information that can translate into something tangible in the future. The fundamental importance of prospecting and networking is encapsulated by the saying, 'It is not what you know, but who you know'.

Direct mail and outbound telemarketing are also useful in soliciting for more customers. To be effective, the soliciting message should not be a repetition, but rather a variation of the same message. For instance, if the first email is based on a rational appeal, then the second reminder email should be emotional and vice versa. When the appeals are sequentially different, the amount of leads generated are significantly higher than if the same message, whether rational or emotional, is repeated twice. This is true whether the message is carried out using a single channel (e.g. email only, 7% improvement) or multi-channel (i.e. email and telephone selling, 67% improvement).[7] Fundamentally, repeating the same message twice is boring![8]

Yet another avenue is to gather names of prospects at tradeshows. One early study found that this is especially effective for a new product of woodworking machinery because exposure at tradeshows generates interest even after three months.[9] Attendees to tradeshows tend to buy more (by as much as 24% to 40%) and much sooner, which increases the efficiency of the personal selling by as much as 50%. This makes sense since tradeshows are events in which a firm is most likely to meet (and interest) many potential customers in a single location and time; there is a natural in-built efficiency. It therefore pays to generate pre-tradeshow interest using other IMC tools like direct mail, advertising or PR. The key is to attract potential customers to the firm's sales booth at the tradeshow.

The rise of social media has given sales agents another avenue to look for customers. The strategy is for the sales agent to first find, and then build relationships with prospects through social networks. LinkedIn is a fertile hunting ground for business customers. One tactic is for the sales agent to regularly upload relevant content on their LinkedIn account. If the content is good, it will soon find an audience and hence customers (see chapter 9 on content marketing). It has been suggested that a sales agent should allocate about 5–10% of his or her time to social selling.[10] This involves listening to online conversations on social media and looking for opportunities to engage with potential customers by providing the relevant information at just the right time. The objective is to create familiarity and trust, which we will discuss later.

Step 3: Identifying the most promising leads

Not all prospective buyers are equally likely to buy, and an efficient sales agent decides at this step which buyers to concentrate on first. Although sales agents should generally follow up on all enquiries, they should also prioritise and start with the most promising leads first. To do this well, they need good analytical skills.

In many industrial buying situations, the use of sophisticated analyses (e.g. multi-attribute choice modelling) can establish which product or service attributes different customer segments value. This helps an organisation to understand how best to compete, given its range of products or services and its available resources. By understanding how each segment views the strengths and weaknesses of different competitive offers, appropriate selling strategies can be devised.[11] For instance, research may reveal that there is a greater probability of success if the organisation can:

- understand what benefits new buyers want
- reassure vulnerable customers by emphasising the right benefits
- change the call pattern (e.g. the frequency of sales visits) to reflect the relative importance of different benefits across the segments
- shift the advertising budget to different media combinations to reflect this relative importance.

Finally, it should be noted that when a customer has had a bad experience, the last thing the customer wants is to be sold to more.[12] What is needed instead is a service recovery. This is when a good customer relationship management system, supported by a good service team, will be crucial to the success of the recovery process.[13]

INTEGRATING THE MARKETING TEAM AND THE SALES TEAM USING LEAD SCORING

Lead scoring is one area in which the marketing and sales teams can achieve better integration. It is an objective method of ranking different sales leads so that the sales force can prioritise their activities. But it is not unusual to hear the sales team accusing marketing for not providing enough quality leads because of inappropriate qualification (e.g. the prospect is two years out from buying). The crux of the problem lies in not agreeing what a good lead is. But if an agreement can be reached, then it will significantly improve the alignment and collaboration between the marketing team and the sales team. One solution is for both teams to *jointly* agree at the outset what they consider to be quality leads based on important criteria. As an illustration, if both teams agree that a good lead is a buyer who has high readiness to buy with potentially large revenue, then applying these two criteria will allow the firm to segment their customer base into different groups. For instance, figure 10.3 shows that there is a cluster of potential customers (A) who are both ready to buy and can potentially provide large revenue. Then there are two other clusters who are either ready to buy but have smaller revenue potential (cluster B) or have larger revenue potential but are not quite ready to buy (cluster C). Finally, we have a third cluster who are neither (cluster D).

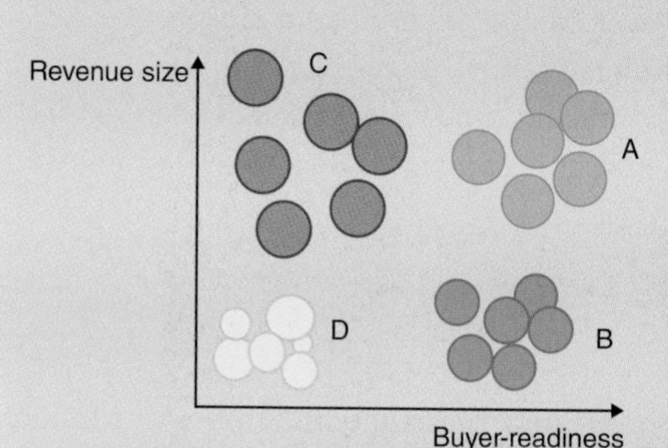

Figure 10.3 Classifying potential buyers into their readiness to buy and potential revenue

This information would suggest that the sales force should prioritise customers in cluster A over those of other clusters. At the same time, the marketing team can nurture relationships with customers of clusters B and C using content marketing like webinars and white papers as well as telemarketing. At the ground level, the sales team can also provide feedback to the marketing team as to the quality of the customers in cluster A. If they turned out to be of poor quality, then the scoring method must be improved or new criteria added. Firms should experiment with different lead scoring criteria,[14] but the point is that an objective lead scoring method that is jointly developed and owned by both teams can serve as a way for closer integration, leading to higher revenue, win rate, and sales.

Step 4: Making the initial contact

The next step is to think of an approach, with the objective not of closing a sale but of gaining an audience. Any approach should include a credible reason for making the initial contact, and so preparation is crucial. The reason must be based on a benefit that the prospective buyer can obtain.

The salesperson can carry out the approach by phone or email. In a referral situation, the salesperson must mention the name of the person who referred the prospective buyer in the opening sentence. Securing a meeting may be more difficult if the sales agent has to get past a 'gatekeeper' (e.g. a personal assistant). Therefore, follow-up calls are essential.

It should be noted that first impressions are important because they are immediate in their effects. People tend to make split-second judgements which are not only powerful but enduring and hence consequential. But these judgements are often biased. For instance, a sales agent with a tattoo may not be perceived to be credible.[15] Unless a customer actively guards against such biases, misleading attributions will be made; but what is the probability of a customer doing this? Therefore, the sales agent must always try to give a good impression when he or she meets a potential customer for the first time. Always.

CORPORATE REPUTATION AND 'OPENING DOORS'

It is easier for a salesperson from a well-known organisation to gain an audience with the key decision maker than it is for a salesperson from a less well-known organisation.[16] This means that it is important to invest in building corporate reputation, for example through image advertising. One study found that with every corporate print ad a prospective customer sees, there is a 25% greater chance of a purchase.[17]

When there is little budget for corporate advertising, a marcoms manager can opt for cause-related marketing, sponsorship or other marketing-oriented PR activities to improve corporate image (see chapter 9).

Step 5: Presentation

The next challenge is for the sales agent to secure a formal presentation. Prior to this though, the potential buyer may request a preliminary meeting. In the preliminary meeting, it is imperative that the sales agent learns as much as possible about this buyer. One way of doing this is to use the SPIN method,[18] which is a series of questions or statements the sales agent can make to create a rapport with the buyer. SPIN is an acronym for the following types of questions a sales agent can make:

- Situation – these are fact-based questions about the buyer's background (e.g. How many widgets are you current producing?)
- Problem – these are questions about the buyer's dissatisfaction or difficulties (e.g. Why are you unhappy with your current machinery?)
- Implications – these are questions about the negative consequences of the buyer's problems (e.g. Will this affect your bottom line?)
- Need-payoff – these are the questions that will steer the buyer to see the benefits when a right (i.e. supplier's) solution is found (e.g. If you can improve the efficiency of throughput, how would it help the bottom line?)

After this preliminary meeting, the sales agent may be invited to give a presentation. This represents the first formal step towards a buying decision. It also represents the culmination of hard work, and so the opportunity should not be wasted. Below are some suggestions for making a successful presentation.[19]

TIPS FOR THE PRESENTATION

- Present an agenda so that buyers know where you are heading.
- Establish your credibility at the beginning of the presentation (not at the end) but do so in a humble way.[20]
- If one's credibility is not as high, then persuade through careful argumentation.[21]
- Cite credible evidence to support your argument.[22]
- Use the names of people in the audience throughout the presentation, because this makes them feel important.
- Dress formally to signify authority.
- Present a well-groomed image, to increase liking.
- Smile and maintain eye contact to increase liking, especially to make the most of your physical attractiveness.
- Use visual aids to assist with comprehension. Be organised.
- Show key information only – keep it simple.
- Speak in a low-pitch voice; do not shriek.[23]
- Speak fast if your argument is weak, to deter and disrupt counterargument from the buyer.
- On the other hand, if your argument is strong, use slow, deliberate speech.
- Pause just *before* making key points, to make their delivery more dramatic.
- Pause again *after* making key points, so that the audience can reflect on them.
- Ask the audience questions whose answers will naturally lead to one of your key points.
- Avoid humour, because this will distract the audience from processing any complex information in your presentation (e.g. in industrial selling).
- Use persuasive body language like leaning forward and adopting an open body stance (i.e. arms away from the body).[24]
- Send a summary of buyer action steps after the presentation.

Step 6: Handling objections

It is common for prospective buyers to raise objections or concerns during the presentation. Objections also often form part of the negotiation process. So, it is important to learn to handle and respond to objections effectively.

Broadly, there are four ways to handle objections:

1. Meet the objection head-on by suggesting that the buyer is wrong. For instance, if the buyer complains the price is too high, the sales agent can reply, 'No, not really, this price represents good value'.
2. Make an indirect rebuttal. This means listening to the objection with sympathy and then replying in a way that does not directly contradict what the buyer has said, but nevertheless implies that the buyer's opinion is wrong. For example, if the buyer claims that an aspect of the product or service is inadequate, the sales agent can refer to evidence (such as a research study) that establishes the opposite position.
3. Offer a solution without explicitly stating that the buyer is wrong. This is a variation or extension of the second method. For example, in consultative selling, it is common for a sales agent to follow up an objection with additional information for the buyer, particularly when the product or service is complex and the purchase cycle is long. Buyers typically appreciate sales agents who are willing to invest extra effort to address their concerns.
4. Agree with the objection and then present a compensatory counterargument – this is known as the compensation method. Typically, this takes the form of a 'Yes, but . . .' statement. For instance, if the buyer complains that the price is too high, the sales agent can say, 'Sure, the price is higher, but it's more durable, so in the long run it will save you more money'.

A further consideration arises if the objection arises specifically in the context of a negotiation. In that case, the overriding rule is to strive for a 'win–win' outcome (i.e. an outcome that can be presented as a compromise that benefits each party). This is likely to appeal to the buyer's sense of fairness and thus help to keep the negotiation process on course.

Although these four methods of handling objections are useful, they do not solve all problems or risks. If the sales agent says, 'No' (or even 'Yes, but . . .'), the buyer may experience psychological 'reactance' – this means the buyer will feel that his or her choices or freedom are suddenly being restricted.[25] If that happens, the buyer may well terminate the sales process. Another issue is that in most cases a sales agent has to decide the precise information to use to support his or her rebuttal. This is an important point and we will return to it in the section on multi-attribute reframing.

Step 7: Closing the sale

The penultimate stage is to close the sale or ask for the order. This is called the 'close'. Sales agents are often reluctant to ask for the order for fear of rejection. Below are three common kinds of sales closure:

1. 'Direct close' means simply asking for the order. This can be effective if the buyer has already signalled that he or she is interested.
2. 'Summary-benefit close' means reminding the buyer of all the accepted benefits of the product or service before asking for the order.
3. 'Assumptive close' means the sales agent deliberately assumes that the buyer is ready to buy and therefore makes an indirect form of close such as 'How many do you want us to deliver?' or 'When do you want us to start?'

If there is an impasse in the negotiations, the sales agent may provide other incentives to try to nudge the deal across the line, such as better service terms, a trial period or an extended warranty.

Step 8: Following up after the sale

Once the sale is made, it is important to ensure that all the loose ends are tied up. In some industries, such as real estate, there may be a cooling-off period that allows the buyer to pull out if they reconsider their decision. A sales agent can reduce the risk of a buyer pulling out by following up with a phone call. Further, post-purchase follow-up can also give the sales agent intelligence for future upsell or cross-sell opportunities. It is generally a good idea to follow up because it helps build the relationship.

CASE STUDY 10.1 SYNCHRONISING ADVERTISING AND YOUR SALES FORCE[26]

What happens when your advertising is so good that your sales force cannot cope with the massive amount of leads generated? Consider the case of a US home improvement retailer. The organisation specialised in installing new windows in homes. But to do this properly, a quote had to be given, which could only be done onsite when the salesperson visited the home. This meant that appointments had to be made between the salesperson and the homeowner. Once the meeting was set up, the salesperson did his best to close the deal on the spot. On the other hand, if a meeting could not be set up quickly, the homeowner was likely to lose interest, and a potential sale was lost. The longer the delay, the more likely the homeowner lost interest. But setting up the appointment, visiting the home and closing the sale took time.

The crux of the problem was that the home improvement company spent too much on marcoms (e.g. direct mail, newspaper advertising and exhibitions), which generated so many leads (i.e. from in-coming enquiries) that the sales force could not cope. The leads coming in were also not constant. Instead, there were wide variations, which made planning difficult. This was quite apart from the seasonality effects observed. Worse still, this unevenness of incoming leads led to tension between the marketing team and the sales team. It also created much anxiety within the sales force because the leads generated were not likely to be optimally taken advantage of, due to the delay in setting up the meeting onsite.

To solve this problem, Smith, Gopalakrishna, and Chatterjee studied (and then modelled) the company's data, and this was what they discovered:

- Sales leads for in-home appointments mostly arrived via telephone calls.
- Although the company used nine sources for lead generation (i.e. radio and TV advertising, direct mail, home shows, retail showroom, internet, referrals, repeat business and directories), the most effective were direct mail, newspaper advertising, home shows and radio advertising.
- There were significant interaction effects. Both radio advertising and direct mail boosted the leads generated from newspaper advertising: doubling radio advertising and increasing newspaper advertising by 50%, which increased the number of leads by 7.6%.
- The newspaper leads resulted in almost full in-home appointments, if there was no delay in making contact. However, if the delay was seven days, only 86% of the leads wanted an in-home appointment, which dropped to 76% if the delay was three weeks.
- The quality of the salesperson improved sales by 9%.

Several optimisations were explored, but one option was to reduce overall advertising by 10%, as well redistributing the spend so that there would be more radio advertising (increased by 30.6%), and less direct mail (decreased by 40%). This would result in fewer leads, but more closures and hence more sales. This also would lead to a significant drop in the variability of the delay by 26%, resulting in less stress among the sales force.

This case study illustrates the ironic situation where advertising is so good in generating leads (see step 2 in figure 10.2) that the sales force cannot cope. It brings home the point that different marcoms tools affect each other, and therefore, it is important to understand their interactions for better optimisation.

DISCUSSION QUESTIONS

1. What is the main lesson in this case? Draw a sales cycle diagram showing how the lack of synchronisation between various marcoms led to problems.
2. In the analyses and modelling carried out by the home improvement company, what was the most interesting finding? Explain your answer.
3. Is there another way to solve this problem outlined here instead of reallocating the budget?

PRESENTATION AND OBJECTION-HANDLING

We have discussed the qualities of an effective presentation and ways of handling objections, which are the most challenging aspects of being a sales agent. For this reason, careful research and preparation are needed before we undertake these two steps.

Figure 10.4 expands on these steps. It shows that the purpose of the formal presentation is to inform and convince the prospective buyer how one or more benefits can be derived from the attributes of the product or service, so that the buyer will receive an 'improved value' – in effect, a reward. As we will see in more detail in chapter 12, the reward can be either utilitarian (e.g. if it solves or prevents a problem) or hedonic (e.g. if it confers a pleasure). This reflects the two basic buying motives, which are sometimes described as 'the avoidance of pain' (i.e. utilitarian motive) and 'the pursuit of pleasure' (i.e. the hedonic motive). Much industrial buying (such as buying equipment) is motivated mainly by the need to avoid pain or solve a problem, while consumer buying can be either utilitarian (e.g. buying insurance) or hedonic (e.g. going on a holiday).

In this section, we will discuss three ways of convincing a prospective buyer that he or she will receive good value from a product or service: multi-attribute reframing, selling the improved value and selling the vision.

Multi-attribute reframing

Multi-attribute reframing means attempting to change the buyer's evaluation of certain attributes for a brand (or that of a competitor), so that the buyer perceives the target brand more positively. Preparation and research are needed so that the sales agent knows what important attributes to present and how to respond to objections fruitfully. The Fishbein–Ajzen equation (1975) shows how to understand the process using a mathematical approach.[27]

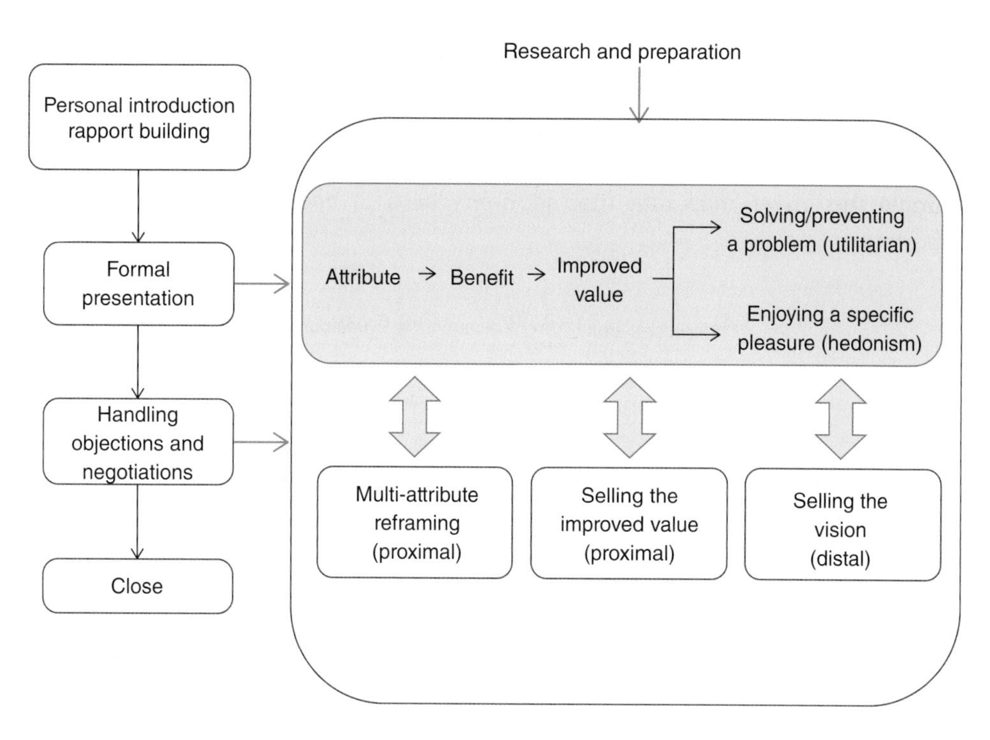

Figure 10.4 Three ways to sell value

The equation in figure 10.5 states that our attitude towards an object 'x' (or event 'x', or situation 'x'), symbolised as A_x, is determined by a number of factors: whether (and to what extent) we believe that object 'x' possesses attribute 'i' (this is 'b' in the equation) and how much we like or value attribute 'i' (this is 'e' in the equation). For instance, consider the attribute of fuel economy in cars. If a buyer assumes that the attribute of fuel economy is a weakness of a Mercedes-Benz car and if he or she places a lot of importance on this attribute, then we can see that the equation tells us the buyer's attitude toward Mercedes-Benz cars would be low. In other words, for this single attribute, Mercedes-Benz will not compare favourably to a more fuel-efficient car brand, such as Toyota.

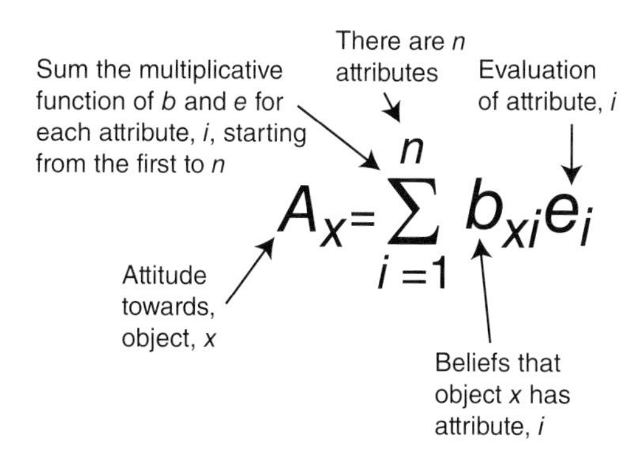

Figure 10.5 The Fishbein–Ajzen equation (1975)

To make this more concrete, let's put some hypothetical numbers into the equation (see figure 10.6), using a scale of 1 to 5 to quantify each element. For 'b', 5 signifies the highest probability of possessing the attribute, so in this example the buyer may rate Mercedes-Benz at 1 and Toyota at 4 for fuel economy. For 'e', 5 signifies the highest level of importance, so in this example the buyer may rate fuel economy as a 5, because they perceive it to be very important.

$$A_{Mercedes\text{-}Benz} = \sum_{i=1}^{1} b_{fueleconomy}\, e_{fueleconomy}$$

Figure 10.6 Hypothetical attitudinal structure for Mercedes-Benz

Applying this equation, Mercedes-Benz (see figure 10.7) will yield an attitude score of 5 (i.e. 1 × 5 = 5), and Toyota (see figure 10.8) will yield an attitude score of 20 (i.e. 4 × 5 = 20).

$$A_{Mercedes\text{-}Benz} = \sum_{i=1}^{1} b_{fueleconomy}\, e_{fueleconomy}$$
$$= 1 \times 5 = 5$$

Figure 10.7 Hypothetical attitudinal score for Mercedes-Benz

$$A_{Toyota} = \sum_{i=1}^{1} b_{fueleconomy}\, e_{fueleconomy}$$
$$= 4 \times 5 = 20$$

Figure 10.8 Hypothetical attitudinal score for Toyota

Of course, this probably does not provide a complete picture of the buyer's attitude towards the two makes of car, because the buyer is likely to value other attributes too, not just fuel economy. We can obtain a fuller picture by including all these other attributes in the equation and summing the result. We can also extend the exercise to cover all the other competing brands (e.g. BMW, Audi and Volvo).

WHAT CAN A SALES AGENT DO?

This way of thinking about the attitude structure of an object (or event or situation) has a long history and evolved from the expectancy–value model of human behaviour. This model postulates that our attitude towards an action is a function of what we expect to achieve with or from that action and how much we value that expected outcome. If we expect an activity (e.g. reading a book) to bring us joy and joy is important to us, then our attitude towards that activity (i.e. reading) will be very high and we will form strong intentions to engage in that activity (see figure 10.9).[28] The Fishbein–Ajzen equation is therefore a useful generalisation of expectancy–value models.

$$A_x = \sum_{i=1}^{n} \text{Expectancy} \times \text{value}$$

Figure 10.9 The expectancy-value equation

What has this model got to do with selling? There are three major implications for a salesperson. First, it lays out the structure of attitudes very clearly, showing the important components of expectancy and value. Second, it assists a sales agent to identify which attributes to emphasise (or de-emphasise) to improve the buyer's attitude towards the brand during the presentation. This second aspect implies that our attitude is not necessarily fixed (or 'invariant') but can be moulded during the sales presentation, for instance, by objection-handling, which causes the buyer to re-evaluate his or her expectations and value. Third, the model highlights the importance of understanding how the target audience perceives the attributes (and hence the benefits) of the brand in relation to the competition, and so reinforces the need to conduct research before the presentation and to listen carefully to buyer feedback during and after the presentation. Once a sales agent understands these implications, they are ready to attempt multi-attribute reframing.

Multi-attribute reframing involves influencing how a buyer perceives a product by attempting to change his or her attitude structure. This typically occurs during the sales presentation or while handling objections afterwards. Figure 10.10 summarises the five strategies[29] a sales agent can employ to improve a buyer's attitude towards the brand (denoted as 'Brand Att_x'):

1. Increase the buyer's belief that the brand possesses the relevant attribute. In our car example above, the Mercedes-Benz sales agent might try to convince the buyer that Mercedes-Benz does indeed possess high fuel economy because it uses the latest technology to manage fuel consumption.
2. Decrease the strength of the buyer's belief that a competing brand possesses the relevant attribute. For instance, the Mercedes-Benz sales agent might try to persuade the buyer that Toyota's fuel economy is overrated because, say, the efficiency is derived not from a better technology but rather from the car's lighter weight.
3. Increase the buyer's positive evaluation of one or more attributes that are unique strengths of the brand. For instance, the Mercedes-Benz sales agent might emphasise and reinforce the buyer's dream of driving a luxury car once in his or her life.
4. Introduce an important attribute that is a unique strength of the brand, and which the buyer might not already have considered. For example, if a Mercedes-Benz car has higher resale value than a Toyota, the sales agent might introduce this attribute into the sales discussion.
5. Change the decision rule for the purchase, to try to tilt the buyer's preference towards your brand. For example, the Mercedes-Benz sales agent might suggest that the most important choice rule for buying a car is its resale value and that a car that does not have a good resale value should not even be considered.

This is an example of changing a compensatory decision rule (where a decision is reached by allowing one attribute to compensate for another) to a non-compensatory conjunctive decision rule (where a brand is rejected if a particular attribute does not meet a minimum cut-off).

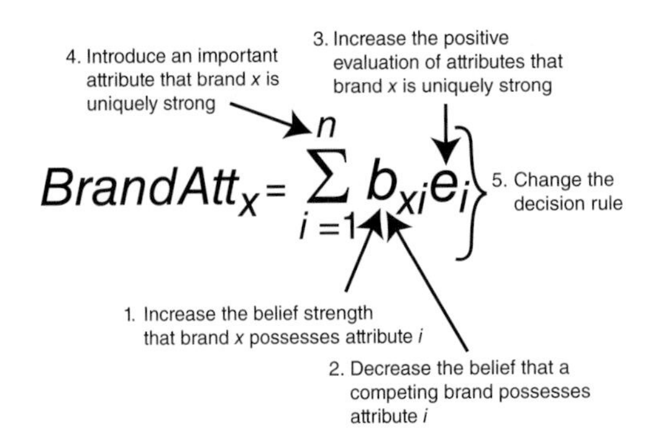

Figure 10.10 Five ways to improve a buyer's brand attitude

FINDING DIFFERENT 'HOT BUTTONS' FOR DIFFERENT SEGMENTS

The equation above assumes that everyone views the target brand (or competing brand) similarly. What if this is not true? What if different buyers value the various attributes differently? This will complicate the selling process, but the principle remains the same. The sales agent just needs to keep track of the different beliefs (i.e. expectancy) and evaluations (i.e. value) that the different buyers or segments hold. Once this is understood, the process of multi-attribute reframing can proceed in the way we have just described. The real value with this method is that the sales agent knows which attributes to emphasise for each buyer or segment – these are sometimes euphemistically called the buyer's 'hot buttons'.

Selling the improved value

Price is often perceived to be an obstacle in the sales process. However, in reality people usually do not buy something based solely on price – if they did, the cheapest goods would always be market leaders, which is clearly not the case. Rather, people buy based on perceived value, which can be conceptually defined as the trade-off between perceived benefits and price (see figure 10.11).

$$\text{Perceived value} = \frac{\text{Perceived benefits}}{\text{Price}}$$

Figure 10.11 A conceptual equation for perceived value

Perceived value is not evaluated in isolation, but rather in comparison with another competing offer. For instance, before making a purchase, a prospective buyer typically compares a new offering to a reference in order to ascertain its worth. The reference can be the current product, or the next best alternative.

Improved value assessment is especially important in industrial buying because certain criteria must be fulfilled before the next step of the purchase can proceed. In the group-buying context that typifies most industrial buying, this is a critical requirement. For instance, the buying group may stipulate that the new equipment must improve output by at least 15% to warrant a changeover.

Let's consider an example of value analysis for an industrial product, say a new machine that makes ball bearings. In table 10.1, the first column (i) identifies the various attributes of a machine. The second column (%) shows the percentage improvement the new machine provides compared to the old one; for instance, the new machine creates 15% more ball bearings per hour and is 40% more energy efficient. The third column (e_i) shows the relative importance the buying group places on each of the attributes, the most important one for them being quantity per hour (a weight of 0.4). By multiplying columns 2 and 3 for each attribute, we get the weighted improvement for each one, as shown in the last column (% * e_i). Adding these weighted improvements yields 16.5% total percentage improvement over the old machine.

Table 10.1 An example of value analysis

1. Attribute (i)	2. Improvement (%)	3. Relative importance (e_i)	4. Weighted improvement (% * e_i)
Quantity per hour	15.0	0.4	6.0
Energy savings	40.0	0.1	4.0
Maintenance improvement	20.0	0.2	4.0
Quality improvement	10.0	0.2	2.0
Ease of application	5.0	0.1	0.5
Total	100.0	1.0	*16.5*

Note: Column 4 = column 2 × column 3

How can a sales agent exploit this figure? At face value, it means that the sales agent can theoretically set the price of the new machine 16.5% higher than the price of the old one. This is only a theoretical number, though, because typically the buyer will resist a price increase of that size and a lower, compromised price will have to be negotiated. This negotiation process actually gives the sales agent a chance to demonstrate an even greater value; for instance, the sales agent could highlight his or her willingness to sell the new machine at a price only 12% higher than the old machine's price, even though the new machine gives a substantial improvement of 16.5%.

In summary, we can see how this form of analysis can be useful for a sales agent. It can also be adapted for use when there are multiple competing brands.

Selling the vision

All the discussion so far about presentation and handling objections has emphasised the importance of evaluating the buyer's perception about the attributes of a product or service and the value the buyer places on each attribute. This form of analysis centres on the immediate (or proximal) value of the offering. But this is not the only approach – consider the following advice:[30]

- Don't sell me books. Sell me pleasant hours and the fruits of knowledge.
- Don't sell me toys. Sell my children happy moments.

- Don't sell me a house. Sell me comfort, contentment, a good investment, and pride of ownership.
- Don't sell me insurance. Sell me peace of mind and a great future for my family and me.

These are examples of selling by reference to future benefits: what we will call vision selling. This involves providing the prospective buyer with a mental picture of a continuous payoff that can extend to the future, which may be utilitarian or hedonistic in nature.

Vision selling introduces the element of time by framing the attributes in terms of achieving long-term benefits or payoffs continuously, rather than in terms of immediate attainment. These continuous long-term benefits tend to be about future positive experiences and value. For instance, a prospective buyer of a house may only focus on its attributes (e.g. number of rooms, size of garage), and may forget about benefits that may arise in the future, such as the potential growth in its value (the utilitarian motive) or its capacity for hosting dinner parties and other events for years to come (the hedonic motive). A sales agent should always paint a mental picture of a continuous payoff that can stretch to the future for the prospective buyer.

There are at least three reasons why vision selling is important. First, it helps remind the sales agent to reinforce the two basic buying motives – utilitarian and hedonic. Second, it encourages the sales agent to use visualisation as a selling technique, often the only way to paint a future. Research has found that high-performing insurance sales agents tend to use visualisation to help prospective buyers understand the advantages of their offerings, while low-performing insurance sales agents tend to rely solely on the product-benefit approach.[31] Third, changing the time frame of how people can see their future can reduce their resistance, especially if it can be couched in a meaningful way – people generally tend to evaluate distant events with greater purpose and meaning.[32]

Now, lest one thinks this tactic only applies to high ticket items (e.g. houses, insurances), consider Ken Helm, the iconic winemaker from Canberra (see figure 10.12). He once complained that it was difficult to sell his Riesling (a white wine) to Chinese tourists who visited his cellar door because they prefer red wine, as the colour signifies luck. One day, he hit upon an idea, why not sell his Riesling as an age worthy wine? Riesling turns to golden yellow as it ages (see figure 10.13), and this colour also signifies luck to the Chinese. Therefore, his solution was to sell to the Chinese the vision that drinking his age worthy Riesling would bring them good luck![33]

Figure 10.12 Ken Helm, the iconic winemaker of Helm Wines

Figure 10.13 The golden yellow hue of Riesling as the wine ages (left to right)

Are salespeople born or made?

How many times have you heard the phrase 'Oh! He is a born salesman'. But is this true? Are some people born with a natural selling ability or is selling ability learned? This is not a trivial question because every year, millions of dollars are spent on sales training and this is not counting the cost incurred by a firm when a salesperson drops out. In the US, the annual dropout rate of a salesperson across the industry is about 28%, at a replacement cost of about US$120 000 per person.[34] If one were to subscribe to the entity theory of abilities, being that people are born with certain predispositions (e.g. optimistic thinking) that makes them a natural salesperson, then it is better to spend resources on selecting and recruiting the right candidates. On the other hand, if we subscribe to the incremental ability theory that people are malleable and can be trained (e.g. to think optimistically), then resources should be spent on training.

But what exactly is selling ability? And can this ability be learned? One perspective says that selling ability is comprised of three dimensions: (1) interpersonal skills (e.g. able to read non-verbal signals), (2) salesmanship skills (e.g. able to prospect), and (3) technical skills (e.g. understanding own products).[35] On the surface, the solution seems quite straightforward. If a person can be trained on these three dimensions, then sales should improve. The only problem is that it is challenging to train someone on interpersonal skills. The sales agent for instance must not only learn to have empathy with the buyer's dissatisfaction but also learn to read subtle cues while interacting and, if necessary, quickly change tack during the selling process.[36] Such skills may not be easy to learn. And what if selling skills are more complex than these three dimensions? For instance, in adaptive selling, the sales agent must also be adept in using seller influence tactics (or SITs) contingently. Some of these are:[37]

- information exchange – where general issues are discussed without the sales agent asking for a request
- recommendations – where a sales agent suggests that the customer will be more profitable if the suggestions are followed
- threats – where a sales agent threatens the customer with a future penalty if there is no compliance
- promises – where a reward is promised if the customer complies
- ingratiation – where a sale agent praises the customer for his or her achievements or for expressing a similar attitude
- inspirational appeal – where the sales agent appeals to the higher-order psychological needs of the customer (e.g. certain values and ideals).

By contingent, we mean that the sales agent must know when to apply these influence tactics, and to whom. McFarland and colleagues[38] discovered that when customers are task-oriented, the sales agent would tend to apply information exchange and recommendations. Such customers just want to get on with completing the buying task, and hence they value getting the right information quickly. On the other hand, for interaction-oriented customers, that is, those who enjoy socialising with the sales agents, ingratiation and inspirational appeals are more commonly applied; somehow a sales agent can intuit that such customers would enjoy interactions that are emotional in nature. Finally, for customers who are self-oriented, that is, those who are preoccupied with their own self-interest, the sales agents tend to entice such customers with promises and ingratiation; such customers tend to get excited with personal rewards, including being praised.

McFarland and colleagues discovered these contingent effects by interviewing 193 sales agents and their corresponding customers.[39] Sales agents were *not* aware of SITs, but somehow still managed to apply these tactics in a seemingly effective way. But how? One could speculate these sales agents must have learnt over the years (through trial and error) the contingent effectiveness of these influence tactics. The feedback they received would have given them greater confidence,[40] and their persistence or tenacity would have ensured that they learned and improved over the years. In the Further Thinking section at the end of this chapter, we will revisit this notion of persistence when we discuss optimistic thinking.[41]

CASE STUDY 10.2 BLENDING HIGH-TOUCH AND HIGH-TECH IN B2B SELLING

Business-to-business (B2B) enterprises generally lag their business-to-consumer (B2C) counterparts in using digital tools to sell. This is because B2B selling is more complicated, often involving consultative selling, and hence face-to-face interaction (i.e. the human touch) is important. However, with increasing digitisation, this dictum may no longer be true. Recent research by McKinsey[42] suggests that a blend of high-tech and high-touch is necessary, but the weightage depends on where the prospect is in their decision journey. Typically, at the start of a new buying process, human-to-human interaction is necessary. Here, a human touch will go a long way at this stage in reducing risk perception, even though the prospect may have started doing their research online. The objective for the supplier is to be in the consideration list of the buyer at this time.

The other extreme end of the journey is when a customer is already satisfied and simply wants to re-order. Here, human touch is less important. What is more valued is an automated streamline repurchase process. If a human touch is needed, it is more as a backup for the automated system. At this stage, there is no need to involve any sales agent, whose time is better spent upfront securing new appointments and presentation to new prospects.

Now, a shrewd sales agent would already know that their time is better spent at the beginning of the buyer's decision journey. Enlightened firms will structure the compensation in such a way that the sales agent is better rewarded when they find new customers. If so, then the sales agent should (1) target larger prospects; (2) attract the attention of the decision maker early in the sales process; (3) ask, listen and uncover their needs; (4) communicate the unique value proposition; (5) justify the cost of the customer's purchase; (6) anticipate and address sales objections; (7) understand the competition thoroughly; (8) cultivate a network of influence (before it is needed); (9) ask for referrals; and (10) retain and upsell to existing customers. These are the 10 best practices that will lead to bigger deals, faster.[43]

Digital tools are also useful at the active consideration stage. For this part of the journey, the suppliers can assist by ensuring all information is easily accessible. The section on FAQ (i.e. Frequency Asked Questions) and product information should always be up to date. If the purchase is complex, there should be an intelligent system which allows a prospect to make product comparison or use configurators to generate new prices. And, if necessary, the prospect should be able to quickly connect to experts. Ideally, technical expertise should be available 24 hours a day (e.g. via webchat). The objective of the supplier is to be included in the final short list, be invited to provide a formal proposal and, eventually, to give a presentation.

As one can see from above, context is important. A B2B supplier should use a blend of high-touch and high-tech to sell but the intensity of each kind (and hence investments) will depend on what the customer needs as they make their journey towards purchase (see figure 10.14). Throughout, the supplier should be transparent, speedy and provide great expertise in their interactions.

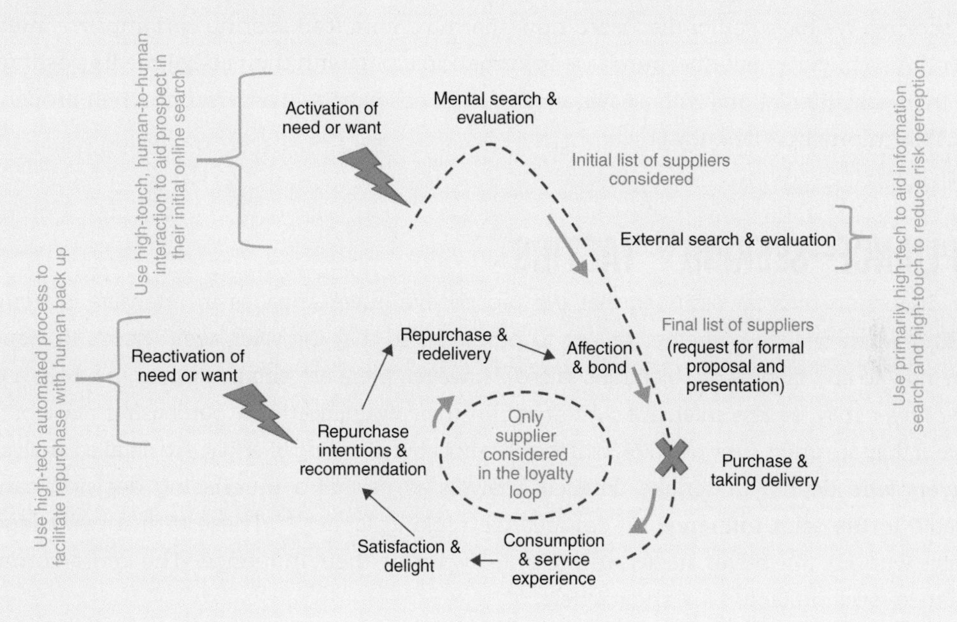

Figure 10.14 How high-touch and high-tech can be useful in the B2B customer decision journey

DISCUSSION QUESTIONS

1. Now that you understand how high-touch and high-tech can be blended in selling, provide an example in which this was, or was not, carried out properly in a recent experience you might have had with a firm. Described what happened.
2. Which part of the decision journey should be devoted to high-touch, and which part to high-tech? Justify your answer.
3. Of the 10 best practices of selling faster, discussed above, which of these is the *most* and *least* interesting to you? Discuss why.

Artificial intelligence and selling

Much of selling requires completing a series of manual tasks. But with artificial intelligence (AI), many of these tasks can be automated. For instance, the rise of virtual assistance means personalised email messaging with automated follow up can be sent to prospective buyers requesting a meeting before handling promising leads to a live sales agent. This frees up the time of the sales agent to concentrate on the actual selling.

AI can also help a company sell more profitably by providing better analysis.[44] First is optimal pricing. Using historical data, algorithms can be built to help a sales agent price optimally during negotiation. This means knowing how much to discount (if at all) and to which buyer. Second is forecasting and managing sales performance. AI-assisted software can help a sales manager forecast what the total sales revenue is likely to be next quarter and with dashboards can see which deals are more likely to be successful, or otherwise. Third is cross-selling and up-selling. AI can identify which customers are more likely to buy a new offering (hence cross-sell) or to a better version of an existing product (hence up-sell). This makes marketing more efficient. Fourth is lead scoring. We have earlier discussed how sharing a joint lead scoring can improve integration. With AI, a buyer's historical purchase information along with their social media postings as well as their past interactions with a sales agent can be collected and assessed for their propensity to buy. This improves efficiency.

COMPLIANCE–SEEKING[45] TACTICS

All our discussion thus far assumes that the prospective buyer engages in intensive, systematic processing when deciding whether or not to purchase, so that the sales agent needs to respond convincingly to any queries or objections raised. However, there are circumstances in which a prospective buyer may be less intensive-systematic in their evaluation of a purchasing decision; for example, if they are under time pressure or if they are not able or willing to engage in detailed analysis.[46]

Buyers who do not undertake detailed analysis as part of a purchasing decision can be vulnerable to the sales influence of 'compliance seeking tactics'.[47] These tactics can trigger a purchase without the buyer necessarily being aware of their influence. The most common compliance–seeking tactics are shown here.

Scarcity

This tactic works on the principle that the value of things tends to be a function of their scarcity. For instance, luxury goods and even goods that are banned generally tend to be perceived as more valuable.[48] Marketers have long known this and exploit it by, among other things, limiting the distribution of goods, limiting access to certain information and giving special privileges only to certain customers. In advertising, scarcity is usually conveyed by portraying that the stock of the goods is running out or its price is discounted for a limited time only. In selling, this is often heightened by also suggesting that such an offer rarely comes along.

Scarcity can also be combined with competition[49] to elicit an even higher level of perceived value – as in a public auction (see figure 10.15). The most dramatic example can be seen in the auctions of paintings of famous deceased artists. These are extra-valuable because the artist is no longer alive to paint another picture. Such paintings can fetch in the hundreds of millions as buyers compete to out-bid each other. The picture *The Scream*, by the Norwegian painter Edvard Munch, was auctioned for a record US$120 million. The auction lasted just 12 minutes.[50]

Figure 10.15 Fine Arts Auction at Christie's, London 1887

Authority

Authority means using the power of coercion or social status to encourage compliance. In marketing, coercion is not appropriate, and instead we tend to rely on social dominance cues or expertise. Social dominance cues are ways of clearly signifying a higher level of status to the other party in order to encourage compliance. Symbols of status include items such as branded clothing, a business suit or luxury products (e.g. cars, watches and jewellery). In a series of non-verbal interactive studies of dyads (i.e. observing how two people interact), researchers found that the presence of power brands, such as wearing a Hugo Boss sweater or having a can of 'Coca-Cola' on the table, is enough to induce non-verbal submissive behaviour (e.g. nodding, smiling) in the other person (i.e. the 'target'). This is more pronounced if the target person has a low social dominance predisposition. Interestingly, women are susceptible to such status cues only if the other party is a male associated with high-status brands (but not low ones).[51]

One clear implication of this is that sales agents should dress well. This helps to give an impression of success, which triggers status heuristics. Studies have shown that clothing that signifies status or formality, especially a specialist uniform such as those worn by police and soldiers, tends to elicit higher levels of compliance. In one meta-analysis, the correlation was found to be 0.46.[52]

Using clothing and other forms of display to suggest status should be done subtly. For instance, the sales agent should not verbally boast about his or her success, because doing so is likely to trigger a negative reaction in the prospective buyer: nobody likes a boastful personality. Erring on the side of humility[53] when it comes to verbal speech probably makes more sense.[54] But always dress for success.

Social proof

This means relying on others as proof that the product or service is good. For instance, the sales agent could say, 'This is one of our best sellers' or 'People have been buying this model a lot lately'. Very subtly, this sort of statement implies that the many people who have bought the product have not been disappointed, and that the current prospective buyer can expect the same result. We see this principle at work most clearly when purchases are publicly ranked. One study found that people tend to download very popular music even if they have not heard of the artist.[55] This is the reason why first-time authors often buy up their own books in the first week after publication, to get into the bestseller list.[56] Social validation can also be combined with scarcity as when the sales agent says, 'This model has been so popular that we will soon run out'.

Consistency and commitment

We typically like to maintain consistency in our beliefs, preferences and behaviour, to keep our world in a neat order. This desire to be consistent varies from individual to individual,[57] but it is also an important drive in order not to unsettle others.

A sales technique that exploits consistency is called 'foot-in-the-door' (or FITD). It typically starts with a small request that may be easily agreed to. Once people agree to the small request, they are more likely to agree to a larger request, which also happens to be the real request. One variation often used by telemarketers is to start each call with some seemingly innocuous questions, solely to induce potential customers to say 'yes' to that question before the actual request follows. For instance, the telemarketer might ask a series of questions about whether it is important to eliminate world hunger, which are designed to evoke a 'yes' answer, and then followed by a request for a donation to a charity that feeds hungry children. In order to appear consistent, people are likely to donate.

Another ethically questionable technique is often used in selling used cars. This is how it works: the sales agent will pretend to have sold you the car at a good price. But once you are committed to buying, he or she will suddenly remember some reason why the sale cannot be completed – for example, because his or her boss has objected to the price (which triggers the authority heuristic too, as discussed above). At this point, what you thought to be a bargain purchase is no longer so. But since you are already committed to, and probably enthusiastic about, buying that car (and may have talked yourself into owning it), it is easier for the sales agent to persuade you to buy the same car, or even a different one, at a higher price.

The tactic is often called a 'low-ball' because the offer is essentially changed. One effective variation of this is the 'lure', more commonly called the 'bait-and-switch'.[58] Here, one might be enticed to buy something (e.g. a vacation to go to New Zealand) because it is such a great offer only to learn that it is sold out. The customer is then encouraged to switch to a *different* product (e.g. a vacation to Vanuatu) often at a higher cost. The difference between a low-ball tactic and that of bait-and-switch is that the latter involves a switch to a different product. Both tactics are unethical because they are premeditated and deceptive.

Reciprocity

Reciprocity is a powerful heuristic that relies on our desire to want to return a favour. Applying this tactic, a sales agent will often do seemingly small favours for a buyer, which create a sense of indebtedness. This will in turn induce the buyer to concede to the sales agent's request later on. One common tactic is to offer the buyer a free trial. For example, a car sales agent might say, 'Why don't you have this car over the weekend before you decide whether to buy it or not?' When Apple first launched its Macintosh computers many years ago, it had great success with a campaign that let consumers take a computer home for a 'test drive' before buying.

Another common application of this principle is the sampling programs seen in supermarkets, where the sales agent offers you a piece of cheese (or chocolate or biscuit) to try. This is designed to create a sense of indebtedness, after which you feel more obliged to buy the product. To maximise the effectiveness of this tactic, the sales agent generally ensures that the product is stocked nearby, so they can hand it over to you immediately.

Another technique that exploits the reciprocity heuristic is called 'foot-in-the-face' (or FITF).[59] This is the opposite of the 'foot-in-the door' technique, because this time the sales agent makes a large request first (as opposed to a small request first). The sales agent expects this large request to be rejected and afterwards comes back with a smaller request, which in this case is the real request. For instance, the sales agent might try to sell you six boxes of sweets for $6. Having rejected this large offer, the sales agent might reduce this request to just one box for $1. Chances are you are more likely to accept this because you have already rejected the agent once.[60]

Likeability

As the saying goes, 'people buy from people they like', and not surprising, we also tend to hang out with people we like. Likeability 'works' because it creates a positive emotion in others, which is a psychological benefit.[61] Therefore, one of the easiest ways for a sales agent to influence a prospective buyer is simply to be likeable. There are many ways of achieving this, including Familiarity, Attractiveness, Compliments and Similarity or 'FACS'. We will examine each of those in turn.

FAMILIARITY

We tend to like familiar things, which is why we tend to repeatedly buy the same brands. In the same way, we tend to socialise mainly with people we know instead of with strangers. That is why we called them friends! Marketers have long known and exploited this in multi-level selling (e.g. Tupperware parties) or members-get-members program (e.g. gym membership).

While this may be common sense, experimental research reveals that the tendency manifests in unexpected ways; for example, it shows that we tend to like or prefer things even after only a very brief exposure to them, and that this liking increases with repeated exposures. More than 40 years ago, in a series of now classic studies, a psychologist by the name of Robert Zajonc[62] discovered this curious effect, which he called the 'mere exposure effect'. First, he showed that we generally prefer more frequently used words than less frequently used words. Second, when he briefly exposed people (for about 2 seconds) to nonsensical words, characters or unknown faces, they grew to like them more as the number of repetitions increased from 0, 1, 2 and 10 to 25 times. Since the objects were nonsensical or unknown, the people's increased liking could not have been due to prior knowledge, and so can be attributed to their repeated exposure.

Hundreds of studies have since replicated Zajonc's results. In a major review, it was found that mere exposure effects tend to be stronger when the stimuli are presented subliminally, but that they decline after between 10–20 exposures.[63] It was also found that the effect even applies to a person whom you meet only briefly; for instance, repeated exposure to a student who happens to be sitting in a classroom will lead you to like them more, even though there is no direct contact.[64] In another experiment, participants who were made to stand next to each other as they moved from one stand to another, ostensibly for a taste-test experiment, reported greater liking when they encountered the same person again, even though they had not talked to each other.[65]

WHAT CAN A SALES AGENT DO TO ENHANCE AND TAKE ADVANTAGE OF FAMILIARITY?

In the sales context, it pays to invest in corporate advertising so that prospective buyers will become more familiar with the corporation. This greater visibility should help the sales agent secure more appointments and get more customers.[66] Alternatively, the sales agent can become more active in the local community, to become more familiar to their potential customer base. Yet another tactic is to adopt a referral system, for example by collecting the names and contact details of buyers' friends. The sales agent can then contact these people and begin by mentioning the name of the referrer, in order to establish an instant sense of familiarity.

ATTRACTIVENESS

We also tend to like physically attractive people more than unattractive ones.[67] One possible (and somewhat controversial) reason for this is that, from an evolutionary perspective, attractiveness signifies having good genes – suggesting good health and reproductive fitness.[68] The effects of attractiveness also flow into income. For instance, taller men not only tend to be associated with greater leadership skills and social standing than shorter men, they actually earn significantly more income too.[69] Obese people, on the other hand, tend to earn less over time.[70] Socially, we also want to be seen with physically attractive friends or romantic partners because being close to them also makes us look more attractive.[71] So if you want to appear 'hot' on social media, it helps to show good-looking friends on social media.[72]

It has long been known that attractive people can literally 'get away with murder'. For instance, physically attractive defendants, compared to less attractive ones, are less likely to be found guilty of crimes like robbery and are more likely to receive more lenient sentences.[73] It is no wonder that defence lawyers always insist that their clients look their best on the witness stand. Physically attractive people also tend to be perceived as more honest, kind, sociable and persuasive.[74] This is often called the 'beautiful is good' halo effect. As a result, we are more likely to donate to a charity if the requester is an attractive person rather than an unattractive one.[75]

Eye contact is another effective tactic because it signals intimacy, which is why lovers tend to gaze into each other's eyes.[76] Also, messages are evaluated more favourably when it is presented by someone who makes eye contact with the audience than otherwise.[77] Generally, eye gaze is attractive, but this effect can be accentuated even more if an attractive person looks at us. When an attractive person makes eye contact, we feel good and the reward centre of our brain (ventral striatum) is activated.[78] Finally, smiling also makes us look more attractive. This is because it signifies warmth and makes us appear kind, sincere and even intelligent; these are appealing qualities. Smiling at someone also puts that person in a good mood, which makes him or her want to help others. It is no wonder that a waitress who smiles more gets greater tips too.[79] But the smile must be genuine (sometimes called a Duchenne smile)[80] or else it will backfire.

WHAT CAN A SALES AGENT DO TO ENHANCE AND TAKE ADVANTAGE OF ATTRACTIVENESS?

The easiest option is to simply groom attractively, make eye contact during interactions and, where appropriate, smile genuinely. A more difficult – if not discriminatory – option is to only recruit attractive-looking sales agents.

Dressing attractively does not mean dressing inappropriately. Since physically attractive people are also perceived to be vain and sexually permissive,[81] it is important to avoid reinforcing this stereotype, which can be counterproductive and alienate prospective buyers. Imagine a sales agent dressed in too showy an outfit while trying to sell a car to a married couple; it could create awkwardness or even envy and jealousy. A dress code should stipulate attractive, but appropriate and professional, clothing.

COMPLIMENTS

Another tactic to increase liking is to use compliments or ingratiation – in other words, praising others. The effect is quite robust and there are at least two reasons for this.

First, it is reciprocal: when someone praises us, we are likely to return the praise in the form of liking. In one early study, researchers found that to increase the response rate to a mail survey, all they needed to do was to compliment the respondents on their kindness in the covering letter.

Even the act of remembering a person's name is perceived to be a compliment: they feel special, important and liked. This in turn makes them more likely to want to return the compliment by complying with a request. This was demonstrated in five studies, where researchers found that if a professor remembered a student's name, the student was more likely to comply with the professor's request of buying cookies for charity.[82]

Second and more intriguing is that it is almost impossible to disagree when someone praises you. To do so would imply that we are not as good as the flattery suggests we are. This would create cognitive dissonance because it contradicts the usual positive self-regard we have for ourselves (what psychologists call a 'self-serving bias'). Thus, when others praise us, we are more likely to accept the statements uncritically,[83] as truthful rather than otherwise.[84] Our susceptibility to flattery is most dramatically illustrated in a study where respondents were told to interact with a computer to improve the algorithm of a game. Feedback given by the computer was deliberately manipulated to be either flattering or generic. Interestingly, even though the respondents knew they were interacting with a pre-coded computer (and so had no reason to fear not reciprocating its flattery), those who received flattering feedback reported more positive feelings, better performance, better interactions and greater regard for the computer than the control condition in which the computer did not give any flattering remarks.[85] The computer had become human-like by simple flattery!

Note that in McFarland and colleagues' study discussed earlier, they discovered that sales agents tend to use ingratiation for customers who are interaction-oriented and self-oriented. Since about two thirds of B2B customers tend to have such orientations, it implies a near universal power of ingratiation as an influence tactic.

WHAT CAN A SALES AGENT DO ABOUT COMPLIMENTS?

Studies have shown that buyers tend to be very suspicious when a sales agent adopts this tactic, and rightly so. When compliments or flattery are too obvious – for example, in a situation such as a sales presentation, when the agent clearly has something to gain from the buyer – they will likely backfire.[86] So, a sales agent should look for more subtle ways of flattering and complimenting, for example, by agreeing with the buyer's opinion and by having modest, self-deprecating and deferential behaviour and demeanour. Such tactics enhance the ego of the buyer and are found to be more effective if there is greater difference in status between the two parties,[87] which is clearly the case between the (lower-status) sales agent and the (higher-status) buyer. Yet another way is simply remembering the name of the buyer, which is a more subtle and yet effective means of paying a compliment.

SIMILARITY

We tend to like others who share our background, opinions, attitudes and values.[88] This is because we like ourselves, and therefore by seeing ourselves in others, we end up liking them too.[89] However, this makes us vulnerable to sales agents who are similar to us or who manufacture a veneer of similarity. One early study found that people tend to buy insurance from sales agents who are similar in age, religion and politics to themselves.[90] Even something as trivial as having similar dress style or being a fellow student can increase our compliance. For instance, we are more likely to sign petitions[91] or contribute to charity[92] if the requester dresses in the same way or belongs to the same campus as us. The similarity effect also extends to coincidence; for instance, as silly as it sounds, sharing the same birthday or first name with the requester will make us more compliant with his or her request.[93]

Research has looked at the phenomenon of mimicry in relation to similarity. It turns out that as human beings, we have an innate tendency to automatically (and subconsciously) mimic the behaviour of others in an interaction. Being behaviourally mimicked by another (e.g. in our gestures, postures and mannerisms) makes us like the other person more, creating the impression that our interactions have gone well. This effect does not arise when there is no mimicry.[94] This insight is extremely useful in building rapport.[95] In the context of psychotherapy, some psychotherapists are much better than others in establishing rapport with their patients; these are the ones that are better mimickers. In the context of a restaurant, the very act of repeating the order back to the diner results in significantly higher tip rates. However, the repetition must be verbatim; paraphrasing the order does not have the same effect.[96] In the context of advertising, participants who mimicked the facial expressions, gestures and head movements of a model in a TV ad liked and wanted to buy the advertised product more than participants who did not mimick the model.[97]

Further, being mimicked creates pro-social feelings in us (i.e. feelings that encourage us to want to help others), which in turn makes us want to help others; this has been shown to result in higher levels of donation to charity[98] and picking up dropped pens.[99] Mimicry can also change your taste perception. In one study, respondents were asked a series of questions about a new brand of soft drink or cheese straws, under the pretext that they were participating in pre-launch market research. One set of respondents had their behaviour mimicked while they responded, while the controlled group was not mimicked. What the experimenters found was startling: the mimicked respondents not only reported a higher likelihood of buying the new product (soft drink or cheese straws), but also bought more of it and reported enjoying it more than did the controlled group. This result suggests that being mimicked can actually cause a significant change in our taste perception! Further, when the participant was told that the interviewer would benefit from the success of the new product, this strengthened the effect even more because it was clear who needed help. So, being mimicked creates pro-social feelings which, in turn, make us want to help others.[100]

HOW CAN A SALES AGENT MAKE USE OF SIMILARITY?

The most obvious starting point is to look for points of similarity with the buyer, which should be real and not manufactured. Used-car salespeople are trained to look into the back or boot of a buyer's car, to try to find something from which they can fabricate similarity with the buyer.[101] For instance, if they see golf clubs, they might tell the buyer how much they love playing golf. This is deceitful and can lead to negative outcomes (e.g. if it erodes their trustworthiness, as discussed in the next section). On the other hand, there is no harm in sending a Chinese sales agent to sell a car to a Chinese buyer – they will probably have genuine points of similarity through shared culture.

Another option is for the seller to mimic the body language and speech rate of the buyer. But this should be done subtly. For instance, in the case of body language, there should be a lag of 1–2 seconds, and what is being mimicked should be the corresponding mirror movement of the buyer. For instance, if the buyer is leaning to the left, the sales agent should lean to the right.

Mimicking can also occur with speech. With speech mimicking, the sales agent should try to slowly converge at a slightly higher rate than the speech rate of the buyer.[102] This is because people who speak fast tend to be perceived as more trustworthy and expert. However, converging on the speech rate of the prospective buyer may be more difficult than mimicking their body language.

Trust and trustworthiness

Trust is an important component of the sales process because the buyer must depend on the sales agent to keep his or her promises. The greater the trustworthiness of the sales agent, the easier the negotiation process will be and the more likely the buyer will make a purchase.[103] Despite this, consumers do not generally trust sales agents. This means most sales agents are constantly battling to earn the trust of prospective buyers. Developing trust in buyers should always be the long-term objective of any sales agent.

But what is trust? Although the concept has been discussed quite extensively across many disciplines, for our purposes there are two central elements: *confident expectations* and a *willingness to be vulnerable*.[104] This means that, for a buyer to trust a sales agent, the buyer must be willing to be vulnerable, while also having a positive expectation that the sales agent will deliver as promised.

What about trustworthiness? This is not the same as trust, but rather refers to the characteristics of the trusted party – in this case, the sales agent. Trustworthiness is conceptualised as made up of three dimensions: 'ability, benevolence, and integrity'.[105]

Ability refers to the 'skills, competencies and characteristics that enable a party to have influence within some specific domain'.[106] In industrial or professional selling, this refers to the technical or professional competence or knowledge of the sales agent. Benevolence, on the other hand, is defined as 'the extent to which a trustee (i.e. the sales agent) is believed to want to do good to the trustor (i.e. the buyer), aside from any egocentric profit motive'.[107] In other words, sales agents who genuinely care about and look after the interests of the buyer will be perceived as trustworthy. Integrity, the third dimension of trustworthiness, is 'a set of principles that the trustor (i.e. buyer) finds acceptable'.[108] In the sales context, this means the sales agent is perceived as fair, honest and reliable, traits that are generally acceptable to the buyer. In short, a sales agent can be deemed to be trustworthy if he or she possesses the following qualities:

- ability: competent, knowledgeable
- benevolence: caring, looks after the interest of the buyer
- integrity: fair, honest and reliable.

WHAT CAN A SALES AGENT DO TO BE PERCEIVED AS MORE TRUSTWORTHY?

First, behave in a way that consistently displays or demonstrates the qualities listed above. And the best way of achieving consistency is to be honest and upright. Strive for a win–win outcome, so that it is also fair for the buyer. All these will signal integrity.

Second, provide information that clearly highlights the sales agent's ability. For example, ensure that presentations (and objections handling) are credible. Adopt non-verbal cues that convey an impression of knowledge and competence; for example, research shows that a person who wears formal clothing and speaks in a measured tone tends to be perceived as more trustworthy;[109] this is the same with the wearing of glasses,[110] although this might be stretching the truth a bit.

Third, strive for benevolence by looking after the buyer. For instance, in real estate, if the market is not buoyant, the sales agent could say, 'This is not necessarily the best time to sell a home, and it might be better to hold off for a few years until the market improves'. Such a statement will clearly signal benevolence.

MANAGERIAL APPLICATION: PUTTING IT TOGETHER

How do we make sense of the various ways of influencing the prospective buyers we have discussed in this chapter? Figure 10.16 summarises the different pathways to influence. First, it shows that a sales agent needs to be trustworthy and likeable. The more the agent possesses these qualities, the better regarded he or she will be; that is, the buyer's attitude towards the sales agent will be more positive. This then influences a buyer's intention to buy, via path A. At the same time, if the sales agent is well regarded, he or she can also influence how a buyer sees the product or service, via path B; that is, all things being equal, people are more likely to buy the product if the sales agent who recommends it is likeable and trustworthy. Of course, if the brand is strong to start with, this can also influence how the buyers see the sales agent (as we discussed earlier, it's easier for a sales agent to secure a sales appointment if he or she works for a well-known organisation). For this reason, path B has a double-headed arrow. Thus, paths A and B summarise the idea that we are more likely to buy from people we trust and like.

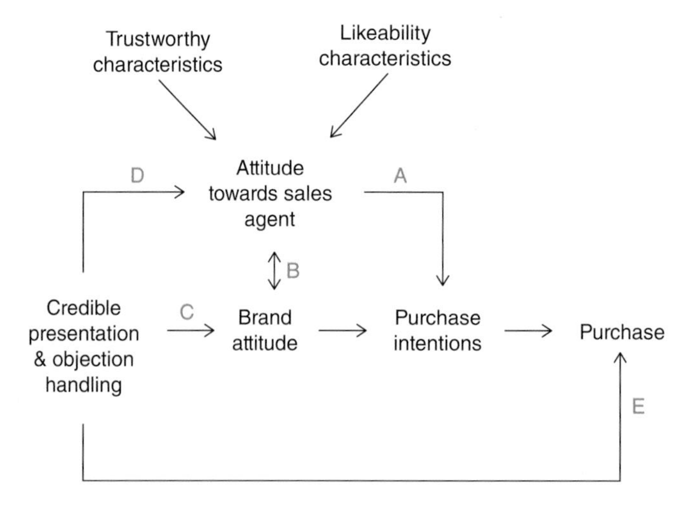

Figure 10.16 A conceptual framework for paths of influence

The sales agent needs to present and handle objections well, via path C. This will affect a buyer's purchase intentions by directly influencing how they feel about the product or service (e.g. during the presentation). While on this path, the sales agent can adopt the tactics of multi-attribute reframing, selling the improved value or the vision. The key is to make the product or service more attractive (i.e. increasing brand attitude).

If the sales agent presents convincingly and handles the objections well, the buyer will also come to regard the sales agent more highly, via path D (i.e. the buyer's positive attitude towards the sales agent will increase).

Finally, compliance can also occur, via path E. On this path, the sales agent can try to influence the purchase directly using compliance-seeking tactics. There is no need to change brand attitude – just the behaviour. But do so ethically.

ETHICS AND A NOTE OF CAUTION

It is very easy for a sales agent who knows these tactics to be tempted to behave unethically. Some of the tactics we have discussed in this chapter are powerful because they can influence people's behaviour in strong but subtle ways, for example by leading people to make decisions they did not initially want to make. For this reason, the tactics are liable to misuse. This can occur where, for example, the sales agent deliberately lies about the veracity of information, or omits important facts, to generate an impression of scarcity (this is one of the compliance-seeking tactics discussed above). For instance, the sales agent could tell the buyer to decide quickly because there are other people very keen to buy the product as well. If this is untrue, then it is unethical. Similar circumstances arise for many of the tactics covered in this chapter.

FURTHER THINKING: ATTRIBUTION STYLES

This section examines one of the perennial questions in sales force management: why do so many sales agents give up and leave their job, while others persist even after repeated failures? The answer lies in how they attribute their success and failure.

LEARNING GOALS

After reading this section, you will understand:

- why some sales agents tend to give up while others persist in the face of rejection
- the attribution styles that differentiate top sales agents from poor ones.

One of the key characteristics of a successful sales agent is tenacity. A survey that asked 215 sales managers to rate 60 characteristics of successful agents (on a scale of 1 to 7)[111] found that tenacity (or persistence) was ranked 4. But what is tenacity? And how does it help us understand why so many sale agents fail?

Seligman and Schulman[112] investigated this question with life insurance sales agents. Selling life insurance is one of the hardest jobs in the selling game: not only are the benefits intangible but they can only be realised if something unfortunate happens. As a result, customers are largely indifferent to the product and life insurance sales agents experience a high level of rejection. It is therefore not surprising that the turnover of life insurance salespeople is high.[113] This becomes a major problem if it means the organisation cannot retain its sales force, since there will be continual costs and disruption associated with having to recruit and train replacement sales agents. Although the problem is serious, the cause Seligman and Schulman identified is quite simple, yet profound.

EXPLANATORY STYLE (OR CAUSAL ATTRIBUTION)

Seligman and Schulman found that the way we explain events influences our persistence. If we think that our success is due to something permanent and pervasive, and we take this success personally we are more likely to persist with what we are doing. High achievers tend to have this kind of explanatory style, known as 'optimistic thinking'. On the other hand, if we attribute our failure to permanent and pervasive causes and we take it personally, then we will probably give up. Low achievers tend to have this kind of explanatory style, known as 'pessimistic thinking'.

But what happens if high achievers encounter failure? Interestingly, they tend to see the failure as only temporary (i.e. it is not permanent), compartmentalise it to only one area of their life or job (it is not pervasive), and do not necessarily take the failure personally (they de-personalise it). This means that an instance of failure does not disturb their optimistic outlook: they think they will once again succeed next time. The same thing can happen in reverse when low achievers experience success: they perceive it as the transient result of luck or coincidence in a discrete aspect of their life or job, and so as something unlikely to be repeated.

Therefore, just as in the case of our cognitive responses (see chapter 7), it is not the events themselves but rather how we interpret or elaborate on them that really matters. In this case, our style or pattern of attributing causes to our successes and failures will influence whether or not we persist in the long term. The diagrams in figure 10.17 summarise these ideas (the ticks signify what high achievers tend to do).

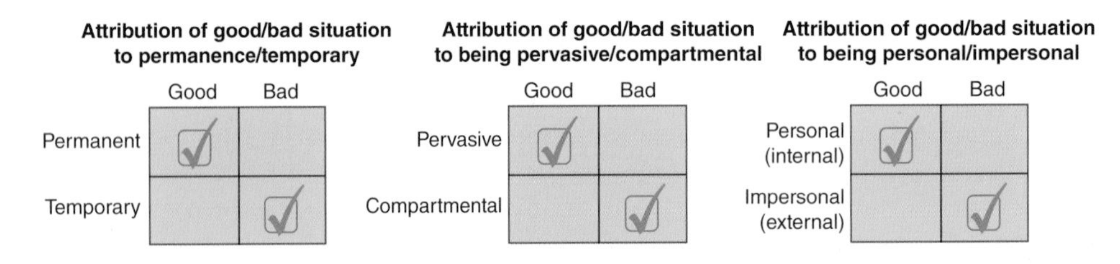

Figure 10.17 How a high achiever attributes good and bad situations

The major insight of Seligman and Schulman's study was that human behaviour (and in particular how persistent, tenacious and determined we are) is strongly influenced by how we perceive and explain events. When we attribute bad events to causes that are stable (or permanent), global (or pervasive) and internal (or personal), we are likely to exhibit symptoms of learned helplessness[114] – because we expect the same outcomes to happen again and again (a pessimistic thinking style). By contrast, if we attribute bad events to causes that are temporary, isolated and impersonal, we are not deterred by the future, and we are more likely to persist with what we are trying to do (an optimistic thinking style).

In their landmark studies of life insurance salespeople, Seligman and Schulman[115] were able to show that optimistic and pessimistic thinking styles not only predict whether a salesperson sells more, but also whether they are likely to quit the profession. In conclusion, Seligman and Schulman found quite a simple, yet profound, answer to the question: why do some persist and others give up? It is all about the way we think!

DISCUSSION QUESTIONS

1. Why do we need salespeople? Why can't we just use advertising to sell?
2. Outline the eight steps of high-involvement selling. Which step may benefit the most from other IMC tools?
3. How does corporate reputation assist or hinder a salesperson?
4. Suggest five ways to create an effective sales presentation. Which of these are the most challenging to you and why?
5. Explain the four common ways of handling objections and give an example of each.
6. Give an example of a multi-attribute framing technique in a sales presentation that you have experienced recently.
7. Will you make a good salesperson? Do you think a salesperson is born or made?
8. Describe how artificial intelligence can be harnessed for personal selling.
9. What are the principles of compliance-seeking tactics? Give examples of how they can be misused.
10. What is the difference between trust and trustworthiness?
11. How is the attribution style for success and failure relevant for a salesperson?

NOTES

1 RL Spiro and BA Weitz, 'Adaptive selling: conceptualization, measurement, and nomological validity', *Journal of Marketing Research*, 27(1), 1990, pp. 61–9.

2 BA Weitz, H Sujan and M Sujan, 'Knowledge, motivation, and adaptive behavior: a framework for improving selling effectiveness', *Journal of Marketing*, 50(4), 1986, pp. 174–91.

3 GR Franke and JE Park, 'Salesperson adaptive selling behavior and customer orientation: a meta-analysis', *Journal of Marketing Research*, 43(3), 2006, pp. 693–702.

4 S Albers, MK Mantrala and S Sridhar, 'Personal selling elasticities: a meta-analysis', *Journal of Marketing Research*, 47(5), 2010, pp. 840–53.

5 G Assmus, JU Farley and DR Lehmann, 'How advertising affects sales: a meta-analysis of econometric results', *Journal of Marketing Research*, 21(1), 1984, pp. 65–74.

6 THA Bijmolt, HJ van Heerde and RGM Pieters, 'New empirical generalizations on the determinants of price elasticity', *Journal of Marketing Research*, 42, 2005, pp. 141–56.

7 E Pöyry, P Parvinen and RG McFarland, 'Generating leads with sequential persuasion: should sales influence tactics be consistent or complementary?', *Journal of Personal Selling & Sales Management*, 37(2), 2017, pp. 89–99.

8 This is similar to the idea of varying the advertising theme discussed in chapter 7.

9 TM Smith, S Gopalakrishna and PM Smith, 'The complementary effect of trade shows on personal selling', *International Journal of Research in Marketing*, 21, 2004, pp. 61–76.

10 L Minsky and KA Quesenberry, 'How B2B sales can benefit from social selling', *Harvard Business Review*, 10 November 2016. Accessed October 2018 at https://hbr.org/2016/11/84-of-b2b-sales-start-with-a-referral-not-a-salesperson?autocomplete=true.

11 In what is now a celebrated classic case study, this is exactly what ABB Electric did in the 1980s, when the market for electric transformers was down. Through clever analyses, they were able to increase both market share and revenue in a difficult market. See DH Gensch, N Aversa and S Moore, 'A choice-modelling market information system that enabled ABB Electric to expand its market share', *Interfaces*, 20(1), January/ February 1990, pp. 6–25.

12 M Kovac, 'Good sales teams know when to stop selling', 21 September 2016. Accessed October 2018 at https://hbr.org/2016/09/good-sales-teams-know-when-to-stop-selling?autocomplete=true.

13 For a more detailed discussion on customer relationship management, see F Buttle and S Maklan, *Customer Relationship management: concepts and technologies*, 4th edition, Routledge, New York, 2018.

14 Oracle presents a different scoring method called buyer engagement and fit using a number of different criteria for each dimension. See Oracle Marketing Cloud, 'Lead scoring, a guide for modern marketers'. Accessed October 2018 at www.oracle.com/marketingcloud/resources/lead-scoring.html.

15 JS Seiter and S Hatch, 'Effect of tattoos on perceptions of credibility and attractiveness', *Psychological Reports*, 96, 2005, pp. 1113–20.

16 T Levitt, *Industrial purchasing behaviour*, Harvard Graduate School of Business Administration, Boston, 1965.

17 JR Morrill, 'Industrial advertising pays off', *Harvard Business Review*, March/April 1970, pp. 4–14, 159–69.

18 The SPIN method was developed by Neil Reckham in *SPIN Selling*, Penguin Australia, 2000.

19 For similar suggestions, see S Armstrong, *Persuasive advertising: evidence-based principles*, Palgrave Macmillan, London, 2010, pp. 312–14.

20 It is better to provide your credentials at the beginning because it will influence how the audience processes your message, especially if they are too lazy to think too much about the subsequent message. See X Nan, 'The influence of source credibility on attitude certainty: exploring the moderating effects of timing of source identification and individual need for cognition', *Psychology and Marketing*, 26(4), pp. 321–32.

21 Credibility works through heuristics (see chapter 7); that is, if the audience thinks you are credible, they are *less* likely to scrutinise your message. They just accept the fact that you are an expert (i.e. using a peripheral route of processing). On the other hand, if you are not credible, then you want your audience to pay attention to your carefully crafted message (i.e. using the central route of persuasion), which should be strong and well argued, and hence persuasive. See RH Gass and JS Seiter, *Persuasion*, 6th edition, Routledge, New York and London, 2018, p. 92.

22 JC Reinard, 'The empirical study of the persuasive effects of evidence: the status after fifty years of research', *Human Communication Research*, 15(1), 1988, pp. 3–59.

23 A low-pitched voice is more credible and persuasive. See M Dubey, J Farrell and L Ang, 'How accent and pitch affect persuasiveness in radio advertising', *Advances in Advertising Research* series, 9, 2018, pp. 117–30, European Advertising Association, Springer.

24 H Mcginley, R Lefevre, P Mcginley, 'The influence of a communicator's body position on opinion change in others', *Journal of Personality and Social Psychology*, 31(4), 1975, pp. 686–90.

25 JW Brehm, *A theory of psychological reactance*, Academic Press, New York, 1996.

26 TM Smith, S Gopalakrishna, and R Chatterjee, 'Integrated marketing communications at the marketing–sales interface', *Journal of Marketing Research*, 43(4), 2006, 564–79.

27 M Fishbein and I Ajzen, *Belief, attitude, intention, and behavior: an introduction to theory and research*, Addison-Wesley, Reading, MA, 1975. Of course, our intention to buy can also be influenced by what others expect of us and our willingness to comply. It is often influenced by our perceived control of the purchase. In social psychology, this is often called the theory of planned behaviour. See I Azjen, 'Perceived behavioural control, self-efficiency, locus of control, and the theory of planned behaviour', *Journal of Applied Social Psychology*, 32, 2002, pp. 665–83.

28 MJ Rosenberg, 'An analysis of affective-cognitive consistency', in CI Hovland and MJ Rosenberg (eds), *Attitude organization and change*, Yale University Press, New Haven, CT, 1960, pp. 15–64.

29 This approach is also suggested in advertising. See JR Rossiter and S Bellman, *Marketing communications: theory and applications*, Pearson Prentice Hall, Frenchs Forest Australia, 2005, pp. 68–9.

30 M LeBoeuf, *How to win customers and keep them for life: revised and updated for the digital age*, Berkeley Books, New York, 2000.

31 S Dwyer, J Hill and W Martin, 'An empirical investigation of critical success factors in the personal selling process for homogenous goods', *Journal of Personal Selling & Sales Management*, 20(3), Summer 2000, pp. 151–9.

32 RR Vallacher and DM Wegner, 'What do people think they are doing? Action, identification and human behavior', *Psychological Review*, 94, 1987, pp. 2–15.

33 Personal conversation with Ken Helm at a Riesling tasting show in Sydney in February 2018 (Riesling Riot, Town Hall Sydney). You can find out more about Ken Helm wines here: http://winetenquestions.com.au/ken-helm-am-helm-wines/. Accessed October 2018.

34 D Hoffmeister and R Rocco, *2012 Sales Effectiveness Survey*, DePaul University, Center for Sales Leadership, Chicago, 2011.

35 JO Rentz, e al., 'A measure of selling skill: scale development and validation', *Journal of Personal Selling & Sales Management*, 22(1), 2002, pp. 13–21.

36 D Mayer and HM Greenberg, 'What makes a good salesman?', *Harvard Business Review*, July–August, 2006. Accessed October 2018 at https://hbr.org/2006/07/what-makes-a-good-salesman.

37 The original taxonomy was developed by Frazier and Summers, which was updated later by McFarland et al. See GL Frazier and J Summers, 'The use of influence strategies in interfirm relationships in industrial channels', *Journal of Marketing*, 48, 1984, pp. 43–55 and RG McFarland, GN Challagalla and TA Shervani, 'Influence tactics for effective adaptive selling', *Journal of Marketing*, 70, 2006, pp. 103–17.

38 RG McFarland, GN Challagalla, and TA Shervani, 'Influence tactics for effective adaptive selling', *Journal of Marketing*, 70, 2006, pp. 103–17.

39 Although McFarland et al. were guided by Kelman's theory of influence in developing their questionnaires, it was the sales agents and their corresponding buyers who confirmed Kelman's theory even though none of them knew anything about Kelman's theory. For more information about Kelman's theory of influence, see H Kelman, 'Compliance, identification, and internalization: three processes of attitude change', *Journal of Conflict Resolution*, 2(1), 1958, pp. 51–60.

40 JM Loveland, JW Lounsbury, SH Park and DW Jackson, 'Are salespeople born or made? Biology, personality, and the career satisfaction of salespeople', *Journal of Business & Industrial Marketing*, 30(2), 2015, pp. 233–40.

41 P Schulman, 'Applying learned optimism to increase sales productivity', *The Journal of Personal Selling & Sales Management*, 19(1), 1999, pp. 31–7.

42 C Angevine, CL Lun Plotkin and J Stanley, 'When B2b buyers want to go digital – and when they don't', *McKinsey Quarterly*, August, 2017. Accessed October 2018 at www.mckinsey.com/business-functions/digital-mckinsey/our-insights/when-b2b-buyers-want-to-go-digital-and-when-they-dont.

43 J Boyens, '10 keys to selling bigger deals faster', *Forbes*, 19 September 2018. Accessed 2018 at www.forbes.com/sites/forbescoachescouncil/2018/09/19/10-keys-to-selling-bigger-deals-faster/#d783dff7d0b0.

44 V Antonio, 'How AI is changing sales', *Harvard Business Review*, 30 July 2018. Accessed May 2019 at https://hbr.org/2018/07/how-ai-is-changing-sales.

45 We agree with Gass and Seiter that the term 'compliance seeking' is more a reflection of what influencers try to do instead of the more common term 'compliance gaining'. See RH Gass and JS Seiter, *Persuasion*, 6th edition, Routledge, New York and London, 2018, p. 236.

46 DJ MacInnis, C Moorman and BJ Jaworski, 'Enhancing consumers' motivation, ability and opportunity to process brand information from ads: conceptual framework and managerial implications', *Journal of Marketing*, 55, October 1991, pp. 32–53.

47 The section on compliance-seeking tactics owes much to the original contribution of Robert Cialdini, the father of the modern compliance-seeking tactics used in selling. See R Cialdini, *Influence: science and practice*, 5th edition, Allyn & Bacon, Boston, 2009.

48 MB Marzis, RB Settle and DC Leslie, 'Elimination of phosphate detergents and psychological reactance', *Journal of Marketing Research*, 10, 1973, pp. 390–5.

49 See Cialdini's work for this and other brilliant insights. RB Cialdini, *Influence: science and practice*, Allyn & Bacon, Boston, MA, 2001.

50 A Chakelian, 'Edvard Munch's The Scream sells for a record $120 million at auction', 3 May 2012. Accessed July 2013 at http://newsfeed.time.com/2012/05/03/edvard-munchs-the-scream-sells-for-a-record-120-million-at-auction/#ixzz2b9qJT5V5.

51 BM Fennis, 'Branded into submission: brand attributes and hierarchization behaviour in same-sex and mixed-sex dyads', *Journal of Applied Social Psychology*, 38, 2008, pp. 1993–2009.

52 C Segrin, 'The effects of nonverbal behaviour on outcomes of compliance gaining attempts', *Communication studies*, 44(3–4) 1993, pp. 169–87.

53 SW Martin, 'Seven personality traits of top salespeople', *Harvard Business Review Blog* network, 2011. Accessed March 2013 at http://blogs.hbr.org/cs/2011/06/the_seven_personality_traits_o.html.

54 I once met a real estate sale agent who, within 10 seconds of shaking my hand, began to tell me how much money he had made, how many properties he owned, and how he managed to score a bargain in some real estate deals. He no longer works as a real estate agent.

55 P Dodds, R Muhamad and D Watts, 'An experimental study of search in global social networks', *Science*, 301(5634), 2003, pp. 827–9.

56 'Authors buy way onto best-seller lists', *Wall Street Journal*, 23 February 2013. Accessed March 2013 at http://allthingsd.com/20130223/authors-buy-way-onto-best-seller-lists/?KEYWORDS=book+sales.

57 R Cialdini, M Trost and JT Newsom, 'Preference for consistency: the development of a valid measure and discovery of surprising behavioural implications', *Journal of Personality and Social Psychology*, 68, 1995, pp. 318–28.

58 RV Joule, F Gouilloux and F Weber, 'The lure: a new compliance procedure', *The Journal of Social Psychology*, 129(6), 1989, pp. 741–9.

59 B Fennis and W Stroebe, *The psychology of advertising*, Psychology Press, Hove, East Sussex, UK, 2010.

60 B Fennis, 'Persuasion pleasure and selling stress: the role of non-verbal communication in consumer influence settings', *Advances in Consumer Research*, 35, 2008, pp. 797–8.

61 T Sanders, *The Likeability Factor: how to boost your L-factor and achieve your life's dreams*, Crown Business, New York, 2006.

62 RB Zajonc, 'Attitudinal effects of mere exposure', *Journal of Personality and Social Psychology Monographs*, 9(2), 1968, pp. 1–27.

63 RF Borstein, 'Exposure and affects: overview and meta-analysis of research 1968–1987', *Psychological Bulletin*, 106, 1989, pp. 265–89.

64 RL Moreland and SR Beach, 'Exposure effects in the classroom: the development of affinity among students', *Journal of Experimental Social Psychology*, 28, 1992, pp. 255–76.

65 S Saegert, S Swap and RB Zajonc, 'Exposure, context, and interpersonal attraction', *Journal of Personality and Social Psychology*, 25, 1973, pp. 234–42.

66 See G Dowling, *Creating corporate reputations*, Oxford University Press, Oxford, 2001, pp. 12–13.

67 E Hatfield, and S Sprecher, *Mirror, mirror...: the importance of looks in everyday life*, State University of New York Press, Albany, 1986.

68 JH Langlois et al., 'Maxims or myths of beauty? A meta-analytic and theoretical reviews', *Psychological Bulletin*, 126, 2000, pp. 390–423.

69 TA Judge and DM Cable, 'The effect of physical height on workplace success and income: preliminary test of a theoretical model', *Journal of Applied Psychology*, 89(3), 2004, pp. 428–41.

70 TA Judge and DM Cable, 'When it comes to pay, do the thin win? The effect of weight on pay for men and women', *Journal of Applied Psychology*, 96(1), 2011, pp. 95–112.

71 RE Geiselman, NA Haight and LG Kimata, 'Context effects on the perceived physical attractiveness of faces', *Journal of Personality and Social Psychology*, 20, 1984, pp. 409–24.

72 JB Walther, B Van De Heide, S Kim, D Westerman and ST Tong, 'The role of friends' appearance and behavior on evaluations of individuals on Facebook: Are we known by the company we keep?', *Human Communication Research*, 34(1), 2008, pp. 28–49.

73 R Mazzella and A Feingold, 'The effects of physical attractiveness, race, socioeconomic status, and gender of defendants of victims on judgements of mock jurors: a meta-analysis', *Journal of Applied Social Psychology*, 24, 1994, pp. 1315–44.

74 AH Eagly et al., 'What is beautiful is good but...: a meta-analytic review of research on physical attractiveness stereotype', *Psychological Bulletin*, 110, 1991, pp. 109–28.

75 PH Reingen and JB Kernan, 'Social perception and interpersonal influence: some consequences of the physical attractiveness stereotype in a personal selling setting', *Journal of Consumer Psychology*, 2, 1993, pp. 25–38.

76 Z Rubin, 'Measurement of romantic love', *Journal of Personality and Social Psychology*, 16(2), 1970, pp. 65–273.

77 RV Exline, 'Explorations in the process of person perception: visual interaction in relation to competition, sex, and need for affiliation', *Journal of Personality*, 31, 1963, pp. 1–20.

78 KKW Kampe et al., 'Reward value of attractiveness and gaze', *Nature*, 413(11), 2001, pp. 589, 602.

79 N Gueguen and M Gail, 'The effect of smiling on helping behavior: smiling and good samaritan behavior', *Communication Reports*, 16(2), 2003, pp. 133–40.

80 A genuine smile is one in which 'our eyes also smile' (not just the mouth), that is, with crow's feet forming around our eyes. It is not easy to fake. In a recent study on celebrity endorsements, Ilic et al. found that a celebrity with a genuine smile tends to be more effective. See J Ilic, A Kulczynski and SM Baxter, 'How a smile can make a difference: enhancing the persuasive appeal of celebrity endorsers', *Journal of Advertising Research*, 58(1), 2018, pp. 51–65.

81 Eagly et al. (1991) 'What is beautiful is good, but...', note 74.

82 DJ Howard, C Gengler and A Jain, 'What's in a name? A complimentary means of persuasion', *Journal of Consumer Research*, 22, September 1995, pp. 200–11.

83 D Drachman, A de Carufel and CA Inkso, 'The extra credit effect in interpersonal attraction', *Journal of Experimental Social Psychology*, 14, 1978, pp. 458–67.

84 E Berscheid and EH Walster, *Interpersonal attraction*, 2nd edition, Addison-Wesley, Reading, MA, 1978.

85 BJ Fogg and C Nass, 'Silicon sycophants: the effects of computers that flatter', *International Journal of Human–Computer Studies*, 46, 1997, pp. 551–61.

86 R Gordon, 'Impact of ingratiation on judgements and evaluations: a meta-analytic investigation', *Journal of Personality and Social Psychology*, 71(1), 1996, pp. 54–70.

87 Ibid.

88 D Byrne, *The attraction paradigm*, Academic Press, New York, 1971.

89 GW Allport, *Patterns and growth in personality*, Holt, Rinehart & Winston, New York, 1961; DJ Howard and RA Kerin, 'The effects of name similarity on message processing and persuasion', *Journal of Experimental Social Psychology*, 47, 2011, pp. 63–71.

90 FB Evans, 'Selling as a dyadic relationship: a new approach', *American Behavioral Scientists*, 6(7), 1963, pp. 67–79; cited in Cialdini (2009), *Influence*, p. 151, note 47.

91 P Suedfeld, S Bochner and C Matas, 'Petitioner's attire and petition signing by peace demonstrators: a field experiment', *Journal of Applied Social Psychology*, 1, 1971, pp. 278–83.

92 RK Aune and MD Basil, 'A relational obligations approach to the foot-in-the-mouth effect', *Journal of Applied Social Psychology*, 24(6), 1994, pp. 546–56.

93 JM Burger, 'Fleeting attraction and compliance with requests', in AR Pratkanis (ed.), *The science of social influence*, Psychology Press, Taylor & Francis, New York, 2007, pp. 155–66.

94 TL Chartrand and JA Bargh, 'The chameleon effect: the perception–behavior link and social interaction', *Journal of Personality and Social Psychology*, 76(6), 1999, pp. 893–910.

95 M La France, 'Nonverbal synchrony and rapport: analysis by the cross-lag panel technique', *Social Psychology Quarterly*, 42(1), 1979, pp. 66–70; M La France, 'Posture mirroring and rapport', in M Davis (ed.), *Interaction rhythms: periodicity in communicative behavior*, Human Sciences, New York, 1982, pp. 279–98.

96 RB van Baaren et al., 'Mimicry for money: behavioral consequences of imitation', *Journal of Experimental Social Psychology*, 39(4), 2003, pp. 393–8.

97 M Stel, J Mastop and M Strick, 'The impact of mimicking on attitudes towards products presented in TV commercials', *Social Influence*, 6(3), 2011, pp. 142–52.

98 RB van Baaren et al., 'Mimicry and prosocial behavior', *Psychological Science*, 15(1), 2004, pp. 71–4.

99 Chartrand and Bargh (1999), 'The chameleon effect', note 94.

100 RJ Tanner et al., 'Of chameleons and consumption: the impact of mimicry on choice and preferences', *Journal of Consumer Research*, 34(6), April, 2008, pp. 754–66.

101 Cialdini (2009), *Influence*, note 47.

102 Rossiter and Bellman (2005), *Marketing communications*, note 29.

103 P Schurr and J Ozanne, 'Influences on exchange processes: buyers' preconceptions of a seller's trustworthiness and bargaining', *Journal of Consumer Research*, 11, 1985, pp. 939–53.

104 DM Rousseau et al., 'Not so different after all: a cross-discipline view of trust', *Academy of Management Review*, 23, 1998, pp. 393–404.

105 RC Mayer, JH Davis and FD Schoorman, 'An integrative model of organizational trust', *Academy of Management Review*, 20(3), 1995, pp. 709–34. Note that others have more dimensions, but I have opted for these three dimensions because of the simplicity of this model – see also JE Swan et al., 'Measuring dimensions of purchaser trust of industrial salespeople', *Journal of Personal Selling & Sales Management*, 8, May 1988, pp. 1–9.

106 Mayer, Davis and Schoorman (1995), 'An integrative model of organizational trust', p. 717, note 105.

107 Ibid., p. 718.

108 Ibid., p. 719.

109 T Leigh and JO Summers, 'An initial evaluation of industrial buyers' impressions of salespersons' nonverbal cues', *Journal of Personal Selling & Sales Management*, 22(1), Winter 2002, pp. 41–53.

110 G Thorton, 'The effect of wearing glasses upon judgments of personality traits of persons seen briefly', *Journal of Applied Psychology*, 28, 1944, pp. 203–7.

111 GW Marshall, DJ Goebel and WC Moncrief, 'Hiring for success at the buyer–seller interface,' *Journal of Business Research*, 56, 2003, pp. 247–55. The other top characteristics are listening skills, follow-up skills, ability to adapt sales style, organisation skills, verbal communication skills, and the ability to interact well with people at all levels.

112 M Seligman and P Schulman, 'Explanatory style as a predictor of productivity and quitting among life insurance sales agents', *Journal of Personality and Social Psychology*, 50(4), 1986, pp. 832–8. The simple illustrations of the principle are taken from M Seligman, *Learned optimism: how to change your mind and your life*, Pocket Books, New York, 1998.

113 According to the Life Insurance Market Research Association, this can be as high as 78% within three years of hiring a new sales agent. This statistic is cited in Seligman and Schulman (1986), 'Explanatory style as a predictor of productivity and quitting among life insurance sales agents', note 112.

114 C Peterson and M Seligman, 'Causal explanations as a risk factor for depression: theory and evidence', *Psychological Review*, 91, 1984, pp. 347–74.

115 See Seligman and Schulman (1986), 'Explanatory style', note 112.

CHAPTER 11
DIRECT RESPONSE MARKETING AND SALES PROMOTION INTEGRATION

CHAPTER OVERVIEW

This chapter covers two topics. The first topic is direct response, a tactic designed to trigger a response by making an offer to the target audience. The aim of this section is to understand how to conduct a good direct response marketing campaign. We will also discuss the various methods for delivering an offer, and how if applied carefully, direct response marketing can build brand equity.

The second topic is sales promotion. Like direct response marketing, the objective of sales promotion is to trigger an immediate response, but this time with sales at both trade and consumer levels. This chapter will discuss the various types of trade and consumer promotion and examine how promotions can be negatively or positively oriented. It ends by suggesting some clever uses for consumer promotion.

Learning goals

After reading this chapter, you will understand:

- what direct response marketing is
- the principles underlying a good direct response marketing campaign
- the different methods for delivering the offer
- what sales promotion is
- how trade and consumer promotions are different yet related
- types of trade and consumer promotion
- the difference between positive- and negative-oriented sales promotions
- when to use monetary or non-monetary consumer sales promotion
- the notion of congruency benefits in promotion and the reasoning behind it
- how to use consumer sales promotions more effectively.

Although this chapter covers two topics – direct response marketing and sales promotion – they are in fact intimately related. A direct response marketing offer (e.g. a subscription to a magazine) often includes an incentive (e.g. a 20% discount). This incentive is the sales promotion. Likewise, many sales promotions (e.g. a closing down sale) are often delivered using direct response marketing (e.g. a letter drop). We will discuss direct response marketing first.

DIRECT RESPONSE MARKETING

Direct response marketing or, more commonly, direct marketing can be defined as the use of non-personal media (e.g. mail, telephone or TV) to design and deliver a profitable offer to the right person at the right time, in order to secure that person's immediate behavioural response.

There are therefore two important distinguishing characteristics in direct response marketing: (1) making direct contact with potential customers and (2) encouraging an immediate response. Making direct contact means getting in touch with the best prospect while the immediate response could be a purchase, a click-through to a website, a new enquiry or a visit to a showroom. For example, an art gallery could send out a direct mail invitation to prospective customers inviting them to attend an exhibition. While the gallery's ultimate aim is to sell a painting, it may be difficult to do this in a single step using direct mail. Rather, by inviting prospective customers to visit the gallery first, the selling task may be made easier and more efficient, since only those interested will turn up for the exhibition and the gallery director has a greater opportunity to persuade buyers in person. This is called a 'two-step approach' because two different media are used in the selling process – direct response marketing and personal selling. This simple two-step approach can be applied to other settings.

Unlike in public relations or image advertising, where there is no explicit behavioural component, in direct response marketing there is an explicit call to action. Further, as the art gallery example shows, direct response marketing can be combined with other IMC tactics to achieve greater efficiency. As direct response marketing is a versatile tool, a marcoms manager should be able to use it effectively, and this means understanding its underlying principles. In the next section we describe those principles.

Principles of direct response marketing

PRINCIPLE 1: BUILD A GOOD CUSTOMER DATABASE

Building a good customer database is extremely important. In fact, for businesses that exclusively use direct response marketing as a means of selling, a good customer database is the key to success. When carefully selected, a response rate as high as 40 or 50% can be achieved in a direct response marketing campaign.[1] Some well-known organisations, such as Reader's Digest, rely almost exclusively on direct response marketing to find new subscribers. With advanced customer analytics, companies can also mine their loyalty program data to help develop more suitable offers for the right segment.[2]

But what if a business does not have a customer database? A database can be developed from a list of names that are publicly available (e.g. from a telephone directory or through an association's membership). This is called a 'compiled list'. Such lists are widely available but are generally not responsive to a business' offer since we are only guessing that these people are interested. The best lists are those that have names of people who have responded to similar offers before. For instance, if you are selling books through direct response marketing, you need a list of people who have bought books before in response to a direct response marketing campaign. List brokers, who sell all sorts of response lists, can help. The people on these lists are potential buyers, and they become our customers when they buy our product. All names on the new list need to be de-duplicated to ensure that they do not overlap with those on our current customer list. Then, over time, by turning these prospects into customers, we can build up our own database of customers and form relationships with them. By forming a relationship, we get to know them better. The more we know about our customers (e.g. geo-demographics, preferences, purchase history, and monetary value of past purchases), the more we can segment and present them with a timely, customised offer.

This is where the value of direct response marketing lies – in understanding our customers intimately enough to make the right offer directly to them at the right time. This is the basis of customer relationship management (CRM), which allows us to manage the relationship (starting from customer acquisition, retention and development) in order to achieve long-term profitably for the firm.[3]

In social media, new target audiences can be quickly developed if we want to grow our market through social media. One prominent example is Facebook. This social media giant has a wealth of data about its users which can be exploited when developing Facebook ads for a social media campaign. For instance, one can build a 'look alike' audience, using available profile information on Facebook users. Through a series of drop-down menus and tick boxes, a group of Facebook users who are like our own customers can be found. We then target these Facebook users with our ads.

PRINCIPLE 2: MAKE A PROFITABLE OFFER

Making a profitable offer means that, before sending out an offer, the marcoms manager must estimate the likely financial returns. Some of the important items to consider in the estimation include estimate response rate, total units sold, total revenue, total cost of goods, cost of mailing and printing. To complicate the issue, we also need to factor in customer service and support.

So, by working through the numbers (and making certain assumptions), one can quickly check the viability of a campaign – will it be profitable? Direct response marketing is generally more appropriate for high-involvement goods. The economics for low-involvement goods, such as snack foods, does not add up.

But how do we know if our assumptions are correct? We conduct a test run first, and then embark on the actual campaign, which typically involves sending offers to millions of homes. We can also use data from earlier campaigns to model the propensity of certain households to respond to our offer. Traditionally, the segmentation technique in direct response marketing uses the recency–frequency–monetary value model (RFM) to classify homes into degrees of propensity to buy. Recency refers to the time period since the last purchase; frequency refers to number of purchases made (in a given period); and monetary value refers to the amount of money spent (in the same period). By regressing these variables to response, we can see which of the RFM variables has the greatest predictive weight for purchase. Knowing the weight then allows us to rank and group customers (and so to segment the database) in terms of their propensity to respond. Although there are other, more sophisticated ways to optimise the selection,[4] with the availability of large datasets to model effectiveness the RFM model is the most basic.

PRINCIPLE 3: ADJUST THE OFFER

Adjusting the offer means tweaking the deal so that it will become more attractive to the target audience (yet still profitable). For instance, one can increase the warranty period or offer a better discount for multiple purchases. Unlike in image advertising, where the effect of advertising on sales is not instantly discernible, in direct response marketing the result is known quickly because the target audience is invited to respond to the offer. With digital technologies like smartphones – which the target audience carries around in their pockets – there is virtually no lag between the offer and consumer response. If a consumer wants to accept the offer, he or she will usually do so almost immediately. This speed of response means adjustments can be made quickly and a new direct response campaign created. Compare this to a TV ad, which is extremely difficult to change once it has been made.

PRINCIPLE 4: TEST TO FIND THE MOST PROFITABLE OFFER

Testing to find the most profitable offer refers to one of the most desirable aspects of using direct response marketing: with enough investment devoted to systematic testing, we can eventually find the most profitable offer. For instance, if an offer was unable to triple the response rate from 1% to 3%, then the marcoms manager could experiment with several things. There are usually five variables to test and potentially change, which are (using an example of selling figurines):

- The creative execution – for example, allowing for a two-page instead of a one-page cover letter or producing a four-colour instead of a two-colour sales brochure for the figurines.
- The nature of the offer – for example, instead of just making a straight offer of $180, we can include a letter of authentication for each figurine (which does not cost too much but is highly valued among collectors).
- The payment method – for example, instead of asking customers to fork out $180 at once, we can offer a payment plan of two $90 instalments.
- The timing – for example, instead of sending out the offer in August, we can send it out during the Christmas period in December.
- The target segment – for example, instead of targeting older women (aged 55 years and over), the database manager can target younger, professional Asian women (aged 35 or over), who are also collectors of figurines.

As you can imagine, there are many permutations for testing the offer, but the objective is finding the most profitable one through systematic controlled testing and modelling. This is sometimes called A/B testing, where one element is tested at a time (although multiple tests can be done concurrently as well). In chapter 12, we will revisit this idea of A/B testing in assessing synergy in different channel combination. Once we have identified this, it becomes the one to beat – this is called 'beating the control'. That way, there will always be a motivation to improve with each new campaign.

PRINCIPLE 5: RETARGETING

In the online world, retargeting is the most efficient way of increasing revenue. This is because with retargeting, one is re-contacting those who already showed an interest in our offer. Their interest is manifested by their online behaviour (visits to the website), their submission of a purchase order without finalising it (the abandoned cart) or their online enquiry and so on. In other words, people who showed an interest are those who have entered the brand's ecosystem. These people can be easily identified using tracking methodology, and because they have previously considered the offer, as witnessed by their online behaviour, they are the ones most likely to buy, and hence should be retargeted. One can simply re-present the order or modify the order to make it more appealing. With increasingly sophisticated technology, the process of retargeting can be automated. We will revisit this issue in chapter 13.

Methods of delivery

The five principles above were illustrated using one form of direct response marketing – that of direct mail. But the offer can be delivered in other ways as well, including the use of mass media or digital interactive technologies such as the smartphone. We will consider the pros and cons for each delivery method.

DIRECT MAIL

As illustrated above, this is a well-known form of delivery due to consumer exposure to 'junk mail' (i.e. mail without an addressee). With geo-demographic data, this delivery mode allows us to make a highly personalised and selective offer. For instance, a removalist company can target consumers who are moving, because information about houses bought and sold in an area is readily available. We can also time our delivery so that it reaches the target audience who are readiest to buy (see chapter 4 on media planning for growth). Direct mail also gives the marcoms manager almost unlimited design options, in terms of the size, colour and format of the collateral produced. This flexibility has allowed firms to integrate its brand image into the offer. For instance, if a customer has not visited a pool store for a while, the firm can send a postcard as a gentle reminder (e.g. 'We missed you'), but with the design of a pool on the postcard (see figure 11.1). And as an added incentive to re-visit the store, the postcard is also a coupon that can be redeemed for any product bought. This is a clever use of direct mail.

Figure 11.1 A creative postcard that serves as a reminder as well as a coupon

The downside of direct mail is that consumers perceive it as clutter, and this brings with it image problems. Consumers do not like their mailboxes to be filled with junk mail, and this makes it more likely that one's direct mail will not even be opened. Once opened, however, there is little competition for the consumer's attention.

CATALOGUE

These are magazine-like publications about products. A catalogue is very effective in reaching customers who are highly involved in the product category. When combined with a loyalty program, some customers look forward to each new edition in order to use their points. Traditionally, the catalogue has also been particularly effective for consumers living in the country, who find it difficult to visit shops, although online shopping has now overcome the tyranny of distance. However, catalogues from supermarkets are still common, and these are often delivered unaddressed to people's homes – a common form of junk mail. Paper-based catalogues may soon be a relic of the past, as we move into digital catalogues (or e-catalogues), which are much quicker to produce and distribute.

EMAIL

The main advantages of email over ordinary mail or catalogue are its low cost and high speed of delivery. As with direct mail, it is important to get a list of email addresses – without this, there is no campaign. However, this presents a problem because consumers are usually more sensitive about their email address being targeted for a direct mail campaign than about their home address. This is partly because of the amount of spam people receive and partly because email addresses are often not publicly available information (unlike residential addresses, which are listed in phone books). A marcoms manager must ensure that all consumers targeted via email have opted in; that is, they have agreed to be contacted by email. This means that a consumer must first register their willingness to be contacted and then the organisation must send an email that requires some action (e.g. clicking on a link) to confirm their agreement. It is only on confirmation that the organisation can use their email address. This is sometimes called 'permission-based marketing'.

Even with opt-in customers, the marcoms manager may still be tempted to indiscriminately send consumers countless offers. This will only increase their annoyance. The question then becomes how often should one send the offer? It depends on the rate of purchase for the specific goods or service. If the firm has intimate detail of the customer's shopping habits, it should be leveraged to optimise the best timing to send out the offers. For instance, if a wine purveyor knows that a particular customer likes champagne and often buys this for the weekend, then it makes sense to send the offer on Thursday or Friday. With improved customer data analytics and email capability that can integrate into the firm's inventory, the age of personalisation offer is now upon us (see chapter 13). A firm should not indiscriminately email offers because it will not maximise profit.[5]

TELEMARKETING

This form of direct response marketing uses outbound telephone calls to make a sales pitch to customers. Telemarketers can significantly increase the effectiveness of their outbound calls by using a good database showing the purchase history of customers. For instance, if a direct-sale wine company knows that a particular customer only likes pinot noir, then there is little point trying to sell this customer something else. Another advantage with telemarketing is that it comes closest to face-to-face personal selling, because it is highly interactive and adaptive. It is also personal in nature – there is a human being at the other end of the phone line.

Similarly, the telephone can also be used for upselling and cross-selling. This may be more effective for inbound calls. Here, the person may be calling the organisation to make an enquiry or complaint. If this signals dissatisfaction, then it has to be resolved immediately. If it signals an opportunity to cross-sell or upsell, then that opportunity should be taken.

The disadvantage of telemarketing is that outbound calls irritate consumers. The medium is extremely intrusive, especially if the telemarketer calls at an inconvenient time (e.g. at dinner-time). With the rise of the call centre, the use of telemarketing has exploded, and this has created a backlash. In some countries, such as Australia, telemarketers cannot call homes that have opted out of receiving such calls (e.g. by registering their phone number on a Do Not Call register). Telemarketing companies caught violating this exclusion rule can be fined.

TELEVISION

On TV, direct response marketing can take the form of infomercials. These are long commercials (often around 20 minutes), often shown in the early hours of the morning, when the cost of buying airtime is relatively low. Infomercials usually use a demonstration format to show how good the product is, then display a telephone number or website for consumers to order the product. Such ads often try to communicate with a sense of urgency, in order to increase arousal – the higher the arousal, the greater the probability of purchase.[6]

Cable TV or subscription-based networks (e.g. Foxtel), with their better profiled consumers, are also seeing a rise in direct response marketing. For instance, if we are selling home exercise equipment, it is probably more effective to place an infomercial on a sports cable channel such as ESPN, rather than on the Disney Channel. There are also dedicated shopping channels such as QVC (US), Ideal World (Britain) and TVSN (Australia) which sell direct to consumers.

DIRECT RESPONSE TV

Direct response TV (or DRTV) means using TV advertising to sell directly to consumers, often at the time when the cost of media buy is cheap (e.g. daytime or late nights or during non-rating seasons, sometimes called remnant airtime). These ads can be of the short form (e.g. 30s, 60s, 90s or 120s) or of the long form (e.g. 30 minutes). The short-form is for low-priced goods while the long-form is for more expensive goods. The advantage with using DRTV is the response is immediately trackable. Even so, most direct response TV campaigns fail for a whole host of reasons. The following principles should be borne in mind in planning a DRTV campaign:[7]

- The product should have mass appeal and its benefit should be visually demonstrated on TV.
- It should be priced profitably, and the sales-to-cost ratio should be at least four times.
- If appropriate, develop various upsell offers or some sort of subscription, continuity or automatic shipment program (e.g. new titles) to generate future revenue.
- Ensure that the telemarketing support is optimal for answering questions, collecting orders, and so forth.
- Publicise internet links with the DRTV ad so that viewers can also buy directly from the firm's website.
- Test all backend fulfilment operations so that customers can quickly receive their order, outsourcing this operation to a third party, if necessary.
- The DRTV ad itself should create a sense of urgency (e.g. the best home gym in the market), provide incentive/s for viewers to respond (e.g. free steak knives), and have an effective call to action (e.g. ring now!).
- Consider advertising on cable networks (e.g. ESPN) or subscription-based networks (e.g. Foxtel) whose niche audience may be appropriate for the product (e.g. home gym).

With the rise of other digital avenues, the direct relationship between DRTV and sales is no longer as straightforward. For instance, the viewer may search for more information on the internet (e.g. using a search engine) or contact their friends on social media before making a decision. This in turn will affect media planning because the firm now has to optimise its search engine (see chapter 5) to drive more web traffic, as well as increasing its content marketing (see chapter 8) to facilitate more conversation on social media. Thus a marcoms manager needs to understand how responses are connected[8] to each other (e.g. see the POSSE model in chapter 5), even though, on the surface, it may look like a straightforward direct response marketing campaign.

ONLINE VIDEOS

Creating online videos on YouTube is now a popular way of selling direct to consumers. This format is suited to selling a product because you can tell a story; it is sometimes called storyselling. To grab attention, the story is often humourous. The direct response function is incorporated by including a link within the video and encouraging viewers to click and buy the product. Encouraging viewers to click on the video can also be done humorously. If well executed it can lead to a significant increase in sales, as in the case of PiperWai, a natural deodorant, which had a 70% lift in sales on Amazon.[9]

RADIO

Radio can also be used for direct response, although it is less commonly used. It is less intrusive than TV because many people tend to use radio as a background while they engage in another activity. It is also more difficult for a consumer to contact the marketer; for example, if a person is driving it can be hard to find a way of copying down the details of the offer. In response to this problem, the use of vanity numbers (e.g. 1800-FLOWERS or 1800-PIZZAHUT) has become popular; they act as mnemonics to help people remember how to recontact the organisation at a more convenient time. In fact, any form of mnemonic or repetition is a serious creative option here.

NEWSPAPERS

Newspapers are a commonly used mass medium for direct response marketing. The offer can be printed on special sections of the newspaper (e.g. the sports section) for better targeting (e.g. selling exercise equipment). It can also take the form of a free-standing insert (FSI). This means that the advertisement is printed on a postcard or a separate document and inserted between the pages of the newspaper. This is a very effective means of gaining attention because the materials tend to drop out of the newspaper's pages. However, it is expensive to implement because of the extra effort needed to put inserts into the paper – so, if this tactic is used, the product should appeal to a large audience.

MAGAZINES

While newspapers tend to reach a broader audience, magazines have the advantage of reaching niche audiences. FSI can also be used effectively here, for the same reason as with newspapers. Further, since magazines have a longer readership life, the direct response offer can be printed as an ad on the pages of the magazine.

WEBSITES

In the current digital era, the websites of organisations have now become the portal through which prospective customers can make direct contact. This is also an inbound source for obtaining interested consumers and should be carefully followed up. The advantage with websites is that the reach is now greater. However, prospective customers are much better informed and demand faster responses to their enquiries. For companies that are digitally proficient, this is an opportunity.

However, the digital frontier also creates its own woes. For instance, when a person visits a website, an unrelated pop-up ad can appear on their screen. When clicked, it takes the consumer away from the company's website. For this reason, many organisations use blocking technologies to prevent pop-up ads from occurring and thus prevent their customers from being lured away.

SOCIAL MEDIA MICRO-TARGETING

A direct response ad can also appear on an organisation's social media page. Micro-targeting can be very effective because the offer only appears on the social media pages of people who have expressed an interest in the category. For instance, if five mothers have been having a social media discussion about babies, then a pram manufacturer can drop a direct response text ad for a pram on their personal pages. We have already encountered this in chapter 8. This is also called behavioural targeting. This technique is controversial because of privacy issues, since users' personal information is collected without permission. It also gives consumers a 'creepy' feeling of being followed. Furthermore, behavioural targeting does not stop even after a purchase is made.

Direct response marketing and brand equity

Misuse of direct response marketing can hurt the equity of the brand, for instance, when the privacy of customers is violated. Another issue is the irritating, continual bombardment of customers with offers. Further, the flexibility of direct response marketing can result in a number of variations in the message. This can create confusion if the 'look and feel' is not consistent. So, although direct response marketing is a powerful IMC tool, it should not be misused.

Finally, at a minimum, the entire firm's inbound marketing assets (e.g. websites and microsites, e-commerce facilities, social media pages, 1300 or 1800 telephone numbers and apps) should be well branded in order to achieve a consistent look, feel and voice of the brand as discussed in chapter 1.

CASE STUDY 11.1 OLD SPICE DIRECT RESPONSE MARKETING CAMPAIGN[10]

Old Spice is a body wash product that practically invented the category, but with increased competition the brand needed a change of image to differentiate itself. A straight brand-building campaign targeting men would probably not work because up to 50% of men's body wash products are bought by wives or girlfriends. The challenge was not only to target men, but also the women who buy for them. Then there was another added complication – women tended to buy body wash that was female scented. So how do you create a campaign that can target both genders and then convince the wives and girlfriends that female-scented body wash is not desirable and that only Old Spice will do for their men? This was a real challenge.

Old Spice's advertising agency, Weiden and Kennedy, first came up with the strategy that it was important to encourage the male and female partners to start a conversation about body wash. They then sought to create a centrepiece that could serve as the partners' point of conversation. They came up with an idea of an ideal man whom all women could fantasise about, secretly wishing that their partners could be that man. Old Spice could make this happen, even if only by association through using the same brand.

Launched online in 2010 on Super Bowl weekend and also on TV in subsequent weeks, the ad featured the handsome Isaiah Amir Mustafa, an actor and a former NFL footballer, speaking shirtless (and with a towel around his waist) on camera, teasing the female audience that if she were to buy Old Spice for her partner, he too could smell like him. The ad, called 'The Man Your Man Could Smell Like', was witty, sensuous (to the female audience!) and well executed, with some special effects thrown in. Isaiah's tongue-in-cheek delivery style was simply brilliant and critical to the success of the ad. An other, less capable actor might not have been able to pull this off. The media placement of the campaign was also important. The ad was placed in primetime TV programs that couples were more likely to watch together (e.g. *Lost*, *American Idol*).

The ad quickly became a sensation. Within three months, it generated 75% of all conversations for the category, half of these initiated by women. There was tremendous buzz spawning countless parodies on YouTube. It created such interest that even celebrity hosts like Oprah Winfrey and Ellen DeGeneres clambered to interview the gorgeous star, Isaiah, much to the delirium of their largely female studio audiences.

After this initial success, Old Spice wanted to go one step further, and that was to develop a closer relationship with their customers. With the help of digital specialists, the agency came up with an interactive campaign using both the internet as well as the TV. This is what they did:

1. They created a follow-up TV ad using the same theme and starring the same actor, Isaiah.
2. Then over two days, they created 186 video clips in response to questions from the public posted in social media (e.g. Facebook and Twitter), including questions from fans and celebrities. Isaiah delivered all these responses in his signatory shirtless, tongue-in-cheek style.

The video responses, which were often very short yet witty, were then posted on YouTube. The result was nothing short of phenomenal. On the first day, the campaign registered more than 5.9 million views. Two days later, this climbed to more than 20 million views, and by the seventh day, more than 40 million views. During this period, Old Spice's Twitter following increased by 2700%. Interactions among their Facebook fans went up by 800% and online traffic to the Old Spice website increased by 300%. The brand's YouTube channel became the most viewed brand channel in history, and six months after launch, the campaign generated 1.4 billion impressions.

Finally, in terms of business outcome, sales of Old Spice went up by 27% (compared to 12 months prior), while in the last three months of the campaign this rose to 55%. By the last month, sales had increased by 105%. The campaign cemented Old Spice's #1 position in the category.

Figure 11.2 Old Spice direct response campaign

DISCUSSION QUESTIONS

1. Generally, it is a challenge to address two target audiences in a campaign. Why do you think this is so, and how did Weiden and Kennedy mitigate this problem?
2. This case study shows how online videos when combined with social media can be used as a direct response tactic. This integrated approach is seldom used. Why aren't more brands adopting this tactic?
3. In terms of creative execution, what lessons did you learn from this case study, if any?

SALES PROMOTION

Sales promotion, like direct response marketing, is one of the oldest weapons in the marketing arsenal. It is defined as a temporary incentive used to encourage consumers to buy the product or service now (or in their next purchase cycle) and to gain the support of channel members (i.e. resellers and others involved in selling to end users). Therefore, in terms of action, sales promotion is like direct response marketing – it seeks an immediate response. This has the effect of changing buying behaviour by making the consumer or channel member buy sooner (called the 'acceleration effect'). It also encourages a consumer or channel member to buy more (called 'stockpiling'). Such effects are well documented.[11] And it is devastatingly effective in the short term, causing consumers to switch brands.[12] Note, the price elasticity of sales promotion is substantial. One estimate puts it as −2.62[13] compared to advertising which is only 0.22.[14] But the long-term effects of sales promotion, especially with the constant price discounting, will damage the brand's equity (see Further Thinking section towards the end of this chapter).

Achieving push and pull synergy with trade and consumer promotions

Sales promotions take two main forms: trade and consumer promotions. Trade promotions are those that help manufacturers gain support from channel members. Consumer promotions, on the other hand, are those that appeal to the consumers. In recent years, the budget devoted to sales promotions has been steadily increasing. In fact, sales promotions on average accounts for up to two-thirds of the marketing budget in US companies. The other third is for general advertising.[15] This is because of the growing distribution power of retailers and the rise of their private labels.

Although the two kinds of promotions serve different marketing functions, they are related, as shown in figures 11.3 and 11.4. In figure 11.3, we see how trade promotions (a1) help manufacturers 'push' the products through the channel (a2).

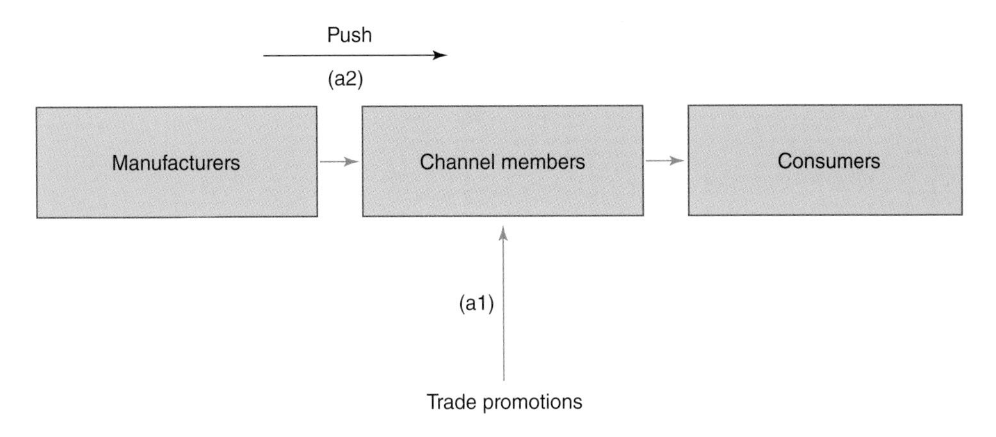

Figure 11.3 Where trade promotions fit in

This is different from consumer promotions, shown in figure 11.4. These appeal to the consumers (b1), who then help 'pull' the products through the channel by demanding them from retailers (b2).

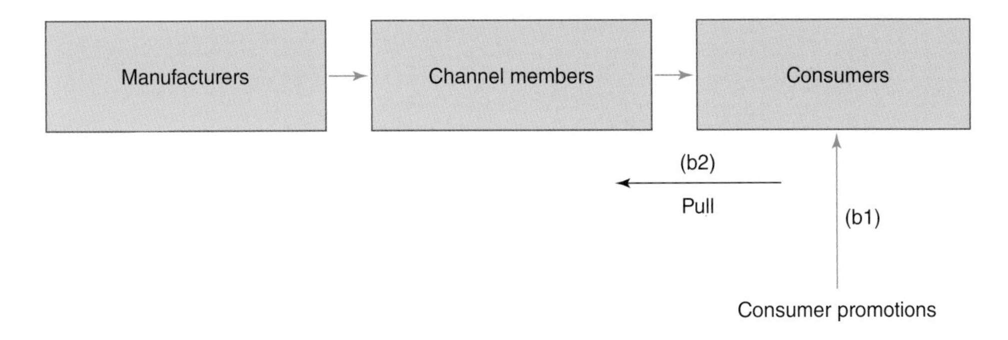

Figure 11.4 Where consumer promotions fit in

Together, the figures illustrate the idea of 'push' and 'pull' strategies. If the company intends to execute both strategies then it is more logical to gain the support of channel members first before appealing to the consumers; that is, 'push' before 'pull' (or a2 before b2). This is because products have to be readily available (i.e. in stock at the channel members) before the consumer promotions start.

The exception to this rule occurs when we want to deliberately create scarcity or win distribution. When this is the case, the consumer promotion campaign occurs first at b1, usually accompanied by advertising or direct response marketing. The demand and hype created then encourages channel members to stock and distribute the products. What all this implies is that all the promotional push and pull activities should be closely coordinated in order to achieve the desired synergistic effects.[16]

Types of trade promotion

Since trade promotions usually occur first, we will discuss them first. Although there are many types of trade promotion, they all fall roughly into four categories, as shown in figure 11.5. While these categories will give you some general ideas of what trade promotions are, the details of how much companies actually spend on each kind of tactics are a closely guarded secret.

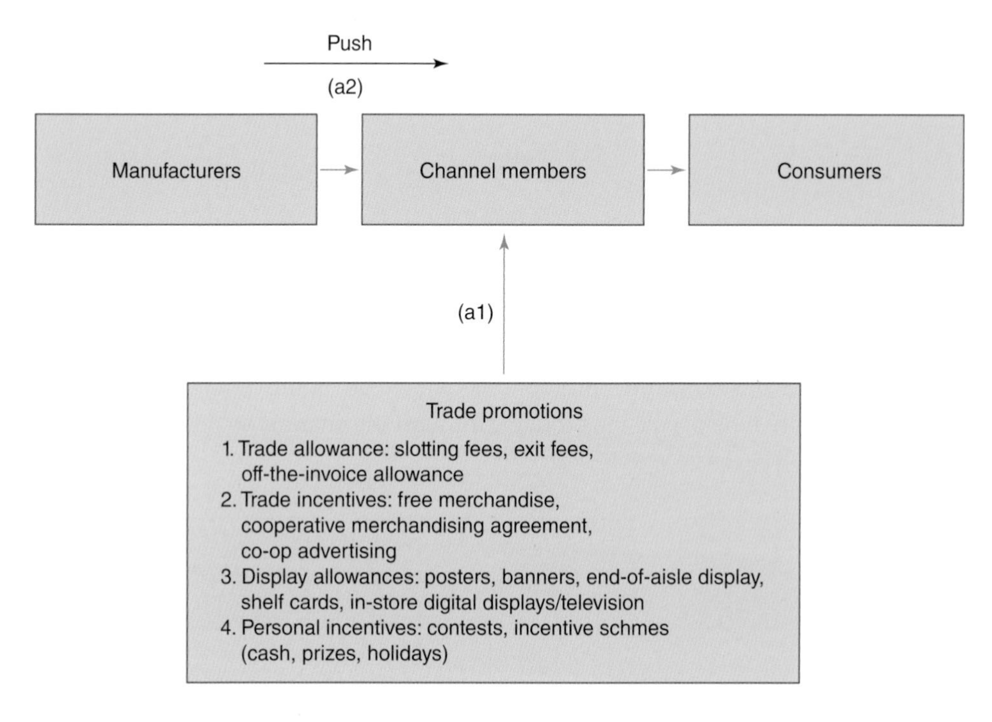

Figure 11.5 The different kinds of trade promotion

TRADE ALLOWANCE

These are financial incentives channel members demand in return for the work they have to do for manufacturers. For instance, retailers might charge slotting fees for putting new products on the shelves and exit fees when they remove them (e.g. when the new product fails to sell its expected quantity). Manufacturers are often not happy to pay these fees, likening them to extortion. Retailers, on the other hand, argue that they have a huge inventory to look after, and the fees help defray their costs. Nevertheless, all these fees go straight to the bottom line of the retailers.

An off-the-invoice allowance is a discount demanded by retailers for the goods they buy. Usually, these are volume-based, so that the more stock a retailer buys, the more discounts it receives. Retailers like this form of promotion because it is straightforward and simple to execute. However, manufacturers dislike it because the savings are usually not passed onto the end consumers. These savings also go straight to the bottom line of the retailers. Further, retailers may take advantage of this discount by stocking up in advance or diverting stock to other retail locations.

TRADE INCENTIVES

As an alternative to financial incentives, manufacturers can also incentivise channel members with free products. Again, this may be a volume-based deal – the more a retailer orders, the more free merchandise the retailer gets. Trade incentives can also be agreed in advance.

A cooperative merchandising agreement between the manufacturer and retailer formally spells out how the two parties will cooperate with each other to improve sales. Manufacturers generally like such agreements because they clearly state what a retailer has to do in exchange for the incentives. Retailers also favour such agreements because they allow them to plan ahead (usually 12 months).

The agreement may specify cooperative ('co-op') advertising, which means the manufacturer shares the advertising cost with the retailer. The manufacturer will contribute to a pool of money every time the retailer buys the product. The retailer then uses these monies for advertising the manufacturer's products. For instance, if a retailer buys $200 000 worth of goods, the manufacturer may contribute 2% (or $4000) of this to the retailer's advertising pool. The retailer can use this money to defray part of the cost of their advertising, on the approval of the manufacturer. Usually, this means that no competing brand (from the same category) will appear on the same ad.

DISPLAY ALLOWANCE

Since 70% of purchase decisions are made at the point of sale (POS),[17] in-store displays are important in triggering impulse purchase in retail. There are many kinds of display: banners, posters, end-of-aisle displays, racks and even computerised shopping trolleys that can signal which products are on offer as shoppers go past.

However, not all displays are equally effective. Generally, displays that are at eye-level or near the products (e.g. shelf talkers) are effective. Prominent displays that interrupt our vision, such as those at the end of the aisle, are also effective. Overhead banners are generally not effective because shoppers seldom look up towards the ceiling when shopping or entering a fast-food joint. The exceptions are banners or posters displayed behind the checkout counter or next to a cashier – shoppers waiting to pay will have time to read this signage.[18] Regardless, retailers demand an allowance for putting up such displays.

Digital screens in retail stores are now becoming very popular because retailers can influence their captive audience in-store. For instance, US retail giants such as Walmart have 127 million shoppers a week and now have hundreds of digital screens in-store, allowing manufacturers to advertise.

PERSONAL INCENTIVES

This class of incentive targets personnel who work in the channels. This could be the salesperson, sales manager, retail or wholesale manager, merchandising officer, wholesaler or reseller. To spur them on, various schemes are designed to reward their achievements. One common scheme often seen in high-involvement goods (e.g. automobiles) is a contest, in which the salesperson who sells the most of the manufacturer's products wins a holiday, prize or cash, sponsored by the manufacturer.

Types of consumer promotion

Sales promotion can also occur at the consumer level, and its objective is to stimulate demand from end users. There are essentially eight different kinds of consumer promotion, as shown in figure 11.6. These are also the forms of promotion we are most familiar with as consumers, since we encounter them every day.

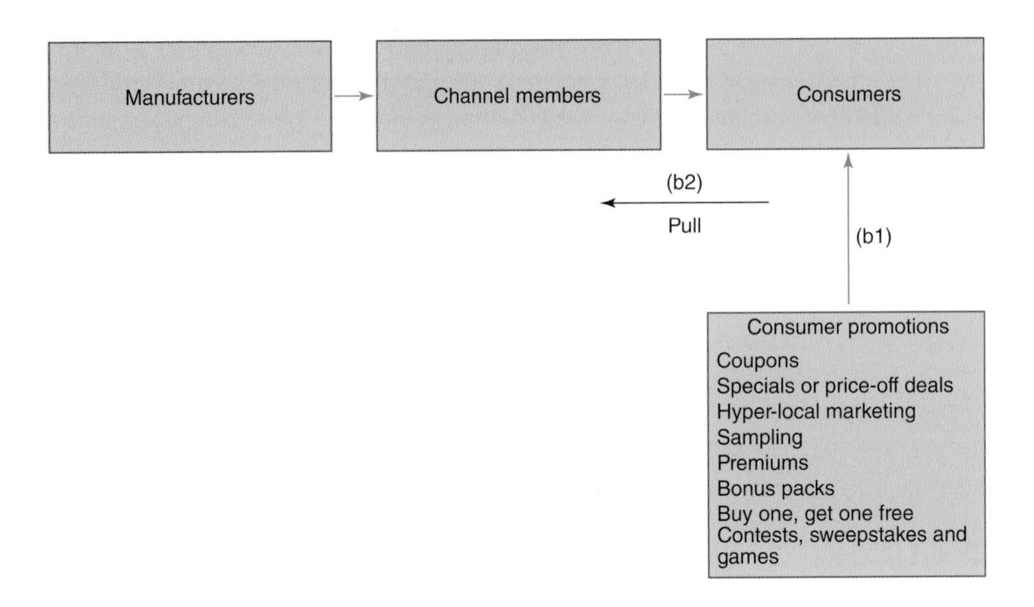

Figure 11.6 The different kinds of consumer promotion

COUPONS

This is the oldest and commonest form of consumer promotion. It is usually in the form of a price discount which consumers can redeem simply by presenting the voucher or docket in the store. It is also very effective for consumer-packaged goods because the reward is immediate. Studies have shown that brands that use coupons tend to enjoy higher consumer brand preference even when the promotion has ended.[19] One reason is that consumers are actively involved in cutting out the coupons and in the process convince themselves that the effort is worthwhile; in other words, the consumer may subconsciously think, 'This brand must be good because I have put in all this effort to get it'. Another reason is that cutting out the coupon also involves learning: at the very least, it helps consumers remember the brand. So, it is the brand-related activities that consumers engage in that caused them to like the brand. One early study shows couponing to be even more effective if it is combined with another form of promotion like sampling (discussed later this chapter).[20]

The disadvantage of coupons is that it is difficult to predict how many will be redeemed or who will redeem them. Ideally, we want only new customers to redeem our coupons so that we can grow our customer base, but this is generally not the case – existing brand users are the ones who tend to use these coupons most. This in turn decreases the overall profitability of the firm.[21] Printing coupons also costs money, which further eats into profit. However, with the advent of e-coupons and more precise targeting of particular consumers, the cost of coupons has dropped dramatically.

SPECIALS OR PRICE-OFF DEALS

This is the easiest (and laziest) form of sales promotion, which is why it is so easily abused. Unlike most other forms of sales promotion, price-off deals require very little planning, effort or management time. But consumers like price-off deals because the reward is immediate. The greater the discount, the more consumers will take up the offer.[22]

If we execute a price-off promotion, the regular price should be shown so that consumers can use it to assess the value of the discount.[23] In Australia, the use of unit pricing in consumer-packaged goods makes it easy for consumers to compare price-off deals across competing offers and package size. For instance, if four toilet rolls of brand A at the regular price costs $2.00 (unit pricing of $0.50 per roll), during promotion the price may drop to $1.60 (unit pricing of $0.40 per roll). Brand B may have a similar promotion under way, but in a bigger pack (e.g. nine rolls) – unit pricing, however, makes the comparison straightforward.

Price promotion should always be accompanied by display advertising because it will increase its effectiveness several folds.[24] Such advertising can occur in newspapers (called run of press), in the form of brochures of leaflets inserted in newspapers (called free-standing inserts or FSIs), or even through direct mail to households. Generally, the larger the pictorial elements, the greater its ability to attract attention. The size of the text has very little effect in gaining attention.[25]

Although price-off deals are very effective, they have a major weakness. If used too frequently, consumers will learn never to buy at full price (see the Further Thinking section below). Smaller brands who are at the mercy of retailers generally tend to allocate more of their budget for price-off deals. Brand leaders, however, are less susceptible to this.[26] But even so, brand leaders still suffer from heavy discounting inflicted by retailers through the practice of loss leadership which is very common. This means the retailer will purposefully evoke a deep discount on a leading brand (e.g. 'Coca-Cola') in order to attract more customers into the store to buy it. In the process, the retailer is hoping customers will end up buying other products to more than offset the loss incurred. This accounts for 45% of the bump in retail sales.[27] The loss leader tactic is extremely effective for the retailer seeking to increase its profit[28] although it will erode the leader's brand equity, a hazard of being a market leader!

HYPER-LOCAL MARKETING

With the use of infra-red technologies, retailers can now send offers to a customer's smartphone (enabled with the app) who is in close proximity to the product. Sometimes called proximity marketing or location-based advertising (as discussed in chapter 5), it is said to be able to enhance the experience for the consumer.[29] With the pervasiveness of (Bluetooth enabled) smartphones, retailers can now use location detection technology to send the offers in the form of text or images or even videos. Consumers generally do not mind being 'interrupted' by notifications of offer and in fact say they are more likely to shop more.[30] This is because they are already interested in the product as evidenced by their downloading of the app; and they are also in the mood for shopping as evidenced by being in the vicinity. In other words, such forms of advertising are relevant and valuable.[31] Furthermore, for some product categories, like clothing or shoes, the same technology can also inform shoppers if the stock of the desired size, colour or style is available. Hyper-local marketing is effective because not only does it deliver the offer to interested customers, but also when they are about to buy!

SAMPLING

Sampling is an effective consumer promotion because consumers actually get to try before buying. While the brand name, advertising and pricing can evoke cues about quality, sampling allows the consumer to experience the product directly, the most powerful way for them to evaluate its intrinsic qualities. This also means that it only makes sense to use this tactic if (and only if) the product has a clear superiority. If it does not, then sampling actually makes the situation worse. To provide better value, price-off deals often accompany sampling.

For sampling to work, the product must be divisible. For indivisible products, such as cars, sampling takes the form of limited trial usage, such as taking a car for a test drive. It is interesting to note that in consumer-packaged goods, trial means purchase (to try), but in high-involvement goods, trial means a limited trial usage, not a purchase.

Sampling can be expensive if there are too many hurdles. For instance, even for an innocuous product like shampoo, retooling of the production process is necessary to produce smaller versions of the pack. This disrupts the usual production process. To minimise disruption, a third-party sales promotion agency can be subcontracted to produce and distribute the samples. However, product sampling has proven to be very effective in stimulating WOM (see chapter 8), boosting conversation by as much as 20%. This is because it gives the consumer the full experience of using the product. A cheaper option is using non-product options like T-shirts and hats which can also boost WOM, although less effectively at 15%.[32]

Sampling also induces the reciprocity heuristic, a subtle pressure to want to return the favour by buying the product after sampling it (see chapter 10).

PREMIUMS

Premiums are gifts or prizes that a consumer receives when they buy a product. For example, for children, the premium could be a toy; for men it could be a leather bag, and for wine lovers it could be wine glasses. The gift may come packaged with the product (i.e. packaged bundled) in which case it is likely to be free, or the consumer may have to pay a little extra for it, in which case it is 'self-liquidating'.

Of all the consumer promotions, premium is the most effective in enhancing the brand image because it can be used to evoke positive associations about the brand. This is because, unlike price-off deals, premiums do not undermine perceptions of quality. If anything, premiums actually enhance the value of the brand because consumers are not focusing on a discounted price.[33] However, to achieve this, premiums must be:

- carefully selected to fit the brand image
- creatively integrated into the campaign theme
- desirable for the target audience
- non-faddish, since that would be likely to overwhelm the brand image
- branded with the logo or brand name, to increase brand awareness and attitude.

One of the problems with premiums is the low redemption rate. If the premium is desirable for the target audience, we can avoid being left with too much unredeemed stock. One recent report shows that even with digital products (e.g. software) where the manufacturers give away limited versions of the product (called 'freemiums'), hoping that consumers will upgrade after the initial free trial, the redemption rate is about 1–2%. Freemiums turned out to be an expensive sales strategy.[34]

BONUS PACKS

In a bonus pack, the target audience receives more for the same price, thus benefiting from greater financial value. For instance, we might offer a 20% bigger pack or bundle two products for the same price. Bonus packs are more likely to appeal to current users than new customers. This is because current users are more likely to understand the value proposition. This is not necessarily a negative, because it encourages our customers to stock up and thereby takes them out of the market for a period of time, so they do not have the opportunity to switch to another brand. It is a loading tactic.

However, the cost of this privilege is an increased cost of goods. Bonus packs can also be expensive to execute because of the need to change the packaging format. Further, the loading function does not necessarily mean that the consumption behaviour of the consumer will change. For instance, a bonus pack of toilet rolls does not mean we go to the toilet more often.

BUY ONE, GET ONE FREE

In a large-scale study across four countries (Mexico, Colombia, Brazil and Argentina), consumers were asked to rank and rate 21 different types of promotions for breakfast cereals and laundry detergents.[35] The key measures were the incidence of these promotions and the likelihood the promotion (once considered) will cause them to switch to another brand. Not surprisingly the most popular promotion is that of buy one, get one free (or BOGOF); followed by three for the price of two; and free samples. These promotions are powerful because they are so simple for consumers to work out the value, it's immediate, easy and does not require any change in consumer behaviour. In contrast, the least effective promotions are those that do not provide enough value (e.g. 10% price discounts), are not immediate and require extra effort to obtain (e.g. rebates), and have elements of uncertainty (e.g. sweepstakes). BOGOF are so popular that we now see them for travel holidays. Consumers can research and buy these holidays over the internet, either with the assistance of a travel agent or not.

But BOGOF-like promotions are expensive, so one must be fairly certain that they are worth it. The upside is that consumers will get to experience the brand more than once, which implies that the intrinsic quality of the product better be good!

ESTIMATE THE COST-BENEFIT OF A PROMOTION

Some promotions are more expensive than others and so it is important to estimate whether the promotion being contemplated is worth it. Assume that one is launching a new product (e.g. a new chocolate bar) and is willing to spend $1 million dollars on a sampling campaign. If the profit earned per product is $1, assuming that each new customer buys 10 products per year. This means that each new customer will turn a profit of $10 (i.e. $1 × 10 units bought per year). Assuming this is reasonably true – that is, each new customer will bring in a profit of $10 – then: how many new customers are needed to recoup the $1 million spent in the sampling campaign? The answer is 100 000 new customers (i.e. $1 000 000/$10 = 100 000). The breakdown is as follows:

1. Cost of promotion campaign (including cost of goods, agency fees and ancillary expenditure)	$1 000 000
2. Profit per unit	$1.00
3. Number of units each customer is willing to buy in a year	10
4. Number of customers needed to break even in a year	100 000

The tricky part will be estimating the number of units a customer is willing to buy per year after the promotion is over (i.e. item 3). This estimate will determine the number of new customers needed to break even (i.e. item 4). Now assuming item 3 is reasonable, the question is whether finding 100 000 new customers is reasonable? Likewise, different sorts of promotions will affect the cost (i.e. item 1). A BOGOF campaign, for instance, will double the cost. Judgement is therefore needed.

CONTESTS, SWEEPSTAKES AND GAMES

Manufacturers usually like this form of sales promotion because it has the potential to create buzz if it is imaginative. Contest requires some skill and the winners are selected according to particular criteria (e.g. consumers might be asked to write an essay, with the best essay winning the contest). Winners of sweepstakes, on the other hand, are chosen at random.

Consumers tend to favour sweepstakes because they are easier to enter. For instance, a soft-drink company can create a sweepstake promotion in which all consumers need to do is to collect six bottle caps that have the winning insignia. No skills are required, but it can still be good fun because consumers have to build up a collection. The marcoms manager needs to be mindful of legal requirements when implementing contests and sweepstakes.

Interactive games via the internet are all the rage now. As the cost of graphics and computer technology drops, game suppliers can now quickly design a cost-effective, online, interactive game that includes a sales component for the brand. For instance, if a gamer manages to solve a number of problems, he or she becomes eligible for a free product. This form of sales promotions appeals to 14–25-year-olds because of their gaming mentality. These consumers are also difficult to reach using traditional mass media. Games as a form of sales promotion are also a good way to creatively integrate the brand into the promotion and so to strengthen the brand image.

REFUNDS AND REBATES

This form of sales promotion means the consumer will receive a portion of the money back at a later time after the purchase. (The term 'rebate' usually refers to white goods.) The promotion comes from manufacturers, which tend to like this form of promotion because it offers better control and they know who the customers are.

However, consumers may not necessarily favour this form of promotion because to claim the refund later means they have to show proof of purchase, which takes effort.[36] For more expensive goods (e.g. refrigerators), the retailers can fill in the paperwork on behalf of the consumer during the purchase, and the refund can be obtained immediately. Retailers also find this form of promotion troublesome because of the administrative need to keep track of the various refund or rebate programs for different brands.

LOYALTY OR VIP PROGRAMS

This is a very popular form of sales promotion with both consumers and companies and can be seen in a range of industries, including department stores, cafes, airlines, hotels and bookstores. Consumers like a loyalty program because it allows them to accumulate points. Since they are going to buy the product or service anyway, they might as well be rewarded for it. Companies like it because it encourages their customers to buy continually and keeps sales up. It also helps them retain their customers and improve their database, which in turn allows them to be more efficient in their direct response (see the discussion on direct response marketing above). Although loyalty programs started life as a means of differentiating to gain competitive advantage, it can become a liability, with added cost, if all competitors also have one.[37]

However, Qantas, the Australian airline, has managed to turn its huge frequent flyer membership program into a profit powerhouse. They do this by selling an allocated amount of frequent flyer membership (at a profit) to firms who want to partner with Qantas. For instance, a bank may buy an allocated amount every year to use as incentives. Because the membership is so desirable to consumers, these firms can use this as an effective incentive for their own business (e.g. a bank can use this to entice new customers). Qantas is now making more profit from this endeavour than from its international business.[38] This is ironic since selling frequent flyer points is not strictly an airline business, but it only works because the points are desirable. Cynically, one can argue whether consumers are loyal to the airline (i.e. brand) or to its frequent flyer program (i.e. marketing program).[39] Research has shown that consumers can differentiate between these two forms of loyalty. Loyalty to the marketing program, like Qantas' frequent flyer program, is driven more by our utilitarian needs (e.g. value, special treatment and social benefits), while that of the brand (e.g. Qantas) is driven more by our global evaluation (e.g. commitment, trust and satisfaction).[40] Finally, consumers can also communicate with each other about the benefits of loyalty programs through social media (e.g. Tripadvisor, Yelp). If firms were to be involved in this discussion, their *style* of communication should be friendly, but still provide accuracy.[41] In so doing, the loyalty of consumers is likely to increase.

The VIP program is a more refined variation of the loyalty program, designed to reward important customers. Since the profitability of an organisation is often derived from a small segment of its customers, it makes sense to treat this group differently. To do this form of promotion well, organisations have to segment their customer base into different tiers and reward each tier accordingly. For instance, if a person is an American Express Platinum customer, he or she can get access to special luxury privileges (e.g. access to top restaurants, special airline deals for first-class cabins, personal concierge services and other offers) that are not available to ordinary American Express members. Likewise, in casino businesses, high-rollers are given special room rates for their accommodation, chauffeured from the airport, treated to top restaurants and, most importantly, given a line of credit for their gambling – in short, full VIP treatment.

NEGATIVE- AND POSITIVE-ORIENTED PROMOTIONS

We can now ask why we need sales promotions at all. In a perfect world, there would be no need for them, since all products would be well made, well known, well priced, effectively advertised and optimally produced and distributed. However, we do not live in a perfect world – things go wrong. Further, our competitors are constantly trying to steal our customers with better deals. Sales promotions are therefore needed to correct a bad situation or avoid a downturn; for instance, when we want to reduce or redistribute excess stock, defend our distribution, defend our market share, disrupt the initiatives of competition (e.g. new product campaign) and so on. We call these negative-oriented promotions.

Negative-oriented promotions

Negative-oriented promotions (NOPs) are often short term, reactive and driven by oversupply, and they rely almost exclusively on financial incentives (e.g. price cuts or discounts or coupons) because this is the quickest and most responsive way of increasing sales.

However, if NOP is frequently practised, it changes the buying behaviour of consumers – they learn never to buy the product at full price. In other words, the reference price shifts to a lower point for the consumers.[42] We can explain this shift in terms of attribution theory. If the only emphasis of the sales promotion is monetary value – that is, on its price discount – then price becomes the most salient thing on a consumer's mind. This diverts attention away from other intrinsic qualities of the brand. Further, the lower reference price now signals a drop in quality.[43]

Worse still, if a competitor also engages in the same price-cutting strategy in order to defend their market share, then both brands will suffer, falling into a promotion trap, because neither brand dares to stop price promotion. The focus of management is now exclusively on price. Consumers, on the other hand, will benefit enormously by simply 'cherry-picking' the best deals, especially if they have the time and inclination to visit multiple stores (e.g. retirees).[44]

There is another major downside to constant promotions – it is administratively expensive. Imagine a big corporation, such as Procter & Gamble (P&G), which owns countless brands of consumer-packaged goods. Keeping track of constant promotions, dealing with retailers who constantly buy forward and diverting become difficult to manage. That is why, in the 1990s, P&G implemented Everyday Low Pricing (EDLP), under which the manufacturer charged retailers the same price for each order. Six years after P&G adopted EDLP, it was found that across 118 brands (in 24 product categories), both trade and coupon expenditures were substantially reduced, resulting in greater profit for P&G. The downside was that they also lost market share to competitors who continued to use sales promotion.[45]

Figure 11.7 Coles' 'Down, Down' campaign

In Australia, major retailers like Coles and Woolworths have also moved towards a hybrid form of EDLP. This means not all products are at constant everyday low prices, but only some (e.g. milk and bread). This is because EDLP pricing is generally not as profitable for the retailer compared to the normal discounting practice of high-low pricing.[46] Part of the reason for this shift is to combat Aldi, the German retailer which practises EDLP; many of the products they sell are their own (i.e. private labels).[47]

Positive-oriented promotions

Instead of cutting price to prop up sales, management should be thinking of how promotions tactics can be used to enhance the experience of the consumer. Candon, Wansink and Laurent noted that sales promotion does not always have to be about monetary benefits.[48] If it were, how can we explain why coupons are more effective than a similarly advertised price discount? Or why consumers bother with an insignificant price discount, or why they cut out coupons and yet fail to redeem them? They argued that something else is happening. They suggested that sales promotion could also be exciting and fun, like receiving a premium or winning a sweepstake. If so, consumers would be more likely to attribute such hedonism to the brand, which would help to build brand equity. This approach is thus less reactive and more long term in orientation. So, in comparison to NOPs, we can characterise positive-oriented promotions (POPs) as more proactive and long term, focusing more on the demand side of the equation, using non-financial incentives (e.g. premiums, sweepstakes, contests, games) to create hedonic benefits for the consumers. To consumers, POPs are non-instrumental or play-oriented ('paratelic'), while NOPs are instrumental or work-oriented ('telic'). In short, POPs are generally more fun, leading to more favourable thoughts than NOPs.[49]

CASE STUDY 11.2 EXPERIENTIAL PROMOTION: THE CASE OF CADBURY AUSTRALIA[50]

The rise of the experience economy[51] has raised the importance of customer experience. When applied to promotion, it often takes the form of giving consumers an unforgettable experience with the brand. One way is to create live events, at which consumers can have fun and be entertained. One can call this tactic experiential promotion (or more commonly, experiential marketing[52]). The objective is very simple. Give consumers a brand-integrated experience that is memorable, usually multi-sensory and interactive in nature (e.g. taste, smell, sight, sound, touch, and even virtual reality). When well executed, positive brand associations will be developed,[53] leading to higher brand attitude, brand equity[54] and purchase intentions.[55] And as we discussed earlier, it will also generate very powerful positive word-of-mouth.[56] But for this to work, consumers must like the event, so that positive emotions can be generated, which then transfers onto the brand. The greater the fit between the event and the brand, the more effective it will be.[57] This tactic is different from a visual stunt, which is often executed at a distance and a one-off. In experiential promotion, consumers get to experience the brand more intimately.

In 2017, Cadbury Australia wanted the brand to become synonymous with the joy of gift-giving and the festive Christmas lights. Their marketing agency, XPO Brands, came up with the idea of using virtual reality (VR) headsets to give consumers an animated journey on a sleigh, as it wings across the night sky at 35 000 feet in the air.[58] The virtual sleigh ride, called the Joy Ride VR experience, was very popular with long queues. At the same time, free samples of Cadbury chocolates were given away at these events by Santa's elves (dressed in Cadbury's colour of course).

Figure 11.8 Cadbury's Christmas experiential promotion

The event was no small feat; it took place over six weeks, in eight premium shopping centres, at six popular streetlight locations, and during two iconic Christmas events in Sydney (Carols in the Domain) and Melbourne (Federation Square Christmas Lights). It was supported by more product sampling in retail as well as personalised gift tags created in special pop-up booths. The campaign was an overwhelming success.

ASKHAM BRYAN
COLLEGE
LEARNING RESOURCES

Experiential is becoming increasingly popular because it gives the brand an opportunity to create a face-to-face 'wow' experience, which traditional media lacks. However, its reach is poor and the campaign can be expensive. A marcoms manager should always evaluate its effectiveness, by tracking outcome changes and carrying out control group studies (see chapter 12). This will help inform the accuracy of the cost-benefit estimate discussed earlier, and hence improve learning for the next campaign (see the PEEL principle in chapter 1).

DISCUSSION QUESTIONS

1. After reading this case study, do you think this is a positive- or negative-oriented promotion? Justify your answer.
2. Why does Cadbury Australia bother to go to all this trouble with experiential promotion? Why not just cut price which is simpler? Justify your answer.
3. Can experiential promotion build brand equity? Justify your answer.

When do we use NOPs?

We might now ask whether there is any place at all for NOPs. In theory, managing the brand well minimises the need for them, but since brands are not always managed well, sometimes for reasons beyond our control, there will always be a need for NOPs.

NOPs are also useful when the product is utilitarian in nature. For instance, products such as flour, AAA batteries or laundry detergent tend to benefit more from monetary forms of sales promotion (e.g. coupons and price-off deals) than non-monetary forms (e.g. sweepstakes and premiums).[59] This is because when consumers buy utilitarian products, they place more weight on attaining utilitarian benefits – so, monetary promotions, which can be characterised as being instrumental, are more effective. On the other hand, when consumers buy hedonic products, they place more weight on the attainment of hedonic benefits – so, promotions that appeal to their hedonism tend to be more satisfying.

Congruency of benefits in promotions

Table 11.1 summarises the changes in market share that occur when different kinds of promotion are paired with different types of product.[60] Observe that when the product matches the promotion type the market share tends to rise *after* the promotion. This is shown as shaded boxes in table 11.1. For instance, when a marcoms manager uses coupons with utilitarian products such as flour, AAA batteries or laundry detergent, the market share jumps to 26% on average. But if the coupons are paired with hedonic products (chocolate, nuts and bubblebath), the market share drops dramatically to an average of −5%. The use of coupons actually destroys the market share of hedonic products. For hedonic products, it is more effective to use non-monetary forms of sales promotion, especially premiums, which raise the market share by an average of 26%. So, premiums can permanently enhance brand image and improve brand preference even after the promotion is over.[61] This result suggests that for sales promotions to be effective, their benefits must match the purchase motivation of the product. This is known as the congruency of benefits in promotion.

Table 11.1 Changes in market share after promotion

Promotion type	Utilitarian products	Hedonic products
Coupons (monetary)	26	-5
Bonus product (monetary)	21	1
Premiums (non-monetary)	17	26
Sweepstakes (non-monetary)	-9	7

There are two caveats. First, this congruency result only works for high-equity brands. Brands with low brand equity show few changes in market share regardless of the types of promotion used. This is understandable since high-equity brands will be perceived as being more of a bargain when there is a promotion than low-equity brands; or, to put it another way, promotion price elasticity is higher for high-equity brands than for low-equity brands.

Second, when brands of higher equity have a substantial price promotion, they attract more customers from lower-quality brands. However, the opposite is not true; that is, promotions from lower-quality brands do not steal customers of higher-equity brands.[62]

The above result does not mean that products should always be on constant price promotion in order to gain market share. To do so will lead to a decline in profitability, decrease the reference price and possibly fall into the sales promotion trap, as discussed earlier. This is the second caveat.

Dangers of POPs

POPs are not without their dangers either. POPs can only enhance the brand image if we choose those that work creatively. Let's look at a hypothetical example of a premium. Imagine a toy manufacturer approaches McDonald's for a promotional tie-in using their toys. Two options are suggested as a premium:

(a) McDonald's racing-car toy
(b) McDonald's hamburger toy.

To build brand equity, we should go with premium option (b), because this is more closely related to what McDonald's stands for. It is more likely to enhance its brand image even though option (a) may be more popular with boys. In fact, there is a real danger that if the racing-car toy proves too popular, the equity of the McDonald's brand will be transferred to the toy. In other words, people might buy McDonald's not because the food is good but because they want the racing-car toy.

Many years ago, in Singapore, McDonald's had a promotional tie-in using six-limited editions of the 'Hello Kitty' toy (see figure 11.9). It became so popular as a collector's item that people were buying the burgers and then throwing them away because all they wanted was the toy! There was also a riot in one store, the frenzy causing seven Singaporeans to be injured as frantic shoppers shattered a glass door.[63] This illustrates how easy it is for promotions to obscure the reason why people buy the product. In fact, some researchers have argued that the more prominent the promotion, the more likely it will 'overshadow the benefits of the brand and undermine brand preference'.[64]

Figure 11.9 Six limited editions of the Hello Kitty toy

Therefore, advertising remains important. It must still be used to remind the target audience the original reason why we should buy the brand. Unless this reason is constantly reinforced consumers will forget or, to put it another way, advertising is needed to maintain the goodwill or 'adstock' for the brand, which will otherwise decay over time. Further, if we cut our advertising while our competitors continue to advertise, the image of the competing brands will grow at our expense. This means that competitors' promotions will more deeply affect our brands, if and when competitors decide to promote. Table 11.2 summarises the key differences between NOPs and POPs.

Table 11.2 Table outlining the difference between NOPs and POPs

Negative-oriented promotions (NOPs)	Positive-oriented promotions (POPs)
Short term	Long term
Reactive	Proactive
Business focused, concerned more with supply side of the equation	Consumer focused, concerned more with demand side of the equation
Financially based (e.g. price-off deals, coupons, bonus)	Non-financially based (e.g. premiums, contests, sweepstakes)
Instrumental	Non-instrumental
Utilitarian benefits	Hedonic benefits
Work-oriented (telic)	Play-oriented (paratelic)
Lowers brand equity, reference price and quality with repeated use	Undermines brand equity if promotion is unrelated to the brand and allowed to overshadow it

MANAGERIAL APPLICATION: PUTTING IT TOGETHER

Now that we understand the basic theory behind sales promotions, we can use the tactic in some clever ways. Below are some recommendations.

ADVERTISE TO BUILD BRAND EQUITY, THEN PROMOTE

If advertising helps give people reasons to buy our brand, then it must occur first in order to build the brand's image, before sales promotion can take place. This is the reason why sales promotions have been found to be less effective for unfamiliar brands: such brands have very little brand equity. When these brands have a sales promotion, consumers' preference actually drops when the promotion is over.[65] This is also the reason why, as we have seen, the principle of congruency of benefits in promotion does not apply to low-equity brands. More importantly, a manager must remember that to prosper in the long term, the brand equity must be built and maintained. Here, the laying down of emotional memories is important. Straight sales promotion cannot do this; it is primarily good for activating a quick sale. (One exception might be experiential promotion - see case study 11.2.) For this reason, one recommendation is set a limit of 40% of the media budget for short-term sales activation as discussed in chapter 4.

SIGNAL THAT THE SALES PROMOTION IS ONLY TEMPORARY

All promotions should be perceived as temporary; this is, in fact, the definition of a sales promotion. Supporting this recommendation is the observation that unannounced price cuts tend to have a negative effect on brand preference after the promotion is over.[66] This is because consumers interpret an unannounced price cut as a *permanent* drop in price, which in turn signals a drop in quality, and this erodes brand equity.

Usually sales promotion is accompanied by some form of restriction, generally in terms of purchase limit (e.g. each person is only limited to two items), time limit (e.g. this weekend only) or purchase precondition (e.g. only if you spend more than $40). This 'restriction effect' increases the perception of value of the brand and is found to be very robust in increasing purchase intentions as well as sales.[67] However, not all restrictions are equal. A restriction based on purchase limit is most likely to signal high brand quality because it implies that the product is so good that consumers are most likely to stock up if no restrictions to quantity are made. And depending on how quantity restrictions are phrased, it can also create competition among consumers. For instance, if the company was to say that the offer was only limited to first 100 customers, it would create a sense of scarcity, driving up purchase intentions.[68]

SALES PROMOTION SHOULD NOT BE PREDICTABLY CYCLICAL

Sales promotion should also be unpredictable. It should not be perceived as part of a cyclical game, to fulfil the sales objective of the organisation at the end of the financial year, for instance. If it is predictable, consumers will simply defer their purchase until the next promotion; they also become price sensitive.[69]

Keeping the timing of the promotion somewhat unpredictable prevents these problems. For instance, in the US, Costco sporadically have upscale products available at deep discounts (e.g. a grand piano). This drives foot traffic into the stores. Similarly, in Australia, the liquor chain Vintage Cellars periodically have a triple point bonus weekend. Consumers do not know when such promotions will occur.

THE VALUE OF THE PROMOTION

How much should the value of the promotion be? Recent research shows that if the promotion value is more than 20% of the regular product price, it will hurt the brand when the promotion is over.[70] In other words, it cheapens the brand too much. Further, if price discounts are used, it is important to reassure consumers that quality will not suffer as a result.[71]

MATCH THE BENEFIT OF THE SALES PROMOTION WITH THE PURCHASE MOTIVATION

We have seen how important it is to match the right kinds of promotion tactics with the right kinds of products. With hedonic products, use non-monetary promotional tactics that trigger hedonic benefits such as excitement or fun. This includes tactics such as premiums and contests, sweepstakes or games. For utilitarian products, on the other hand, use monetary tactics to trigger a sense of value. This includes tactics like bonuses and price-off deals. Such tactics will only work for high-equity brands.

THE PROMOTION SHOULD NOT OVERSHADOW THE BRAND

It is very tempting for a marcoms manager to dream up a sales promotion that is so exciting that it threatens to overwhelm the brand. When this occurs, the benefits of the brand will become less salient.[72] Instead, the benefits will shift to the promotion itself, instead of with the brand.

INTEGRATE THE BRAND'S POSITIONING INTO THE THEME OF THE PROMOTION

The previous recommendation does not mean that a marcoms manager should not strive for eye-catching, dramatic sales promotions that could potentially create viral contagion (see chapter 8) or free publicity (see chapter 9). Rather, the buzz and publicity created should be relevant and clearly linked to the positioning of the brand. We have seen how the same logic applies in sponsorship (chapter 8). One way of achieving this is to think of sales promotion as part of a larger positioning of the brand. The brand's positioning then guides the theme of the promotion. Or to put it another way, the marcoms manager should creatively integrate the positioning of the brand into the theme of the promotion.

FURTHER THINKING: PRICE DISCOUNTING

In this section we explore why discounting is so prevalent in the consumer-packaged goods industry. It shows how to diagnose the health of a brand using baseline sales data as well as price variability due to promotions. It concludes with three suggestions on how to avoid the temptation of price discounting.

LEARNING GOALS

After reading this section, you will understand:

- how price discounting can become a vicious circle
- how to avoid the temptation of price discounting.

Consumers are not stupid – once they learn they do not have to pay full price for a product because of frequent sales promotion, they will simply wait for the next price promotion to come along before buying again (called 'lie-in-wait'). And they will then buy in bulk to stock up, as is often observed in the case of consumer-packaged goods.[73] When this occurs, there is no net increase in sales – consumers simply bring their purchases forward.

This can set up a vicious cycle, in which consumers will buy from one promotion cycle to the next and never pay the full price. This in turn erodes the profitability of the brand. And seeing this erosion, a marcoms manager will be tempted to cut advertising, which in turn makes the brand less differentiated from its competition. Soon, consumers can think of no other reason to buy the brand other than its price, which leads to the commoditisation of the brand, and, as with most commodities, people will buy based almost solely on price. The lack of profitability then leads to further price discounts to boost sales, which then leads to stockpiling and the vicious cycle starts all over again (see figure 11.10). Repeat this cycle over several years and the brand will soon not exist.

Figure 11.10 The vicious cycle of constant price-discounting

So, what can we do to avoid the vicious cycle? Before offering a solution, we might ask why it occurs in the first place. Leonard Lodish and Carl Mela asked precisely this question in 1997, and what they discovered is unfortunately still true today.[74] A large part of the problem stems from taking a short-term perspective. This happens because the performance of companies and hence managers are judged quarterly. Given the often-short tenure of managers, there is no long-term perspective on how brands should be managed. Further, price promotions tend to fuel a false sense of confidence, which in the long run may cause managers to become short-sighted.

This is the advice. First, care about the long-term health of the brand. Do not be tempted by short-term gains in sales generated by price discounts. However, since the tenure of brand managers is often short (which means they may not be motivated to take a long-term perspective), careful monitoring of key measures in brand health must be the responsibility of the higher levels of management. Profitability should be the main criterion. Quality marketing data must also be assiduously collected over many years to help better understand the dynamics of the market.

Second, invest in advertising in order to differentiate the brand. Differentiation not only allows us to charge more but is also less susceptible to competitive price discounting. As advanced advertising pre-testing research methodologies are now available, managers can no longer use the excuse that advertising does not predict short-term sales. It can: ads that generate short-term sales over a year are also likely to continue to generate sales over two years even after advertising has stopped. In fact, in a study of 24 brands in Europe, Lodish and Mela found that advertising turns out to have a 60% *greater* long-term effect than its short-term effect. However, with sales promotion, its long-term effect is 20% *less* than its short-term effect. In other words, advertising on average has positive long-term effects for the brand, while sales promotion has negative long-term effects.

Third, and in the same vein, innovate in order to differentiate. In some product categories, such as electronics, this is mandatory for a firm to survive. In the consumer-packaged goods industry, this is also critical, especially given the increasing threat from private labels. National brands no longer have any choice. Innovation allows the creation of different (i.e. distinctive) brands that, when distributed through leading retailers, result in lower consumer price-sensitivity.

Fourth, if a marcoms manager wants to use sales promotions then it is vital to use them cleverly, drawing on the recommendations in the preceding section.

DISCUSSION QUESTIONS

1. Why is it important to have a good customer database in direct response marketing?
2. Explain how direct response marketing, unlike general advertising, is immediately accountable, adjustable and testable.
3. How might direct response marketing undermine brand equity?
4. How can we use mass media in making a direct response marketing offer?
5. What is hyper-local marketing (sometimes called location-based advertising)? Would you employ this tactic if you are a marcoms manager? Explain your answer.
6. Using a diagram, explain the difference between trade and consumer promotions. Show how they are related to each other.
7. What is the difference between positive- and negative-oriented sales promotions (POPs and NOPs)?
8. Explain the notion of congruency benefit in promotion and give reasons for its effect.
9. What are the dangers of regularly using price discounts as a form of promotion?
10. How would you conduct a sales promotion without undermining brand equity?
11. Although experiential promotion can increase brand equity, it suffers from poor reach. How would you mitigate against this if you plan to do this?
12. How does advertising combat the dangers of price promotion?

NOTES

1 R White, 'Direct marketing', *Admap*, 431, 2002, pp. 14–15.

2 M Felgate, A Fearne, S DiFalco and MG Martinez, 'Using supermarket loyalty card data to analyse the impact of promotions', *International Journal of Market Research*, 54(2), 2012, pp. 221–40.

3 For a good solid exposition of what CRM should be, see F Buttle, *Customer relationship management: concepts and technologies*, 2nd edition, Elsevier, Oxford, 2009.

4 For example, one approach is to optimise for profitability by using other variables – see JR Bult and T Wanseek, 'Optimal selection for direct mail', *Marketing Science*, 14(4), 1995, pp. 378–94.

5 For instance, half of the offers were sent out to customers who were more than happy to pay full price! Progressive Grocer, '52% of promotions go to customers who would pay full price: Study', 25 May 2018. Accessed October 2018 at https://progressivegrocer.com/52-promotions-go-customers-who-would-pay-full-price-study.

6 K Yoon, P Bolls and A Lang, 'The effects of arousal on liking and believability of commercials', *Journal of Marketing Communications*, 4, 1998, pp. 101–14.

7 M Medico, 'Principles of direct response television', American Marketing Association Best Practice, World Advertising Research Centre (Warc). Accessed October 2018 at www.warc.com/content/paywall/article/principles-of-direct-response-television/82099.

8 D Beale, 'TV strategy: Make a direct connection', *Admap*, December, 2014. Accessed October 2018 at www.warc.com/content/paywall/article/admap/tv-strategy-make-a-direct-connection/103328.

9 T Chambers, 'Forget storytelling. 2019 will be the year of storyselling', Think with Google, 2019. Accessed May 2019 at www.thinkwithgoogle.com/advertising-channels/video/direct-consumer-response-marketing/.

10 For more details of this case study, go to www.contagious.com/blogs/news-and-views/five-great-advertising-case-study-videos-or-how-to-wow-awards-juries. Accessed May 2018.

11 RC Blattberg, R Breisch and EJ Fox, 'How promotion works', *Marketing Science*, 14(3), 1995, G122–31.

12 B Sun, Baohong, SA Neslin and K Srinivasan, 'Measuring the impact of promotions on brand switching when consumers are forward looking', *Journal of Marketing Research,* 40(4), 2003, pp. 389–405.

13 THA Bijmolt, HJ Van Heerde and RGM Pieters, 'New empirical generalizations on the determinants of price elasticity', *Journal of Marketing Research,* 42, 2005, pp. 141–56.

14 G Assmus, JU Farley and DR Lehmann, 'How advertising affects sales: a meta analysis of econometric results', *Journal of Marketing Research*, 21(1), 1984, pp. 65–74.

15 Promo Industry Trend, 'Cutting the promo pie', 2007. Accessed August 2012 at https://faculty.nipissingu.ca/denyseh/home/save_word_documents_here/MKTG%203437%20Fall%2009/Promo%20Trend%20REport%202007.pdf.

16 Oliver and Farris were to first to point out that in trying to understand how distribution affects market share, one should consider how consumers are influenced by the push and pull factors of promotions. See JM Olver and PW Farris, 'Push and pull: A one-two punch for packaged goods', *Sloan Management Review,* 31(1), 1989, pp. 53–61. Ailawadi et al. also outlined much of the push and pull effects in their review paper. See KL Ailawadi et al., 'Communication and promotion decisions in retailing: A review and directions for future research', *Journal of Retailing*, 85(1), 2009, pp. 42–55.

17 M Bellas, 'Shopper marketing's instant impact', *Beverage World*, 126(11), 15 November 2007, p. 18.

18 P Underhill, *Why we buy: the science of buying*, Simon & Schuster, New York, 2008, p. 67.

19 D Del Vecchio, DH Henard and TH Freling, 'The effect of sales promotion on post-promotion brand preference: a meta-analysis', *Journal of Retailing*, 82, 2006, pp. 203–13.

20 D McGuiness, M Brennan and P Gendall, 'An empirical test of product sampling and couponing', *Journal of the Market Research Society,* 37(2), 1995, pp. 159–170.

21 K Bawa and RW Shoemaker, 'The effects of direct mail coupon on brand choice behaviour', *Journal of Marketing Research*, 24, November 1987, pp. 370–6.

22 BA Alvarez and RV Casielles, 'Consumer evaluations of sales promotion: the effect on brand choice', *European Journal of Marketing*, 39(1/2), 2005, pp. 54–70.

23 K Monroe, *Pricing: making profitable decisions*, 2nd edition, McGraw-Hill, Boston, MA, 1990.

24 THA Bijmolt, HJ van Heerde and RGM Pieters, 'New empirical generalizations on the determinants of price elasticity', *Journal of Marketing Research,* 42, 2005, pp. 141–56.

25 Ibid.

26 MI Gomez, V Rao and E McLaughlin, 'Empirical analysis of budget and allocation of trade promotions in the U.S. supermarket industry', *Journal of Marketing Research,* 44(3), 2007, pp. 410–24.

27 K Ailawadi, B Harlam, J Cesar and D Trounce, 'Retailer promotion profitability: The role of promotion, brand, category, and market characteristics', *Journal of Marketing Research*, 43(4), 2006, pp. 518–35.

28 DK Gauri, D Talukdar and B Ratchford, 'Empirical investigation of the impact of loss leader promotion on store and category performance in grocery industry', Working Paper, Syracuse University, 2008.

29 D Girish, 'What is proximity marketing and how does it work?', Beaconstac, 6 January 2015. Accessed October 2018 at https://blog.beaconstac.com/2015/01/what-is-proximity-marketing-and-how-does-it-work/.

30 M da Silva, 'Proximity marketing: How to attract more shoppers with beacon technology', Shopify, 12 April 2017. Accessed October 2018 at www.shopify.com/retail/the-ultimate-guide-to-using-beacon-technology-for-retail-stores.

31 AE Hühn et al., 'Does location congruence matter? A field study on the effects of location-based advertising on perceived ad intrusiveness, relevance and value', *Computers in Human Behavior,* 73, 2017, pp. 659–68.

32 J Berger and EM Schwartz, 'What drives immediate and ongoing word of mouth?', *Journal of Marketing Research*, 48, 2011, pp. 869–80.

33 PR Darke and CMY Chung, 'Effects of pricing and promotion on consumer perceptions: it depends on how you frame it', *Journal of Retailing*, 81(10), 2005, pp. 35–47.

34 SE Needleman and A Loten, 'When freemium fails', *Wall Street Journal*, 22 August 2012. Accessed July 2013 at http://online.wsj.com/article/SB10000872396390443713704577603782317318996.html?mod=djemMGMTNEWS_t.

35 A Tello, G Losschilder and L Salano, 'The most effective promotion: a comparative study across Latin American markets', *ESOMAR Latin America*, Buenos Aires, April 2014. Accessed October 2018 at www.warc.com/content/paywall/article/the-most-effective-promotion-a-comparative-study-across-latin-american-markets/101632.

36 P Tat, WA Cunningham III and E Babakus, 'Consumer perceptions of rebates', *Journal of Advertising Research*, 28(4), 1988, pp. 45–50.

37 G Dowling and M Uncles, 'Do customer loyalty programs really work?', *Sloan Management Review*, 38(4), 1997, pp. 71–82.

38 A Whitely, 'Qantas frequent flyer program turning into airline's biggest money spinner', *Sydney Morning Herald*, 12 May 2017. Accessed October 2018 at www.smh.com.au/business/companies/qantas-frequent-flyer-program-turning-into-airlines-biggest-money-spinner-20170512-gw34wq.html.

39 MD Uncles, GR Dowling and K Hammond, 'Customer loyalty and customer loyalty programs', *Journal of Consumer Marketing*, 20(4), 2003, pp. 294–316.

40 H Evanschitzky et al., 'Consequences of customer loyalty to the loyalty program and to the company', *Journal of the Academy of Marketing Science*, 40, 2012, pp. 625–38.

41 C Raab, O Berezan, AS Krishen, and S Tanford, 'What's in a word? Building program loyalty through social media communication', *Cornell Hospitality Quarterly*, 57(2), 2016, pp. 138–49.

42 Blattberg, Breisch and Fox (1995), 'How promotion works', note 11.

43 Darke and Chung (2005), 'Effects of pricing and promotion on consumer perceptions', note 33.

44 EJ Fox and SJ Hoch, 'Cherry picking', *Journal of Marketing*, 69, January 2005, pp. 46–62.

45 KL Ailawadi, DR Lehman and SA Neslin, 'Market response to a major policy change in the marketing mix: learning from Procter & Gamble's Value Pricing Strategy', *Journal of Marketing*, 65, January 2001, pp. 44–61.

46 R Lal R and R Rao, 'Supermarket competition: the case of every day low pricing', *Marketing Science*, 16(1), 1997, pp. 60–80.

47 T Osegowitsch and A McCabe, 'Aldi supermarket strategy is unlikely to challenge Woolworths and Coles', ABC News, August 2018. Accessed May 2019 at www.smartcompany.com.au/industries/retail/why-woolworths-and-coles-should-follow-aldis-lead-and-keep-it-simple/.

48 P Candon, B Wansink and G Laurent, 'A benefit congruency framework of sales promotion effectiveness', *Journal of Marketing*, 64(4), 2000, pp. 65–81.

49 E Delgado-Ballester and M Palazón-Vidal, 'Sales promotions effects on consumer-based brand equity', *International Journal of Market Research*, 47(2), 2005, pp. 179–204.

50 I would like to thank Bianca Ellershaw, strategist at XPO Brand, for bringing this case to my attention.

51 J Pine and J Gilmore, *The Experience Economy*, Harvard Business School Press, Boson, MA, 2011.

52 BH Schmitt, *Experiential Marketing*, Free Press, New York, 1999.

53 E Delgado-Ballester and M Palazón-Vidal, 'Sales promotions effects on consumer-based brand equity', *International Journal of Market Research*, 47(2), 2005, pp. 179–204.

54 L Zarantonello and BH Schmitt, 'The impact of event marketing on brand equity', *International Journal of Advertising*, 32(2), 2013, pp. 255–80.

55 J Sneath, RZ Finney and AG Close, 'An IMC approach to event marketing: the effects of sponsorship and experience on customer attitudes', *Journal of Advertising Research*, 45(4), 2005, pp. 373–81.

56 J Berger and EM Schwartz, 'What drives immediate and ongoing word of mouth?" *Journal of Marketing Research*, 48, 2011, pp. 869–80.

57 A Martensen, L Grønholdt, L Bendtsen and MJ Jensen, 'Application of a model for the effectiveness of event marketing', *Journal of Advertising Research*, 47(3), 2007, pp. 283–30.

58 You can watch a video of the case study here: www.xpobrands.com.au/v3/portfolio/cadbury-christmas/. Accessed October 2018.

59 Candon, Wansink and Laurent (2000), 'A benefit congruency framework of sales promotion effectiveness', note 48.

60 Ibid.

61 D DelVecchio, DH Henard and TH Freling, 'The effect of sales promotion on post-promotion brand preference: a meta-analysis', *Journal of Retailing*, 82(3), 2006, pp. 203–13.

62 SM Nowlis and I Simonson, 'Sales promotions and the choice context of competing influence on decision making', *Journal of Consumer Psychology*, 9(1), 2000, pp. 1–16.

63 This riot happened in 2000. See coverage of the story at the BBC news website: http://news.bbc.co.uk/2/hi/asia-pacific/603932.stm. Accessed September 2013.

64 SA Neslin, *Sales promotion*, Marketing Science Institute, Cambridge, MA, 2002, p. 13; see also DelVecchio, Henard and Freling (2006), 'The effect of sales promotion on post-promotion brand preference', note 61.

65 DelVecchio, Henard and Freling (2006), 'The effect of sales promotion on post-promotion brand preference', note 61.

66 Ibid.

67 JJ Inman, AC Peter and P Raghubir, 'Framing the deal: The role of restrictions in accentuating deal value', *Journal of Consumer Research,* 24(1), 1997, pp. 68–79.

68 P Aggarwal, YJ Sung and HH Jong, 'Scarcity Messages', *Journal of Advertising*, 40(3), 2011, pp. 19–30.

69 CF Mela, S Gupta and DR Lehmann, 'The long-term impact of promotion and advertising on consumer brand choice', *Journal of Marketing Research*, 34, 1997, pp. 248–61.

70 DelVecchio, Henard and Freling (2006), 'The effect of sales promotion on post-promotion brand preference', note 61.

71 Darke and Chung (2005), 'Effects of pricing and promotion on consumer perceptions', note 33.

72 Neslin (2002), *Sales promotion*, note 64.

73 CF Mela, K Jedidi and D Bowman, 'The long-term impact of promotions on consumer stockpiling', *Journal of Marketing Research*, 35(2), 1998, pp. 250–62.

74 L Lodish and CF Mela, 'If brands are built over years, why are they managed over quarters?', *Harvard Business Review*, July–August, 2007, pp. 104–12.

CHAPTER 12
ADVERTISING TESTING, CAMPAIGN TRACKING AND SYNERGISTIC EFFECTS

CHAPTER OVERVIEW

This chapter is about evaluating the effectiveness of an ad and the subsequent campaign. This is an important chapter because a bad ad can hurt a brand even with a single exposure,[1] and a good ad of the same brand can outsell a bad one by about four times, even with the same media expenditure.[2] Therefore, at the very least, we should think of ad evaluation as a risk-reduction exercise!

We discuss how to formally evaluate one's ad, first *in situ*, when we assess the ad in a strict experimental control condition, and then *in vivo*, when we track the effectiveness of the ad in the field. But before either of these, a marcoms manager can systematically judge (guided by theory) whether the ad is easy to understand, whether the ad elicits the right brand and associations and, finally, whether it is persuasive. We will discuss how to do this, including assessing the ROI of ad pre-testing, and the synergistic effects.

Learning goals

After reading this chapter, you will understand:

- the difference between concept exploration and quantitative advertising pre-testing
- how to use principled evaluation in subjective judgement of ads
- the four persuasion styles and their executional requirements
- criticisms and best practices of ad pre-testing
- estimating ROI of ad pre-testing
- the Starch methodology for post-testing print ads
- how campaign tracking works, and the difference between ad-diagnostic measures and outcome measures
- the concepts of brand awareness, brand consideration, and brand associations
- the uses of measuring ad recognition and ad recall
- benefits of, and issues in, campaign tracking
- how to evaluate synergistic effects.

How do we evaluate an ad? Figure 12.1 shows that quantitative ad pre-testing occurs after a long series of preparations, starting with research (for detailed discussion, see chapter 2). Research is an important step because, as we saw in chapter 6, if an ad is poor then virtually nothing will save the campaign.

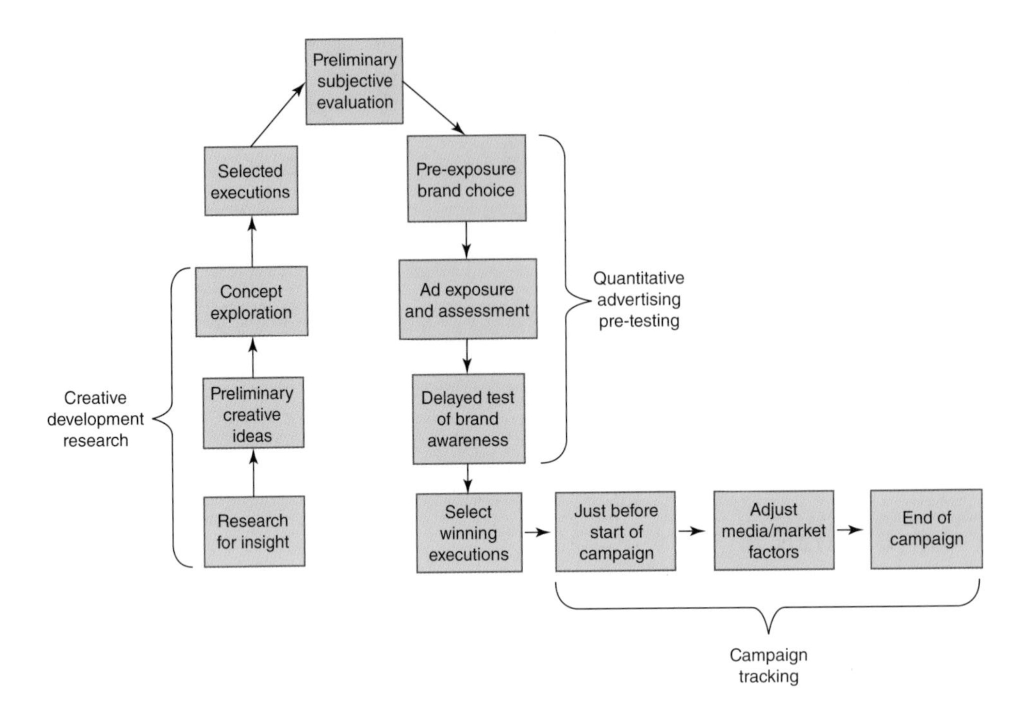

Figure 12.1 An overview of advertising research

CONCEPT TESTING AS EXPLORATION

Before discussing quantitative pre-testing, it is important to distinguish concept testing from quantitative advertising pre-testing (sometimes called 'copytesting'). Concept testing uses qualitative exploratory research to gain insights about various concepts, and it does not test an actual ad. Its objective is to explore whether some preliminary hunches have potential. At the concept-testing stage, it is all about exploring concepts, not evaluating them. As figure 12.1 shows, this is part of creative development research.

Let's take the example of a beer brand, to make this point clearer. Imagine we are working on a campaign for a German beer, Warsteiner. We might initially think that Warsteiner beer would sell more if it emphasises its German heritage (since Germany is one of the biggest consumers of beer in the world, per capita). Further research tells us that a German heritage positioning may limit the future growth of the brand. An international image might be better, perhaps emphasising the beer's world-class quality. So, there are two potential positionings – one that focuses on German heritage and another that underlines world-class quality. Which concept will appeal more to consumers? Since we are not sure, it is prudent to conduct some exploratory research. Note that, at this stage, we are still exploring and not formally testing anything.

Further, there may be many ways of expressing each positioning concept. For instance, with the German heritage positioning, we might choose to say 'Only the Germans know their beer', or 'Warsteiner – brewed in the mystical Arnsberg Forest of Germany'. Likewise, with the world-class quality positioning, we might choose to say, 'Warsteiner – quality since 1753' or '250 years of quality brewing' (see figure 12.2). It is not unusual to explore half-a-dozen different positioning concepts (with accompanying visuals) in a focus group, using concept boards (remembering that these are *not* ads).

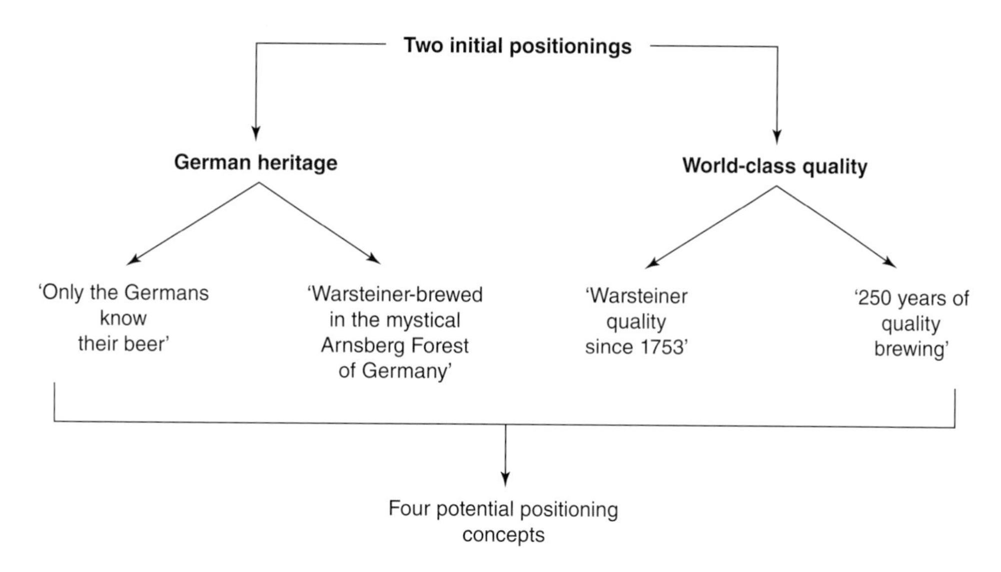

Figure 12.2 Four positioning concepts from two initial positionings

What is more, we may also recruit different consumer groups (e.g. lapsed users, whom we may try to convert) to explore different viewpoints. Such exploration of initial concepts is (misleadingly) called concept 'testing'. A better term is concept 'exploration'. All this exploration may eventually lead to a better positioning claim for the brand. For instance, in our beer example, the account planner, after much exploration, may suggest this slogan: 'Warsteiner Quality – still German after 250 years.' Thus, the value of qualitative exploratory research lies in the insights gleamed from consumers (see chapter 2). More broadly, we can also think of this search as looking for the 'creative frame' from which the final creative idea will emerge (see chapter 6).[3]

PRELIMINARY SUBJECTIVE EVALUATION

Once we have found the creative idea, the next step is to actualise it in one (or a number of) rough executions.[4] Now we are moving towards the actual evaluation. It is no longer exploration, but evaluation based on principles. But where do these principles come from? We already discussed them in chapters 6 and 7, where we learnt that some executions tend to be more effective under some circumstances. However, to be systematic, we can ask these questions.

1. Which execution is easiest for people to understand?
2. Which execution will elicit the desired associations?
3. Which execution will elicit the brand?
4. Which execution (and its message) is more persuasive?

These roughly correspond to the following four criteria: (1) comprehension; (2) desired positioning; (3) branded attention and (4) acceptance. Of the four criteria, the easiest to judge is the first.

The first objective is to assess how well each execution (of the same concept) will perform, relative to the others, in terms of comprehension. This means that the selling point of the branded message is judged to be clearly communicated and not confusing. This is important because if it is not understandable, viewers will be spending half their time wondering what the point of the ad is. This inevitably leads to negative outcomes.[5] And as we saw in chapter 6, having a single-minded message helps. The more you try to say within a 30-second TV ad, the more comprehension will suffer. Below is a simple example of how the principles we outlined in chapters 6 and 7 can be used to evaluate comprehension of a TV ad. One can think of this as a hygiene check.

> The TV ad should use simple, concrete, unambiguous consumer language. The brand should appear early in the ad so that the relevance of the ad is quickly grasped. If information is important, the ad should not have too many scenes. The storyline of the ad should be easy to follow. The message should be single-minded.

The second objective is to assess how well each execution (of the same concept) is 'on message', relative to the others, in delivering the desired positioning as outlined in the creative brief. The key is to assess if the right associations can be triggered. More often than not, viewers do not remember exactly what is being said in the ad, but only the gist of it. Below is an example of how the principles in chapter 6 can be applied.

> For each execution, quickly ask what comes to mind. Try not to censor one's thoughts. Ask whether (i) the dominant association of the conveyor supports the desired positioning, (ii) no other conflicting associations are triggered and (iii) there is creative unity so that all the elements reinforce each other.
>
> For instance, if the positioning of a brand of ice-cream is about its exotic flavour, then the picture, headline, brand name, slogan and copy of its print ads must all convey similar notions of 'exoticness' without necessarily creating conflicting associations. This also applies to the celebrity if one is used.

The third objective is to assess how well each execution can capture and sustain the attention of the target audience, and in a way that involves the brand in a positive way. The following principles from chapters 6 and 7 should help you make a judgement.

> For each execution, quickly assess whether surprise and joy are elicited. Check if these emotions occur at the beginning of the ad (for eliciting initial attention), and throughout the ad (for sustained attention). Look for scenes that use evocative cues and/or whether they are executed in high intensity. Once an overall emotional assessment is made, ask whether the brand is the hero in those emotional scenes. It should be an integral part of the story line or narrative. Play two mental experiments for each execution:
>
> - the substitute game: mentally insert the competitor's brand into the ad. If the ad still 'works', then chances are, creative integration has *not* occurred.
> - the creative magnifier game:[6] ask which two scenes are the most memorable for each execution; for these scenes ask whether (i) it is portraying the main selling point, and (ii) the brand has a role in it.

The fourth objective is to assess its (short-term) persuasive powers. This is the most difficult subjective assessment to make because it requires one to walk in the shoes of the target audience. To be sure, it *must* be double-checked against the results of quantitative pre-testing (which we discuss below).[7] Broadly, a framework of different generic persuasion styles can guide our assessment of persuasion because, under some circumstances, one form of persuasion style may be more effective than another. Figure 12.3 shows one such framework, called the 'dual-motive, dual-processing' model (DMDP), which describes four persuasion styles.

	Utilitarian motives (telic mindset)	Hedonic motives (paratelic mindset)
Intensive–systematic processing	**1. Convincing argumentation** Convincing *argument* with supporting pictures (e.g. deciding on changing retirement funds)	**2. Hedonistic immersion** Hedonistic *imagery* with supporting argument (e.g. deciding which holiday resort to go to)
Easy–heuristic processing	**3. Entertaining argumentation** Entertainment using *utilitarian* values (e.g. buying a washing detergent)	**4. Hedonistic entertainment** Entertainment using *hedonic* cues (e.g. craving a beer)

Figure 12.3 Four generic persuasion styles

The four persuasion styles are based on two dimensions. The first dimension is the target audience's buying motives, which may be either utilitarian or hedonic in nature (for more on these motives, see chapter 7). A utilitarian motive is characterised by a 'work' (telic) mind-set, where the target audience is motivated to solve a problem or avoid pain. A hedonic motive, on the other hand, is characterised by a 'play' (paratelic) mindset, where the target audience is motivated to seek pleasure or recognition.

The second dimension is the target audiences' processing predisposition. This can be intensive (and systematic) or it can be easy (or heuristic).[8] Intensive–systematic processing means that the target audience will devote considerable resources to the purchase decision. People do this for many reasons – maybe the purchase risk is high, the brand or category is new, or the personality of the person desires close scrutiny (e.g. the person has a high need for cognition).

Easy–heuristic processing means that consumers use simple rules of thumb, or mental shortcuts, to come to a purchase decision. For example, a person may think, 'This brand is well known and so it must be good', even though this person has no prior experience with it. Relatively few resources are devoted to the purchase decision in this case.

When we cross the two different kinds of processing with two different kinds of purchase motives, we end up with four different persuasion styles (see figure 12.3). The first persuasion style, called 'convincing argumentation', occurs when purchase is driven by utilitarian–telic motives, and the processing is likely to be intensive–systematic. A typical situation is when one is thinking of switching to a new retirement fund. The second persuasion style, called 'hedonistic immersion', occurs when the purchase is driven by hedonistic–paratelic motives, but the processing is still likely to be intensive–systematic. A typical situation is when a person is weighing up which new holiday resort to go to.

The third persuasion style, called 'entertaining argumentation', occurs when purchase is driven by utilitarian motives, and the processing is likely to be easy–heuristic. A typical situation is the purchase of washing detergent. People are not likely to spend much time thinking about it, as long as the product works (i.e. it removes dirt from dishes). Finally, the fourth persuasion style, called 'hedonistic entertainment', occurs when purchase is driven by hedonistic desires, and the processing is likely to be easy–heuristic. A typical situation is when a person feels like having their favourite beer.

These four persuasion styles imply that certain basic executional requirements are necessary for each of these conditions. For the persuasion style of convincing argumentation, the quality of the argument must be convincing. If pictures were to be used, it should be to support the argument. For the persuasion style of hedonistic immersion, the imagery used should mentally transport the person to the desired time and place, so that the person is totally immersed in what is being depicted in the ad. The imagery should also be supported by information to assist in the purchase decision since the target audience too engages in intensive–systematic processing. Note that both of these persuasion styles are intensive–systematic. The difference is that with utilitarian–telic buying motives, the target audience is likely to hone in on the verbal argument (which is why the argumentation has to be convincing), while in the case of hedonic–paratelic buying motives, the target audience is likely to hone in on the imagery (which is why the imagery must have high immersion values).

In the same way, the persuasion styles of entertaining argumentation and hedonistic entertainment share a common style of processing; both are easy-going, relying more on easy–heuristics than on intensive–systematic thinking. This is likely to occur when there is nothing worthwhile to know about the brand. For instance, what is there new to learn about washing detergent or ice-cream (unless it is a new product with new benefits)? So, what becomes important for these two persuasion styles is not so much *what* you say but *how* you say it. Entertainment holds the key in these two persuasion styles. In the case of utilitarian buying motives, we want the entertainment to revolve around the brand's key utilitarian value. That is why this persuasion style is called 'entertaining argumentation'. When the buying motives are hedonic, the entertainment should revolve around using hedonic cues to depict enjoyment. That is why this persuasion style is called 'hedonistic entertainment'.

This framework allows a marcoms manager to make a more informed judgement about the persuasive powers of the executions, and helps him or her to prioritise the executions that are more persuasive under certain circumstances. For instance, if the purchase decision of a beer is motivated by hedonic–paratelic motives coupled with easy–heuristic processing then, theoretically, the most effective persuasion style for the brand will be hedonistic entertainment. On the other hand, if we are advertising a low-carb beer, where the purchase motive is more utilitarian–telic then the persuasion style of entertaining argumentation will theoretically be more persuasive.

QUANTITATIVE ADVERTISING PRE-TESTING

We have suggested how guidelines and frameworks can be used to help us with preliminary evaluation of the ad. However, all the guidelines and framework can only go so far. In the end, it is still important to pre-test the ad with the target audience before the campaign is launched. Besides, managers are generally poor at predicting the success of ads.[9] So pre-testing allows our learning to be continually refined.

In quantitative advertising pre-testing ('copytesting'), we test the ad execution using large numbers of respondents. This occurs before the launch of the campaign as a final check, either using the finished execution or a prototype version (e.g. animatic).

We use three essential classes of metrics in quantitative advertising pre-testing. They are designed to assess the cognition (i.e. thoughts and memory), affect (i.e. intensity of feelings) and conation (i.e. behavioural predispositions) of the target audience. We do these assessments in a controlled condition, and very often we test different executions. The aim is to find the most promising one for the campaign. Here, we do not measure the behaviour of the target audience, such as purchase (online or in-store), telephone enquiries or click-through rates. These can be tracked when the campaign is in progress, as we will discuss later in the chapter.

CASE STUDY 12.1 THE MOST INTERESTING MAN IN THE WORLD (AND ASSESSING THE RETURN ON INVESTMENT FOR AD PRE-TESTING)

As we discussed in the introduction, advertising pre-testing is a way to reduce risk. When used in a 'go'/'no-go' decision, the test ad must exceed a certain score. This is called action standard. Sometimes the test ad has to exceed the category norm. But sometimes the reverse can also occur. Pre-testing results can be used to convince nervous managers that an ad should be run, especially one that is based on a 'big idea'. This is what happened to Dos Equis, a Mexican beer in the US in 2007. Within five years of the campaign, the little-known brand with no personality achieved a continuous double-digit sales growth and became a premium beer in the US market.

In 2007, Dos Equis was in trouble; no one heard about the brand, and among those who were aware, it is considered a cheap Mexican beer. The beer category was also cluttered with 261 beer brands advertising on TV alone. The closest competitor also outspent Dos Equis 3 to 1 in advertising spend, and to add to the challenge, the American consumers were also drinking less beer. The category was in decline.

Therefore, to achieve any cut-through, a radically new idea was needed. The advertising agency EuroRSGC New York (now Havas Worldwide) decided on a user positioning (see chapter 3) where people who drink the beer will become socially adventurous. Their target was American men in their late 20s. It centred around a dashing character (played by the actor Jonathan Goldsmith) having various adventures in exotic locations but always impeccably dressed (a la James Bond!). The ad would end with him drinking the Dos Equis beer among beautiful girls, with the tag line 'Keep Thirsty My Friends'. As you can imagine, this is a very different creative strategy to a typical beer ad, which made the executives at Heineken (the parent company) nervous, since the media spend was around US$30 million. In fact, the vice-president of sales said that the ad was no good after showing it to 5000 salespeople.

RESULTS

Three executions were created and pre-tested using Kantar's Link™ pre-testing system. With a persuasion action standard and category norm of 17, the three executions exceeded this criterion with scores of 50, 41 and 29. Likewise in terms of awareness, the index was 14, 14 and 16, against an action standard and category norm of 6. The three 30-second ads scored in the top 6% of all ads ever tested.[10] With this positive result, the campaign was launched; sales increased by 18% in the first year, with increases in brand awareness (+6%) and consideration (+4%). The brand is now perceived to be different, cool and worth the price. Average weekly consumption of the brand increased from 2.5 beers to 3 among Dos Equis drinkers.

ROI ASSESSMENT

How would a marcoms manager go about assessing the ROI of the pre-test? Since the marcoms manager has no information on future sales, the only figures he or she can rely on is that of pre-test data, like the short-term persuasion score. The average pre-test persuasion scores of the three ads were 40 (i.e. [50 + 41 + 29]/3 = 40). Now this is 2.35 times above the action standard of 17 (i.e. 40/17 = 2.35). This is more than double the benchmark, which in this case also happens to be the industry norm. This means that for a US$30 million campaign, this effectiveness has more than doubled to US$70.5 million (i.e. 30 × 2.35 = 70.5). This equates to US$40.5 million worth of *extra* free advertising (i.e. 70.5 - 30 = 40.5). Assuming that the total pre-testing cost for the three ads was US$300 000, then the ROI from the pre-testing would be 135 to 1 (i.e. 40 500 000/300 000 = 135).

Of course, this is an extreme example of a successful 'big idea', which unfortunately is very rare. Furthermore, the cost of ad pre-testing has dropped considerably since 2007. So, what is the best intelligence one can use as benchmarks? Since Kantar is the pre-eminent leader in this area, we will use their figures to make an informed guess. According to Nigel Hollis, consistent pre-testing can improve a brand's advertising by 20%.[11] This suggests that for a $100 000 campaign, one would expect an improvement of $120 000. This means our pre-testing cost should *not* exceed $20 000. This is achievable with online testing (see endnote 21). With more media spend, the ROI will improve.

DISCUSSION QUESTIONS

1. What is an action standard used in advertising pre-testing?
2. The vice president of sales showed the ad to 5000 sales reps and concluded that the ad was no good. What is wrong or right with this pre-testing method?
3. If advertising pre-testing can consistently improve effectiveness by 20%, what is the most pre-testing should cost for a $500 000 campaign to make it worthwhile?

Pre-testing broadcast ads

Pre-testing broadcast ads, especially that of TV ads, is much more involved than pre-testing a print ad. This is because, unlike print ads, TV is much more difficult (and expensive) to modify once it is completed. For these reasons, pre-testing of TV ads often uses a rough-finished product (animatic).

Different research companies have different methods of pre-testing TV ads. Nowadays the internet is commonly used for the pre-testing of TV ads because it is inexpensive. Instead of respondents visiting a central location, a link of the ad can be emailed to them (or it can appear on their social media newsfeed).[12] By clicking the link, respondents can watch the test ad online and then answer the questions.

The questions asked after the exposure to the test ad can include: cognitive response, purchase predisposition, brand attitude, brand beliefs, ad attitude, ad distinctiveness, ad comprehension, branding, adjectival descriptions and brand awareness after one day. Table 12.1 lists some suggested questions and outlines the main purpose of each of them. The results from the test ad can be compared to ads from previous campaigns, to norms the research agency may have, to a control group or to an alternative ad.

One day later, they can also be re-contacted (via email) to assess their brand awareness. The ease in which ads can be pre-tested has now made it very cost effective, and there is *no* reason why a manager should not do this. One market research outfit even allows firms to set up their own study and upload the video they want to test, and within a day, obtain the top-line results.[13]

Table 12.1 Questions that can be used for quantitative advertising pre-testing

Questions	Comments
What thoughts and feelings come to mind when you see this ad? And what words would you use to describe the brand?	This is open-ended question, sometimes called a 'cognitive response question'. It allows the researcher to gauge what the respondent thinks and feels about the test ad by carefully coding the responses in terms of positive, neutral or negative sentiments directed at the brand, execution, source and self.[14] When we talk about assessing counterarguments, this is the measure we use. One should include a more specific open-ended question about the brand. Here, using word cloud, we can summarise the brand's dominant associations created by the ad.
If you have to buy a [product], how likely are you to buy this brand? What other brands would you consider?	This question evaluates the buying predisposition and brand considerations of the respondent towards the brand after the exposure. (For low-involvement goods, avoid purchase intention measures since they are likely to overstate behaviour.)[15] Alternatively, a respondent can indicate their preference for brands they would want from product categories if they were to win a basket of free goods.[16] We can also ask what other actions the respondent is willing to engage in if this is the objective of the ad (e.g. recommending or visiting the showroom).

Table 12.1 *(cont.)*

Questions	Comments
Below are some characteristics that can be used to describe the brand. In your opinion, does the brand have such characteristics?	Using a rating scale for a list of brand beliefs, this question evaluates the strength of these beliefs.
Based on what you just saw, which of the following choices – ranging from extremely bad to extremely good – best describes your feelings about the brand?	This question is about brand attitude. The objective is to compare the test ad with the control (or before exposure).
How much do you like this ad?	This question measures ad attitude which evaluates the respondent's liking of the ad.
Please rate to what extent this ad stands out from other ads.	Attention is difficult to test. It is not ecologically valid to test attention if a respondent has just seen it. But this question is a good proxy because it is asking the respondent to compare the distinctiveness of the test ad with all the other ads that he or she can remember.
Apart from asking you to buy the product, what do you think the message of the ad is?	This question assesses the respondent's comprehension of the message.
And tell me, what was the brand?	This assesses if the ad is well branded.
Based on what you just saw how much do you like or dislike the brand?	This assesses brand attitude, which evaluates the respondent's liking of the brand.[17]
Please rate this ad using the following adjectives [lists adjectives].	This question assesses other aspects of the ad using a list of adjectives (e.g. interesting, original, entertaining, confusing, pointless, irritating, appealing, amusing, lively, informative, new, thought-provoking, exciting, different, intriguing, clever, surprising and sexy). This is a useful ad diagnostic when we want to compare why one test ad (execution 1) creates a higher level of purchase predisposition than another (execution 2). We can examine the relationship between these descriptors to brand attitude, ad attitude and purchase intentions, to better understand how different executions are working.[18 19]
Please rate how likely are you to pass along this ad to someone you know.	This question assesses the viral potential of the ad.

TESTING OF DIGITAL ADS ON YOUTUBE USING PRE-ROLL

With the rise of the internet, ads can now be shown on different screens across a number of platforms. One popular platform is the social media channel YouTube. One procedure[20] of pre-testing is as follows: First, upload the test video. Second, allow the target audience to select the video among many from YouTube, as they normally would when they log on. Third, when they do click on the test ad, check if they watch it right to the end or skip halfway through. This behavioural data will give us an unbiased result of the actual viewing behaviour of the respondent in their natural environment. Fourth, show the video again, this time as a pre-roll which cannot be skipped. Fifth, invite the target audience to answer the survey questions.

The strength of this methodology is that it captures both the behavioural data in a natural environment (i.e. 'skippable') as well as survey-based data in a forced-exposure situation (i.e. 'non-skippable'). We can compare these results with other videos or norms as benchmarks of performance.

It should be noted that there are many ways of testing and measuring a TV ad – generally, the more complex the design, the higher the cost. However, the main weakness with most pre-testing methodology is that its effects on sales cannot be directly gauged, although we can make a probabilistic guess through the use of norms.[21] But, now that we have single-source panel data and cable TV, we can check whether households that received ad A will buy more of the brand than households that received ad B. By designing a split-test experiment, in which different ads can be sent to different households whose purchase data is available, we can conduct a real-life test of ad effectiveness.

Criticisms of ad pre-testing

Although ad pre-testing is intended to reduce risk in advertising, advertising agencies do not generally view it positively. Of course, nobody likes to have their work evaluated, but a number of other criticisms have also been levelled at ad pre-testing:

- It is a cookie-cutter method of assessing all ads in the same way without due consideration for different strategies – a one-measure-fits-all syndrome.[22]
- Although pre-testing an ad can predict sales,[23] there is a lack of evidence to show that it will result in better quality creative ads.[24]
- It encourages advertising agencies to 'game' the system instead of producing genuinely high-quality work.[25]
- It is too reductionist without taking into account the holistic meaning of the ad.[26]
- It is carried out in an unrealistic setting (e.g. sitting in front of a computer watching the TV online) and therefore has no external validity.
- It relies too heavily on norms that are not independently verified.[27]
- It does not provide suggestions on how the ad can be improved, only a simple 'go'/'no-go' decision.
- It does not reflect how buying decisions are made in real life.

The best ad pre-testing practices try to overcome the limitations discussed above.[28] Likewise, a progressive marcoms manager should also use pre-testing intelligently. For instance, one should not rely just on one number (or action standard) to decide a go/no-go decision but instead examine a set of metrics and interpret the results holistically. This requires clear thinking upfront and the marcoms manager should brief the research agency thoroughly on the communication objectives, other than sales! (see chapter 1).

While pre-testing does not necessarily improve creativity, it is not meant to be used as such. The main strength (and weakness) of pre-testing lies in its ability to predict sales, assuming that the norms are valid.[29] To this end, all marcoms managers should insist that the norms are valid in predicting sales and that only the right norms are used. This includes using relevant country norms for the right channel. For instance, if the campaign is to be run primarily on digital channels (e.g. Facebook and YouTube, and not TV) in Australia (and not India), then the correct norms should be used for comparison. Similarly, the results of the pre-tested ad should be compared against a control, to a close alternative, previous executions, or competing ads. All these will provide a better context for the marcoms manager to evaluate the pre-test results.

Pre-testing results therefore should be used to improve the ad, because once improved, it can make a big difference to its effectiveness.[30] For example, certain detrimental scenes of the ad can be eliminated, or a better music used. The use of psycho-physiological methods for pre-testing (to be discussed later) can greatly improve the accuracy of this assessment and such methods are better reflections of intuitive decision-making.

But to optimise, it means there should be enough time devoted for testing. This is especially true for a global campaign where different variations of the same ad are to be used around the world. This principle also applies if the firm is testing the foundation of a new communication strategy like a new 'big idea' where a large number of new story boards and executions have to be pre-tested. This can take up to a year. Enough time should be given for in-depth analyses by the research agency, so that a more considered reporting can occur.

Finally, one should not forget that on average, we are poor predictors of good advertising, often only achieving chance level (about 51%), unless we are in the insight business, in which case our prediction improves (to about 61%).[31] In some ways, being a poor predictor is not a surprise since we know our ability to forecast anything is poor even among experts.[32]

POST-TESTING AND CAMPAIGN TRACKING

Post-testing means testing the effectiveness of an ad after a campaign is launched. In broadcast advertising, we often track the campaign, while in print advertising, we assess its readership.

Starch methodology for post-testing print ads

The earliest and best known method for post-testing print ads was developed by Daniel Starch (1883–1979) and is still widely used today.[33] The ad we wish to post-test must be placed in the publication (e.g. a magazine) in such a way that it appears to be a regular ad in the publication. This can be done by replacing an existing print ad in the publication.

The test starts by asking a representative group from the target audience if they have recently read the publication. This is a filtering question, as we wish to include only people who read certain targeted publications. If they have read the target publication, we then ask which issue of it they have read, and then which ads they noticed in that issue. This is a measure of ad recall and is not limited to any category, so any ads for any product categories can be included in the answer. It is also unaided, which means that respondents have to retrieve information from their memory.

The next step, becoming more interesting, is for the interviewer to produce the issue and ask the target audience to have a look at it. After each respondent has done this, the researcher turns to the print ad being tested and asks if each respondent (i) remembered seeing this ad, and (ii) if so, whether they saw or read the brand or logo, and (iii) read at least half of the ad. This tests ad recognition. By tabulating the percentage of respondents who answered these questions, we obtain the following scores:

i. Noted score – percentage who remembered seeing this specific ad.
ii. Associated score – percentage who saw or read the brand or logo of the ad.
iii. Read most score – percentage who read at least half of the ad.

Figure 12.4 shows the Starch results for a print ad for lamb in the *Australian Women's Weekly*. Understand that these three indices are based on visual recognition because respondents see the test ad while answering these questions. This means that the test essentially assesses the visual memorability of the ad. These scores allow the marcoms manager to compare the ad with others.

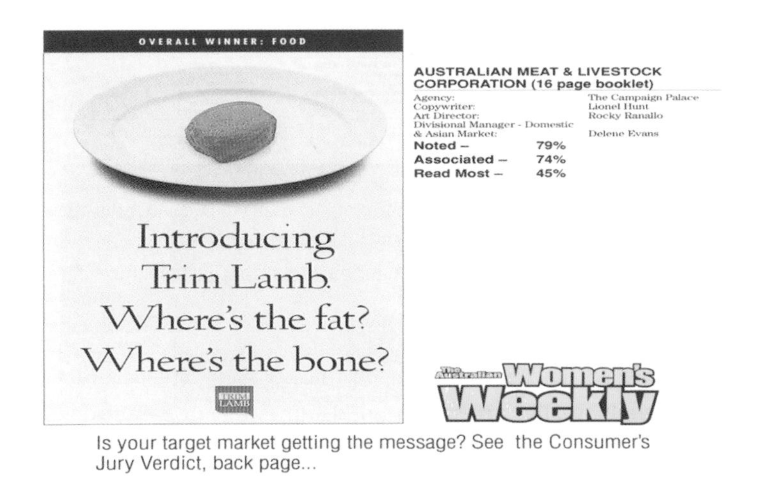

Figure 12.4 The Starch methodology (Meat and Livestock Australia)

Campaign tracking

Tracking a campaign essentially means assessing how well a broadcast ad performs in the field. It allows us to quickly diagnose what is wrong (or pinpoint what is right) and therefore guides us in making adjustments to our marketing mix and media schedule in order to optimise the campaign while it is still in the field. This is the value of campaign tracking.

There are many ways of evaluating a campaign in the field. For instance, we can carry out a day-after recall, where we contact a group of target audience the day after the ad is broadcast and ask them if they have seen the ad and remembered the brand. By tabulating the number (or percentage) of people who respond one way or another and then comparing these numbers to previous campaigns or norms, we can infer how well the campaign is going. This is the classic Burke's day-after recall test, invented in 1952 by Don Miller of Burke Marketing Research in the US (a company founded in 1931 by Alberta Burke). This method, however, tends to be limited in its diagnostic value because it is a one-shot survey.

Another simple method is use of a pre–post difference measure, or what one might call a 'dipstick' approach.[34] In its simplest form, it means evaluating the campaign at only two points in time – once just before the campaign starts (called a 'pre-measure') and another after the campaign ends (called a 'post-measure'). If a campaign works, then one would expect the post-measure of key indicators like market share or purchase intentions (at time 2) to be higher than during the pre-level (at time 1); in other words, after the campaign, we would expect all these key indicators to go up. But what happens if they do not, as in the case of figure 12.5a, which shows no difference in market share (20%) between time 1 and time 2? Does this necessarily mean that the ad is not working?

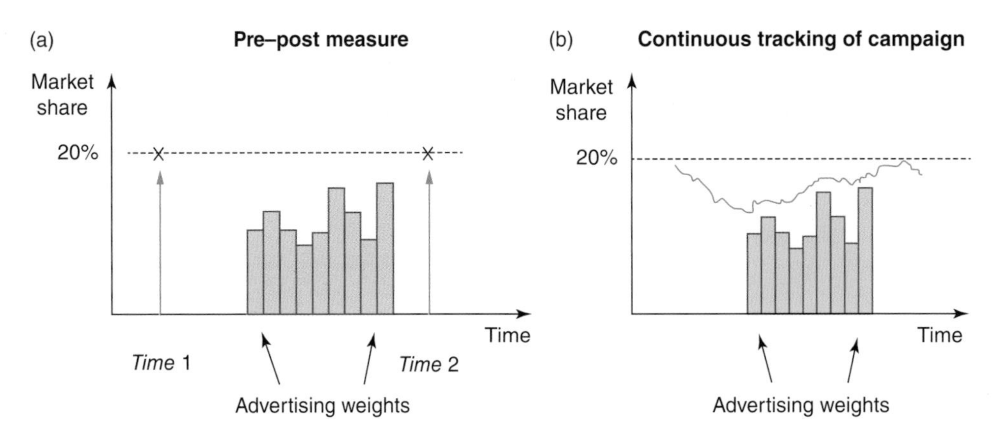

Figure 12.5 Pre-post (a) and continuous (b) approaches to campaign tracking

This is not necessarily so. This is because the market share may in fact be declining, and the campaign may have actually arrested this decline in preparation for turning things round. This is depicted in figure 12.5b. We can only tell by assessing the market continuously. On the other hand, by only taking the pre–post difference (as in figure 12.5a), we would completely misinterpret the dynamics of the market. Doing so could lead to some major consequences:

- the abandonment of a good ad, implying we have lost an opportunity (whereas the solution is already found)
- the loss of media dollars (since we assume that the campaign has failed)
- additional expense and delays incurred while we develop another campaign.

Therefore, we recommend always evaluating the campaign continuously, starting just before the campaign begins (in order to obtain a pre-campaign benchmark) and running until the campaign ends; that is, tracking from start to finish.

CONTINUOUS TRACKING

The gold standard in campaign tracking is to use a single-source panel. As discussed in chapter 4, this means that we can observe whether advertising to a panel of households will influence its purchase pattern. If the advertising is effective, then its pattern of purchase will change. However, this is often expensive and the results slow.

A more practical way is to randomly sample the target audience, say 50 people per week. By combining the sample responses with others over a fixed period, and using this as the unit of analysis, we can begin to smooth the trend line. For instance, if we combine two weeks of interviews with 50 people per week, we will have a sample of 100 respondents per week. We then do the same for the next two weeks, always combining the data from the previous week with the most current. We can typically 'roll' four weeks of data together, combining the data from the most recent three weeks with this week's data.

The key to interpreting continuous tracking results is to examine the changes in the pattern of the trend, taking into consideration the time sequence and competing hypotheses. As an illustration, consider the following scenarios.

From which of these scenarios would you conclude that your advertising is working (i.e. that advertising has increased your market share)?

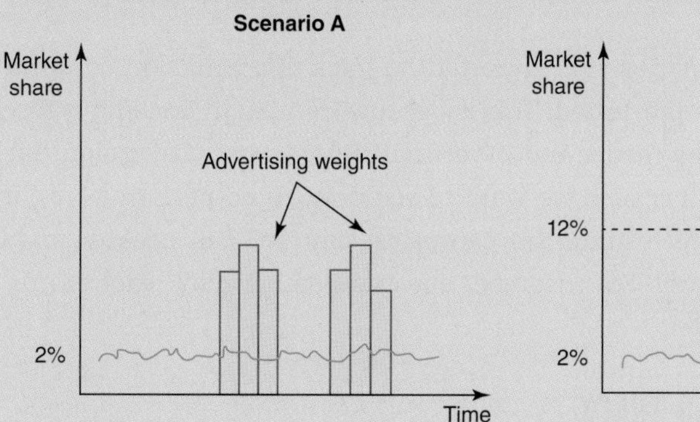

Figure 12.6 Scenario A – small changes in market share

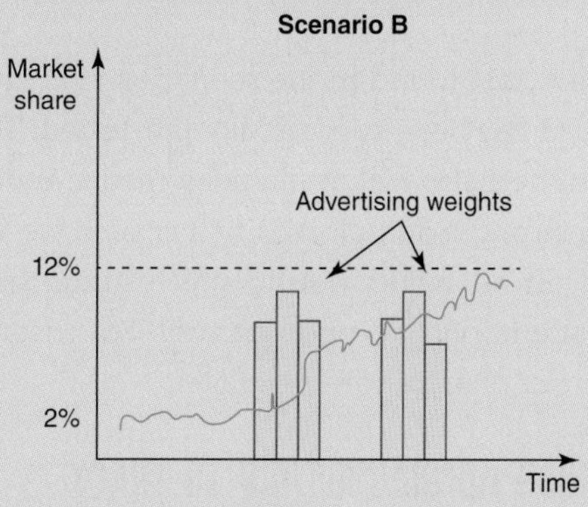

Figure 12.7 Scenario B – one type of change in market share

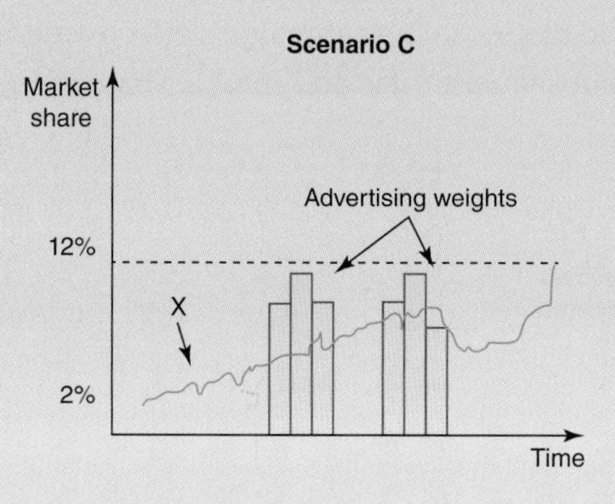

Figure 12.8 Scenario C – another type of change in market share

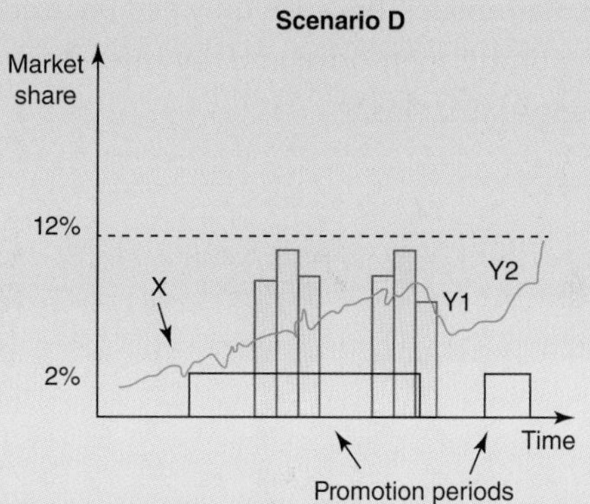

Figure 12.9 Scenario D – the importance of examining all possible causal factors

Let's examine each of these in turn. First consider scenario A. Here, we see that market share has not moved; it remains at 2% after two months of the campaign. In scenario B, on the other hand, we see that the market share started at 2%, but two months into the campaign, has increased to 12%. So, advertising has obviously worked here. How about scenario C? Market share has increased here, too, but would you conclude that advertising has caused the increase in scenario C? Perhaps not.

If you examine scenario C carefully, you may notice that market share was in fact already increasing at point X a full month before the advertising campaign started.

You later discover that there was a sales promotion around this time (see scenario D). On investigation, you conclude that it is more likely that sales promotion has caused market share to increase. Notice, too, how the market share drops off at point Y1, when the sales promotion ends, and then kicks up again at Y2, when it starts.

As you have just found in the scenarios, it is important to track the campaign continuously even after an ad has been successfully pre-tested. This is because campaign tracking is research carried out in the field, which includes media and other marketing issues. Campaign tracking therefore has strong external validity, because we want to see how an ad performs 'live' in the field. Even if an ad works during pre-testing, the campaign can still fail because of many unforeseen factors outside one's control. For instance, our competitors may react to our new campaign, or our distribution may falter.

KNOWING WHICH AD DIAGNOSTICS TO TRACK

How do we work out what to track? Let's start at the beginning. Figure 12.10 illustrates the logic of campaign tracking. There are two important kinds of measure: outcome measures and ad diagnostics. The outcome measures assess sales and market share, while ad diagnostics assess ad awareness, brand associations (including brand awareness) and purchase intentions. They are called 'ad diagnostics' because they can be used to diagnose the campaign's effectiveness in strengthening brand memories and, by inference, subsequent sales and market share (barring other extraneous variables).

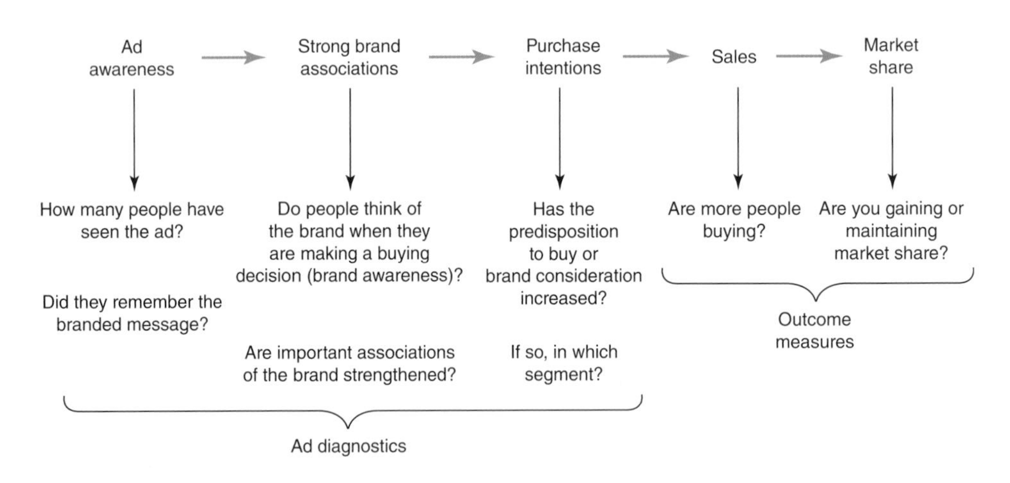

Figure 12.10 A framework for selecting an ad diagnostic for campaign tracking

If the objective of advertising is to create strong brands, then at a minimum the ad has to be seen. This means that ad awareness becomes an important diagnostic in tracking. The target audience must also learn something about the brand through the advertising, or else why bother? This means that we can also assess whether the target audience remembers the branded message. If the branded message is also well conceived and executed (see chapter 6 and 7), it should translate to higher brand awareness and stronger brand associations, which will lead in turn to an increased purchase predisposition and brand consideration.

One key index to track is brand awareness, which is the associative strength between the brand and the product category. For instance, by asking the question 'What brands come to mind when you think of soft drink?', the following brands might be evoked in the following order:

1. 'Coca-Cola'
2. Pepsi
3. 7-Up
4. Fanta
5. Mountain Dew

This set of recalled brands is called the 'evoked set'.[35] In this example, 'Coca-Cola' is the top-of-mind brand; that is, it is the first brand mentioned. As the campaign progresses, we can track the percentage of target audience who include the target brand in their evoked set (sometimes also called the 'consideration set'). If the campaign is successful, we would expect these indices to improve, or at least be maintained at a high level, for a strong brand. Then, all things being equal, we should see a higher purchase predisposition. If this is increasing (for the right group of customers) as the campaign progresses, then sales and market share should follow (barring other market-related issues like poor distribution).

ORDER OF AD-DIAGNOSTIC MEASURES

Although figure 12.10 outlines the logic of tracking, the order in which the measures are implemented in a tracking survey is different. We change the order to avoid biasing the respondent. Below is the suggested order for the main measures (after the usual screening questions).

1. Brand awareness

Since advertising is meant to create strong brand associations, the first diagnostic is to check if brand awareness has increased over time. We ask, 'When thinking about [product category X], what brands come to mind? This way of assessing brand awareness is cued by the product category. This is the traditional method.

But there is another way, one that is cued by needs. This is called need-based brand awareness where respondents are first asked what they look for in a product and then for each need elicited, they are then asked the first brand that comes to mind. As an illustration for champagne, we might ask, 'When you choose a champagne, what are the three main things you want from it?' The person might answer, 'prestige', 'freshness' and 'value for money'. Then for each attribute, ask what is the *first* brand that comes to mind. For example, 'When you think of prestige, what is the first brand of champagne that comes to mind?' Need-based awareness is said to be 30% more accurate in predicting survey-based market share than category-based brand awareness.[36]

2. Purchase intentions[37]

We next assess buying predisposition by asking, 'Suppose you were about to buy [product category X], which one brand would you most likely buy?'

3. Brand considerations

Since consumers are likely to consider a repertoire of brands, we can also assess this by asking, 'What other brands would you consider buying?'

4. Ad recall

Ad recall means asking the target audience to describe any ad he or she can remember for that product category. For instance, we might ask, 'Please describe any TV ads you have seen for [product category X]'.

This is a very stringent way of assessing ad memory because the respondent has to retrieve the ad from their memory and then correctly describe it, including the identity of the brand. Essentially, the ad-recall measure assesses competitive cut-through. If, for instance, no respondents can recall our ad but instead recall the competitor's, it means that our competitor's advertising is more successful in dominating the respondents' minds. Or, to put it another way, our ad is not able to cut through the competitive clutter. We can say that our ad has low *executional* cut-through.

Sometimes, a sizeable number of the target audience gives an accurate description of the ad (i.e. we achieve high executional cut-through) but get the brand wrong. In this case, we have not achieved a comparable level of *branded* cut-through. When this occurs, it essentially means that the (named) competitor has benefited from our advertising!

Recall that in chapter 6 we emphasised the importance of the branded message. Therefore, a well-branded ad is one in which the person who recalled the ad also recalled its brand. When this occurs, the aggregate tracking pattern will show a close correspondence between executional cut-through and branded cut-through levels (see figure 12.11a).

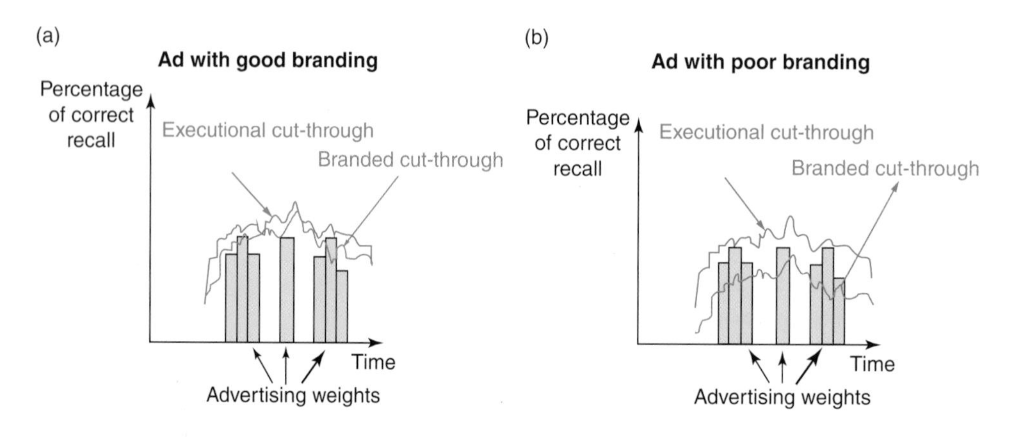

Figure 12.11 Cut-through is easier using good branding (a) than poor branding (b)

On the other hand, if the percentage of branded cut-through is lower than that of executional cut-through, then it means that the ad is not well branded – fewer people got the brand correct (see figure 12.11b). Generally, ads that are better branded tend to have higher sales (see figure 12.12), and they do not necessarily lead to a drop in attention despite the fear of some creatives.[38] Poor branding also opens the possibility that we end up advertising for our competitor since the target audience will most likely misattribute the advertising to them.

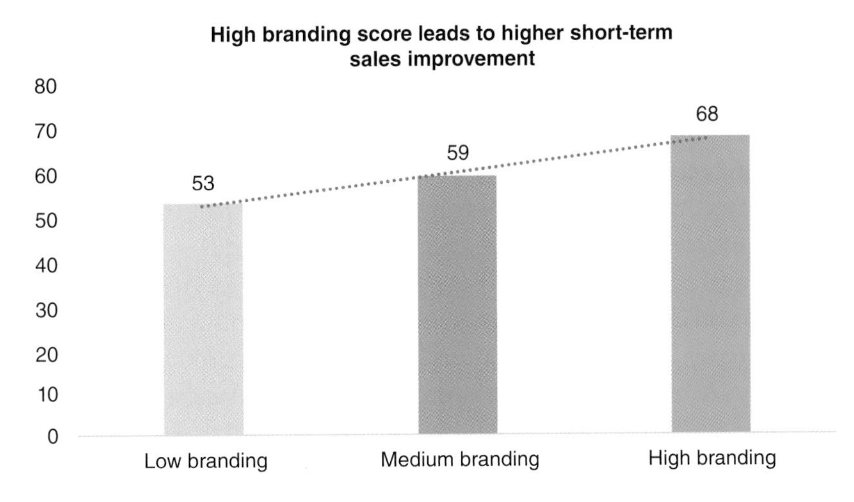

Figure 12.12 A chart showing the relationship between sales and branding[39]

5. Ad recognition

Besides ad recall, we also assess ad recognition. The easiest way to assess this is to show or describe the ad (without the brand) to a person and ask if he/she recognises it, like this: 'Have you seen this ad?' and 'What is the brand?'

This is not a very stringent way of assessing memory since our recognition memory (especially the visual kind) is almost perfect.[40] If so, why then do we use such a measure? In fact, it is precisely because of this near-perfect retrieval that we use ad recognition.

Consider the following. If few people say that they have seen the ad, then it is a pretty safe bet that it is not registering in the marketplace. The ad did not 'register' because it did not rise above the noise to impress on respondents' memory. For instance, we can lose up to 30% of a TV audience to competing activities during commercial breaks (e.g. as they go to make a cup of coffee, take a bathroom break or talk to friends or family).[41] Even if the person does not leave the living room, up to 40% will not have their eyes on the screen.[42] Thus, we can potentially lose up to 40% of our audience during a commercial break. If our visual recognition is near perfect, then the recognition question allows us to gauge if such situations occur. This means if our TV ad is good, we should be able to achieve at least 60% recognition.

The use of recognition, however, has one pitfall. There is a potential for confusion if the ad contains generic images. For instance, many years ago, while tracking a campaign for a major airline, we found that it registered a recognition score of 60% even though the campaign had not started! This was because the ad contained all the iconic images of Australia, such as the Sydney Harbour Bridge, Uluru, the Great Barrier Reef, sandy beaches and kangaroos. It is therefore always important to take a pre-campaign assessment, so that any false recognition (called 'false positives') can be taken into account.

We can also supplement the recognition question by asking where, and how often, people have seen the ad. This allows us to assess media integration and effective reach. For instance, if people say they only saw the TV ad but not the print ad, even though print ads are used in this campaign, then it means that the print campaign may not have enough media investment. Likewise, by asking people how many times they have seen a particular ad, we can measure the number of people who report seeing the ad at the intended frequency (e.g. 3+). This can then be checked against the media plan (see chapter 4).

6. Message take-out and image tracking

If the advertising is influencing brand image, then the target audience should be able to remember its branded message. We assess this by asking this question, 'Apart from encouraging you to buy, what do you think is the main message of the ad for this brand?'

For image-type ads, such a question may be difficult to answer. Therefore, for such ads, we can use a closed version of the question by giving the respondents a list of image attributes to rate. The same principles apply for the continuous tracking of corporate image (discussed in chapter 9). We simply ask respondents to check off the corporate image attributes that apply to the focal organisation (and to the competition).

Table 12.2 shows the image attributes of business schools in a tracking questionnaire. If we are tracking the image of a business school, we can ask this question:

> This question is about getting your impression of the various business schools, even if you have not dealt with them. For each statement below, please indicate whether it applies to each of the business schools. You can indicate as many or as few as you like, or none at all.

Table 12.2 Image attributes of business schools

	Business school A	Business school B	Business school C	Business school D	Business school E	None of these schools
Is a leader in business education	1	1	1	1	1	98
Friendly and customer-oriented	2	2	2	2	2	98
Offers a rich learning experience	3	3	3	3	3	98
Has an international reputation	4	4	4	4	4	98
Has highly qualified academics with extensive industry experience	5	5	5	5	5	98
Has mature and experienced students	6	6	6	6	6	98
Has a flexible curriculum with various progression paths towards the MBA	7	7	7	7	7	98
Offers option of completing the MBA in a shorter period of time	8	8	8	8	8	98

7. Personal characteristics (e.g. demographics and media habits)

The last section of the survey evaluates respondents' personal characteristics and media habits. This information is most useful for segmental analysis and media planning.

MORE USES FOR CAMPAIGN TRACKING

By now you will understand that tracking of a campaign using ad diagnostics is predominantly about assessing the associative memory strength of a brand and how it changes, if at all, during the campaign. The key is to check the effects of this on the outcome or other behavioural measures. Tracking is not about assessing changes in emotions that an ad may generate; advertising pre-testing is more appropriate for that purpose.

Thinking about ad diagnostics in this way is also consistent with Colley's idea[43] that advertising is first and foremost a communication task and should be evaluated as such (see chapter 5). However, the diagnostic perspective advocated here goes one step further than Colley because, in campaign tracking, we try to link the intermediate effects – such as ad recognition or purchase intentions – to sales. This will tell us, at least, if the advertising is a cause of the outcome (good or bad).

Note that ad diagnostics are also useful even when the ad is working (e.g. sales are moving up). After all, we still want to know *why* it is working, for the following reasons. First, we want to confirm whether the main drivers of purchase intentions are still valid. For instance, by running regressions between brand associations and purchase intentions, we can ascertain which associations are the main drivers and if they have changed at all. Second, by simultaneously monitoring the ads of other competitive brands and assessing their performance, we can discover which competitors our campaign is hurting most. For instance, in a McDonald's campaign, we may discover that every time a McDonald's ad is run, the brand considerations for Hungry Jack's drop but those for Subway do not. Figure 12.13 is a simple hypothetical example showing how every time brand B advertises (at periods P), the percentage of people considering buying brand A decreases. But when brand B stops advertising (at period Q), the percentage increases.

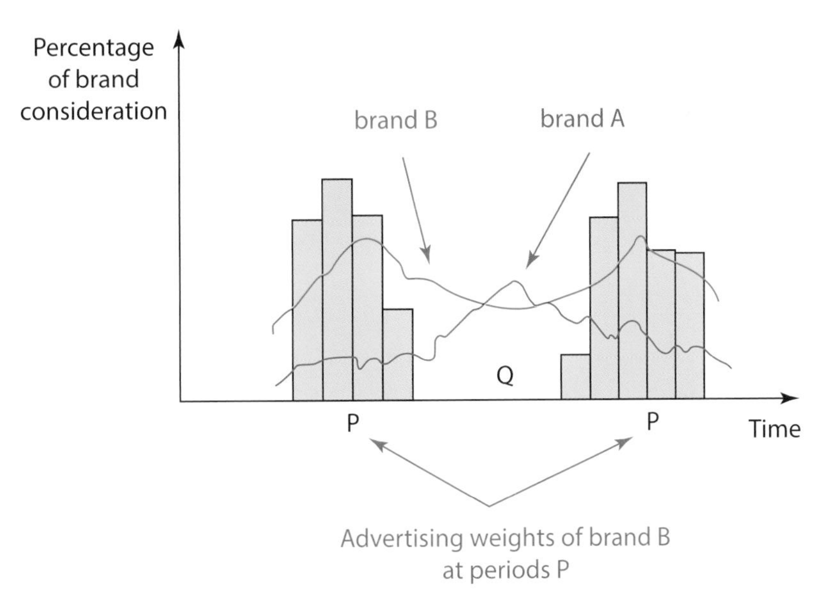

Figure 12.13 A hypothetical example – how brand B's advertising is hurting brand A

Campaign tracking often creates unforeseen benefits for the advertiser. It forces the marcoms manager to collate all the important information so that he or she can evaluate a more complete picture of the campaign. This includes changes in sales, market share, media expenditure and schedules, other promotions that may be simultaneously occurring and changes in pricing or distribution, as well as concurrent competitive activities. Through systematic analyses such as these, we can often find important insights.

In terms of assessing cross-media effects, the data from campaign tracking can be analysed among both people who have seen the ad and those who have not. If the campaign is effective, we would expect those who have seen the ad to have higher scores on key indicators than those who have not seen it. Cross-media synergy is often assessed this way, by observing which media combination yields the greatest effect (if any). For instance, table 12.3 shows that the combination of TV and print ads yielded the greatest effect (see column E; column A is the control). This is often called split (or A/B) testing, but there are other ways of assessing synergy (see below).

Table 12.3 Cross-media synergy analysis

	Did not see any ad for brand [A]	Saw TV ad only [B]	Saw print ad only [C]	Saw banner ad only [D]	Saw TV ad + print ad [E]	Saw TV ad + banner ad [F]	Saw print ad + banner ad [G]
1. Brand recall (top of mind)	35%	55%	39%	35%	60%	36%	35%
2. Purchase intention (among those who recall the brand)	42%	56%	43%	43%	60%	42%	45%
3. Agree that brand has image attribute X (among those who are aware)	20%	23%	21%	22%	28%	21%	20%

We can also collate for assessment a range of other online activities, such as website traffic, click-through rates (CTR),[44] number of visits and abandonment, enquiries and complaints, cost-per-click (CPC) and cost-per-order. We can also examine the amount of social chatter on social media (see chapter 8).

Finally, there will come a time when the campaign wears out – it is no longer effective in delivering the desired effects. We will be able to tell this is happening because, for example, all the ad diagnostics (including web traffic) will trend down despite having the same media weight as before. Instead of waiting for this decline to be translated into lower sales, and let competitors gain the upper hand, the marcoms manager can institute a new campaign (or execution), assuming of course that the market segment has not changed, and drivers of purchase remain the same.

DETECTING SYNERGISTIC EFFECTS

So how do you detect synergy in one's campaign? There are essentially three ways: split (or A/B) testing, multiple regression analysis and using advertising elasticities. The last two forms can be called econometric modelling.

SPLIT (OR A/B) TESTING

Table 12.3 shows the effectiveness of various media combinations in delivering different communication objectives (e.g. brand recall, purchase intention). These results are obtained by asking a sample group of consumers whether they have seen the specific ads in various media. For instance, cell E shows the percentage of the target audience who have seen the ad on TV *and* print, while cell B shows those who saw the ad on TV only, and cell C, print only.

Let's consider purchase intention. The difference in purchase intention between cell E and cell B is 4% (i.e. cell E minus cell B or 60 – 56 = 4) which represents the additional (i.e. synergistic) contribution of ad print to TV. Likewise, the difference between cell E and cell C represents the additional (i.e. synergistic) contribution of TV or 17% (i.e. 60 – 43 = 17). But is this difference greater than those who have not seen any advertising at all (i.e. control group, cell A)? One must still make the comparison with the control group in order to take into account of people who were simply guessing. In this case, the difference is 18% (i.e. 60 – 42 = 18). A judgement is then made as to whether 18% is managerially significant. Split testing is often used in evaluating direct marketing campaign as well (see chapter 11).

INTERACTION EFFECTS

Statistical interaction in a regression analysis is another way of assessing synergy. But first, let's understand what an interaction is using a simple example. Figure 12.14 shows how delicious a cookie can be if it is baked properly. The best result is either when the temperature is low, but the cookie is baked for a longer time, or when it is baked for shorter time, but at a higher temperature. So, it is not just the temperature and timing that are important, it is the *combination*. Or to put it another way, the right combination of temperature and timing, has an effect *above and beyond* the individual additive effects of either temperature or timing.[45] In a (linear) multiple regression equation, this is represented by a multiplicative factor (timing × temperature). This can be represented conceptually as follows:

Deliciousness = timing + temperature + (timing × temperature).

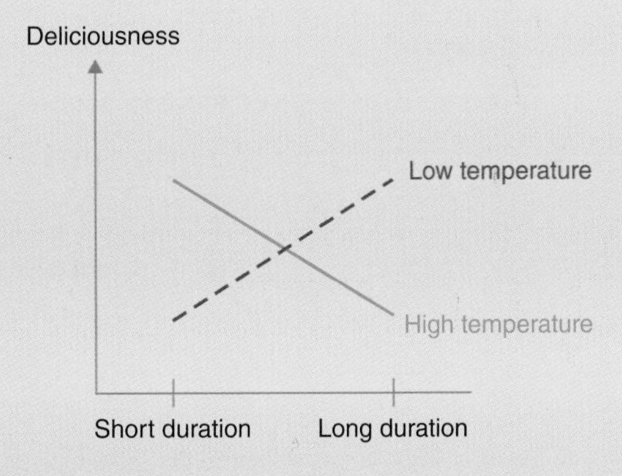

Figure 12.14 An interaction effect between temperature and time

Formally, the equation will look something like the one in figure 12.15, where Y represents the criterion (or dependent variable) of deliciousness; and x_1 and x_2 are the predictors (or independent variable) of timing and temperature respectively. The multiplicative term ($x_1 \times x_2$) represents the *joint* effect of timing and temperature. This is the interactive term.

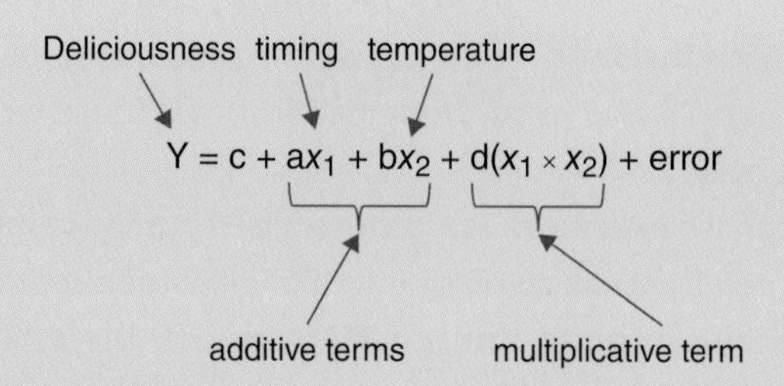

Figure 12.15 A multiple regression equation showing the factors influencing deliciousness

A few other terms in the equation need explanation. The letter c represents the constant or baseline level. The error refers to a random variable whose value is the difference between Y and its expected value. The letters a and b refer to the coefficients of their respective predictor variables (i.e. timing and temperature). They represent the slope or change in the criterion variable, Y (i.e. deliciousness), when its associated predictor variables change. For instance, if $a = 1.45$, it means the deliciousness of the cookie (Y) increases by 1.45 units when x_1 (i.e. timing) increases by one unit. Note, these coefficients (i.e. a, b and d) can be positive or negative. If the coefficient is negative, it means the change in Y is in the negative direction. For instance, if x_1 is price and Y is number of cookies people buy (instead of deliciousness and timing), then the coefficient a is most likely to be negative (e.g. −1.45). This means, every time we increase x_1 or price by one unit, Y or the amount bought drops by 1.45 units.[46]

Now that we understand what interaction means, we can extend the logic to evaluating the *joint* effects of various media. Figure 12.16 illustrates a simple interaction effect between two media: TV and outdoor. We can see that on average TV advertising is more persuasive than no TV advertising. Similarly, having outdoor advertising is more persuasive than no outdoor advertising. However, it is the combination of the two media that cause persuasiveness to soar.

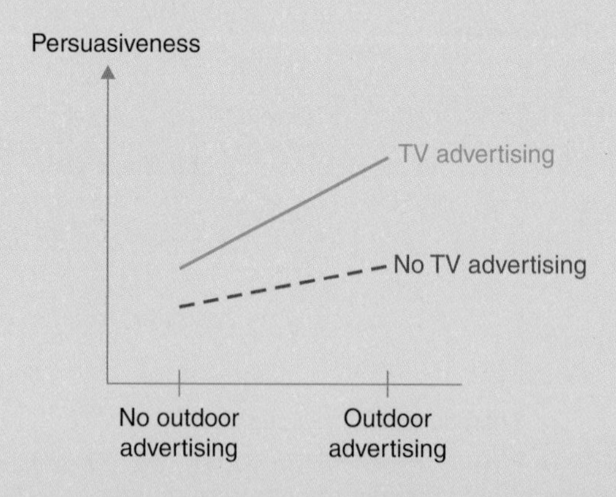

Figure 12.16 An interaction effect between TV and outdoor advertising

In this example, we would expect the coefficient d for the multiplicative term of TV and outdoor advertising (i.e. $x_1 \times x_2$) to be positive and statistically significant (see figure 12.17). If so, we would have synergy. If this is negative, we would have antergy (see chapter 1).

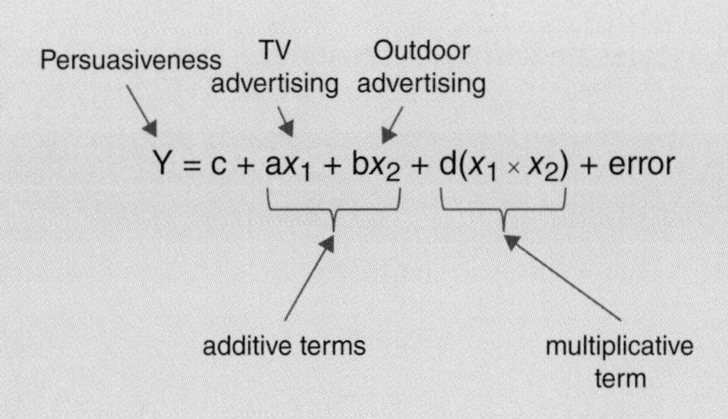

Figure 12.17 A multiple regression equation showing the factors influencing persuasiveness

ADVERTISING ELASTICITIES

Advertising demand elasticity refers to the percentage change in the amount of goods (or services) sold every time there is an incremental amount of advertising spend. This is usually benchmarked at 1%. For instance, advertising elasticity of 0.22 means that a 1% change in advertising spend leads to 0.22 increase in sales. This is miniscule. Sales promotion is slightly better (see table 12.4). Not surprisingly, pricing elasticity has an even larger effect, albeit a negative one.

Table 12.4 Elasticities for different promotion types and price

Promotion types	Elasticities
Advertising	0.22[47]
Sales promotion	0.31[48]
Pricing	−2.62[49]

One reason why the advertising elasticity is so small is because at the aggregate level, the effects of advertising on sales are influenced by a host of factors, affecting the strength of its causal relationship. Also, aggregate results do not allow one to examine the elasticities for different media, nor its profitability. The ideal is to collect individual-level data. For instance, by surveying the media habits of members of a loyalty program and knowing their expenditure, we can track the amount of dollars they've spent during the campaign period. With this data, we can calculate the individual elasticities of each medium.

Table 12.5 is an example of this form of analysis. It shows that the elasticity of TV advertising (i.e. 0.078) is slightly lower than that of direct mail (0.095), which implies that as a means of closing sales, direct mail is superior. Of course, TV advertising may be superior in delivering other communication objectives not evaluated here (e.g. creating a brand image). To calculate synergy, we just add the two elasticities together (i.e. 0.078 + 0.095 = 0.173). Thus, although the effects of advertising on sales is low (i.e. 0.078), together with promotion (i.e. 0.095) the joint effect is much higher (0.173). With such data, we can test which combination is best in dollar sales, or better still, profitability! (see table 12.6). Note that elasticities for profitability is lower (as you would expect).

Table 12.5 Elasticities of sales dollar for different advertising mediums[50]

Mediums	Dollar sales	
	Elasticities	*Standard error*
Television	0.078***	0.0230
Newspaper	0.011*	0.0065
Radio	0.022**	0.0102
Magazine	-0.004	0.0103
Online display	-0.011	0.0132
Search	0.036*	0.0210
Social media	0.02	0.0357
Catalogue	0.104***	0.0350
Direct mail	0.095*	0.0527
E-mail	0.054*	0.0328

(*significant at the 10% level; **significant at the 5% level; ***significant at the 1% level)

Table 12.6 Elasticities of profit for different advertising mediums[51]

Mediums	Profit	
	Elasticities	*Standard error*
Television	0.042**	0.0166
Newspaper	0.010**	0.0045
Radio	0.019**	0.0074
Magazine	-0.001	0.0072
Online display	-0.009	0.0093
Search	0.014	0.0146
Social media	0.021	0.0250
Catalogue	0.052**	0.0253
Direct mail	0.067**	0.0336
E-mail	0.038*	0.0233

(*significant at the 10% level; **significant at the 5% level; ***significant at the 1% level)

SPLIT (OR A/B) TESTING VERSUS INTERACTION VERSUS ADVERTISING ELASTICITIES

Since there are three methods of detecting synergy, which method should one use? If the organisation has access to large amounts of past data of campaigns, then one should use multiple regression and advertising elasticities to search for synergistic effects. Finding such effects can help inform future campaigns, by knowing which promotional combination would yield the highest effect. It also implies how the budget can be reallocated.

If no such data exists, then one should experiment with split testing. Then when enough data is accumulated, econometric modelling (i.e. regression and elasticity calculations) can be used to supplement the split test findings. In some forms of promotions, like website banner advertising or direct marketing or email campaigns, split testing can be easily implemented, yielding large amounts of data quickly. Combined with econometric modelling, it improves the efficiency of the campaign with very little mistakes.

MANAGERIAL APPLICATION: PUTTING IT TOGETHER

In summary, continuous campaign tracking has many advantages for marcoms managers. It serves an early warning system, helping us to check:

- whether advertising (and not something else like sales promotion) is the likely cause for the movements of sales and market share
- whether the campaign is increasing (or in the case of market leader, maintaining) purchase predisposition
- whether there is enough media investment (i.e. repetition) for the campaign and the level of media integration
- whether the ad has broken through the competitive clutter and, if so, whether the advertised brand (and not the competitor's brand) is creatively integrated in the ad
- whether the message of the ad is remembered and, if so, whether it is creating the right associations
- which competitors, if any, our campaign is hurting
- which cross-media synergy effects are occurring
- whether our campaign is wearing out
- that we have the complete picture of market dynamics, by collating important information.

The last point needs a little more elaboration. Although this chapter is about assessing the effectiveness of advertising, campaign tracking can also be expanded to assess the effectiveness of a marketing strategy in business-to-business. For instance, figure 12.18 shows a 'push–pull' marketing strategy for selling a new digital copier, which has a unique printing capability and hence can provide new services to print-shop owners. We have already discussed the idea of 'push–pull' in chapter 11.

The marketing strategy in this example is to 'push' the new digital photocopying services through the channel by targeting print-shop owners with trade promotions (A) so that they will recommend that end users use the new service (B). At the same time, advertising will target the end user customers (C) so that they will enquire about the service and hence 'pull' the demand across the channel (D). By carefully tracking the activities at each point, using different target segments, we can check whether this marketing strategy is increasing purchase intentions of the copier (E) and, if not, diagnose where the problem lies.

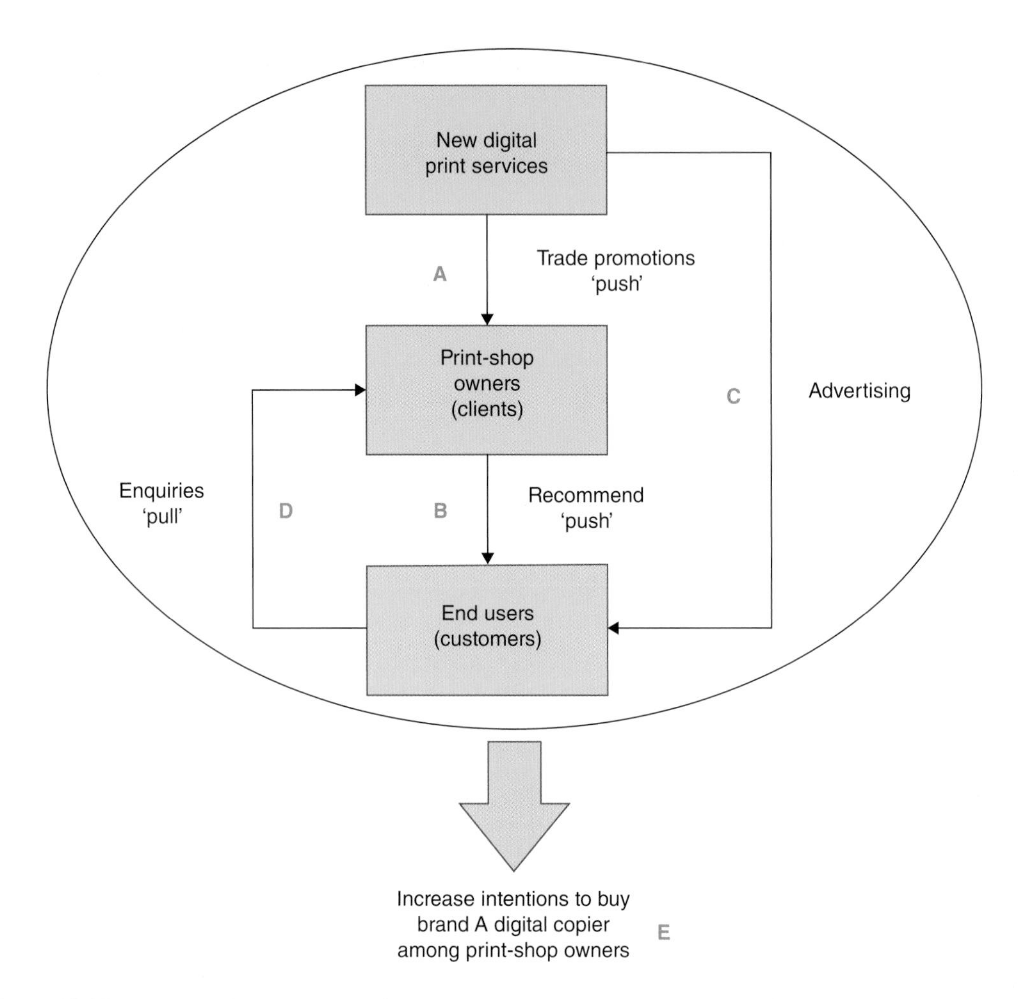

Figure 12.18 A push-pull strategy can be continuously tracked at various points

FURTHER THINKING: ADVANCED KNOWLEDGE METHODOLOGIES

This section deals with the more advanced knowledge methodologies, like the use of Implicit Response Testing (IRT) and neuroscience in advertising pre-testing. The strengths and weaknesses of different psycho-physiological methods are discussed, including functional magnetic resonance imaging (fMRI), electroencephalography (EEG), eye-tracking (ET), galvanic skin response (GSR) and facial coding and electromyography (facial EMG).

LEARNING GOALS

After reading this section, you will understand:

- system 1 and system 2 thinking
- biases and implicit response testing
- the weakness of using a traditional self-report questionnaire for assessing TV advertising
- the characteristics of a range of psycho-physiological methodologies used in ad pre-testing.

We've known for a long time that humans suffer from a host of biases ranging from that of anchoring to that of the Zeigarnik effect.[52] All these biases can affect our decision-making. In marketing, the classic one is mental availability, where we tend to buy the brands we know. This is because we are cognitive misers, not willing to spend too much time or effort thinking(!), which is why brand awareness is so important. It is also the reason we tend not to opt out of any default option.[53]

Two psychologists, Kahneman and Tversky,[54] have studied how these biases affect our decision-making. Their main finding is that most of our decisions are made in the face of uncertainty, and to be efficient, we rely on heuristics. This means we use 'short cuts', allowing us to make decisions quickly, which Kahneman[55] dubbed system 1 thinking. In this mode, we are in cognitive ease, and our decisions are impulsive and intuitive, influenced for instance by our perceptions and emotions which are automatically activated. This is opposed to system 2 where decision-making is more deliberate and effortful, and we apply our analytical skills before deciding. Here, we are in cognitive strain, and tend to be slower in making up our minds.

So what has this got to do with advertising pre-testing? The issue is that much of the pre-testing methodology is based on system 2 thinking, where respondents are put into a 'cognitive strain'; for instance, when they are asked to answer survey questions in response to an ad. In real life, however, consumers tend to make their purchase decisions automatically based on perceptions and emotions (and then post-justify that decision with a rational or acceptable answer).

IMPLICIT (REACTION TIME) MEASUREMENTS OR IMPLICIT RESPONSE TESTING

One way around the problem is to capture the intuitive way in which decisions are made using the Implicit Association Test (or IAT).[56] This is a reaction time measure based on our tendency to associate two similar constructs together. For instance, we are more likely to say 'cat' in response to the stimulus word 'dog'. Similarly, 'nurse' in response to 'doctor'. In devising such tests, we can check the natural bias a person might have towards certain issues without directly asking them. For instance, if a person has a strong positive bias towards thin people, this person will be quicker in categorising positive words (e.g. joy, happy) with images of thin people than images of fat people and vice versa for negative words (e.g. terrible, awful).

This difference in the reaction time, measured in milliseconds, is called the IAT effect and reflects a person's implicit preference. Note, the person may not necessarily want to admit to any preference in an interview (because of social desirability,[57] or may lack true insight,[58] or may even deceive themselves[59]), but the difference in reaction time does not lie, assuming the test was conducted correctly. The IAT is therefore assumed to be a test capable of tapping into our unconscious, bypassing our filtering system. It is equivalent to indirect questioning in qualitative research (see chapter 2). For over 20 years, social psychologists[60] have successfully used this method to study a whole range of social biases (e.g. racial attitudes, stereotyping), and even political affiliations.

In marketing, the IAT has been used to study consumer cognitions[61] and seems to have some predictive validity for brand preferences in consumer-packaged goods (e.g. yogurt, fast food, or cola brands)[62] as well as personal computers (i.e. Mac versus PC).[63] The method has also been used in brand image research. Here, the images of the brand name, logos, products, and packaging can be used as stimuli and the speed in which they are categorised with certain descriptors (e.g. premium, good, cheap, inferior, quality, budget, bargain, great, superior, imitation, traditional, old and original) can be collected and analysed.

In advertising pre-testing, one can use this same method, here sometimes called Implicit Response Testing or (IRT), to see if an ad (or a celebrity or a spokesperson) has an effect on the reaction time compared to a control group. One recent study into an eBay TV ad (using animatic) showed that using IRT is more sensitive in detecting image change than when using explicit survey.[64] Another study found that although an ad for consumer-packaged goods did evoke the intended association of sensuality and indulgence, it also evoked a negative impression of dominance and humility because of a male character in the ad.[65] Such 'unholy' feelings are difficult for consumers to verbalise while IRT can detect then.

For this to happen, the descriptors must be carefully chosen to align with what the intended message is meant to convey. For instance, in one recent pre-test for the Smart car, IRT showed that the top three intuitive associations were cool, fun and comfort, but not agility, which is a shame since this is an important attribute for this car.[66] The deficiency of the ad can only be detected if the descriptor of agility is used. If the right descriptor is not used, one will be none the wiser.

IRT is now one of the fastest growing 'neuro' research techniques because it is versatile, scalable, easy to use, fun to respond and cost effective.[67] Some research outfits have developed this method to an extraordinary degree of proficiency by providing an online platform for one to quickly design the test, recruit the target audience, track progress of their research and analyse the results.[68]

PSYCHO-PHYSIOLOGICAL MEASUREMENTS

This is the application of psycho-physiological methods to monitor how a person is reacting to an ad without the need to ask questions. This includes the use of functional magnetic resonance imaging (fMRI), electroencephalography (EEG), eye-tracking (ET), facial coding and facial electromyography (facial EMG), and galvanic skin response (GSR).

There are four reasons for this rise in the use of this technology. First, the cost of this equipment has dropped, including its associated computing cost. Second, our knowledge of cognitive neuroscience has exploded, which makes the use of this methodology less speculative (though not perfect). Third, there is a growing awareness among advertisers that our subconscious can affect our human behaviour. Fourth, there is a need to capture moment-to-moment reactions to an ad to help with diagnosis.

WEAKNESS OF THE TRADITIONAL SELF-REPORT QUESTIONNAIRE

Traditional ad pre-testing methods have long used a questionnaire as a tool. The answering of the questions typically occurs *after* the viewers have finished viewing an ad (not while they are viewing). There are a number of limitations to this method: it means that the subject needs to rely on his or her memory to assess the ad; subtle but important cues that are present in certain scenes may not be remembered; the intensity of emotions generated by a particular scene may have dissipated. The biggest contribution of cognitive neuroscience to advertising pre-testing is that it can isolate and quantify the emotional reactions of the person while they are viewing the ad. The person is not necessarily conscious of such reactions or able to easily verbalise them.[69]

By time-locking these reactions to an ad, we can infer which scene is generating these effects, millisecond by millisecond, and understand how the emotions change as the ad progresses. This is specificity at a different order of magnitude compared to a traditional static self-report questionnaire. Using neuroscience methodologies, the ad is assessed at the point of exposure, and reactions are measured instantaneously, moment to moment. This means that the emotional responses we capture are unadulterated by bias, peer pressure, political correctness or social desirability and cannot be easily faked.

Although psycho-physiological methods have grown in popularity they are not perfect. It is complex and still a young science. Different software or 'neuro' methodology can yield different results even with the same ad.[70] Therefore, all results need to be carefully interpreted. The methods used should be theoretically robust, including the appropriateness of the research sample. Special attention should be paid to the reliability of the measures,[71] and their validity in predicting in-market performance. And the recommendations given by the research agency should also be evidence-based. A marcoms managers should not be afraid to ask these pointed questions to the research agency, when using these methods.[72] Let's look now at the various methods and evaluate their pros and cons.

PSYCHO-PHYSIOLOGICAL METHODS OF ADVERTISING PRE-TESTING

There are many psycho-physiological methods, and each has its strengths and weaknesses. The following section discusses five methods used in advertising pre-testing.

Electroencephalography

One psycho-physiological method that is increasingly popular is electroencephalography (EEG). The brain is made up of millions of brain cells called 'neurons'. Neurochemical changes in these cells can be detected in minute electrical activities. EEG detects changes in their firing activity across the scalp, by wearing an EEG cap and using hardware that can amplifies these signals.

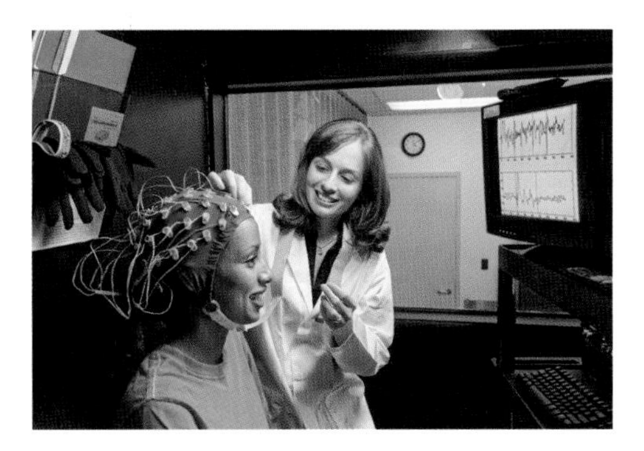

Figure 12.19 A person wearing an EEG cap to detect neuronal firing on the scalp

One promising application of EEG for ad pre-testing is to check if a scene is encoded into our long-term memory.[73] When a scene is encoded into a long-term memory, our left lateral prefrontal hemisphere of our brain, but not the right, emits a faster electrical impulse. In subsequent recognition tests, those scenes tend to be remembered better.[74] Now if those scenes also happen to contain the brand (i.e. branding scenes), then it will shift our choice to that brand.[75]

Functional magnetic resonance imaging

Functional magnetic resonance imaging (fMRI) relies on changes that take place in the metabolic process of the brain when someone watches an ad. One version of fMRI relies on the changes in the oxygenated blood flow (called 'BOLD fMRI') to the local area of the brain when that area is active. This is detected by looking for changes in the magnetic properties in the area since our blood haemoglobin possesses magnetic properties.[76] Using this method, three studies[77,78] have found that the reward-related area of our brain (i.e. the ventral striatum) is mostly associated with our desire to buy. This could very well be our 'buy button' (see figure 12.20).

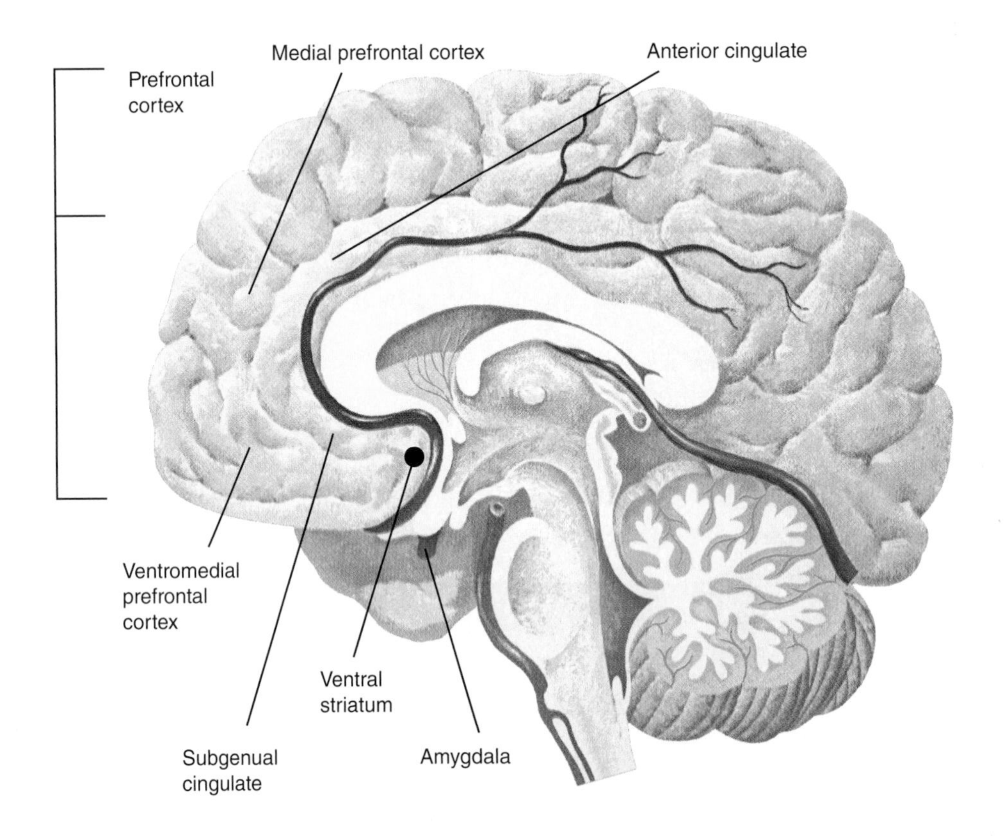

Figure 12.20 The human brain, showing the location of the ventral striatum (our 'buy button')

Galvanic skin response

Galvanic skin response (GSR) measures the arousal state of a person. Since our skin is a good conductor of electric current, it is possible to assess how well a small electric current is being conducted between two electrodes on the skin, usually measured at the fingertips or palm. Since our sweat glands are directly connected to our (peripheral) nervous system, any changes in our arousal level are quickly registered in our sweat glands, which then influence the conductance level of the skin – the greater the arousal, the greater the electrical conductance between the two electrodes.

Arousal is easy to understand, and some early studies show that ads that are highly arousing tend to predict sales.[79] However, valence (i.e. extent of positivity or negativity) is not captured. An individual can still be aroused in a negative way (i.e. anxious), which we do not know; and this may occur in some scenes but not in others. Therefore, to be diagnostically useful, GSR should be used in conjunction with a valence-capturing method, time-locked to the exposure of the ad.

Facial coding and facial electromyography

Facial coding involves examining the facial expressions of a person in order to gauge how they are feeling as they watch the ad. Using a scheme called the Facial Coding Action System (FACS),[80] researchers can deduce which of the seven basic emotions a person is feeling. By analysing which facial muscles are contracting simultaneously, it is possible to detect which of the seven basic emotions of joy, sadness, surprise, anger, disgust, fear and contempt a viewer is experiencing.[81] For instance, if a person's inner eyebrows are raised while the corner of their lips are depressed, he or she can be said to be sad or in distress (see figure 12.21).

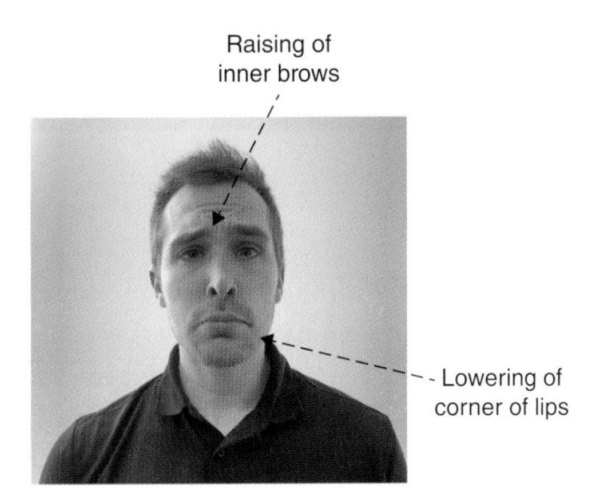

Figure 12.21 How to decode sadness (or distress) from facial expression

However, coding a person's face while he or she is watching a TV ad is time-consuming. It is difficult to time-lock changes in facial expression to changes in the advertising scenes; indeed, advertising scenes often do not trigger the kind of discernible changes in facial expressions that may be reliably coded.[82] One solution is to detect the minute changes in the contraction of facial muscles directly, using facial electromyography (facial EMG). This is more intrusive than facial coding and involves attaching electrodes on specific groups of facial muscles so that electrical signals (from the contractions) can be detected quickly.

This limitation is overcome, however, with facial recognition software where changes in our facial expression and hence our emotions can be automatically captured using a camera while we are watching an ad.[83] This is achieved by dynamically mapping the changes of feature points on our face. In research, we obtain the consent of the participants before capturing their facial reactions.

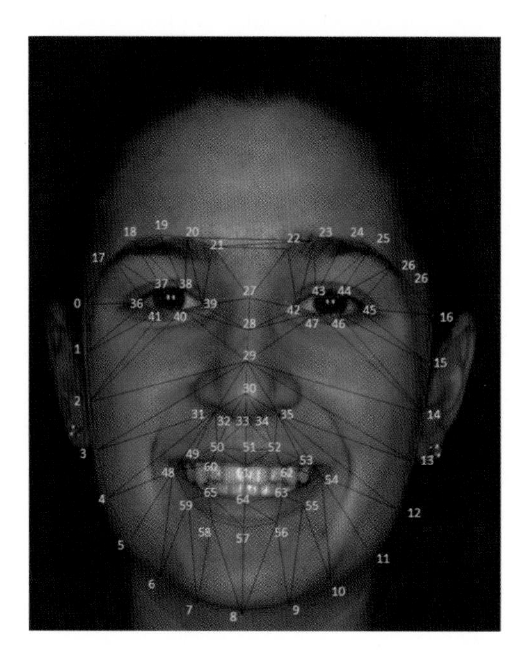

Figure 12.22 Feature points on a face[84]

Using this methodology, one can now time-lock our emotional response to any scene of the ad, and as the ad progresses, the software can capture these changes forming a trace. For example, figure 12.23 shows the smiling trace of 57 people (averaged) for an Amazon ad, called the Priest and Imam. The green line indicates those who especially enjoyed the ad (17 people, or 29%) and from the trace, we can see that three scenes were especially evocative for this group. If we want to evaluate if the ad can continue to elicit a positive emotion, we can show the ad twice and compare the two traces. A good ad will be able to evoke the same level of intensity as the first time.[85] Many humorous ads may not be as funny the second time you watch them! This methodology also allows us to decide which scenes to cut to create a shorter ad (e.g. by reducing an ad from 30s to 15s). That way, only the most effective scenes will be included in the shortened ad.[86]

Another advantage with automatic facial recognition software is its scalability. The camera on the computer can automatically capture the facial changes of the individuals while they are watching an ad online. Using this methodology, one multi-category study of over 140 ads across four countries (i.e. the US, the UK, France and Germany) found that amusement

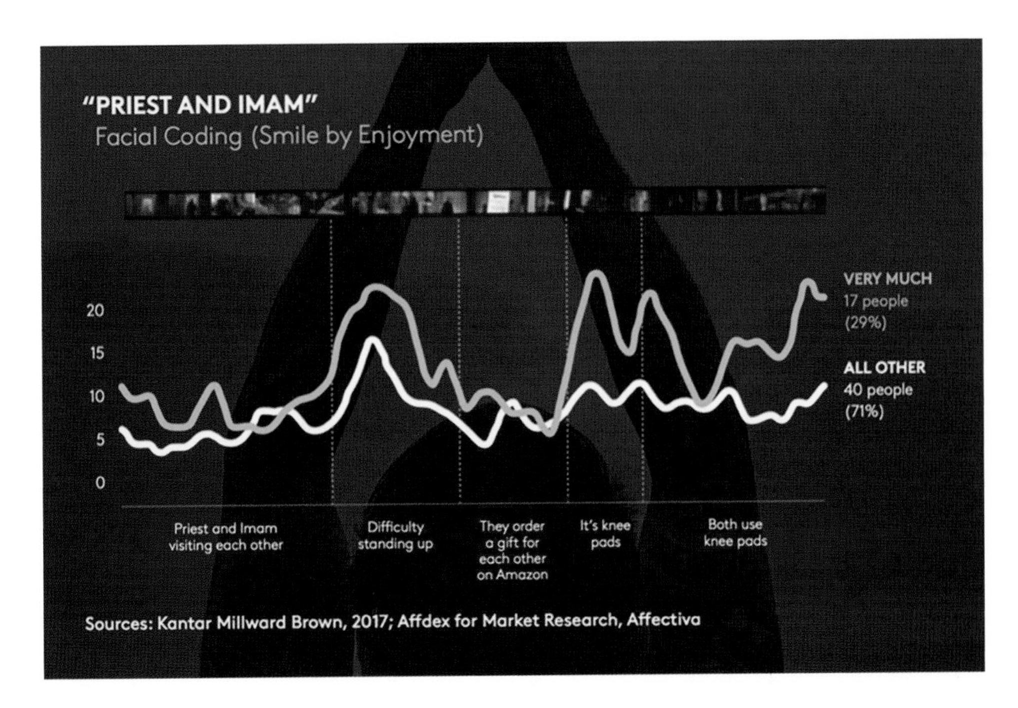

Figure 12.23 Moment-to-moment changes in the intensity of enjoyment using automatic facial coding

was the strongest predictor of sales.[87] This study demonstrated the true scalability of this measure.

Eye-tracking

None of these methods can tell us at which part of the ad the person is looking. This is where eye-tracking (ET) methodology using infrared technology is useful. Research shows that our eyes do not move smoothly over a scene but rather dart around (this fast movement is called a 'saccade'). At points of interest in a scene, our eyes stop for a fraction of a second (about 200–300 milliseconds) as they take in the information (this tiny pause is called a 'fixation'). Such fixations can be aggregated across people to obtain 'heat maps'. For instance, figure 12.24 is the heat map of a TV scene showing that viewers are looking at the logo at the steering wheel of a car. The greater the number of fixations, the redder is the image. (This can be predetermined as our 'area of interest' in the analysis.) It is an objective way of assessing which parts of the ad are creating interest, on the assumption that we look at what we are interested in.[88]

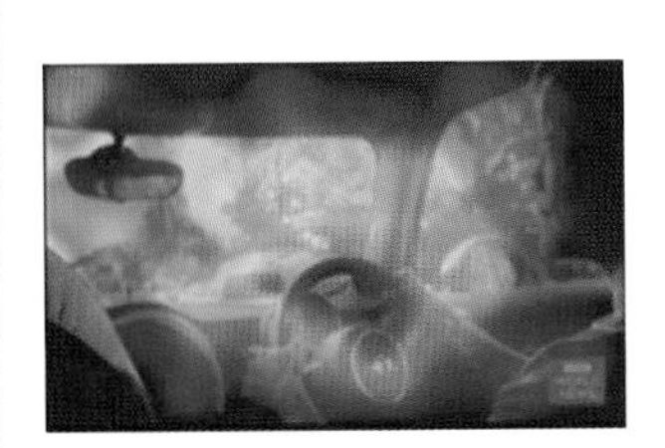

Figure 12.24 A heat map showing a person driving a car with the fixation on the steering wheel and logo

Each of these psycho-physiological methods has its pros and cons, summarised in table 12.7.

Table 12.7 Advantages and disadvantages of psycho-physiological methods

Psycho-physiological method	Advantages	Disadvantages
fMRI	It has great spatial resolution (1–3 mm) and can provide information about which deep structure of the brain is activated while a person is watching the ad. Since we know which part of the brain is responsible for each emotional state, this allows us to infer which emotional state is being activated by certain scenes.[89]	It has poor time resolution (5–8 seconds) compared to EEG (discussed below), making it more difficult to time-lock the quick changes in the ad scenes with changes in blood flow. It is also the most expensive method because of the sophistication of the equipment. A high level of expertise is also needed to interpret the data. It is better suited to measuring stationary stimuli such as logos and packaging.
EEG	It has high time resolution, meaning that it can detect changes in firing activities of the neurons in the order of milliseconds (instead of seconds). By time-locking this to changes in ad scenes, researchers can infer which scene: (i) is being encoded into long term memory;[90] (ii) is personally relevant;[91] (iii) is inducing approach or avoidance tendencies;[92] (iv) is eliciting active attention.[93]	There is large amount of noise in the data, which requires 'cleaning up' using a mathematical algorithm.[94] One form of EEG, called 'Steady State Topography' (SST), has a higher signal-to-noise ratio and can be used to monitor changes in brainwaves.[95]
GSR	This technology has been around for a long time. It is easy to set up and measure, requiring only two electrodes on the hand.	It measures arousal but does not measure valence. It must be used in conjunction with other methods.
Facial coding and facial EMG	This can capture changes in specific emotions triggered by specific scenes in the ad, which the other methods cannot.	Facial coding, which relies on human coders, does not have the precision to time-lock which ad scene is responsible for generating the specific emotions. This is overcome with facial recognition software. Facial EMG can also achieve this, but it is intrusive since the electrodes have to be placed on the face.
ET (Eye-tracking)	It allows us to know which part(s) of the ad the person is watching. By examining patterns of fixation, researcher can infer which part of ad arouses the person's interest.	Examining eye movement only reveals if there is visual contact and hence interest. It does not tell us how a person is feeling while viewing the ad.

Although psycho-physiological methods have many advantages, they can also suffer from difficulties in interpretation. For instance, although GSR measures our physiological arousal to a scene, it does not measure the psychological meaning we attach to it. Figure 12.25 shows that we may be aroused, and yet we can feel either anxious or excited.[96] Some researchers argue that, in the end, we still need to use self-report measures to assess psychological meaning.[97]

	Not aroused	Aroused
Positive	**Relaxed**	**Excited**
Negative	**Bored**	**Anxious**

Figure 12.25 The different psychological states

Each psycho-physiological method has its own limitations, but some market research companies are combining different methods to compensate for them.[98] For instance, although EEG measures brainwave activities, it does not pinpoint at which part of the ad the person is looking. But by combining ET with EEG, researchers can ascertain whether the area the person is looking at (called 'areas of interest') is also evoking the desired EEG response.[99] Of course, more than one method can be used in combination, as shown in figure 12.26.

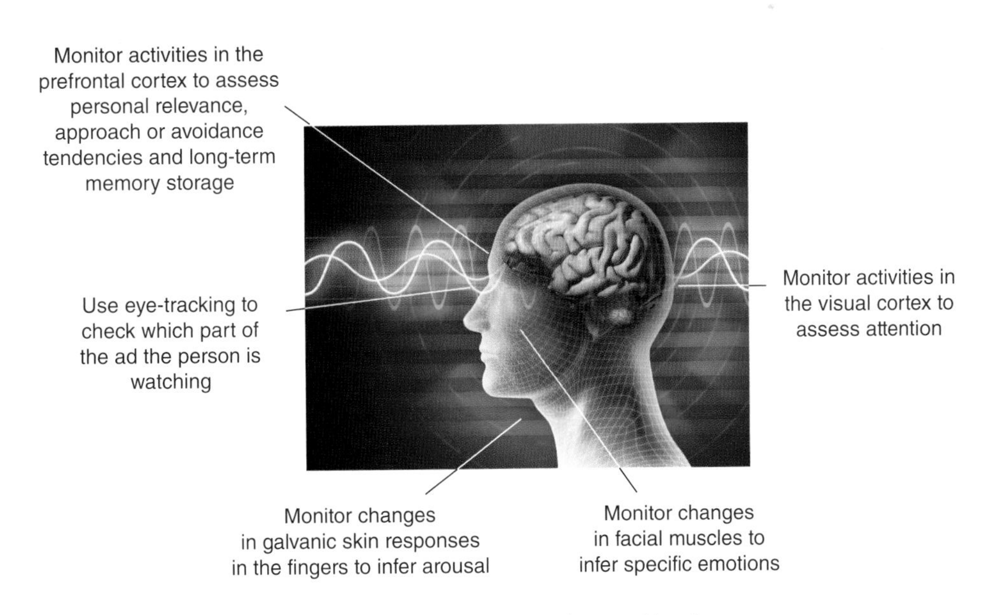

Figure 12.26 How the psycho-physiological methods can be combined

To increase the validity of the interpretation, we should also analyse the data of different groups of consumers (e.g. customers versus non-customers) who watched the same ad. The pattern should display some internal logic. For instance, one study found that an ad for Nespresso coffee, featuring the actor George Clooney, tended to generate more approach tendencies in women than in men.[100]

CASE STUDY 12.2 SELLING MINIS TO THE BRITISH: THE CASE OF COMBINING DIFFERENT PSYCHO-PHYSIOLOGICAL MEASURES WITH SUBGROUP ANALYSES

Subgroup analyses can be applied to other forms of psycho-physiological analyses. A recent BBC study found that certain scenes in a film can surprise viewers, which they tend to remember.[101] And if those scenes happen to show a brand, it will be encoded into their long-term memory, leading to greater brand consideration. For instance, figure 12.27 shows that viewers experienced a peak emotion of surprise about 50 seconds into film. This is when the protagonist talked about her experience.

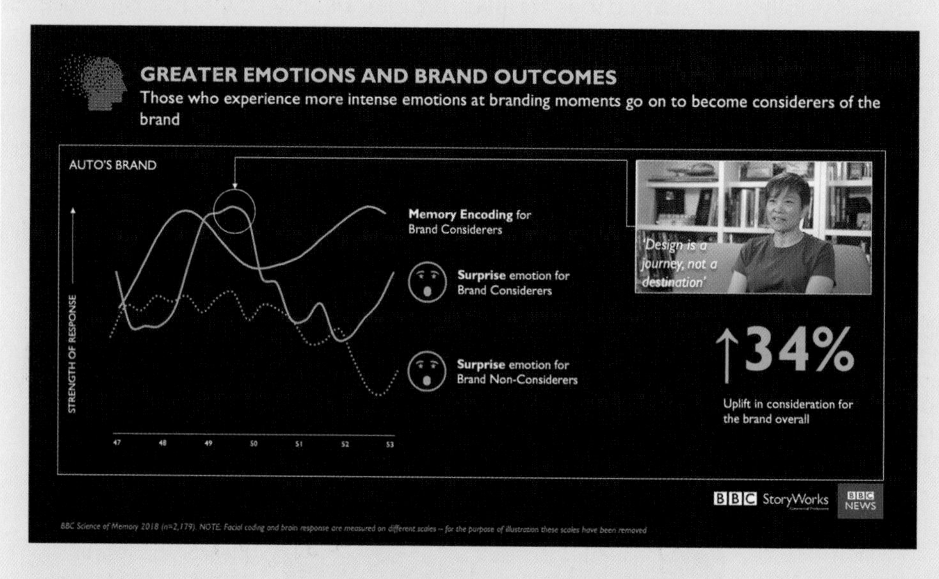

Figure 12.27 A scene showing a peak emotion of surprise

When this data was divided into those who would consider buying a Mini car versus those who wouldn't, a more interesting picture emerged (see figure 12.28). Among considerers, the surprise scene led to better memory encoding for the Mini car brand. Non-considerers on the other hand were not affected by this scene. Considerers were also more likely to encode the brand of the car into memory. Eye-tracking data (heat map) confirmed this, showing that considerers towards the end of the ad were also more likely to notice the label on the steering wheel.

This is a good example of using different psycho-physiological measures (i.e. EEG and eye-tracking) coupled with subgroup analyses (i.e. brand considerers and non-considerers) to interpret the result.

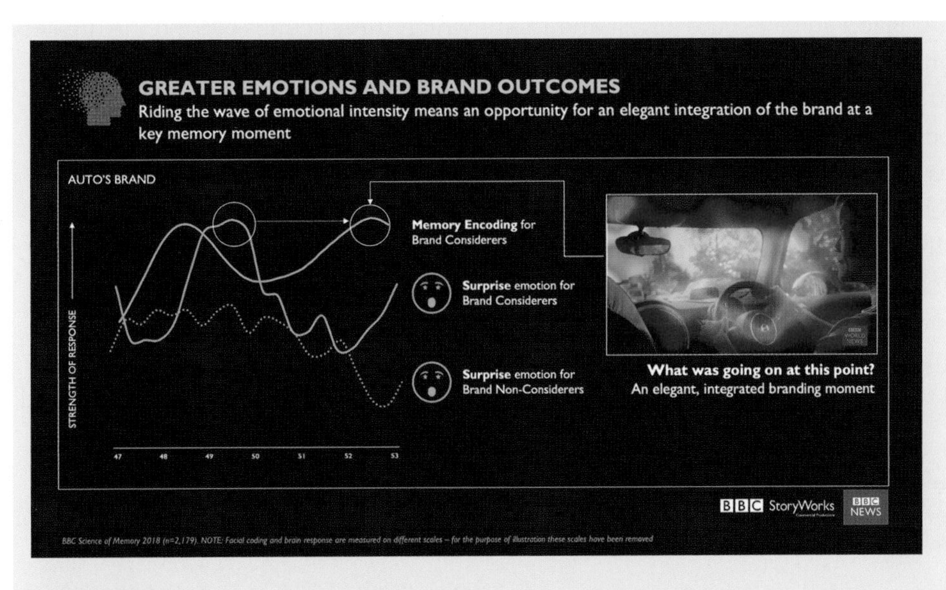

Figure 12.28 Sub-analyses of EEG activations among brand considerers and non-considerers, plus heat map of brand considerers

DISCUSSION QUESTIONS

1. Of the two subgroups, which do you think is more important? The considerers or non-considerers? Why?
2. Do you think it is possible for considerers or non-considerers to verbally express which scene of the ad is surprising? Or which scene captures their attention? Or whether they are attracted to the label or brand?
3. What is the managerial significance of knowing which scene is more effective for different subgroups of consumers? Does it or does it not matter?

DISCUSSION QUESTIONS

1. Why do we pre-test an ad before a campaign begins? Why is it best not to simply launch the ad once it is finished?
2. What is the difference between concept exploration, quantitative advertising pre-testing and campaign evaluation?
3. If an advertising campaign has started, why might we want to track it?
4. What are the typical outcome measures and ad-diagnostic measures used in campaign evaluation? Why is it important to measure these, rather than only the outcome?
5. What is the difference between category-cued brand awareness versus need-based cue brand awareness?
6. Looking at table 12.7, which three advertising mediums should one use to get maximum synergy for profits?
7. What are the limitations of using a standard self-report questionnaire for testing a broadcast ad such as a TV commercial?

8. In the Amazon ad called the 'Priest and Iman', which three scenes evoked the greatest amount of happiness? You can watch the ad here: https://youtu.be/UGS4HMqoNqM.
9. What is system 1 and system 2 decision-making? Give examples of research methodologies that tap into these two kinds of decision-making.
10. What is IRT? Why do you think it has grown in popularity among advertising researchers?
11. Recently, scientists may have found our 'buy button' in our brain. What is this called, and what method did they use to establish this? Does it matter from a managerially viewpoint where this button is? Explain your answer.
12. Each psycho-physiological method has strengths and weaknesses. Suggest how you would take advantage of each method in an integrated manner when testing a TV ad.

NOTES

1 LD Gibson, 'What can one exposure do?', *Journal of Advertising Research*, 36(2), 1996, pp. 9–18.

2 B Biteau and D Brandt, 'Pre-testing and sales validation', *Admap*, 35(2), 2000, pp. 23–6.

3 Once we have something promising, we can still go into large-scale testing of the concept (not the ad), although in my experience this seldom occurs.

4 It is not advisable to create a finished ad, since we are not sure which executions are easier to process and more motivating.

5 DW Stewart, 'The moderating role of recall, comprehension, and brand differentiation on the persuasiveness of television advertising', *Journal of Advertising Research*, April/May, 1986, pp. 43–7.

6 A Green and C Aubury, 'Global copy testing – lessons from experience', *Admap*, October, 1997. Accessed November 2018 at www.warc.com/content/paywall/article/global-copy-testing—lessons-from-experience/4804.

7 However, newer methods of testing now allow objective consumer feedback to be used as input during the concept development phrase. See later discussion on the criticisms of pre-testing.

8 This follows Petty and Chaiken's work – see RE Petty and DT Wegner, 'The elaboration likelihood model: current status and controversies', in S Chaiken and YT Trope (eds), *Dual-process theories in social psychology*, Guilford Press, New York, 1999, pp. 37–72.

9 Haydn Northover, Senior Account Director, Kantar, Sydney, personal communication, September 2018.

10 Effie Worldwide, 'Dos Equis / Heineken USA – The Most Interesting Man in the World, Gold, Beverages – Alcohol', Effie Awards 2009. Accessed November 2018 at www.warc.com/content/paywall/article/dos-equis—heineken-usa—the-most-interesting-man-in-the-world/89434.

11 N Hollis, 'One thing that LinkNow pre-testing will not fix', Kantar Blog, 18 February 2015. Accessed November 2018 at www.millwardbrown.com/global-navigation/blogs/post/mb-blog/2015/02/18/one-thing-that-linknow-pre-testing-will-not-fix.

12 A Gallagher and B Earle, 'Permission to launch: Why insight and research is the missing ingredient in successful digital creative', *ESOMAR Congress*, 2018. Accessed November 2018 at www.warc.com/content/paywall/article/permission-to-launch-why-insight-and-research-is-the-missing-ingredient-in-successful-digital-creative/123732.

13 For example, Katar has created a fast and cost-efficient way for a firm to test their ads in different formats like television, social media (e.g. Facebook), online video (e.g. YouTube), online display, and mobile ads. The cost starts from around US$3000, and you can get the results within six hours. You can watch the promotional video of LinkNow at: www.youtube.com/watch?v=Kz9v0xks4Xs. Accessed November 2018.

14 M Blackston, 'Copy-testing and brand equity: what's the connection?', *Journal of Advertising Research*, 35(1), 1995, RC2–7.

15 See K Clancy, RS Shulman and M Wolf, *Simulated test marketing: technology for launching successful new products*, Lexington Books, New York, 1994.

16 Assessing differences or changes in brand preference is one way of getting at the persuasiveness of the ad. The comScore ARS method relies on the respondent choosing the brand before and after watching the ad. In this example, it will be the percentage difference in respondents choosing the target brand before and after watching the ad.

17 Brand attitude is sometimes labelled as brand liking or brand affinity. With the latter, it is measured using a rating scale, in conjunction with ranking of other competitive brands using a love–hate seven-point bipolar scale. See J Alagon and J Samuel, 'The meaningfully different framework', *Millward Brown*, 2013.

18 A Mehta, 'How advertising response modelling (ARM) can increase ad effectiveness', *Journal of Advertising Research*, 34(3), 1994, pp. 62–74.

19 One study found that ads that are enjoyable and involving tend to have adjectives like thought-provoking, exciting, different, intriguing, clever, surprising and sexy. See D Twose and D Smith, 'How effectively can ad research predict sales?', *Admap*, 487, October 2007, pp. 42–4.

20 The method is described in a Kantar webinar: see K Malcom and P Albert, 'LinkNow'. Accessed November 2018 at www.millwardbrown.com/global-navigation/news/news-events/webinars/2015/linknow-webinar.

21 To date, Kantar has tested more than 107 000 ads worldwide, and 40% of these are in rough finish, using their Link methodology. They claimed their three key measures of Persuasion, Awareness Index (or AI) and Short-term Sales Likelihood (or STSL) have been validated against actual sales of the brand. This forms the database of norms against which an ad is compared. This is reported in the topline results they provide. (For an example, see case study 12.1 The Most Interesting Man in the World). For a discussion of their Link method, see www.millwardbrown.com/solutions/slick-sheets/millwardbrown_link.aspx. Accessed November 2018.

22 C McDonalds, 'Point of view: the key is to understand consumer response', *Journal of Advertising Research*, 33(5), 1993, pp. 63–9. Rossiter and Percy are the only researchers I am aware of who advocate a contingency approach to advertising pre-testing. It is too complex to explain the nuances in this text, but interested readers may wish to look up chapter 19 in J Rossiter and L Percy, *Advertising communications and promotion management*, 2nd edition, McGraw-Hill, New York, 1997.

23 R Haley and AL Baldinger, 'The AFR copy research validity project', *Journal of Advertising Research*, 40(6), 2000, pp. 114–35.

24 S Koslow, S Sasser and EA Riordan, 'Do marketers get the advertising they need or the advertising they deserve?', *Journal of Advertising*, 35(3), 2006, pp. 81–101.

25 Ibid.

26 C Young, 'Neuroscience and advertising: the essence of an ad', *Admap*, May, 2012, pp. 40–1.

27 T Ambler, 'Copy testing: practice and best practice – a review of UK ad research procedures', Warc Monographs, August 2003.

28 D Poole, 'How to use copy testing or pre-testing', Warc best practice, 2016. Accessed November 2018 at www.warc.com/content/paywall/article/how-to-use-copy-testing-or-pre-testing/107800.

29 Kantar, the pre-eminent advertising pre-testing research agency, has one of the most extensive advertising pre-testing norms developed since the 1970s. The firm has pre-tested more than 107 000 ads from over 92 countries. And the norms through their Link pre-testing system have been validated with sales. See Link™ Copytesting, www.millwardbrown.com/solutions/slick-sheets/millwardbrown_link.aspx. Accessed November 2018. See also D Twose and D Smith, 'How effectively can ad research predict sales?', *Admap*, 487, October 2007, pp. 42–4.

30 Haydn Northover, Senior Account director, Kantar, Sydney, personal communication, September 2018.

31 Ibid. Haydn also told me that Kantar had tested more than 175 000 ads worldwide.

32 J Armstrong, 'The seer-sucker theory: the value of experts in forecasting', *Technology Review*, June/July, 1980, pp. 16–24.

33 GfK research conducts magazine research using this methodology. See https://mri.gfk.com/solutions/magazine-research/. Accessed November 2018.

34 Max Sutherland has long advocated the importance of continuous tracking, and this is an example he uses to powerfully demonstrate its importance. Personal communication, M Sutherland to the author.

35 P Nedungai, 'Recall and consumer consideration sets: influencing choice without altering brand evaluations', *Journal of Consumer Research*, 17 December 1990, pp. 263–74.

36 See J Alagon and J Samuel, 'The meaningfully different framework', Millward Brown, 2013, pp 7.

37 Although this example is about purchase intentions, it can also be about consumption intentions, willingness to recommend, or any behavioural actions we want to assess. Generally, purchase intention is more suited to high-risk purchase because they tend to be less overstated. See Clancy, Shulman and Wolf (1994), *Simulated test marketing*, note 15.

38 K Nelson-Field and E Riebe, 'How advertising attracts attention', *Admap*, September, 2018. Accessed November 2018 at www.warc.com/content/paywall/article/how-advertising-attracts-attention/123122.

39 See Kantar, 'Advertising: Making a lasting impression', p. 19. Accessed November 2018 at www.millwardbrown.com/Documents/Reports/Make_a_Lasting_Impression/default.aspx?access=yes.

40 R Shepard, 'Recognition memory for words, sentences, and pictures', *Journal of Verbal Learning and Verbal Behavior*, 6(1), February 1967, pp. 156–63.

41 S Byfield, 'Watching people, watching television: how people really behave during commercial breaks', *ESOMAR Audience Research*, Miami, May 2000.

42 E Thorson and X Zhao, 'Television viewing behaviour as an indicator of commercial effectiveness', in WD Wells (ed.), *Measuring advertising effectiveness, Lawrence* Erlbaum, Mahwah, NJ, 1997. See especially chapter 13, p. 227 – about 60% of people who have eyes on screen (or EOS) when the ad is on recognise it later.

43 RH Colley, *Defining advertising goals for measured advertising results*, Association of National Advertisers, New York, 1961.

44 CTR may not always be the online advertising objective. For instance, if the objective is to raise brand awareness rather than say increasing sign-up rates, then CTR may be less important.

I thank Melissa Airs, Senior Account Manager (Media & Digital) Kantar, for pointing this out to me. September 2018, personal communication.

45 We can also call this moderated regression since a moderator is a variable that strengthens (or lessens) the relationship between two variables. So, in this example, timing acts to moderate the relationship between deliciousness and temperature. Alternatively, temperature acts to moderate the relationship between timing and deliciousness.

46 The explanation given here is based on standardised or mean-centred units. This makes comparison across variables easier.

47 G Assmus, JU Farley and DR Lehmann, 'How advertising affects sales: a meta-analysis of econometric results', *Journal of Marketing Research*, 21(1), 1984, pp. 65–74.

48 S Albers, MK Mantrala and S Sridhar, 'Personal selling elasticities: a meta-analysis', *Journal of Marketing Research*, 47(5), 2010, pp. 840–53.

49 THA Bijmolt, HJ van Heerde and RGM Pieters, 'New empirical generalizations on the determinants of price elasticity', *Journal of Marketing Research,* 42, 2005, pp. 141–56.

50 The table of data is obtained from PJ Danaher and TS Dagger, 'Comparing the relative effectiveness of advertising channels: a case study of a multimedia blitz campaign', *Journal of Marketing Research,* 50(4), 2013, pp. 517–34.

51 Ibid.

52 Wikipedia listed six classes of cognitive biases, totalling 190. Accessed November 2018 at https://en.wikipedia.org/wiki/List_of_cognitive_biases.

53 In behavioural economics, this is known as the default effect where the chooser will end up with the choice without making any decision. This can make a difference in some situations; for example, in organ donation where one can become an automatic donor when we die, for instance in an accident (unless we opt-out) or we only become a donor when choose to (i.e. opt-in). See EJ Johnson and D Goldstein. 'Medicine: Do defaults save lives?', *Science*, 302(5649), 2003, pp. 1338–9.

54 A Tversky and D Kahneman, 'Judgment under uncertainty: heuristics and biases', *Science*, New Series, 185(4157), 1974, pp. 1124–31.

55 D Kahneman, *Thinking, Fast and Slow*, Penguin Publisher, 2011.

56 AG Greenwald, DE McGhee and JLK Schwartz, 'Measuring individual differences in implicit cognition: the implicit association test', *Journal of Personality and Social Psychology* 74(6), 1998, pp. 1464–80.

57 JEM Steenkamp, MG de Jong and H Baumgartner, 'Socially desirable response tendencies in survey research', *Journal of Marketing Research*, 47, 2010, pp. 199–214.

58 AG Greenwald, 'The totalitarian ego: fabrication and revision of personal history', *American Psychologist*, 35, 1980, pp. 603–18.

59 TD Wilson, *Strangers to ourselves: discovering the adaptive unconscious*. Harvard University Press, Cambridge, MA, 2002.

60 AG Greenwald and MR Banaji, 'Implicit social cognition: attitudes, self-esteem, and stereotypes', *Psychological Review*, 102, 1995, pp. 4–27.

61 CV Dimofte, 'Implicit measures of consumer cognition: a review', *Psychology and Marketing*, 27, 2010, pp. 921–37.

62 D Maison, AG Greenwald and RH Bruin, 'Predictive validity of the implicit association test in studies of brands, consumer attitudes, and behavior', *Journal of Consumer Psychology* 14(4), 2004, pp. 405–15.

63 FF Brunel, BC Tietje and AG Greenwald, 'Is the implicit association test a valid and valuable measure of implicit consumer social cognition?', *Journal of Consumer Psychology* 14(4), 2004, pp. 385–404.

64 D Penn, 'True lies and true implicit – how priming reveals the hidden truth', *International Journal of Market Research*, 58(2), 2016, pp. 175–99.

65 G Page, 'Neuroscience: a new perspective', Millward Brown, Point of View, 2010. Accessed November 2018 at www.millwardbrown.com/docs/default-source/insight-documents/points-of-view/MillwardBrown_POV_NeurosciencePerspective.pdf.

66 N Hollis, 'Why marketers must adapt video to media channel', Kantar Blog, 22 March 2017. Accessed November 2018 at www.millwardbrown.com/global-navigation/blogs/post/mb-blog/2017/03/22/why-marketers-must-adapt-video-to-media-channel.

67 T Noble, 'How neuroscience is advancing consumer insights', *Admap*, August, 2017. Accessed November 2018 at www.warc.com/content/paywall/article/how-neuroscience-is-advancing-consumer-insights/111903.

68 One outfit called CloudArmy claimed that one can report the results of a study within 24 hours. See their promotion video here: https://cloud.army/explainer-videos/. Accessed November 2018.

69 At a more fundamental level, Libet et al. found in 1983 that there is a lag of up to 800 milliseconds between our brain activity signalling what we plan to do and the actual action. In other words, our brain activity, which is unconscious, precedes our conscious actions. See B Libet et al., 'Time of conscious intention to act in relation to onset of cerebral activity (readiness-potential) the unconscious initiation of a feely voluntary act', *Brain*, 106, 1983, pp. 623–42.

70 For a detailed critique, see HJ Northover, 'Assessing the value of neurophysiological measurement for advertising pre-testing', PhD thesis, Ehrenberg-Bass Institute for Marketing Science, The University of South Australia, 2012. See also S Bellman et al., 'What makes a television commercial sell? Using biometrics to identify successful ads', *Journal of Advertising Research*, 57(1), 2017, pp 53–66.

71 D Varan et al., 'How reliable are neuromarketers' measures of advertising effectiveness: data from ongoing research holds no common truth among vendors', *Journal of Advertising Research*, 55(2), 2015, pp. 176–191.

72 R Kennedy and H Northover, 'How to use neuromeasures to make better advertising decisions: questions practitioners should ask vendors and research priorities for scholars', *Journal of Advertising Research*, 56(2), 2016, pp. 183–92.

73 Richard Silberstein from Neuro-insight is the first to discover this using a more sophisticated form of EEG called Steady State Topography (or SST). See https://neuro-insight.com/. Accessed November 2018.

74 JR Rossiter, RB Silberstein, PG Harris and G Nield, 'Brain-imaging detection of visual scene encoding in long-term memory for TV commercials', *Journal of Advertising Research*, 41(2), 2001, pp. 13–20.

75 RB Silberstein and GE Nield, 'Brain activity correlates of consumer brand choice shift associated with television advertising', *International Journal of Advertising*, 27(3), 2008, pp. 359–80.

76 S Ogawa et al., 'Intrinsic signal changes accompanying sensory stimulation: functional brain mapping with magnetic resonance imaging', *Proceedings of the National Academy of Science of the USA*, 22(1), 1992, pp. 210–16.

77 For instance, using fMRI Venketraman et al. found that the activation of ventral striatum is the best predictor of the effectiveness of the advertising tested (measured via its elasticity), even after

taking more traditional advertising survey-based pre-test (i.e. pencil-and-paper) into consideration. See V Venkatraman et al., 'Predicting advertising success beyond traditional measures: new insights from neurophysiological methods and market response modeling', *Journal of Marketing Research*, 52, 2015, pp. 436–52.

78 Using three years of sales data of music, Berns and Moore found that songs that activated the ventral striatum of adolescences tend to have greater sales. See GS Berns and SE Moore, 'A neural predictor of cultural popularity', *Journal of Consumer Psychology*, 22(1), 2012, pp. 154–60; See also B Knutson, S Rick, GE Wimmer, D Prelec, and G Loewenstein, 'Neural predictors of purchases', *Neuron*, 53(1), 2007, pp. 147–56.

79 P LaBarbera and J Tucciarone, 'GSR reconsidered: a behavior-based approach to evaluating and improving the sales potency of advertising', *Journal of Advertising Research*, 35, 1995, pp. 33–53; R Hopkins and J Fletcher, 'Electrodermal measurement particularly effective for forecasting message influence on sales appeal', in A Lang (ed.) *Measuring Psychological Responses to Media*, Lawrence Erlbaum Associates, Hillsdale, 1994.

80 P Ekman, WC Friesen and JC Hager, *Facial Action Coding System (FACS) manual on CD ROM*, A Human Face, Salt Lake City, UT, 2002.

81 Later, Ekman added other emotions, such as amusement, contempt, contentment, embarrassment, excitement, guilt, pride in achievement, relief, satisfaction, sensory pleasure, and shame. See P Ekman, 'Basic emotions', in T Dalgleish and M Power (eds), *Handbook of cognition and emotion*, John Wiley & Sons, Chichester, 1999.

82 JL Graham, 'A new system for measuring nonverbal responses to marketing appeals', in *AMA Educator's Conference Proceedings 1980*, American Marketing Association, Chicago, 1980.

83 The company Affectiva is the leader in this field. It was spun out of MIT. Accessed November 2018 at www.affectiva.com/product/affdex-for-market-research/.

84 T Baltrusaitis, *Automatic facial expression analysis*, PhD thesis Oxford University, 2014, p. 58.

85 Haydn Northover, Senior Account Director, Kantar, Sydney Australia, personal communication, September 2018.

86 Damaris Chevalier Boisne, Kantar, Senior Account Manager, Kantar, personal communication, September 2018.

87 D McDuff, R El Kaliouby, E Kodra and L Larguine, 'Do emotions in advertising drive sales? Use of facial coding to understand the relation between emotional ads and sales effectiveness', ESOMAR, Congress, Istanbul, September 2013. Accessed November 2018 at www.warc.com/content/paywall/article/do-emotions-in-advertising-drive-sales-use-of-facial-coding-to-understand-the-relation-between-emotional-ads-and-sales-effectiveness/100222. See the video here: https://martechtoday.com/official-smiling-ad-means-sales-wiFll-go-196533.

88 For a demonstration of how eye-tracking can be used to evaluate print ads, go to the Tobii website, which supplies eye-tracking equipment: www.tobii.com/en/eye-tracking-research/global/library/videos/all/ad-testing. Accessed April 2013.

89 For instance, the *nucleus accumbens*, deep in the middle part of the brain, is active when people feel excitement, anticipation and wanting. See D Ariely and GS Berns, 'Neuromarketing: the hope and hype of neuroimaging in business', *Nature Review Neuroscience*, 11(4), 2010, pp. 284–92.

90 J Rossiter, et al., 'Brain-imaging detection of visual scene encoding in long-term memory for TV commercials', *Journal of Advertising*, 41(2), 2001, pp. 13–21.

91 For example, parts of the orbito-frontal cortex are activated when we see stimuli that are personally relevant and involving. See JB Nitschke et al., 'Orbitofrontal cortex tracks positive mood in mothers viewing pictures of their newborn infants', *Neuroimage*, 21, 2004, pp. 583–92.

92 R Ohme et al., 'Application of front EEG asymmetry to advertising research', *Journal of Economic Psychology*, 31(5), 2010, pp. 785–93.

93 This means allocating resources to processing the ad, not just visual contact. This shifting of resources can be mapped. See R Naatanen and PT Michie, 'Early selective-attention effects of the evoked potential: a critical review and reinterpretation', *Biological Psychology*, 8, 1979, pp. 81–136.

94 H Stipp and RP Woodard, 'Uncovering emotions: using neuromarketing to increase ad effectiveness', Advertising Research Foundation, 2011. Accessed April 2013 at https://thearf-org-aux-assets.s3.amazonaws.com/research/NeuroStandards_WhitePaper_Oct262011_Pre-Production_Version.pdf.

95 RB Silberstein, 'Steady state visually evoked potentials, brand resonances and cognitive processes', in PL Nunez (ed.), *Neocortical dynamics and human EEG rhythm*, Oxford University Press, New York, 1995, pp. 272–303.

96 This basic framework is from the Reversal Theory of British psychologist MJ Apter, *Reversal theory: the dynamics of motivation, emotion and personality*, 2nd edition, Oneworld Publications Oxford, UK, 2007; for a more detailed coding of other emotions using this basic framework, see K Nelson-Field and E Riebe (2018), 'How advertising attracts attention', note 38.

97 RF Potter and PD Bolls, *Psycho-physiological measurement and meaning*, Routledge, New York, 2012.

98 R Ohme, M Matukin and B Pacula-Lesniak, 'Biometric measures for interactive advertising research', *Journal of Interactive Advertising*, 11(2), 2011, pp. 60–72.

99 M Matukin and R Ohme, 'What do we feel when we look? Eye tracking and brain waves help to better understand the advertising processing', paper presented at the 10th International Conference of Research in Advertising, Berlin, 2011.

100 Personal communication from Michal Matukin of Human Mind and Brain to the author. The Applied Research Center (HMB-ARC) in Warsaw, Poland conducted the Nespresso study featuring George Clooney.

101 S Wu, H McPharlin and C Harley, 'The neuroscience of memory: emotion and memory in branded content', Research on Warc, November 2018. Accessed November 2018 at www.warc.com/content/paywall/article/the-neuroscience-of-memory-emotion-and-memory-in-branded-content/124134.

CHAPTER 13
INTEGRATIVE REVIEW, IMC IMPLEMENTATIONS AND MARKETING TECHNOLOGIES

CHAPTER OVERVIEW

We have now come to the end of the book, with much discussion and a lot to absorb along the way. As we noted in chapter 1, the philosophy that marcoms campaigns must be both effective and efficient underpins this book. To be effective and efficient, many elements need to work together. This integrative review chapter provides an overview of the lessons you have learned, summarised into different core themes. Yet this knowledge is useless if it cannot be implemented. In this chapter, we also discuss why IMC implementations have often failed. Finally, we conclude with a word on ethics in IMC and a look into the future of marketing as it becomes more technologically driven.

Learning goals

After reading this chapter, you will understand:

- important underlying themes of IMC efficiency and effectiveness
- IMC implementation and its barriers
- marketing technologies and activation engines
- ethical issues in IMC
- a future, driven by data and technology, underpinned by understanding human psychology.

INTEGRATING THEMES

Several themes underpin the philosophy of being effective and efficient in IMC. Figure 13.1 will help guide your reading of these themes.

Theme 1: Overcoming communication barriers with direct and indirect means

Chapter 1 introduced the notion of communication barriers. The basic idea is that it pays to know what barriers we need to overcome in order to get the branded message across to our target audience. These barriers include noise and clutter (see point A in figure 13.1); consumer apathy (see point B), often caused by inertia or lack of need (C); and lack of brand equity and preference

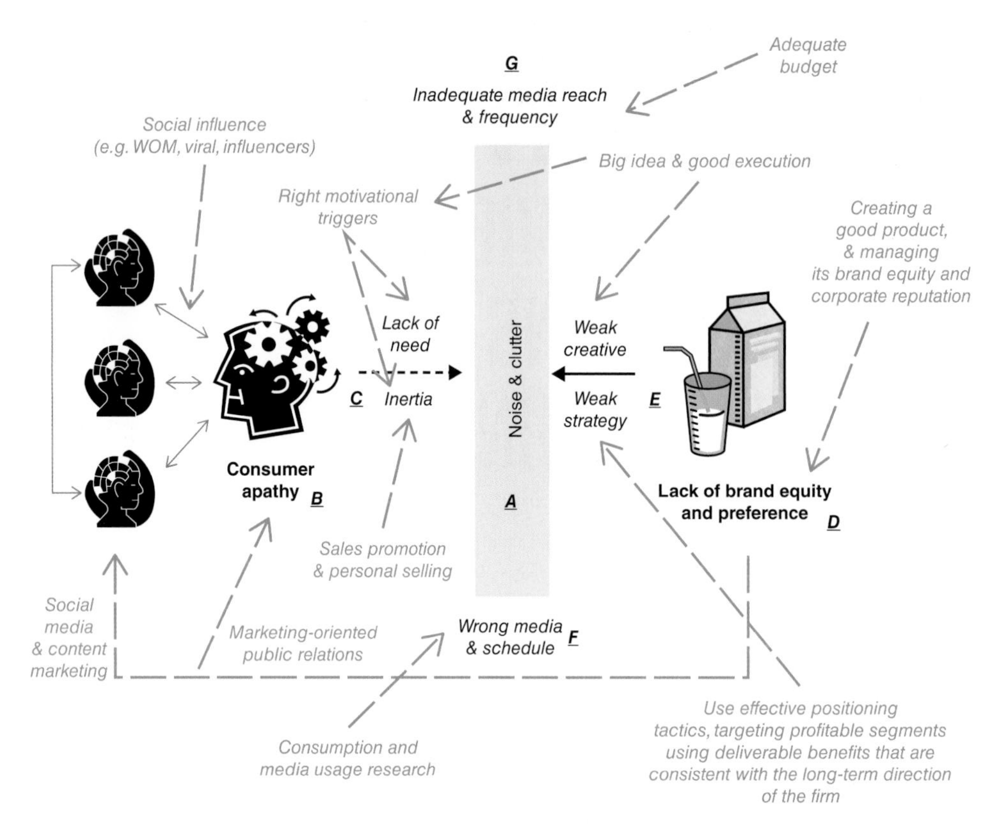

Figure 13.1 Communications barriers and some suggested solutions

(D), which are all exacerbated by not having a strong creative idea or strategy (E), and hampered by using the wrong media and schedule (F) or having inadequate media reach and frequency (G). The main communication barriers, depicted in figure 13.1, were first encountered in chapter 1. However, this version of the figure now shows the various ways in which these barriers can be overcome. As you read through the themes in this section, the figure's depiction of the barriers and suggested solutions should fall into place.

Given the number of impediments to modern-day marcoms, the discipline rests on the idea of integration. In this book, IMC is defined as a research-based, audience-focused, result-driven communication planning process that aims to execute a brand communication program over time so that there is clarity and consistency in the positioning of the brand. This is achieved by coordinating different communication tools and channels, and integrating multiple pieces of creative content across different media in order to create synergistic effects. The aim is to achieve short-term financial gain and long-term brand equity.

Marketing's reason for being is to be able to influence consumers; for marcoms, it is to be able to communicate a message in an influential way. This book has considered two routes of influence. First, the direct route where organisations try to convince the target audience to buy its goods or services. The classic examples are advertising (chapters 6 and 7), sales promotion, direct response marketing (chapter 11) and personal selling (chapter 10). Second, the indirect route where the influence comes from other people in the community through word-of-mouth or recommendations (chapter 8), sometimes heightened by marketing-oriented PR (chapter 9). It is indirect because consumers generally think there is no vested interest involved in these forms of communication.

DIRECT INFLUENCE

The main problem with direct influence is that consumers will resist it, which we can see in their level of counterargument when they respond to an advertisement. This is why even weak arguments can be persuasive if the target audience is distracted from mentally arguing with the message. Generally, if a person is motivated or has the opportunity or ability to process a message, the arguments had better be strong to combat such counterarguments (see the Further Thinking section in chapter 7).

Sales promotion and direct marketing (see chapter 11) are also obvious forms of direct influence. The objective of direct marketing, like promotions, is to stimulate an immediate response, but unlike promotions, in direct marketing we need to very tightly define not only the addressability of the target audience but also how to personalise the offer and what money-back guarantee to provide. And unlike consumer promotions, in which the offer of a reward or incentive is typically for inexpensive goods (such as a bottle of salsa), in direct marketing, more often than not, the offer is for expensive ones (such as a PC). Therefore, more is at stake, and the objective is to create a sense of urgency so that the consumer will take immediate action.

The direct route of influence also creates the greatest resistance. That is why, for complex and high-involvement goods, the use of personal selling is essential – it is flexible, and the salesperson can handle complex questions on the spot. The downside is its high contact cost. For this reason, each contact a salesperson makes is precious, which makes the framing of the selling message extremely important. In a selling situation, the main task of the salesperson is to frame the benefit in a convincing way and to overcome any objections the consumer raises.

However, direct influence does not mean the buyer is always fully conscious of being manipulated. In chapter 10, we first discussed the six principles of persuasion in personal selling: scarcity, authority, social proof, consistency, commitment, reciprocity and likeability. It is important to understand these principles because they are very powerful in creating compliance, sometimes even without the buyer's knowledge. But not everyone can be a good salesperson. More than just knowledge, it is the ability to combat pessimistic thinking that defines a good salesperson. How we think about a particular event influences our subsequent action.

INDIRECT INFLUENCE

The rise of ad blockers has raised serious concerns for marketers, who have no choice but to look for ways of influencing consumers indirectly. Chapter 8 is about indirect influence, specifically between friends. Social influence is important because even in the offline world it has long been known that friends affect us. It is human instinct. With the growth in social media, however, social influence has now become digitised. Marketers have become quite excited about this, but they also have little control over it.

With social media, the main sphere of influence now occurs between consumers, principally in the form of digitised word-of-mouth, sometimes called electronic word-of-mouth (eWOM). It is true that word-of-mouth has always existed, but what is different now is that its speed is now greatly accelerated, and this can make it very powerful. Chapter 8 outlined some principles of how viral effect can be achieved. This is essentially turbo-charged eWOM. But beware, eWOM has a long memory which cannot be easily erased! Once a consumer has criticised a brand, that criticism's digital footprint lives forever unless it is somehow removed by the firm. The rise of digital influencers (or micro-celebrities) on social media also suggests one more way to influence the social narrative apart from trying to influence opinion leaders, market mavens, brand loyalists, brand advocates and online communities.

However, organisations should not see social influence as a short-term exercise confined to a campaign. Rather, social influence should be viewed as managing the long-term conversations among consumers. Ultimately, for these conversations to continue the organisation needs to have a great – not just a good – product or service, which indicates the importance of being continually innovative. Then there is a reason for consumers to spread the good word online (and offline).

Theme 2: Synergy and stretching the media dollar

A second major consideration for the marcoms manager is how to drive the media dollar further. In fact, the whole idea of integration is to create synergies so that consumers' interest for the brand can be compounded. In chapter 1, we discussed in detail the many tactics (e.g. interlinking and sequencing) of creating synergy with our creative assets that go beyond just 'luggage matching'. And in chapter 5, we saw how paid, owned, searched, shared and earned media (the POSSE framework) can be combined in a campaign, sometimes using dynamic, digital technologies to amplify the synergistic effects. Chapter 12 showed how synergistic effects can be estimated across different media in a campaign, yielding useful information on how such media should be combined to achieve the largest synergistic effects.

But what happens if there is little budget for developing multiple creative assets or indeed advertising, as is often the case for small business, small brands or non-profit organisations, or if advertising is prohibited, as is the case for political parties (during a non-election period) or pharmaceutical brands (in some countries)?

One option is to use marketing-oriented PR (see chapter 9). This should be considered first because it can be very cost-efficient. This is especially useful when the organisation has a new marketing initiative and does not want to pay (or pay too much) for its exposure. PR activities become useful because they can lead to free publicity for the brand. Usually, topics that are both deviant and socially significant tend to be picked up by media organisations, since they want this kind of story for their content in order to attract viewers and help sell their advertising space. The key, however, is to be able to weave the brand creatively into the story for the media. There is therefore a symbiotic relationship between the media and the stories about brands (or organisations). This is something Richard Branson understood and has consistently practised with his Virgin brand, and so has the US President Donald Trump with his tweets. In fact, Donald Trump may very well be the first US president that has understood marketing.

Yet another option is to practise content marketing (see chapter 9). By consistently putting out useful material, firms can influence the narrative in the marketplace and in the process build strong and favourable associations for the brand. Good content would also stimulate eWOM. However, we do not advocate the use of native advertising which is unethical.

Theme 3: Creativity

Another way of driving the media dollar further is creativity. In fact, one could argue that it is the lack of budget that often forces us to come up with a creative solution! This is especially important for a mass medium, such as TV, where the cost is high. Without a great creative idea, it does not matter how much we spend on media as it is unlikely to cut through the clutter. But if it is effective, the extra share of voice (eSOV) we have spent on the campaign will in fact increase the brand's market share (see chapter 6).

What then is a creative idea? It is a compelling way of selling the branded message. This branded message is usually some benefit the target audience desires (although, as we saw in chapter 6, the message can also emphasise brand elements, attributes, consequences or actions). But how does one incorporate this benefit into the ad and yet be compelling? Chapter 6 discussed the theory of remote associative matching (RAM). The idea here is to search for a conveyor – for example, a celebrity, a brand name, a cultural icon – that is not normally associated with the brand and yet has a dominant association that will convey the intended meaning without creating any conflict in our minds. When this is found, the ad is likely to be unexpected and yet relevant. To increase the probability of finding the conveyor that is relevant, we should explore the principles of convergent and divergent thinking, also discussed in chapter 6.

Related to creative ideas is their execution (chapter 7). Execution means effectively translating the idea into reality – making it come into fruition with great skill. It is important to draw a distinction between a creative idea and its execution because an idea can be executed in many ways, and if it is not well executed, it will come to nothing. Consumers do not see an idea – they only see its execution. Therefore, we want to choose the most effective way of depicting the creative idea. While the aim of a creative idea is to enhance the benefit, the aim of execution is to enhance the idea with great skill.

Chapter 7 also discusses the important strategic decision of whether to have one or many executions. The advantages and disadvantages of different kinds of execution are also discussed and the circumstances under which they are most likely to be effective, including celebrity endorsement. The use of celebrity is common in a campaign, but its usage is plagued with issues (e.g. its expense, lack of 'fit' or credibility, celebrities' misbehaviour and power to distract from the brand). The chapter provides a framework for how to navigate through these issues. In a similar vein, chapter 8 discusses the issues of using social media influencers.

Theme 4: Research

Great creativity (and execution) is hard to achieve without first understanding the target audience and their relationship with the brand, including the decision journey (see chapter 1). Understanding the consumer journey is important because this will allow marcoms managers to see where to improve. For instance, if research shows that a large proportion of consumers have not considered buying a particular brand, even if it is well known, then strategies can be developed to translate this awareness into purchase consideration. For instance, this might require a better buy-back plan (see case study 1.2) or increased human-to-human interactions (see case study 10.2).

There are many kinds of research. The thrust of chapter 2 was that research can yield insights for creative development. Special emphasis was paid to different qualitative research techniques. However, regardless of the chosen technique, the objective is to unearth a key insight which can be translated into a creative idea that will trigger the desired behaviour; in short, to find the right motivational trigger that will create a need and move consumers. This will unlock growth for the brand.

The sort of research discussed in chapter 2 is different from the evaluation-based research discussed in chapter 12. One form of evaluation-based research is advertising pre-testing.

Pre-testing is required to ensure that what is communicated is 'on message'. Fundamentally, it is about testing a promise. This is carried out before the campaign starts to check its effectiveness; that is, before media dollars are spent on it. Since a bad ad can hurt sales, it is also a form of risk reduction. The use of psycho-physiological techniques has grown in popularity; they allow researchers to gauge the ongoing reaction of the target audience as they watch or hear the ad. This helps pinpoint which part of the ad is communicating best or worst, and whether the branded scenes are transferred to long-term memory. As the validity of ad pre-testing has improved, together with the lowering of its evaluation cost, the ROI of ad pre-testing has improved dramatically in recent years.

Research is also needed for media plans and personal selling. In media planning (see chapter 4) it pays to know where and when to best reach the target audience. This means understanding their buying behaviour and media usage habits. This will help decide which media vehicles to use and how to schedule them to maximise reach and help trigger purchase. This is very much needed as the number of channels continues to grow (see chapter 4) and budgets are reallocated accordingly to achieve the best synergy. For personal selling (see chapter 10), research is needed to prioritise customer visitations, so qualification of leads can improve performance significantly. In terms of sales presentation, research seeks to better understand customer needs, which are especially important when selling expensive or complex goods or services. Knowing the needs of customers will give the salesperson the advantage of knowing what 'hot buttons' to press during the sales interaction. Without this understanding, the salesperson will only be guessing and therefore be less convincing.

The availability of quality research also means we can now quickly tell whether marcoms activities are likely to be effective. This means the pressure to succeed is now greater. However, research should not be used as a stick to punish a manager with when something fails; rather, it should be used as an incentive to understand why the failure happened, so that the mistake can be avoided next time. This is the basis of the plan, execute, evaluate and learn (or PEEL) cycle (see chapter 1).

Accountability is therefore not about success or failure but about understanding why certain (good or bad) outcomes occur. For this reason, we advocate continuous tracking of a campaign from start to finish (see chapter 12). That way, if the campaign is not performing well, it can be quickly fixed. Further, the knowledge gained in tracking a campaign can help support budget submission the next time. This is especially important if the campaign did not go as well as expected, as a documented reason can be given. In fact, even if a campaign is working well, it still pays to understand why because similar tactics may be used in the future.

While continuous tracking of campaign supports accountability, the budget itself still needs to be carefully justified. By far the most logical and yet the most challenging is the objective-and-task method of setting a budget. It is highly logical because it breaks the objective down into smaller tasks, on the assumption that these tasks can, on the whole, help achieve the objective. This method is especially relevant when different communication disciplines are used, because many different tasks need to be coordinated. However, for this method to work, assumptions about conversion ratios between input of different marcoms tools (such as advertising) and its output (such as sales) must be accurate. The same logic goes with planning the reach and frequency of a campaign (see chapter 4). The method forces us to test our assumptions when we succeed or fail, so allowing us to learn from the experience. With the rise of AI and marketing technologies, the results of a digital campaign can be known even quicker and with greater transparency.

Theme 5: Brand-building and equity destruction

It is sometimes easy to forget that the job of a marcoms manager is still fundamentally to build brands (or brand equity). If this were not the case, then all that would be needed to increase sales would be price discounting (see chapter 11). We should remember that brand equity, in essence, means the value of a brand. In chapter 3, we discussed different perspectives of conceptualising and measuring brand equity including financial, price-elasticity, revenue-premium, consumer-based and the BrandAsset Valuator®.

But what is a brand? We defined a brand as an imprint of associations. Therefore, when we build a brand, we are essentially strengthening a set of desirable associations in consumers' minds that can set the brand apart from competition. Chapter 3 discussed the many tactics a marcoms manager can use to position the brand in the target audience's mind. It fundamentally requires two elements: (i) associating the brand with the right conveyor and (ii) repetition.

A conveyor can be defined as any entity – a celebrity, suggestive brand name, cultural icon – that has desirable dominant associations a brand can appropriate for the purpose of creating the desired positioning. By repeatedly pairing the brand with this conveyor, the desired associations of the conveyor are transferred to the brand. This is known as evaluative conditioning. Ideally, we should choose conveyors that will impart to the brand associations that are strong, favourable, unique and relevant. Positioning can thus be defined in these terms: creating strong and favourable associations in the mind of the target audience so that it comes to represent something unique and relevant and hence stands apart from competition. Chapter 3 discussed the pros and cons of different positioning tactics for a brand. Trade-offs must be made when choosing these tactics.

Differentiation is important because if consumers cannot see any difference between brands, they will buy on price. It follows that if we do *not* want consumers to buy on price, we must remind consumers of these differences, so that these differences become *salient* when triggered by purchase cues (e.g. it is Christmas). This is where advertising becomes important – it helps remind consumers that the brand stands for something meaningfully different. Then when promotions are used, it will be perceived as having greater than normal value (although for only a short period). The temporal increase in value will motivate the target audience to accelerate their purchase decision for the brand. It will also be more protected from a competitor's promotion; that is, customers will be less likely to switch. Or, to put it another way, the aim of advertising is to give the customers enough reasons for them to buy and not switch.

The same logic holds with the use of corporate image advertising, cause-related marketing, corporate social responsibility initiatives, advocacy advertising and sponsorship (see chapter 9). They all help build the reputation of the firm. But a firm's reputation is fragile. What takes years to build up can be instantly destroyed when there is a crisis such as product failure. Products or services that use their corporate name as their brand name are especially vulnerable in this area. For this reason, a marcoms manager needs strong crisis-management skills.

We have also warned of the dangers of undermining brand equity with excessive use of price discounts. Constant price promotion (and especially without an image-building program) makes price the most salient attribute of the brand, and in time the target audience will come to view the brand as a discount brand. It is for this reason that we encourage marcoms managers to adopt non-price sales promotions such as premiums, contests and games. These are especially effective for hedonic products (see chapter 11).

IMC IMPLEMENTATION

Knowing the principle of IMC is one thing; being able to implement the plan is quite a different story. Even the best laid plans can fail because of mediocre implementation. One recent study found that about 54% of IMC campaigns failed at some aspects of integration.[1] And as the world becomes ever more complex, with rising consumer expectations, the failure rate is likely to go higher. Traditional ways of implementing marcoms activities based on months of planning are becoming redundant. We are moving to a digital-enabled era of agility where consumers are expected to be served immediately. Unfortunately, not all organisations are agile. Most are constricted by traditional silo-like structures which limits transformation. What also complicates implementation issues are disruptive changes including evolving customer-facing technology, rising consumer expectations, and new digital ecosystems and channels. All these innovative changes have profound implications for IMC and its implementation. The issue, however, is not the lack of tools; there are plenty of tools and consultants to help. Often, the stumbling blocks are the current mind-sets of stakeholders, work processes, and the lack of analytical corporate culture.

Consumers expect the organisation to deliver on all its promises. Therefore, when implementations are poorly carried out, especially for high-profile events, it will damage the brand, no matter how simple the implementation may have initially seemed. For instance, in the 2018 World Cup soccer competition in Russia, Optus' live streaming of a Friday night match between Egypt and Uruguay failed due to poor streaming, low buffering and playback issues. The telecommunications giant had the sole licence to broadcast all 64 matches in Australia but the poor service resulted in a severe backlash from its subscribers, who took to social media. In the end, the Prime Minister had to step in. Optus agreed to let a free-to-air channel (SBS) broadcast six extra matches for free. Optus' mistake was an embarrassment and adversely affected its credibility in its aim to become a multimedia company.[2]

So that deadlines can be met, implementation should be guided by clear objectives and milestones, with regular progress checks. The latter includes daily reviewing of task-related data, updating of performance charts and holding progress 'scrum' meetings. It is also important to optimise internal lead-time with efficient workflow. This means the roles of team members, task expectations and delivery times have to be clear so that everyone knows what to do and by when. If the team fails to move at the right speed or in the right direction, then corrective actions must be taken immediately by the project leader. Implementation is the act of completing a series of task-related activities necessary to progress towards a planned end-goal, underpinned by clearly stated objectives and deadlines.

Barriers to IMC implementation

As early as 1993, Duncan and Everett observed that it was hard to implement IMC even at the tactical level. They found that internally 'turf wars' and externally 'agency egos' to be chief barriers to the adoption of IMC practices.[3] This is quite apart from the added difficulty of implementing IMC at a strategic level for the whole business. At a more strategic level, seven barriers to IMC implementations are often discussed:[4]

1. organisational structure (e.g. functional silos)
2. organisational culture (e.g. HQ differs from sub-branch)
3. processes (e.g. poorly designed operational management)

4. organisational behaviour (e.g. ego)
5. communication (e.g. poor internal marketing)
6. managerial economics (e.g. lack of incentives) and technology (e.g. inefficient information flow)
7. mental models of practitioners (e.g. different understanding of IMC).

While the first six types of barriers listed above originate from organisational barriers, often also discussed in organisational psychology, the last type of barrier originates from how practitioners think about IMC or their mental models. To better understand how different mental models of IMC can affect implementation, Otis and Nyilasy[5] interviewed 26 Swedish professionals over a two-year period complemented with participant observation; these respondents were associated with a large retailer who was implementing an IMC program during this time, and besides the retailer, they came from an advertising agency, a media agency, a custom media agency, and three broadcasting networks. Four mental models were uncovered:

1. Efficiency model (often associated with media strategists)
2. Effectiveness model (often associated with marketing managers)
3. Quality model (often associated with creative personnel)
4. Impact model (often associated with consumer researchers).

The authors argued that when IMC implementation fails it was because the different parties (i.e. media strategists, marketing managers, creative personnel and consumer researchers) did not understand each other. Each group suffered from their own self-serving bias (e.g. different compensation system), resulting in mistrust. They were also not able to reflect on their own practice within the larger IMC context because of the rigidity of their mental models. Finally, each constituent also placed different emphasis on different types of analyses. For example, marketing managers, who tended to focus on effectiveness, were less willing to discuss efficiency with media strategists. Their ideals also discouraged collaboration (e.g. creative personnel may fear loss of creative independence).

MARKETING TECHNOLOGIES AND IMPLEMENTATION

Consider the following scenario:

> Imagine you have to run 50 email campaigns this month across different regions, targeting four different customer segments and then evaluating the results to determine if the desired ROI is achieved. You also need to build into the campaign an A/B testing regime with different executions and to trial a new algorithm for an event-based trigger marketing initiative and an automatic sales activation. In terms of reach, you decide to use TV and print advertising.
>
> At the same time, your advertising agency suggests developing a series of YouTube videos to extend the TV campaign online. This will be 'behind-the-scenes' video clips, which the agency argues can also be used for content marketing. This will further amplify the message. To drive more online conversations, your PR agency also suggests holding competitions with these video clips where customers can vote for their favourite on social media. For digital advertising, you plan to use a display banner ad for the platforms of desktops and mobile devices. To increase efficiency, you plan to buy some key words for the campaign and to optimise the search results. Similarly, you adopt programmatic media buying so that the exposure of these messages across the various channels are automatically optimised. Now further imagine that you delegate some of these tasks to two of your team members since you cannot manage everything yourself.

ASKHAM BRYAN
COLLEGE
LEARNING RESOURCES

The above scenario may seem complicated, but many large corporations routinely run such campaigns throughout the year. However, the complexity and scale of such campaigns is made easier with the help of marketing automations. Such technologies are on the rise because of lowering computing costs, cheaper storage power and more powerful analytics, including artificial intelligence.

Marketing technologies (or martech) is a class of software or operating systems that blends marketing and IT technologies to improve the marketing and its supporting functions. Some of these functionalities include the (i) automatic capture and analysis of customer data from multiple channels, (ii) automating the delivery of campaign messages, (iii) coordinating workflow among team members, (iv) automatic optimising of media buying for ad placements and (v) tracking marketing performance. It is therefore broader than AdTech which is more focused on media buying.[6]

Fundamentally, all these marketing technologies (martech) essentially have two overarching objectives: effectiveness and efficiency, leading to an increase in productivity and accountability. Efficiency means getting the right tasks completed quicker and preventing implementations being held up. Therefore, one of the key benefits of martech is that it helps the streamlining of tasks and workflow so that team members know exactly what to do and by when; and if there is a delay, everyone knows where the bottleneck is. Streamlining of workflow is especially helpful for someone new in the role. Another example of efficiency is the automatic allocation of campaign messages. This is especially useful in email marketing because creative content can be pre-set for different segments. This technology facilitates the process of saying the right thing in the right way, to the right person, at the right time. With programmatic media buying (see chapter 4) all this can be automatically implemented.

Martech can also have an in-built intelligence to help evaluate the ROI of its campaign quickly. This means full transparency. Gone are the days where the marketing director has all the information, or no one is quite sure if a campaign had been effective. For instance, with live tracking, in-field assessment can occur instantaneously. One extreme example is that of Amazon. It is capable of rapidly and frequently changing prices on millions of items on its website. For its bestsellers, Amazon routinely undercuts its competitors, but for less popular items it maintains its margins. The results are known immediately. This takes dynamic pricing to a whole new level!

In summary, when properly applied, martech aids workflow, helps identify weaknesses, and prompts corrective actions (e.g. adjusting the marketing mix, or quickly dropping unpromising initiatives, diverting resources to promising initiatives). The speediness and transparency of the feedback increases responsiveness and cooperation. But for these to work, quality data and interpretation are needed. They are so important that they can change the whole industry, as in the case of Netflix.

CASE STUDY 13.1 NETFLIX: A DATA-DRIVEN MOVIE COMPANY[7]

Netflix was founded in 1998 by Reed Hasting and Marc Randolph. It started life as a video subscription home delivery service in the US. A household paid a monthly fee, choosing from a range of packages. These movies would be booked on Netflix's website. Once available, they were mailed to the household. The most popular package was three DVDs at a time. There were no due dates or late fees, just a monthly subscription. By 2010, Netflix had become the largest video rental subscription service in the US. Their single most important reason for their success was their ability to harness data that can serve both customers and suppliers.

On the customer side, Netflix developed a sophisticated recommendation software, called Cinematch, which allowed users to rate the movies they watched. The more customers rated, the more accurate the recommendation became for their next rental. This not only increased their enjoyment of their viewing experience but also 'locked' them into the recommended movies. Operationally, this allowed Netflix to only recommend movies they stocked and, hence, maximised the utility of their existing inventory. About 60% of subscribers' choice came from Netflix's recommendation.

In 2006, Netflix offered a prize of US$1 million to anyone or any team who could come up with a better algorithm than Cinematch and beat its current efficiency by at least 10%. Netflix was prepared to release the database of 100 million customer ratings. The competition generated a lot of interest worldwide. It was eventually won by the BellKor team, but Netflix also benefited from the all the intellectual input harnessed from the competition. Eventually, this technology allowed Netflix to predict with 90% accuracy whether a movie will be a hit with their subscribers. This was a giant leap forward.

At the same time, Netflix developed an advanced search system that allowed subscribers to search up to 200 subgenres of movies. This greatly expanded the range of movies for subscribers to watch, which created new audiences. About 85% of films never made it to the theatres, but Netflix provided an alternative outlet for these movies and their producers. With a ready-made audience, Netflix could also negotiate with the studios a faster release of their movies for rental after their theatre showing. This kept the Netflix subscribers happy. Furthermore, by knowing their customer base, Netflix could estimate how much to pay for the rights of a particular movie. For instance, if Netflix knew that one million customers had rented the sci-fi movie *Star Trek*, and another 600 000 rented *Star Trek 2*, with 300 000 renting both, then it could assume that 300 000 would be likely to rent *Star Trek 3*. These are the hard-core fans. Netflix could then pay for the DVD rights accordingly for *Star Trek 3*. In short, data analytics had helped Netflix win customers and manage their pipeline of movies.

In 2011, Netflix decided to get into online streaming because the rent-by-mail DVD business was in decline and the internet was becoming ever more pervasive. However, this meant it was limited to areas where there was broadband; that is, households with high-speed internet. Although this market continued to grow within the US, Netflix had to expand internationally in order to grow faster. This made sense as there was very little variable cost in streaming the content worldwide. However, to succeed, it also meant Netflix had to shift its movie mix to appeal to a much wider audience. This meant going up against new competitors (e.g. Hulu and cable TV) who provided their own content. The solution was for Netflix to stream blockbuster movies and popular TV programs, as well as to provide its own content, some of which became worldwide hits (e.g. *House of Cards, The Crown*). This strategy seems to be working. In 2017, Netflix's international streaming revenue grew by 58%. It now has 125 million subscribers and is vying for the Indian market which has 1 billion viewers.[8]

DISCUSSION QUESTIONS

1. Give an overview of how Netflix uses data to improve its communications to its customers.
2. If data can predict our liking of movies, why haven't Hollywood studios made use of such data before to make better movies?
3. What aspects of this case are of most interest to you? Discuss why.

ACTIVATION ENGINES

As discussed above, there are many aspects to martech, but in the context of IMC, two applications have gained prominence: programmatic media buying and activation engines. We have already discussed programmatic media buying in chapter 4. We will now touch on activation engines.

One marketing function martech excels in is the automatic activation of offers, which comes in three forms: retargeting, reminding and recommending. Retargeting means re-contacting consumers with an ad. The most obvious example is customers who visited one's website but never bought anything. Using cookie technologies, an e-commerce organisation can study the browsing behaviour of their shoppers and retarget each shopper with an ad for the product (or service) that they previously viewed. One can also be as specific as retargeting shoppers who did not complete their transaction online.[9] For instance, one study of over 200 global brands found about 74% of shopping carts were abandoned without completing payment.[10] So a gentle reminder email with a compelling image and an accompanying link can help return the shopper to the cart, as seen with the example in figure 13.2.[11] Such retargeting efforts can recover 16% of sales, which is substantial.[12]

Figure 13.2 An online retailer's reminder to complete the online sale

Another way of activating sales is to simply remind customers to buy again at the appropriate time. For example, if we know when a customer is likely to run out of a product (e.g. ink cartilages, water filter or dog food) or when a contracted service is likely to be terminated (e.g. insurance), then a reminder email can be sent. Automated trigger-based reminder emails can be set up when a specific amount of time has lapsed (e.g. 12 months of insurance). Reminding email (or sometimes called replenish email[13]) is the easiest personalisation facility to set up because the data is very simple, but it is important to get the timing correct.

But what happens if customer data cannot be captured automatically or is cumbersome? If this is the case, then investments would have to be made. Recently, the food delivery firm Menulog launched a campaign featuring Jeff Goldblum encouraging consumers to order takeout through their smartphone using the Menulog app (see figure 13.3). They did this because only 20% of their customers order online.[14] Most still rely on the traditional telephone. Strategically, this is an important move because it saves labour costs (i.e. no need to man the telephone), and the automatic capturing of customer data on the app will give the firm a better understanding of the customers' consumption habits and cuisine preferences, allowing it to proactively personalise the next offer.

Figure 13.3 Celebrity Jeff Goldblum spruiking the Menulog app

Recommendation of a related product (or service) is another form of sales activation and can greatly increase revenue because it brings to attention another product (or service) not considered before. Called the 'Next best offer' recommendation, it has to be relevant to be effective. It is essentially a form of personalised suggestion system and is complex to execute. This is because the engine has to make the right recommendation based on customer preference and yet must take the firm's inventory into consideration. The greater the number of customers and inventory, the more complicated the process becomes because the engine has to learn how to rank the order in which the recommendation occurs. The two leaders in this functionality are Amazon and Netflix.

Amazon uses the algorithm-ranking method called item-to-item collaborative filtering to achieve a high level of customer relevance.[15] This means matching the item purchased or rated by a target user to similar items others have rated (which the target user has not rated), and combining those similar items to form a recommendation list.[16] The recommendation usually comes in the following statement: 'Customers who bought this item also bought ...' (see figure 13.4). Of all Amazon sales, 35% originate from their recommendation engine.

Customers who bought this item also bought

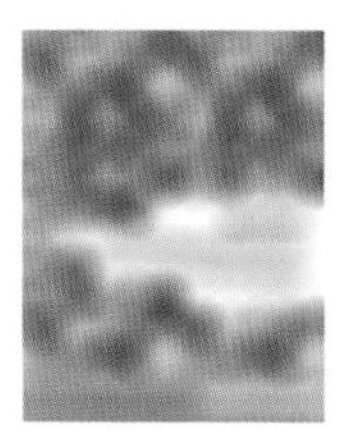

Communication - eBook: Core Interpersonal Skills for Health Professionals
Gjyn O'Toole
5
Kindle Edition
$64.59

Psychiatric & Mental Health Nursing
Katie Evans
4
Kindle Edition
$55.49

Clinical Reasoning eBook
Tracy Levett-Jones
3
Kindle Edition
$32.86

Yatdjuligin: Aboriginal and Torres Strait Islander Nursing and Midwifery...
Odette Best
1
Kindle Edition
$54.22

Figure 13.4 Amazon's 'Next best offer' recommendation

This form of data-activated recommendation can also be extended for use on other platforms. For instance, after having bought a product (e.g. yoga pants) a week earlier using a personal computer, the individual can be retargeted for another product (e.g. sports bag) on their mobile app. Leveraging on previous purchase data, such time-sensitive offers, based on an individual's related needs and interests, can open new revenues of growth. It can increase sales by 15% to 20%.[17]

CASE STUDY 13.2 NETFLIX'S AUTOMATIC DATA CAPTURE AND PROCESSING USING ARTIFICIAL INTELLIGENCE

In the case study earlier, we saw how Netflix used data to help dominate the delivery movie business in the US. Now it wants to dominate the world with its on-demand streaming. Netflix now has over 182 million users worldwide, and more so than Amazon they rely on their recommendation platform to be successful – more than 80% of its TV shows are discovered through this recommendation system by its subscribers.[18] To improve their recommendation, Netflix uses sophisticated machine learning and algorithms, as follows:

First, they have records of their subscribers' viewing habits. This information is automatically captured, and it includes what show they are currently watching, the previous show they watched, the next show they watched, and the show they watched a year ago. Overlaying this information is the time of their viewing. This represents the behavioural data.

Second, Netflix then codes each show on several creative elements like whether it is humourous, intellectual, whether there is an ensemble cast, or has corrupt police in the story line and so forth.

Third, using sophisticated machine learning algorithms, Netflix figure out which creative elements were most important in influencing the viewing behaviour of the individuals and weigh them accordingly in terms of its prediction. From this, segments or 'taste communities' are created. But since a viewer could fit into multiple taste groups with varying preferences, this information will influence the order of visual titles (and genre display) shown on the individual's screen.

So, the next time you log onto Netflix, be reminded that the visual titles you see have been cleverly engineered to tempt you! This AI-assisted recommendation system is said to save Netflix $1 billion per year.

DISCUSSION QUESTIONS

1. Since Netflix relies on data to improve its business, its automatic capture of data is critical to its success. How does Netflix capture viewers' data? And how does the combination of viewers' data and creative elements of the movie help Netflix improve its offerings?
2. Netflix's algorithm implies that the order in which you see the visual titles (and genre display) influences your choice. Do you think this is a good assumption? In what other circumstances in marketing would you see the same assumption being made?
3. With General Data Protection Regulation (GDPR), Netflix technically seeks consent and protects your viewing data. Is this good or bad for Netflix? And is it good or bad for you as a subscriber of Netflix? (See Ethics below on GDPR.)

The deployment of martech will become commonplace in the future; and if properly deployed, will improve the efficiency and effectiveness of marketing. Already one study has shown that 73% of top performing companies, that is those that outperform the market, have increased their martech spending by 16% over the previous year. Of these outperformers, 49% had used the right martech tools to assist them, compared to 16% of firms that did not outperform the market.[19] Thus early evidence seems to suggest that martech tools can help. But the scope and choice of myriad software and operating systems are bewildering.[20] A marcoms manager needs clear thinking before implementation. Figure 13.5 is one simple way of thinking how martech can be used and the benefits derived if properly implemented.

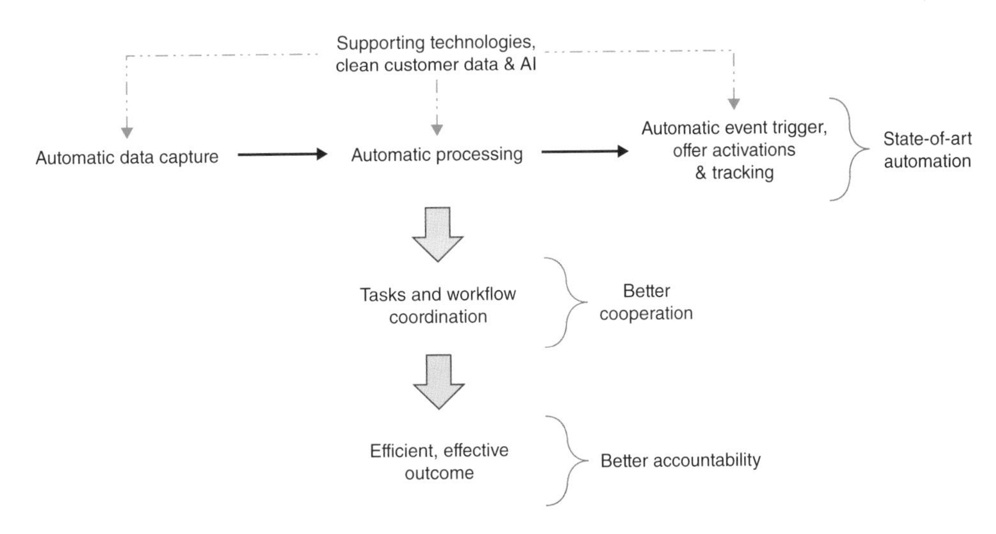

Figure 13.5 Conceptual way of thinking about marketing technologies and their benefits

ETHICS

Ethics is no longer an afterthought. In chasing after profits, it is sometimes easy to forget about ethics. For instance, we might be tempted to lie during a sales negotiation to close the deal; we might make false claims in advertising to appear convincing; we might violate the privacy of consumers in social media to raise sales; or we might contact prospects in direct marketing without gaining their permission first.

There are many opportunities to engage in unethical behaviour, which can involve deceitful or under-handed behaviour or the omission of important information. This kind of behaviour may lead to harmful consequences, although what is considered harmful, and to whom, may be debated. However, it should be noted that telling untruths is not the same as exaggerating an attribute or benefit (hyperbole) as illustrated in this 'piece of puff': 'The tastiest vegetable soup in the world.' Such statements do not affirm any objective fact and any reasonable person can understand that. However, if there were a factual claim – as in 'the vegetable soup that contains more anti-oxidant than any other' – the claim would need to be supported. If this claim were found to be misleading (because, for example, antioxidants are destroyed in heating the soup), then this would constitute lying about the material facts. Often, when a claim to superiority is made, a brand's vigilant competitors are the first to challenge it in court.

A note of caution: in this digital age, when information is freely available and brands are constantly scrutinised, unethical behaviour is quickly found out. Although marcoms managers can undertake ethics training, perhaps the greatest deterrent to unethical behaviour remains the fear of being caught out and being at the receiving end of consumers' anger – now amplified virally through social media. Unethical behaviour risks destroying whatever goodwill the brand has built over time. Why take the risk?

But companies skirt on the fringes of unethical behaviour when it comes to the protection of consumer privacy, as seen in the recent Cambridge Analytica scandal with its 'harvesting' of Facebook profiles.[21] But no more. Protecting consumers' privacy is now a major requirement for all organisations. In Europe, a new law called General Data Protection Regulation (GDPR) has now come into force (25 May 2018).[22] Among other things, a firm must seek and gain approval from the visitor to its website if user identification technology (e.g. cookie files) were to be used. Failure to comply will attract heavy fines. For serious infringements, firms can be fined either €20 million or 4% of the previous year's turnover.

A LOOK TO THE FUTURE

We conclude this chapter (and book!) by boldly making two predictions. First, a new breed of marketing professionals will be required – marketing technologists – because marketing has become a technology-driven discipline. Such a person should understand both the languages of IT and marketing. However, this person should *first* be a marketer with a deep understanding of consumer needs but still imaginative enough to see what technologies can be deployed in service of this need and finding a profitable solution. Forward-looking organisations will have an MTO (marketing technology officer) in their ranks.[23]

Second, the speed of implementation, iterative learning and a strong analytical corporate culture will be paramount for the future. This is because the speed of change will become quicker and the environment more complex. If an organisation cannot learn fast enough, supported by an analytical culture, it will not prosper.[24] One contribution the MTO can make is to have a vision of a new future and then suggest ways in which technology (with fast iterative learning and analytics) can help shape consumer preference. Ultimately, the MTO needs the conviction of such a belief. Without this, the organisation will stagnate.

DISCUSSION QUESTIONS

1. Several integrative themes are discussed in this chapter. Which of these themes resonated most with you? Please justify your answer.
2. Define implementation. Relate how this definition can assist you in your next group project.
3. What are the common barriers to IMC implementation? Discuss how different mind-sets of stakeholders can affects its implementation.
4. Relate an online shopping incident when you were re-contacted to buy something. How did you feel about being re-contacted? Explain your answer.
5. How does being retargeted to buy the same product differ from recommendations to buy other similar products? Is there a difference? Explain your answer.
6. How does reputational harm occur in an online context? What can you do as a manager to mitigate this?
7. What are the conceptual benefits of using martech? Discuss this in the context of figure 13.5.
8. Marketing is going to be more technology and data driven. Discuss what this means in terms of your current and future education needs.

NOTES

1 Kantar Millward Brown, 'AdReaction: the art of integration', Global Report, 2018. Accessed May 2019 at www.millwardbrown.com/documents/reports/The_art_of_integration/default.aspx?access=yes.

2 T McLlroy, 'World Cup fail: Optus gives SBS games', *Australian Financial Review*, 19 June 2018, p. 3.

3 TR Duncan and SE Everett, 'Client perceptions of integrated marketing communications', *Journal of Advertising Research*, 33(3), 1993, pp. 30–9.

4 For a good summary see, M Otis and G Nyilasy, 'Integrated Marketing communications (IMC): Why does it fail? An analysis of practitioner mental models exposes barriers of IMC implementation', *Journal of Advertising Research*, 55(2), 2015, pp. 132–45.

5 Ibid.

6 Advertising technologies and marketing technologies are already merging into a new class of technologies called MadTech (Marketing-Advertising Technologies). See M Wlosik, 'What is MadTech? The Convergence of AdTech and MarTech', https://clearcode.cc/blog/what-is-madtech/. Accessed December 2018.

7 R Walker and M Jeffrey, 'Netflix leading with data', Kellogg School of Management, 2010; S Chatterjee, W Barry and A Hopkins, *Netflix Inc: Proving the skeptics wrong*, Ivey Publishing, 2016.

8 V Sharma, 'Netflix turns to Bollywood to script India growth story', *Reuter Business News*, 5 July 2018. Accessed July 2018 at www.reuters.com/article/us-netflix-india/netflix-turns-to-bollywood-to-script-india-growth-story-idUSKBN1JU2MM.

9 Abandoned checkouts, Shopify: https://help.shopify.com/manual/orders/abandoned-checkouts. Accessed July 2018.

10 This study was conducted by SalesCycle in 2013 and the information is summarised in this visual graphic: https://visual.ly/community/infographic/technology/cart-abandonment-stats-q3–2013. Accessed July 2018.

11 D Wang, '13 Amazing abandoned cart emails (and what you can learn from them)' Shopify Blog, 2014. Accessed July 2018 at www.shopify.com/blog/12522201-13-amazing-abandoned-cart-emails-and-what-you-can-learn-from-them.

12 See infographic by SalesCycle based on a study of 200 leading brands in 2013: https://visual.ly/community/infographic/technology/cart-abandonment-stats-q3–2013. Accessed July 2018.

13 J Daly, 'The replenishment email: an e-commerce hack guaranteed to drive sales', Vero, 2 April 2015. Accessed July 2018 at www.getvero.com/resources/replenishment-email.

14 L Bennett, 'Jeff Goldblum stars in campaign for Menulog by Y&R', AdNews, 15 May 2017. Accessed July 2018 at www.adnews.com.au/news/jeff-goldblum-stars-in-campaign-for-menulog-by-yandr#VhYz6W2pp2HsCErE.99.

15 S Arora, 'Recommendation engines: how Amazon and Netflix are winning the personalization battle', MTA Martech Advisor, 28 June 2016. Accessed July 2018 at www.martechadvisor.com/articles/customer-experience-2/recommendation-engines-how-amazon-and-netflix-are-winning-the-personalization-battle/.

16 B Sarwar, G Karypis, J Konstan and J Riedl, 'Item-based collaborative filtering recommendation algorithms', Proceedings of the 10th international conference on World Wide Web, 2001, pp. 285–95.

17 J Boudet, B Gregg, J Heller and C Tufft, 'The heartbeat of modern marketing: data activation & personalization'. Accessed December 2018 at www.mckinsey.com/business-functions/marketing-and-sales/our-insights/the-heartbeat-of-modern-marketing.

18 L Plummer, 'This is how Netflix's top-secret recommendation system works', *Wired*, 23 August 2017. Accessed July 2018 at www.wired.co.uk/article/how-do-netflixs-algorithms-work-machine-learning-helps-to-predict-what-viewers-will-like.

19 J Heller and K Robinson, 'Meet your new MOM (Marketing Operating Model)', McKinsey, 2017. Accessed July 2018 at www.mckinsey.com/business-functions/marketing-and-sales/our-insights/meet-your-new-mom.

20 According to Clearcode, an adtech/martech custom software platform developer, there are over 1800 and growing vendors across 43 different categories. Accessed November 2018 at https://clearcode.cc/.

21 You can read all about the scandal here: C Cadwalladr and E Graham-Harrison, 'Revealed: 50 million Facebook profiles harvested for Cambridge Analytica in major data breach', March 2018. Accessed December 2018 at www.theguardian.com/news/2018/mar/17/cambridge-analytica-facebook-influence-us-election.

22 'EU data protection rules', European Commission, 2018. Accessed July 2018 at https://ec.europa.eu/commission/priorities/justice-and-fundamental-rights/data-protection/2018-reform-eu-data-protection-rules_en.

23 J Gordon and J Perrey, 'The dawn of marketing's new golden age', *McKinsey Quarterly*, February 2015. Accessed July 2018 at www.mckinsey.com/business-functions/marketing-and-sales/our-insights/the-dawn-of-marketings-new-golden-age.

24 P Bisson, B Hall, B McCarthy and K Rifai, 'Breaking away: the secrets to scaling analytics', *McKinsey Analytics*, May, 2018. Accessed December 2018 at www.mckinsey.com/~/media/McKinsey/Business%20Functions/McKinsey%20Analytics/Our%20Insights/Breaking%20away%20The%20secrets%20to%20scaling%20analytics/Breaking-away-The-secrets-to-scaling-analytics.ashx.

INDEX